ROSTER

of

SOLDIERS and PATRIOTS

of the

AMERICAN REVOLUTION

BURIED IN

INDIANA

Compiled and Edited by
Mrs. ROSCOE C. O'BYRNE, *Chairman*

CLEARFIELD

Originally published by
Indiana Daughters of the American Revolution
1938

Reprinted with permission
Genealogical Publishing Company, Inc.
Baltimore, Maryland, 1968

Reprinted for
Clearfield Company, Inc. by
Genealogical Publishing Co., Inc.
Baltimore, Maryland
1994, 1999

Library of Congress Catalogue Card Number 68-18632
International Standard Book Number: 0-8063-0266-6

Made in the United States of America

TABLE OF CONTENTS

Foreword 7, 8
List of Revolutionary Soldiers and D. A. R. Chapters in Counties   9–31
Abbreviations 32
Records of Revolutionary Soldiers.................................... 33–395
Col. Archibald Lochry Massacre.. 396–398
List of men whose service has not been verified.................. 399–403
Revolutionary Pensioners who later transferred to other States.. 404, 405
Indiana Pensioners in other Wars.. 405–407

THIS BOOK IS DEDICATED TO THE FLAMING AND ENDURING SPIRIT OF PATRIOTISM IN INDIANA WITH EVERY GRATEFUL APPRECIATION.

MRS. WILLIAM H. SCHLOSSER
State Regent 1937-1940

MRS. ROSCOE C. O"BYRNE
Chairman of Roster
State Regent, 1931-1934

FOREWORD

This volume of Revolutionary Soldiers buried in Indiana is presented with the hope that it will materially assist in increasing the membership in D. A. R. Chapters in the State. Within these pages will be found authentic service for 1394 soldiers and patriots. The compilation of these records has been the project of Indiana Daughters for the past four years, during the administrations of Miss Bonnie Farwell and Mrs. William H. Schlosser, Indiana State Regents.

This volume is not the work of one person, but the work of many. Chapter members have read all the D. A. R. Lineage volumes, Probate Court Records, Wills, Deeds, and Marriage Records, prior to the date 1850; also early newspapers of the counties and County Histories. Cemeteries have been searched for the graves.

Many persons, not D. A. R.'s, have contributed records of their ancestors. The Indiana State Library, through Dr. C. B. Coleman, State Librarian and Miss Anna Poucher, Librarian Genealogy Section, have furnished much valuable help. Mrs. Harvey Morris, Genealogist, Salem, Indiana, has assisted in several genealogical tangles and has supplied further data. The Indiana S. A. R. turned over their records. Members of the Indiana Historical Society have been helpful in counties where there are no D. A. R. Chapters. The assistance given has been praise-worthy and much appreciated, and is hereby gratefully acknowledged.

All of the names on the Indiana Pension Rolls have been traced and service secured for those who remained in the State. When the date of death and location of grave has not been obtained, that soldier has been placed in the county from which he applied for a pension. In some instances the date of last payment of pension has been secured and this is stated to show the approximate death date.

Information is given for 31 men, whose services are indefinite. With further research these may prove revolutionary services.

When the grave has been reported as marked by a family monument, this is indicated by the use of the word "stone", in the record. If the grave is otherwise marked, that is so stated. Individuals and chapters are given credit for the material they collected. If no name or chapter name is given, then that soldier's record has been secured by the editor of this volume.

Because of the variations in the different lists of the men who were in Col. Archibald Lochry's Company, when he with 36 others were massacred by the Indians, on Aug. 24, 1781, in what is now Dearborn County, Indiana, the entire list is given. This list is a copy of the original which is to be found in the British Museum. A few of the surnames have been supplied.

We do not claim that this volume contains all the Revolutionary soldiers and patriots buried in Indiana. We hope, however, that the publication of this number will bring forth not only additional data on these, but also on soldiers not listed.

ESTELLA A. O'BYRNE, Chairman.

MRS. ROSCOE C. O'BYRNE,
Brookville,
Indiana.

ROSTER BY COUNTIES

ADAMS COUNTY

Archibald, Thomas

Emory, George

ALLEN COUNTY
MARY PENROSE WAYNE CHAPTER

Andre, Jacque
Ball, James
Berry, William
Bird, Samuel
Bryant, David
Burnham, Gurdin
Cardinal, Millett
Clark, Robert
Cronz, Michael
De La Balm, Augustus Mottin
Duplacy, Joseph

Ewing, Alexander
Fontaine, James
Frothingham, Ebeneezer
Griffis, Zachariah P.
McMurtrey, John
Saunders, James
Thorp, Timothy
Threlkeld, Thomas
Tucker, William
Warren, George
Weeks, Charles

Wyllys, John Palsgrave

BARTHOLOMEW COUNTY
JOSEPH HART CHAPTER

Alcorn, George
Carney, John
Campbell, William
Chenoweth, Arthur, Jr.
Cook, Thomas
Crittenden, Richard Hazelwood
Goble, Stephen

Green, Thomas
Hart, Joseph
Lash, Adam
McQueen, Thomas
Moore, Jonathan
Redman, Benjamin
Steinberger, John

Tracy, Solomon

BLACKFORD COUNTY
NANCY KNIGHT CHAPTER

Kirkpatrick, David
Miles, Thomas

Mills, John
Saxon, John

BOONE COUNTY
JAMES HILL CHAPTER

Aldridge, John
Ferguson, John
Foreman, Jacob
Gipson, William
Hill, James
Johns, Henry
Kersey, John
Leap, John
McMannis, John
Pauley, William
Plew, Elias
Robertson, Jesse
Utter, Abraham
Wayman, Harman
Wheatley, Joseph

BROWN COUNTY

Hamblin, Job
Wilkerson, William

CARROLL COUNTY
CHARLES CARROLL CHAPTER

Farmer, Nathaniel
Johnston, James
Nichols, Willibe
Olinger, John

CASS COUNTY
OLDE TOWNE CHAPTER

Bowyer, Peter
Butler, James
Douglass, David
Krider, Christian
Pulee, John
Scott, Alexander
Ward, John

CLARK COUNTY
ANN ROGERS CLARK CHAPTER
GREEN TREE TAVERN CHAPTER

Allstott, John
Arbuckle, Thomas
Armstrong, John
Austin, Philip
Biggs, Robert
Brenton, John
Brenton, Robert
Brenton, William
Brown, James
Bullard, Isaac
Burritt, Zalmon
Calloway, Samuel
Carl, Elijah
Carr, Elisha
Carr, Thomas
Covert, Daniel
Dailey, Philip
Ditzler, Peter
Dolph, Stephen
Drummond, James, Jr.
Fislar, John
Garnsey, Daniel
Goben, William
Goodwin, William

Harrod, William	McDonald, Peter
Holman, Isaac	Pierce, Charles
Huckleberry, George	Pile, Richard
Jenkins, Ezekiel	Ramsey, Samuel
Johnson, Daniel	Reese, John
Kelley, Elias	Robinson, Joseph
Kestler, Frederick	Russell, John
Kuntz, George	Sanborn, Richard
Lawrence, William	Shadburn, Richard
Littell, Absalom	Sullivan, Daniel
Mikesell, Jacob	Summers, George
McAfee, Mathew	Teeple, Jacob
McBride, Isaac	True, Robert
McClelland, James	Tuttle, Enos
McComb, William	Ward, Zebediah
McCoy, William	Willey, Barzillai

Young, John

CLAY COUNTY
WILLIAM OARD CHAPTER

Dannor, David	Thompson, Lawrence
Oard, William	Wheeler, Benjamin
Sampson, Samuel	Yocum, John

CLINTON COUNTY
CAPTAIN HARMON AUGHE CHAPTER

Aughe, Harmon	Shaffer, Frederick
Carter, William	Wells, John
Ragin, Thomas	Wright, Robert
Reed, John	Young, Matthias

CRAWFORD COUNTY

Black, Alexander	Pendock, Samuel
Chapin, Samuel	Pierson, James
Denbo, Elijah	Reed, Thomas
Kemp, Reuben	Williams, Constant

Wright, Jeremiah

DAVIESS COUNTY
WHITE RIVER CHAPTER

Allen, John	Cannon, James
Baldwin, William	Chapman, William

Chumblay, John
Culbertson, Josiah
Fuller, William
Hammond, Job
Horrall, William
Hunter, John

Kilgore, Charles, Jr.
Lashley, George
Peachee, Bejamin
Scudder, John A.
Tisdale, Cudbard
Veale, James Carr

Wallace, John

DEARBORN COUNTY
COL. ARCHIBALD LOCHRY CHAPTER

Abell, John
Bailey, Lewis
Baker, John
Bisbee, Charles
Blasdel, Jacob
Brasher, Henry
Calhoun, John
Case, John
Cherry, Aaron
Cook, Charles
Cooper, John
Corbach, Peter
Crandon, John
Dickinson, Zebulin
Dunn, Hugh
Durham, John
Ehler, Michael
Elsbury, Jacob
Flake, Adam
Goodwin, John
Guard, Alexander
Hall, David
Haney, David
Hayes, Joseph
Hayes, Solomon
Henderson, William
Hendrickson, Moses
Hill, Eli

Judd, Job
Kelsey, Thomas
Kerr, William
Lawrence, Volantine
Loder, Daniel
Lindly, Moses
Leeds, James
Marsh, Samuel
Mason, George
Percival, Jabez
Pike, Zebulon
Plummer, Samuel
Porter, David
Powell, Nathan
Ramer, Henry
Rand, Thomas
Rich, Elijah
Scott, James
Shed, Daniel
Slanson, Ezra
Smithers, William
Stone, Samuel
Taylor, Jacob
Tower, Gideon
Welch, Daniel
Whetstone, Daniel
White, William
Wright, Robert

DECATUR COUNTY
LONE TREE CHAPTER

Alley, Samuel
Barnes, Elijah

Boyer, John
Collins, Josiah

Demoss, John
Dogan, Jeremiah J.
Donnell, Thomas
Dunkan, Edward
Falconbury, Jacob
Foster, James
Gosnell, Benjamin
Gray, John
Horton, Thomas
King, George
Lee, Joseph

Lloyd, Samuel
Lovejoy, Samuel
Meek, Thomas
Menefee, Spencer
Montgomery, Hugh
Pemberton, John
Piles, Elijah
Pritchard, John
Robbins, William
Weston, Levi
Yarbaugh, John

DELAWARE COUNTY
PAUL REVERE CHAPTER

Dougherty, William
Gilbert, Sewell
Pollen, Willam

Wallace, Benjamin
Whicker, William
Williams, William

DUBOIS COUNTY
DUBOIS COUNTY CHAPTER

Adams, Luther
Anderson, William
Harbison, James

Hills, John
Powers, Lewis
Rodman, Hugh, Sr.

Stillwell, Richard

ELKHART COUNTY
WILLIAM TUFFS CHAPTER

Cathcart, John
Denny, Walter

Leer, Jacob
Proctor, John

Tuffs, William

FAYETTE COUNTY
JOHN CONNER CHAPTER

Byrd, John
Conner, Philomen
Ellis, Benjamin
Garretson, John
Gillam, Jonathan
Goodlander, Henry or Jacob
Harry, Charles
Johnson, Othniel

Justice, James
Kimmer, Nicholas
Milner, Amos
McCormick, John
Pearce, Benjamin
Perin, Lemuel
Pigman, Jesse
Roots, Benajah Gurnsey

Seward, Samuel
Shaw, Jonathan

Sleeth, Alexander
Wright, James

FLOYD COUNTY
PIANKESHAW CHAPTER

Bateman, William
Bell, Joseph
Boyll, Charles
Buckman, Benjamin
Chesshire, John B.
Cole, Jacob
Dauchy, Jeremiah
Deal, Daniel
Fannin, Daniel
Floyd, Abraham
Fowler, Joshua
Garretson, Jacob

Gratsty, George
Hiested, Abraham
Ingram, Andrew
Jones, Epaphras
Jones, Richard Lord
Poindexter, Gabriel
Smith, Asa
Smith, Reuben
Steelman, John
Stewart, James, Jr.
Stodard, Philo
Toney, Jesse

Wells, William

FOUNTAIN COUNTY
OUIBACHE CHAPTER
RICHARD HENRY LEE CHAPTER
VEEDERSBURG CHAPTER

Bake, John
Birch, Thomas
Blue, John
Cook, Isaac
Davis, Enos
Gunsallis, John
Mosier, Tobias

McConnell, Hugh
Osborne, William
Pearson, Mahlon
Redden, George
Rosseau, Antoine
Stotts, Michael
Ward, William

Youngblood, Jacob

FRANKLIN COUNTY
TWIN FORKS CHAPTER

Adair, James
Alley, John
Barrickman, Jacob
Cooksey, Zachariah
Cotton, William
Curry, Thomas
Deakins, James

Eads, Henry
Fordyce, Henry
Fordyce, James
Glidewell, Robert
Gray, David
Griner, Peter
Jackson, Andrew

John, Jehu
Kever, James
Masters, John
Myers, Jacob
Nithercut, William
Portlock, John
Reynolds, John
Samuels, Gilbert
Seal, Joseph
Shirk, Andrew
Skinner, Thomas
Sliker, Lucas
Smith, Richard

Snow, Lemuel
Stout, Job
Taylor, Jacob
Templeton, Robert
Trusler, James
Tullis, Michael
Updike, Isaac
VanWinkle, John
Vincent, John
Wiggins, William
Winchell, Robert Ruggles
Winship, Jabez Lathrop
Woodworth, Dyer

FULTON COUNTY
MANITOU CHAPTER

Johnson, John

Lane, Samuel

GIBSON COUNTY
GEN. JOHN GIBSON CHAPTER

Archer, Robert
Bell, Thomas
Grigsby, Moses
Holbrook, George, Sr.
Jerauld, Dr. Gorton
Kimbal, Jesse
Lucas, Francis
Montgomery, Samuel
Montgomery, Thomas
McEntire, William

Neely, Joseph
Pritchett, John
Redman, Aaron
Sample, Thomas
Simpson, ———
Smith, James
Stilwell, David
Wheeler, James
Witherspoon, John
Woods, Joseph

GRANT COUNTY
GENERAL FRANCIS MARION CHAPTER

Campbell, James
Grimes, William

Sudeth, Isaac
Ven Devanter, Barnabas

GREEN COUNTY

Abbott, John
Blevins, James
Burnett, Joshua
Chaney, John

Clenny, William
Ellis, Robert
Ferguson, Thomas
Lang, Francis

Lawrence, Joseph
Lemon, Matthias
May, Abraham
Rainbolt, Adam

Woodworth, Daniel

Reany, Joseph
Storm, John
Slucer, William
Westfall, Cornelius

HAMILTON COUNTY

Abney, George
Cutts, William

Torrons, Samuel

Hair, John
Holloway, Levi

HANCOCK COUNTY

Childers, Mosby

Hatton, William

HARRISON COUNTY
HOOSIER ELM CHAPTER

Acre, Philip
Allin, John
Applegate, Garrett
Armstrong, George
Baldwin, John
Bennett, Joshua
Blunt, Andrew
Boone, Squire, Jr.
Case, James
Charley, George
Claine, John
Cooper, Michael
Cromer, John
Deatrick, Peter
Funk, Henry
Gaither, John
Gardner, John
Gilmore, Alexander
Grant, Daniel
Hogan, Prosser
Hunter, Patrick
Irvin, Samuel
Johnson, Henson
Kirkham, Robert
Keithley, John

Lefler, George
Lemmon, John
Long, John
Lunsford, Mason
Madden, William
Mannon, John
Marsh, William
Mitchell, James
Payton, Lewis
Pell, William
Purcill, Lawrence
Ransom, Isreal
Reed, Joseph
Reneau, Thomas
Sampson, William
Sappenfield, Michael
Shuck, Philip
Sipes, Daniel
Smith, Edward
Steinsuffert, Henry
Sterrit, Stewart
Stine, Philip
Trout, Anthony David
Vandeventer, Peter
Weaver, Philip

Williams, Isaac

16

HENDRICKS COUNTY
WAPAKEWA CHAPTER

Barnes, Richard
Faucett, John
Fitzimmons, Thomas
Flathers, Edward
Florence, William
Garrison, Joel
Harding, Thomas
Higgins, Daniel

Jones, Matthew
Lawrence, Isaac
Masten, Mathias
Miller, Mordecai
Ramsay, William
Turpin, Obedieth
Vanarsdall, Lawrence
Wiley, William

HENRY COUNTY
MAJOR HUGH DINWIDDIE CHAPTER
SARA WINSTON HENRY CHAPTER

Colturn, Revel
Conway, Richard
Craig, Rodrick
Dille, Caleb
Dunn, Aaron
Harper, Ebenezer
Healey, Hugh
Hedrick, Philip
Hilman, Thomas
Hubbell, John

Ice, Andrew
Isham, George J.
Keesling, John
Lee, John
Leonard, Nathaniel
Long, Christopher
Morris, Jacob
Rinker, George
Simmons, Joel
Wimmer, Jacob

HOWARD COUNTY
GENERAL JAMES COX CHAPTER

Gullion, John O.

HUNTINGTON COUNTY
HUNTINGTON CHAPTER

Mitchell, Elijah

JACKSON COUNTY
GEN. JACOB BROWN CHAPTER

Benton, David
Boas, Henry
Breneman, Christian
Byarlay, Michael
Chambers, William
Daniel, Buckner

Downing, Michael
Edwards, John
Guffy, James
Hagan, Charles
Johnson, David
Keiphart, George

Lockman, Vincent
McCormick, John
Phelps, Asahel
Prather, Thomas
Walker, Obadiah

Ross, Daniel
Scott, Benjamin
Shuemaker, Leonard
Sparks, James

JASPER COUNTY
GENERAL VAN RENSSELAER CHAPTER

Moore, George

JAY COUNTY
MISSISSINEWA CHAPTER

Collins, Joseph
Counkle, Michael

Mason, Peter
Phelps, Abijah

JEFFERSON COUNTY
JOHN PAUL CHAPTER

Bassett, Elisha
Baxter, James
Bell, James
Benefiel, George
Bishop, Job
Blake, George Kennett
Booth, John
Brown, Johnston
Brown, Patrick
Burk, George
Campbell, William
Chambers, Alexander
Chute, James
Chysman, Jacob
Cloyer, Henry
Conner, John
Cope, Jonathan, Sr.
Crawford, James
Custer, Arnold
Davis, Francis
Dickerson, John
Eastin, Philip
Edens, Elias
Fewell, Nathan
Field, John
George, Thomas
Glover, Thomas J.

Griffin, Ralph
Guess, George
Hall, William
Hillis, William
Jackson, James
Jackson, Solomon
Jameson, Thomas
Jines, Jacob
Jones, David
King, James
Lawler, Nicholas
Lott, John
May, John
Maxwell, Bezeleel
Medock, Emmanuel
McCasland, William
McClellan, Daniel, Sr.
McCune, Joseph
McKay, Alexander
McKay, Robert
McKay, Thomas
Patrick, Robert
Paul, John
Ramsay, Thomas
Rea, Robbin
Rowland, Thomas
Ryan, George

Ryker, John
Scott, John
Shannon, George
Spann, Jesse
Stewart, Charles
Suggan, James
Taylor, David
Taylor, Joseph
Thom, Joseph
Tilford, William

Tull, Handy
Vancleave, John
Vawter, Jesse
Wallace, Nathaniel
Welch, Samuel
West, John
Williams, Rememberance
Wilson, Nathaniel
Wilson, William
Wyatt, William

JENNINGS COUNTY

Butler, Joel
Carson, Walter
Conner, Philip
Courtney, Michael
Elliott, William
Grinstead, John
Harraway, Owen
Hill, Thomas
Hood, William
Howlett, William
Hughes, John
Hurlbut, Caleb
Johnson, Philip

Kendrick, Heth
Kyser, Frederick
Messerve, William
McGannon, Darby
McGill, Robert
New, Jethro
Smith, Samuel
Spencer, Amasa
Stagg, John
Story, John
Thomas, Evan
Watts, Mason
Wilkerson, Joseph

Wright, James

JOHNSON COUNTY
ALEXANDER HAMILTON CHAPTER

Adams, David
Barnett, John Perry
Bell, Nathaniel
Carr, James
Carrol, Bartholomew
Hammer, John
Hanks, Abner
Harrell, Jeremiah

Harris, Joshua
Isreal, John
Jacobs, Samuel
Nay, Samuel
Parr, John
Parr, Mathias
Poe, John
Smith, Thomas

KNOX COUNTY
FRANCIS VIGO CHAPTER

Alton, John
Anderson, James
A'Sturgus, Minard
Baird, Thomas

Boneaux, Pierre
Bonneau, Charles
Bowman, Joseph
Brouillette, Michell

Buntin, Robert
Busseron, Francois
Cardinal, Nichlas
Catt, George
Catt, Philip
Chambers, Alexander
Claycomb, Frederick
Cuerre, Pierre
Danis, Honoré
Decker, John, Sr.
Decker, Joseph
Decker, Luke
Dunn, Samuel
Fitzgerald, Charles
Ford, William
Godere, Louis
Grimard, Pierre
Henry, Moses
Holmes, William
Huffman, John
Jennings, Augustin
Johnson, James
Knight, Moses
Langdon, Daniel, Jr.
Languedoc, Charles La Coste Dit
LeGrand, Gabriel Christopher
LeGras, Jean Marie Philippe
Lindsay, William
Mahle, Frederick
Merry, Cornelius

Miller, Abraham
McAnelly, Peter
McClure, Daniel
McClure, George
McClure, John
McClure, William
McCord, William
McCoy, Robert
McKinzey, Jesse
Pagé, Guillaume
Piety, Thomas
Plough, Jacob
Polk, Charles
Purcell, Jonathan
Purcell, William
Racine, Francois
Setzer, John
Shannon, William
Snapp, George
Snyder, John
Snyder, Leonard R.
Snyder, William
Stork, John
Thompson, John
Thorn, Michael, Jr.
Turpin, Francois
Vanderburgh, Henry
Vigo, Francis
Welton, Jonathan
Young, Jaret

LA GRANGE COUNTY
LA GRANGE DE LAFAYETTE CHAPTER

Cowan, David

Young, Morgan

Harding, Micajah

LAKE COUNTY
CALUMET CHAPTER
JULIA WATKINS BRASS CHAPTER
MARGARET BRYANT BLACKSTONE CHAPTER
OBADIAH TAYLOR CHAPTER
POTTAWATOMIE CHAPTER

Taylor, Obadiah

LA PORTE COUNTY
ABIJAH BIGELOW CHAPTER
MIRIAM BENEDICT CHAPTER

Bigelow, Abijah
Otis, Edward

Wheeler, Simeon

Smith, Ezekiel
Van Dalsem, Henry

LAWRENCE COUNTY
JOHN WALLACE CHAPTER

Boone, Jeremiah
Boyles, David
Boyd, John
Burton, John Pleasant
Carlton, Ambrose
Evans, Edward
Fleetwood, Isaac
Haggerty, William
Hall, Robert
Hammersley, John
Henderson, John
Herring, Isaac

Hurt, James, Jr.
Jennings, Isreal
Miller, Henry
Mitchell, Abraham
Post, Ebenezer
Reid, Alexander
Short, John
Smith, John Andrew
Todd, Thomas
Williams, Richard
Wilson, James
Younger, Joshua

MADISON COUNTY
KIKTHEWENUND CHAPTER

Hobaugh, Philip
Mingle, John

Richmond, Nathaniel
Wall, William

MARION COUNTY
CAROLINE SCOTT HARRISON CHAPTER
CORNELIA COLE FAIRBANKS CHAPTER
GENERAL ARTHUR ST. CLAIR CHAPTER
IRVINGTON CHAPTER
JONATHAN JENNINGS CHAPTER

Bryan, Samuel
Carr, Robert
Dickerson, Robert
Dobbins, James
Foster, Samuel
George, John
Hall, Edward
Harding, Ede

Harding, Henry
Hume, John
Linn, Patrick
Mitchell, John
Monroe, Alexander
Morrow, John
Murphy, Butler
McClure, Robert.

Newland, Harrod
Ray, Jonathan
Reddick, William

Smith, Hezekiah
Taff, James
White, Robert

Wilson, Isaac

MARTIN COUNTY

Demoss, Andrew
Hunt, Josiah

Raney, Jeremiah
Voorhees, Garret

MIAMI COUNTY
NINETEENTH STAR CHAPTER

Martindale, William

Rector, Charles

Wiseman, James

MONROE COUNTY
BLOOMINGTON CHAPTER

Alexander, Agnes Brewster
Armstrong, Alexander
Back, John
Blain, James
Campbell, John
Dowell, George
Dunn, Elinor Brewster
Ferguson, Andrew
Hall, Moses
Henderson, Joseph
Hooke, George

Irvin, Jennette Brewster
Leabo, Isaac
Mathers, William
Parks, George
Price, Thomas
Rogers, Henry
Ross, Thomas
Roush, Joseph
Sanders, Henry
Van Buskirk, Isaac
Weir, Markham

MONTGOMERY COUNTY
DOROTHY Q CHAPTER

Alexander, Joseph
Bower, Andrew
Bunn, Barnes
Foster, Alexander
Fruits, George

Gregory, Samuel
Hardy, John
Mason, Thomas
Miller, Jacob
Simms, Presley

Stonebraker, Sebastian

MORGAN COUNTY

Baker, George
Cutler, Benjamin
Duke, John
Graves, Francis

Hight, Thomas
Jones, Williamson
Kellar, Devault
Kelso, Alexander, Jr.

King, Cornelius
Lacy, Elijah
Orme, Charles
Utterback, Benjamin

Steele, John
Townsend, William
Tramel, Sampson

NOBLE COUNTY
FRANCES DINGMAN CHAPTER

Galloway, Joseph

Prentice, Nathaniel

OHIO COUNTY

Dixon, John
Elliot, John
Fulton, John
Fulton, Samuel
Losey, Moses
Miller, Noah
Ward, Timothy

North, Lot
Ricketts, Robert
Robbins, Ephraim
Rollins, Hannaniah
Saurman, Peter
Turner, Robert

ORANGE COUNTY
LOST RIVER CHAPTER

Atkinson, Thomas
Bowling, Joseph
Case, William
Chandler, William
Duncan, George
Henton, George H.
Irvine, William
Lewis, David
Lindley, Jonathan
Moore, William
Murphy, James
McKinney, Alexander, Sr.
Wilson, Joseph

McKinney, David
Nichols, Joshua
Pinnick, James
Reed, David
Reed, Joshua
Reiley, John
Shields, James
Shively, Henry
Sparling, George
Urton, Peter
Wells, Joseph
Wells, Nathaniel

OWEN COUNTY

Ashbrook, Thomas
Asher, Bartlett
Bryant, James
Carpenter, John
Clements, David
Evans, Andrew
Fortner, Emanuel

Greenwood, Philip
Hopper, John
Kelley, Joshua
List, John
Moderell, Adam
McCullough, John
Newell, Samuel

Night, Jacob
Pearson, Shadrach

Withan, Peter

Snoddy, John
Wallace, John

PARK COUNTY
ESTABROOK CHAPTER

Allen, Isaac
Davis, William
Duncan, Jesse
Ephland, David
Evins, David
Hedger, Stephen Thomas
Hines, Jacobas
Judd, John

Lane, Larkin
Mitchell, William
Musgrove, Samuel
Shaw, James
Stringham, Daniel
Tucker, John
VanSante, John
Wilkins, George

PERRY COUNTY
LAFAYETTE SPRINGS CHAPTER

Alvey, Thomas Green
Avit, Richard
Bolin, Thomas
Connor, Terrence
Ewing, George

York, Jeremiah

Hiley, Abraham
Lamb, John
Lanman, James
Mallory, Lemuel
Weatherholt, Jacob

PIKE COUNTY
CRADLE OF LIBERTY CHAPTER

Arnold, Josiah
Black, William
Brenton, James
Chambers, John
Coonrad, John

Dedman, Samuel
Fisher, Isaac
Johnson, Robert
Mead, Thomas
Palmer, John

PORTER COUNTY
WILLIAM HENRY HARRISON CHAPTER

Batton, Henry

POSEY COUNTY
GENERAL THOMAS POSEY CHAPTER
NEW HARMONY CHAPTER

Bainbrook, Ezekiel
Black, James

Bradley, Cornelius
Calvin, Job

Carson, Charles
Gamble, David
Jaquess, Jonathan
McReynolds, Joseph
Palmer, William

Walker, John

Pelham, Dr. William
Price, Joseph
Price, Thomas
Rowe, George
Six, John

PUTNAM COUNTY
WASHBURN CHAPTER

Albion, William
Armstrong, Isaac
Banks, William
Bowen, Charles
Buck, John
Burnside, John
Cornell, William
Cunningham, Nathaniel
Denny, Samuel
Denny, William
Glazebrook, Julius
Hammer, George
Haslet, Samuel
Highnote, Philip
Jones, Thomas

LaFollette, Joseph
Mahorney, Benjamin
Moore, Samuel
McGahey, William
Norman, John
Piercy, Jacob
Rhoten, Thomas
Shepherd, William
Slavens, Isaiah
Stoner, Peter, Sr.
Tucker, Thomas
Walden, John, Sr.
Walls, John
Westfall, Jacob
Whitehead, Robert

RANDOLPH COUNTY
WINCHESTER CHAPTER

Amburn, Samuel L.
Borders, Christopher
Cline, William
Evans, John
Fitzgerald, William E.

Ward, Thomas

Kepler, John
Lumpkin, John
McKinney, Joseph
Porter, Eli
True, Arthur

RIPLEY COUNTY

Arnold, James
Babbs, John
Bassett, William
Baumgardner, Daniel
Beall, Ninian
Boldrey, John
Burchfield, John
Burchfield, Robert

Buskirk, John
Chapman, Lemuel
Collins, William
Cruzan, Benjamin
Davis, Philemon
Delap, James
Dowers, Conrad
Dowers, Jacob

Gibson, Wilbourne
Gookins, Samuel
Grimes, James
Hall, Benjamin
Hamilton, Benjamin
Hennegin, Joseph
Hodges, Richard
Johnson, James
Johnson, Roswell
Johnston, Thomas
Levi, Isaac
Lipperd, William
Mavity, William
Mitcheller, Jacob
Myers, Henry
McDonald, Joseph

MacMillen, Daniel
Newcomer, Peter
O'Neal, John
Overturf, Martin
Pendergast, Edward
Pennetent, John
Pratt, Jonathan
Rolff, James
Rutledge, Peter
Stevens, Samuel
Tucker, John, Sr.
VanBibber, Peter
Ward, John
Whittaker, John
Wilson, Ephraim
Wycoff, Jacob

RUSH COUNTY
RUSHVILLE CHAPTER

Aldridge, John Simpson
Berry, Joel
Brown, George
Brownlee, James
Caldwell, Robert
Carson, John
Cassady, Thomas
Clark, Ebenezer
Cox, Isaac
David, Henry
Finney, John
Gregg, Mathew
Groves, Robert
Hackleman, Jacob
Hite, Jacob, Sr.
Iles, Samuel
James, Thomas

Lane, James
LeGore, John
Lewis, John
Logan, Patrick
Mauzy, William
Miller, John
Mizner, Henry
Posey, Zephaniah
Reiley, John
Richey, Gilbert
Robinson, John, Sr.
Smith, Henry
Smith, Michael
Smith, William
Thomas, Henry
Tibbetts, George
Watson, John

Wyatt, John

SCOTT COUNTY

Clark, John
Dean, John
Harrod, William
Hopper, William

Kinney, Richard
Michell, Amasa
Parks, Hugh
Spader, Bergen

Spencer, Walter

SHELBY COUNTY
MARY MOTT GREEN CHAPTER

Applegate, Benjamin
Barlow, Lewis
Brown, Matthew
Christian, Allen
Cole, Benjamin
Daniel, William
Field, Ansel
Glidewell, William

Goodrich, Nathan
Gordon, Robert
Harsin, Garret
Hoskinson, Josiah
Miller, Edward
Pope, Samuel
Ray, Thomas
Thomas, John

Young, Philip

SPENCER COUNTY
SPIER SPENCER CHAPTER

Blair, Thomas
Briant, Zachariah
Chancellor, David
Davis, Lodowick
Hornback, Abraham
Jones, James

Jones, Thomas
Kelly, William
Overlin, William
Pollard, James
Rasor, Peter
Shaw, Henry

Turnham, Thomas

STEUBEN COUNTY
POKAGON CHAPTER

Rogers, Ethan

ST. JOSEPH COUNTY
MISHAWAKA CHAPTER
SCHUYLER COLFAX CHAPTER

Druliner, Frederick
Mead, John
Ranstead, Joseph

Roof, Peter
Ross, Isaac
Thompson, David

SULLIVAN COUNTY
NATHAN HINKLE CHAPTER

Armstrong, Alexander
Bailey, Alexander
Balch, James
Batson, Mordicia
Bedwell, Robert

Bemis, Levi
Dougherty, William
Handly, Handy, Jr.
Hart, Adam
Hinkle, Nathan

Hinkle, Wendle
Hopewell, John
Houck, Michael
Hunt, Mesech
Johnson, Abraham
Mayfield, Michajah
McCammon, Matthew

Neeley, Joseph
Plough, Albert
Purcell, Edward
Ransford, Joseph
Reid, James
Spence, James
Williams, James

SWITZERLAND COUNTY

Ayres, Thomas
Bassett, Joseph
Bray, John
Burns, John
Coy, William
Critchfield, John
Cross, Ebenezer
Davis, David
Deisky, Leiman
DeWitt, William
Dickenson, Griffith
Dumont, Peter
Gullion, Robert
Hannis, Henry
Harris, Daniel
Harris, Robert
Heath, Daniel
Hufman, Henry
Humphrey, Ebenezer
Kelly, William
Lancaster, William
Landers, Kimbrow
Lewis, Thomas
Magruder, Norman Bruce

Moore, Roderick
Morgan, Nathan
Mounts, Thomas
Norris, Daniel
North, Thomas
Parkinson, Abraham
Peak, Nathan
Porter, Thomas
Protsman, John
Reamer, David
Ricketts, Nathan
Robert, John
Robinson, Winthrop
Rogers, Stephen
Scudder, Abner
Shadday, John
Shaver, John
Shupe, John
Smyth, Philip D.
Stepleton, Andrew
Todd, Joseph
Turner, Smith
Warden, Barnard
Wilson, Michael

TIPPECANOE COUNTY
GENERAL DE LAFAYETTE CHAPTER

Crose, Philip
Dawson, Edward
Herbert, Thomas
Kesler, Jacob
Lane, Jacob

Lee, David
Miller, Henry
Morris, Cornelius
Rank, George
Stingley, George

White, Nathaniel

UNION COUNTY
BENJAMIN DUBOIS CHAPTER

Colson, James
Davis, Jonathan
Folger, Latham
Fosher, Daniel
Hanna, Robert
Harvey, Henderson
Haynes, Richard
Logan, William

Meredith, Samuel
Murphy, William
McMillon, Rowley
Ogden, Jedediah
Rose, Ezekiel
Rose, William
Sims, William
Thomas, David

Ward, Daniel

VANDERBURG COUNTY
VANDERBURG CHAPTER

Stinson, Elijah

VERMILLION COUNTY
BROUILLET CHAPTER

Coleman, Jacob
Groendyke, John
Hamman, Abraham
Hannaman, William
Mack, Richard

Malone, Francis
Stone, Nimrod H.
White, Abraham
Williams, James
Zabirskie, Christian

VIGO COUNTY
FORT HARRISON CHAPTER

Caldwell, John
Dickerson, Walter
Dixon, Joseph
Hall, Laban
Hamilton, John
Jeffries, Gowin

McDaniel, William
Patrick, Joshua
Pomeroy, Ethan
Ray, William
Solsby, Daniel
Stevens, Isaac

Thomas, William

WABASH COUNTY
FRANCES SLOCUM CHAPTER

Burdge, Samuel

WARREN COUNTY

Beckett, Humphrey
Biddlecomb, Richard

Dixon, George
High, Jacob

High, John
High, Henry

Pearson, Thomas
Wilkerson, David

WARRICK COUNTY

Alexander, John
Baker, John
Campbell, William
Cook, Daniel
Frisbie, Jonah
Hinman, Asabel

Musgrave, Samuel
Osborn, William
Reed, George
Richardson, Thomas
Stucky, John Frederick
Williams, William D.

WASHINGTON COUNTY
CHRISTOPHER HARRISON CHAPTER

Alvis, Jesse
Beck, George
Berry, George
Boyden, Jonathan
Brewer, Benjamin
Bridgewater, Levi
Callaway, Micajah
Chambers, Nathaniel
Colglazier, David
Davis, Enoch
Denny, Robert
DePauw, Charles
Flowers, Thomas
Garrison, James
Grace, William
Hole, Daniel

Johnson, Archibald
Keyte, John
Langdon, Philip
Mahoney, James
Martin, Jacob
Moore, William
McKnight, John
McPheeters, John
Parr, Arthur
Payne, John
Smith, Thomas
Still, Murphy
Trinkle, Christopher
Vest, Samuel
Williams, John
Wood, John

Wright, William

WAYNE COUNTY
RICHMOND CHAPTER

Alexander, William
Ashby, Bladen
Benbow, Edward
Bishop, Benjamin
Bonine, Daniel
Boyd, Samuel
Bradbury, David
Bundy, Christopher
Burk, John

Burrows, Thomas
Cain, John
Case, Isaiah
Commons, Robert
Cook, William
Cull, Hugh
Dougan, John
Eperly, George
Fell, John

Forrey, Jacob
Fox, Stephen
Gay, John
Hancock, Joseph
Hendershot, Abraham
Holman, George
Hoover, Andrew
Jester, Nimrod
Jones, Francis
Kepler, Matthias
King, Jesse
Ladd, Joseph
Lamb, James

Marlatt, Abraham
Meek, Jacob
McWhinney, Thomas
Railsback, David
Reed, Isaac
Robbins, John
Rue, Richard
Stevenson, James
Taylor, Ignatius
Townsend, John
Ulrich, John
Walker, Samuel
Wasson, Joseph

IN INDIANA

Asher, William
Buchanan, George
Depositer, John
Flynn, Thomas
Ferguson, Samuel
Fiscus, Adam
Ghormley, Joseph
Heaton, Ebenezer
Hoffman, Henry

Keith, Alexander
Minnear, Abraham
Parks, Samuel
Reddington, Daniel
Shores, Christian
Swaim, Isaac
Thurston, Jason
Wardell, Robert Fowler
Way, Isaac

Wilson, William

LIST OF ABBREVIATIONS

States, Months and Military Titles as usual.

B. or b.	born
Ch.	child or children
Co.	county
CO.	company
D. or d.	died
M. or m.	married
Pri.	private
Regt.	regiment
Twp.	township
w.	wife

RECORDS OF REVOLUTIONARY SOLDIERS

ABELL (ABLE), JOHN   Dearborn County
Born—About 1758.
Service—9 mos. as a pri. in Capt. Hollinshead's CO., Col. Shreve's 2nd N. J. Regt.
Proof—Pension claim S. 35760. Borne on pension roll as John Able. He signed John Abell.
Married—Elizabeth ——, aged 59 in 1820.

ABBOTT, JOHN   Green County
Born—Feb. 16, 1755, Dorchester Co., Maryland.
Service—Enlisted June 1, 1781, while a resident of Guilford Co., N. C., served as pri. in Capt. William Little's CO., Col. Dixon's N. C. Regt. and in Capt. Rudolph's CO., Col. Lee's Regt. Was in the battles of Eutaw Springs and Dorchester, S. C., and was discharged June 1, 1782.
Proof—Pension claim S. 32089.
Died—1836. Buried in Bloomfield Cemetery. Government Marker.

ABNEY, GEORGE   Hamilton County
Born—Feb. 10, 1752, Lunenburg, now Halifax Co., Virginia.
Service—While residing within 18 miles of Ninety-Six, S. C., he enlisted July 3, 1775, served as pri. in Capt. Henry Foster's CO., Col. LeRoy Hammond's S. C. Regt. He was marched through the mountains to the head of Savannah River against the Indians who were then invading the frontiers of S. C., and while on this tour was in two engagements with the Indians and was discharged after having served 4 mos. Later served as pri. and 2nd Sergeant in Capt. Henry Foster's CO., Col. LeRoy Hammond's S. C. Regt., length of this tour not less than 12 mos. Enlisted in 1780 or 81 as pri. under Capts. William Butler, Samuel Sinfield and Tolls in the S. C. troops, scouting and ranging against the Tories. In the siege of Augusta and Ninety-Six and was discharged after having served on this tour 16 mos.
Proof—Pension claim S. 16591.
Died—Last payment of pension was made April 5, 1838. In 1822 he referred to his wife, then aged 66, but does not give name.

ACRE, PHILIP   Harrison County
Born—Aug. 20, 1754, Pennsylvania.
Service—Drafted Frederick Co., Md., in CO. of Capt. George Perry,
    Regt. of Col. Tim Greene. Served 3 mos. Was not at any time
    with regular troops. Again drafted for 3 mos.
Proof—Pension claim W. 9690.
Died—Aug. 8, 1843, in Harrison Co., Indiana.
Married—March 14, 1788, to Catherine ———. Ch. Anna Acckerin
    (German spelling), b., Dec. 15, 1789; Maria Magdelina Acckerin;
    Anna Barbara Acckerin, b., Sept. 12, 1790.

ADAIR, JAMES   Franklin County
Born—May 8, Bucks Co., Pennsylvania.
Service—Name appears on a return for the regiments of the Ninety-Six
    District, S. C.—showing the amount due him was 566 pounds cur-
    rency. Return made by Col. Robert Anderson.
Proof—Historical Commission of S. C.
Died—March 23, 1831. Buried in Old Brookville Cemetery. Stone.
    S. A. R. bronze marker placed by Judge Charles Remy, a descendant.
Married—Rebecca Montgomery (1751-1835). Ch. Margaret 1784-1866,
    m. John Ewing; Rebecca 1786-1875, m. James Remy; John 1787, m.
    first to Lucy Trusler, second to Susanna Thomas, third to Sally
    Trusler; Jean, m. ——— Eads; Joseph; Isaac 1792-1852, m. Jane
    Holland; Lucretia 1795-1870, m. John Wildridge; Benjamin.
Collected by Mrs. Z. R. Peterson, Detroit, Michigan.

ADAMS, DAVID   Johnson County
Born—1762, in Donegal, Ireland.
Service—Drafted from York County, Penn., in August, 1780, served
    in Capt. Coverhafer's CO., under Major Bailey. Served from Nov.
    1780 to Feb. 1781, as a substitute for Jacob Staley in the same CO.
Proof—Pension claim.
Died—May 1, 1839, in Morgan Co. Indiana, where he had lived but is
    buried across the county line in Johnson Co. in the Bethlehem
    cemetery. Family stone.
Married—Mary———. Ch. Henry; John; Hugh; Jacob; Elizabeth; Mary;
    Tenna; Isabelle.
Collected by Mrs. I. E. Tranter, 448 E. Madison Street, Franklin, Ind.

ADAMS, LUTHER   Dubois County
Born—About 1753, England.
Service—Private in Houghton's CO., P. Denny's Mass. Militia. Also in
    Capt. Jothan Houghton's CO., Col. Samuel Denny's 2nd. Regt.,
    Gen. Fellows' brigade. Enlisted Oct. 24, 1779, and discharged
    Dec. 1, 1779, at Claverack. Also with West Point men 1781.

Proof—Mass. S. & S. of Rev. War, p. 62; Muster Roll of Soldiers
N. H. 1781; U. S. War Documents; N. H. War Record.
Died—At age of 94. Buried Wilhoits Graveyard, 2 miles W. of Jasper,
Ind. Government marker placed by Luther A. Parker.
Collected by George W. Wilson, Historian of Dubois Co. Indiana.

ALBION, WILLIAM   Putnam County
Born—1764, Westmoreland Co., Penn.
Service—Private and Ensign in Capt. John Van Meter's Westmoreland
    CO., Penn. Troops.
Proof—D. A. R. No. 107680 and No. 139622.
Died—1849, near Greencastle, Ind.
Married—Jane —— (1777-1839). Ch. William; Joseph 1794-1863, m. Rosannah Sheeks.

ALCORN, GEORGE   Bartholomew County
Born—March 25, 1760, Pedee River, N. C.
Service—Enlisted Fairfield Dist. S. C. Volunteered 1780 in militia under
    Capt. Thomas Hanna, served 10 days. 1781, under Capt. Thomas,
    Col. Hammond, served 2 mos., went to Augusta. Later served 3
    mos. under Capt. Davis.
Proof—Pension claim S. 31516.
Died—Dec. 27, 1833. Buried west of Columbus.

ALDRIDGE, JOHN SIMPSON   Rush County
Born—Feb. 9, 1761.
Service—Enlisted 1776, 1777, in Vir., now Greene Co., Penn., and served
    under Capt. James Hook, Col. Russell's 13th Vir. Regt.; Capt.
    Uriah Springer, Col. John Gibson's 9th Vir. Regt.
Proof—Pension claim W. 9698.
Died—Nov. 17, 1842. Buried on his farm in Anderson Twp. Name appears on the bronze tablet in the Rush Co. Court House, Rushville, Ind.
Married—1783, Mary Lakin (1760-1843). Ch. Joseph Lakin 1784-1815;
    Rachel Plumm, b. 1786, m. —— Stiers; Rauzy, b. 1789, m. Sarah
    ——; Eliza, b. 1791, m. Rafe Stiers; Mary b. 1793, m. —— Smith;
    Sarah b. 1795; John b. 1798; Delilah b. 1799, m. —— Layton;
    Erasmus b. 1801; Nathan b. 1803.

ALDRIDGE, JOHN   Boone County
Born—1762.
Service—Enlisted Westmoreland Co., Penn. June 1781. Served with
    Penn. Troops as drummer and private under Capt. Holmes and
    Thomas Stokley. Discharged July 1783.

Proof—Pension claim W. 25342.
Died—Feb. 2, 1835, in Boone Co., Ind.
Married—Elizabeth Wees. In 1855 widow was living in Boone Co., Ind., with grandson, whose name was not given.
Collected by Mrs. Minnie McClaine, 210 W. Royal Street, Lebanon, Indiana.

ALEXANDER, AGNES BREWSTER   Monroe County
Born—April 25, 1763, Virginia.
Service—A Patriot. Aided soldiers with food, clothing and bullets.
Proof—Revolutionary Services of the Brewster Sisters by Ann S. Alexander.
Died—Aug. 25, 1830. Buried Cemetery on Indiana University Campus, Bloomington, Ind. Stone.
Married—William Alexander. Ch. William; James; John; Robert; Henry; Rachel; Mary.
Collected by Bloomington Chapter D. A. R.

ALEXANDER, JOHN   Warrick County
Born—1759 N. C.
Service—Drafted as pri. in cavalry N. C., commanded by Capt. James Stinson, Col. Samuel Isaac, at Salisbury. Volunteered for 3 mos.; for 1 mo. in Vir.
Proof—Pension claim R. 89. Soldier allowed pension. Widow's application rejected because marriage occurred after service.
Died—June 2, 1842.
Married—1795, Susannah Katharine ——. Ch. Randolph.

ALEXANDER, JOSEPH   Montgomery County
Born—1756 County of Tyrone, Ireland.
Service—Enlisted about Christmas 1777, under Capt. Hugh White, Penn. Militia. Northumberland Co. Penn. Was at Philadelphia, Trenton, and Princeton. Was in 10 skirmishes in tour of Ash Swamp, Camrons Hills. Was elected ensign on this tour. Enlisted in fall of 1778 under Capt. James McMahon of Penn. Militia. Discharged spring of 1779. Served again in 1779 for 5 mos.
Proof—Pension claim S. 32091.
Death—Last payment of pension made to soldier on March 6, 1838, at which time he certified he had lived in Indiana for six years. No family data given on pension application.

ALEXANDER, WILLIAM   Wayne County
Born—1752, North Carolina.
Service—Enlisted in Carlisle, Penn., in Dec. 1775, as a pri. in Capt. James Wilson's CO., Col. Irvine's Penn. Regt. Was in battle of Three Rivers and discharged March, 1777.

Proof—Pension claim W. 9697.
Died—Jan. 5 or 6, 1821.
Married—1789, Margaret Cull. Ch. William Jr., m. Elizabeth Parks.
Collected by Mrs. Glenn Beeson, Cambridge City, Indiana.

ALLEN, ISAAC   Park County
Born—March 15, 1755, Scott Co., Virginia.
Service—Pri. under George Rogers Clark—16 mos. 18 days. He received 33 pounds and 4 shillings. Enlisted again May 30, 1780, served until Nov. 30, 1781, under Capt. Richard Brasheas, Col. John Montgomery.
Proof—Ill. Reg. and the Western Army—Doc. No. 32, under the command of George Rogers Clark. Doc. No. 12, p. 1, on file in Vir. State Library.
Died—Dec. 15, 1831, Fountain Co., but buried in Wolf Cemetery, Sugar Creek Twp. Park Co., Ind. Stone.
Married—First to Frances Petitt. Ch. Thomas; Isam; David; Jane; William; Anna M. second to Mrs. Poplett. Ch. James; Isaac; Peggy.
Collected by Richard Henry Lee Chapter at Covington, and Veedersburg Chapter D. A. R. at Veedersburg.

ALLEN, JOHN   Daviess County
Born—1760, Hunterdon Co., New Jersey.
Service—Pri. in Capt. John Philip's 1st CO., Col. David Chambers' 3rd Regt. Hunterdon Co., N. J. Militia, Oct. 20, 1777.
Proof—Stykers' Official Register of the Officers and Men of N. J., p. 487.
Died—1837. Buried Sugarland Cemetery, N. of Washington, Ind. Government marker placed by White River Chapter D. A. R.
Married—First, about 1787, Rachel Wykoff. Ch. Hannah, m. Robert Wykoff and Elijah Burnett and John Rhodarmel; Sarah, m. Robert D. Majors; William b. 1792, m. Elizabeth Eads; John, m. Emily Manning; Rachel, m. Charles Wildridge and Zachariah Wood; Firman; Moses b. 1800, m. Mary Small; Mary b. 1802; m. Emanuel Gephart; Charity b. 1804, m. Dudley Johnson. Soldier, m. second to Sarah Jones and third to Mary Bruce.
Collected by Mrs. Roy Bogner, Washington, Indiana.

ALLEY, JOHN   Franklin County
Born—July 8, 1764.
Service—Served as Spy with his brother-in-law, Samuel Porter, under Col. Alexander Barnett of Russell Co. Virginia—about 7 mos. Received 5 shillings Vir. Currency per day for his service.

Proof—Pension claim R. 152. Claim rejected because he did not serve by order of competent authority and in a military capacity for 6 mos.
Died—After 1841. Probably buried in Butler Twp.

ALLEY, SAMUEL   Decatur County
Born—June 25, 1761 Henrico Co., Virginia.
Service—Enlisted in May 1777, served 4 mos. as pri. under Capt. McLanahan (mcClanahan) and Snody in Vir. Troops against the Indians at Moore Fort. Enlisted June 1, 1779, for 1 mo. in Capt. Alexander Ritchie's Vir. CO., against Indians in Powell's Valley. Oct. 1, 1782, enlisted from Ky. in Capt. Adam's CO., Col. Benjamin Logan's Vir. Regt. served 5 weeks
Proof—Pension claim W. 9694.
Died—Aug. 12, 1847, in Shelby Co. Ind. Buried in Alley Cemetery near Milford, Decatur Co. Stone.
Married—1786, Mary Osborne (Osburn), died 1856. Ch. Jonathan b. 1787, m. Catherine ——; Doddridge b. 1788, m. Jane ——; Cyrus b. 1791, m. Charity Nelson; Thursey b. 1793, m. —— McCarty; Joydey b. 1795, m. —— Gant; Sampson b. 1797; Lanzel b. 1800, m. William Fowler; Elihu b. 1803; Azby C. b. 1806; Samuel b. 1808; Soloman b. 1810.
Collected by Mrs. H. S. McKee, Greensburg, Indiana.

ALLIN (ALLEN), JOHN   Harrison County
Born—1759.
Service—Name appears on records in office of Comptroller, Raleigh, N. C., as having received pay for military service. Served three tours in N. C. against the Indians.
Proof—Pension claim R. 135. Pension rejected because failure to prove 6 mos. service.
Died—Dec. 28, 1832, Harrison Co., Ind.
Married—Polly (Mary) —— in 1779, in Caswell N. C. Dau. Nancy, m. Francis Wright.

ALLSTOTT, JOHN   Clark County
Born—1755.
Service—Enlisted April 1776, Burke Co., Penn. in company of Capt. Lewis Farmer, for a term of 1 yr., 9 mos. In battles of Long Island, Brandywine, Germantown, and Trenton.
Proof—Pension claim W. 9695.
Died—Dec. 31, 1837, Clark Co., Ind.
Married—1783, Margaret Williams (1763-1845). Ch. Robert b. 1784; Jacob b. 1786; Elizabeth b. 1788; John b. 1789; Domel b. 1791; Nicholas b. 1793; Rease b. 1795; William b. 1801; Thomas b. 1808; Joseph b. 1810.

ALTON (ALLTON), JOHN   Knox County
Born—May 22, 1759, Maryland.
Service—Pri. Rangers of the Frontiers 1778-83, in Capt. John Dean's
   CO.; pri. Continental Line, Westmoreland Co. Militia; pri. 8th
   class under Capt. Wm. Parr's CO., Sept. 15, 1782; Also Capt. John
   Wall's 2nd. Battalion, 1782.
Proof—Penn. Archives, 3rd Series, vol. 23, p. 321; 5th Series, vol. 4,
   pp. 428 and 734; 6th Series, vol. 2, pp. 68 and 52.
Died—July 18, 1823. Buried Alton cemetery, 6 miles from Vincennes.
Married—1784, Catherine Adams, b. 1764. Ch. Joseph (1785-1858) m.
   Rachel Jones; John b. 1799; Cynthia (1798-1867) m. David Richey;
   Mary, m. George Stipes; William, m. Jane ——; James b. 1815.
   All these names taken from Will and dates from cemetery.
Collected by Mrs. S. G. Davenport, Vincennes, Indiana.

ALVEY, THOMAS GREEN   Perry County
Born—About 1750.
Service—Enlisted for 3 yrs., April 24, 1778, to April 24, 1781, under Capt.
   Chew, Col. Ramsey's Regt. Md. Line Continental Establishment.
   Discharged at Annapolis, Md. In battles of Monmouth, Stony
   Point.
Proof—Pension claim S. 35766.
Died—Feb. 12, 1824, at Tobansport, Indiana.

ALVIS, JESSE   Washington County
Born—Aug. 1757.
Service—Pri. in Capt. Holman Rice's CO., Col. Francis Taylor's Regt.
   of Vir. Militia. Served from March 1778 to April 1780.
Proof—Pension claim S. 35765.
Died—After 1840. Buried Mt. Washington Cemetery near Pekin. Government marker.
Married—Mary Mallory. Ch. David; Patsy; Mary; Jesse.
Collected by Mrs. Mabel Johnson, Sullivan, Indiana.

AMBURN, SAMUEL L.   Randolph County
Born—May 4, 1765 or 1761, Philadelphia, Penn.
Service—Enlisted 1776, as substitute for his father, Jacob Amburn.
   Pri. in Capt. Stephen Bloom's CO., Col. Faris' Penn. Regt. In battle
   of Trenton. Served 6 mos. Enlisted 1777 as pri. in Capt. Henry
   Shipe's Penn. CO. In battles of Brandywine and Germantown.
   Was chosen captain of volunteers and as such served 15 mos.
Proof—Pension claim S. 32095.
Died—1860. Buried Union Cemetery, Stoney Creek Twp. Stone.

Children—Samuel (1789-1881). In 1853 five children were living in Indiana.
Collected by Mrs. James P. Goodrich, Winchester, Indiana.

ANDERSON, JAMES   Knox County
Born—Oct. 22, 1743, Delaware.
Service—He lived in the early part of the Revolution on the South Branch of the Potomac in Hampshire Co. Vir., and served at various times guarding the country and in pursuit of Tories, until 1780, when he moved near the Falls of the Ohio in Ky. Joined a company under Capt. Peter Sturges in Col. George Rogers Clark expedition. Assisted in building a Block House near Cincinnati, then marched against the Indians at Little Miami. He served in 1782, as sergeant in Capt. Peter Hines, CO., Col. George Rogers Clark. In 1786 was taken prisoner by the Shawnee Indians and held until purchased by a French trader who released him.
Proof—Pension claim S. 32096.
Died—April, 1835. Buried Anderson graveyard at Sandborn, Vigo Twp.
Married—Inez Lavarro (a Cuban). Had 5 ch. but only Rachel and James came to Indiana. Rachel b. Aug. 5, 1777, m. Thomas Anderson (no relation) and had Peggy b. 1796; Pressley b. 1806; James b. 1808; Thomas Jr. b. 1811; Lewis b. 1813; Clark b. 1817; Alexander b. 1822.
Collected by Mrs. S. G. Davenport, Vincennes, Indiana.

ANDERSON, WILLIAM   Dubois County
Born—Nov. 21, 1763, Penn.
Service—Muster Roll of 2nd. class 6th Battalion, Lancaster Co. Militia, on tour of duty at Lancaster, 1781.
Proof—Penn. Archives, Series V, vol. VII, pp. 578, 585.
Died—April 22, 1836. Buried Hobb's graveyard, Ireland, Ind. Stone and Government marker.
Married—Jane Bell (1771-1844). Ch. William Jr.; Thomas; Andrew; James; John; Matilda; Jane; Melissa; Lucinda.
Collected by George W. Wilson, Historian Dubois Co., Indiana.

ANDRE, JACQUE   Allen County
Service—Listed in a company of volunteers of Infantry in Vir. under Capt. Francois Busseron from Oct. 27, 1778, to Dec. 17, 1778. Later he went with George Rogers Clark to Kaskaskia. Later in 1780, he enlisted with Col. Augustus Motin de la Balm to march north to quell the Indians.
Proof—Wisconsin Historical Society, Drapers Papers 5-J-77-1780. Indiana Historical Society Papers; Vital Records of Vincennes.
Died—Killed Nov. 3, 1780, on banks of Aboite River, Allen Co.

Married—Josette Dumay. Ch. Therese, m. 1796 Michel Teraque; Pierre.
Collected by Mrs. T. J. Hindman, Fort Wayne, Indiana.

APPLEGATE, BENJAMIN   Shelby County
Born—About 1763.
Service—Enlisted April, 1779—Northampton Co., Penn., as pri. under
   Capt. Whetherly and Col. Spencer—N. J. Troops. Discharge
   signed by Gen. Washington.
Proof—Pension claim W. 9706.
Died—April 4, 1832, Shelby Co., Ind., according to statement made by
   widow in her application for pension.
Married—Phebe Grimes. Had 9 ch. Richard (oldest son); Catherine
   (oldest daughter); Benjamin; Hannah; John; James.

APPLEGATE, GARRETT   Harrison County
Born—Nov. 2, 1752, Berkeley Co., Vir.
Service—Enlisted May 30, 1778, for 3 mos. as pri. under Capt. Hall—
   8th Regt., in Sept. 1778, for 6 mos. under Capt. Isaac Pearce, Col.
   Joseph Beler. May 1, 1779, for 3 mos. under Capt. Zadick Wright,
   Col. Daniel Brodhead. Was in Gen. McIntosh's Campaign.
Proof—Pension claim—Inv. File 32098.
Died—Sept. 21, 1837. Probably buried Heth Twp.
Married—Mary Johnson. Ch. Isaiah, m. Hannah ——.

ARBUCKLE, THOMAS   Clark County
Born—May 2, 1747, Augusta Co., Vir.
Service—Enlisted in Botetourt Co., Vir. Served 15 days as Lieut. in
   Capt. George Givens' Vir. CO. in expedition against Indians at Big
   Island on Holston River. Enlisted April, 1780, for 6 mos. as pri.
   in Capt. John Bowles' CO., Col. Benjamin Logan's Vir. Regt. In
   battle with Indians at Pickaway. Enlisted 1782, in same CO. for
   6 mos. and was in battle at Big Miami. Was stationed at Whitley's
   Station, Ky.
Proof—Pension claim S. 16609; Family records of J. C. Jefferds, "Kanawha Drug Co.," Charleston, W. Vir.
Died—1843. Buried Adams graveyard, New Washington, Ind. (Last
   pension paid Sept. 4, 1843, to son John. Lived in Jefferson Co.,
   Ind., with son John, but buried across county line in Clark Co.)
   Stone.
Married—Elizabeth Lawrence. Ch. Ann, m. 1797, Henry James; Elizabeth, m. 1798, John Smith; Margaret, m. 1800, Daniel F. McKinney;
   John, m. 1801, Susanna Smith; Fanny, m. 1805, Samuel Lawrence,
   and 1815 Capt. James Arbuckle, and later Philip Rendenbaugh;
   Polly, m. 1808, James McCroskey; Sally, m. 1809, Robert Robertson.
Collected by John Paul Chapter D. A. R.

ARCHER, ROBERT   Gibson County
Born—1748, Chester District, S. C.
Service—Private in Capt. John Steele's CO. of Mounted Rangers, S. C.,
    for which service and the loss of a gray mare, the said State of
    S. C. paid.
Proof—Indent No. 577, Book P., in office of the S. C. Historical Commission.
Died—1818, Princeton, Indiana. Buried in Archer Cemetery.
Married—1775, Mary Steele (1749-1817). Ch. Thomas b. 1777, m. Mary
    McCalla; William b. 1779, m. Anna Peters; Mary b. 1782, m. Vincent Woods; Isabella b. 1784, m. George Taylor; Catherine b. 1786,
    m. Purnel Fisher; Margaret b. 1790, m. John McMillan; Nancy
    Agnes b. 1793, m. Robert Milburn; Rosa b. 1795, m. James W.
    Hogue.
Collected by Miss Anne Huddleson, Princeton, Indiana.

ARCHIBOLD, THOMAS   Adams County
Born—1752, Ireland.
Service—Enlisted July 1777, served 5 mos. as pri. under Samuel Shannon. Enlisted 1778, served 8 mos. as pri. under Samuel Shannon,
    and 2 mos. under Bell. Service in Penn.
Proof—Pension record.
Died—1837. Buried Reynolds Cemetery near Decatur, Ind. Stone.
Married—Mary Kent. Ch. Paterick; Thomas b. 1800; Sarah Ann; William; Martha; Rebecca; Sabietha.
Collected by Roy Archibold (great-grandson), Decatur, Indiana.

ARMSTRONG, ALEXANDER   Sullivan County
Born—1756, Ireland.
Service—Enlisted 1776, in Cumberland Co., Penn. Served 2 mos. as a
    sergeant in Capt. Thomas Clark's CO.; in fall 1776, served 2 mos.
    with Capt. William Black's CO., Col. Ourdy's Penn. Regt.
Proof—Pension claim S. 16033.
Died—1833. Probably buried Fairbanks Twp.
Children—Benjamin; Abel; Mary Ann; Margaret; Thomas.
Collected by Mrs. James R. Riggs, Sullivan, Indiana.

ARMSTRONG, ALEXANDER   Monroe County
Born—1752, Bedford Co., Virginia.
Service—Enlisted 1776, in Vir. Militia from Bedford Co. under Capt.
    James Bluford, against Cherokee Indians. Went to Long Island
    under Col. Charles Lewis. Served 3 mos., May 1777, enlisted for
    6 mos. in Capt. Henry Bluford's Regt., Col. Shelby. In 1778 volunteered for 6 mos., and was made first sergeant. 1781 enlisted in
    Ky. militia for expedition to Bryant's Station. June, 1781, volun-

teered Ky. Militia in expedition to Big Benson Creek. Total service 21 mos.
Proof—Pension claim S. 31525.
Died—May 27, 1833.
Married—Abigail.

ARMSTRONG, GEORGE   Harrison County
Born—Before 1760 in New York.
Service—Volunteer in a N. Y. Regt. early in the War. Served almost the entire time.
Proof—Revolutionary War Record of N. Y. Regents; Eminent and Self Made Men of the State of Indiana, Vol. I, p. 2.
Died—About 1808. Buried at Corydon, Indiana.
Married—1784, Sarah Faix. Ch. John; Hannah; Anna; James Faix b. 1809, m. Frances Brown.
Collected by Mrs. W. R. Davidson, 810 E. Powell Ave., Evansville, Indiana.

ARMSTRONG, ISAAC   Putnam County
Born—July, 1762, near Baltimore, Maryland.
Service—Enlisted 1777, 1778, 1781, Augusta Co., Vir. Served 9 mos. 6 wks., under Capt. Robert Craven and Cols. Nilson and McCleary. In militia near Richmond, Vir. Also served under Capt. Looney.
Battles—Hotwater, Jamestown.
Proof—Pension claim S. 16312.
Died—Probably buried Jefferson Twp., Putnam Co., Ind.
Collected by Miss Minnetta Wright, Greencastle, Indiana.

ARMSTRONG, JOHN   Clark County
Born—April 20, 1755, New Jersey.
Service—Served in 12th Penn. Regt. in fall of 1776. A sergeant in Brady's CO. and was promoted to ensign and to 2nd. Lieut., Dec. 11, 1777. Made First Lieut. May 12, 1779, in 3rd. Penn. Regt. In battles of Stony Point, Trenton, Monmouth and Yorktown. Usually spoken of as Colonel, having gotten the title in the Ohio Militia after leaving regular army.
Proof—Penn. Archives, Series II, Vol. 10, p. 761.
Died—Feb. 4, 1816. Buried on his farm in Clark Co. Stone.
Married—Tabitha Goforth (1774-1848). Ch. Ann; Catharine; William Goforth b. 1797; Mary Gano; John Gano; Thomas Pool; Eliza; Viola Jane Hamilton; John Hilditch b. 1809.
Collected by Ann Rogers Clark Chapter D. A. R.

ARNOLD, JAMES   Ripley County
Born—1755 or 1756.
Service—Enlisted as a pri. in Capt. Gillison's CO. of the 10th, subsequently the 6th Vir. Regt. commanded by Col. Edward Stevens,

Maj. Samuel Hawes, Col. John Green and Col. William Russell. On the roll for 1779, he is reported as a corporal.

Proof—War Department Records. He applied for a pension while living in Woodford Co., Ky., in 1832.

Grave—In Old Cemetery near Napoleon, Ripley Co., Ind. Many descendants are living in Ripley Co.

Collected by Mrs. A. B. Wycoff, Batesville, Indiana.

ARNOLD, JOSIAH   Pike County
Born—1755, Virginia.
Service—Enlisted as pri. in Capt. William Croghana CO., Col. Muhlenberg's Regt., Vir. Militia, March 12, 1776. Served two years.
Proof—Pension claim S. 35708.
Died—After 1829. Buried Arnold Cemetery, Jefferson Twp. Stone.
Married—Judith Daughtery. Ch. Jeremiah, m. Jemima Keith; Names of others not known.
Collected by Cradle of Liberty Chapter D. A. R.

ASHBROOK, THOMAS   Owen County
Born—1758, Hampshire Co., Virginia.
Service—Enlisted June 20, 1781, under Capt. Ed. McCarty, Col. Drapes' 2nd Rifle Regt. of Vir., served 6 mos. Reenlisted for 3 mos. in Capt. Voss' Vir. CO. as substitute for John Been or Bein. Later served 3 mos. in Capt. Elisha Bell's Vir. CO., as substitute for Matthew Pigon. Served again as substitute for William Johns.
Proof—Pension claim S. 31528.
Died—Aug. 24, 1848. Buried Old Secrest Cemetery near Romona, Ind.
Married—Agnes ———. Ch. Isaac; Anda; Elizabeth Canada; Hannah Hiatt; Frances; Rachel, m. William Wilson.
Collected by Miss Ura Sanders, Gosport, Indiana.

ASHBY, BLADEN   Wayne County
Born—1759, Bladensburg, Maryland.
Service—Enlisted as pri. in Capt. John Lemond's CO. 13th Vir. Regt., Sept., 1777, under Col. Russell. Also served in Capt. Uriah Springer's CO. of Light Infantry 9th Vir. Regt. under Col. John Gibson. And with George Rogers Clark at capture of Vincennes.
Proof—Will H. Henton, 704 College St., Canton, Mo., and Mrs. H. B. Stauffer, Nappanee, Ind.
Died—1828. Buried on farm now owned by Mrs. Pearl Beck Clark, near Middleboro. Government marker placed by Richmond Chapter D. A. R.
Married—Catherine Van Meter. Ch. Milton, m. 1811 Poly White; Abraham, m. 1824 Mariah Jones; Eleanor, m. 1813 Joseph Pemberton; Lavena, m. 1828 Wm. Auston; Lettice, m. 1827 Andrew Penland;

Elizabeth, m. 1805 Amos Smith; David; Gideon; Elijah; Hankerson; Thomas.
Collected by Mrs. Paul Ross, Richmond, Indiana.

ASHER, BARTLETT   Owen County
Born—1764 or 1767, Virginia.
Service—Enlisted at Culpepper Co., Vir., as pri. 1779, under Capt. Benjamin Roberts, Col. Crocket, Gen. Clark. Served with Clark's army in Ohio Valley.
Proof—Pension claim W. 23465.
Died—1841. Buried Gass Cemetery, N. of Gosport. Government marker placed by Miss Ura Sanders.
Married—1791, Margaret Curry. Ch. John, m. Sarah Omer; William (War of 1812), m. Mary Woolett; Daniel, m. Sarah Risley; Levi, m. Mary Newkirk; Thomas, m. Julia Woolett; Bartlett, m. Drucilla Holbert; Edmund, m. Elizabeth 'Rysinger; Allie, m. John Johnson; Caroline, m. George Thompson; Nancy, m. Peter Hays; Jane, m. Frederick Stirewalt; Catherine, m. Wm. Walters.
Collected by E. O. Asher, New Augusta, Indiana.

ASHER, WILLIAM   Indiana
Born—Said to have been born in Scotland.
Service—Enlisted 1779, Culpepper Co., Vir., under Capt. Benjamin Roberts, Col. Crocket, Gen. George Rogers Clark. Was referred to as ensign, corporal and private.
Proof—Pension claim W. F. 23465.
Died—July 23, 1870—Killed by Indians near Shippingport, Ky., and buried somewhere near the Falls of Ohio in Indiana.
Married—Ann ——. Ch. Bartlett, m. Margaret Curry; John, m. Jane Curry; Lotta, m. Joe Workman; William.
Collected by E. O. Asher, New Augusta, Indiana.

A'STURGUS (A. STURGIS, STURGIS), MINARD (MINER, MINOR,
  MAINARD, MINART)   Knox County
Born—Jan. 26, 1759, Virginia.
Service—In Capt. Wm. Harrod's CO., in 1780, at the station near the Falls now in Jefferson and Shelby Counties, Ky.
Proof—Revolutionary Soldiers and Pensioners, who settled and lived in Kentucky Counties, page 3.
Died—March 23, 1786—Killed by Indians, S. E. of Post Vincennes. No trace of grave. Wife buried in Indiana Church Cemetery on Monroe City Road.
Married—Ann Mayes b. 1762. Ch. Mary b. 1781, m. Daniel Smith; Robert b. 1782; Elizabeth b. 1784; Margaret b. 1785, m. John Johnson, son of Rev. Soldier James Johnson.
Collected by Mrs. S. G. Davenport, Vincennes, Indiana.

ATKINSON, THOMAS Orange County
Born—Sept. 18, 1741, Orange Co., N. C.
Service—Voucher 2768, p. 39, Book W., No. 1. Accounts of War of Revolution, on file at Raleigh, N. C., states that sums of money (English) were issued to him for rendering material aid. He was a Quaker, hence opposed to active service in the army.
Died—Sept. 29, 1784. Buried on his farm, S. of Paoli, Ind.
Married—First to Ruth Cruze. Second to Ruth Harvey. Ch. John; Thomas; Mary; Ann; Robert; William; Elizabeth.
Collected by Mrs. May L. Hollingsworth, Paoli, Indiana.

AUGHE, HARMON Clinton County
Born—Aug. 9, 1759, Penn.
Service—Drafted June, 1776, for 3 mos. in Capt. Peter Hartman's CO., Daniel Shimer. Was ensign under Col. Thomas Bull. Was guard at Brandywine. Served in wagon brigade under Wm. Evans and was stationed at Valley Forge, where he spent the winter hauling forage. Discharged April, 1777.
Proof—Pension claim R. 312. Rejected as pension authorities claimed Col. Thomas Bull was a Col. of the Continental Line and not of the Militia in which Aughe served. Later records show Col. Bull to have been of the militia.
Died—May 19, 1846. Buried Old South Cemetery, Frankfort, Ind. Stone. Bronze tablet placed by Margaret V. Sheridan.
Married—1793 Mary Munger (1771-1829). Ch. John Fertick; Polly; Elizabeth; Jacob; Samuel; Judith Lisle (1806-1874), m. John Pence; Nancy; Jesse.
Collected by Miss Martha B. Aughe, Frankfort, Indiana.

AUSTIN, PHILIP Clark County
Born—Nov. 18, 1765, Berkshire Co., Mass.
Service—Entered April 1, 1782, from Columbia Co., N. Y., in Capt. Cannon's CO., Col. Willet's Regt. Guarded Ft. Plain for 9 mos. Discharged. Enlisted Berkshire Co., Mass., under Capt. Joseph William's 3rd Mass. Regt., Col. John Grafton. Marched with Gen. Howe from West Point to Phila. then to Springfield, Mass. Discharged July 4, 1784.
Proof—Pension claim S. 16035.
Died—Aug. 7, 1838. Buried Old Cemetery, Jeffersonville, Ind. (now abandoned).
Married—Martha, b. 1793. Ch. Albert Gallatin b. 1809; Alice b. 1812; Alfred b. 1814; Susanna Anne b. 1816; Samuel b. 1819.

AVIT, RICHARD Perry County
Born—About 1738.
Service—Enlisted Jan., 1776, Philadelphia, Penn., under Capt. Courtney, Col. Proctor, Continental Establishment Penn. Line—until Jan..

1780. Discharged, Trenton, N. J. Again enlisted as orderly-sergeant for 3 yrs. In battles of Brandywine, Germantown, and White Springs. Served in Navy for 6 mos.
Proof—Pension claim S. 36404.
Died—June 12, 1826. Probably buried in Tobin Twp.
Married—Jane ——. Ch. Nancy; James.

AYRES (AYERS), THOMAS   Switzerland County
Born—Aug. 31, 1755, Somerset Co., N. J.
Service—Entered from Sussex Co., N. J., 1776, 2 mos. pri. under Capt. Countrymon; 1777, 1 mo. pri. under Capt. Key Kendall; 1778, 1 mo. under L. Westfall; 1778-79, 1 mo. under Capt. Key Kendall; 1778, 1 mo. under Capt. Sheaver; 1779, 1 mo. under Capt. Key Kendall; 1780, 1 mo. under Capt. Kane; 1781, 1 mo. under Capt. Harkness; 1782, 1 mo. under Capt. Bunnell.
Proof—Pension claim S. 17245. Lived at Patriot, Posey Twp., and is probably buried there.
Married—After the Rev. in Penn., and continued to live in Penn. 5 yrs. Lived in Ohio 25 yrs., then moved to Indiana.

BABBS, JOHN   Ripley County
Service—Enlisted in Annapolis, Md., in 1776; pri. in Capt. Scott's CO., Col. Smallwood's Md. Regt. In the battle of Long Island and White Plains. Wounded in latter battle. While recovering in the hospital, he served as orderly sergeant. Later served in Capt. Ford's CO. of 3rd Md. Regt.
Proof—Pension claim S. 45241.
Died—About 1842. Buried in Booher Graveyard near Napoleon, Ind.
Daughter—Hannah, m. John Glass.
Collected by John Babbs Glass, Toulume Co., California.

BACK, JOHN   Monroe County
Born—1760, Culpepper Co., Virginia.
Service—Enlisted March, 1778, from Washington Co., Vir.; pri. under Capt. Thomas Quick, Gen. George Rogers Clark; 1 yr. Vir. Line under Col. John Montgomery.
Proof—Pension claim S. 32103.
Died—1840. Buried Old Cemetery Simpson's Chapel, Gosport, Ind.
A daughter Nancy, m. Allen Sims.
Collected by Miss Ura Sanders and Miss Josephine Demarcus, Spencer, Indiana.

BAILEY, ALEXANDER   Sullivan County
Born—1751, Ireland.
Service—Served with N. C. Troops. 1776, 6 wks. in Capt. David Caldwell's CO., Col. Alexander Martin. 3 mos. in Capt. Caldwell's CO.

Marched against the Indians. 1780, 3 mos. Capt. Thomas Kennedy's CO., Col. Charles McDowell's Regt. Was in battle of King's Mt. In 1782, 20 days in Capt. Thomas Kennedy's CO., Col. Joseph McDowell's Regt.
Proof—Pension claim S. 32101.
Died—1835. Buried in Gill Twp.
Collected by Mrs. James R. Riggs, Sullivan, Indiana.

BAILEY, LEWIS   Dearborn County
Born—Feb. 12, 1754, West Haverhill, Mass.
Service—Pri. in Lexington Alarm, roll of Capt. Richard Ayre's CO., Col. Johnston's Regt., which marched on the alarm of April 19, 1735; length of service 5 days. Pri. on muster and payroll of Capt. Samuel Merrill's CO., Major Gage's Regt.; served Sept. 30, 1772-Nov. 6, 1772.
Proof—Military Archives of Mass., vol. 1, pp. 99-101; vol. 2, p. 187; vol. 21, p. 71.
Died—Sept., 1817. Buried Riverview Cemetery, Aurora, Ind. Stone. D. A. R. bronze marker placed by Col. Archibald Lochry Chapter D. A. R.
Married—1778, Mary Barnard (1758-1819). Ch. Mary; Abraham Lewis; Elizabeth; Barnard; Richard 1787-1833, m. Marie Addison; Judark; Jonathan; Hezekiah Smith; Amaziah; Arena; Mary; Thomas Jefferson; John Langdon.
Collected by Mrs. Dorothy G. Butterfield Talbott, Greencastle, and Mrs. Freda Barricklow Gibson, Rising Sun, Indiana.

BAINBROOK (BENBROOK), EZEKIEL   Posey County
Born—Dec., 1748.
Service—Enlisted 1779 in Montgomery Co., N. C.; pri., Lt. and Capt. with N. C. Troops under Capt. Thomas Child, Cols. Culp, Wade, Childs. In several skirmishes and battle at Drowning Creek. Also assisted Commissary Morse in collecting provisions for the Army.
Proof—Pension claim R. 397. Pension rejected for lack of 6 mos. proof of service.
Died—March 10, 1840. Probably Mais Twp.
Married—Mary. Ch. Ezekiel; Mary Sneed; Lucy Reeder.

BAIRD, THOMAS   Knox County
Born—1749, Penn.
Service—Served as pri. in Lieut. Daniel Smith's CO. of 6th class of the Cumberland Co. Penn. Militia, under Col. Samuel Culbertson.
Proof—Penn. Archives, Series 3, vol. 23, pp. 619 and 660.
Died—Oct. 24, 1834. Buried Upper Indiana Cemetery, Knox Co. Stone.

Married—First, 1777, Esther Kilgore. Ch. Nancy, b. 1787. Second, W. ——, Jane Johnson, d. 1850. Ch. Martha, m. William Adams; Archibald G., 1797-1847; Andrew, 1800-1856.
Collected by Mrs. Frances Lloyd, Vincennes, Indiana.

BAKE, JOHN   Fountain County
Born—1748, Hunterdon Co., N. J.
Service—Volunteered Aug. 20, 1776, Hunterdon Co., N. J. Served until Aug. 28, 1778, under Capts. John Phillips and Cornelius Hanbock, Cols. Chambers and Chamberlain, N. J. Regt.
Proof—Pension claim S. 31538.
Died—1835. Buried Baptist Cemetery, Richland Twp. Government marker.
Children—Christopher; Rebecca.
Collected by Mrs. A. S. Dolch (deceased), Attica, Ind.

BAKER, GEORGE   Morgan County
Born—Oct. 14, 1759, Granville, N. C.
Service—Enlisted 1775, and served as a pri. for 3 years. in N. C. Militia under Cols. Joseph Phillips and Livingston.
Proof—Pension claim S. 17249.
Died—1841. Buried Burns Cemetery, S. of Martinsville, Ind.
Married—Elizabeth Morris d. 1837. Ch. Martha 1788-1859, m. Wilson Moore.

BAKER, JOHN   Dearborn County
Born—1752.
Service—Pri. 3rd Penn. Regt.. under Col. Richard Butler. Was in battles of Brandywine and Monmouth.
Proof—Penn. Archives, Series 2, vol. 10, p. 455.
Died—1843. Buried at Wilmington, Dearborn Co.
Children—Thomas; John; Elizabeth; George; William, m. Tabitha Bruce; Sarah.
Collected by Mrs. Walter Kerr, Aurora, Indiana.

BAKER, JOHN   Warrick County
Born—1762, N. C.
Service—Entered service in 1780, and continued thru 1781. Served under Gen. Pickney, Col. Anderson, and Capt. Joseph Pickney. Was a volunteer. In several skirmishes, but only one regular battle at Abbeville, S. C.
Proof—Affidavit for pension to be found in Clerk's Office, Order Book 3, p. 182, Warrick Co., Ind.
Died—Oct. 7, 1835. Buried Haines cemetery, S. of Boonville, Ind. Stone. Government marker placed by Vanderburg Chapter D. A. R.

Married—First, Rachel McCoy, d. 1813. Ch. John Jr., m. Mary Johnston; Mary 1790-1818, m. Fleming Thurman. Second, W. ——, 1815, Chelly Esom.
Collected by Mrs. H. K. Forsythe, Newburgh, Indiana.

BALCH, REV. JAMES   Sullivan County
Born—Dec. 25, 1750, Deer Creek, Maryland.
Service—A Patriot. Advocated the adoption of the resolution of the Mecklenburg, N. C., Declaration of Independence.
Proof—G. B. Balch, Genealogy of Balch Family, pp. 451-453; 461-465.
Died—Jan. 12, 1821. Buried Mann Cemetery, Turman Twp. Stone.
Married—Susannah Lavinia Garrison, 1758-1843. Ch. Amos Prido 1775; Ann Wilks b. 1776; Mary Martha; Elizabeth Roe b. 1788; Ethelinda; Albina Bloomer b. 1797; John Luther b. 1800; Calvin; Jonathan b. 1803.
Collected by Mrs. Emma Billman (deceased), Sullivan, Indiana.

BALDWIN, JOHN   Harrison County
Born—April 12, 1763, Washington, Penn.
Service—Ranger on frontier in Penn. 1778-1783.
Proof—Penn. Archives, Vol. 23, p. 212; D. A. R. No. 56285.
Died—1838. Harrison Co., Ind.
Married—Jane House. Ch. Robert, 1785-1863; Amos; Hannah; Elizabeth, m. John Rhoades, Jr.
Collected by Mrs. Gertrude T. Rosenbarger, New Albany, Indiana.

BALDWIN, WILLIAM   Daviess County
Born—Dec. 27, 1750, Prince Edward Co., Virginia.
Service—Enlisted Prince Edward Co., Vir., April 30, 1776; private in Capt. Charles Allen's CO., Col. Wm. Meredith's Vir. Regt. Discharged about Christmas 1776. Served 3 mos. in Capt. Henry Walker's CO., and 3 mos. in Capt. Cunningham's Vir. Troops.
Proof—Pension claim S. 16313.
Grave—In Reeve Twp., S. E. of Washington, Ind. Government marker placed by White River Chapter D. A. R.
Collected by Mrs. Roy Bogner, Washington, Indiana.

BALL, JAMES   Allen County
Born—1751, Maryland.
Service—While a resident of Fredericktown, Maryland, he enlisted Aug. 1, 1776, in Capt. Philip Mowery's CO., Col. Shryock's Maryland Regt. Discharged, Dec. 25, 1776. Enlisted 1777. Served 4 mos. as sergeant in Capt. Ralph Hillery's CO., Col. Baker Johnson's Maryland Regt. In the battle of Germantown. Served two mos. as pri. guarding prisoners at Fredericktown and 2 mos. guarding Magazine.

Proof—General Accounting Office, Washington, D. C.
Died—After 1834. Bronze tablet placed by Mary Penrose Wayne Chapter D. A. R.
Children—Daniel; Vachel; James.
Collected by Mrs. Joseph Hanna (deceased).

BANKS, WILLIAM   Putnam County
Born—June 3, 1761, or June 23, 1762, Culpepper Co., Virginia.
Service—While residing in Amherst Co., Vir., he enlisted March, 1781, and served as sergeant for 6 mos. in Capt. James Pamplain's CO., Col. Richardson's Vir. Regt.
Proof—Pension claim W. 10376.
Died—Sept. 5, 1839. Buried Old Cemetery, Greencastle, Ind. Stone.
Married—1801, Elizabeth Brown (1781-1865). Ch. Nancy b. 1802; Frances b. 1805; Mary b. 1807; Elizabeth b. 1809; Daniel P. b. 1810; William S. b. 1814; Emily A. b. 1815; Almirium b. 1818; John Smith b. 1820; Josephine R. b. 1823; Wesley J. b. 1825.
Collected by Miss Minnetta Wright, Greencastle, Indiana.

BARLOW, LEWIS   Shelby County
Born—1755, Culpepper Co., Virginia.
Service—Enlisted in Staunton Co., Vir., Sept., 1776, and served to Oct., 1779, under Capt. Michael Bowyer, Col. James Wood, 12th Vir. Regt. and was discharged at West Point, N. Y. Engaged in battles of Iron Hill, Brandywine, Germantown, and many skirmishes.
Proof—Pension claim S. 16619.
Died—Nov. 27, 1836, Shelby Co., Ind.
Married—Judah. Ch. Elizabeth; George; Bluford.

BARNETT, JOHN PERRY   Johnson County
Born—July 23, 1764, Orange Co., Virginia.
Service—Enlisted in January, 1779, and served as a fifer under Capt. Ambrose Madison, Col. Francis Taylor, Virginia Troops. Discharged April 11, 1781.
Proof—Pension claim W. 9718.
Died—Sept. 8, 1829. Buried Freeman Cemetery, Blue River Twp. Stone. Bronze marker placed by William Donaldson Chapter D. A. R.
Married—Elizabeth Self, 1783. Ch. James; William; Spencer; George; Lucy; Thomas; John; Elizabeth; Ambrose.
Collected by Mrs. I. E. Tranter, Franklin, Indiana.

BARNES, ELIJAH   Decatur County
Born—About 1755.
Service—Pri. in CO. of Capt. Dorsey, Col. Hal, Maryland Regt. 7 mos. Enlisted July 20, 1776, in Ann Arundal, Maryland. Taken prisoner Nov. 16 and held till Jan., 1777.

Proof—Pension claim W. 9717.
Died—Aug. 13, 1840.
Married—Catherine Shipley, 1784. Ch. Absolam b. 1786.

BARNES, RICHARD   Hendricks County
Born—Feb. 20, 1763, Baltimore, Maryland.
Service—Enlisted as a pri. in 1781 for 3 mos. under Capt. Owen Reubel, and Col. Colleway from Vir. Then he served 10 mos. as a Minute Man under Edward Eggleston, Col. Davison. He lived in Henry Co., Vir., when he enlisted. He applied for pension on Oct. 6, 1845, but died before pension was granted.
Proof—Deposition of service on record in Rev. War Records, Ref. 526.
Died—Nov. 7, 1845. Buried East Cemetery, Danville, Ind. Stone.
Daughter—Lydia, b. 1792; d. 1836.
Collected by Mrs. H. C. Sears, Danville, Indiana.

BARRICKMAN, JACOB   Franklin County
Born—Feb. 17, 1763, Penn.
Service—Private in Penn. Volunteers, Westmoreland Co., Penn.
Proof—Penn. Archives, Series 6, vol. 2, p. 331.
Died—Feb. 23, 1842—Buried Fairfield Twp. on Corey Farm.
Married—Jane Swan, 1767-1833. Ch. Martha b. 1785; Mary b. 1786; Sarah b. 1791; Jane b. 1794; Keturah b. 1803; Nancy b. 1805; John b. 1796; Jacob b. 1799; James b. 1808; William b. 1810; Eliza b. 1813.
Collected by Mrs. Charles Masters, Brookville, Indiana.

BASSETT, ELISHA   Jefferson County
Born—Feb. 11, 1760, Sandwich, Mass.
Service—Pri. in Capt. Nathan Tobey's CO. on the Rhode Island alarm in 1780.
Proof—D. A. R. No. 110974.
Died—1814, Jefferson Co.
Married—First to Elizabeth West 1793 (1770-98). Ch. Elisha Jr. 1796-1860, m. 1816, Elizabeth Foster. Soldier's second W., Elizabeth ——. Ch. Hannah Ann b. 1829, d. 1848; Ancel C. b. 1832, d. 1859.
Collected by John Paul Chapter D. A. R.

BASSETT, JOSEPH   Switzerland County
Born—1760, Raynham, Mass.
Service—Enlisted in spring of 1776 for 1 yr. under Capt. Perry in Col. Sargent's Regt. Mass. Line, Cont'l. Establishment. Enlisted within 2 or 3 mos. after this term expired in Capt. Perkins CO., Col. Crane's Regt. in Gen. Knox's Brigade of artillery on the Cont'l. Establishment for 3 yrs. Discharged at Morristown, N. J., under

Capt. Calendar from the hands of Maj. Shaw; aid to Gen. Knox. Was in Brandywine, Monmouth, and Rhode Island.
Proof—Pension claim S. F. 35770.
Died—Sept. 8, 1822. Probably buried in Pleasant Twp., near Benington.
Married—Mary ——. Ch. Ebenezer, m. Elizabeth Mapes; Mary, m. 1823, David Blodgett; Ard. D. A. R. Lineage, vol. 32, p. 249, gives wife, Lydia Jones and son, Daniel.
Collected by Mrs. A. V. Danner, Vevay, Indiana.

BASSETT, WILLIAM   Ripley County
Born—1754.
Service—Entered service from Virginia in 1776 under Col. George Bailor. Served 2 yrs. 9 mos.
Proof—Pension claim W. 9739.
Died—Feb. 6, 1840. Buried on farm in Brown Twp. Government marker and name on bronze tablet in Versailles Court House.
Married—1780, Margaret. Many descendants still living in Ripley Co.
Collected by Mrs. A. B. Wycoff, Batesville, Indiana.

BATEMAN, WILLIAM   Floyd County
Born—1757, Penn.
Service—Enlisted from Cecil Co., Penn., as pri. in Capt. John Rudolph's CO., Light Horse in Lee's Legion of Cavalry. Enlisted June, 1776, in a corps called "Flying Camp" as pri.; 6 mos. under Lt. Stogden, Col. Richardson, Gen. Lee. Was in battle of White Plains. Discharged at Philadelphia. In fall of 1777, enlisted as pri. in Lee's Legion for duration of War. Was at Stony Point and Eutaw Springs.
Proof—Pension claim S. 32099. Pensioned from Floyd Co., Ind.
Collected by Mrs. G. R. Anderson, Mrs. V. R. Conner, New Albany, Indiana.

BATSON, MORDICIA   Sullivan County
Born—1755, Virginia.
Service—Enlisted 1776, was a private for two years in Capt. Stephen Ashby's, Col. Woods' Regt., Virginia. Was in battles of Brandywine and Germantown.
Proof—Pension claim S. E. 31184.
Died—Jan. 6, 1829. Buried Gill Twp., Sullivan Co.
Married—Rachel Marney. Ch. William; Jonathan; Mary; Robert; Ann; John; Rebecca.
Collected by Mrs. Theodore Craven, Indianapolis, Indiana.

BATTON, HENRY   Porter County
Born—1750, Chester Co., Penn.

Service—Served as sergeant from Aug., 1776 to Feb., 1777, under Capt. Wm. Harrod; from April, 1777, 4 mos. under Capt. Wm. Cross; 8 mos. under Capt. Theo. Philips; 2 mos. under Lt. McKinnley; 4 mos. under Capt. Philips. Left the service in 1778.
Proof—Pension records.
Died—Feb. 1, 1845. Buried Cemetery in Liberty Twp. Stone. Government marker and bronze marker placed by William Henry Harrison Chapter D. A. R.
Collected by Miss Ruth Richards, Valparaiso, Indiana.

BAUMGARDNER, DANIEL   Ripley County
Service—Enlisted from N. C. in March, 1779.
Proof—Pension claim S. 32150.
Died—1835. Name on bronze tablet in Versailles, Court House.
Collected by Mrs. A. B. Wycoff, Batesville, Indiana.

BAXTER, JAMES   Jefferson County
Born—June 6, 1765, Gathenaysay, Tyrone, Ireland.
Service—Served as pri. in 7th Battalion of Cumberland Co. Penn. Militia under Capt. James Fisher, 1778-1782. Also pri. in Capt. William Black's CO. Cumberland Co. Rangers. Also in 1st and 4th Penn. Line in Capt. James Wilson's CO.
Proof—Penn. Archives, Series 5, vol. 4, pp. 278, 620; vol. 6, pp. 362, 454, 466, 624, 654; Series 3, vol. 3, p. 268.
Died—Aug. 31, 1828. Buried Craig Cemetery. Stone.
Married—Rachel Riddle (1765-1859). Ch. Daniel b. 1794 m. Susan Wilson; William; James; Nancy.
Collected by John Paul Chapter D. A. R.

BEALL (BELL), NINIAN (NING)   Ripley County
Born—1761, Maryland.
Service—Enlisted from Maryland in April, 1778, under Col. Wm. Washington.
Proof—Pension claim W. 9722.
Died—June 13, 1836. Buried Washington Cemetery, near Versailles, Ind. Stone. Government marker and name on bronze tablet in Versailles Court House.
Married—Christine Stull. Many descendants living in Ripley Co., Ind.
Collected by Mrs. A. B. Wycoff, Batesville, Indiana.

BECK, GEORGE   Washington County
Born—1762, North Carolina, probably Rowan Co.
Service—Served in Continental Army in N. C., some of service on Yadkin River, N. C.

Proof—Roster of N. C. Revolutionary Soldiers (published 1932 by D. A. R.), pp. 198-225. Other references in this volume may not have been this soldier.)
Died—Aug. 16, 1847. Buried Beck's Cemetery in Howard Twp. Stone.
Married—Elizabeth Claver. Ch. John; George; Andrew; William; Jacob; David; Susannah m. John Colglazier.
Collected by Mrs. Harvey Morris, Salem, Indiana.

BECKETT, HUMPHREY   Warren County
Born—June 24, 1760.
Service—Enlisted May 24, 1778, 7th Md. Regt. In battles of Camden, S. C.; Cowpens, Guilford Court House, Eutaw Springs, Siege of 96. Promoted Dec. 21, 1780, to Corporal; Sept. 8, 1781, to Sergeant; to Sergt. Major; to Surgeon's Mate; to Quartermaster Sergt.
Proof—Pension claim W. 9726.
Died—April 2, 1830. Buried Mound Cemetery. Stone.
Married—Mary ——, 1763-1839 m. 1786. Ch. Elizabeth b. 1787, m. James Beckett; Benjamin; Anna b. 1796; William b. 1798; Carle b. 1801; Eliza b. 1803; Maria; Egbert; Alfred; Polly.
Collected by Mrs. Elmer V. Smith, Williamsport, Indiana.

BEDWELL, ROBERT   Sullivan County
Born—Feb. 10, 1759.
Service—Enlisted May, 1780; pri. for 4 mos. in Capt. Snoddy's CO., Maj. Fields N. C. Battalion. Enlisted Nov., 1780, 3 mos. in Capt. Smith's N. C. CO. Enlisted Aug., 1781, in Capt. Lopp's N. C. CO., 2½ mos.
Proof—Pension claim S. 16321.
Died—Sept. 13, 1842. Buried Moody Cemetery near Pleasantville, Sullivan Co. Stone.
Married—Elander ——. Ch. John; Elisha; Thomas; Hannah.
Collected by Charles Bedwell, Sullivan, Ind.

BELL, JAMES   Jefferson County
Born—Sept. 9, 1763, probably Augusta Co., Virginia.
Service—A Revolutionary soldier.
Proof—Ky. Historical Register, Vol. 23, p. 67.
Died—Jan. 6, 1844. Buried Valley Graveyard, Graham Twp.
Married—Elenor Henderson b. 1776, m. 1793. Ch. Elizabeth m. Francis Hinds; James H., m. Jane H. Boggs; Sarah; Henderson, m. Frances Brown; Samuel, m. Emma Flint; Mary Ann; Lucinda, m. Samuel W. Newman; Francis, m. Eliza Willson; John Gray, m. Ann Rice; Archibald H., m. Harriet T. Baker; Elenor, m. Henry Flint.
Collected by John Paul Chapter D. A. R.

BELL, JOSEPH   Floyd County
Born—1761, Chester Co., Pennsylvania.
Service—Entered service in Westmoreland Co., Pennsylvania, about May,
    1781; served 3 mos. in Capt. Stockley's CO., Aug. 1, 1781, 60 days in
    Capt. Smith's Co., 3 mos. in Capt. Casiday's CO., May 1, 1782, 40
    days under Lt. Perry. Wounded in arm at Hannah's Town, Aug.,
    1782. All service in Col. Gibson's Regt., Indian service.
Proof—Pension claim R. 722½.
Died—Jan. 27, 1851. Buried Fairview Cemetery, New Albany, Ind.
    Grave not marked, but burial recorded in cemetery records as
    Plat A.
Married—Anna, about 1780. Ch. Elizabeth D.; Robert F.; Sarah T.;
    Dickey S.; John E.; Agnes F.
Collected by Mrs. V. R. Conner, New Albany, Indiana, and Mrs. Leo
    Schultheis, Vincennes, Indiana.

BELL, NATHANIEL   Johnson County
Born—1757, Berkeley Co., Virginia.
Service—While residing in Washington Co., Pennsylvania, he volun-
    teered in 1778, 3 mos. in Capt. William Harrod's CO., Col. Cannon's
    Penn. Regt. Assisted in building a fort on Fishing Creek near the
    Ohio River and was in Ft. Wheeling when it was attacked by In-
    dians. He was engaged by Col. Crooks to watch the Indians and
    Tories in 1780 and 1781—served 2 mos. as sergeant under Capt.
    James Archie and Col. Morgan.
Proof—Pension claim R. 724. Pension rejected because he did not
    serve 6 mos. in an embodied military organization.
Died—about 1845. Buried in Lowe Burying Ground, Johnson Co.
Married—Mary Timmons about 1784. Ch. Elizabeth; Robert; Polly;
    Jane; Benjamin; Hannah; Jacob; Nathaniel; James; Samuel; Katie;
    Ruth.
Collected by Mrs. I. E. Tranter, Franklin, Indiana.

BELL, THOMAS   Gibson County
Service—Received pay for 116 days on horseback in Militia and 14 days
    on foot as private in Capt. Wm. Strain's CO., S. C., commencing
    May 13, 1780, to March 8, 1783.
Proof—Indent 621 Book L, p. 17-11-5, S. C. Historical Commission.
Died—Buried Bell Cemetery near Gibson-Pike Co. Line.
Married—Nancy, daughter of Capt. John and "Witty" Kate Steele.
Collected by Miss Anna Hudelson, Princeton, Indiana.

BEMIS, LEVI   Sullivan County
Born—1757, Vermont.
Service—Enlisted in Battlenoro, Windham Co., Vermont, March 2, 1781.
    Pri. in Capt. James Blakeslee's CO., Col. Samuel Fletyher's Ver-
    mont Regt. Discharged Dec. 20, 1781.

Proof—Pension claim S. 32116.
Died—1837. Buried Gill Twp., Sullivan Co.
Collected by Mrs. James R. Riggs, Sullivan, Indiana.

BENBOW, EDWARD   Wayne County
Born—Aug. 22, 1761, Cumberland Co., N. C.
Service—Served in S. C. Militia under Gen. Francis Marion and was a member of Capt. Snipe's CO. He received pay for his service and for supplies furnished.
Proof—Stub Entries to Indents Issued in payment of claims against S. C. growing out of the Revolution. S. C. Historical Commission, p. 218.
Died—April 12, 1829. Buried West Grove Graveyard.
Married— ——. Ch. Barclay (oldest son), m. 1st Mary McClure and had ten ch; Barclay, m. 2nd Sarah Hickman and had five ch.
Collected by Mrs. Paul L. Ross, Richmond, Indiana.

BENEFIEL, GEORGE   Jefferson County
Born—Dec. 25, 1759, York Co., Penn.
Service—Pri. in Capt. James Patton's Company, 4th Battalion, Cumberland Co. Penn. militia, Col. Samuel Culbertson's Regt. Aug. 19, 1780.
Proof—Penn. Archives 3rd Series, Vol. 23, p. 704.
Died—April 1, 1832. Buried Jefferson Church Cemetery. Government marker placed by John Paul Chapter D. A. R.
Married—1787, Mary Buchanan (1754-1857). Ch. Robert b. 1787, m. Ann Stewart; Martha b. 1789, m. John West; William b. 1791, m. Phebe Conner; Esther b. 1793, m. Robert McClelland; George b. 1795, m. first to Ann Ryker, second to Marjorie Van Cleave; Mary b. 1797, m. first to James McCarty, second to Isaiah Stewart; Jane b. 1798; Jesse b. 1800, m. Sarah ——; Wilson b. 1802, m. Eliza Buchanan; James b. 1806, m. Eliza Taylor; Samuel b. 1806, m. Elizabeth Stewart; Eliza b. 1808, m. —— Russell.
Collected by John Paul Chapter D. A. R.

BENNETT, JOSHUA   Harrison County
Service—Name appears in an Alphabetical List of discharged soldiers of two battalions of militia raised to serve the Continental Army in the year 1781, Charles Co., Md.
Proof—Records of Md. Troops in Cont'l service, 1775-83, in Md. Archives, Vol. 18, p. 406.
Died—About 1840. Buried in Rehoboth Cemetery, Boone Twp. Crude cedar stakes mark the grave.
Collected from the Indiana S. A. R. Records.

BENTON, DAVID   Jackson County
Born—Dec. 2, 1763. Salisbury, Conn.
Service—Served from July to Nov., 1780, in Capt. Warner's CO. of Col. John Brown's Regt. from Berkshire Co., Mass. He was present at an engagement with Tories and Indians under Sir John Johnson Oct. 19, near Ft. Plant, Montgomery Co., N. Y., in which Col. Brown and about 40 soldiers were killed. In July, 1781, he enlisted at New London, Conn., as a marine on the Brig "Favorite" of 16 guns. Taken prisoner and confined on prison ship "Jersey" until exchanged in Jan., 1782.
Proof—Pension records; Benton Genealogy, p. 13.
Died—1845. Buried in Old Fairview Cemetery near Brownstown, Ind. Government marker.
Married—1784, first to Sarah Bingham (1765-1825). Ch. Henry b. 1784, m. second to Hannah Dickenson; Sarah; Mary; Walter b. 1799, m. Hetty Benks; William David; Norman. Soldier, m. second to Thankful R. McKane. Ch. Elizabeth.
Collected by Gen. Jacob Brown Chapter D. A. R.

BERRY, GEORGE   Washington County
Born—1764, Fauquier County, Virginia.
Service—First Lieut. 13th Vir. Regt., Dec. 16, 1776; 9th Regt. Sept. 14, 1778. Served several times as Lieut. under Capts. Beall and Moore, Cols. Russell and Gibson, Vir. Troops; also served as quartermaster.
Proof—Revolutionary Soldiers of Virginia by Eckenrodes, p. 44; Heitman's Historical Register, p. 101; D. A. R. No. 130249.
Died—1838.
Married—First to Sarah Conway. Ch. Atalanta (1797-1876), m. Lawson Hathaway Owens.
Collected by Mrs. Harvey Morris, Salem, Indiana.

BERRY, JOEL   Rush County
Born—1754, King George Co., Virginia.
Service—Enlisted 1775, and served at various times, amounting to about 5 yrs. 1 mo. as minute man and private under Capts. Joseph Rogers, Garrett, Wm. Berry (soldier's brother), Brunty and Davis, Col. Stith, Vir. Troops. Also served as an Artisan in the Public Armory at Fredericksburg, Vir., under Col. Lewis.
Proof—Pension claim S. 30265.
Died—Feb. 28, 1843. Probably buried East Hill Cemetery, Rushville, Ind.
Married—Anne ——. Ch. Holesworth b. 1794, d. 1871.

BERRY, WILLIAM   Allen County
Service—The name appears on the 1840 census for Allen County, as a pensioner but no service has been found for him to date. He came to Allen Co. in 1836, deed records show he transferred property in Oct. 21, 1839, and again in Feb. 27, 1847.
Died—Probably 1847 or 1848. Is listed on a bronze tablet erected by Mary Penrose Wayne Chapter D. A. R.
Married—Mary ——. Ch. Alfred; Archlinda; David; Michael.
Collected by Mrs. T. J. Hindman, 1214 W. Jefferson St., Fort Wayne, Ind.

BIDDLECOMB, RICHARD   Warren County
Born—Feb. 15, 1760, West Greenager, Rhode Island.
Service—Enlisted in Bennington, Vt., 1779; pri. in Capt. Hutchin's CO., Col. Warner Regt., 9 mos. 21 days, Vt. Line.
Proof—Pension claim W. 9736.
Died—Aug. 23, 1835. Buried West Lebanon Cemetery, Warren Co. Stone.
Married—1783, Ruth Hendrix b. 1767. Ch. Francis b. 1783; Ruth b. 1785; Hendrix b. 1788; Asher b. 1789; Richard b. 1791; Cornelius b. 1794; John b. 1796; Daniel b. 1798; Louisa b. 1800; Ruth b. 1802; Esther b. 1803, m. James J. McAlilly; Nathan b. 1806; Lucinda b. 1809.
Collected by Mrs. Elmer V. Smith, Wiliamsport, Indiana.

BIGELOW, ABIJAH   LaPorte County
Born—April 16, 1756, Waltham, Mass.
Service—Enlisted April 19, 1775, as a pri. under Capt. Abraham Pierce and Cols. Gardner and Thatcher, in Mass. Troops. Served until March 17, 1776. Enlisted in fall of 1777 for 5 or 6 mos. under Capt. Brooks and Col. Brooks. In battle of Bunker Hill.
Proof—Pension records.
Died—Oct. 22, 1848. Buried Greenwood Cemetery, Michigan City, Ind. Stone. Bronze marker placed by Indiana S. A. R.
Married—Mercy Amelia Spring. Ch. Marshall, m. Olive Sparhawk-Barre; Nabby; Lucy b. 1797, m. Herbert Williams; Sumner; Increase Sumner; Nabby; Zibi b. 1787, m. Rev. John Nelson; Jacob, m. Eliza Southgate; Abijah m. —— Phelps; Amelia, m. M. Dickinson; Sally, m. Rev. Luther Wilson.
Collected by Miss Edna P. Kitchell, Michigan City, Indiana.

BIGGS, ROBERT   Clark County
Born—About 1753.
Service—Enlisted in Penn. in Aug., 1776, served 18 mos. as a pri. in Capts. Eli Myer's and Huffnagle's Companies, Col. McCoy's 8th

Penn. Regt. Was in the battles of Woodbridge and "Bomburg on the Raritan River" and was in various skirmishes.
Proof—Pension claim W. 9733.
Died—Nov. 9 or 13, 1831, Clark Co., Ind.
Married—1778, Jane, d. 1839. Ch. John; Andrew b. 1782; William Millar b. 1783; Robert b. 1785; Elizabeth b. 1789, m. Henry Crist; Nancy b. 1791, m. Nicholas Crist; Joseph b. 1793; Samuel b. 179-; Thompson Hay b. 179-; Abner b. 1798; Melindy Jane b. 1821, m. Wm. Crist; Mary, m. George Wellman; Hannah, m. Robert Cairns.
Collected by Ann Rogers Clark Chapter D. A. R.

BIRCH (BURCH), THOMAS   Fountain County
Born—May 9, 1751, Prince George Co., Maryland.
Service—Pri. Hardy Co., Vir.; Capt. John Winston's CO., 14th Regt. of Foot; also 10th Regt. Vir., Col. Com. Davis. Name last on muster roll. Camp Middlebrook, Jan., 1776.
Proof—War Department.
Grave—In Birch Cemetery, Fountain Co.
Married—First to —— Clark, an Indian. Ch. Jesse, 1778-1843; William b. 1779; m. second to Susanna Talbert. Ch. Jonathan, 1782-1849. Third W., Linney Harvey. Ch. Thomas William, 1789-1856; Anson; Roseanna b. 1791; Benjamin 1795-1861; Deborah 1793 or 1796; John.
Collected by Miss Lydia Melinda Earl, Attica, Indiana.

BIRD, SAMUEL   Allen County
Born—1751, Virginia.
Service—Name appears on a record of Virginia Soldiers under heading, "A list of state soldiers and seamen, who have received certificates of their full pay." Shows that on April 14, 1783, the sum of 1.33 S. 18 D. 8 was drawn by one Capt. Wright for Samuel Bird.
Proof—Virginia Records.
Died—March, 1829. Buried in Broadway Cemetery now McCollough Park, Fort Wayne, Indiana. Name on bronze tablet erected by Mary Penrose Wayne Chapter D. A. R.
Collected by Mrs. T. J. Hindman, 1214 W. Jefferson St., Fort Wayne, Indiana.

BISBEE, CHARLES   Dearborn County
Born—About 1757.
Service—Enlisted 1775, under Capt. Freedom; 8 mos. in 1776 under Capt. John Reed, Col. Bailey's Regt.; 1 yr., 1777, 4 mos. Cont'l. Mass.
Proof—Pension claim S. 16642.

Died—June 11, 1833. Dearborn Co.
Children—John; Ezra; Charles; Desire Egelston; Harriet Walker.
Collected by Mrs. Walter Kerr, Aurora, Indiana.

BISHOP, BENJAMIN   Wayne County
Born—April 5, 1759, Kingwood, New Jersey.
Service—While a resident of Rahway, Middlesex Co., N. J., volunteered
    in 1776 or 1777; 1 mo. as pri. in Capt. Craig's CO., N. J. militia,
    and was in an engagement in Blazing Star. Enlisted 1778, 2 mos.
    in Capt. Harriman's N. J. CO., and was in a skirmish with British.
    Later served 6 mos. in Capt. Soudder's CO., Col. Dayton's N. J.
    Regt., and was in engagement at Elizabethtown and Springfield.
    Enlisted in fall of 1780 or 81, served 5 mos. in Capt. Potter's CO.,
    Col. Crane's N. J. Regt., and on Dec. 23 in battle at Elizabeth-
    town was wounded in the thigh.
Proof—Pension claim S. 32119.
Died—1838. Buried at Webster, Wayne Co.
Married—Anna Hawkins. Ch. John.
Collected by Mrs. Paul L. Ross, Richmond, Indiana.

BISHOP, JOB   Jefferson County
Born—1755.
Service—Served from New Jersey.
Proof—Marker at grave.
Died—1845. Buried Methodist Cemetery at Canaan, Jefferson Co.
    Government marker placed by John Paul Chapter D. A. R.
Ch. —— Joel.
Collected by John Paul Chapter D. A. R.

BLACK, ALEXANDER   Crawford County
Born—Feb. 22, 1760, Berkeley Co., Virginia.
Service—Enlisted Augusta Co., Vir., about March 1, 1780; served in
    Capt. John Preston's CO., Maj. Taylor, Vir. Troops; they marched
    to Clinch Station, which was commanded by one Crockett, and
    while there went out on numerous scouting parties. Discharged
    Dec., 1780.
Proof—Pension claim R. 881. Pension rejected because he failed to
    furnish proof of six mos. service.
Died—After 1835.

BLACK, JAMES   Posey County
Born—1759. New York State.
Service—Commissioned Ensign Jan. 5, 1776, in Capt. Stephen Bayard's
    CO., promoted to Lieut. July 4, 1776, 2nd Penn. Battalion under
    Col. Arthur St. Clair.

Proof—Penn. Archives 2nd Series, Vol. 10, p. 93.
Died—1830. Buried in Private Cemetery near Wabash River, Posey Co., Ind.
Married—Eleanor McMillan.
Collected by Mrs. Charles T. Johnson, Mt. Vernon, Indiana.

BLACK, WILLIAM   Pike County
Born—Dec., 1753, Pennsylvania.
Service—Entered Georgia Militia under Col. Elijah Clark, Capt. Joseph Neal, 1776, for 2 yrs. At the siege of Savannah. Then in the army of N. C. under Gen. McDowell.
Proof—Pension claim W. 9730.
Died—April 2, 1837, Pike Co.
Married—1786, Elizabeth, d. 1846. Ch. Cortez b. 1787; Nancy b. 1790; John b. 1792; Robert b. 1794; David b. 1797; William b. 1799; Henry b. 1802; Mary Barrett b. 1807; Samuel b. 1810.

BLAIN, JAMES   Monroe County
Service—Enlisted 1776, March 27 for 1 yr. as pri. in Vir. Line. Discharged Feb. 10, 1777, Middlebrook, N. J. Served under Capt. Stevenson, Col. Nevil, Gen. Scott.
Proof—Pension claim S. 35780.
Died—June 9, 1841. Buried on Dr. Walker farm near Stinesville, Ind.
Never married.

BLAIR, THOMAS   Spencer County
Service—Enlisted in Penn., Aug., 1776. Served as pri. in Capt. John Finley's CO., Col. Daniel Brodhead's 8th Penn. Regt. until spring of 1778, when transferred to Gen Washington's Life Guard, under Maj. Caleb Gibbs, and was discharged Aug. 25, 1779, at West Point, N. Y.
Proof—Pension claim S. 35781.
Died—Jan. 1, 1833. Buried Brown Cemetery, near Dale, Ind.
Married—Mary Ann Jones. Ch. James; Sarah.
Collected by Miss Helen Posey, Rockport, Indiana.

BLAKE, GEORGE KENNETT   Jefferson County
Born—1751, Chester Co., Pennsylvania.
Service—Served 3 mos. with Capt. Robertson and Lieut. Givens in Augusta Co., Vir. Was baggage waggoner under Capt. Lewis without pay; drafted in Staunton, 1778; Capt. McCreary, 6 mos.; 1779 with Capt. Cartmill.
Proof—Virginia Records.

Died—1842. Buried Pisgah Cemetery. Government marker placed by John Paul Chapter D. A. R.
Son—Charles N. Blake.
Collected by John Paul Chapter D. A. R.

BLASDEL, JACOB   Dearborn County
Born—April 8, 1754, Salisbury, Mass.
Service—Pri. in Capt. Philip Filton's CO., Col. Poor's Regt. Date of entry May 25, 1775. Served 2 mos. 12 days. Was Lieut. in Capt. Enoch Page's CO., Lt. Col. Joseph Senter's Regt., from Aug. 25, 1777, to July 6, 1778.
Proof—New Hampshire Rev. Rolls, vol. 1, pp. 112, 146, 195; vol. 2, pp. 250, 251, 256.
Died—April 25, 1831. Buried Cambridge Cemetery near Guilford, Ind. Stone. Bronze marker placed by Col. Archibald Lochry Chapter D. A. R.
Married—Ruth Morse, 1755-1804. Ch. Enoch; Jacob; Nabby; Polly; Ruth; Jonathan; Sally; Elijah; Betsey.
Collected by Stephen H. Bundy, Aurora, Indiana.

BLEVINS, JAMES   Greene County
Born—Dec. 25, 1762, New England.
Service—While residing in Montgomery Co., Vir. Volunteered in summer 1780, as pri. in Capt. Wm. Love's CO., Col. Wm. Campbell's Vir. Regt. Was in battle of King's Mt. after which he guarded prisoners taken. Discharged April 7, 1781; re-enlisted in N. C. as pri. in Capt. John Carroll's CO., Col. Cleveland's N. C. Regt., served 9 mos.
Proof—Pension claim S. 32121.
Buried—Scotland, Greene Co.

BLUE, JOHN   Fountain County
Born—1750, Lancaster Co., Pennsylvania.
Service—Enlisted Lancaster Co., Penn., Aug. 2, 1777, pri. in Capt. Scott's Co., Penn. Troops. Wounded in head at battle of Brandywine, taken prisoner and conveyed to Wilmington, Del. Later taken to Philadelphia and imprisoned until exchanged June 14, 1778. Discharged June 16, 1778.
Proof—Pension claim S. 16646. Applied for pension from Tippecanoe Co., Ind., 1832, and the last payment was sent to him at Corydon, Ind.
Died—Thought to be buried in a cemetery (now a field) in Richland Twp., Fountain Co., Ind.
Son—John b. Sept. 11, 1777, in S. C.
Collected by Miss Lydia Melinda Earl, Attica, Indiana.

BLUNT, ANDREW Harrison County
Service—Enlisted for 3 yrs. 1776 in Co. of Westmoreland, Penn., under Col. Brodhead, 8th Penn. Regt. In battle of Brandywine.
Proof—Pension claim R. 967. (Widow's application rejected.)
Died—May 6, 1821. Buried Blunt Cemetery, Webster Twp.
Married—Mary Calhoon, 1784.

BOAS, HENRY Jackson County
Born—Oct. 30, 1760, Germany.
Service—Enlisted from Lancaster Co., Penn., for 6 mos. on July 1, 1776, as pri. under Capts. Jacob Koltz and Ludwig Meyer in the 1st Battalion, Flying Camp. In battles of Long Island and White Plains.
Proof—Pension claim S. 16053.
Died—1838. Buried Ridge Cemetery, near Medora, Ind.
Married—1785, Dorotha Baumgartner (1756-1839). Ch. Mary 1791-1883, m. Thomas Carr; Peter; Elizabeth; John; Henry; Jacob.
Collected by Gen. Jacob Brown Chapter D. A. R.

BOLDREY, JOHN Ripley County
Born—1756.
Service—Entered service from Mass. in April, 1775, under Col. Walker.
Proof—Pension claim S. 35785.
Died—June 12, 1821. Probably buried in Franklin Cemetery, Ripley Co. Name on bronze tablet in Versailles Court House.
Collected by Mrs. A. B. Wycoff, Batesville, Indiana.

BOLIN, THOMAS Perry County
Born—1766, Orange Co., N. C.
Service—Enlisted 1781 or 82 in Wilkes Co., N. C., as pri. in Capt. Lytle's CO., Col. Lytle's Regt., N. C. Militia, 11 mo. 17 days.
Proof—Pension claim S. 32126.
Died—After March 26, 1851

BONEAUX, PIERRE Knox County
Born—Feb. 4, 1761, Vincennes, Indiana.
Service—A Patriot. Furnished supplies to the army belonging to Virginia, June 2, 1779, and received pay for the same.
Proof—General Clark's Account Claimants, Record No. 7912, U. S. Court of Claims, Dec. term 1873.
Died—1832. Buried Old Cathedral Cemetery, Vincennes, Ind.
Married—Second W. Mary Ann De Noyan, b. 1771, m. 1805. Ch. Mary Ann b. 1806, m. Jean Francis Bayard.
Collected by Frances Lloyd, Vincennes, Indiana.

BONINE, DANIEL — Wayne County
Born—Nov. 11, 1736, Pennsylvania.
Service—Served under Capt. Robert McKeen, 7th Battalion of Lancaster Co. Militia, commanded by Alexander Lowry, 1782.
Proof—Penn. Archives Series 5, vol. 7, pp. 768, 782.
Died—July, 1817, Wayne Co.
Married—First to Elizabeth ——. Ch. Mary; Hannah; Elizabeth; Susanna. Second W., Sarah Miller. Ch. Sarah. Third W. Mary Copeland. Ch. Rachel; David; Rebeccah; Isaac.
Collected by Miss Susanna Wright Stamp, Roachdale, Indiana.

BONNEAU (BONO, BAUNAUX), CHARLES — Knox County
Born—About 1750, Post Ouiatauons.
Service—A Patriot. Signed the oath of allegiance to the Republic of Virginia as a free and independent state at Post Vincennes, July 20, 1778.
Proof—Ill. Hist. Coll. 1771-1778, Gen. George Rogers Clark Papers, vol. VIII, p. 57; no. 52 on list of signers.
Died—Before 1784. Probably buried in St. Francis Xavier Cemetery.
Married—Genevieve Du Devoire. Ch. Genevieve b. 1773; Nicholas b. 1795; Francoise b. 1784. (Found in Register of Old Cathedral.)
Collected by Mrs. Leo Schultheis, Vincennes, Indiana.

BOONE, JEREMIAH — Lawrence County
Born—Feb. 29, 1760, Pennsylvania.
Service—Served in Capt. Samuel Kirkham's CO. with Col. Daniel Boone (a cousin), and Gen. George Rogers Clark in the Northwest Indian War. Mustered out in Oct., 1782.
Proof—Illinois Pay Roll, D. 79; Records of "Boone Family Association."
Died—Oct., 1832. Buried in Boone Cemetery on Indian Creek. Stone.
Married—Joice Nevil, 1787. Ch. Sarah; Elijah; Simeon; Charlotte; Mahala; Hannah; Noah.
Collected by Miss Frances Lloyd, Vincennes, Indiana.

BOONE, SQUIRE JR. — Harrison County
Born—Oct. 5, 1744, Bucks Co., Pennsylvania.
Service—A Patriot. Was a pioneer of Kentucky who gave valuable civil service and was wounded in the defense of Boonesborough.
Proof—The Boone Family, by Haxel Atterbury Straker, pp. 72, 82-6.
Died—1815. Buried in a natural cave on east bank of Buck Creek, Harrison Co., Ind.
Married—1765, Jane Van Cleve (1749-1829). Ch. Jonathan b. 1766; Moses b. 1769; Isaiah b. 1772; Sarah b. 1774; Elizabeth b. 1776, m. James Nelson; Enoch Morgan b. 1777.
Collected by Ft. Harrison Chapter D. A. R.

BOOTH, JOHN Jefferson County
Born—1768.
Service—Inscription on government marker reads "Virginia Militia."
Buried—Dry Fork. Government marker placed in Manville Cemetery, the nearest one to the place where buried, by the John Paul Chapter D. A. R.
Married—1793, Sally Kinder.
Collected by John Paul Chapter D. A. R.

BORDERS, CHRISTOPHER Randolph County
Born—1763, near Schuylkill River.
Service—Pri. in Company of Virginia Militia under Capt. Mansfield, 6 mos.
Proof—Pension claim S. 9104.
Died—1847. Buried in Spartansburg, Greensfork Cemetery. Stone.
Collected by Mrs. James P. Goodrich and Mrs. Oran E. Ross, Winchester, Indiana.

BOWEN, CHARLES Putnam County
Born—Sept., 1749, Virginia.
Service—Served as pri. 2 yrs. under Capt. Reese Bowen, his brother; Capt. John Campbell, Capt. Wm. Edmonson; Col. Wm. Campbell's Vir. Regt. In battle of King's Mt., commissioned there July 2, 1785. Captain of 2nd CO., 2nd Regt., Washington Co. Militia, serving on frequent tours against the Indians, these services amounting to 2 yrs.
Proof—Pension certificate 3146.
Died—After 1834, Putnam County.
Children—William; Charles Jr.
Collected by Miss Minnetta Wright, Greencastle, Indiana.

BOWER (BOWEN), ANDREW Montgomery County
Born—Feb. 16, 1753, York Co., Pennsylvania.
Service—Entered service Berkley Co., Vir., 1777, as fifer under Capt. Isaac Evans for 3 mos.; 1781 as pri. under Gen. Muhlenburgh for 3 mos., and later for 3 mos. under Capt. Porter.
Proof—Pension claim S. 16324.
Died—Nov. 7, 1833, in Montgomery Co.
Children—Son, Henry.

BOWLING (BOLLING), JOSEPH Orange County
Born—About 1753.
Service—Enlisted in Virginia, pri. in Capt. Peyton Valentine's CO., Col. William Heth's 3rd Vir. Regt. Wounded in battle of Monmouth. Served until June 18, 1780, when he was discharged at Philadelphia, having served 3 yrs.

Proof—Pension claim W. 25257.
Died—Jan. 30, 1836. Probably buried in Jackson Twp.
Married—Martha Williams (2nd W.). Ch. Sally, m. Enoch Stone; William. A daughter of the soldier by former marriage, married James Belcher.
Collected by Mrs. N. B. Mavity, French Lick, Indiana.

BOWMAN, JOSEPH   Knox County
Born—About 1752, Frederick Co., Virginia.
Service—Captain in Clark's army at capture of Fort Sackville. Commission of Major arrived two days later, at time Clark was promoted to General. In celebrating event of capture, Bowman was injured by an explosion of gun powder, and eventually died from the effects of his accident.
Proof—English's Conquest of North West Territory, p. 108. Photostatic copy of pay-roll of Clark's men.
Died—Aug. 14, 1779. Buried either on site of Fort or on river bank. History states that Major Bowman left his family in Virginia. That may mean his father's family or a wife and children of whom there is no record in Knox County.
Collected by Mrs. S. G. Davenport, Vincennes, Indiana.

BOWYER, PETER   Cass County
Born—Oct. 10, 1760, in France.
Service—Was a Matross in Capt. Turnbull's CO. of 2nd Penn. Regt. of Artillery under Col. Procter.
Proof—Penn. Archives, Series 5, Vol. 3, p. 1014.
Died—Oct. 10, 1850. Buried Mays Cemetery, Tipton Twp. Government marker placed by Olde Towne Chapter D. A. R.
Married—Second W. 1793, Catherine Shelman, b. 1773. Ch. John; Daniel (War of 1812); Pauline; Frederick; Lewis; Magdalene; Nancy Mays, 1805-1883; Catherine; Peter; Catherine; Adam; Susannah.
Collected by Miss Laura D. Henderson, Logansport, Indiana.

BOYD, JOHN   Lawrence County
Born—Jan. 9, 1760, near Martinsburg Co., Virginia.
Service—Enlisted in 1777 as a pri. in Capt. George Wall's CO., Col. Thomas Elliot's 4th Vir. Regt. Re-enlisted in 1778 as a wagoner in Capt. Gabriel Long's CO., Col. Daniel Morgan's Regt.
Proof—D. A. R. No. 69497; War Department.
Died—1829. Buried Old Shiloh Church Cemetery, near Bedford, Ind. Government marker.
Married—Nancy Martin, b. 1773. Ch. William b. 1792; Sarah b. 1794; Charlotte b. 1795; John b. 1797; Elijah; Nancy; Elisha b. 1803, m. Phoebe Kern; Polly Ann; Jennie b. 1806, m. Isaac Callahan; Isaac

b. 1808, m. Mahala Evans; Juliana b. 1810, m. Jacob Fisher; Ann
Rebecca b. 1812; Charles; Lucinda.
Collected by Mrs. L. C. Cox, Bedford, Indiana, and Mrs. Harvey Morris,
Salem, Indiana.

BOYD, SAMUEL   Wayne County
Born—May 20, 1763, Bedford Co., Virginia.
Service—Enlisted 1780, 1 yr. under Capt. Thomas, Col. Roebuck; re-
enlisted 1781 under Col. Hays; engaged in Battle of Bush River,
at the capture of Augusta, Georgia, and siege of Ninety-Six.
Proof—D. A. R. Lineage, vol. 57, p. 81; Pension record; Young's Hist.
of Wayne Co., pp. 238 and 239.
Died—Nov 27, 1835. Buried Jacksonburg, Wayne Co., Ind. Govern-
ment marker.
Married—Isabella Higgins, 1785. Ch. James; John; William d. 1846;
Elizabeth, m. Elisha Martindale; Samuel K.; Lard; Robert d.
1853; Martha 1800-1882, m. Joseph Lewis; Mary, m. Abner M.
Bradbury; Isabella Ladd, d. 1834.
Collected by Mrs. Paul L. Ross, Richmond, Indiana.

BOYDEN, JONATHAN   Washington County
Born—1741, Groton, Mass.
Service—Enlisted for 9 mos., April 4, 1775, in Mass. under Capt. Asa
Lawrence, Col. William Prescott, Continental Army. Discharged
Cambridge, Mass., May 4, 1777. Re-enlisted for 9 mos., Groton,
Mass., under Capt. Benjamin Warren, Col. Brooks. Discharged at
White Plains, N. Y. Enlisted again under Sylvanus Smith, Col.
Sprout, Mass. Line. Discharged at Valley Forge. In battles of
Bunker Hill, White Plains, and at taking of Burgoyne.
Proof—D. A. R. Lineage, vol. 40, p. 223. Application for pension found
in Washington Co., Ind., Minute Book A., 1818-1822, p. 398.
Died—1833. Probably buried Brown Twp.
Children—Jonathan Jr. and perhaps David.
Collected by Mrs. Harvey Morris, Salem, Indiana.

BOYER, JOHN   Decatur County
Born—Oct. 17, 1760, Palatine, Albany Co., N. Y.
Service—Enlisted Sept., 1777, for 3 mos. as pri. under Capt. Sam. Gray,
Col. Peter Billinger, N. Y. Enlisted Jan., 1780, and Dec., 1780,
as pri. under Capt. Sam. Gray, N. Y. Enlisted April, 1781, 9 mos.
as pri. under Capt. Garret Putnam, Col. Willett, N. Y.
Proof—Pension claim W. F. 522.
Died—Oct. 14, 1836, in Decatur Co., Ind.
Married—First to Margaret Ritter, 1778-1812. Second to Elizabeth
Wilson, 1824. Soldier's Will names the following children: Daniel,
Leonard, Jacob, Samuel, John Jr. (m. Margaret Eyserman); Rob-

ert; Peter; Harmon; Benjamin, 1809-1884; and Nancy Boyer Pickart. John Jr. and Benjamin are known to be children of first wife.
Collected by Mrs. H. S. McKee, Greensburg, Indiana.

BOYLES, DAVID   Lawrence County
Born—1747.
Service—Enlisted 1779, for 4 years as pri. under Capts. Lewis Booker, Singleton, Col. Harrison's Artillery. In battle at Gambee River where he was wounded in the hip, and at the siege of York.
Proof—Pension claim W. F. 12322; D. A. R. No. 111704.
Died—June 17, 1845. Buried at Proctor Cemetery, near Ft. Ritner, Lawrence Co. Stone.
Married—Dec. 1, 1825, at Bedford, Ind. Polly Sappington. Ch. Columbus; Peny; David b. 1828, m. Catherine Lane; George W.; Melissa.
Collected by Mrs. Ellen Hoover, Bedford, Indiana.

BOYLL (BOYLS), CHARLES   Floyd County
Born—About 1741.
Service—Private in Regt. commanded by Col. Harrison of Virginia for a term of 4 years.
Proof—Pension claim S. 35784 B. L. Wt. 1455, 100.
Death—The last payment of pension was made to the pensioner on April 23, 1838, at Bedford, Indiana.

BRADBURY, DAVID   Wayne County
Born—1760.
Service—Essex County Militia, New Jersey.
Proof—Office of Adjutant General of N. J., MSS No. 205 and printed Roster p. 519.
Died—1824. Buried Jacksonburg Cemetery. Stone.
Married—Susanna Craig, 1782. Ch. Abner Marshall.
Collected by Mrs. Paul L. Ross, Richmond, Indiana.

BRADLEY, CORNELIUS   Posey County
Born—1755, Ireland.
Service—Enlisted June 10, 1778; served as pri. in Capt. Henry Dobson's CO., Col. Otho Williams' 6th Maryland Regt. Was in battle of Monmouth and was discharged March 14, 1779.
Proof—Pension claim S. 35798.
Died—Aug. 26, 1840. Buried on Saltzman Farm, Posey Co.
Married—Hannah McFadin. Ch. John; David B.; Hiram; Lavina.
Collected by Mrs. Charles T. Johnson, Mt. Vernon, Indiana.

BRASHER, HENRY Dearborn County
Born—1742, New York City.
Service—Commissioned Lieut. in Capt. James Alner's CO. "Prussian Blues," Col. John Lashen, 1st N. Y. Battalion, Sept. 14, 1775. Capt. in Second Regt. N. Y. Levies, commanded by Col. William Malcom. Name appeared in Record Sept. 28, 1776. In battles of White Plains, Long Island and King's Bridge.
Proof—N. Y. in the Revolution, 1887 by Fernow; War Department; N. Y. Gen. and Biog. Record, vol. 27, pp. 37-42.
Died—1824, Lawrenceburg, Ind.
Married—Lucy Clark, 1764. Ch. John b. 1765 (a Rev. S.); Jacob; Lucy; Robert; Charles; Susan; Sarah; Elizabeth; Abraham.
Collected by Mrs. Helen Barnett Matthews Shirk (a descendant), Richmond, Indiana.

BRAY, JOHN Switzerland County
Born—About 1762.
Service—Enlisted Sept., 1777, in Romney, Hampshire Co., Vir. Private in Capt. Wm. Voss' CO., Col. James Woods' Regt. Was in battles of Brandywine (wounded), Monmouth and Stoney Point. Discharged at end of three yrs. service.
Proof—Pension claim W. 4145. Land warrant No. 8178.
Died—April 10, 1832. Buried McKay Cemetery, Craig Twp. Stone.
Married—First W. unknown. Ch. John; Daniel; Samuel; Jane; Nancy; Elizabeth. Second W., Mrs. Elizabeth Coonies. Ch. Amelia; George Washington; Sophia.
Collected by Mrs. A. V. Danner, Vevay, Indiana.

BRENEMAN, CHRISTIAN Jackson County
Born—1758, Montgomery Co., Pennsylvania.
Service—Volunteered July 1, 1776, in the Penn. Militia, at York, Penn. in CO. of Capt. George Deal, Lt. Barnet Zeigler, Col. Smith; marched to Philadelphia, to Trenton, N. J., to Elizabethtown and there in July volunteered in the Flying Camp Troops for 6 mos. under Capt. John McDonald, Lt. Robert Patterson and Lieut. Wm. Scott, Maj. Wm. Bailey, Col. Swope and Gen. Evans. Discharged Jan., 1777. In the fall of 1777, drafted and served 2 mos. in Penn. Militia.
Proof—Pension claim S. F. 16060.
Died—June 4, 1842. Buried Liberty Cemetery, W. of Brownstown. (Soldier and wife died the same day and buried in same grave.)
Married—Mary Cresner, 1765-1842. Ch. Jacob b. 1786; Rebecca b. 1788; Cety b. 1790; Elizabeth b. 1795; Abraham b. 1801; William b. 1812; James b. 1813; Walas b. 1816.
Collected by Mrs. J. D. Cummings, Brownstown, Indiana.

BRENTON, JAMES   Pike County
Born—1754, Virginia.
Service—Aug. or Sept., 1780, 1 mo. under Capt. Peter A. Sturgus, Col. George Rogers Clark. 1781, 1 mo. Capt. John Cowan. 1 mo. Capt. Ambrose Gordon and 1 mo. Capt. Ellison. Oct., 1782, under Capt. Joseph Kincaid, Col. Benjamin Logan. In battle of Piqua and Gen. George Rogers Clark's expedition.
Proof—Pension claim S. F. 2518.
Died—June 15, 1836. Buried Indian Mound graveyard, Washington Twp. Bronze marker placed by Cradle of Liberty Chapter D. A. R.
Married—First to Ellen. Second to Mrs. Mary Ansley. Ch. Peter, others unknown.
Collected by Cradle of Liberty Chapter D. A. R.

BRENTON, JOHN   Clark County
Born—About 1755.
Service—While residing in Monongahela Co., Penn. Enlisted in 1778, served in Capt. Andrew Swearingen's CO., marched to Pittsburgh, and went on Gen. McIntosh's expedition to what was later the state of Ohio; assisted in building a fort at Tuscarawas, after which he marched to Ft. McIntosh, on the Ohio River, and was discharged, having served 4 mos.; in 1779 he served 2 mos. at the Fall of the Ohio; enlisted 1782 in Col. Benjamin Logan's Regt.
Proof—Pension claim S. 16059.
Died—March 21, 1847. Buried Old Antioch Graveyard.
Married—Pension application states wife died before soldier. In 1853 Ursula West and Mary McCleery, Clark Co., Ind., stated that they are sole heirs of the soldier.
Collected by Ann Rogers Clark Chapter D. A. R.

BRENTON, ROBERT   Clark County
Born—About 1758.
Service—Entered service 1778, as a substitute for Henry Brenton, "who was drafted in Monongahela Co. in the state of Penn.," served in Capt. Swearingen's CO. under Cols. Wm. Crawford and Brodhead, went on Gen. McIntosh's expedition to Ohio against the Indians; service 4 mos.; in 1779, 1 mo under Capt. Peter Sturgus; in 1781, 1 mo. under Capt. John Dougherty; 1782, 1 mo. under Capt. Sam. Kirkham.
Proof—Pension claim S. 16062.
Died—After March 4, 1833. Buried Old Antioch Graveyard.
Collected by Ann Rogers Clark Chapter D. A. R.

BRENTON, WILLIAM   Clark County
Born—1760.
Service—Enlisted in Monongahela Co., Penn., in 1777, for 4 mos. as a
    Spy under Capt. James Brenton, Penn. Troops; 1778, 3 mos. under
    Capts. Jacob Bowman, Andrews, Lot Leonard; 1781, 6 mos. as
    pri. under Capt. Jeremiah Johnson, Col. Morgan Vir. Troops;
    1782, 1 mo. as pri. under Capt. Kirkham, Vir. Troops.
Proof—Pension claim S. 16061.
Died—Nov. 21, 1838. Buried Old Antioch Graveyard. Stone.
Married—Fanny ——, d. 1841. Ch. John b. 1797; William; James;
    Sarah.
Collected by Ann Rogers Clark Chapter D. A. R.

BREWER, BENJAMIN   Washington County
Born—April, 1755, Pennsylvania.
Service—In Penn. Militia in 1776, 1777; 4 mos. as a pri. under Capt.
    Huston, 3 mos under Capts. Shannon and Ratuni.
Proof—Pension claim S. F. 46025.
Died—May 6, 1834. Buried Cooley Cemetery, Washington Twp. Stone.
Married—About 1781, Caty Mellenger, 1768-1839. Ch. William;
    Sammy; Peter; John, 1788-1863, m. Elizabeth Cooly; Katy, m.
    Charles Nuckles; Benjamin; Hannah, m. —— Monicle.
Collected by Mrs. Harvey Morris, Salem, Indiana.

BRIANT, ZACHARIAH   Spencer County
Born—1765.
Service—Entered service 1779 as pri. in company of Capt. Burton, Col.
    Francis Taylor's Regt. Vir. Troops, 2 yrs.
Proof—Pension claim S. 16326.
Death—The last payment of pension was made on March 19, 1849.

BRIDGEWATER, LEVI   Washington County
Born—1761. Probably in Pennsylvania.
Service—Enlisted Jan. 20, 1776, Uniontown, Penn., under Capt. James
    Neil, 13th Vir. Regt., Col. Wm. Russell for 3 yrs. 2 mos. Discharged at Pittsburg by Col. Richard Campbell.
Proof—Pension claim W. 9752.
Died—Sept. 30, 1831. Grave not located.
Married—1785, Patience Stilwell, b. 1769. Ch. Elias b. 1785; Eleanor
    b. 1787; Jack b. 1789; Isaac b. 1790; Daniel b. 1792; Polly b. 1794;
    Rebecca b. 1797; Joseph b. 1800; Solomon b. 1803; Elisha and
    Elijah b. 1805; John b. 1807.
Collected by Mrs. Harvey Morris, Salem, Indiana.

BROUILLETTE, MICHELL Knox County
Born—In Canada.
Service—Soldier and Patriot. Took oath of allegiance under Father
  Gibault, then served in Clark's army, June 24, 1779, as Captain
  of Militia of the District of St. Vincents, County of Illinois.
  Sept. 29, 1779, as Captain under George Rogers Clark.
Proof—Descendant has copy of both commissions.
Died—Jan. 6, 1797. Buried Old Cathedral Cemetery, Vincennes.
Married—Barbe Boneaux. Ch. Michel, b. 1774; Laurent b. 1776; Barbe
  b. 1778; Marie Louise b. 1781; Pierre b. 1782; Genevieve b. 1785;
  Ursule b. 1788; Laurent (2nd) b. 1792 killed in battle of Tippecanoe.
Collected by Miss Mary A. Brouillette, Vincennes, Indiana.

BROWN, GEORGE Rush County
Born—June 22, 1760, Hardy Co., Virginia.
Service—Enlisted 1777, for 3 yrs. Capt. Jacob Valentine's CO., Col.
  George Gibson's Regt. Served to close of war, was given land
  grant in Mason Co., Ky.
Proof—D. A. R. No. 75856.
Died—Sept. 21, 1825. Buried on Charles Fisher Farm, Richland Twp.
  Government marker and name on bronze tablet in Rush Co. Court
  House by Rushville Chapter D. A. R.
Married—Rebecca Conrad and had 6 daughters. Second W., Hannah
  John and had 5 children; Ryland Thomas, m. Mary Reeder.
Collected by Rushville Chapter D. A. R.

BROWN, JAMES Clark County
Born—1755.
Service—Was in Cavalry at battle of Cowpens and Yorktown.
Proof—Grandson, James Ambrose Brown, gave affidavit of Rev. Service;
  S. A. R. Year Book, 1918.
Died—1837. Buried Pleasant Ridge Cemetery. Government marker.
Son—James (1787-1857), buried Pleasant Ridge Cemetery.
Collected by Indiana S. A. R.

BROWN, JOHNSTON Jefferson County
Born—Oct. 2, 1760, Mifflin Co., Penn., on Juniata River.
Service—New Jersey service. Statement in Madison Courier, on March
  14, 1867.
Died—Oct. 12, 1869, age 109 years and 10 days. Buried on farm in
  Milton Twp.
Married—Kezia ——. Ch. Nathaniel; Samuel; Minerva Jane; and six
  others.
Collected by John Paul Chapter D. A. R.

BROWN, MATTHEW   Shelby County
Born—1752, County Wexford, Ireland.
Service—While residing in Ninety-Six District, S. C., enlisted and
    served as a pri. with S. C. Troops as follows: from June 29, 1776,
    3 mos. in Capt. Benjamin Kilgore's CO. of rangers and spies, under
    Col. James Williams; 3 mos. in Capt. Thomas McCrary's CO.;
    from March 4, 1779, in Capt. Benjamin Kilgore's Co. Discharged
    June 5, 1779.
Proof—Pension claim S. 32135.
Died—1839. Buried Little Blue River Cemetery.
Son—David, who had a son, John W.

BROWN, PATRICK   Jefferson County
Born—1760, Hanover Co., Virginia.
Service—Served with Vir. Troops, May, 1778, to Oct., 1782; 6 mos. as
    pri., 4 mos. as Sergeant, 2½ mos. as Sergeant-Major. Was with
    Gen. Clark in expedition on Little Miami.
Proof—Pension record S. 16325; Filson Club Historical Qt., vol. 4, p.
    165; Collins Hist. of Ky., p. 646.
Died—Nov. 29, 1835. Buried on farm near Madison, Ind. Stone.
Married—Elizabeth Paul (a sister of Col. John Paul), d. 1844. Ch. Ann
    Parker; Elizabeth, m. 1822, James E. Bacon; William, m. 1820,
    Alice Crafford; John Parker. See Will record in book B. 368.
Collected by John Paul Chapter D. A. R.

BROWNLEE, JAMES   Rush County
Born—1745, Scotland.
Service—Pri. in Capt. Abner Howell's CO. of Washington Co., Penn.
    In service on the frontier 1782.
Proof—Penn. Archives, Series 2, vol. 14, p. 757.
Died—1828. Buried in Flatrock Cemetery.
Married—Jean Rankin (1771-1783). Ch. John; Hugh, m. Rebecca
    Vicent; Jane; Elizabeth, m. Platt Bayless Dickson; James, m.
    Kate Ewing.
Collected by Schuyler Colfax Chapter D. A. R.

BRYAN, SAMUEL   Marion County
Born—May 6, 1756, Rowan Co., N. C.
Service—Enlisted in July, 1775, in Vir. Served at various times under
    Capts. Wm. Bailey, Smith, John Holder, Wm. Hogan, James Stinson, and Cols. Ben. Logan, Isaacs and Johnson. Vir. and N. C.
    Troops. Was in Gen. George Rogers Clark's expedition. In July,
    1779, was in skirmishes against the Indians in Ky. under Col.
    Logan. In May, 1780, was with his father, Capt. Wm. Bryan,
    when latter was killed by Indians.

Proof—Pension claim 9366-2; Boone Family, pp. 128 and 129; The Bryan Families of Fayette Co., Ky.
Died—March 1, 1837. Buried Baptist Cemetery, Perry Twp. Stone.
Married—Mary Hunt, d. 1842. Ch. Ann; Phebe; William; Abner; Luke; Thomas; Sarah; Daniel; Mary; Hampton; Samuel.
Collected by Indiana S. A. R.

BRYANT, DAVID   Allen County
Born—May 22, 1756, Springfield, New Jersey.
Service—Served several short terms of enlistments from 1776 to 80, under different commands in N. J. Militia. Was at Marines, Springfield, Connecticut Farm, Elizabethtown.
Proof—Bryant Genealogy, pp. 32-36; Jerseymen in the Rev. War, p. 523.
Died—Aug., 1835. Buried on East bank of Eel River, 15 miles N. W. of Fort Wayne, Ind. Name on bronze tablet by Mary Penrose Wayne Chapter D. A. R.
Married—Catherine Wooley (1759-1835). Ch. Sarah b. 1783; Elias b. 1784; Isaac b. 1786; Joseph b. 1788; Samuel b. 1790; Abraham b. 1791; Mary b. 1793; Simeon b. 1795; David b. 1797; Hanah b. 1799; Elizabeth b. 1801; Jacob b. 1803; John b. 1805; Nancy b. 1807; Jane b. 1810.
Collected by Mrs. Joseph E. Brown, Crown Point, Indiana (a descendant).

BRYANT, JAMES   Owen County
Born—1753, Amherst Co., Virginia.
Service—In winter 1780 or 81, he was drafted into service as pri. under Capt. Shaw in a company of Infantry, Vir. Militia. Later he was attached to Col. Wm. Washington's Cavalry and marched to Brushy Mt. At battle of Jamestown. And Yorktown. Total service 15 mos.
Proof—Pension claim S. F. 31568.
Died—Nov. 3, 1853. Buried Spencer Cemetery.
Married—1836, Ruth Dyer.

BUCHANAN, GEORGE   Jefferson or Ripley County
Born—1721, Pennsylvania.
Service—In 4th Penn. Cont'l. Line as pri. 1777-1781, 4 years.
Proof—A. L. Buchanan, Larned, Kansas; Penn. Archives.
Died—1818. There is a question as to his exact grave. A government marker placed by Ripley Co. Hist. Society in McLaughlin Cemetery in 1935. John Paul Chapter D. A. R. had placed one in Jefferson Church Cemetery in 1924.

Married—Esther Campbell. Ch. Mary b. 1764, m. George Benefiel (Rev. S.); Harriet b. 1768, m. —— McLaughlin; Margaret b. 1770, m. John Cowan; William b. 1771; David b. 1774; Wilson b. 1775; John b. 1778.
Collected by Mrs. A. B. Wycoff, Batesville, Indiana, and John Paul Chapter D. A. R.

BUCK, JOHN   Putnam County
Born—1752, in Hanover, Europe.
Service—While residing in Cumberland Co., Penn., he enlisted in Penn. Troops. Served 5 mos. in 1776, as Sergeant under Capt. James McConnell in the "Flying Camp"; 2 mos. in 1778, as pri. under Capt. Merchant in the "Flying Camp"; 1780-81, 4 mos. as Lieut. under Capt. Merchant and Col. Laughery. He was taken prisoner by Indians and held 4 mos.
Proof—Pension claim S. 32155.
Died—Last payment of pension was made on Nov. 21, 1836.
Collected by Miss Minnetta Wright, Greencastle, Indiana.

BUCKMAN, BENJAMIN   Floyd County
Born—April 16, 1759, Hadley, Massachusetts.
Service—Sergeant in Mass. Line. Was a prisoner at Quebec for 6 mos. and was with Washington when he crossed the Delaware.
Proof—Pension record; Indiana Mag. of History, vol. VIII, p. 15; vol. 1, p. 139; Indiana S. A. R. records.
Died—Oct. 1, 1842. Buried Fairview Cemetery, New Albany, Ind. Stone.
Married—Second, W. Eunice Judd, d. 1850.
Collected by Mrs. V. R. Conner, New Albany, Indiana.

BULLARD, ISAAC   Clark County
Born—About 1752.
Service—Entered service July, 1776, at Bury, Worchester Co., Mass., for 5 mos. under Capt. Benjamin Gates, Col. Holman's Regt. Mass. Line. Discharged at Cortland River, N. Y. Enlisted Dec., 1776, for 2 or 3 mos. under Capt. Oliver, Col. Sparhawk, Mass. Regt. Discharged at Boundbrook, N. J. Enlisted April 17, 1777, under Capt. Benj. Gates, Col. Rufus Putnam. Discharged in West Point, N. Y., April 17, 1780.
Proof—Pension claim S. 35801.
Died—1832.
Married—Martha —— Ch. Isaac; Anna.

BUNDY, CHRISTOPHER   Wayne County
Born—1759, Pasquotank Co., N. C.
Service—Enlisted while residing in Guilford Co., N. C., 1779, and served as pri. in Capt. Enoch Davis' CO., Col. Matthes Lock's N. C. Regt. Was transferred to Capt. William Gilriennes' Guard at the Magazine to Two Sisters, Ga. Served 6 mos.

Proof—Pension claim S. 17309.
Died—March 6, 1835. Buried probably in "Starr Park," Richmond, Ind.
Married—Margaret Hill. Ch. William; Martin L., m. Amanda Bundy.
Collected by Mrs. Paul L. Ross, Richmond, Indiana.

BUNN, BARNES   Montgomery County
Service—Served as pri. in Col. Lamb's Artillery. Pensioned for a wound, nature not known, under Act of April 23, 1782. Pension commencing Dec. 31, 1775, at rate of $24.00 per annum and increased to $38.40, under Act of April 24, 1816. Resided in N. J. and Ind.
Proof—Papers on his claim were destroyed when War Office burned in 1814.
Died—About 1823. May be buried in Montgomery Co. or Montgomery Twp., Owen Co., Indiana.

BUNTIN, ROBERT   Knox County
Born—1757, Ireland.
Service—Ensign or Lieut. in Rev. War; also Lieut. in St. Clair's defeat; Quartermaster under Harrison at Tippecanoe.
Proof—Copied from letter written to Hon. Jeff. Davis, Sec. of War, Washington, D. C., dated Nov. 20, 1855, by a living daughter of Robert Buntin. History of Freemasonry in Indiana by Dan McDonald, p. 45. Ind. Hist. Mag., vol. XX, p. 150.
Died—Feb. 18, 1839. Buried Greenlawn, Vincennes, Ind. Stone.
Married—First W. unknown. Ch. Robert, Jr. Second W., 1793, Mary Shannon (1775-1840). Ch. Eliza, b. 1794; Mary Ann 1796-1877, m. first to Dr. Robert Allison, second to Alexander Massey, third to A. E. Lyons; Elizabeth b. 1798; Frances, b. 1799; Francis William, 1802-1803; James Mortimer, b. 1805; Jane, 1809-1875; m. Thomas J. Beeler; William, b. 1812; John Francis, 1814-1878; Campbell, 1815-1892; Henry Shanon, 1818-1847; Nancy, b. 1820; Elizabeth, b. 1810, m. Isaac Whittlesey.
Collected by Mrs. S. G. Davenport, Vincennes, Ind., and Mrs. Francis L. Zollinger (a descendant), Tulsa, Oklahoma.

BURCHFIELD, JOHN   Ripley County
Born—June 6, 1765, Guilford Co., North Carolina.
Service—Entered service from N. C. in 1779. Served 15 mos. and 24 days.
Proof—Pension claim W. 8175.
Died—Dec. 28, 1849, in Ripley Co. Name on bronze tablet in Versailles Court House.
Married—1815, Polly Patterson.
Collected by Mrs. A. B. Wycoff, Batesville, Indiana.

BURCHFIELD, ROBERT　　　　　　　　　　　　Ripley County
Born—1759.
Service—Enlisted from N. C. in April, 1775. Served at different times to March, 1783. Total service, 18 mos.
Proof—Pension claim R. 1444.
Died—Oct. 29, 1844. Buried Whitham Cemetery, Brum Twp. Name on bronze tablet in Versailles Court House.
Child—A daughter, m. Daniel Kelly. Descendants still living in Ripley Co.
Collected by Mrs. A. B. Wycoff, Batesville, Indiana.

BURDGE, SAMUEL　　　　　　　　　　　　　Wabash County
Born—Aug. 21, 1751, Cumberland Co., Pennsylvania.
Service—Pri. in Penn. Militia. On Capt. Daniel McClelland's payroll Sept. 1—Nov. 2, 1780. On pay roll of 6th class, 7th Battalion, Cumberland Co. Militia, commanded by Col. James Purdy, May, 1780.
Proof—Penn. Archives, Series 5, vol. 6, pp. 492 and 619; vol. 4, p. 621.
Died—Nov. 21, 1844. Buried in Burdge Cemetery, near Roann. Stone. And marker by Francis Slocum Chapter D. A. R.
Married—Nancy McGartney about 1811; second W., Agnes Ann Johnson (1788-1845) Ch. James, b. 1815; Johnson McGartney, b. 1819; Elizabeth; Ezra.
Collected by Gen. de Lafayette Chapter D. A. R.

BURK, GEORGE　　　　　　　　　　　　　　Jefferson County
Born—1763.
Service—While living in Shenandoah Co., Vir., enlisted Sept., 1779, as pri. in Capt. Abraham Tipton's CO., Col. Joseph Crockett's Vir. Regt.; guarded prisoners at Albemarle Barracks, went against the British and Indians in District of Ky. Discharged 1781, at Falls of the Ohio.
Proof—Pension claim S. 32152.
Family—In 1831, wife living and a daughter aged 44, names not given.
Collected by John Paul Chapter D. A. R.

BURK, JOHN　　　　　　　　　　　　　　　　Wayne County
Born—July 23, 1760, Rockbridge, Co., Virginia.
Service—Enlisted, while living on the Yadkin River, in Wilkes Co., N. C., in 1776, and served 3 mos. as Orderly-Sergeant in Capt. Jesse Walton's N. C. CO. of Light Horse. In 1779, he served several tours as Indian Spy under Capt. Amos Bird. In 1780, he served in Capt. Wm. Ritchie's S. C. CO. and in Capt. Samuel Johnston's N. C. CO. He enlisted 1781, in Capt. Alexander Gordon's CO., Col. Francis Lock's N. C. Regt. Was in battle at Eutaw Springs. Discharged Sept. 26, 1781.

Proof—Pension claim S. 16332.
Died—Feb. 1, 1836. Buried in Elkhorn Cemetery.
Married—1781, Alcy Robinson. Ch. James; William; Mary; Benjamin; Jesse; Dorcas; John; Lewis, 1799-1877.
Collected by Mrs. Paul L. Ross, Richmond, Indiana, and Mrs. Mary G. Elrod, 2233 Park Ave., Indianapolis, Indiana.

BURNETT, JOSHUA   Green County
Born—April 10, 1753, Elizabethtown, New Jersey.
Service—May 1, 1779, while living in Georgia, was drafted, Capt. Richard Herd, Col. John Dooly—served 3 mos., Sept. 18, 1780, under Gen. Elijah Clark; entered Augusta and marched against the British Army. Retreated through N. C. Was discharged by Gen. Clark in S. C. Served in all about 15 mos.
Proof—Pension claim S. 32154.
Died—About 1858. Probably buried in Taylor Twp.
Family—Had wife and sons but names not given.

BURNHAM, GURDIN   Allen County
Born—Feb. 13, 1756, East Hartford, Connecticut.
Service—Enlisted May 19, 1775, served to Dec. 10, 1775, as drummer in Capt. Pitkin's CO. Also served under him as Lieut. in Capt. Ozias Bissela CO., Col. Hinman's Conn. Regt.
Proof—Pension claim S. 31585.
Died—Oct. 16, 1844. Name placed in bronze tablet by Mary Penrose Wayne Chapter D. A. R.
Married—Polly. Had four children.
Collected by Mrs. Sue Vesta Hanna (deceased), Fort Wayne, Indiana.

BURNS, JOHN   Switzerland County
Born—About 1763.
Service—Entered service 1777, in King and Queen Co., Vir., under Col. Richard Parker. Served until 1780. In battles of Savannah and Charlestown.
Proof—Pension claim W. 9372, B. L. Wt. 71127-160-55.
Died—July 13, 1827, Switzerland Co. Probably buried Slawson Graveyard.
Married—Lucretia Vanosdol, 1810. Ch. David; Robert; Jane; Elizabeth, m. Harrison Harris; George; John.
Collected by Mrs. A. V. Danner, Vevay, Indiana.

BURNSIDE, JOHN   Putnam County
Born—Sept. 10, 1752, Lancaster Co., Pennsylvania.
Service—Entered service in Orange Co., Penn. Pri. in company commanded by Capt. Farmer of Regt. by Col. Ramsay in N. C. Line— 4 mos., 24 days. Infantry, 2 mos.

Proof—Pension claim S. 16333.
Died—Feb. 17, 1838. Buried Portland Mills, Ind. Lived in Scott County, 21 yrs. prior to June 1, 1837.
Married—Mary Denton. Ch. John (lived in Greencastle, Ind., 1871); Thomas; William; Samuel; Isaac.

BURROWS, THOMAS   Wayne County
Service—Pri. Feb. 23, 1776, in Capt. William Washington's CO., 3rd Vir. Regt. of Foot; name on roll of this regt. to July, 1777. In Capt. John Mercer's CO., to May, 1778. In Capt. Robert Powell's CO., 3rd and 7th Consolidated, May, 1778, to Oct., 1778. Again in Valentine Peyton's CO., 3rd Vir. Regt., to Nov., 1779. Name is on Muster Roll as Corporal.
Proof—Pension record.
Grave—Thought to be buried on his farm near Dalton or in Jacksonburg Cemetery.
Children—Charles, b. 1794, m. 1826, Jane Harris; Philip; Barthney; Thomas, Jr.; John.
Collected by Mrs. Paul L. Ross, Richmond, Indiana.

BUSKIRK, JOHN   Ripley County
Born—1757, Frederick Co., Maryland.
Service—Enlisted from Virginia in 1775, served one wk. Re-enlisted in 1777, as a substitute for 3 mos. In 1780, for 3 mos. Again in 1781, for 3 wks.
Proof—Pension claim S. 32148. Soldier's brother, Isaac Van Buskirk, testified that soldier had dropped the Van from his name.
Died—In Ripley Co. Name on bronze tablet in Versailles Court House.
Married———— Little. Ch. George Abram, b. 1783, m. Anna Boswell.
Collected by Mrs. A. B. Wycoff, Batesville, Indiana.

BURRITT, ZALMON   Clark County
Born—March 20, 1750, Newton, Fairfield Co., Connecticut.
Service—Enlisted July, 1777, and served 1 mo. as a pri. in Capt. Elijah Botchford's CO., Col. Barsley's Conn. Regt. and again enlisted in July, 1779, served 2 mos. Enlisted June, 1780, in Col. Sherman's Conn. Regt. Marched to West Point, there placed in Capt. Munson's CO., Col. H. Swift's Conn. Regt., served until Christmas, 1780. He afterward joined the quartermaster department and served as a wagoner; was then attached to the hospital at Fishkill, N. Y., and discharged April, 1781.
Proof—Pension claim S. 16331.
Grave—Probably buried in old cemetery now abandoned in Jeffersonville, Indiana.
Collected by Ann Rogers Clark Chapter D. A. R.

BURTON, JOHN PLEASANT   Lawrence County
Born—July 3, 1758, Virginia.
Service—Pri. in Capt. Levin Joyne's CO., 9th Vir. Regt. of Foot, commanded by Col. George Mathew. He served as John Burton.
Proof—Record in office of Adjutant General; Pension record.
Died—July 4, 1836. Buried Burton Cemetery near Mitchell, Ind. Stone. Bronze marker placed by John Wallace Chapter D. A. R.
Married—Susanah Stamper (1767-1845), m. 1779. Ch. Richard; Patsy; Allen; John; Mary; David; William; Hutchins Hardin; Zachariah; Ann; Isom; Eli.
Collected by Mrs. Mary Ingalls, Bedford, Indiana.

BUSSERON, FRANCOIS (FRANCIS) RIDAY   Knox County
Born—1748, Old Post Vincennes.
Service—Soldier and Patriot. Assisted Col. Clark as follows: Commissioned Captain. Major Busseron in command at one time of Fort Patrick Henry (Fort Sackville). Lowered the British Flag and hoisted Flag of Virginia. Signed the Oath of Allegiance. Major in 1780.
Proof—Letters of Col. Clark, vol. I, p. 91; Cawthorn's Hist. of Vincennes, Dunn's history, Green's Hist. of Knox Co., pp. 132-133.
Died—1791. Buried Francis Xavier Cemetery, Vincennes, Ind.
Married—Sept., 1773 or 4, Francoise Drouet de Richarville. Ch. Suzanne m. Nicholas Fortin; Rosalie; Charles; Ursule, m. Antoine Marchal; Julie, m. Hyancinthe Lasselle.
Collected by J. A. Reincke, New Orleans, La., and Mrs. S. G. Davenport, Vincennes, Indiana.

BUTLER, JAMES   Cass County
Service—Soldier in the Rev. War.
Proof—History of Cass County, p. 127; One Hundred Years of Tipton Lodge No. 33, F. and A. M., p. 155. These are considered authentic.
Collected by Miss Laura Henderson, Logansport, Indiana.

BUTLER, JOEL   Jennings County
Born—1752.
Service—Pri. in Col. Joseph's Regt., 1777—Vermont Militia.
Proof—Vermont Militia Rolls by Goodrich, p. 28; D. A. R. No. 142333.
Died—1822. Buried in old cemetery near Scipio, Jennings Co.
Married—Mabel Thompson, b. 1749. Ch. Sally, 1806-1870, m. Spencer Thayer; Chauncy, b. 1775.

BYARLAY (BYERLY), MICHAEL   Jackson County
Born—July 7, 1758, Shepardtown, Pennsylvania.
Service—Pri. July 10, 1777, to June, 1781, under Captains Morrow and McIntire, Cols. Pendleton, Scott and Darke—Vir. Line.

Proof—Pension claim S. F. 16065; Virginia State Library—List of Rev. S. in Vir.
Died—Aug. 20, 1844. Buried Seymour, Ind.
Married—1781, Rebecca Pitcock. Ch. Hannah; Elizabeth; Nancy; Michael; Mary; Samuel M.; Rebecca; Margaret.
Collected by Caroline Scott Harrison Chapter D. A. R.

BYRD, JOHN   Fayette County
Born—About 1759.
Service—Enlisted 1776 in Capt. Jonathan Clark's CO. Col. Muhlenburgh 8th Vir. Regt. for 2 yrs. Discharged Valley Forge. In battles of Brandywine and Germantown.
Proof—Pension claim S. 35807.
Died—1829 or 1830 in Connersville, Ind.
Married—1780 Elinor. Had two children.

CAIN, JOHN   Wayne County
Born—June 22, 1760, North Carolina.
Service—While residing in Union District, S. C., he served as a pri. in S. C. Troops as follows: In the spring of 1776 or 1777, 4 mos. in Capt. Joshua Palmer's CO. under Gen. Williamson. 1 mo. in Capt. William Fair's CO., Col. Thomas' Regt. In 1779, 3 mos. in Capt. Joshua Palmer's CO. and was at the battle of Stone River. Served at various times under Capts. William Fair, Hughes, Woodson and Jolly, amounting in all to 15 mos. He served 3 mos. in 1781 under Major Benj. Jolly and was at the battle of Eutaw Springs.
Proof—Pension claim W. 3510.
Married—First Miss Pearson. Ch. Robert; Joseph; Barbara; Rebecca. Second 1795, to Susanna Henley. Ch. Elizabeth, b. 1798; John, b. 1802; Abijah, b. 1808; Jonathan, b. 1813; Letty, b. 1818; Nancy, b. 1800; William, b. 1805; Sarah, b. 1809; Susanna, b. 1815.
Collected by Mrs. Paul L. Ross, Richmond, Indiana.

CALDWELL (COLWELL), JOHN   Vigo County
Born—1755, Prince Edward Co., Virginia.
Service—Entered 1779, under Col. Scott, Gen. Nelson, 3 mos. Virginia Militia. Drafted in 1780 and 1782. 6 mos. service.
Proof—Pension claim S. 16344.
Died—Aug. 19, 1838. Buried in Caldwell Cemetery. Stone.
Married—Jane ——, d. July 25, 1834.

CALDWELL, ROBERT   Rush County
Born—June 1, 1757, Fayette Co., Pennsylvania.
Service—Enlisted July, 1776, for 3 yrs., pri. in Capt. Wendel Curry's CO. and Cols. Mackay and Daniel Brodhead's 8th Penn. Regt. Also under Capts. Van Swearinger and John Findley.

Proof—Pension claim S. 35814.
Died—July 31, 1846. Buried in Concord Cemetery, Rushville Twp. Government marker. Name on bronze tablet in Rush. Co. Court House.
Married—Sarah Fryer. Ch. Nancy, m. —— Smith; William; Elizabeth, m. —— Scott; Robert; James; Polly; Peggy; Joseph; David; Jane, m. —— Ploughe; Sally, m. ——Foster; Tabitha, m. ——McVey.
Collected by Rushville Chapter D. A. R. and Caroline Scott Harrison Chapter D. A. R.

CALHOUN, JOHN   Dearborn County
Service—Drew pay for military duty as horseman 1781-82. Wagon service, 1780-81.
Proof—Pension claim W. 9777.
Died—1823. An old church record states he was buried at Hardintown.
Married—Violet ——.
Collected by Mrs. Walter Kerr, Aurora, Indiana.

CALLAWAY, MICAJAH   Washington County
Born—1755, Lynchburg, Virginia.
Service—1777, people of Boonesboro, Ky., needing salt, it was arranged that Daniel Boone and 80 men should go to lower Blue Licks on the Licking River and manufacture salt. Micajah Callaway and his brother Flanders were of this number. The party set out Jan. 1, 1778, and by Feb. had enough salt to send 3 men back. Boone was captured by Indians the same day and persuaded his men to surrender. Callaway was prisoner 3 yrs. and 7 mos., and was able to tell of the work of the British with the Indians. He was used later as interpreter in exchange of prisoners. He was at one time chief of scouts.
Proof—Pension application. Washington Co. History by Stevens.
Died—April 11, 1849. Buried Peugh Cemetery, Washington Twp. Stone.
Married—First to Mary Arnold, 1796. Ch. James; Edmund; Second Wife Frank Hawkins. Ch. John Hawkins; Noble.
Collected by Mrs. Harvey Morris, Salem, Indiana.

CALLOWAY, SAMUEL   Clark County
Born—About 1753.
Service—Enlisted at Pittsburgh, Penn., in March, 1779; as pri. in Capt. Uriah Springer's CO., Col. John Gibson's 9th Va. Regt. Was at capture of Muncy Indiantowns, also at Fts. Laurens and McIntosh, and at Fort Pittsburgh, guarding the attacks of the Indians. Discharged Oct. 21, 1780.
Proof—Pension claim S. 35813.
Died—Last payment of pension was made Sept. 4, 1822. Had a wife and 8 children but gave no names in pension application.
Collected by Ann Rogers Clark Chapter D. A. R.

CALVIN, JOB Posey County
Born—About 1755.
Service—Served from S. C. in the same company with Samuel Parks, under Capt. John Virgin.
Proof—Posey Co., Ind., Probate Court Records C. and D., p. 255.
Collected by Mrs. Charles T. Johnson, Mt. Vernon, Indiana.

CAMPBELL, JAMES Grant County
Born—April 16, 1763, Blandford, Berkshire, Co., Massachusetts.
Service—Enlisted March, 1781, and served until Dec., 1783, as a pri. under Capt. Job Wright and Col. Marinus Willett of N. Y. Enlisted at Nobletown, N. Y.
Proof—Certificate 3045.
Died—1859. Buried Maple Grove Cemetery, 2 miles N. of Sweetser. Marker placed by Gen. Francis Marion Chapter D. A. R.
Married—Mahala McPherson. Son, William Lauson Campbell.
Collected by Mrs. Charles A. Priest, Marion, Indiana.

CAMPBELL, JOHN Monroe County
Born—March 7, 1756, Belfast, Ireland.
Service—Private in Regt. of Col. Muhlenburg, Vir. Line, 2 yrs.
Proof—Pension claim S. 35824.
Died—Dec. 18, 1838. Buried Rosehill Cemetery, Bloomington, Ind. Stone.
Married—Isabella Blakely. Ch. James; Archibald; Rachel; Sally; Jane; Mary; Anna; Rebecca; Cynthia.
Collected by Alice Worley Carpenter, Tampa, Florida.

CAMPBELL, WILLIAM Bartholomew County
Born—1760, Philadelphia, Pennsylvania.
Service—Pri. in company under Col. Moore in Penn. Militia, 13 mos.
Proof—Pension claim W. 9773.
Died—June 30, 1834. Probably buried in Columbus Twp.
Married—1791, Rachel Robinson. Ch. Martha, b. 1792; Eley, b. 1795; Alexander, b. 1797; Elizabeth, b. 1800.
Collected by Mrs. Laura D. Fix (deceased), Columbus, Indiana.

CAMPBELL, WILLIAM Jefferson County
Born—1732, Ireland.
Service—Was with Arnold and Montgomery in 1776, when they made an unsuccessful attack on Quebec.
Proof—Robert's N. Y. in the Revolution, p. 31. D. A. R. No. 110974.
Died—1826. Buried on B. F. Law's farm near Deputy, Ind. Government marker.

Married—Elizabeth Wellen. Ch. George; James; William; Wellen; Parmelia, m. 1790, Gabriel Foster; Hannah; Sarah.
Collected by John Paul Chapter D. A. R.

CAMPBELL, WILLIAM Warrick County
Born—1759, near Charlotte, North Carolina.
Service—Enlisted 1775, York Co., S. C., under Capt. Peter Clinton, Capt. How, Cols. Neal, Polk, Bratton and Roberts, Gen. Williamson. Served, in all, 18 mos.
Proof—Pension claim W. 9774.
Died—April 21, 1837. Warrick Co.
Married—1785, Elizabeth Bogan, b. 1766. Ch. James, b. 1786; Jennet, b. 1788, m. Wm. Webb; Thomas, b. 1790; Rachel, b. 1792; Lettice, b. 1796; Cynthia, b. 1798; Polly Ann, b. 1801; Elizabeth, b. 1803; Samuel, b. 1806.

CANNON, JAMES Daviess County
Born—June 5, 1755, Ninety-Six District, South Carolina.
Service—Volunteered in Dec., 1775, for 9 mos. Served in Capt. Jared Smith's CO. S. C. Troops, marched to Smith's Station on the frontier of S. C., where he was stationed the 9 mos. Engaged in guarding the frontier against attacks of Cherokee Indians. Volunteered again in May, 1777, and served in Capt. James Grear's CO., Col. McCreary's S. C. Regt., marched to Augusta, Georgia, from there to St. Mary's river in Florida; served 3 mos. He volunteered in Dec., 1778, served 3 mos. in Capt. Sexton's CO., Col. James William's S. C. Regt.
Proof—Pension claim S. 32166.
Died—After 1843.
Married—In Montgomery Co., N. C., but names of wife and children not given.
Collected by Mrs. Roy Bogner, Washington, Indiana.

CARDINAL, MILLETT Allen County
Service—Volunteered with 400 others, under Col. Augustus Motin de la Balm to march north to Post Miami (Fort Wayne), to quell Indian atrocities and depredations. Eighty men left Post Vincennes in advance, reached Miami villages and destroyed the store house of Baubine on Nov. 3, 1780. Returned toward Vincennes to meet reinforcements, and camped on the banks of the Abute (Aboite) river and was ambushed in the night by the Miami Indians led by Little Turtle. About 30 or 40 men were killed. Among them was Millett Cardinal.

Proof—References at Vincennes St. Francis Xavier Cathedral; Draper's
MSS 50-J-77; Wisconsin Historical Society.
Died—Nov. 3, 1780. The Aboite River is in Allen County.
Collected by Mrs. T. J. Hindman, Fort Wayne, Indiana.

CARDINAL, NICHOLAS   Knox County
Born—Aug. 25, 1723, Montreal, Canada.
Service—A Patriot. Signed the Oath of Allegiance to the Republic of
Virginia, July 20, 1778.
Proof—Next to the last name in the list of signers as found in George
Rogers Clark's Papers 1771-1781; Ill. Historical Collections, vol.
VIII, pp. 52-59.
Died—Aug. 24, 1789. Buried St. Francis Xavier Cemetery, Vincennes.
Married—1761, Marie Joseph Girard. Ch. Marie Joseph Cardinal, b.
1776, m. Vital Bunche; Celeste Cardinal, b. 1769, m. Joseph Leveron;
Francoise; Nicholas; Joseph; Medars; Genevieve, m. Francoise
Avelin.
Collected by Mrs. Leo Schultheis, Vincennes, Indiana.

CARL, ELIJAH   Clark County
Born—March, 1763, New Jersey.
Service—Pri. in company under Capt. Chamburg, Col. Scudder's N. J.
Regt. Militia for 2 yrs.
Proof—Pension claim S. 1724.
Death—Last payment of pension was made to the pensioner on Sept.
4, 1843, at the Pension Agency, New Albany, Ind. He lived with
a daughter in Clark Co., Indiana.

CARLTON, AMBROSE   Lawrence County
Born—March 28, 1763, England.
Service—Enlisted at age of 17, serving 3 mos. under Capt. James
Henderson and Col. Brandon. In summer of 1780, he enlisted for
7 mos. under Capt. Keyes, Capt. Beverly and Col. Lewis. From
1781 until Aug., 1782, he served as sergeant under Capt. Alexander
Gordon and Col. Malmady, and later under Capt. James Stations
and Col. James Jackson in the celebrated "Georgia Legion."
Proof—Pension record.
Died—Dec. 23, 1823. Buried Carlton Cemetery. Stone. Bronze marker
placed by John Wallace Chapter D. A. R.
Married—1789, Jean Montgomery (1769-1835). Ch. Cynthia; Elizabeth;
Esther; Catherine; Mary; Thomas Lewis; Robert Montgomery.
Collected by Mrs. Julia Wallheiser, Bedford, Indiana.

CARNEY, JOHN   Bartholomew County
Born—April 15, 1757. Frederick Co., Virginia.
Service—Enlisted Botetourt Co., Vir. Served under Capts. Wm. Mc-
    Clanahan, and Henry Paulding and Cols. Wm. Christian and John
    Bowman, 1 year.
Proof—Pension claim S. 1607. Applied from Jennings Co., Ind.
Died—After Sept. 4, 1840. Probably buried S. of Columbus, Ind.
Married—Margaret Floyd. Son, Pleasant, b. 1786.

CARPENTER, JOHN   Owen County
Service—Private in Vir. Line. Enlisted 1777 for 3 years in 12th Vir.
    Regt., under Col. Nathaniel Guest, Capt. Alexander Breckenridge.
    In Battles of Monmouth and Stony Point.
Proof—Pension claim S. 35812.
Grave—In Hick's Cemetery near Freedom, Owen Co.

CARR, ELISHA   Clark County
Born—Fayette Co., Pennsylvania.
Service—Pri. in Penn. Militia. Enlisted Westmoreland Co., Penn.
Proof—Penn. Archives, Series 5, vol. 14, pp. 734 and 431.
Grave—Silver Creek Cemetery, Clark Co.
Children—Joseph, b. 1782; John, b. 1784; Elijah; Elisha, b. 1792.

CARR, JAMES   Johnson County
Born—1756, Ireland.
Service—Enlisted in Berkley Co., Vir., as a private the last of May
    or first of June, 1776. Served 6 mos. in Capt. Robert Jackson's
    Virginia CO. Served 3 mos. in 1777, in Capt. George Scott's
    Va. CO., and was in the battle of Piscataqua and a skirmish
    near Quibbletown.
Proof—Pension claim S. 32157.
Grave—On Luyster farm S. of Franklin. Government marker placed
    by Alexander Hamilton Chapter D. A. R. Died March 15, 1842.
Married—Elizabeth.
Collected by Mrs. I. E. Tranter, Franklin, Indiana.

CARR, ROBERT   Marion County
Born—1759 in Ulster District, Ireland.
Service—Enlisted March, 1780. Five mos. as pri. under Capt. Trimble,
    Vir., and Feb., 1781, 2 mos. as pri. under Capt. David Mary, Vir.
    In battle of Guilford Court House 1781, under Gen. Green.
Proof—Pension record.
Died—July 4, 1833. Buried New Bethel Cemetery.

Married—Nancy Craig, 1793 (1773-1836). Ch. David, b. 1793; Arthur,
b. 1799; George, b. 1796, b. Mary Ohr; Robert, b. 1805; A. Craig,
b. 1808, m. first to Sarah Williams, second to Mary Sample.
Collected by Miss Marion May Carr, Indianapolis, Indiana.

CARR, THOMAS   Clark County
Born—June 23, 1755, Maryland.
Service—Served as a Captain from Westmoreland Co., Penn.
Proof—Penn. Archives, Series 5, vol. 4, p. 737.
Died—Oct. 26, 1822. Buried Silver Creek Cemetery near Sellersburg,
Ind. Stone.
Married—Hannah Cooms (1766-1829). Ch. Absolom; Elizabeth Carr
Bowell; Nancy Carr Parr; John; Joseph; Hannah Carr Parr;
Thomas; Rachel; Jefferson; Rebecca Carr Athen; Elisha.
Collected by Mrs. J. H. Grimes, Danville, Indiana.

CARROLL, BARTHOLOMEW   Johnson County
Born—1722.
Service—Enlisted in New London, Vir., June 1, 1780. Pri. in Capt.
Stribling's and Capt. Stephen's CO., Col. Haws' Vir. Regt. He
was in the battles of Camden, Guilford Court House and Eutaw
Springs and was discharged Jan. 1, 1782.
Proof—Pension claim S. 35827.
Died—Will probated March 18, 1828. Buried Union Twp., Johnson Co.
Married—Catharine ——. Son, Bartholomew, Jr., and other children,
names not known.
Collected by Mrs. I. E. Tranter, Franklin, Indiana.

CARSON, CHARLES   Posey County
Born—Oct. 22, 1761.
Service—Served 5 yrs. in Rev. War.
Proof—Information given on tombstone.
Died—Oct. 5, 1816. Buried West Franklin Cemetery, Posey Co. Stone.
Married—Rachiel ——. Had 4 sons and 2 daughters. Sons, John;
Charles; Hamilton; David.
Collected by Mrs. Charles T. Johnson, Mt. Vernon, Indiana.

CARSON, JOHN   Rush County
Born—May 3, 1761, Virginia.
Service—Enlisted July, 1780, for 3 mos. as pri. under Capt. Masterson,
Virginia. Enlisted fall of 1780 for 7 mos. under Capt. Morgan,
Cols. Mumford, Davis, Archibald Campbell; was detailed in Lee's
Corps; was in skirmish on James River.
Proof—Pension claim S. F. 32167.

Died—1845. Buried Alger Graveyard, Union Twp., Rush County. Stone.
Married—Hester ——, d. 1852, aged 85.
Collected by Mrs. Williard Amos, Rushville, Indiana.

CARSON, WALTER   Jennings County
Born—1758, York County, Pennsylvania.
Service—Enlisted in July or August, 1776, and served 3 mos. as a pri. in Capt. William McClelland's CO., Col. David Kenedy's Penn. Regt. Also served 3 mos. from Dec. 1, 1777, in Capt. David Wilson's CO., Col. John Andrew's Penn. Regt., and was in the battle of Whitemarsh. He moved to Camden District, S. C., in 1779, and in 1780 served 6 mos. as Captain in Col. Andrew Neel's S. C. Regt., and was in the battles of Williamson's Plantation, Camden Ferry, on the Wateree River, Rocky Mount, Hanging Rock and Sumter's Defeat at Fishing Creek.
Proof—Pension claim S. 32165.
Died—March 3, 1834. Buried in Graham Church Cemetery near Vernon. Stone.
Married—Mary ——. Ch. Walter; Felix; Daniel C.; James P.; Louisa A.; William; Mary.
Collected by John N. Graham, Franklin, Indiana.

CARTER, WILLIAM   Clinton County
Born—May 22, 1748, Chester Co., Pennsylvania.
Service—Enlisted July or August, 1781, and served 6 mos. as pri. in Capt. John Ralston's CO., Col. Thomas Hawkley's Penn. Regt. He again enlisted and served 4 mos. as teamster under Owen Thomas, Wagonmaster.
Proof—Pension claim S. 31592.
Died—Sept. 21, 1840. Buried Bunnell Cemetery, 2 miles from Frankfort. Stone. Marker in Courtyard of Clinton Co. placed by Col. Harmon Aughe Chapter D. A. R.
Son—Jesse, d. 1871.
Collected by Daisy Heavilon, Frankfort, Indiana.

CASE, ISAIAH   Wayne County
Born—Jan. 19, 1759, Morris, New Jersey.
Service—Volunteered from Morris Co., N. J., for 6 wks. as pri., under Lieut. Currian in N. J. troops and assisted in building a fort at Pompton Plains, N. J. Again served 6 wks. as pri. in Capt. Solomon's (Salmon's) CO., N. J. troops; moved to N. C., where he volunteered and served at different times on tours for 12 mos. in Capt. Cleveland's N. C. CO. and for a like time on tours in Capt. Jackson's N. C. CO. In battle of King's Mountain.

Proof—Pension claim S. 16692.
Died—Last payment of pension was made Oct. 2, 1849.
Collected by Mrs. Paul L. Ross, Richmond, Indiana.

CASE, JAMES   Harrison County
Born—Sept. 12, 1760.
Service—Pri. in company under Capt. Paddox of Regt. under Col. Williamson, Penn. 10 mos. 21 days.
Proof—Pension claim S. 16694.
Died—Feb. 8, 1850. Buried Salem Cemetery, Washington Twp.

CASE, JOHN   Dearborn County
Born—1754, near Flemington, N. J.
Service—Pri. in Capt. Nathan Stout's CO. 3rd Regt. N. J. Militia.
Proof—D. A. R. No. 143745.
Died—Oct. 18, 1838. Buried Braysville Cemetery. Stone. Bronze tablet placed by Col. Archibald Lochry Chapter D. A. R.
Married—Nancy ———. Son, John P., 1794-1880.
Collected by Mrs. Walter Kerr, Aurora, Indiana.

CASE, WILLIAM   Orange County
Born—1755. Probably Pennsylvania.
Service—Enlisted at Winchester, Vir., in July, 1776. Served in Capt. Abraham Shepherd's CO., Col. Rawling's Regt. He was taken prisoner at Fort Washington, Nov., 1776. After 9 weeks, released. Joined wagon service under Jacob Hillismer and Biddle, 4 mos. Returned to his father's home at Redstone Settlement, Penn., and served 4 campaigns against Indians.
Proof—Pension record—pension allowed 1820, while a resident of Washington Co., Ind.
Died—Nov. 1, 1827. Buried Trimble Graveyard in Northeast Twp. Stone.
Married—Rebecca Glover, 1798. Ch. James; Squire; Malinda; Hannah; Betsey; Washington; Ruth; Sally; Uriah; Rebecca; William.
Collected by Mrs. N. B. Mavity, French Lick, Indiana.

CASSADY THOMAS   Rush County
Born—1757, Virginia.
Service—Served as a private in the Vir. Continental Line.
Proof—Adjutant General's Office, Doc. 44; Doc. House of Delegates, Virginia, 1834; D. A. R. No. 54238.
Died—1825. Buried Kelly Cemetery.
Married—Margaret McGriff Hart, d. 1823. Ch. Wear, 1780-1831; Thomas; William; Sampson, 1797-1882; Simon; Elizabeth, 1787-1834; Elenor.
Collected by Miss Emma Cassaday, Rushville, Indiana.

CATHCART, JOHN   Elkhart County
Born—1740, Scotland.
Service—Pri. in 6th CO., 9th Battalion, Lancaster Co. Militia. Name
    appears in list for the year 1782.
Proof—Penn. Archives, 5th Series, vol. 7, p. 958; 6th Series, vol. 3,
    p. 381.
Died—After 1830. Buried cemetery back of Washington Twp. School.
Children—James (War of 1812), m. Pennot Leonard.
Collected by Mrs. F. C. Wherly, Elkhart, Indiana.

CATT, GEORGE   Knox County
Born—Virginia.
Service—Pri., May 25 to July 25, 2 mos. 2 days. Pay per month, 6-2/3 S.
Proof—From Pay Abstract of Capt. John Whitsell's CO. of rangers
    from Monogalia and Ohio Counties; in W. Va. Archives and History, 3rd biennial report, p. 122.
Died—Oct., 1816. Buried in Johnson Twp.
Names of children taken from Will are: George; Elizabeth Pea;
    John; Catherine Johnson; Solomon; Moses; Mary; Susannah;
    Nancy Decker.
Collected by Mrs. S. G. Davenport, Vincennes, Indiana.

CATT, PHILLIP   Knox County
Born—1750, in Virginia.
Service—While residing at Brownsville, Penn., enlisted in 1776 or 77
    in Capt. John Whitsell's CO., under Col. Brodhead in Penn.
    Troops. Established a station at mouth of Fishing Creek on
    the Ohio River and went out as a ranger from this station as
    far as the mouth of the Kanawha; served 6 mos. Returned to
    Brownsville and served on several tours against the Indians under
    Capts. Kincaid and Wilson. Enlisted in 1777 or 78, in Capt.
    Morgan's CO. In 1782, enlisted in Capt. Jacob Tevibaugh's CO.,
    marched to Sandusky Plains, where he was in battle with Indians
    under Col. Crawford, in which the Americans were defeated and
    Col. Crawford taken a prisoner.
Proof—Pension claim S. 16072.
Died—1844. Buried West Salem Church Cemetery, Johnson Twp.
Married—Sarah. Had five daughters according to will, but no names
    were given.
Collected by Mrs. S. G. Davenport, Vincennes, Indiana.

CHAMBERS, ALEXANDER   Jefferson County
Born—1756, Rockbridge, Virginia.
Service—Enlisted in 1776 or 1777; transferred to Continental Army
    1777.

Proof—"Chambers History" found in State Library.
Died—June 29, 1857. Buried White River Cemetery near Kent, Ind.
Government marker placed by John Paul Chapter D. A. R.
Married—Rachel Ann Monroe. Ch. William; Sanders; John; Avery; George; Nancy; Mary; Rachel.
Collected by John Paul Chapter D. A. R.

CHAMBERS, ALEXANDER   Knox County
Born—1753, Ireland.
Service—Pri. in Virginia, 3 mos. in 1777. In N. C., 3 mos. in 1780.
Proof—Pension record; D. A. R. Lineage, vol. 101, p. 268.
Died—1834. Buried near Edwardsport in Chambers Cemetery.
Married—Polly ——. Ch. Thomas; Dave; James; John Alexander; Levi; Joseph.
Collected by Mrs. S. G. Davenport, Vincennes, Indiana.

CHAMBERS, JOHN   Pike County
Born—About 1749, Virginia.
Service—Enlisted Dec., 1776, at the forks of the Cheat on the Monongahela River in Vir., and served as a pri. in Capt. David Scott's CO., Col. John Gibson's Vir. Regt. Discharged Dec. 28, 1779, but served until March 1, 1780.
Proof—Pension claim S. 35834.
Died—June 22, 1824. Buried Hornbrook Farm, 1 mile from Union, Pike Co.
Married—Rachel ——, b. 1765. Son, George, 1794-1842. Possibly other children.
Collected by Mrs. C. R. Emery, Bloomington, Indiana, and Mrs. Margaret Jean, Petersburg, Indiana.

CHAMBERS, NATHANIEL   Washington County
Born—1762, Probably North Carolina.
Service—While residing in Surry Co., N. C., he enlisted at Surry Court House, fall 1778, served 6 mos. in Capt. Henry Smith's CO., Col. Armstrong's N. C. Regt. In battle of Brier Creek. 1781, on Hunting Creek, Wilkes Co., N. C., 3 mos. under Capt. Johnson, Col. Cleveland's Regt.
Proof—Pension claim S. 32171; Court Records, Washington Co., Ind.; Cemetery and Family records.
Died—Feb. 11, 1848. Buried Monroe Cemetery, Washington Co. Family tombstone states aged 100 yrs., which would indicate he was born 1748. Also a government marker placed by G. A. R.
Married—Mary ——. Ch. John; William; Mary; Milly; Catherine; James.
Collected by Mrs. Harvey Morris, Salem, Indiana.

CHAMBERS, WILLIAM   Jackson County
Born—About 1746, Virginia.
Service—Pri. in company under Capt. Smith, Col. John Armstrong's
    N. C. Regt. 9 mos.
Proof—Pension claim S. 16078.
Died—Last payment of pension made to the pensioner on March 25,
    1836, at the State Bank of Ind., Bedford, Indiana.

CHANCELLOR, DAVID   Spencer County
Born—Oct., 1749, probably in Virginia.
Service—Enlisted in the state of Virginia in Jan., 1779, in Capts. Holman Rice's and Merriwether's CO., Col. Francis Taylor's Vir. Regt., guarding prisoners at Albemarle and Winchester Barracks and was discharged May 1, 1781.
Proof—Pension claim S. 35833.
Died—After 1832. Buried Chancellor graveyard, Hammond Twp. Government marker.
Son—Thomas M. There were other children.
Collected by Miss Laura M. Wright, Rockport, Ind., and Irvington Chapter D. A. R.

CHANDLER, WILLIAM   Orange County
Service—Enlisted in Buckingham Co., Vir., in 1776, and served as a pri. under Capt. Franklin and Capt. Shelton, Col. Steven's Virginia Regt. Was in the battles of Brandywine, Germantown, Monmouth and others. Discharged, having served 3½ yrs.
Proof—Pension record.
Died—Feb. 10, 1837. Buried graveyard at Danner's Chapel, Stampers Creek Twp.
Married—First wife unknown. Ch. Elizabeth; Robin; Catherine; Sarah; Isaac; Rachel; William. Second W., Polly Goff, a widow.
Collected by Mrs. N. B. Mavity, French Lick and Mrs. Harvey Morris, Salem.

CHANEY, JOHN   Greene County
Born—1757, Orange Co., N. C.
Service—Enlisted with Capt. James Sepham. Volunteered 1786 to serve in S. C. for 7 yrs. Was promised 100 pounds sterling and lands. Marched toward Georgia. Later joined Col. Middleton. Enlisted in cavalry under Col. Wm. Washington, one year. Was in battle of Eutaw Springs.
Proof—Pension claim S. 32177.
Died—Sept. 12, 1845. Buried near Ooley's Mill, N. E. of Worthington, Indiana.
Had wife and children but names not given in pension application.

CHAPIN, SAMUEL   Crawford County
Born—1760, Granby, Mass.
Service—While residing in Bennington, Vt., he served as pri. with the
    Vt. Troops, as follows: 5 days guarding ammunition from Ben-
    nington to North River, N. Y.; about   1 mo. in Capt. Samuel
    Robinson's Co., Col. Moses Robinson's Regt. and marched to Ticon-
    deroga; 6 mos. in Capt. Parmalee Allen's Co., Col. Samuel Her-
    rick's Regt.; 1 mo. and 2 wks. in same regt.; 1 mo. at Rutland
    in Col. Ebenezer Walbridge's Regt. In Battles of Lake George
    Landing, Mount Defiance, Mount Hope, and the "Mills" at the
    outlet of Lake George.
Proof—Pension claim S. 16706.
Died—Feb. 13, 1842.
Son—Gad Chapin, m. Margaret White in 1825.

CHAPMAN, LEMUEL   Ripley County
Born—1759, Conn.
Service—Entered service from N. Y. in 1777, under Col. Swift and Capt.
    Strong. Served 5 mos.
Proof—Pension claim S. 35831. Pensioned first in Vermont. Moved to
    Ripley Co., Ind., in 1837.
Died—Sept. 17, 1847. Thought to be buried near Versailles, Ind. Name
    is on bronze tablet in Versailles Court House.
Had a daughter, Alvina, aged 14, in 1820.
Collected by Mrs. A. B. Wycoff, Batesville, Indiana.

CHAPMAN, WILLIAM   Daviess County
Born—1752, New Jersey.
Service—He was from Sussex Co., N. J., and received Certificate No.
    691, dated May 1, 1784, signed by Joseph Gaston, for depreciation
    of his Continental pay for services as private, Sussex Co., N. J.,
    Militia.
Proof—Adjutant General's Office, N. J.; Stryker's Roster of N. J. Rev.
    War, p. 537.
Died—In fall of 1823. Buried in Reeve Twp.
Married—1786, Hannah Smith. Ch. Elijah, m. Elizabeth Miller; Han-
    nah, m. Henry Weaver; Elizabeth, m. Edward McKinley; William,
    m. Ruth Miller; Mary, m. James Broades, and James Richards;
    Jesse, m. Betsey Wallace; Rachel, m. Patrick McKinley, and Wes-
    ley Wallace; Thomas, m. Sarah Stringer; Sarah, m. Coleman Wal-
    lace. Charles, m. Eleanor Morgan; Cynthia, m. Solomon Cox;
    Enoch.
Collected by Mrs. Roy Bogner, Washington, Indiana.

CHARLEY, GEORGE   Harrison County
Born—About 1763.
Service—Pri. in company under Capt. Wallace, Regt. of Col. Campbell in Vir. Line, 3 yrs., 1779.
Proof—Pension claim W. 9781.
Died—Aug. 6, 1833. Buried on David Charley farm, on Indian Creek, N. E. of Corydon, Indiana.
Married—Christina ——, 1790. Ch. Peter b. 1791; Polly b. 1794; Elizabeth b. 1796; Sarah b. 1798; Anna b. 1801; Lydia b. 1803, m. Philip Brandenburg; George b. 1805; Jacob b. 1807; Christena b. 1811; Susannah b. 1813; Joseph b. 1815.

CHENOWETH, ARTHUR JR.   Bartholomew County
Born—July 16, 1752, Baltimore, Maryland.
Service—He enlisted with his brother John in Maryland Line, Sept. 16, 1776, and was discharged July 1, 1779, a Corporal. They were in Rawling's Regt. and were captured at Fort Washington when the Fort was compelled to surrender. They were soon exchanged and returned to their regiment.
Proof—Samuel S. Sargent, an S. A. R.; and County Records.
Died—1829, in Columbus, Indiana.
Married—1773, Elspa Lawrence. Ch. Absolem b. 1774; Jane b. 1776; Mary b. 1778; John b. 1780; Arthur b. 1784; Margaret b. 1786; Rachel b. 1789; Eleanor; Anna; Elias; William.
Collected by Mrs. Laura D. Fix (deceased), Columbus, Indiana.

CHERRY, AARON   Dearborn County
Born—Penn.
Service—Received depreciation pay for services in Westmoreland Co. Militia. Name appears as a ranger on Frontiers from Westmoreland Co., and on muster roll of Navy and Line, militia and ranger. He was a member of Capt. Thomas Moore's CO. and of Capt. Archibald Leech's CO.
Proof—Penn. Archives, Series 5, vol. 4, p. 432; Series 3, vol. 23, pp. 223, 322, 324.
Died—In Dearborn Co. Buried Georgetown Cemetery.
Married—Mary Phillips. Dau. Honor, b. 1778, d. 1847.
Collected by Mrs. Hattie S. Whittaker, Tiskilwa, Illinois.

CHESSHIRE, JOHN B.   Floyd County
Born—About 1753.
Service—Pri. in company commanded by Capt. West, Regt. of Col. Howes in Vir. Line, 1 yr.
Proof—Pension claim S. 35829.
Died—Estate probated Aug. 27, 1836.

Married—Sarah ———. Ch. Baptiste. (In pension application the soldier stated he had 4 children.)
Collected by Mrs. V. R. Conner, New Albany, Indiana.

CHILDERS, MOSBY   Hancock County
Service—Enlisted Charlottesville, Vir., in 7th Vir. Regt., under Capt. Mathew Dewitt. In battles of Brandywine and Monmouth.
Proof—Pension record.
Died—Aug. 3, 1843, Hancock Co.
Children—John; Hammel; William; Mosby; Robert; Henry; Andrew; Martin; Nancy; Joseph; Abraham.

CHRISTIAN, ALLEN   Shelby County
Born—May 22, 1754, Cumberland Co., Virginia.
Service—While residing in Bedford Co., Vir., he enlisted April 1, 1780. Served as a pri. in Capt. Nathaniel Tate's CO., Col. Calloway's Vir. Regt., marched to N. C. to join the army under Gen. Gates, was ordered to act as a guard to the wagons which were sent out for provisions, had reached Deep River, when it was learned that Gen. Gates had been defeated at Camden; the wagons with the guards then retreated to Hillsboro, N. C., where soldier was discharged having served at least 4½ mos.; he enlisted July, 1781, under the same officers, served 3 mos. and was discharged in Cumberland Co., Va.
Proof—Pension claim S. 32170.
Died—Last payment of pension was made on Sept. 17, 1842.

CHUMBLAY (CHUMBLEY), JOHN   Daviess County
Born—Dec. 4, 1760, Amelia Co., Virginia.
Service—Enlisted in Amelia Co., Va., Sept. 1, 1778. Served 3 mos in Capt. Richard Oglesby's CO., Maj. Joseph Scott's Brigade, Va. Troops. Enlisted July, 1779, served 3 mos. as pri. in Capt. Wm. Crosscrarrick's CO., Maj. James Jenkins' Brigade. Enlisted Feb. 1781, served as pri. in Capt. Robert Hutson's CO., Col. Randolph's Vir. Regt., for 6 wks. In battle of Guilford Court House. Enlisted June 1, 1782, served 8 wks. in Capt. Philip Williams' Vir. CO.
Proof—Pension claim S. 32169.
Died—About May, 1835. Buried in Reeve Twp.
A son was buried in Fountain Co., Ind.
Collected by Mrs. Roy Bogner, Washington, Indiana.

CHUTE, JAMES   Jefferson County
Born—Feb. 16, 1751, Newburry, Mass.
Service—Minute-man at Lexington, Alarm. Pri. in Capt. Jacob Gerrish's CO., which marched on the Alarm of April 19, 1775, to Cambridge. Served 6 days.

Proof—Curries' History of Newbury, Mass., p. 587; Mass. Soldiers and
Sailors, vol. 111, p. 464; Chute Genealogy; Brooks-Houghton's
Genealogy, by Thomas J. Brooks III.
Died—1823. Buried Old Cemetery, now a park, in Madison, Ind.
Married—1775, Mehitable Thurston. Had 8 children.
Collected by Mrs. Thomas J. Brooks (deceased) Bedford, Indiana.

CHYSMAN, JACOB   Jefferson County
Born—1761, German Flats, near Fort Herkimer.
Service—While residing in German Flats, enlisted in 1779, served under
Capt. Frank at Fort Herkimer for 2 yrs.; 9 mos. under Capt. Mc-
Gregor at Fort Herkimer. Service 4 years. In skirmish with
Indians at Shaaran; in battle of Canada Creek under Col. Willett;
at battle of Johnstown.
Proof—Pension claim S. 31608.
Died—June 19, 1837, in Graham Twp., Jefferson Co.
Collected by John Paul Chapter D. A. R.

CLARK, EBENEZER   Rush County
Born—About 1762.
Service—Enlisted about first of May, 1775, at Roxbury, Mass., as pri.
in Capt. Jonathan Bardwell's Mass. CO. and was discharged Jan.
1, 1776. Enlisted Jan. 12, 1776, as pri. in Capt. William King's
CO., Col. Ward's Mass. Regt. Was in the battle of Long Island
in which he was wounded. Was at the taking of N. Y., in 1776,
the battle of White Plains. Discharged Jan. 12, 1777. Enlisted
April, 1780, as pri. in Col. Tupper's Mass. Regt. and discharged
Jan. 1, 1781.
Proof—Pension claim W. 9788.
Died—March 29, 1837.
Married—1789, Rachel Chapin, b. 1768. One child living in 1798—name
not given in pension application.
Collected by Mrs. Williard Amos, Rushville, Indiana.

CLARK, JOHN   Scott County
Born—1759.
Service—Pri. in company commanded by Capt. Williams of Regt. of
Col. Penticott, Penn. Line, 2 yrs. Entered service from Washing-
ton Co., Penn.
Proof—Pension claim W. 9789, B. L. Wt. 8905, 160-55.
Died—April 18, 1846, Scott Co.
Married—Julia Ann Hooker.

CLARK, ROBERT   Allen County
Born—1755, Lancaster Co., Penn.
Service—Served in 1st Regt. Lancaster Co., 1780, and his name also
appears as a Capt. in Lancaster Co., in 1790.

Proof—State Library, Penn.
Died—Oct. 22, 1790. Killed in Indian massacre at Miami Town (Fort Wayne). Probably buried in a trench along the Maumee River.
Collected by Mrs. T. J. Hindman, Fort Wayne, Indiana.

CLAYCOMB, FREDERICK   Knox County
Born—1758, Penn.
Service—While residing in Berkley Co., Vir., enlisted in April or May, 1781, and served 6 mos. in Capt. Jarret's CO., Col. Dart's Vir. Regt.
Proof—Pension claim S. 16083.
Died—1846. (Will probated Nov. 17, 1846.) Buried Johnson Twp.
Married—Eliza ———. Ch. Frederick 1787-1849; Elias, m. Elizabeth ———; Mary Couchman; Elizabeth Rudle.
Collected by Mrs. S. G. Davenport, Vincennes, Indiana.

CLEMENTS, DAVID   Owen County
Born—1755.
Service—Pri. in Regt. of Col. Thaxter of N. C. Line, 9 mos.
Proof—Pension claim S. 35840.
Died—July 16, 1840. Buried in White Hall Cemetery, 6 miles W. of Bloomington, Ind. Stone.
No family according to pension application.
Collected by Miss Ura Sanders, Gosport, Indiana.

CLENNY (CLENEY), WILLIAM   Green County
Born—March 18, 1758, near Wilmington, Delaware.
Service—Pri. in company under Capt. Williams, Col. Ramsey's N. C. Regt., 1 yr.
Proof—Pension claim S. 32182.
Died—Last date of pension paid, Oct. 25, 1851. Buried Bloomfield, Indiana.

CLINE, JOHN   Harrison County
Service—Enlisted for 3 yrs. in Va., under Capt. Stephen Ashly, Regt. of Col. James Wood. In battle of Brandywine.
Proof—Pension claim S. 35837.
Died—1821. Buried on his farm in Harrison Co.
Children—Nancy; Peggy; Bennett; Jesse; Polly.

CLINE, WILLIAM   Randolph County
Born—Jan. 23, 1747, New Jersey.
Service—Enlisted at Taneytown, Md., in the spring of 1777, was attached to Capt. Key's CO., who died and Capt. William Pepple succeeded him. The company was organized to guard the in-

habitants and was confined to certain counties in Md. and Penn. In 1780, he was ordered to N. C., and detailed to drive a wagon loaded with baggage and camp equipage and drove the same to the headquarters of Col. Otho H. Williams in N. C., returned to his company and served to the close of the war.
Proof—Pension claim R. 2050 (claim rejected).
Died—Aug. 23, 1853. Buried in Pleasant Hill Cemetery on the Randolph Co. side. Bronze marker placed by Mississinewa Chapter D. A. R. of Portland.
Married—Susannah Lance. Ch. Anna Mary; William Jr.; Elizabeth; Abram; Mary; Sarah; Margaret; Conrad. Second W., Jane Woten. Ch. Susannah b. 1828, m. John Bird; Cynthia b. 1830, m. David Bird, and Charles Rice; Alexander H. b. 1832, m. Elizabeth Cochran, and Lucinda Pinny; Jerushia A. b. 1834, m. Henry C. Mongar; Lydia A. b. 1836 (Real Daughter), m. Thomas W. Simmons; Jacob b. 1838; Charles b. 1841. (His pension application states he had 11 children by first wife and 7 by second.)
Collected by Mrs. Oscar T. Finch, Portland, Indiana.

CLOYER, HENRY   Jefferson County
Born—1744.
Service—Enlisted in year 1776, at Warm Springs, Va. Private in Capt. Andrew Hines' CO. in Col. Rawling's Regt. Discharged in Phila., Penn. Length of service, 10 mos.
Proof—Pension claim S. 35838.
Died—Feb. 12, 1821.
Marriage—Records in Jefferson Co. give Margaret Cloyer and John Campbell, 1837; Warden Cloyer and Elizabeth Loughridge, 1836.
Collected by John Paul Chapter D. A. R.

COLE, BENJAMIN   Shelby County
Born—June 30, 1750, Dutchess Co., N. Y.
Service—Served in Capt. Bigelow Lawrence's CO., Col. Walbridge's Regt., also in Capt. Jonas Galusha's CO., Col. Herrick's 1st Regt., Vermont Militia, also in Capt. John Pratt's CO., Col. Walbridge's Regt.
Proof—The Descendants of James Cole of Plymouth, 1633, pp. 77, 78.
Died—Oct. 25, 1822. Buried in Hanover Cemetery.
Married—1778, Prudence Hard. Ch. Abel b. 1779; Anna b. 1782; Calvin b. 1783; Arvilla b. 1785; Eddy; Almena b. 1789; Arletta b. 1792; Seth b. 1795.

COLE, JACOB   Floyd County
Born—About 1740.
Service—Captain in New York Militia.

Proof—D. A. R. No. 42888.
Died—1827. Buried New Albany Cemetery now abandoned.
Married—Dinchey ——, d. age of 104 yrs. in Putnam Co., Ind. Ch. Nancy; Letitia, m. John Jennings.
Collected by Mrs. V. R. Conner, New Albany, Indiana, and Mrs. Harvey Morris, Salem, Indiana.

COLEMAN, JACOB   Vermillion County
Born—About 1754.
Service—Enlisted, Virginia 1776, under Col. Wm. Russell, Capt. Benjamin Harrison's CO. Served to 1779. His regiment became the 9th under Col. John Gibson. In 1779 commissioned an Ensign in 7th Regt., later a Lieut. In battles of Brandywine, Germantown and White Marsh.
Proof—Pension claim S. 35848, B. L. Wt. 1206-200.
Died—Last payment of pension made to attorney for pensioner on March 9, 1828, at Corydon, Indiana. Thought to be buried in Vermillion Co.
Son—John M., grandson, Sam. M.

COLGLAZIER, DAVID   Washington County
Born—1764, where Pittsburgh, Penn., now located.
Service—Served with Rangers of the Frontiers, 1778-1783. Lt. in Capt. John Van Meter's CO. of Militia, 4th Westmoreland Battalion, W. C. Benj. Davis's CO. Called out for running the line between Penn. and Vir. He served from June 6 to 14, 1782. (Huntington Twp.)
Proof—Penn. Archives, 3rd Series, vol. 23, and 5th Series, vol. 4, pp. 738 and 433; 6th Series, vol. 2, p. 288.
Died—1855. Buried Old Mill Creek Cemetery, W. of Salem, Ind.
Married—1788, Cynthania (Cinthania) May (1762-1851). Ch. John (1790-1863), m. Susanna Beck; Abraham (1791-1885), m. Sarah Brittain; David b. 1803, m. Christina Fultz; Jacob b. 1805, m. Elmy Kyte; Lewis b. 1815, m. Rebecca Hauger; Elizabeth; Rebecca; Catherine.
Collected by Mrs. D. C. Atkinson, 2611 East 73rd Street, Chicago, Illinois.

COLLINS, JOSEPH   Jay County
Born—Probably Penn.
Service—History of Jay County by Dr. M. T. Jay, vol. 1, p. 265, states Joseph Collins was a revolutionary soldier.
Died—In late 1840's. Buried in Winters Cemetery.
Collected by Mississinewa Chapter D. A. R.

COLLINS, JOSIAH   Decatur County
Born—April 19, 1757, Worcester Co., Md.
Service—Volunteered in autumn of 1777. He served 13 days under Capt. John Ratliff, guarding a magazine at Salisbury; served in same company as a pri. for 5 days near Annapolis in 1778. In 1779, he moved to Washington Co., Penn. Enlisted there in "harvest time" 1781, and served 10 days in Capt. Joshua Right's CO., and 3 days under Capt. John Wall's CO., against Indians. Enlisted May, 1782, as sergeant in Capt. Jas. Munn's CO. in expedition against Indians. Was in battle of Sandusky and taken prisoner day after, delivered to English traders, carried to Canada thence to N. Y., and was discharged Dec. 8, 1782, at Dobb's Ferry.
Proof—Pension claim S. 16730.
Died—Jan. 4, 1841. Buried Presbyterian Church Cemetery at Kingston. Stone.
Married—Eleanor Hopkins. No known descendants now.
Collected by Miss Emma A. Donnell (deceased) Greensburg, Indiana.

COLLINS, WILLIAM   Ripley County
Born—1763.
Service—Enlisted Nov. 1, 1780. Entered and left service four times. Final discharge was Nov. 8, 1781. Entire time, 8 mos. 3 days.
Proof—Pension claim S. 31613.
Died—1838. Name is on bronze tablet in Versailles Court House.
Collected by Mrs. A. B. Wycoff, Batesville, Indiana.

COLSON (COLSTON), JAMES   Union County
Born—May 30, 1743.
Service—Pri. in Capt. Joseph J. Anderson's CO., 3rd N. J. Regt. commanded by Col. Elias Dayton. He enlisted May 22, 1777, at Cumberland, for 3 yrs. Name last appears on a company roll for Aug., 1780.
Proof—Records in Adjutant General's Office, Washington.
Died—March 27, 1829. Buried Bath Springs Cemetery, Union Co. Stone.
Married—Abigail ———. Ch. Harriet, m. Ezekiel Rose; Mary, m. Lewis Mullin; William; John.
Collected by Mrs. Elnora P. Campbell, Liberty, Indiana.

COLTURN, REVEL   Henry County
Born—Sept. 16, 1764.
Service—Volunteered in 1780, when 16 years old. Served as Lieut. in Capt. Polk's CO.
Proof—Genealogy of the Current and Hobson Families, by Mark Waters, p. 197.

Died—Feb. 24, 1844. Buried 9th Street Cemetery, New Castle, Ind.
(A church has been erected on the grounds now.)
Married—Mary ——, 1768-1832.
Collected by Mrs. G. K. Hewit, New Castle, Indiana.

COMMONS, ROBERT   Wayne County
Born—1748, Ireland.
Service—Served in 2nd Battalion of Chester Co. Militia, under Col.
  Evan Evans. April 24, 1778, in Capt. Samuel Evans' CO.
Proof—Penn. Archives, 5th Series, vol. 5, p. 526; Bond Genealogy, vol.
  12, pp. 29, 59, 125.
Died—Dec. 19, 1837. Buried West Grove Cemetery.
Married—1780, Ruth Hayes (1755-1845). Ch. Lydia, m. Adam Davis;
  Phoebe, m. Jesse Bond; Isaac, m. Mary Townsend; William, m.
  Sarah Brady; John, m. Elizabeth Mote; Ezekiel, m. Sarah Julian;
  Hannah, m. Greenbury Cornelius; Nathan, m. Martha Beard;
  David b. 1800.
Collected by Mrs. Paul Ross and Mrs. Fred Gennett, Richmond, Indiana.

CONNER, JOHN   Jefferson County
Born—1757, Philadelphia, Penn.
Service—Enlisted in Guilford Co., N. C., in 1775, and served at various
  times in the N. C. Militia under Capt. John McDowee or McAdoo
  in Col. William Calhoun's Regt. Was in the battle of Gates
  Defeat, length of service 28 mos.
Proof—Pension claim W. 3659.
Died—May 25, 1847.
Married—Sarah Knight, 1793. Son, John Jr.
Collected by John Paul Chapter D. A. R.

CONNER, PHILIP   Jennings County
Born—July 11, 1754, England.
Service—Pri. in Capt. Charles West's CO. under Col. Thomas Marshall,
  Capt. Briscoe, Col. Weeden, 3rd Vir. Regt.
Proof—Pension claim S. 42134 and D. A. R. No. 88287.
Died—After 1836.
Married——. Wife died 1815. Ch. Willoughby b. 1785, m. Rachel
  Johnson; John.
Collected by Kentland Chapter D. A. R.

CONNER, PHILOMEN   Fayette County
Born—June 29, 1763, Orange Co., Va.
Service—Enlisted 1779, from Va. as a pri. as follows: From Sept.,
  1779, 2 mos. in Capt. Robert Miller's CO., in Col. Francis Taylor's
  Regt., and served as a substitute for his father, John Conner;

Nov., 1779, 2 mos. in Capt. Roebuck's CO., Col. Francis Taylor's Regt.; Aug., 1780, 2 mos. in Capt. Wm. Buckner's CO.; Feb., 1781, 2 mos. in Capt. Robert Miller's CO.; June, 1781, 2 mos. in Capt. James Hawkin's CO., in Col. Mathew's Regt.
Proof—Pension claim S. 17364; Fayette Co., Ind., Court Records, Book C, p. 201.
Married—Nancy Ann ——.
Collected by Mrs. Wright Holter, Connersville, Indiana.

CONNOR, TERRENCE   Perry County
Born—1757, Virginia.
Service—Enlisted Sept., 1776, Prince William Co., Vir., in Vir. Line, Continental Troops under Col. Daniel Morgan in Brigade commanded by Gen. Woodford. Served 3 yrs., 2 mos. Discharged at Bush Encampment on North River.
Proof—Pension record.
Died—Dec. 16, 1841. Buried in Connor Graveyard, on Groves Farm, Rome, Ind. Stone.
Married—Sarah Speaks. Ch. Dade; Samuel; William; John; Terrence Jr.; Elizabeth; Margaret; Jane.
Collected by Mrs. D. S. Conner, Cannelton, Indiana.

CONWAY, RICHARD   Henry County
Born—1762, Queen Anne Co., Maryland.
Service—Served as a pri. in Capt. Meal's CO. of Col. Michael Cresap's Vir. Regt. In 1781, re-enlisted for 6 mos. under Capt. Meal in Col. Holmes' Regt. On March 1, 1782, reenlisted for 6 mos. under Capt. John Simeral in Col. Holmes' Regt.
Proof—Pension claim S. 16731.
Died—1854. Kissinger Cemetery, S. of Mooreland, Ind. Government marker and S. A. R. marker.
Collected by Mrs. R. M. Cluggish, Knightstown, Indiana.

COOK, CHARLES   Dearborn County
Born—About 1755.
Service—Enlisted March, 1781, Charlottesville, Albemarle Co., Vir., under Capt. Harris, Regt. of Infantry, Col. Gaskins. Served until July or Aug., 1781, transferred to Regt. under Col. Posey and served until Sept. 1, 1782. Discharged by Gen. Chas. Scott. At Yorktown.
Proof—Pension claim S. 35857.
Died—Jan. 7, 1825. Dearborn Co., Ind.
Married—Priscilla ——. Son, Thomas.
Collected by Mrs. Walter Kerr, Aurora, Indiana.

COOK, DANIEL   Warrick County
Born—1760, Wilmington, N. C.
Service—Member of Militia, Edenton District, N. C.
Proof—From Accounts of U. S. with N. C., War of Revolution, Book
    C, p. 38.
Died—1846. Buried in cemetery at Selvin, Warrick Co.
Married—Nancy McNeeley. Ch. Hiram b. 1802; Curtis b. 1804; Fannie
    b. 1806; Tilda b. 1809.
Collected by Mrs. Phoebe De Motte Norman, Jasper, Indiana.

COOK, ISAAC   Fountain County
Born—1761, Penn.
Service—In Jan., 1781, he enlisted as a pri. in Capt. Thomas Austin's
    CO., in a Philadelphia Militia. On Feb. 4th the same year he
    was made Sergeant in Capt. William Bowers' CO., and later promoted to Captain in the Sixth CO., 4th Regt.
Proof—Records from the Adjutant General's Office.
Died—Feb., 1837. Buried Family graveyard, E. of Covington, Ind.
    Government marker placed by Richard Henry Lee Chapter D. A. R.
Married—Ann (Stephen) Masterson, 1796; Ch. Mary; Elizabeth; Rebecca; Isaac N.; Gilbert; Susannah; Hannah.
Collected by Mrs. Worth Reed, Covington, Indiana.

COOK, THOMAS   Bartholomew County
Born—1756, North Carolina.
Service—Sergeant, Cook's CO., 9th Regt., N. C., enlisted Dec., 1777, 3
    yrs.
Proof—Adjutant General's Office, Raleigh, N. C.
Died—1844. Buried Friends' Cemetery near Azalia, Ind.
Married—Jane Hallowell.
Collected by Mrs. Gertrude A. Barber, 50 East 78th Street, New York
    City.

COOK, WILLIAM   Wayne County
Born—Jan. 15, 1761, Rowan Co., N. C.
Service—While a resident of Surry Co., N. C., he enlisted and served
    as a pri. with the N. C. Troops as follows: from Dec., 1779, 3
    mos. in Capt. Lalathiel Martin's CO., in Col. Hampton's Regt.;
    from about Sept. 1, 1781, 3 mos. in Capt. Minor Smith's CO., in
    Col. Smith's Regt.
Proof—Pension claim S. 31612. Moved to Wayne Co. 1817.
Died—Soldier's Will probated Aug. 28, 1836.
Children—Named in Will, Isaac; William; Nathan; James; Mary; Margaret; Martha; Sarah; Lyda.
Collected by Mrs. Voyle Martindale, Cambridge City, Ind., and Mrs.
    Fred Gennett, Richmond, Indiana.

COOKSEY, ZACHARIAH   Franklin County
Service—In a sworn statement before the Judge of Franklin Court on
    Nov. 13, 1832, he states that he was drafted in service in 1778,
    and served in Regt. of Col. Darke, under Capt. Jennings, and Col.
    Allen, for 3 wks. About a year later he was again drafted and
    served more than 2 mos. under Capt. Riggins, and Col. Netherton,
    afterwards served in Col. Darke's Regt., about 4 mos. Was at
    Yorktown. Served as a guard to Cornwallis' army until they
    arrived at Nolen's ferry where he (Cooksey) was discharged.
Proof—Pension record.
Buried—In Franklin County, Ind.
Married—Martha Utsier. Ch. Mary, m. William Rockwell 1870.

COONROD, JOHN   Pike County
Born—Sept. 5, 1757, Lancaster Co., Penn.
Service—Enlisted as pri. in June, 1776, and served 3 mos. under Lieut.
    Contee, Flying Camp, Penn.; enlisted in June, 1777, 3 mos. under
    Capt. Snider; Oct., 1777, 4 mos. under Capt. Shafer.
Proof—Pension records.
Died—June 22, 1824, Pike Co., Ind.
Children—John; George; Henry; Daniel; Mary Barbara; Elizabeth.
Collected by Cradle of Liberty Chapter D. A. R. and Mrs. Harvey
    Morris, Salem, Indiana.

COOPER, JOHN   Dearborn County
Born—About 1748.
Service—Drummer in CO. commanded by Capt. Marshall, Regt. of Col.
    Adley, Penn. Line, 3 yrs.
Proof—Pension claim W. 6715.
Died—Nov. 7, 1825, Dearborn Co., Ind.
Married—Anna Barbara Trout. Ch. Jacob.
Collected by Mrs. Walter Kerr, Aurora, Indiana.

COOPER, MICHAEL   Harrison County
Born—About 1753.
Service—Pri. in Regt. of Capt. Jos. Erwin, Col. George Nagle, Penn.
    Line, 3 yrs., 1776-79.
Proof—Pension claims W. 22857.
Died—Jan. 19, 1831. Probably buried Hancock's Chapel, Harrison Co.,
    Indiana.
Married—1783, Mary Griffin (1765-1845). Ch. Jane b. 1785; William R.
    b. 1788; John C. b. 1790; James C. b. 1794; Solomon b. 1796;
    Moses b. 1799; Mary b. 1801, m. Isaac LaFavor; Betsy b. 1803;
    Sarah b. 1807; Celia b. 1810.

COPE, JONATHAN SR.   Jefferson County
Service—Served in Penn. under Capt. William Brisben, 1780-81; also pri. in 7th Battalion, 1777, Lancaster Co., Penn.
Proof—Penn. Archives, Series 5, pp. 32, 45, 74, 76, 651; Tax List of Salisbury Twp., Lancaster Co., Penn., 71-78.
Died—1819. Buried Hebron Cemetery, Jefferson Co.
Children—Soldier's Will in Book A, Jefferson Court Records, gives Jonathan; David; Jesse; Sarah Denny; Betsey Hinton; Polly Hill; Caby Cahill.
Collected by John Paul Chapter D. A. R.

CORBACH (CARBAUGH, CARBEL), PETER   Dearborn County
Service—Pri. Penn. Cont'l. Line, Capt. John Paul Schott CO. Enlisted in Lancaster, Feb. 27, 1777. Discharged there 1783.
Proof—Pension claim S. 16691.
Died—Feb. 4, 1844, Dearborn Co.
Married—Mary ——.
Collected by Mrs. Walter Kerr, Aurora, Indiana.

CORNELL, WILLIAM   Putnam County
Born—Feb. 25, 1762, New York.
Service—Battle of Yorktown 1779. Guide under General St. Clair, 1780, 3 mos. under Pat McKinsty and John Malcolm, March 17, 1781, to end of war.
Proof—Pension records and family records.
Died—Nov. 3, 1850. Buried Bainbridge Cemetery, Putnam Co. Stone.
Married—Mary Cornell. Ch. Sarah 1799-1863, m. Thomas Batman.
Collected by Dorothy Q. Chapter D. A. R.

COTTON, WILLIAM   Franklin County
Born—Feb. 28, 1750, Virginia.
Service—While residing in Guilford Co., N. C., he volunteered and served as a pri. in the N. C. troops in Capt. John Leek's CO., Col. Martin's Regt., as follows: from March, 1780, 6 mos. in battle at Cross Creek; from Nov., 1780, 6 mos. and was in battle of Guilford Court House; from July, 1781, 6 mos. in an expedition against the Cherokee Indians.
Proof—Pension claim S. 32187.
Died—Estate settled in 1836.

COUNKLE, MICHAEL   Jay County
Born—March 9, 1763.
Died—May 10, 1851. Buried Daugherty Cemetery. Stone bears the inscription: "A Revolutionary Soldier". A bronze tablet has been placed on the grave by the Mississinewa Chapter D. A. R.
Collected by Mississinewa Chapter D. A. R.

COURTNEY, MICHAEL   Jennings County
Born—About 1761, Virginia.
Service—Enlisted Greenbrier Co., Va., under Capt. Wm. McKee.
Proof—Pension claim S. 35836.
Died—Last payment of pension was made on Sept. 7, 1842.
Married—Sally ——.

COVERT, DANIEL   Clark County
Born—Monmouth Co., N. J.
Service—Pri. in Capt. Thos. Hunn's CO., 1st Regt., Monmouth Co.,
    N. J., Militia.
Proof—D. A. R. No. 133072.
Died—1803. Buried Family cemetery, 6 miles N. E. of Charlestown,
    Indiana.
Married—Catherine ——, d. 1835. Ch. Peter d. 1857, m. Catherine
    Jones; Henry.

COWAN, DAVID   LaGrange County
Born—March 12, 1762, Gloucester Co., Rhode Island.
Service—Pri. in CO. commanded by Capt. Burlingame, Regt. of Col.
    Mory, R. I. Troops, 19 mos.
Proof—Pension claim S. 32183.
Died—1851. Buried Shafer Cemetery, VanBuren Twp. Stone.
Married—Esther Smith (1767-1848). Ch. Esther b. 1790; Celinda b.
    1792; Elisha b. 1794, m. Elmira Tucker; John b. 1796, m. Sarah
    Harding; Jonathan b. 1798; Phoebe b. 1799, m. Enos Leighton;
    Lucy b. 1802; Amy Angel b. 1804; Marenus b. 1806.
Collected by Alta Crampton McClaskey, LaGrange, Indiana.

COY, WILLIAM   Switzerland County
Born—March 10, 1756, Somerset Co., Md.
Service—Enlisted July, 1777, Montgomery Co., Md., under Capt. Na-
    thaniel Pigman, Col. Mordock, Gen. Smallwood's Brigade, served
    5 mos. in the battle of Germantown, discharged. Drafted Oct.,
    1781, served 5 mos. Guard over Cornwallis' men, Hessians at
    Frederickstown.
Proof—Pension claim S. 31614.
Died—July 10, 1833. Buried on Ted Carver farm on Homeney Ridge,
    near Delhi School. Tree marks grave.
Married—Mary Ann Dennis, m. Nov. 25, 1779. Pension gives children,
    Thomas; Nancy; Susannah; Samuel; Esther; Elizabeth; Ann; Wil-
    liam; Sarah; Mary; Seely; Francis.
Collected by Mrs. Raymond Carnine and Mrs. A. V. Danner, Vevay,
    Indiana.

COX, ISAAC   Rush County
Born—About 1755.
Service—Enlisted for 1 yr., Nov., 1775, in Washington Co., Md., under
    Capt. Andrew Hines, Col. Smallwood. Discharged Dec., 1776, in
    Philadelphia.
Proof—Pension claim S. 32186.
Died—After 1834. Grave on Matney farm, Noble Twp., Rush Co.
Wife—Died before 1818.
Collected by Mrs. R. M. Cluggish, Knightstown, Indiana.

CRAIG, RODRICK   Henry County
Born—1740, London, England.
Service—Pri. in Capt. Elijah Williams CO., Col. Belford's N. C. Regt.
Proof—D. A. R. Lineage, vol. 134, p. 243.
Died—1844, buried Cadiz, Ind., (West of New Castle).
Married—1780, Becky ——. Son, John, 1781-1835.
Collected by Mrs. G. K. Hewit, New Castle, Indiana.

CRANDON, JOHN   Dearborn County
Inscription on tombstone—"A Revolutionary Soldier—1775. Born
    Plymouth, Mass., 1769. Died, Lawrenceburg, 1841. Served in
    Navy". His Will in Dearborn Co. left estate to Wife, nieces, and
    nephews.
Buried—In Old Cemetery, Lawrenceburg, Ind. Bronze marker placed
    by Col. Archibald Lochry Chapter D. A. R.
Collected by Mrs. Walter Kerr, Aurora, Ind., and Mrs. Harvey Morris,
    Salem, Indiana.

CRAWFORD, JAMES   Jefferson County
Born—1758, Augusta Co., Virginia.
Service—Pri. from Botetourt Co. Served 3 mos. under Capt. Wm. Col-
    bert and Col. Patrick Lockhart; 3 mos. under Capt. Alex Henley
    and Col. Morgan. Served in battle of Camden and in skirmish
    at Yadkin River.
Proof—Pension claim S. 1191.
Died—1836. Buried Hebron Cemetery. Stone. Government marker
    placed by John Paul Chapter D. A. R.
Married—Rebecca Anderson. Ch. Polly, m. William Guthrie; Elizabeth,
    m. Beverley Vawter; Anne, m. Robert Creath; James Maxwell, b.
    1790. (Eight children altogether.)
Collected by John Paul Chapter D. A. R.

CRITCHFIELD, JOHN   Switzerland County
Born—1752, Sussex Co., N. J.
Service—Entered Capt. Wm. Underwood's CO., Surry Co., N. C., then
    Capt. Woolridge's CO. county militia.

Proof—Pension claim R. 2547. Pension rejected because he did not serve 6 mos. D. A. R. Lineage, vol. 50, p. 294.
Died—Dec. 31, 1841. Buried Vevay Cemetery. Stone.
Married—Silvia Randolph. Daughter Mary, m. John Francis Dufour.
Collected by Mrs. A. V. Danner, Vevay, Indiana.

CRITTENDEN, RICHARD HAZELWOOD   Bartholomew County
Born—March 6, 1761, Charles City County, Virginia.
Service—Father was drafted as a pri. in Vir. Troops, March 15, 1778. Richard Hazelwood Crittenden, then a resident of Amherst Co., Vir., entered service as substitute for his father and served 3 mos. as pri. under Capt. James Dillard and Col. Patrick Rose. He afterwards enlisted and served as pri. under Capt. Isaac Parker and Col. Nicholas Cavell in Vir. Troops. He was in battle of Guilford Court House. Served 18 mos. Served 3 mos. as pri. in Capt. Charles Christian CO., and was in the siege of Yorktown.
Proof—Pension claim R. 2491.
Died—June 22, 1841.
Married—1789, Sally Tanner, b. 1773. Ch. Josiah b. 1789; John b. 1790; Charles b. 1793; Mary W. b. 1794; Matthew b. 1797; Samuel b. 1798; Martha b. 1801; Nancy b. 1803; Richard Hazelwood b. 1806.
Collected by Mrs. Roscoe Haymond, Columbus, Indiana.

CROMER, JOHN   Harrison County
Born—April 22, 1758, Lancaster Co., Penn.
Service—Enlisted 7th Penn. Regt. Served 2 mos. at a time as pri. under Capt. Hollinger, Col. Hoover.
Proof—Pension claim S. 17338.
Died—April 3, 1839, in Harrison Co., Ind.
Married—Sophia ——.

CRONTZ, MICHAEL   Allen County
Born—1753, Orange Co., N. Y.
Service—Enlisted from Orange Co., N. Y., serving with N. Y. Troops, 4 mos. under Capt. Burrens late in 1775, 8 mos. in Capt. Wm. Falkendeis' CO., Col. Hornbeck's Regt.
Proof—Pension records.
Died—March 17, 1841. Buried McColloch Park. Name on bronze tablet by the Mary Penrose Wayne Chapter D. A. R.
Married—Dorcas. Married twice and had children by second wife.
Collected by Mrs. Joseph T. Hanna (deceased) Fort Wayne, Indiana.

CROSE, PHILIP   Tippecanoe County
Born—1757, Hampshire Co., Virginia.
Service—Enlisted 1780, for 6 mos. as pri., in Capt. Daniel Richason's
    Vir. CO. In battle of Guilford Court House. Enlisted again in
    same CO. July 20, 1781, and discharged Oct. 25, 1781.
Proof—Pension claim S. 32193.
Died—Last payment of pension made to pensioner, Sept., 1839.

CROSS, EBENEZER   Switzerland County
Born—About 1754.
Service—Enlisted May, 1780, in Conn. Capt. Nathaniel's CO., Col. Levi
    Will's Regt., Continental Establishment, served 9 mos. In 1781,
    under Jonathan Little, conductor of teams, for 9 mos. Discharged
    by Little.
Proof—Switzerland County, Ind., Civil Order, Book 1820, p. 375.
Married—Hannah ——.
Collected by Mrs. A. V. Danner, Vevay, Indiana.

CRUZAN (CRUIDSON), BENJAMIN   Ripley County
Born—About 1758.
Service—Pri. in company commanded by Capt. Fauntleroy, Regt. of
    Col. A. W. White, Vir. Line, 1780-1783. Discharged in S. C.
Proof—Pension claim S. 35868.
Died—June 5, 1848, in Ripley Co., Ind. Had children living in Ripley
    County.

CUERRE, PIERRE   Knox County
Born—About 1740.
Service—A Patriot. Signed the Oath of Allegaince to the Republic
    of Virginia as a free and independent State at Post Vincennes,
    July 20, 1778.
Proof—Vol. VIII, p. 56, Ill. Historical Collections. George Rogers Clark
    Papers, 1771-1778, by James.
Died—About 1780. Buried Francis Xavier Cemetery, Vincennes, Ind.
Married—Marie Joseph Peltier, 1763. Son, Pierre b. 1766, m. Angelique Bonneau.
Collected by Mrs. Leo Schultheis, Vincennes, Indiana.

CULBERTSON, JOSIAH   Daviess County
Born—About 1748, Ninety-Six District, S. C.
Service—Enlisted fall of 1775, served as pri. at various times in each
    year amounting to more than 3 yrs. with S. C. Troops. He was
    in Snow campaign of 1775; a tour against the Cherokee Indians
    in 1776; Stone campaign 1777; a tour against Indians with Capt.

Parsons, 1778; in the siege of Savannah, Battle of Ramson's Mills, King's Mt., Cowpens.
Proof—Pension claim S. 16354.
Died—About 1839. Buried Maysville Cemetery, 3 miles S. W. of Washington, Ind. Government marker placed by White River Chapter D. A. R.
Married—Jane Thomas. Ch. John; Josiah Jr.; Samuel; Adeline, m. James Robinson; another dau. m. —— Funston.
Collected by Mrs. Roy Bogner, Washington, Indiana.

CULL, HUGH   Wayne County
Born—Oct., 1759, Havre de Grace, Maryland.
Service—Pri. 7th Penn. Regt., Cont'l Line, Dec. 27, 1776; transferred to chiefs guards.
Proof—Penn. Archives, Series 2, vol. 10, p. 630.
Died—Aug. 31, 1863, aged 104 yrs., 10 mos. Buried Elkhorn Cemetery. Stone.
Married—1785, Rachel Meek.
Collected by Mrs. Paul L. Ross, Richmond, Indiana.

CUNNINGHAM, NATHANIEL   Putnam County
Born—1768, Petersburg, Virginia.
Service—Enlisted in Prince Edward Co., Vir., Sept., 1775; March, 1776; fall of 1776. Served 1 yr. 6 mos., 2½ yrs., and some service till 1780. Under Capts. Robert Ballard, John Morton, and Cols. Patrick Henry, Robert Lawson, 4th Vir. Militia; later transferred to Gen. Washington's Life Guard; under Col. Parker in 1st Vir. Militia. Battles, Trenton, Princeton, Brandywine, Monmouth, Gates Defeat, Yorktown.
Proof—Pension claim W. 9821.
Died—Aug. 16, 1832. Buried on Goldsberry Farm, E. of Greencastle, Ind.
Married—1790, Elizabeth Sneed, b. 1772. Ch. Alexander; Amelia; Elizabeth 1798-1866, m. Absalom Brown; John W.; Benjamin; Lucinda; Susan.
Collected by Miss Minnetta Wright, Greencastle, Indiana.

CURRY, THOMAS   Franklin County
Born—1762, Ireland
Service—While residing in Loudoun Co., Vir., he enlisted in 1779, and served two years as pri. in Capt. John Chapman's CO. in Col. Crockett's Vir. Regt. and marched to the Falls of the Ohio against the Indians.
Proof—Pension claim S. 16747.

Died—Oct. 16, 1840. Buried Ebenezer Cemetery, Franklin Co., Ind.
Stone. Government marker placed by Twin Forks Chapter D. A. R.
Married—Alsie Gordon. Ch. James; Thomas, b. 1811, d. 1895, m. 1830, Katharine Whitacre; Rachel; Polly; Martha; Elsie; Betsy; John S.

CUSTER, ARNOLD   Jefferson County
Born—1756, Virginia.
Service—Private in Virginia Troops.
Proof—D. A. R. No. 132993; No. 136385; No. 140494.
Died—1840. Buried Hebron Cemetery. Government marker placed by John Paul Chapter D. A. R.
Married—1788, —— Schull. Ch. Reuel 1790-1880, m. Martha Allen; William 1792; Sarah 1794, m. Mathew Robinson; James 1796, m. Katherine Ross; Polly 1798; Jesse 1800, m. Nancy Spurgeon; Rachel 1802, m. Gid Jackson; Elizabeth 1805, m. Jackson Denny; Arnold 1808, m. first —— Moore, second Malinda Jane New; Isaac 1814.
Collected by John Paul Chapter D. A. R.

CUTLER, BENJAMIN   Morgan County
Born—Sept. 4, 1725, Lexington, Mass.
Service—Private and Sergeant in Rev. War.
Proof—Listed in "Mass. Soldiers and Sailors."
Died—1814. Buried near Martinsville, Ind.
Married—1776—Second W. Mary Cozad Coons (widow of J. Coons). Ch. Benjamin; Mercy; Martha; Jacob; John.
Collected by Miss Jessie B. Mead, Spencer, Indiana.

CUTTS, WILLIAM   Hamilton County
Service—Enlisted 1779, Chesterfield Co., Vir., under Capt. Wright, 13th Vir. Regt., Col. Dick.
Proof—Pension claim W. 25458, B. L. Wt. 85060-160-55.
Died—July 28, 1849. Buried Gibson Family Cemetery, Jackson Twp.
Married—First W. Mrs. Mullins. Ch. Robert; Paschal; Elizabeth; James. Second W. Elizabeth Bentley. Ch. William.
Collected by Perry A. Bray, Noblesville, Indiana.

DAILY, PHILIP   Clark County
Born—1762.
Service—Pri. in 3rd Maryland Regt. under Capt. Horatio Claggett and Col. Nathan Ramsey.
Proof—D. A. R. No. 111597.
Died—1830, in Charlestown, Ind.
Married—Mary Wise (1769-1845). Son, David (1798-1878).
Collected by Mrs. W. R. Davidson, Evansville, Indiana.

DANIEL, BUCKNER   Jackson County
Born—1761, Dinwiddie Co., Virginia.
Service—Drafted 1779 from Dinwiddie Co., Vir. Joined army at Petersburg, served under Col. Waggoner, Col. James, Gen. Malenburg, 3 mos. 1780, drafted, served under Col. Falkner, Gen. Lawson. 1781 drafted, served under Gen. Lafayette.
Proof—Pension claim S. 17372.
Died—1840. Buried near Medora in Heighton Hill Cemetery.

DANIEL, WILLIAM   Shelby County
Born—May 12, 1761, Orange Co., Virginia.
Service—Enlisted while residing in Orange Co., Vir., May, 1778. Served as pri. 3 mos. in Capt. Garland Burnley's CO. Col. Francis Taylor's Regt. Vir. Troops. In spring 1779 served 3 mos. in Capt. Richard Graves CO. In summer of 1780 served 3 mos. under Lt. William Thomas and 1781-3 mos. in Capt. Richard Webb's CO.
Proof—Pension Record. Applied 1834 from Boone Co., Ky.
Died—April 13, 1855. Buried Keith's Cemetery near Boggstown, Ind.
Married—Mollie Pendleton Gaines. Ch. Baxter, m. —— Miller; Abner, m. first, Susan Cross; second, —— Meyers; third, —— Jennings; William; John, m. Nancy Bogguss; Margaret, m. —— Mallady; Nancy Mathews, m. —— Cross.
Collected by Miss Susan Ray Wilson, Shelbyville, Indiana.

DANIS, HONORE   Knox County
Born—About 1732, Villa Marie, Canada.
Service—A Patriot. Signed the Oath of Allegiance to the Republic of Virginia, July 20, 1778.
Proof—No. 149 on the list of signers of oath as found in Clark's Papers, 1771-1781, and Ill. Hist. Coll., vol. VIII, pp. 52-59. In list name is spelled "honores Dannie."
Died—Oct. 22, 1792. Buried St. Francis Xavier Cathedral Cemetery, Vincennes, Ind.
Married—First W. Marie Louise Butos (half Indian). Ch. Marguerite b. Oct., 1767. Second W. Marie Joseph Godere (1767-1793). Ch. Ursule, b. 1789.
Collected by Mrs. Leo Schultheis, Vincennes, Indiana.

DANNOR, DAVID   Clay County
Born—March, 1759, Frederick Co., Maryland.
Service—Enlisted Aug. or Sept., 1779. Served 6 mos. as pri. under Capt. Patrick Watson, Col. Bruce's Maryland Regt. Enlisted from Frederick Co.
Proof—Applied and received a pension from Clay Co., Ind., 1833.

DAUCHY, JEREMIAH   Floyd County
Born—1755, Ridgefield, Connecticut.
Service—Enlisted 1776 as private in Capt. Mill's CO., Col. Philip Burr
    Bradley's Conn. Regt.
Proof—Conn. Military Record 1775-1848, p. 418.
Died—1823, Floyd County.
Married- -Sarah Hull.
Collected by Piankeshaw Chapter D. A. R.

DAVID, HENRY   Rush County
Born—March, 1760.
Service—He was living in Shenandoah Co., Vir., when he enlisted.
    1777, 3 mos. under Capt. Crookshank, Col. Brown of Vir. Drafted
    3 mos. under Col. Fry of Vir. and again for 3 mos. under Col.
    Downer, Brown, Gen. Morgan of Vir.
Proof—Pension claim R. 2686, Ind. Cert. 7691.
Died—July 20, 1844, Rush County.
Married—Nancy —— 1792 or 1793.

DAVIS, DAVID   Switzerland County
Born—About 1754.
Service—Enlisted at Lebanon, Penn., as pri. May 10, 1777, under Capt.
    Amos Wilkinson of Col. Thos. Proctor's Artillery. Discharged
    at Carlisle, Penn., in 1783, by Major Lukens. Allowed 100 acres
    of land, 1801.
Proof—Pension claim S. 35878, B. L. Wt. 252-100.
Died—Last payment of pension made March 27, 1829.
Married—Anne ——. Ch. Alace; David; John; Spencer.

DAVIS, ENOCH   Washington County
Born—Feb. 14, 1740, near Philadelphia, Penn.
Service—While a resident of Guilford Co., N. C., about 1778, made
    Captain of a CO. in Col. Paisley's Regt. of drafted militia and
    rendered various services until 1779.
Proof—Pension record; Affidavit of grandson, Andrew B. Davis, living
    in 1917. D. A. R. No. 139385; 144556; 241139.
Died—1837. Buried Crown Hill Cemetery, Salem, Ind. Stone.
Married—About 1774, Elizabeth Hawkins. Ch. Elias; Enoch, b. 1777;
    Abner.
Collected by Mrs. Harvey Morris, Salem, Indiana.

DAVIS, ENOS   Fountain County
Born—1760.
Service—Enlisted July 5, 1778, as a pri. in Capt. Henry Gates CO.,
    Md. Militia and was discharged Dec., 1779.
Proof—Pension claim S. 35877.

Died—Feb. 26, 1841. Buried "Davis Burying Ground," Wabash Twp. Government marker placed by Veedersburg Chapter D. A. R.
Married—1790, ——. Son, James.
Collected by Miss Edith Miller, Veedersburg, Indiana.

DAVIS, FRANCIS   Jefferson County
Born—In Virginia.
Service—His name appears as an invalid pensioner who was paid at the Virginia Agency but whose place of residence could not be ascertained by the reason of destruction of papers in the War Department in 1814. Served as a private and was paid $60.00 per annum from March 4, 1792.
Proof—On roll of pensioners for Albemarle Co., Vir., 1835.
Died—His will was offered for probate June 2, 1818, in Jefferson Co., Ind. Buried in orchard on Malcomson farm at top of Hanover Hill.
Married—Mildred Dollins. Ch. Thomas, m. Sarah Reese; Sarah, m. Benjamine Reese; Mildred; and other children.
Collected by Mrs. I. E. Tranter, Franklin, Indiana.

DAVIS, JONATHAN   Union County
Born—Jan., 1761.
Service—Enlisted in N. J. line of Continental Army under Gen. Maxwell, 3rd Regt. Col. Daton, Capt. Patterson for 9 mos. In battle of Monmouth.
Proof—Pension claim S. 35873.
Died—Oct. 26, 1845, in Union Co.
Children—William; Polly; Elijah; Huldah Davis Monger.

DAVIS, LODOWICK   Spencer County
Born—Feb., 1764, Montgomery Co., Md.
Service—Enlisted in Fredericktown, Md., June 23, 1781, served as a pri. in Capts. John Reid, Nathaniel Beall Magruder's and David Lynn's Md. CO. and was discharged Dec. 10, 1783.
Proof—Pension claim R. 2713.
Died—Aug. 13, 1841, Spencer Co., Ind.
Married—Dolly Ann, 1790. Ch. Hezekiah, b. 1790; Sally, b. 1792; Lucey, b. 1794; Polly, b. 1796; Amos, b. 1797; Jemima, b. 1799; Joshua, b. and d. 1801; Dicky, b. 1802; Leroy, b. 1804; Forrest, b. 1807; Harper, b. 1808; Miranda, b. 1810.
Collected by Irvington Chapter D. A. R.

DAVIS, PHILEMON   Ripley County
Born—1750.
Service—Enlisted in Maryland in Aug., 1775. Served 1 year and 7 mos.

Proof—Pension claim S. 31640.

Died—1841, Ripley Co., Ind. Name on bronze tablet in Versailles Court House.

Collected by Mrs. A. B. Wycoff, 219 Maplewood Ave., Batesville, Indiana.

DAVIS, WILLIAM   Parke County

Born—Jan. 12, 1761, Worcester Co., Maryland.

Service—While residing in Worcester Co., Md., he enlisted in March, 1780, and served 3 years as a pri. under Capts. John Stewart and Bartley Townsend, Col. Samuel Handy's Md. Regt. Served as a ranger guarding the shores of the rivers and protecting the inhabitants of Worcester and adjoining counties from the Tories.

Proof—Pension claim S. 32202.

Died—Last payment of pension was made Sept. 13, 1834. Had a son living in Parke Co. in 1834.

DAWSON, EDWARD   Tippecanoe County

Born—1755.

Service—Pri. in Capt. Samuel Montgomery's CO., 7th Penn. Line, 1776.

Proof—Penn. Archives, Series 5, vol. 3, p. 221.

Died—Aug. 28, 1833. Buried on the Jack Bryan Farm, ¾ mile from Warren Co.

Married—Hannah —— (1759-1839). Ch. Elizabeth 1777-1861, m. Enos Moore, 1785-1845; Leonard.

Collected by Miss Sarah Lank, Greencastle, Indiana.

DEAKINS, JAMES   Franklin County

Born—Nov. 14, 1754, Prince George County, Virginia.

Service—Enlisted as a pri. from Westmoreland, Vir., in Capt. Richard Parker's CO., Col. Spotswood's Regt., in Sept., 1775; he was in the battle of Long Bridge and was discharged at Williamsburg, Vir., Aug. 20, 1776.

Proof—Pension claim W. 9833.

Died—July 20, 1834, Fairfield Twp., Franklin Co., Ind.

Married—Martha Brand, 1782 (1765-1835). Ch. John, b. 1783; Alice, b. 1785; William, b. 1796; Mary, b. 1800; Martha, b. 1802; Elizabeth, b. 1804; Nicholas, b. 1807.

DEAL, DANIEL   Floyd County
Born—About 1760, Lancaster, Pennsylvania.
Service—Entered from Lancaster, Penn., as pri. for 2 mos. under Capt.
    Stevens, 6 mos. under Capt. Anthony Frecker, Col. Klotts and
    Gen. Mercer.
Proof—Pension claim W. 6999, B. L. Wt. 36640-160-55.
Died—July 4, 1839, Floyd County.
Married—Catherine Shake, 1801.

DEAN, JOHN   Scott County
Born—July 31, 1757.
Service—While residing in Dorchester Co., Md., enlisted 1776, for 6
    mos. as pri. under Capt. Joseph Richardson, Col. William Richardson and Gen. Bell. Shipped 1777 under Capt. Wm. Bedloe. 1778
    shipped under Capt. Lockley. 1780 shipped under Capt. Wm.
    Derry. 1782 shipped under Capt. Hill. In battle of White Plains.
Proof—Pension claim S. 16100.
Died—Last payment of pension was made Sept. 7, 1838.

DEATRICK, PETER   Harrison County
Born—Augusta Co., Virginia.
Service—Served under Gen. Marion.
Proof—D. A. R. application of Mrs. Margaret Payton's.
Died—1863. Buried Deatrick Cemetery, Boone Twp.
Married—Mary Beard. Ch. Mrs. Margaret Payton; David.
Collected by Piankeshaw Chapter D. A. R.

DECKER, JOHN (JOHANNES) SR.   Knox County
Born—Baptized March 9, 1712.
Service—Pri. 7th class in Capt. George Gieslman (Gyselman) CO.,
    1780. Later was listed among Associators and Militia from Aug.
    24, 1782, to Oct. 24, 1782, under Capt. Thomas Clingan. Both
    services from York Co., Penn.
Proof—Penn. Archives, Series VI, vol. 11, pp. 571 and 660.
Died—Before Jan. 10, 1791. Buried in Decker Graveyard, Decker Twp.
Married—Diana Kuykendall. Ch. Barbary; Isaac; Joseph; Abraham;
    Moses; John; Luke; Tobias; Elizabeth.
Collected by Miss Helen Decker and Mrs. S. G. Davenport, Vincennes,
    Indiana.

DECKER, JOSEPH   Knox County
Born—Hampshire County, Virginia.
Service—Private—Associators and Militia under Capt. Edmund Baxter,
    Chester Co. Muster Roll of the 4th CO., for the spring of 1785,
    under Capt. Will Martin, York Co., Penn.

Proof—Penn. Archives, Series 5, vol. 5, p. 682, and Series 6, vol. 3, pp. 1469 and 1473.
Died—Will probated Jan. 20, 1810. Buried Decker Graveyard, Decker Twp.
Married—Florinda ——. Ch. Isaac; Abraham; and a daughter who married —— Johnson.
Collected by Mrs. S. G. Davenport, Vincennes, Indiana.

DECKER, LUKE   Knox County
Born—About 1760, Pennsylvania.
Service—Pri. under Capt. Edward Baxter in militia of Chester Co., Penn.
Proof—Penn. Archives, Series 5, vol. 4, p. 682. Records on Knox Co., Ind.
Died—About March, 1825. Buried Decker Graveyard, Decker Twp.
Married—First Sarah Kuykendall. Ch. John; Dr. Hiram; Asa. Second W. Trenny Claypool.
Collected from records of Registrar of Francis Vigo Chapter D. A. R.

DEDMAN, SAMUEL   Pike County
Born—1749.
Service—Enlisted Feb. 7, 1777, as Serg. under Capt. John Marks, Col. Charles Lewis, Virginia. Served 3 yrs. In battles of Brandywine, Germantown and Monmouth.
Proof—Pension claim S. 35887.
Died—Aug. 18, 1818.
Collected by Cradle of Liberty Chapter D. A. R.

DEISKY (DEASTY, DESKY), LEIMAN (LEAMON, LEEMON)
                                                Switzerland County
Born—About 1758.
Service—Enlisted 1780 as pri., N. J. Battalion, 3 yrs. Discharged by Gen. Washington, June 5, 1783. He was honored by a badge of merit for faithful service.
Proof—Pension claim S. 35886.
Died—Feb. 15, 1829. Probably buried near Old Bethel Church now in York Twp.
Married—Hannah ——. Ch. Malinda, m. Joel Heron 1824; Samuel; Polly, m. Chas. F. Krutz 1830; James; Sarah, m. Thomas Hatton 1823.
Collected by Mrs. A. V. Danner, Vevay, Indiana.

DE LA BALM, AUGUSTUS MOTTIN   Allen County
Service—Served as Colonel in the French army, came to this country
    with Marquise de la Fayette and served with him in the service
    of the state of Virginia. Went with George Rogers Clark to Post
    St. Vincentores. In 1780 he organized a company of 400 men from
    Vincennes to go north to quell Indian distrubances at Post Miami
    (Fort Wayne). He, in command of an advance company of 80
    men, destroyed the store house of Baubine on Nov. 3, 1780, and
    returned toward Vincennes to meet the reinforcements and
    camped on the banks of the Abute (Aboite) river and were am-
    bushed in the night by Miami Indians led by Little Turtle, and
    was killed.
Proof—Drapers Mss. 50-J-77, Wisconsin Historical Society; Original
    letter of LaGras reporting the massacre; Histories of Allen Co.,
    Ind.
Collected by Mrs. T. J. Hindman, Fort Wayne, Indiana.

DELAP, JAMES   Ripley County
Born—1755, Burlington, N. J.
Service—Entered service from N. J., under Col. Robert Taylor in
    1777. Served 9 mos.
Proof—Pension claim S. 32215.
Died—July 10, 1840. Buried near Versailles, Ind. Stone and govern-
    ment marker and name on bronze tablet in Versailles Court
    House.
Married— ——Sidney, b. 1763. Son, Nathaniel, 1793-1841, m. Mary
    Kindle.
Collected by Mrs. A. B. Wycoff, Batesville, Indiana.

DEMOSS, ANDREW   Martin County
Born—July 2, 1753, Berkley Co., Virginia.
Service—Pri. enlisted 1776, under Capt. Nevil, 12 Vir. Regt. Was in
    Battles of Brandywine, Germantown, Monmouth and Gates De-
    feat. Discharged at Winchester, Vir. Entered service at Martin-
    burg, Vir.
Proof—Pension claim rejected—R. 2869.
Son—Andrew, Jr.

DEMOSS, JOHN   Decatur County
Born—Sept. 16, 1758.
Service—Enlisted in infantry in company under Andrew Waggoner in
    12th Vir. Regt., Col. James Wood, 1776. Battles of Camden,
    S. C., and after this he was transferred to 4th Regt. of Virginia
    Line. Employed as a wagoner to transport the baggage of the

French under command of Lafayette. Was also in battle of Brandywine, Germantown and Monmouth.
Proof—Pension claim W. 9832. B. L. Wt. 60-100.
Died—Aug. 12, 1844. Buried on Milton Byer's farm, Clay Twp. Decatur Co. Bronze marker placed by Lone Tree Chapter D. A. R.
Married—Lucy Chapel, b. 1765, m. 1787. Ch. Peter, b. 1788; Dorothy, b. 1790; Susanna, b. 1793; Sarah, b. 1796; John, b. 1798; Charley, b. 1800; Lucy, b. 1803; Mary, b. 1807.

DENBO, ELIJAH   Crawford County
Born—1738, Durham, New Hampshire.
Service—Four yrs. in Col. Meserve's N. H. Regt., French and Indian War. Entered the Rev. War. at Lee, N. H., April, 1775, as a Captain of N. H. Troops. Fought at Bunker Hill, Portsmouth, Cambridge and in Canada. Served in Col. Burnham's and Gen. Poor's Regts. Was Captain of N. H. Scouts during the Indian War, 1781-85.
Proof—Pension record; N. H. Adjutant General's Report of 1866.
Died—1823. Buried Denbo Cemetery, English, Ind. Government marker.
Married—Sarah Willey. Only child, Joseph, 1779-1851, m. Jane Lowry, dau. of John Lowry a Rev. S. and g. dau. of Alexander Lowry, a. Rev. S.
Collected by Francis J. Denbo (Capt. U. S. Army, A. E. F., France) Terre Haute, Indiana.

DENNY, ROBERT   Washington County
Born—1753, Berks Co., Pennsylvania.
Service—Enlisted Frederick Co., Vir., 1779. Recommended for Lieut. in this year, as shown by notes of Military Services in Frederick Co., Vir., 1779.
Proof—Chronicles of the Scotch-Irish Settlement in Virginia, Augusta Co., 1745-1800; Chalkley, vol. 2, p. 505; Genealogy of Denny Family in England and America, by C. C. Denny, p. 237.
Died—April 17, 1826. Buried Sharon Cemetery, S. E. of Salem, Ind. Government marker placed by Christopher Harrison Chapter D. A. R.
Married—1778, Rachel Thomas (1758-1808). Ch. David; Elisha; Samuel; Joseph; William; John; Mary; James; Sally.
Collected by Mrs. Harvey Morris, Salem, Indiana.

DENNY, SAMUEL   Putnam County
Born—Aug. 28, 1755, Chester Co., Pennsylvania.
Service—Enlisted Frederick Co., Vir. Served March 6, 1777—June 20, 1777, under Capt. Peter Babb and Col. John Smith; Summer 1777, 2 mos., 3 days as 2nd Lieut. under Capt. Aaron Mercer and Col.

Smith; Aug., 1777, 2 mos. as pri. under Capt. Mercer and Col. Smith; 1778, 6 mos. under Capt. Mercer and Col. Alex Skotts Wood, 2nd Vir. Militia. In the battles of Brandywine, Germantown.
Proof—Pension claim S. 32212.
Died—July 4, 1843. Buried Deer Creek Baptist Cemetery, Warren Twp.
Married—Elizabeth ———. Had no children of their own, but reared 13 orphan children.
Collected by Miss Minnetta Wright, Greencastle, Indiana.

DENNY, WALTER   Elkhart County
Born—March 3, 1756, Lancaster Co., Pennsylvania.
Service—Captain of 7th CO., 2nd Battalion, Cumberland Co. Militia 1777, under Col. Davis. Pri. in 5th CO., 2nd Battalion, Cumberland Co., Penn., Sept. 10, 1781. Was commissioned Captain for bravery at Yorktown. He was also in War of 1812 and cited for bravery at Harrisburg, Penn., on March 29, 1814.
Proof—Penn. Archives.
Died—March 31, 1842. Buried Jackson Cemetery, Haw Patch, Ind. Stone.
Married—Elizabeth McConnell, 1761-1820. Ch. John; William; Elizabeth, 1788-1864, m. Thomas Nisbet.
Collected by Mrs. F. C. Wherley, 800 Garfield Ave., Elkhart, Indiana.

DENNY, WILLIAM   Putnam County
Born—1748 Chester Co., Pennsylvania.
Service—Frederick Co., Virginia—enlisted early in war. Served as 2nd Lieut. in Capt. Peter Babb's CO., Col. John Smith's Regt. In a campaign against Indians. After 1777, was 1st Lieut. in Capt. Aaron Mercer's CO. Assisted in guarding prisoners taken at surrender of Cornwallis.
Died—April 5, 1832. Buried private cemetery E. of Greencastle, Ind.
Married—Mary Shields, 1792. Ch. Martha, b. 1795; John, b. 1797; Nancy, b. 1800; Isabel, b. 1802; Mary, b. 1804, m. James Denney; Eliza, b. 1808, m. Hiram Gaither.
Collected by Miss Minnetta Wright, Greencastle, Indiana.

DE PAUW, CHARLES   Washington County
Born—March 11, 1753, Ghent, Europe.
Service—Was a boyhood friend of Lafayette. Joined his fortunes with Lafayette expedition and came to America. Fought throughout the war. Was with Lafayette at the battle of Brandywine. Was wounded in the siege of York.
Proof—Family records Appleton's Cyclopedia of Am. Biography, p. 144 of vol. 2; Representative Men in Indiana, vol. 2, p. 10.

Died—Aug. 31, 1814. Buried Crown Hill Cemetery, Salem, Ind. Stone.
Son—N. B. De Pauw.
Collected by Mrs. Harvey Morris, Salem, Indiana.

DEPOSITER (DEPOYSTER), JOHN   Warrick or Posey County
Born—1754, Kent Co., Delaware.
Service—Entered service 1775, under Capt. Jonathan Caldwell—1st Del. Regt. for 12 mos., Geo. McCall was First Lieut. Marched to N. Y. through Philadelphia. Later became ill and was sent to Wilmington, where he was discharged.
Proof—Pension claim S. 32214.
Died—1843.

DEWITT, WILLIAM   Switzerland County
Born—March 18, 1763. Frederick Co., Maryland.
Service—Enlisted and served in a company of Penn. Militia, under Capt. Thos. Clugedge, Maj. Robert Clugedge, Maj. Poper. Was drafted in Bedford Co., Penn. Served 9 mos.
Proof—Pension claim W. 729 B. L. Wt. 26609-160-35.
Died—Jan. 31, 1838. Probably buried in Cotton Twp., Switzerland Co.
Married—Elizabeth White Conner, m. Dec. 4, 1804. Ch. (named in soldier's will) Polly Bradford; Nancy; Betsey Palmerton; John m. Mary Jane Potter; Phoeby b. John Johy; Judith m. Simeon Shattick; Marie; Isabelle.
Collected by Mrs. A. V. Danner, Vevay, Indiana.

DICKENSON, GRIFFITH   Switzerland County
Born—Dec. 25, 1762. Hanover Co., Virginia.
Service—Enlisted 1777 under Capt. Richard Anderson, 5th Vir. Regt., Col. Ball, Gen. Hand's Brigade, for 3 yrs. Was at Valley Forge. Discharged near Williamsburg.
Proof—Switzerland County, Ind., Civil Order Book, Sept., 1832, p. 68.
Collected by Mrs. A. V. Danner, Vevay, Indiana.

DICKERSON, JOHN   Jefferson County
Born—1755, Maryland.
Service—Captain 3rd Regt. of N. Y.
Proof—Stryker's Officers and Men of N. J. in the Rev.
Died—May 15, 1828. Buried Marling Cemtery, S. of Hanover, Ind. Stone and Government marker placed by John Paul Chapter D. A. R.
Married—Grace Lindsley, Aug. 15, 1780, d. March 13, 1836.
Collected by John Paul Chapter D. A. R.

DICKERSON, ROBERT — Marion County
Service—Pri. in Capt. Moss's 2nd Vir. Regt. Enlisted in war on the condition of receiving 160 acres of land and $10.00 bounty. Received the bounty and no land.
Proof—Pension claim S. 46355 B. L. Wt. 1385-100. Records in the General Accounting Office, Washington, do not show that any payments were ever made to this pensioner.

DICKERSON, WALTER — Vigo County
Born—June 17, 1763, Morris County, New Jersey.
Service—Pri. in Capt. Thomas Dickerson's CO. under Major Hutchins in N. J. Troops.
Proof—Office of Adjutant General; D. A. R. No. 205783.
Died—Oct. 8, 1855. Buried Dickerson Family burying ground—Lost Creek Twp.
Married—Penelope Heaton, 1762-1849. Ch. Caleb; Elizabeth, m. Joseph Graham; Samuel; John, m. Rhoda Holland; Ruth; Walter; Penelope; Martha, m. John S. Tiley; Nancy, m. Matthew Gray; Daniel. Soldier married second time—no issue. Third time to Sarah Garthwait.
Collected by Fort Harrison Chapter D. A. R.

DICKINSON, ZEBULIN — Dearborn County
Born—1761. New York.
Service—Pri. under Capt. Ephraim Woodworth in the Regt. of Albany Co. Militia, district of Saratoga, N. Y. Fifer under John Thompson.
Proof—D. A. R. No. 96900 and No. 210454.
Died—1835, Dearborn County.
Married—Elizabeth Brush. Ch. Townsend, b. 1795, m. Sophia Stearns; Amos, b. 1818, m. Indiana Talmerton; Mary, m. John Underwood; Deborah, m. S. P. Palmer; John Calvin.
Collected by Mrs. H. S. McKee, Greensburg, Indiana.

DILLE, CALEB — Henry County
Born—1759, Washington Co., Pennsylvania.
Service—Private. Received depreciation pay Washington Co. Militia, Continental Line. Pri. in 2nd class, Capt. John Millers' CO., 1st Battalion, Washington Co. Militia, Lieut. Col. Henry Enoch, Maj. Samuel McCollough.
Proof—Penn. Archives, Series 6, vol. II, p. 8.
Died—1839. Buried Old Graveyard, N. E. part of Knightstown, Ind. Government marker placed by Maj. Hugh Dinwiddie Chapter D. A. R.

Married—Rebecca Martin. Ch. David; Daniel; Rebecca; Noahdiah; Phoebe; Abigail; Absolam; Joseph; Caleb; Martha.
Collected by Mrs. Roy A. Mayse, Goshen, Indiana.

DITZLER, PETER Clark County
Born—About 1756, Pennsylvania.
Service—Living in Penn. when enlisted. Drafted 1776, in Lancaster Co., Penn., in Capt. Steven's CO. of militia, Col. Philip Greenewalt, 2 mos. Enlisted at Powel Hook, N. J., Capt. Andrew Freckey. 6 mos. under Col. Klotz. Discharged at Trenton. Again drafted and served for over 1 yr.
Proof—Pension claim S. 16102.
Died—July 18, 1837. Buried Union Chapel Cemetery.
Child—George Y.

DIXON, GEORGE Warren County
Born—1754, Augusta Co., Virginia.
Service—Volunteered Sept. 5, 1777. 3 mos. private under Capt. Armstrong, Gen. Hann. Drafted Feb., 1778, 6 mos. private under Henderson, Gen. Clark. May 1, 1779, 1 year, 2 mos., private under Col. Brown. Called into service from Greenbrier Co., Vir.
Proof—Pension claim S. 16764.
Died—Feb., 1840. Warren Co.
Children and heirs of soldier—Peter Dixon; Unice Davis; Jesse Dixon; Henry Dixon; Oliver Stover.

DIXON, JOHN Ohio County
Born—Nov. 12, 1763, Frederick Co., Maryland.
Service—Pri. in Capt. Hopkins CO. in cavalry of Regt. of Penn. Line. Helped build Ft. Washington, now Cincinnati, and was at Ft. Vincennes during Indian raid.
Proof—Pension claim W. 9835.
Died—Widow states in her application for pension that soldier died March 24, 1846, but his will was probated March 30, 1840. Buried in Dixon Graveyard near Rising Sun, Ind.
Married—1791, Elizabeth Garrison, 1774-1848. Ch. Tamson, b. 1792, m. John Hunter; Lydia, b. 1793, m. Benjamin McQueen; Elizabeth, b. 1796, m. William M. Orr; Sara, b. 1800, m. James Clement; Rhoda, b. 1802, m. William Babbs; Nancy, b. 1807, m. James Clark; Rebecca, m. John McCullum; Annie; Palta; William.
Collected by Mrs. Walter Kerr, Aurora, Indiana.

DIXON, JOSEPH   Vigo County
Born—1760. Probably Pennsylvania.
Service—Acct. of 5th, 6th, and 7th classes of the 8th Battalion of the
    Cumberland Co., Penn., Militia, called upon to perform a love
    of Duty by an order of the Council Aug. 1, 1780.
Proof—Penn. Archives.
Died—1827. Buried in Grandview Cemetery, Terre Haute, Ind. Government marker.
Married—Elizabeth Hurst. Ch. John and Joseph.
Collected by Richmond Chapter and Ft. Harrison Chapter D. A. R.

DOBBINGS, JAMES   Marion County
Born—About July 11, 1760, Baltimore, Maryland.
Service—In 1774 or 1775 "impressed" at Baltimore by Capt. Samuel
    Smith to serve as a marine or sailor on board the schooner Polly,
    then employed in carrying the public mail from Annapolis to
    Head of Elk, Md., it being unsafe to carry it by land. Served 1
    yr. 10 mos., acting as mate the greater part of the time and sometimes
    sailing the schooner in the absence of the commander,
    James Lynch. Was discharged at Baltimore by Col. Zebulon
    Hollingsworth of Md. A year later he enlisted as a substitute
    for his father, James Dobbings, and served as a pri. 6 mos. in
    the Flying Camp under Capt. Samuel Smith, Lieut. Wm. Butler,
    Ensign Jacob Rogers, Col. Zeb. Hollingsworth. In the battle of
    Brandywine.
Proof—Pension claim R. 2979. Pensioned while living in Center Twp.,
    Marion Co., Ind.

DOGAN, JEREMIAH J.   Decatur County
Born—1764.
Service—Resident of Fauquier Co., Vir. Enlisted April, 1780, to serve
    as drummer in company under Capt. Stewart in Regt. of Col.
    Blackwell in Vir. Line for 2 years.
Proof—Pension claim S. 32219. B. L. Wt. 26367-160-55.
Died—April 14, 1857. Buried in Mt. Pleasant Cemetery. Government
    marker.
Children are mentioned in pension application but no names given.

DOLPH, STEPHEN   Clark County
Born—1737.
Service—Enlisted 1781, under Capt. John Buell, 1st Regt. Conn., Col.
    Govenor. Discharged Nov., 1782.
Proof—Pension claim S. 35897.
Died—Jan. 14, 1824, Clark Co.
Married—Emma ——. Ch. Mary; Sarah; Phebe.

DONNELL, THOMAS   Decatur County
Born—June 1765, Cumberland Co., Pennsylvania.
Service—As a frontier ranger in Westmoreland Co., Penn., between 1178-83. Also private in militia of Westmoreland Co.
Proof—Penn. Archives, Series 3, vol. 23, p. 283; Series 5, vol. 4, p. 435.
Died—1833. Buried Kingston Cemetery. Stone.
Married—Nancy Barr, 1771-1833. Ch. James, 1790-1863; Sarah, 1792-1846; Catherine, 1794; Robert Barr, 1797-1882; Samuel, 1799-1846; Margaret, 1800-1817; Nancy, 1804-1846; Thomas, 1806-1863; Luther A. and Eliza J. (twins), 1809; John R., 1812-1890.
Collected by Miss Emma A. Donnell (deceased), Greensburg, Indiana.

DOUGAN, JOHN   Wayne County
Born—Jan. 9, 1763, Lancaster Co., Pennsylvania.
Service—While living in Randolph Co., N. C., he enlisted in 1778 and served 3½ years as a pri. in Capt. Thomas Dougan and William Gray's CO. of horse, and under Col. Edward Sharp, Col. John Collier, Col. James Dougan and Col. Sanders. He was in a number of skirmishes with the Tories.
Proof—Pension claim W. 9836.
Died—Jan. 25, 1842. Buried in Earlham Cemetery. D. A. R. marker placed by Richmond Chapter D. A. R.
Married—Margaret Collier, 1764-1855. Ch. Margaret, 1785-1819, m. John F. Fryas; Mary, b. 1788, m. John McWhinney; Susannah, b. 1790; Thomas, b. 1792; Rebecca, b. 1795, m. John Walker; Ellen, b. 1797, m. David Adams; John C., b. 1801, m. Rebecca Homes; Martha Kerr, b. 1804, m. Thomas Little; Sarah, b. 1807; Jane, b. 1811.
Collected by Mrs. Paul L. Ross and Mrs. John Eudaley, Richmond, Indiana.

DOUGHERTY, WILLIAM   Sullivan County
Born—June 7, 1762, Rowan Co., North Carolina.
Service—Volunteered Feb., 1780, served 1 mo. in Capt. Kuyendol's N. C. CO. Dragoons; volunteered March, 1780, served 3 mos. in Capt. Enoch's CO., Col. Moffett's N. C. Regt. Was in siege of Charleston, taken prisoner for 14 mos. then exchanged. Volunteered Aug., 1781, served 1 mo. in Capt. Mackafee CO. in Aug., 1782, served 1 mo. in Capt. Wood's CO.
Proof—Pension claim W. 10315.
Died—Jan. 26, 1842. Buried Gill Twp., Sullivan Co.
Married—Mary —— 1785, d. 1862. Ch. Agnes, b. 1785, m. Thomas Baker; Jane; John; William; Martha; Thomas.
Collected by Mrs. James R. Riggs, Sullivan, Indiana.

DOUGHERTY (DAUGHERTY), WILLIAM   Delaware County
Born—1754, Chester Co., Pennsylvania.
Service—Private in company commanded by Capt. Swindler of Regt. under Col. Gates in Penn. Line. Served 7 mos. 21 days.
Proof—Pension claim W. 4182.
Died—Aug. 31, 1841. Buried on bank of White River below Yorktown, Delaware Co.
Married—1777, Lydia Cox, d. 1851. Ch. Hannah Reed; James; Bridget Bell; William, Jr. (soldier of 1812); Elizabeth Reed; Lydia Somers.

DOUGLASS, DAVID   Cass County
Born—1756, Lock Co., Pennsylvania.
Service—Commissioned Ensign 2nd CO., 8th Battalion, York Co., Penn., Militia, June 7, 1779, Capt. Thomas Warren, John Laird commanding officer. In active service until close of war. In battles of Brandywine, Kingston and Yorktown.
Proof—Penn. Archives, Series 2, vol. 14, p. 2, Muster Rolls and Papers Relating to the association of the County of York, Penn.
Died—1839, Logansport, Ind. Buried Old Cemetery. Government Marker.
Married—First to Jean Buchanan (no children); second to Elizabeth Reay. Ch. David (soldier of 1812); Joseph, m. first to Susan Roath, second to Henrietta Pugh; William, 1815-1904, m. first to Amanda Thomas, second to Rosanna Trapp, third to Sarah Neff; Nancy, 1809-1896; Rebecca, 1811-1896; Rachel.
Collected by Miss Laura D. Henderson, Logansport, Indiana.

DOWELL, GEORGE   Monroe County
Service—Enlisted in spring of 1781 as a pri. under Capt. John Sumter and was placed in Capt. Wm. McKinsie's CO. and served under Cols. Henderson and Hill, Gen. Sumter's Brigade S. C. Troops, 10 mos.
Proof—Pension claim S. 32222.
Died—Oct., 1845. Buried in Moore Cemetery, W. of Elliottsville, Ind. Stone.
Married—Jane ———. Had at least one child.
Collected by Mrs. Laura Esarey, Bloomington, Indiana.

DOWERS, CONRAD   Ripley County
Born—1764, Philadelphia, Pennsylvania.
Service—Enlisted from Penn., in March, 1778, and served as pri. in Capt. Bunner's CO., Col. Weltner's German Regt. for 9 mos. In battle of Monmouth. Discharged Nov., 1778.
Proof—Pension claim W. 9839.

Died—Feb. 27, 1844, Ripley Co. Name on bronze tablet in Versailles Court House.
Married—Mary Shields, 1788, d. 1853. Ch. Sarah; Catherine.
Collected by Mrs. A. B. Wycoff, Batesville, Indiana.

DOWERS, JACOB　　　　　　　　　　　　　　　　Ripley County
Born—1760, Philadelphia, Pennsylvania.
Service—While a resident of Lancaster Co., Penn., enlisted in Aug., 1780, served in Capt. Bartley's CO., Col. Johnston's Fifth Penn. Regt., and was discharged by Col. Mentges after 6 mos. service.
Proof—Pension claim S. 16371.
Died—Jan. 9, 1847, Ripley Co., Ind. Name on bronze tablet in Versailles Court House.
Children—Azariah; Henry; Isaac; Sally; Jolly; Purlina Sams; Nancy Johnson.
Collected by Mrs. A. B. Wycoff, Batesville, Indiana.

DOWNING, MICHAEL　　　　　　　　　　　　　　Jackson County
Born—About 1760, Ireland.
Service—Enlisted at age of 15 and served during the war and afterwards under Wayne. Served 11 yrs. in war as a volunteer from Virginia.
Proof—D. A. R. No. 11096. Also Lineage 43, p. 100.
Died—1852. Buried Downing Cemtery, Grassyfork Twp. Government marker.
Married—Mary Ann Wells. Ch. John.
Collected by Gen. Jacob Brown Chapter D. A. R., Brownstown, Indiana.

DRULINER, FREDERICK　　　　　　　　　　　St. Joseph County
Born—June 18, 1754, Salem County, New Jersey.
Service—Enlisted from Salem Co., N. J., as a pri. in Capt. Abner Penton's CO., Col. Benjamin Holmes's N. J. Regt., commanded part of the time by Maj. Edward Hall, as follows: from June 17, 1776, 2 mos. 2 wks.; early in 1777, 3 mos.; from July 1, 1777, 3 mos.; from Jan., 1778, 3 mos.; the greater part of this service was rendered at Fort Mercer, in Gloucester Co., N. J.
Proof—Pension claim S. 16106; Stryker's Officers and Men of Rev. War, p. 579.
Died—June 3, 1841. Buried Hamilton Cemetery, St. Joseph Co. Government marker and bronze table placed by Schuyler Colfax Chapter D. A. R.
Married—Hannah Summers. Ch. Gabriel, b. 1777, d. 1851, m. Catherine Hornell; Joseph.
Collected by Miss Amanda McComb, South Bend, Indiana.

DRUMMOND, JAMES, JR.   Clark County
Born—1764, Pennsylvania.
Service—Pri. and Ensign in Capt. James Poe's CO., 8th Battalion,
    Cumberland Co. Militia, Oct. 23, 1777, Col. Abraham Smith.
Proof—Penn. Archives, Series 5, vol. 6, p. 520, and Series 3, vol. 23,
    p. 618.
Died—July 19, 1843. Buried Silver Creek Cemetery, W. of Charlestown,
    Ind. Stone. Bronze tablet placed by Piankeshaw and Green Tree
    Tavern Chapters D. A. R.
Married—Nancy Griffith. Ch. Margaret, 1790-1845, m. John Carr;
    Nancy; Nellie; Mary; Lettia; Malinda; Rebecca; Hannah; Matilda; David; James; John.
Collected by Miss Mary Carr Guernsey, Charlestown, Indiana.

DUKE, JOHN   Morgan County
Born—June 25, 1756, England.
Service—Enlisted as a pri. in Capt. Charles Craig's CO., 1st Penn.
    Line, Col., Edward Hand, May 5, 1776. Was in battles of Brandywine, Trenton, Princeton, Fort Washington and White Plains.
    Name is recorded among pri. in Penn. invalid Regt. at Phil. in
    Oct. and Nov., 1777. Sept. 12, 1778, he reenlisted to serve under
    Capt. John Pearson at Phil., Col. Walter Stewart's 2nd Regt., Col.
    Richard Butler's 9th Regt.
Proof—Penn. Archives, Series 2, vol. 10 and 11, and Series 3, vol. 23.
    Pension claim W. 9841.
Died—April 9, 1841, Johnson Co., Ind. Buried across the county line
    in Morgan Co., near Banta. Stone.
Married—Sally McNeal 1789. Ch. Hugh; George; John; William;
    James; Robert; Mary; Elizabeth; Washington; a dau. m. John
    Jordan; a dau. m. Robert Branch.
Collected by Mrs. I. E. Tranter, Franklin, Indiana.

DUMONT, PETER   Switzerland County
Born—1744, New York.
Service—Captain in 2nd Battalion Somerset, N. J. His services in
    the cause were even more outside the ranks than as a soldier.
    Gen. Washington often consulted him. Certain accounts still in
    existence indicate that he may have been in the commissary department. It is also said that at Washington's request he ran
    his mills day and night to help the soldiers at Valley Forge and
    that this resulted in irretrievable loss financially. Due to overwork his health failed and he became blind. He refused to apply
    for a pension.
Proof—Tales of Our Forefathers by Eugene McPike, pp. 55-152;
    Stryker's Register of N. J. Officers and Soldiers, p. 289.

Died—1821. Buried Cemetery at Vevay, Ind. Stone.
Married—Mary Lowe, 1750-1841. Ch. Lydia Guest; Catherine Anderson; Jane Murphy; John; Abraham.
Collected by Mrs. A. V. Danner, Vevay and Miss Ellen Graydon, Indianapolis, Indiana.

DUNCAN, GEORGE   Orange County
Born—March 8, 1758, Albemarle Co., Virginia.
Service—Served three different enlistments as a pri. in the Vir. Troops.
Proof—Pension claim W. 9845.
Died—Nov. 2, 1838. Buried Stampers Creek Cemetery. Stone. Government marker.
Married—1790, Elizabeth Phillips, 1770-1850. Ch. John b. 1791; George Jr. b. 1792; Fleming H. b. 1794; Lisa b. 1796; Livina b. 1799; Sally b. 1801; Elizabeth b. 1806; Rolly b. 1807; Mary b. 1810.
Collected by Mrs. I. E. Tranter, Franklin, Indiana, and Mrs. N. B. Mavity, French Lick, Indiana.

DUNCAN, JESSE   Parke County
Born—About 1754, N. C.
Service—Enlisted in Caswell Co., N. C., in 1778; served 11 mos. as a pri. in Capt. William Lytle's CO. and in Col. Thackston's N. C. Regt., and was in battles of Brier Creek and Stono. Also served in Capt. Robert Moore's CO., Col. Archibald Lytle's and James Sander's N. C. Regt.
Proof—Pension claim S. 16774. Moved to Parke Co., Ind., 1840 to live with a daughter.
Died—Feb. 10, 1848. Buried in Rockville Cemetery.
Had children living in Virginia and Indiana. Theodore Whitted is a great-grandson.

DUNKAN, EDWARD   Decatur County
Born—1759, Frederick Co., Maryland.
Service—Drafted into service 1778, in Rowan Co., N. C., where he was living, under Capt. Joseph Craig, Gen. Rutherford, 3 mos. In 1781 again drafted, in Brigade commanded by Gen. Davison.
Proof—Pension claim S. 17395.
Died—Last payment of pension was made Aug. 5, 1836.

DUNN, AARON   Henry County
Born—March 7, 1763, Pennsylvania.
Service—1781 drafted in CO. of Capt. Andrew Millikin's in Ulster Co., N. Y. Discharged 4 mos. later. In 1782 again drafted in Goshen, Orange Co., N. Y., in Capt. John Wood's CO. of Militia for 3 mos.
Proof—Pension claim S. 32223.
Died—Last payment of pension made Sept. 25, 1843.

DUNN, ELINOR BREWSTER　　　　　　　　Monroe County
Born—Jan. 25, 1754, Augusta Co., Virginia.
Service—A Patriot. One of the Brewster Sisters who are on records as having given loyal aid to the soldiers of the revolution. They spun, wove, knit, sewed, and cooked to supply the needs of soldiers, contributing to the utmost from their possessions. They melted their household utensils of pewter, molded them into bullets and sent them to the soldiers for their use.
Proof—Article entitled "Revolutionary Service of the Brewster Sisters" by Ann A. Alexander; D. A. R. No. 93983.
Died—Nov. 3, 1841. Buried in cemetery on Indiana University Campus, Bloomington, Ind. Stone.
Husband—Samuel Dunn. Ch. James, m. Elizabeth Hopkins; John, m. Margaret Kerr; Sarah, m. John Maxwell; William m. Mariam Wilson; Nathaniel, m. Sophia Irwin; Samuel Jr., m. Elizabeth Grundy; Mary, m. David Henry Maxwell, M. D.; Martha, m. William Alexander.
Collected by Mrs. S. G. Davenport, Vincennes, Indiana.

DUNN, HUGH　　　　　　　　　　　　　Dearborn County
Born—Curry County, Ireland.
Service—Captain of 1st Regt., Middlesex Co., N. J., Militia.
Proof—N. J. Archives; Collins History of Ky., vol. 1, p. 5; S. A. R. Yearbook of Ky., 1896.
Died—1804. Buried near Lawrenceburg, Ind.
Married—Mercy ——. Son, Isaac.
Collected by Mrs. Walter Kerr, Aurora, Indiana.

DUNN, SAMUEL　　　　　　　　　　　　Knox County
Born—1754, Ireland.
Service—Pri. 5th Class, Chester Co., Penn. Militia under Capt. Reed.
Proof—Penn. Archives, Series 5, vol. 5, p. 647.
Died—Nov. 2, 1847. Buried Upper Indiana Cemetery, Vincennes, Ind.
Married—1789, Anna Stagg, 1770-1846. Ch. Rachel; John; Leah; Elizabeth; Mary; Sarah; Joseph; James; Andrew; Anna; Margaret; Samuel.
Collected by Mrs. E. A. Billman, Sullivan, Indiana.

DUPLACY, JOSEPH　　　　　　　　　　　Allen County
Service—Volunteered at Post Vincennes with 400 others under Col. Augustus Mottin de la Balm to quell the Indians at Post Miami. Killed by Miami Indians on banks of Aboite River.
Proof—Drapers Mss., 50-J-77; Wisconsin Historical Society. Original letter of LeGras reporting the massacre.
Collected by Mrs. T. J. Hindman, Fort Wayne, Indiana.

DURHAM, JOHN   Dearborn County
Born—1759, King and Queen County, Virginia.
Service—Served at various times in Virginia Army from 1777-1783.
Proof—Revolutionary Soldiers of Virginia, Supplement, p. 99.
Collected by Mrs. Walter Kerr, Aurora, Indiana.

EADS, HENRY   Franklin County
Born—1755. On the Waters of the Shenandoah River in Virginia.
Service—Volunteered in 1776, while a resident of Kent Co., Maryland, and served on short tours on alarms, from that year until 1782—3 yrs. and 2 mos. in all. All of his service was as a guard for the shores of Baltimore Bay and Elk River. He was in a number of skirmishes, several of them quite severe and the British were frequently prevented from landing at the point of the bayonet.
Proof—Pension claim S. 32226.
Died—Aug. 23, 1843. Springfield Twp., Franklin Co.
Married—Sarah Elizabeth Sailors. Ch. Jonathan; Henry, Jr.; Mary, b. 1784, m. John Quick.

EASTIN, PHILIP   Jefferson County
Born—1755, Virginia.
Service—Pri. 8th Virginia, 27th Feb., 1777; Ensign. May 20, 1777; 2nd Lieut. Oct. 1, 1777; 1st Lieut., Aug. 10, 1778; transferred to 4th Virginia, Sept. 14, 1778; retired Jan. 1, 1783.
Proof—Heitman's Historical Register, p. 210. Inscription on stone.
Died—1817. Buried Rykers Ridge Cemetery, near Madison, Ind. Stone.
Married—1782, Sarah Anna Smith (1762-1843). Ch. Sarah, m. James Kelley Read; David, m. Nancy Griffin; Rebecca, m. Leonard Barnes; Charles, m. Sarah Swearinger; Frances, m. Benjamin Stevens; Philip, Jr., m. Elizabeth Green; Lucy, m. Eleanor Raylings; Rachel, m. Elmore Cheek; Mahala, 1799-1882, m. Elisha Gale English.
Collected by W. G. Walling, 105 W. Madison St., Chicago, Ill., and John Paul Chapter D. A. R.

EDENS, ELIAS   Jefferson County
Born—1753.
Service—Pri. in Capt. Francis Boykin's CO., Col. Wm. Thompson's 3rd S. C. Regt. In battle of Eutaw Springs. Served 3 yrs. and 6 mos.
Proof—Pension claim W. 11092 and Order Book B.-315, Jefferson Co., Ind.
Died—April 29, 1839, in Milton Twp., Jefferson Co., Ind.
Married—First to Sally ——, b. 1750. Had one son, b. 1797, who m. Mary, b. 1802. Second to Nancy Ann Bradshaw, m. 1831. After death of Elias Edens, Nancy Ann married three times and after

death of her fourth husband, applied and received a pension on Elias' service.
Collected by John Paul Chapter D. A. R.

EDWARDS, JOHN   Jackson County
Born—1762.
Service—Enlisted June, 1778, in Lancaster, Penn., served until Oct., 1783, as a drummer in Capt. Van Swearingin and Clark's CO., Col. Daniel Brodhead's Penn. Regt. Served as drummer in 8th Penn. Regt., mustered April 29 (no yr.), and was paid to Jan. 1, 1782, to Jan. 1, 1783, and to Nov. 3, 1783.
Proof—Pension claim W. 8685.
Died—April 18, 1836, in Jackson Co., Ind.
Married—Mary Jackson (1770-1846), m. 1790. Ch. John, b. 1792; Jesse, b. 1793; David, b. 1795; Margaret, b. 1796, d. 1801; Polly, 1798-1836; Drewery, b. 1800; Margaret, b. 1803, m. Henry Greeg; Rebecca, b. 1804; Martha, b. 1806, m. William D. L. Haney; Joel, b. 1807; Aaron W., b. 1809, d. 1844; Nancy, b. 1811, m. Alexander Burlhanner.
Collected by Mrs. Roy Bogner, Washington, Indiana.

EHLER, MICHAEL   Dearborn County
Born—August 2, 1760, Lancaster, Pennsylvania.
Service—Volunteered 1776, for 2 mos. as private under Capt. Boyd, Col. Ross, Penn. Enlisted 6 mos. under Capt. Grafe, Col. Cunningham, Gen. Hand; 1777, 2 mos. under Capt. Petrie, Col. Clots; 1779, 2 mos. under Capt. Davis, Col. Davis; 1781, under Capt. Boyd, Col. Ross.
Proof—Pension claim S. 16377.
Died—April 23, 1838. Probably buried in Old Cemetery in Jackson Twp., Dearborn Co.
Collected by Mrs. Walter Kerr, Aurora, Indiana.

ELLIOT, JOHN   Ohio County
Born—1761, Chester, New Hampshire.
Service—Pri. and Serg. in N. H. Cont'l Line 1775, for 2 yrs. service. First enlistment under Capt. John Hile, Col. Starke, in N. H. Discharged by Col. Weston. Second enlistment in Rockingham Co., N. H., under Capt. Durbin, Gen. Starke. Next as sergeant in Col. Peabody's Regt.
Proof—Pension claim S. 16784 and D. A. R. No. 142489.
Died—Last payment of pension was made Sept. 18, 1841. Buried in Old Cemetery, Rising Sun, Indiana.
Married—Bathsheba Fields, 1770-1836. Daughter, Harriet, 1810-1838.
Collected by Mrs. Walter Kerr, Aurora, Indiana.

ELLIOTT, WILLIAM   Jennings County
Born—May 12, 1752, Cumberland Co., Pennsylvania.
Service—Ensign, 1779, under Capt. Todd, Bedford Co., Penn., Col. Davis,
    Maj. John Woods. Ensign 1780, under the same officers, against
    the Indians. Left service in Oct., a total of 10 mos. June, 1781,
    drafted.
Proof—Pension claim S. 16378.
Died—Aug. 20, 1838.
Wife died before the pensioner. Robert Elliott was an heir of soldier.

ELLIS, BENJAMIN   Fayette County
Born—May 7, 1751, Sunderland, Mass.
Service—While residing at Ashfield, Mass., he enlisted May 3, 1775,
    and served 9 mos. as pri. in Capt. Simeon Hazeltine's CO., a part
    of the time under Major Tupper and immediately after served
    1 mo. under Col. Ward, Mass. Troops.
Proof—Pension claim S. 16107; Archives Division, The Commonwealth
    of Mass.
Died—1835. Buried in Bentonville Cemetery.
Married—First to Ruth Pike, 1774. Ch. Stephen, b. 1775, m. Susannah
    Coburn, and Mrs. Martha Huntington; Lurenca, b. 1777, m. John
    Phelps; Moses, b. 1780, m. Elizabeth Judd, and Desire Harris;
    Daniel, b. about 1782; Benjamin, b. 1784, m. Abigail Howard.
    Soldier, m. second time to Lois Mann. Ch. Ruben, b. 1786, m.
    Elizabeth King; Mehitable, b. about 1788, m. Lawrence Kemp;
    Chelometh, b. about 1790, m. Walter Avery, Jr. Soldier, m. third
    time to Mrs. Zilpha Mills.
Collected by Mrs. Edna Mount and Miss Harriet Williams, Conners-
    ville, Indiana.

ELLIS, ROBERT   Greene County
Born—1753. Ireland.
Service—Pri. 2nd. Regt., N. C. Cont'l Line, Sept. 3, 1776, Feunies' CO.,
    3 yrs. service. Also pri. in 10th Regt., N. C. Line, Coleman's Co.,
    Jan. 15, 1782, for one year.
Proof—N. C. State Records, p. 1049, vol. 16. Roster of Cont'l Line
    for N. C., 1783, p. 1054, vol. 16.
Died—Dec. 25, 1849. Buried in Moss Cemetery, near Dugger, Green
    Co. Stone.
Married—Eliza Robertson, m. May, 1783. Child, William, b. 1803.
Collected by Mrs. Leo Schultheis, Vincennes, Indiana.

ELSBURY (ELLSBURY), JACOB — Dearborn County
Born—Nov. 11, 1763, Maryland.
Service—In N. C. Line, March, 1780, 9 mos. pri. under Capt. Jones, Col. Armstrong; Dec., 1780, 8 mos. under Col. Wm. Armstrong; 1781, 3 mos. under Capt. Scott, Gen. Washington; 1781, 3 mos. under Capt. Daniel Wright, Col. Robert Smith.
Proof—Pension claim W. 10,016.
Died—March 15, 1844, Lawrenceburg, Ind.
Married—1788, Mary Hudspeth, b. 1769. Ch. Elizabeth, b. 1789, m. Wm. Sefton (Lefton); Nancy; another dau. m. —— Chrismon.
Collected by Mrs. Walter Kerr, Aurora, Indiana.

EMORY (EMREY), GEORGE — Adams County
Born—Oct. 2, 1752, Frederick Co., Virginia.
Service—In March or April, 1777, at Leesburg, Loudoun Co., Vir., he entered the service as Quartermaster in Col. Andrew Russell's Vir. Regt. Marched in Capt. George Johnson's CO. to Penn., was stationed at Chad's Ford at the time of the battle of Brandywine, served as pri. at his own request. In the battle of Germantown under Col. Weedon, wintered at Valley Forge. The summer following marched to various points in Penn. Was later ordered to Leesburg, Vir., served there as Quartermaster in 1780, under Capt. Thomas Respass. Engaged in housing the soldiers and remained in service until the troops were disbanded in 1783. It was stated that he was called upon to act as captain of, a company in Col. Smallwood's Md. Regt.
Proof—Pension claim S. 32236.
Died—July 3, 1841. Buried in Loofburrow Cemetery, Adams Co. Stone. Bronze marker placed by Mississinewa Chapter D. A. R.
Children—Elizabeth Lownes; Margaret Page; Olivia Shepherd; Stephen; Thomas; Celina Kingrey; Andrew J.
Collected by Mrs. Philp Obenauer, Decatur, Indiana, and Mississinewa Chapter D. A. R.

EPERLY, GEORGE — Wayne County
Born—March 2, 1760, Lancaster Co., Pennsylvania.
Service—While residing with his father in Frederick Co., Md., he enlisted Dec., 1776, served as a substitute for his father, as a pri. in Capt. Snowdenbarger's CO., Col. Joseph Wood's Md. Regt. Marched to Trenton, N. J., where he served 3 mos. as a guard and on scouting parties; he enlisted in Aug., 1778, in Capt. Tarr's CO., Col. Johnson's Md. Regt., was ordered to join Gen. Wayne at Chestnut Hill, Penn., but before arriving there, was attacked by British at White Horse Tavern and had a sharp encounter with them and was not able to join Gen. Wayne. He again enlisted

in Jan., 1782, served 6 wks. in Capt. Wilson's Md. CO. and was stationed at Frederick, Md., as a guard to the British prisoners taken with Lord Cornwallis.
Proof—Pension claim S. 32238.
Died—Last payment of pension made April, 1840.
Collected by Mrs. Paul L. Ross, Richmond, Indiana.

EPHLAND, DAVID   Parke County
Born—About 1751, probably in N. C.
Service—Served in company of Capt. Goodman 1st N. C. Regt., Col. Jackson. Enlisted for 3 yrs. in Orange Co., N. C., where he resided. Was on several short tours. Length of service, 2 yrs. 6 mos.
Proof—Pension claim S. 32239.
Died—Pension paid to Sept. 4, 1837.

EVANS, ANDREW   Owen County
Born—Sept. 28, 1759, Mecklenburg Co., N. C.
Service—Enlisted in Vir. Militia under Col. Wm. Campbell, served 4 mos. Engaged in battle of King's Mt. Served 3 mos under Col. Sevier in campaign against Cherokee Indians.
Proof—Pension claim 17254. King's Mountain and its Heroes by Draper.
Died—Dec. 5, 1840. Buried Asher graveyard, 5 miles N. of Gosport, Ind. Government marker.
Married—1781, Elizabeth Fain (1764-1850). Ch. David; Nathaniel; Jesse; John Fain; Elizabeth Taylor Evans; Nancy; Samuel; Andrew; James; William; Mary; Rachel (1805-1885), m. James Burcham.
Collected by C. C. Tucker, Greencastle, Indiana.

EVANS, EDWARD   Lawrence County
Born—June, 1758, Virginia.
Service—Enlisted Feb., 1778; served 18 mos. under Capts. Thomas Dillard, Jesse Herd, and Isaac Clement, Col. Morgan's Vir. Regt. Present at Yorktown.
Proof—Pension claim R. 3382; widow received 160 acres of land on warrant No. 43878.
Died—Oct., 1837, or 1838. Buried Shiloh Cemetery. Government marker.
Married—Second time, 1801 or 1804, Elizabeth Howard, b. 1784. Soldier is reported to have had 22 children. William, son of first marriage. Those known of second marriage are: Mahala (3rd

Ch.); Walter Ann (9th Ch.), b. 1820, m. Oliver Witsman; Elbert; Susan; Lina; Eliza; Lucinda; Edward; Sanders; James.
Collected by Mrs. L. C. Cox, Bedford, Ind., and Mrs. S. G. Davenport, Vincennes, Indiana.

EVANS, JOHN   Randolph County
Born—1761, South Carolina.
Service—Enlisted as pri. in the 1st S. C. Regt., April 19, 1776, commanded by Col. C. Pickney.
Proof—War Department; Randolph Co. History; Lineage, vol. 65, p. 197.
Died—1831, Randolph Co., Ind.
Married—Judith Bunker. Ch. Dianah, d. 1904, m. William E. Moore. (Dianah was a Real Daughter.) Soldier, m. second time, 1885, to Rhoda —— (1767-1800). Ch. John Jr., b. 1786.
Collected by Mrs. James P. Goodrich and Mrs. Oren Ross, Winchester, Indiana.

EVINS, DAVID   Parke County
Born—May 23, 1763, Augusta Co., Virginia.
Service—Served in Virginia. 1780, volunteered 6 days, pri. under Capt. Campbell. 1782, about 5 mos. as spy under Col. Logan in Vir. 1782, about 40 days as pri. under Gen. Clark, Col. Logan, in Ohio.
Proof—Pension claim S. 32695.
Died—Aug. 11, 1838. Probably buried in Florida Twp., Parke Co.
Widow claimed remainder of pension but her name was not shown.

EWING, ALEXANDER   Allen County
Born—May 28, 1760, Pennsylvania.
Service—Pri. in Capt. John McConnel's CO., Lieut. Col. Samuel Cuthbertson's 4th Battalion, Cumberland Co. Association, Aug. 10, 1780, till the close of the war. Served in the War of 1812 under Capt. W. Griffith.
Proof—Penn. Archives, Series 3, vol. 23, p. 753.
Died—Jan. 1, 1827. Buried Lindenwood Cemetery, Fort Wayne, Ind. Stone. Bronze tablet by Mary Penrose Wayne Chapter D. A. R.
Married—Charlotte Griffith, 1795. Ch. Sophia C.; Charles W.; William G.; Alexander H.; George; Lovena; Louise.
Collected by Ruth B. Knorr, Fort Wayne, Indiana.

EWING, GEORGE   Perry County
Born—March 18, 1754. Greenwich, N. J.
Service—Enlisted Nov. 11, 1775, Fifth CO., 2nd Battalion, First Establishment, N. J. Cont'l Troops. Commissioned Ensign, Feb. 5, 1777. Was in battles of Germantown, Brandywine and at Valley Forge and with Montgomery at Quebec.

Proof—War Department; his own "Journal"; Heitman's Register, p. 220.
Died—Jan. 15, 1824. Buried Cliff Cemetery, Cannelton, Ind. Stone.
Married—Rachel Harris, 1778. Ch. George Jr., 1779-1850; Abigail, 1781; Sarah d. 1835; Rachel, 1785-1833; Hannah Harris, d. 1860; Thomas, 1789-1871; Jane Hunter, 1792-1877.
Collected by Mrs. D. S. Conner, Cannelton, Indiana.

FALCONBURY, JACOB   Decatur County
Born—Feb. 14, 1757, Anson Co., N. C.
Service—Volunteered 1776, for 2 mos., 21 days, as private under Gen. Redderford, Capt. Hay, Col. Lone. 1780, under Col. Wade, Capt. Deganett. Drafted 1781, for 12 mos. under Col. Wade. Engaged in battle of Beaty's Bridge. All N. C. service.
Proof—Pension claim S. 167789.
Died—Nov. 2, 1844, Decatur Co., Ind.
Married—Levina ——, who survived the pensioner.

FANNIN (FANNING), DANIEL   Floyd County
Born—1759.
Service—Enlisted in 1776 or 1777 in Montgomery Co., Vir. Served in Regt. of volunteers, commanded by Capt. John Montgomery.
Proof—Probate book 1830-1836, p. 93, Floyd County records.
Collected by Mrs. V. R. Conner, New Albany, Indiana.

FARMER, NATHANIEL   Carroll County
Born—About 1757.
Service—Enlisted 1778 in Maryland under Capt. Griffin in Regt. commanded by Col. Anderson. Served until last of July, 1780. Discharged near Wilmington, Delaware.
Proof—Pension claim S. 35917.
Died—Dec. 11, 1838. Buried in Deer Creek Cemetery, Washington Twp. Stone. Bronze tablet placed by Charles Carroll Chapter D. A. R.
Married—Wife living at the time of application for pension in 1827.
Collected by Mrs. Julia H. Irelan, Delphi, Indiana.

FAUCETT, JOHN   Hendricks County
Born—Aug. 10, 1752, Greenbrier Co., Virginia.
Service—Volunteered as a militiaman and served 1 mo. as guard and ranger to prevent surprise from Indians on the frontiers. In the summer 1778, he substituted 1 mo. for Jacob Beason, under Lt. John Springer, whose company was later attached to a company of the regular Vir. Line under Capt. Farrill; marched to Fort Wheeling where they were stationed 7 wks.; marched to Ft. Pitt under Lt. Springer and was discharged. Summer of

1779 volunteered as pri. under Capt. James Dougherty in company of Rangers and Indian Spies to protect farmers on the frontier. Served 65 days and later 1 mo. at Van Meter's Fort. Summer of 1780, volunteered as pri. under Lt. Springer, and served 2 mos. Served 6 mos. under Capt. Pierce, Col. Robert Bell, in 1781, clearing ground, erecting Ft. McIntosh, acting as spy and guard. Later drove pack horses to Ft. Pitt under Wm. Gahagin.
Proof—Pension claim S. F. 32240.
Died—1838. Buried Shiloh Cemetery, N. E. of Avon, Ind.
Married—Eve —— (1762-1851). Ch. Joseph, b. 1797; Cynthia, b. 1802, m. —— Fryer; David, b. 1803, m. Martha McCalment; Sibelene, b. 1805, m. Aaron Homen; Lydia, b. 1808, m. Wilson McCalment.
Collected by Miss Helen McCalment, Danville, Indiana.

FELL, JOHN   Wayne County
Born—Sept. 8, 1763, Bucks Co., Pennsylvania.
Service—Served 2 years as a pri. in Capt. Jacob Bennett's CO. of Light Dragoons. His name appears in a muster roll of June, 1781, in the official muster published by the State of Penn., found at the General Registrar Office in Phila. He was in several battles, one being Brandywine.
Proof—Penn. Archives, vol. 2, p. 214, and Bucks Co. History, pp. 253-258.
Died—1845. Buried Doddridge Chapel, Wayne Co., Ind. Government marker.
Married—Elizabeth Mason, d. 1831. Ch. Mary, m. John Connelly; Hannah, m. Benjamin Stevens.
Collected by Mrs. Paul Ross, Richmond, Indiana, and Mrs. Lora Larson, Cambridge City, Indiana.

FERGUSON, ANDREW (Colored-Man)   Monroe County
Born—July, 1765, Dinwiddie Co., Virginia.
Service—Pri. in company commanded by Capt. Harris of the Regt. commanded by Col. McCormack in Vir. Line. In battles of King's Mt., Camden, S. C., Cowpens and Eutaw Springs. Applied for bounty land which was granted a few months after his death.
Proof—Pension claim S. 32243, B. L. Wt. 26076.
Died—1855. Buried in Cemetery at Bloomington, Indiana.
Wife—Died before the soldier. No children.

FERGUSON (FORGASON, FORGUSON), JOHN   Boone County
Born—Jan. 15, 1755, York County, Virginia.
Service—While a resident of Brunswick Co., Vir., he enlisted about Sept., 1777, and served 3 mos. as a pri. in Capt. Charles Lucas' CO., Col. Grey Jenkins' Vir. Regt., and was stationed as a guard

at Smithfield, Vir. Later he moved to Guilford Co., N. C., and served 3 tours in N. C. Troops. Two of these tours were for 3 mos. each in Capt. John Mackeden's CO., Col. John Bausley's Regt., and the other was for 5 mos. in Capt. Wm. Bethel's Regt., Col. Abram Phillips. During this time he marched to Camden, S. C., and joined the army under Gen. Gates and was in the defeat at that place; he stated that he was also in a skirmish at Eutaw Springs.

Proof—Pension claim W. 10777.

Died—Feb. 14, 1828. Buried Cox Cemetery, Boone Co. Stone.

Married—1828, in Union Co., Ind., to Bethand Dickens or Bethena Deacons (probably a second marriage). Ch. of the soldier, Mary Chimault; Mary Knott; Rebecca Knott; William; David; John; Elizabeth Young; Joseph; Benjamin; Hannah Green; Moses; Sarah Hill; Jonathan b. 1829; Bethany b. 1831.

Collected by Mrs. Minnie McClaine, Lebanon, Indiana.

FERGUSON, SAMUEL   Indiana
Born—About 1752.

Service—Enlisted in Lancaster Co., Penn., as pri. in Col. Hazen's Regt., Penn. Line, for 3 yrs.

Proof—Pension claim S. 35924. Made application in 1818, in Cambria Co., Penn. In 1820, he appeared in court in Indiana Co., Penn. In Sept. 1822, asked for a transfer to Indiana.

FERGUSON, THOMAS   Greene County
Born—Nov. 25, 1756, Virginia.

Service—Pri. in Capt. Benjamin Spiller's CO., Capt. Augustine Tobb's CO., 2nd Vir. Regt., commanded successively by Col. Gregory Smith and Col. Wm. Brent. Enlisted for 3 yrs.

Proof—Portrait and Biographical Album of Sedgwick Co., Kansas, pp. 351-2.

Died—June 19, 1836. Buried Hobbieville, Greene Co. Stone.

Married—Nancy Young, 1773-1850. Ch. William and Andrew (twins), b. 1794; Gus; Rolse; Jim; J. Wesley; Sam; Benjamin; Hyrum; Thomas; Rose.

Collected by Mrs. Elvenah F. Miller, Vincennes, Indiana.

FEWELL, NATHAN   Jefferson County
Born—Virginia.

Service—Revolutionary Soldiers of Virginia by the State Librarian of Virginia, gives the name Nathaniel Fewell, Aud. Acct. Bk. 15, p. 533. This man died while visiting his daughter, Mrs. Willis Sullivan in Jefferson Co., Ind. Buried on Ford farm west of Volga. Mrs. Edwin Corrie, North Madison, Ind., is a descendant.

Collected by John Paul Chapter D. A. R.

FIELD, ANSEL   Shelby County
Born—Jan. 5, 1749, Hanover, Virginia.
Service—While residing in Guilford Co., Vir., he volunteered in July,
    1780, served as sergeant in Capt. John Leek's CO., Col. James
    Martin's N. C. Regt., went on an expedition against the Cherokee
    Indians. Was in several skirmishes with the Indians and burned
    one of their towns; length of service 3 mos. He again volunteered,
    Nov., 1780, and served one tour of 3 mos. and another of 6 mos.
    under same officers. Was in battle of Guilford Court House.
Proof—Pension claim W. 10021.
Died—Oct. 1, 1834. Probably buried in Sugar Creek Twp., Shelby Co.
Married—Martha Dodd, 1781. Ch. Mary, b. 1783; Sarah, b. 1784;
    Nathaniel, b. 1786; Allen, b. 1789; John, b. 1793; Catharine, b.
    1795; Abner, b. 1797; Noah, b. 1801; Redmon, b. 1804; Patsey, b.
    1808. There were two more children whose names were not given.

FIELD, JOHN   Jefferson County
Born—1752.
Service—Enlisted in Bedford Co., Vir., 1778; served 2 yrs. as pri. in
    Capt. Joseph Crockett's CO., in 7th Vir. Regt.; was in the battle
    of Brandywine, some skirmishes and discharged about June, 1780.
Proof—Pension claim S. 35937.
Died—1839, Jefferson Co., Ind.
Married—Lavina Shortridge (1755-1857). Ch. Margaret, 1800-1884, m.
    Hiram Newlon, 1794-1887.
Collected by John Paul Chapter D. A. R.

FINNEY, JOHN   Rush County
Born—Dec. 25, 1751, County Antrim of Ireland.
Service—Drafted from Chester Co., Penn. He guarded Tories. Pri. in
    CO. commanded by Col. Jenkins with Penn. Line for 9 mos.
Proof—Pension claim W. 10025.
Died—July 11, 1836, Rush Co., Ind.
Married—Sarah McDaniel, 1768-1848. Ch. Mary, b. 1788; James, b.
    1789; Edith, b. 1792; Ann, b. 1798; Amos, b. 1800; William, b.
    1801.

FISCUS, ADAM   Indiana
Born—Sept. 25, 1759, Lancaster Co., Pennsylvania.
Service—Entered service at "Moravian Town," N. C., as volunteer for
    9 mos., in 1778 in Capt. Henry Smith's CO., Col. Locke's Regt.
    Went to Ky. with Daniel Boone in 1779, joined Capt. William
    Hay's CO. for 18 mos. in Col. B. Logan's Regt., under Gen.
    George Rogers Clark. Later in battle of Guilford Court House.

Proof—Pension claim S. 16115. Made application in Washington Co., Ind., and his Will is recorded there in 1832, but probated in Owen Co., Ind. Last payment of pension made Feb. 27, 1839.
Children—Peter; Henry; Frederick; Jacob; Sussy Fulk; Elizabeth Fulk.
Collected by Mrs. Harvey Morris, Salem, Indiana.

FISHER, ISAAC   Pike County
Born—1753.
Service—Pri. in company under Capt. Meade, in Regt. of Col. Shreeves, N. J., Militia. Was a resident of town of Pompton, Burgin Co., N. J., when he entered service.
Proof—Pension claim W. 10598, B. L. Wt. 105513-160-55. Moved to Pike Co., Ind., 1841.
Died—Dec., 1844 or 45.
Married—Fanny Jones, 1833. Ch. Thomas, b. 1834; Jane, b. 1836; Gennet, b. 1838; Isebel, b. 1840; Peter, b. 1842; Flavil, b. 1844. Widow of soldier, m. Joseph Chance in 1854.

FISLAR, JOHN   Clark County
Born—April 25, 1862, Middlesex Co., New Jersey.
Service—Pri. under Capt. Perrine, N. J. Militia, 1 year.
Proof—Pension claim S. 32247.
Died—June 28, 1833. Buried Old Pleasant Cemetery, near New Bethlehem.
Married—First W., 1783, Sarah Plaskett (1764-1806). Second W., Sophia Neddgit (Liggett). Ch. John, b. 1785; James, b. 1787; Jacob, b. 1790; Joseph; Elizabeth, b. 1800; Sarah Ann, b. 1805; Jesse; William, b. 1807.
Collected by General Jacob Brown Chapter D. A. R.

FITZGERALD, CHARLES   Knox County
Born—About 1761.
Service—While living in Caroline Co., Maryland, he enlisted in 1779 or 1780; served 3 years and 3 days as private with Maryland Troops under Capts. Richard Andrew, Sheppard, Smith, and Price, and Lt. Col. Stewart and Col. Williams. Was wounded in the battle of Eutaw Springs.
Proof—Pension claim S. 17950.
Died—July 2, 1836, Knox Co., Ind.
Married—Wife unknown. Son, James was administrator of estate and was living in Knox Co., in 1839. From marriage records of Knox Co., Johnston Fitzgerald, m. Margretta Eyers, 1812. This may be a son.
Collected by Mrs. S. G. Davenport, Vincennes, Indiana.

FITZGERALD (FITZJERREL), WILLIAM E.   Randolph County
Born—1746, Maryland.
Service—Enlisted in "Newtown, Chester," Maryland, and served as pri. under Capts. Shepher, Price, and Hugo, Cols. Smith, Gist, Stewart, and Eccleston in the Md. troops; was in the battle of Hobkirk's Hill, Siege of Ninety-Six, and Eutaw Springs, following which he was stationed on James Island until "Peace was made." Was wounded in the elbow.
Proof—Pension claim S. 16796. Randolph County histories give the name as Fitzjerrel. The grave stone says "Jerrels."
Died—Feb. 15, 1851. Buried in Mt. Zion Cemetery, Washington Twp.
Married—Sarah ——, d. 1852, age 92 years.
Collected by Mrs. James P. Goodrich and Mrs. Oran E. Ross, Winchester, Indiana.

FITZIMMONS, THOMAS   Hendricks County
Service—Enlisted 1778 from Virginia. Served three yrs. as pri.
Proof—Pension record.
Died—Buried in Regan cemetery, S. of New Winchester, Ind.
Collected by Mrs. J. H. Grimes, Danville, Indiana.

FLAKE (FLECK, FLICK, FLACK), ADAM   Dearborn County
Service—Listed as pri. in Capt. Samuel Rogers CO. of the 1st Battalion, Cumberland Co., Penn., Militia, Aug. 16, 1780-1781.
Proof—Penn. Archives, 5th Series, vol. 6.
Died—1836. Buried near Aurora, Indiana.
Married—Elizabeth Stuff. Ch. Catharine, b. 1785; William, b. 1794; Elizabeth; Susanna, b. 1796; Mary; Sarah, b. 1798; Nancy, b. 1809.
Collected by Mrs. Viola Flake Rawalt, Corpus Christi, Texas, and Miss Marguerite Rawalt, 1725 N. Hampshire, N. W., Washington, D. C.

FLATHERS, EDWARD   Hendricks County
Born—1755, England.
Service—Enlisted as a substitute 1781, and served 2 mos. as pri. under Capt. John Britt. Marched to Occoquan Creek and engaged in clearing road for Washington's troops. Again served 2 mos. under Capt. Will Patton. Was at Yorktown. Discharged at Princetown, Virginia.
Proof—Pension claim S. F. 17418.
Died—May 6, 1847. Buried Gentry Cemetery, N. W. of Danville, Indiana. Stone.
Married—Clary (Clara) Legg (1754-1848). Ch. Isaac, d. 1815; Benjamin, m. Ann Shackleford.
Collected by Mrs. J. Harold Grimes, Danville, Indiana.

FLEETWOOD, ISAAC Lawrence County
Born—About 1732.
Service—Pri. in company commanded by Capt. Smith, Regt. of Col. Febiger in Virginia; 1776 for three years.
Proof—Pension claim S. 35942.
Died—Last payment of pension was made Oct. 3, 1832. Grave in Pleasant Run Cemetery.
Pension application mentions wife and three children, names not given. Last pension was paid to Isaac Fleetwood, Jr.; relationship to soldier not shown.

FLORENCE, WILLIAM Hendricks County
Born—1761, Prince William County, Virginia.
Service—Drafted into service in Prince Williams Co., Vir.; marched to Alexandria and continued there for his term of 3 mos., then back to Prince Williams Co. In July or August, 1778, again drafted at Culpepper Co. for 6 mos. Marched to Richmond and was in one small skirmish. 1780, he enlisted in the service and was marched to Yorktown for the siege.
Proof—Pension claim W. 25599, B. L. Wt. 34279-160-55.
Died—Jan. 28, 1840. Grave in Cartersburg Springs Cemetery. Stone.
Married—Elizabeth Hufford in 1829.

FLOWERS, THOMAS Washington County
Born—About 1761.
Service—Served in 9th Penn. Regt., 6 mos. under Lt. Col. George Nogle. Drafted into 5th Penn. Regt., under Col. Richard Butter. Discharged Philadelphia, Penn., 1783. Granted 100 acres bounty land. The original discharge is filed with his pension application.
Proof—Pension claim S. 35944, B. L. Wt. 1201-100.
Died—Sept. 10, 1840. Buried Flowers Gap Cemetery, Polk Twp. Government marker.
Married—Elizabeth ———. Ch. Jane, m. James Welch.
Collected by Mrs. Harvey Morris, Salem, Indiana.

FLOYD, ABRAHAM Floyd County
Born—May 10, 1755, Camden, S. C.
Service—Volunteered March 31, 1776; served as a pri. in Capt. Wm. Byer's CO., Col. Thomas Neil's, S. C., Regt., was in an expedition against the Cherokee Indians. Was in several skirmishes and an engagement with the savages at a place called the Black Hole on the French Broad River and was discharged Oct., 1776; he enlisted latter part of Feb., 1779. Served in Capt. Wm. McCullough's CO., under Maj. Thomas Ross. Was in the battle of Brier Creek, where he was captured, carried to Savannah, Geor-

gia, from which place he made his escape about July, 1779, and returned home.
Proof—Pension claim S. 32251.
Died—Floyd Co., Indiana, 1844.
Married—Eve Julen. Ch. Abraham, b. 1787, m. Jane Chaney.

FLYNN, THOMAS   Indiana
Born—About 1753.
Service—Enlisted in New Castle Co., Delaware, and served 2 yrs. as pri. in Capt. John Smith's CO., Col. Edward Veazy's Md. Regt., and was in battles of White Plains, Trenton, and Brandywine. Re-enlisted 1779, served to end of war in Delaware Troops under Capt. John Learmonth, Lt. Col. Joseph Vaughn, and Cols. David Hall and Williams and was in battles of Camden, Guildford, and Eutaw Springs.
Proof—Pension claim S. 35943.
Died—About 1830. Allowed pension 1819, while living in Sullivan Co., Indiana; 1820, he was in Posey Co. Received his last pension in 1830, Harrison Co.
Children—Jacob; Polly; Augustine; Charles; Solomon and David (twins).

FOLGER, LATHAM   Union County
Born—Dec. 17, 1749, Nantucket Island.
Service—A Patriot. Released some prisoners held by the British in Stokes County, N. C.
Proof—D. A. R. No. 202167.
Died—Nov. 9, 1833, Union Co., Ind.
Married—Matilda Worth, 1748-1843. Ch. Reuben; Judith Lydia; Eunice; Rebecca, m. Paul Gardner; Asa Lydia; Dinah; Elizabeth George; Asa Jethro; Mary; Paul. (Judith Lydia and the first Asa died in infancy).
Collected by Anderson Slade Gardner, 1148 Hancock St., Brooklyn, New York.

FONTAINE, JAMES   Allen County
Born—1757. Probably Hanover Co., Virginia.
Service—At an early age entered on a military career, became a member of the first expert rifle company raised in Buckingham District, for the defense of the colony in 1775. Later this company was attached to the 2nd Vir. Regt., Oct. 21, 1775. Served till March, 1776, near Williamsburg. Major of a volunteer regt. of cavalry in Ky. Wounded by Indians at Miami town. Killed at Harmers defeat.

Proof—Huguenot Magazine; Virginia State Library, Kennedy's Seldons of Virginia and Allied Families; Griswold's History of Fort Wayne.
Died—Oct. 22, 1790. Probably buried in a trench along Maumee River, Ft. Wayne, Ind. Never married.
Collected by Mrs. T. J. Hindman, Fort Wayne, Indiana.

FORD, WILLIAM   Knox County
Service—Letter from Office of Quartermaster General gives the following: "The only record on file in this office shows that in 1902 a government headstone was furnished to mark the grave of one Wiliam Ford, soldier of the Revolutionary War, who died ——."
Died—Jan. 22, 1850. Buried in Upper Indiana Cemetery, Knox Co.
Collected by Mrs. S. G. Davenport, Vincennes, Indiana.

FORDYCE, HENRY   Franklin County
Born—Nov. 12, 1744, Essex Co., New Jersey.
Service—He enlisted sometime in Oct., 1775; served in Capt. Andrew McMyer's CO., Col. William Wind's N. J. Regt.; was in the expedition to Canada and the battle of Three Rivers, and was discharged Nov. 13, 1776. He enlisted Dec. 1, 1776, and served at various times in the N. J. Militia under Capts. Patten and Wharton in Col. Scudder's Regt. He was in the battle of Elizabethtown and Connecticut Farms, and many "severe skirmishes"; continued in this service until about Nov. 1, 1781.
Proof—Pension claim S. 32256.
Died—Last payment of pension was made Sept. 15, 1836.

FORDYCE, JAMES   Franklin County
Born—1752, Morris County, New Jersey.
Service—While residing in Morris, Co., N. J., he enlisted and served four tours in the N. J. Troops, as follows: from June (yr. not given), 1 mo. in Capt. Jacob Gard's CO.; from Dec., 1778, 2 mos. in Capt. Peter Salmon's CO.; from June, 1779, 3 mos. in Capt. Samuel Morris' CO.; from April 1, 1780, 1 mo. in Capt. Scott's CO. All of the service was under Col. Jacob Drake. He was in three skirmishes, two of Springfield, N. J., and one at Elizabethtown, N. J.
Proof—Pension claim S. 17961.
Died—Last payment of pension was made Jan. 11, 1845.
Married—Jane ——, d. Sept. 6, 1835, Blooming Grove Twp., Franklin Co.

FOREMAN, JACOB   Boone County
Born—1758 or 1759, Lancaster Co., Penn.
Service—While residing in Lancaster Co., Penn., he enlisted and served as a pri. with the Penn. Troops as follows: in the summer of the 2nd yr. of war, 2 mos. in Capt. Ream's CO., and guarded

the powder magazine at Lancaster. The following summer, 2 mos. in Capt. Michael Overly's CO., and guarded British prisoners at Lancaster. In the 4th yr., 2 mos in Capt. John Uplinger's CO., and guarded Hessian prisoners at Lancaster. The next summer, 2 wks. in Capt. Michael Overly's CO.
Proof—Pension claim S. 322540.
Died—Last payment of pension was made Sept. 5, 1836.
Collected by Mrs. C. M. McClaine, Lebanon, Indiana.

FORREY, JACOB   Wayne County
Born—1757.
Service—Private in Penn. Troops. Enlisted in Lancaster, Co., Penn. Served under Capt. Jacob Klotz CO. of the Flying Camp. Served in the Jersey's in summer of 1776. Was in Battles of Long Island and Brandywine.
Proof—Pension records.
Died—1840. Buried Doddridge Chapel, Wayne Co. Original stone and new granite stone placed by great grandson, George C. Forrey, Jr.
Children—Stricklin; Henry; Isaac; and possibly others.
Collected by George C. Forrey, Jr., 3261 N. Penn. St., Indianapolis, Indiana.

FORTNER, EMANUEL   Owen County
Born—Sept. 20, 1760, Butte Co., N. C.
Service—Private, N. C. Militia. Enlisted 1779, from Butte Co., N. C., under Capt. Aaron Fuzzell, Lt. Buffort, Col. Johnson.
Proof—Pension claim S. 32258.
Died—Aug. 20, 1839, Owen Co., Indiana.

FOSHER (FORSHIER, FOSHA), DANIEL   Union County
Born—May 12, 1763 or 1762.
Service—Present at surrender of Cornwallis. At the battle of Trenton.
Proof—Mrs. Glen Curtis, Chariton, Iowa; Mrs. Jesse B. Mandleco, Rochester, Ind.; H. D. Bertsch, account in "Old Trails Echo of Centerville."
Died—Aug. 4, 1849. Buried on farm S. of Abington. Stone, inscription states he was a revolutionary soldier.
Married—Mavillis Echols, d. 1832. Ch. John, m. Elizabeth Landis; Susanna, m. —— Pagin; Mathias, m. Mary E. Rife; May, m. David Hale; Elizabeth; Catherine, m. Stephen Hicks; Salona, m. John Drook; Jacob, m. Elizabeth Brewington; Anna, m. Stanton ——; David, m. Elizabeth Tlivibbles.
Collected by Mrs. Paul Ross, Richmond, Indiana and Mrs. Elnora Campbell, Liberty, Indiana.

FOSTER, ALEXANDER   Montgomery County
Born—Feb. 10, 1759, Ireland.
Service—Enlisted in the summer of 1776, for 6 mos. as a pri. in Capt.
    George Greaf's CO., Col. Cunningham's Regt., Lancaster Co.,
    Penn. In 1777, same CO., 2 mos. In battle of Flatbush, Westchester, Eastchester, Rocky Hill, White Plain, and Brandywine.
Proof—Pension claim S. 32252; Penn. Archives, Series 5, vol. 4, p. 229;
    vol. 7, p. 1074.
Died—June 26, 1843. Buried Indian Creek Cemetery, near New Market,
    Ind. Stone.
Married—First w. unknown. Ch. Sarah Casper; Mary Hollman; Ann
    Trailkill; Elizabeth, b. 1788; William, b. 1786. Soldier m. second
    time to Sarah Campbell, 1770-1845. Ch. Phoebe Jones; Sally
    Ramsey; Rebecca Jones; Martha Hindman; George; Robert, 1803-
    71, m. Susanna Jones; Hannah Smith.
Collected by Miss Jesse Watson, Crawfordsville, Indiana.

FOSTER, JAMES   Decatur County
Born—1753, Ireland.
Service—Fought in the battle of Cowpens, 1781. Served as a member
    of the 6th S. C. Regt. Enlisted May 7, 1776.
Proof—D. A. R. Nos. 158492, 201575, 268412.
Died—Sept. 19, 1837. Buried Springhill Cemetery, N. E. of Greensburg, Ind. Stone.
Married—Jane Morrow. Ch. James, m. Mary ——; Samuel; Alexander Morrow, m. first, Jane Crawford, second, Jane N. Adams;
    John, m. Elener Cochran; Isabella, m. Adam Stewart; Mary
    Porter, m. James Bonner; Thomas Thornton, m. Rebecca Hawthorn; William L., m. Sarah Buck.
Collected by Francis May Davis, Troy, South Carolina, and Minnie
    Myrtle Dansey, 6056 Harper Ave., Chicago, Illinois.

FOSTER, SAMUEL   Marion County
Born—Feb. 1, 1763, Prince George Co., Maryland.
Service—Declares that he volunteered his service in 1778, under Jesse
    Pigmon, Capt. John Minor, Col. Joseph Vanmater and gave 4 mos.
    service doing scouting as an Indian Spy. Entered service again
    in the spring of 1779, in a CO. under Capt. Wm. Herod, 3 mos.
    In Aug., 1780, he volunteered under Capt. Wm. Crawford, Col.
    John Minor.
Proof—Pension claim R. 3693. Applied while living in Marion Co.,
    Ind. Pension rejected because service not under competent military authority or organization.

FOWLER, JOSHUA   Floyd County
Born—About 1758, Ann Arundel County, Maryland.
Service—Entered service 1781, having previously been drafted, was
    called out from Washington Co., Md., to Ft. Frederick. Served
    3 mos. under this draft, Capt. Leonard Bilmore; 1st Lt. James
    Patterson; his father, John Fowler, 2nd Lt. He enlisted again
    last of April, or first of May, 1781, for a term of 9 mos., under
    Capt. Joseph Chapline's CO. This company was called the "yellow
    jackets"—they were to guard and keep in check the Tories.
Proof—Pension claim S. 16120.
Died—March, 1839. Buried Fairview Cemetery, New Albany, Ind.
    Stone.
Married—Amelia ——, d. March 26, 1839. Ch. Joshua.
Collected by Mrs. V. R. Conner, New Albany, Indiana.

FOX, STEPHEN   Wayne County
Born—About 1760.
Service—Enlisted about Nov., 1780, in Greenwich, Conn., as pri. in
    Capt. Bulkley's CO., Col. Samuel B. Webb's 3rd Conn. Regt., also
    under other captains, not named, in Col. Zebulon Butler's Conn.
    Regt., and continued until Nov., 1783, when he was discharged
    at West Point, N. Y. He served also in Gen. Harmer's Indian
    War on the western frontier, for three years.
Proof—Pension claim W. 10031.
Died—Feb. 25, 1842. Probably buried in Jefferson Twp., Wayne Co.
Married—Mary Bates 1790 (1776-1844). Ch. Uzal Bates; Samuel;
    Stephen; Enos H.; Jemimah Price; Mary, m. John Baldridge.
Collected by Mrs. Carl Caldwell, Milton, Indiana.

FRISBIE, JONAH   Warrick County
Born—Aug. 12, 1763.
Service—Enlisted in Lanesborough, Mass., Dec., 1781. Served as pri.
    in Capt. Jeremiah Miller's CO., Col. Joseph Vose's 1st Mass. Regt.
    Discharged Oct. 28, 1783; his discharge signed by J. Pettengill.
    Major.
Proof—Pension claim S. 35956.
Died—Aug. 27, 1820. Buried Frisbie Cemetery, Yankeetown, Warrick
    Co. Government marker placed by Vanderburgh Chapter D. A. R.
Collected by Mrs. H. K. Forsythe, Newburgh, Indiana.

FROTHINGHAM, EBENEEZER   Allen County
Born—1758, Middletown, Conn.
Service—Sergeant of Webbs Continental Regt., May 25, 1777; Ensign,
    May 16, 1778; Lieut., May 26, 1779; Regimental Quartermaster,
    May 27, 1779 to June, 1783; transferred to 3rd Conn. Jan. 1,

1781, and served to June, 1783; Lieut. U. S. Infantry Regt., July, 1785; Lieut. 1st Infantry U. S. Army, Sept. 29, 1789.
Proof—Heitman's Historical Register, p. 238.
Died—Oct. 22, 1790. Buried probably in trench along the Maumee River, Fort Wayne, Ind.
Married—Mary Boardman, d. May 25, 1790.
Collected by Mrs. T. J. Hindman, Fort Wayne, Indiana.

FRUITS, GEORGE   Montgomery County
Born—Jan. 2, 1762 or 1763, Baltimore, Maryland.
Service—Under Capt. Kirkwood in latter part of war. Not regularly enlisted. In 1797, Ky. Rifleman under Capt. Kennedy.
Proof—Inscription on gravestone reads "A Remnant of the Revolution."
Died—1876. Buried in Bunker Hill Cemetery, Alamo, Ind.
Married—Katherine Stonebraker. Ch. Jacob; George, Jr.; Sebastion; Lucinda Pate; John; Katherine Phillot; William; Michael; Margaret.
Collected by Miss Jessie Watson, Crawfordsville, Indiana.

FULLER, WILLIAM   Daviess County
Born—1754.
Service—Served in Virginia Infantry. Name appears in list of soldiers of Virginia Line on Continental Establishment, who have received certificates for the balance of their full pay by Act of Assembly passed Nov., 1781, and shows that on Dec. 10, 1783, the sum of 65 pounds was paid.
Proof—War records, Washington, D. C.
Died—Feb. 12, 1850. Buried Maysville Cemetery, S. W. of Washington, Ind. Stone bears words "A Hero of the Revolution."
Collected by Mrs. Roy Bogner, Washington, Indiana.

FULTON, JOHN   Ohio County
Born—Ireland.
Service—He and his wife were taken prisoners by the Indians, 1780.
Proof—See Samuel Fulton service.
Died—At the age of 97. Buried in Fulton graveyard, near Rising Sun, Ind.
Married—Jane Dills. Ch. Samuel, m. Mary Huston; Thomas.
Collected by Mrs. Walter Kerr, Aurora, Indiana.

FULTON, SAMUEL   Ohio County
Born—July 1, 1762, Carlisle, Cumberland Co., Pennsylvania.
Service—In pension application states that he was a resident of Northumberland Co., Penn., in the time of Revolution. Volunteered under Capt. Samuel Dougherty, who was killed by the Indians.

Served 6 mos. under Col. John Kelly and Capt. McGradt or McGrund. While he was in the service his father, mother, one brother and one sister were taken prisoners by the Indians. Two of his brothers were killed. He states that his father was adopted into an Indian family by the name of Montown or Mantoee who took him to Niagara where the British finding that he was a hacksmith bought him and that he afterwards prevailed upon them to buy his wife and children. It was 2 yrs. and 4 mos. from the time his parents, brothers, sister, were captured until they returned home and then after peace was declared they were exchanged. His father's name was John Fulton.

Proof—Pension claim R. 3850. Application was made from Randolph Twp., Dearborn Co., Ind., Sept., 1833. This is now Ohio Co. Pension rejected because department was not satisfied with dates given.

Died—Jan. 15, 1849, Rising Sun, Indiana.

Married—Mary Huston, d. 1834. Ch. Anna; Jennie, m. Peter Allen; Mary, b. 1793, m. Robert E. Covington; Sarah, m. —— Welch; Frances, m. —— Thompson; Eliza, m. —— Peck; John; William; three other daughters, names not found.

FUNK, HENRY II   Harrison County
Born—About 1739.
Service—With Col. George Rogers Clark under Capt. Joseph Bowman. Served 2 yrs., 1778-1779. A pri. from Virginia. Discharged Aug. 8, 1779.
Proof—Pension claim W. 23075; English's Conquest of Northwest, p. 844, 1034.
Died—Nov. 1, 1815. Buried on farm near New Amsterdam, Harrison Co. Government marker placed by descendant Miss Clara Funk.
Married—Elizabeth Miller, 1774. Ch. Henry III; Peter, m. Nancy Padgett; John, m. Rebecca Padgett; Joseph; Elizabeth, m. Rev. Wm. Potter; Isaac, m. Rachel Coates; Daniel, m. Rachel Denbo.
Collected by Mrs. Ed. G. Keller, Corydon, Indiana.

GAITHER, JOHN   Harrison County
Born—1752, Virginia.
Service—1st Lieut., 1st Maryland Battalion of the Flying Camp, July, 1776.
Proof—Heitman's Historical Register, p. 240.
Died—1825, Harrison County.
Married—Mary Perry, 1780. Ch. James W., 1784-1866, m. 1814, Mary E. Hunter.

GALLOWAY, JOSEPH Noble County
Born—Jan. 8, 1757, Cumberland, Co., Pennsylvania.
Service—Cumberland Co. Militia, his name appearing on pay roll in 1779, of a company that had seen service in 1779, in Penn.'s Valley. He also was in service in 1778 in the CO. of Lieut. James Dickson, July, 1778. In 1782 he saw service in the 8th Battalion, called to perform a tour of duty. This class was recruited chiefly in Derry Twp., Cumberland Co., Penn.
Proof—Penn. Archives, Series 5, vol. 6, pp. 337, 569.
Died—Aug. 12, 1838. Buried Griesinger Cemetery, Washington Twp., Noble Co. Stone. Bronze tablet placed by Frances Dingman Chapter D. A. R.
Married—Second W. Agnes "Polly" Cross. Ch. William; John; George; James; Joseph.
Collected by Mrs. H. G. Misselhorn, Kendallville, Indiana.

GAMBLE, DAVID Posey County
Born—Oct. 28, 1752. Lancaster Co., Pennsylvania.
Service—Private in company commanded by Capt. Posey, Col. Crockett in Vir. Line, 10 mos. 15 days.
Proof—Pension claim S. 32264.
Died—Aug. 26, 1846, Posey Co.
Children—A daughter Sally is mentioned in pension application. Arrears of pension was paid to children, Patsy Randolph and Susanna Hughes.

GARDNER, JOHN Harrison County
Born—About 1760.
Service—Enlisted in Maryland 1778, in the CO. under William Buchanan 3rd Regt. Served until June, 1781. Discharged in Philadelphia.
Proof—Pension claim S. 35963.
Died—The last payment of pension was made March 27, 1827.
Married—Mary ——. Ch. Dan; Phebe; Matilda; Horatio; John; William.

GARNSEY, DANIEL Clark County
Born—July 18, 1760, Watertown, Connecticut.
Service—Served in Dutchess County Militia (land bounty rights) 6th Regt. Capt. Elijah Townsend. After the surrender of Cornwallis at Yorktown, was sent there to look up continental soldiers confined in British prison there.
Proof—New York Men in the Revolution, p. 248; Town and City of Waterbury, Conn., vol. 1, pp. 58, 125; History of Dutchess County by Smith, p. 490.
Died—April 28, 1840. Buried family graveyard, Clark Co.

Married—Huldah Seymour. Ch. William; Seymour; Guy; Melliscent; Anna; Polly and Bronson.
Collected by Miss Mary Carr Guernsey, Charlestown, Indiana.

GARRETSON, JACOB   Floyd County
Born—1755, New Jersey.
Service—Pri. in Capt. John Sonner's CO., 3rd Battalion, Gloucester Co., N. J. Wm. Price's 3rd Battalion, Capt. Robert Snell's CO. Sailor, enlisted on armed schooner "Hawk," Capt. Enoch Stilwell. Enlisted on ship "Morning Star" captured at sea, taken to prison at Charleston, S. C., and confined 9 mos. and escaped, arriving home Nov., 1781. Enlisted at Egg Harbor, N. H., under Capt. Enoch Willette, Naval Service.
Proof—Records in Office of Adjutant General, N. J.
Died—April 16, 1836. Buried on old Garretson farm, near Galena. Stone.
Married—1783 Millicent Tomlin, 1768-1854. Ch. George W.; Joseph; Martha; Hudson; Sarah; William; Jacob, Jr.; Gamaliel; Millicent; Experience; Sylvia.
Collected by Mrs. V. R. Conner, New Albany, Indiana.

GARRETSON, JOHN   Fayette County
Born—1757.
Service—Enlisted Georgetown, S. C., for 3 yrs., Aug., 1776-1779, as pri. under Capt. Harry, Col. Moultrie.
Proof—Pension claim S. 35962. Pensioned in Jefferson Co., Tenn., and transferred to Fayette Co., Ind., in 1831.
Died—July 27, 1834.
Married—Anne ———. Ch. Freeborn; Elizabeth; William; Benjamin; Owen; James.

GARRISON, JAMES   Washington County
Born—July 13, 1760, Rowan Co., North Carolina.
Service—Enlisted 1781, Militia N. C., as pri. in Capt. John Lopp's CO., Lieut. Joseph Cunningham, Maj. Grimes, Gen. Rutherford. Served until surrender of Cornwallis, 6 mos.
Proof—Pension claim S. 16123, B. L. Wt. 13203-100-55; Stevens History of Washington Co.. p. 623; Roster of Soldiers from North Carolina, p. 416.
Died—Feb. 3, 1859. Buried Beech Grove Cemetery, Franklin Twp. Stone.
Married—Susannah ——— (probably 2nd Wife), d. 1847. Ch. Margaret, m. Jonathan Charles; others not known.
Collected by Mrs. Harvey Morris, Salem, Indiana.

GARRISON, JOEL   Hendricks County
Born—Feb. 9, 1760, Cumberland Co., New Jersey.
Service—While a resident of Cumberland Co., N. J., he enlisted in
    1776, and served 1 yr. as drummer in Capt. Joseph Bloomfield's
    CO., Col. Dayton's 3rd N. J. Regt. He enlisted in 1778, as pri.
    in Capt. Patterson's CO., Col. Dayton's 3rd Regt., N. J., was in
    the battle of Monmouth and discharged at the expiration of 9
    mos. He served subsequently about 6 mos. in the militia, one
    tour under a Capt. Garrison.
Proof—Pension claim S. 32261.
Died—March 4, 1835. Buried Stilesville Cemetery. Stone.
Married—Christine ———. Ch. Josiah, m. Abiah Bosley.
Collected by Mrs. J. A. Clark, Pueblo, Colorado.

GAY, JOHN   Wayne County
Born—1762, Rockbridge Co., Virginia.
Service—Pri. in 2nd Vir. Regt. and 6th Vir. Regt. Commissioned as
    an Ensign, May 4, 1779. Was with Washington's Army at siege
    of Yorktown.
Proof—Vir. Hist. Mag., vol. 17, p. 324; Hist. of Rockbridge Co., Vir.,
    by O. F. Morton, p. 397.
Died—About 1826. Letters of administration were granted April, 1827.
    Buried Old Cemetery, Centerville, Wayne Co. Bronze marker
    placed by Richmond, Ind., Chapter D. A. R. Family stone.
Married—Nancy McKee. Ch. John; Jane; Betsey; Hetty; Nancy;
    James; Esther, m. first to Samuel P. Booker, second to Gov.
    James B. Ray.
Collected by Mrs. Paul L. Ross, Richmond, Indiana.

GEORGE, JOHN   Marion County
Born—1758.
Service—Enlisted at Raritan, N. J., in Jan., 1777, served 3 yrs. as pri.
    in Capt. John Flahaven's CO., in Col. Matthias Ogden's 1st Bat-
    talion, N. J. Continental Line. Was in battles of Brandywine,
    Germantown and Monmouth. Enlisted Jan. 1, 1780, served as
    Sergt. in Capt. Aaron Ogden's CO., Col. Matthias Ogden's 1st
    Battalion, N. J. Cont'l Line. Was at capture of Cornwallis. Dis-
    charged at New Windsor, N. Y., June, 1783.
Proof—Pension claim S. 16386; also certificate of war records by
    Adjutant General of N. J.
Died—1842. Buried in Round Hill Cemetery, Perry Twp. Stone.
Collected by Mrs. Theodore D. Craven, 4656 Hinesley Ave., Indianapo-
    lis, Indiana.

GEORGE, THOMAS Jefferson County
Born—Oct. 17, 1759, Amelia Co., Virginia.
Service—Enlisted 1778, Lunneburg Co., Vir., served to Dec., 1780, under Capts. William Munford and Sylvanius Walker, Col. Nathaniel Cook. Was in the battles of Guilford Court House, Eutaw Springs.
Proof—Pension claim F. 16821.
Died—Nov. 23, 1843. Probably buried in Wirt Cemetery.
Married—Betty Wrenn (1760-1822), m. 1783. Ch. Sarah, 1783-1855, m. John M. Pugh; Spencer, 1785-1789; Mary W., 1788-1789; Milton, 1790-1851, m. Sally Coleman; Martha, 1792-1825; William, 1795-1836, m. Eliza Locke; Grace, 1797, m. George W. Bantz; Ann 1801, m. George Arnold; Amelia S., 1801-1822, m. Randolph Thomson. (List of children taken from soldier's Bible.)
Collected by Alexander Hamilton Chapter D. A. R.

GHORMLEY, JOSEPH Floyd or Parke County
Born—1758, Cumberland Co., Pennsylvania.
Service—Entered service about Christmas, 1776, 2 mos. Spring of 1777, 2 mos. Fall of 1777, 2 mos. pri. under Capt. Mitchell, Penn. Militia.
Proof—Pension claim S. 16130. Last payment of pension was made Nov. 11, 1843. On Oct. 25, 1843, the pensioner certified that he had resided in Parke Co., Ind., for the space of 2 yrs., and previous thereto he resided in Floyd Co., Indiana.

GIBSON, WILBOURNE (WELLBORN) Ripley County
Born—1763.
Service—Entered service from N. C. in 1781, served 3 mos.
Proof—Pension claim R. 4000.
Died—April 4, 1843, Ripley Co., Ind.
Collected by Mrs. A. B. Wycoff, Batesville, Indiana.

GILBERT, SEWELL Delaware County
Born—Dec. 29, 1765, Cavendish, Vermont.
Service—Enlisted 1780 as private for 9 mos. under Capt. White and Capt. Comstock. In 1781 as pri. for 9 mos. under Capt. Green.
Proof—Pension claim S. 3394.
Died—Nov. 8, 1843. Buried Beech Grove Cemetery, Muncie, Ind. Stone.
Son—William.
Collected by Mrs. Horace G. Murphy, Muncie, Indiana.

GILLAM, JONATHAN　　　　　　　　　　　　　　Fayette County
Born—1753, Lancaster Co., Pennsylvania.
Service—While living in Fayette Co., Penn., he enlisted Aug. 15, 1775, to Nov., 1775, Capt. Miller, Col. Neville; Sept. 1, 1776, 4 mos., Capt. Miller, Col. Crawford; Aug., 1776, 3 mos., Capt. Miller, Col. Williamson; May 20, 1778, 3 mos., Capt. Miller, Col. Crawford; spring of 1779, 1 yr. as Indian Spy, Capt. Duncan, Col. Neville.
Proof—Pension record and Family History by Edward C. Crider, Kokomo, Ind.
Died—March 24, 1835. Buried on homestead, west of Alpine, Fayette County.
Married—First W. unknown. Ch. John M., 1785-1856, m. first to Mary Henderson, second to Mary Overholz; Thomas, 1787-1856, m. Rachel Stoops; David, 1789; Jonathan, 1791-1832, m. Nancy Martin; William, 1793-1826, m. Phoebe Cook; Robert, 1795-1838, m. first to Mary Smith, second to Phoebe Tanner; Mary, 1797; Isaac, 1798-1832, m. Keziah ———; Lettie, 1799-1877, m. Charles Smith; Elizabeth; Rebecca; Soldier m. second time to Mary ———. Ch. Nancy, 1807-1877, m. Samuel Fish; Martha, 1809; Rainey, 1810-1867, m. Margaret Carter; Jane, 1811-1877, m. Edward W. Ricords; Benjamin J., 1814-1869, m. Mary Case; Peter, 1821-1864, m. Mary M. Miller.
Collected by Edward C. Crider, Kokomo, Indiana.

GILMORE, ALEXANDER　　　　　　　　　　　　Harrison County
Born—June, 1764, Rockingham Co., Virginia.
Service—Pri. in company commanded by Capt. Baxter, Col. Boyer in Vir. Line, 6 mos., 18 days, from 1779.
Proof—Pension claim W. 10056.
Died—Oct. 8, 1843.
Married—Rebecca Smith, 1789. Had at least three children, names not given in pension application.

GIPSON, WILLIAM　　　　　　　　　　　　　　　Boone County
Born—Nov. 25, 1753, Monks Corners, South Carolina.
Service—Enlisted from Guilford Co., N. C., June or July, 1777, Capt. James Armstrong's CO., Col. Wm. Armstrong Regt. Served 6 mos. Ordered out March or April, 1778, pri. same CO. and Regt. against the Tories.
Proof—Pension claim S. 17437.
Died—April 9, 1835. Buried on farm near Thorntown, Ind. Stone.
Married—Nancy Roarch, 1795. Ch. Mary, b. 1796, m. William Williams; Delilah, b. 1798, m. James Riley; Jacob, b. 1800, m. Nancy Crawford; Sarah, b. 1802, m. William Williams; Nancy, b. 1801, m.

Stephen Jett; Rachel, b. 1809, m. Andrew Hudson; William, b. 1811; John, b. 1814; Isaac, b. 1816, m. Mary Scott; Ester, b. 1819.
Collected by Mrs. C. M. McClaine, Lebanon, Indiana.

GLAZEBROOK, JULIUS   Putnam County
Born—April 15, 1752.
Service—Enlisted June 10, 1780, and July, 1781, at Charlotte Co., Vir. Served 5 mos. under Capt. Thomas Williams, and 3 mos. under Capt. Andrew Wallace and Cols. Tucker and Holt Richardson, Vir. Militia.
Proof—Pension claim S. F. L6831.
Died—Sept. 14, 1847. Buried Carmel Cemetery, S. W. of Filmore, Ind. Bronze tablet placed by Washburn Chapter D. A. R.
Married—Mary ——. Ch. James Richard, 1787-1847, m. Catherine Snead.
Collected by Miss Minnetta Wright, Greencastle, Indiana.

GLIDEWELL, ROBERT   Franklin County
Born—Oct. 15, 1762, Halifax Co., Virginia.
Service—Virginia Militia, Halifax Co., as a Minute Man, from about Feb. 1, 1781, for 6 wks. under Capt. Joseph Gill, Col. Peter Rogers. Marched last of July, or first of Aug., 1781, and served under Capt. Jno. Falkner, Peter Rogers and Jno. Richardson at the siege of York. Discharged Oct. 20, 1781.
Proof—Pension record.
Died—Aug. 18, 1839. Buried Old Franklin Cemetery, Franklin Co. Stone.
Married—Joanna Lovesy. Ch. William; Sylvania; Sally; Elizabeth; Nash; Robert; Mary; Susie; Nancy m. Samuel Hubbard; Thomas. (All children born in Laurens District, S. C.)
Collected by Mrs. Frank S. Masters, Brookville, Indiana.

GLIDEWELL, WILLIAM   Shelby County
Born—March 4, 1760, Halifax Co., Virginia.
Service—Enlisted from Halifax Co., Vir., in Sept. or Oct., 1778, in a CO. of militia under Cols. Watt Cole and John Boyd, county colonels. Served as pri. in Capt. Peter Roger's CO., marched to Norfolk, where he remained until last of the year. Again called out in March, 1780, for 3 mos. in Capt. William Carr's Vir. CO. From March, 1781, served 3 mos. in Capt. Charles Booker's CO., Col. Peter Roger's Vir. Regt., was in siege at Yorktown.
Proof—Pension claim S. 32271.
Died—Last payment of pension was made April 11, 1836.

GLOVER, THOMAS J.   Jefferson County
Born—About 1760.
Service—Pri. in Col. Thomas Clarke's Regt., Dixon Co., N. C. Enlisted Jan. 20, 1777. Also served in Vir. State Line.
Proof—Roster of N. C. Soldiers, p. 53; Brumbaugh Rev. War Records, vol. 1, p. 203; Vir. State Library, 1912, p. 183; Special Report, 5, 76.
Died—After 1837.
Married—Nancy West (dau. of John West, a Rev. S.). Ch. James, 1792-1856, m. 1813 Elizabeth Vawter; Lucinda, 1805-1857, m. 1823 David Vawter; Ann, m. 1818 —— Coleman; Elizabeth, m. 1820 William Kennedy.
Collected by John Paul Chapter D. A. R.

GOBEN, WILLIAM   Clark County
Born—1758.
Service—From July, 1776-1779, pri. under Col. Mackey in 8th Penn. Pri. in Capt. Samuel Dunningham's CO., 2nd Battalion, Washington Co. Militia 1782. May 1, 1783, was commissioned Ensign in Col. Mabra Evans CO.
Proof—Pension record.
Died—Feb. 26, 1842. Buried near Olisto, Clark Co., Ind. Stone.
Married—First to Rebecks Braudy. Ch. Peggy; Betsey; Rebecka; Katy; Joseph; James William; John. Second W., Unity Durham. Ch. Charles; Mary; Nancy; Hugh; William; Harriett.
Collected by Alice Kennedy, Crawfordsville, Indiana.

GOBLE, STEPHEN   Bartholomew County
Born—March, 1759, Morris Co., New Jersey.
Service—Entered service from Bedford Co., Vir. Volunteered 1781, served to close of war under Gen. Potter, Capt. John Boyd, Penn. troops. 1780, served 7 mos. under Capt. John Moore. In battle of Frankstown.
Proof—Pension claim S. 16388; Civil Order Book "A," pp. 388, 389; Bartholomew Co. records.
Buried—On farm of Chas. F. Delmer, west of Taylorsville, Ind. Had a wife and 4 ch.
Collected by Joseph Hart Chapter D. A. R.

GODERE (CODER), LOUIS   Knox County
Born—Ouantanon (now Fort Wayne, Indiana).
Service—A Patriot. Signed the oath of allegiance, to the State of Virginia, at Post Vincennes, July 20, 1778. Name appears in the list as "loui goden."

Proof—George Rogers Clark's Papers, 1771-1781, Ill. Hist. Coll., vol. VIII, pp. 52 and 59.
Died—Before 1802. Buried St. Francis Xavier Cathedral Cemetery, Vincennes.
Married—Elizabeth Leveron, native of Montreal, m. about 1765. Ch. Agnes Marie Joseph, m. Honore Danis; Louis Coder, d. Jan. 11, 1795, Gibault, priest; Felicite Coder baptized Nov. 20, 1773; Joseph Coder baptized May 22, 1786; Francois, m. 1804; Marie Louise, m. 1802.
Collected by Mrs. Leo Schultheis, Vincennes, Indiana.

GOODLANDER, HENRY or JACOB   Fayette County
Born—Came to America 1751, age 3 yrs. (Berks Co., Pennsylvania).
Service—Pri. in Penn. Continental Line, Berks Co. Militia. Listed on pay roll of Lieut. Nicholas Seybert's detachment for continental pay and bounty from Oct. 17, 1781, to Dec. 18, 1781.
Proof—Penn. Archives, 5th Series, vol. 4, p. 258, and vol. 5, p. 284; Hist. of Fayette Co., Ind., p. 177.
Died—1829. Buried Lick Creek Cemetery. Stone now gone.
Married—Katherine Stump. Ch. Jacob (1779-1836), m. Mary, d. 1862, aged 82.
Collected by Mrs. Fred Gennett, Richmond, Indiana.

GOODRICH, NATHAN   Shelby County
Born—April 13, 1765, Alstead, Vermont.
Service—Enlisted from Sharon, Litchfield Co., Conn., in 1772 in Capt. Benjamin Conklin's CO., of Conn. Militia, and on April 1, 1782, served as pri. in Capts. David Strong, Colfax and Humphrey's CO., Col. Heman Swift's 2nd Conn. Regt., until June, 1783. Then transferred to Capt. Jonathan Heart's CO., and served until late Aug., 1783.
Proof—Pension claim S. 32276.
Died—Last payment of pension was made Sept. 15, 1836. Buried in Shelbyville City Cemetery.

GOODWIN, JOHN   Dearborn County
Service—In Capt. Wadsworth's CO., Col. Cook's Conn. Regt. Marched Aug. 24. Discharged Nov. 3, 1777.
Proof—Conn. Military Record, 1775-1848, p. 511.
Died—Said to be buried in Georgetown Cemetery, Miller Twp.
Collected by Mrs. Walter Kerr, Aurora, Indiana.

GOODWIN, WILLIAM   Clark County
Born—May, 1758, Virginia.
Service—Served under George Rogers Clark for three years. He was allotted 108 acres of land for this service.

Proof—Records of the land grant are to be found in Clark County, Ind., and Department of War, Bounty Land Office.
Died—July 7, 1826, Clark County.
Married—Mary Wallace Eakin (widow). Ch. John; Elizabeth; Willis Wallace; Amos; George.
Collected by Ann Rogers Clark Chapter D. A. R.

GOOKINS, SAMUEL   Ripley County
Born—Sept. 19, 1762, Suffolk, Connecticut.
Service—Enlisted April 26, 1777, for the term of the war in Capt. Samuel Granger's CO., 2nd Regt. Conn. Line, Col. Chas. Webb. Was later in Capt. Roger Well's CO., 3rd Conn. Line, Col. Samuel B. Webb.
Proof—Family records furnished by Mrs. Clara Gookins Scherer.
Died—Dec. 4, 1842. Buried in family cemetery, Delaware Twp., Ripley Co. Stone. Name on bronze tablet in Versailles Court House.
Grandchildren of Soldier—Samuel; Lydia; William.
Collected by Mrs. A. B. Wycoff, Batesville, Indiana.

GORDON, ROBERT   Shelby County
Born—1760, Chester Co., Pennsylvania.
Service—In 1777 moved to Westmoreland Co., Penn. He volunteered to defend Shield's Fort against Indians and served 5 mos. as pri. in Capt. Moore's CO., under Col. John Shield in Penn. Troops; in 1778 he again volunteered and served 2 mos. under Capt. White in Penn. Troops and acted as a guard to a magazine on Mount's Creek, near Chestnut Ridge. Penn.
Proof—Pension claim S. 1853.
Died—Feb. 1, 1841. Buried Davis Cemetery, Morristown, Indiana.
Married—First W. unknown. Son, James. Second W., Mary Hunter. Ch. Robert, b. 1795; John, b. 1799; Mary, b. 1800; William and Andrew, b. 180—; Hannah; Robert, b. 1805; Mathew, b. 1807; Agnes, b. 1808; Betty, b. 1810.

GOSNELL, BENJAMIN   Decatur County
Born—1761, Baltimore Co., Maryland.
Service—Enlisted 1781 in Bedford Co., Vir. Served under Col. Charles Linch, Capt. Wm. Jones, Col. Callaway, Capt. James Bullock, Gen. Lawson's Brigade. Discharged by Col. Tucker.
Proof—Pension claim W. 11060. B. L. Wt. 36757-160-55.
Died—Aug. 28, 1846, Decatur Co., Ind.
Married—Dorcas Farnish Porter 1815. Will in Record A, p. 101, Decatur Co., names the following children: William; John; Joseph; Benjamin; Wilkison; Thomas; Edith Wheeler; Patarine Foot; Nancy Hoshorn; Polly Fry; Delia; George; Alexander; Washington.
Collected by Mrs. H. S. McKee, Greensburg, Indiana.

GRACE, WILLIAM   Washington County
Born—About 1758, Delaware.
Service—Enlisted' May 25, 1778, in Sussex Co., Delaware, served as a
   pri. in Capt. Robert Kirkwood's CO., Col. Hull or Hall, Md. Regt.,
   was in battle of Monmouth and discharged March, 1779. Also at
   Eutaw Springs and surrender of Cornwallis.
Proof—Pension claim W. 10067 Cert. 17558.
Died—June 1, 1824. Probably buried in Old Mill Creek Cemetery, W.
   of Salem, Ind.
Married—1784 Lydia Clows (1756-1852). Ch. Sarah Sloan; Jesse;
   Lydia Pickler.
Collected by Mrs. Harvey Morris, Salem, Indiana.

GRANT, DANIEL   Harrison County
Born—Jan. 2, 1759.
Service—Minute Man in 1775 under Capt. Wm. Pickett of Fauquier
   Co., Vir. In Aug., 1776, enlisted and served as a pri. in Capt.
   Wm. Blackwell's CO., 11th Vir. Regt., and in Capt. Gabriel Long's
   CO. In Col. Daniel Morgan's Vir. Rifle Regt., and was at the
   capture of Burgoyne; the entire length of service was 3 yrs. In
   1780 he enlisted and served as pri. in Capt. Benjamin Lawson's
   CO., Col. Green's Vir. Regt., and was in the battle of Guilford.
   Discharged Jan. 17, 1782.
Proof—Pension claim S. 35985.
Died—Feb. 21, 1831. Buried Hottell Cemetery, Scot Twp.
Married—Jane ——. Ch. George; Betsey; Mahala; Isabel; Daniel;
   James; John; Smith.
Collected by Miss Mabel Claxton, French Lick, Indiana.

GRATSTY (GRASTY, GRASTON), GEORGE   Floyd County
Born—About 1747.
Service—Enlisted in May, 1775 or 76. Served in 4th Regt. Vir. Troops.
   Stationed in New York, Col. Reeves. In battles of Brandywine,
   Germantown. Served 3 yrs.
Proof—Application for pension in Probate Court Records of Floyd
   Co. R. 4202. Widow's application was rejected.
Died—Aug. 28, 1829, New Albany, Ind.
Married—1775, Rutha ——.
Collected by Piankeshaw Chapter D. A. R.

GRAVES, FRANCIS   Morgan County
Born—1746.
Service—Served as a Lieut. and Quartermaster in the N. C. Regt.
   Commissioned July 14, 1779. Name last appears on a record
   dated Feb. 6, 1782, with remark "prisoner of war." Lieut. N. C.,

Oct. 26, 1777; 1st Lieut. July 14, 1779, transferred to 1st N. C. July, 1780, taken prisoner at Charleston, May 12, 1780; exchanged June 14, 1781; served to close of war.
Proof—War Department, Office of Adjutant General.
Died—1845. Martinsville, Ind.
Children—Susie; Sally, m. —— Thomas; Peter; Henry, m. Mary Cobel; Oscar; William; David.
Collected by Mrs. S. G. Davenport, Vincennes, Indiana.

GRAY, DAVID   Franklin County
Born—1752, Antwerp County, Ireland.
Service—Enlisted Aug. 1, 1776, from Bucks Co., Penn., as pri. under Capt. Jemison, Col. Smith in Penn. Militia. Served 11 mos.
Proof—Pension claim S. 32282.
Died—Dec. 27, 1839. Buried on farm owned by Mrs. Lulu Abbott, Bath Twp. Stone and S. A. R. marker.
Married—Nancy Blackburn. Ch. Isabella; Mathew; Nellie; Lizzie; David; Nancy; Whiteford; William, m. Rose Ann Hansel; Martha; Susan; Mary; John.

GRAY, JOHN   Decatur County
Born—Dec. 11, 1759, Augusta Co., Virginia.
Service—Enlisted as pri. in 1777, from Rockbridge Co., Vir. Served under Capt. David Gray (his older brother) and Col. John Boyer. Re-enlisted Jan. 20, 1781, and served under Capt. Charles Campbell and Col. Charles Dawnman of Vir. Was present at Yorktown and because of service rendered here he was granted a pension and 200 acres of land in Virginia.
Proof—Pension record.
Died—April 5, 1836. Buried Old Sandcreek Cemetery.
Married—Nancy Pritchard. Ch. Ruth Ann, m. John Carroll; Sarah Jane; Hamilton, m. America Elder.
Collected by Mrs. H. S. McKee, Greensburg, Indiana.

GREEN, THOMAS   Bartholomew County
Born—1760, Rhode Island.
Service—Enlisted in Rhode Island Regt. Began as an orderly and carrier on Gen. Nathaniel Green's staff; made the trip between the army in the North and the army in the South, passing through the British lines without detection, eighty-five times. Served 8½ years. Was mustered out of service as a Capt. in 1782 and was made Judge Advocate and Land Commissioner of the Territory of Indiana. Was accidentally drowned in a stream called Driftwood in what is now Bartholomew County, Ind., while rescuing one of his surveyors. Swollen condition of the streams and

impassable condition of the roads made it impossible to return the body, so he was buried in a lonely spot. He received pay as Capt. 2 yrs.; as 1st Lieut. 2 yrs.; as 2nd Lieut. 2 yrs. and as Sergeant 2 yrs.
Proof—D. A. R. No. 76864.
Died—1822.
Married—Elizabeth Matthews. Ch. Daniel, b. 1783, m. Nancy ——, second, Peggy Belle Leiw; Elizabeth, b. 1785, m. John Waggoner; Susanna, b. 1787, m. John Scott; Agnes, b. 1788, m. Henry Harmon; Nancy, b. 1790, m. Thomas Hill, second, Wm. Whitcett; Ransbird, b. 1792, m. Ruth Morgan; Drusilla, b. 1793, m. Levi Cooper; James, b. 1795, m. Mary Ewing, second, Martha ——; Samuel, b. 1797, m. Betsy Hittle; Lot, b. 1799, m. Anna Cooper, second, Sarah Heuston; Ascena, b. 1801, m. Thomas Wolverton, second, Stephen Sparks.
Collected by Mrs. H. S. McKee, Greensburg, Indiana.

GREENWOOD, PHILIP　　　　　　　　　　　　Owen County
Born—Nov. 28, 1755, Frederick Co., Maryland.
Service—Pri. in Md. "Flying Camp." Enlisted 1776, Frederick Co., Md., and served under Capt. Voluntine Creiger, Lieut. Wm. Smith, Maj. Man, Gen. Bell.
Proof—Pension claim R. 4289.
Died—Sept. 5, 1842. Buried Dutch Bethel Cemetery, near Freedon, Owen Co.
Married—1788, Sarah —— in Penn.

GREGG, MATHEW　　　　　　　　　　　　　Rush County
Born—July, 1745, England.
Service—Pensioned for service as pri. in Stafford Co., Vir., Troops under Cols. Stevens, Green, and Buford. Enlisted 1776 and served 3 yrs.
Proof—Family History of Gregg Family; Autobiography of Rev. Wilson Thompson; Pension record.
Died—March 30, 1832, Rush County, Ind.
Married—Nancy Gibson, 1750-1832, m. 1769. Ch. Elizabeth Baker; Sarah Rees; Nancy, b. 1781, m. Uriah Edwards; Lucy Thompson; John, 1786-1857, m. Frances Spillman; Mary Thompson; James; Marie Culbertson.
Collected by Mrs. F. M. Harrison, Danville, Indiana.

GREGORY, SAMUEL　　　　　　　　　　Montgomery County
Born—1760, Westmoreland Co., Virginia.
Service—Minute Man from Virginia. Present at surrender at Yorktown.
Proof—Pension claim R. F. 297.

Died—1826. Buried Turkey Run Cemetery near Wingate. Stone. Bronze tablet placed by Dorothy Q. Chapter D. A. R.
Married—Sarah Davis. Ch. James, b. 1788; John; William; Esther McClure; Elizabeth Kerr; Charlotte Clarkson.
Collected by Miss Jessie Watson, Crawfordsville, Indiana.

GRIFFIN, RALPH   Jefferson County
Born—Jan. 5, 1754, Halifax Co., Virginia.
Service—Enlisted Jan. 1779, in Camden District, S. C., served 2 mos. as pri. in Capt. Edward Lacey's CO., Col. Joseph Brown's S. C. Regt.; in July, 1780, served in Capt. Edward Lacey's CO., Col. Patton's S. C. Regt. In battles of Rocky Mount, Hanging Rock, Fishing Creek, Ling's Mt. After a furlough returned to the army and served till April, 1781.
Proof—Pension claim S. 16389. Will in Jefferson Co., Ind. Entered land in 1806.
Died—Late in 1838. Probably buried in Springdale Cemetery in Madison, Ind.
Married—Catherine ——. Ch. Elizabeth, m. Aaron Van Cleave; Sally, m. Allen Munson; David; John; Charity, m. —— Heddon; Wilmoth, m. —— Rodgers; Ruth, m. —— Heddon; Catherine, m. James Pickett; Polly, m. Stephen Green; Nancy, m. David Eastin.
Collected by John Paul Chapter D. A. R.

GRIFFIS, ZACHARIAH P.   Allen County
Service—"I give and bequeth to the first male child which shall be born to my son Thomas Griffis and which child will be called Zachariah after me, three hundred acres of land situated and lying in the Virginia Line No. 36 which was granted me by Congress for my services in the Revolutionary War, and request my son Thomas Griffis to draw and receive all profits, rents, issues and revenues of said three hundred acres of land so bequethed."
Proof—Will in the Allen Co., Ind., Clerk's Office.
Died—1832. Buried along the St. Joseph River on a farm.
Sons—William; John; Thomas, b. 1806.
Collected by Mrs. T. J. Hindman, Fort Wayne, Indiana.

GRIGSBY, MOSES   Gibson County
Born—1763.
Service—Enlisted for a term of 3 yrs. Nov., 1781, under Capt. Abraham Fitzpatrick, Col. Hawes of the Vir. Line.
Proof—Pension claim W. 10069, B. L. Wt. 29728-160-55.
Died—June 16, 1838, Gibson Co., Ind., according to statement made by the widow in her application for pension.
Married—Abigail Fritten (Fritters). Ch. Nancy; Frances, m. Reuben Fritter.

GRIMARD, PIERRE   Knox County
Service—On the "Pay Roll of a company of volunteers of Infantry in
    the service of the State of Virginia, commanded by Capt. Francois
    Busseron on the 27th of Oct., 1788, and ending the 17th of Dec.,
    1778." Name appears as Pierre Grimare. Name of "pierre grimar"
    is in list of signers of oath of allegiance. (At present time this
    name has become Greemore. In one cemetery is it spelled
    Gremour.)
Proof—Pay Roll in existence; Cauthorne's History of Vincennes, p.
    100; Clark's Papers 1771-1781; Ill. Hist. Coll. vol. VIII, pp. 52-59.
Died—Before 1783. Grant of land confirmed to his widow. Buried in
    Old Cathedral Cemetery, Vincennes, Ind.
Married—Genevieve Colon (Colombe), m. about 1761. Ch. Charles,
    baptized Oct. 17, 1776, m. 1809, Rosalie Turpin; Raphael baptized 1786.
Collected by Mrs. Leo Schultheis and Mrs. S. G. Davenport, Vincennes,
    Indiana.

GRIMES, JAMES   Ripley County
Service—Enlisted in Virginia in 1777, 2 yrs.
Proof—Pension claim S. 17455.
Died—Nov. 11, 1833. Buried Old Washington Cemetery near Versailles, Ind. Government marker placed by Ripley Co. Hist.
    Society.
Married—Mary McDonald. Ch. John; Thomas; Henry; and probably
    others.
Collected by Mrs. A. B. Wycoff, Batesville, Indiana.

GRIMES, WILLIAM   Grant County
Service—Inscription on Government marker reads: "Wm. Grimes, U. S.
    Soldier, Rev. War." Buried in Maple Grove Cemetery.
Collected by Mrs. C. A. Priest, Marion, Indiana.

GRINER, PETER   Franklin County
Born—1742, Germany.
Service—In a sworn statement before the Judge of Franklin County
    Court (Indiana) on Feb. 12, 1833, in applying for a pension,
    Peter Griner stated that he was 91 years old and a resident of
    Brookville Twp., Franklin Co. Entered service in 1776 being
    drafted for a month at a time for 8 mos. Served under Capt.
    James Ewing. Once when drafted he could not leave home due
    to illness of his wife—for this he was fined 3 pounds, which he
    paid to Capt. Ewing. Enlisted from New Jersey.

GRINSTEAD, JOHN   Jennings County
Born—About 1756, Henrico Co., Virginia.
Service—Enlisted in 1781 from Henrico Co., Vir., under Capts. Woodson
    and Coverly, Cols. Scott and Posey. Engaged in battles near
    Savannah, Georgia, and Siege of Yorktown. Previously served
    in Col. Buford's Regt. for 18 mos. Two years as Orderly Sergeant.
Proof—Pension claim S. 35988.
Died—First Monday of August, 1840. Buried on farm near Otter
    Creek Church.
Married—Milly ——. Ch. Wesley; Richard; William; John F., m.
    Catherine Waggoner; Edward; Jesse; Jasper H.; Sarah, m. Samuel
    McCallon; Elizabeth, m. Alexander Ross; Subuna, m. John Hudvill;
    Milly, m. Addison Davis.
Collected by Mrs. Zepha M. Weber, North Vernon, Indiana.

GROENDYKE, JOHN   Vermillion County
Born—June 5, 1756, New Brunswick, New Jersey.
Service—Pri. in Middlesex Co., N. J., Militia.
Proof—Adj. General Official Records N. J., p. 612.
Died—Nov. 1, 1824. Buried Groendyke Cemetery, Eugene, Ind. Markers for both soldier and wife placed by Brouillet Chapter D. A. R.
Married—Lucretia Rappleye, m. March 30, 1797. Ch. John.
Collected by Mrs. Ora A. Doyle, Clinton, Indiana.

GROVES, ROBERT   Rush County
Born—1763, Delaware.
Service—Enlisted Feb. 27, 1776, as a musician in David Hall's CO.,
    Col. John Haslet's Regt. Delaware Troops. Served one year.
Proof—D. A. R. No. 130161.
Died—Aug. 25, 1855. Buried in Fairview Cemetery, Union Twp. Stone.
    Name appears on bronze tablet in Rush County Court House.
Married—Martha Miller, d. 1855. Ch. Margaret.
Collected by Mrs. Jessie Spann Gary, Rushville, Indiana.

GUARD, ALEXANDER   Dearborn County
Born—Dec. 20, 1761, Morristown, New Jersey.
Service—Pri. in State Militia, Morris Co., N. J.
Proof—Stryker "Officers and Men of New Jersey in Rev. War," p. 602.
Died—Jan. 18, 1811. Buried Miller Cemetery, Lawrenceburg, Ind. Stone.
    Government marker and D. A. R. bronze marker placed by Col.
    Archibald Lochry Chapter D. A. R.
Married—Hannah Keen. Ch. Timothy; David; Ezra; Bailey; James;
    Mahlon; Sarah; Chalon; Elizabeth; Hannah.
Collected by Mrs. Alta M. Baker, Lawrenceburg, Indiana.

GUESS, GEORGE   Jefferson County
Born—1760.
Service—Pri. in Penn. Line.
Proof—Pension claim, Certificate No. 4770.
Died—1819.
Collected by John Paul Chapter D. A. R.

GUFFY, JAMES (LIEUT.)   Jackson County
Born—May 5, 1758, Hartford Co., Maryland.
Service—While residing at Pittsburgh, Penn., he volunteered and served at the fort there, which was then commanded by Gen. Hand, for 2 yrs.; his service consisted in spying against the Indians, taking care of the wounded brought into the fort, burying the dead and carrying frequent expresses for Gen. Hand. Later he served 1 mo. as an Indian spy for Capt. Rollator's CO., Col. Stinson's Penn. Regt., and assisted in building Fort Crawford on the Allegheny River Later was commissioned Ensign in the Penn. Troops under the same officers and still later Lieut. in Capt. John Turner's Penn. Regt., Col. Crawford. All his service was rendered in or about Pittsburgh.
Proof—Pension claim S. 31718.
Died—Feb. 25, 1837. Buried Gantry Hill Cemetery, Hamilton, Twp.
Married—First Jane ——. Ch. James; Alex; William; John; Henry; Maria; Betsey; Martha; Sally. Second W. Sally. Ch. Thomas; George Patterson; Joshua. These taken from soldier's will.
Collected by Mrs. D. J. Cummings, Brownstown, Indiana.

GULLION (O'GULLION), JOHN O.   Howard County
Born—1760.
Service—Enlisted from Westmoreland Co., Penn., in April or May, 1776, as pri. in Capt. Joseph Erwin's CO., Col. Miles' Penn. Rifle Regt. Was wounded and discharged at Valley Forge after serving 18 mos. Re-enlisted 1778, served 6 mos. in Col. Bayard's Penn. Regt., and 6 mos. in Col. Davis' Penn. Regt. In 1782 he was in Col. Crawford's Regt.
Proof—Pension claim S. 36567. Lived in Switzerland Co., Ind., 1818, 1819. Applied for pension 1831 from Decatur Co., Ind., and was still living there in 1836.
Died—June 29, 1850, in Howard Co., Ind. Proof—Pension record and Probate Court Records of Howard Co., Ind. Buried Twin Springs Cemetery, S. W. of Kokomo, Ind. Stone. There is also a government marker bearing soldier's name erected on Spillman farm, Clinton Twp., Decatur Co.

Married—Mrs. Catherine Riffel Tanner, d. 1845. They had five Ch. but only two known—Thomas; Susan, m. Levi Rayls.
Collected by Mrs. E. C. Crider, Kokomo, Indiana.

GULLION, ROBERT   Switzerland County
Born—Feb. 4, 1764, near Frederick on the Potomac.
Service—Enlisted 1780 or 81 in a company of militia or rangers under Capt. Shearer of Westmoreland Co., Penn. Was stationed at a blockhouse on the waters of Turtle Creek in Penn. for 90 days. In 1782 under Col. Wm. Crawford marched against the Indians on the Ohio River.
Proof—Pension claim S. 16396.
Died—July 23, 1853. Probably buried in York Twp.
Married—Barbara ——. Ch. Henry; John, m. 1815 Elizabeth Jones and 1824 Betsy Scudder; Charles D., m. Lena Dillman; Polly, m. David Miller; Rachel, m. Joseph Fulton; Sallie, m. Wm. McQuiston; Robert, m. Dolly Fulton.
Collected by Mrs. A. V. Danner, Vevay, Indiana.

GUNSALLIS (GONZALES), JOHN   Fountain County
Born—1754, New York.
Service—N. Y. Militia, Col. Phillip Schuyler's Regt. 1777 Capt. Bibbles' CO.; 1777 Capt. Peeta CO.; Lieut. Brass; 1778 Capt. Bloom's CO.; 1778-9 Capt. Moore's CO., 1 mo. in each.
Proof—Pension certificates 29071, 29162, 29125.
Died—Buried in Hatton Cemetery by Government marked placed in Riverside Cemetery, Attica, Ind., by the Ouibache Chapter D. A. R.
Daughter—Rebecca.
Collected by Mrs. A. S. Dolch (deceased).

HACKLEMAN, JACOB   Rush County
Born—July 17, 1752, Maryland.
Service—Shortly after marriage he moved to west side of King's Mt. in Lincoln, N. C., and served in Rev. War from here. Was wounded in the right arm. He then hired John Gant to serve the remainder of this time.
Proof—Hackleman Family Record, vol. 1, pp. 2, 5, and 7.
Died—Jan. 16, 1829. Buried on farm now owned by John Applegate, Rush Co. Stone.
Married—Mary Osborn (1754-1824). Ch. Elizabeth; Abraham; Sarah; Katherine; Isaac; Mary and Margaret (twins); Jacob; John; Susan; Michael; Thomas; Fanny; Riller.
Collected by Mrs. Jessie Spann Gary, Rushville, Indiana.

HAELEY, HUGH   Henry County
Born—1758, on ocean coming to America.
Service—Enlisted Jan., 1776, as pri. Served to May, 1783, under Capt. Jonathan Dayton, Col. Barber of New Jersey. In battles of Long Island, Mud Island, Monmouth and Yorktown.
Proof—Pension record History of Henry Co., Ind., p. 421; Family Bibles.
Died—1824, New Castle, Ind.
Married— —— Hargrave. Ch. Jesse Hargrave Haeley, m. Sarah Bundy; Phoebe, m. Joshua Welborn; Mary, m. David Price.
Collected by Mrs. Harry Beach, Lewisville, Indiana.

HAGAN, CHARLES   Jackson County
Born—April, 1761.
Service—Private in company commanded by Capt. Triplett of Regt. under Col. Grayson, Vir. Line. 3 yrs., Feb., 1777, to Feb., 1780.
Proof—Pension claim S. 36008.
Died—Jan. 30, 1839. Probably buried in Driftwood Twp.
Married—Savannah ——. Ch. Julia Ann, m. Henry Lyster; George; Isaac; John C.

HAGGERTY, WILLIAM   Lawrence County
Born—1754, Ireland.
Service—Enlisted May 12, 1776, Lancaster, Penn., in the First Penn. Regt., under Capt. James Parr. Discharged at Valley Forge, served 2 yrs.
Proof—Pension claim S. 36574.
Died—1836. Buried Springville Cemetery. Stone.
Married—Nancy Hastings Burford. Ch. Sallie; Mary Ann; Nancy; Lucinda, m. —— Helmer.
Collected by Mrs. Ellen Hoover, Bedford, Indiana.

HAIR (HARE), JOHN   Hamilton County
Born—April 25, 1758, Augusta Co., Virginia.
Service—Enlisted and served 3 mos. as pri. in Capt. Robert Craven's CO., Col. Harrison's Vir. Regt., during which period he assisted in building Fort McIntosh. Also pri. in Capt. James Tate's CO., Cols. Moffet and Campbell. In battle of Guilford, 2 mos. 10 days. Next served 2 mos. in fall of 1781 in Capt. Patrick Buckingham's CO.
Proof—Pension claim S. 17469.
Died—Last payment of pension was Oct. 6, 1844. Buried Hair Cemetery. There are numerous descendants in Wayne and Noblesville Twps., Hamilton Co.
Collected by Mr. Perry A. Bray, Noblesville, Indiana.

HALL, BENJAMIN (BENAJAH)   Ripley County
Service—Enlisted from Rhode Island in May or June, 1775. Discharged on Dec. 8, 1775. Re-enlisted April, 1776. Discharged Jan., 1777. Re-enlisted May 12, 1777. Served 1 yr., total service 2 yrs. 5 mos.
Proof—Pension claim S. 32295.
Died—Jan., 1850. Name on bronze tablet in·Versailles Court House.
Collected by Mrs. A. B. Wycoff, Batesville, Indiana.

HALL, DAVID   Dearborn County
Born—About 1768.
Service—Enlisted for a term of 3 yrs. on May 2, 1777, in Lancaster, Penn., under Capt. Taylor, Col. Johnston, Penn. Line. Served until last of Jan., 1781. Discharged at Trenton, N. J. Was in battle of Brandywine and was wounded and taken prisoner in 1778. Joined his Regt. again at Valley Forge.
Proof—Pension claim S. 36572. Penn. Archives, Series 2, vol. X, p. 549.
Died—Last payment of pension paid to March 4, 1845.
Family—Had wife and children, but names not given in pension application.
Collected by Mrs. Walter Kerr, Aurora, Indiana.

HALL, EDWARD   Marion County
Born—June 22, 1760.
Service—Enlisted while a resident of Greenbrier Co., Vir. During the spring and summer of 1776 he was on guard duty at Ft. Jarrett. During 1777, 1778 and 1779, served 24 mos. as a Spy and Ranger under Capts. John Vanbiber and James Graham and Col. Donally in the Vir. Troops and guarded the frontier.
Proof—Pension claim S. 16147.
Died—April 15, 1848. Buried Round Hill Cemetery, Perry Twp. Stone.
Children—Francis B.; Edward S.; Lucinda; John Stuart.
Collected by Indiana S. A. R.

HALL, LABAN   Vigo County
Born—1755, Peekskill, New York.
Service—While residing in Orange Co., Vermont, he enlisted and went to Quebec the year Montgomery was defeated by Capt. Abner Scly on a tour to Ticonderoga, 1776, for 3 or 4 mos. In 1777 enlisted under Capt. Rowell in Col. Reid's Regt.; March, 1778, marched to Portsmouth in N. H. Served 1 yr., discharged by Col. Reid.
Proof—Pension claim S. 48852.
Died—1842. Buried near Otter Creek Bridge, Otter Twp.
Married—First W. Mary ——. Ch. Rebeckah; Abel; Lucy; Allen. Second W. Mercy Daggett (widow of Joseph Daggett, a Rev. S.),

HALL, MOSES Monroe County
Born—May 29, 1760, Roan Co., N. C.
Service—Enlisted 1780, served 18 mos. as teamster under Capt. David Caldwell. In battle at Charlotte. Served under Cols. Wm. Davidson, Francis Locke, Wm. Daire.
Proof—Pension claim W. 10105.
Died—April 10, 1846. Buried in Richland Cemetery. Stone.
Married—Nancy Snoddy (1763-1855), m. 1788. Ch. Samuel, b. 1796, m. Leanna Bitner; Nancy, b. 1802, m. Samuel Hardesty; Moses; William; Eliza, b. 1793; Malinda, b. 1805.
Collected by Mrs. Stella Blakely King, Bloomington, Indiana.

HALL, ROBERT Lawrence County
Born—1761, Albemarle Co., Virginia.
Service—Enlisted in summer of 1778 in Capt. Skelton's CO., Col. Cleveland's Regt., in Virginia, pri. 3 mos. A member of Capt. Trigg's CO., Col. Thomas Merriweather's Regt., 3 mos. in 1779. Served also 3 mos. in Col. Ward's Regt. and 3 mos. in Col. Lee's Regt., 1781. In the Siege of Ninety-Six.
Proof—Pension claim S. 16403; 8th Report of Virginia State Auditor, p. 197.
Died—1836. Buried in an old cemetery near Lawrence, Orange Co. Line.
Married—Nancy Isham. Ch. Isham (Isom); Richard; Robert.
Collected by Mrs. Robert M. Taggart, Orleans, Indiana.

HALL, WILLIAM Jefferson County
Born—1754.
Service—Enlisted in Penn. Served in Capt. Long's Penn. CO.; enlisted April or March, 1778, in Capt. VanSwearingen's CO., Col. Brodhead's Penn. Regt., and was discharged after 18 mos. service. In the battles of Bunker Hill, White Plains, Fort Washington, Fort Lee, Trenton, Brandywine and Paoli.
Proof—Pension claim W. 10072.
Died—April 15, 1844. Buried in Demaree's graveyard. Government marker erected in Manville Cemetery by John Paul Chapter D. A. R.
Married—1781, Sarah ——, d. 1851. Ch. John, b. 1781; Elender, b. 1786; Squier, b. 1789; Catherine, b. 1791; Elizabeth, b. 1793; Poly, b. 1795; Phebe, b. 1797; Nancy, b. 1799; Henry, b. 1801; Sarah, b. 1805; William Standaford, b. —; Sary, b. 1811.
Collected by John Paul Chapter D. A. R.

HAMBLIN, JOB   Brown County
Born—July 14, 1762.
Service—Enlisted March, 1779, Virginia Militia, Capt. John Tabo's CO.,
    Col. Charles Dabney's Regt. Discharged March 10, 1782. En-
    gaged in skirmishes around Point of Fork, Vir., in May, 1781. In
    battle of Jamestown and Yorktown.
Proof—Pension record and D. A. R. No. 92283.
Died—Sept. 1, 1833. Buried Taylor Cemetery, Hamblin Twp. Stone.
Married—1782, Eleanor Mullings. Ch. John, b. 1782, m. Mary Camp-
    bell; Uriah, b. 1787, m. Ruth Camern; George, b. 1789; William,
    b. 1793; Eliakim, b. 1796, m. Nancy Daugherty; Eleanor, b. 1799,
    m. David Lock; Sarah, b. 1802, m. William Taylor; Mary, b. 1805,
    m. Uriah Lock.
Collected by Joseph Hart Chapter D. A. R.

HAMILTON, BENJAMIN   Ripley County
Born—Oct., 1760.
Service—Entered in Penn., Nov., 1776. Four enlistments with total
    service 10 mos. and 24 days.
Proof—Pension claim S. 16400.
Collected by Mrs. A. B. Wycoff, Batesville, Indiana.

HAMILTON, JOHN   Vigo County
Service—Enlisted in 1775 as a 2nd Lieut. in Capt. Benjamin Harrison's
    CO., in 13th Vir. Regt., under Col. William Russell; remained
    until 1778 and resigned. Was in battles of Brandywine and Ger-
    mantown.
Proof—Pension claim S. 36568.
Died—Sept. 22, 1822, Terre Haute, Ind.
Daughter—Mrs. Sarah E. Barkinbile. There were other children.

HAMMAN, ABRAHAM   Vermillion County
Born—1753 or 1754, New Jersey.
Service—Entered service from Rockingham Co., Vir., 1780. 1 yr. 6 mos.
    as pri. under Capt. Oldham, Vir. Line.
Proof—Pension claim W. 10088.
Died—March 2, 1844, in Vermillion Co.
Married—First W. unknown. Ch. Eve, m. Jonathan Downing. Sec-
    ond W. 1783, Charity Hammock. Ch. (named in soldier's Will)
    John; Abraham; George, m. Susannah Rodney; Jeremiah, m. Mary
    Hood; Ruth, m. George Phelnice; Anna Rebecca, m. Nicholas Car-
    ter; Nancy (deceased); another son Isaac is mentioned in widow's
    pension application.
Collected by Mrs. Ora A. Doyle, Clinton, Indiana.

HAMMERSLEY, JOHN   Lawrence County
Born—1761, New York.
Service—Enlisted from Northumberland Co., Penn., March 10, 1778, and served as pri. and corp. in Capt. Jacob Humphrey's and Thomas Doyle's CO., in Col. Josiah Harmar's Penn. Regt., and was in the battle of Monmouth. Was at Tappan when Major Andre was executed. Discharged May, 1781.
Proof—Pension claim W. 421.
Died—March 30, 1836. Buried in Bono Cemetery. Stone.
Married—First W. unknown. Son, James, b. 1783. Second W. 1789, Miss Cochran. Third W. 1799, Sarah McMullen. Ch. Polly; Sally; Jannet; Hannah; Elizabeth; Jacob; John M.; George; Martha C.; Mary Lucinda; William; Charles. Most of these by last marriage. Taken from soldier's first son's (James) Family Bible.
Collected by Mrs. Ellen Hoover and Mrs. L. C. Cox, Bedford, Indiana.

HAMMER, GEORGE   Putnam County
Born—May 4, 1763, near Philadelphia.
Service—While residing in Frederick Co., Maryland, volunteered in April, 1781, as a pri. in Capt. Michael Troutman's CO., Col. John Gregor's Maryland Regt., and was engaged in watching the Tories and in securing provisions for the army. Served until Feb., 1782.
Proof—Pension claim S. 32291.
Died—July 21, 1834, Putnam Co.
No family data available.
Collected by Miss Minnetta Wright, Greencastle, Indiana.

HAMMER, JOHN   Johnson County
Born—Jan. 2, 1761, Mecklenburg Co., Virginia.
Service—From June, 1778, 2 mos. 20 days as a pri. in Capt. Stephen Marberry's CO., Col. Burrell's Regt. From Dec., 1779, 3 mos. under Major James Anderson. From Jan., 1781, 3 mos. and half under Capt. Robert Smith, Cols. Robert Munford and Philip Holcomb's Regt. In battle of Guilford.
Proof—Pension claim W. 10081.
Died—Oct. 28, 1836. Buried in Hammer Cemetery S. of Franklin, Ind. Stone and government marker placed by Alexander Hamilton Chapter D. A. R.
Married—Mary Whobery, m. 1790, d. 1842. Ch. James, b. 1793; Ann, b. 1795; Rebecca, b. 1797; Elizabeth; Mary; John; George.
Collected by Mrs. I. E. Tranter, Franklin, Indiana.

HAMMOND, JOB   Daviess County
Born—June 1, 1740, South Carolina.
Service—He enlisted Nov. 30, 1775, in S. C., served in Capt. Thomas Brandon's CO., Col. John Thomas' Regt., and Capt. Joseph Jolly's

CO., Joshua Palmer's and Benjamin Jolly's S. C. CO., then enlisted in Col. Washington's Regt. of Dragoons. In battles of Cane Brake, Siege of Buck Head, Orangeburg, Congaree, Cowpens, and Siege of Ninety-Six.
Proof—Pension claim S. 36569.
Died—After 1835. Buried in Reeve Twp., Daviess Co.
Married—Martha Palmer. Ch. Nancy, m. James P. Gilley. Possibly other children.
Collected by Mrs. Roy Boger, Washington, Indiana.

HANCOCK, JOSEPH   Wayne County
Born—July 21, 1758.
Service—Pri. in Capt. Nehemiah Stokey's CO., 8th Penn. Regt. Con't'l. Line under Col. Daniel Brodhead. Also served in Capt. Mann's CO., 8th Penn. Regt. On March 16, 1777, he was wounded in his right shoulder by a musket ball in a skirmish at New Brunswick. Served until April 3, 1780, nearly 4 yrs.
Proof—Pension record; Penn. Archives, 5th Series, vol. 3, pp. 339-342, 368.
Died—1834, near Hagerstown, Wayne Co.
Married—First W. Catherine Baltimore. Ch. Mary, m. S. Taylor; Joseph, m. Susan Millman; Nancy, m. Benjamin Warren; Elizabeth, m. Levi Bain; John, m. Elizabeth Pollard; Catherine, m. —— Colvert; Sophia, m. Virgil Tilver; Naomi, m. William Martindale; Cynthia, m. Jonathan Reeder. Second W. Dianah Reeder. Ch. Philip, m. Mahala Adamson; Simeon, d. in childhood.
Collected by Mrs. Paul Ross, Richmond, Indiana.

HANDLY, HANDY, JR.   Sullivan County
Born—1755, Dorchester Co., Maryland.
Service—Pri. in Capt. Lilburn Williams' CO., Col. Peter Adams' 3rd Md. Regt.
Proof—Pension claim S. 16401.
Died—1837. Buried Old Town Cemetery, Carlisle, Ind. Government marker placed by Nathan Hinkle Chapter D. A. R.
Married—First W. Mary. Ch. Planner; Clinton. Second W. Nici Hooper. Ch. Polly; John.
Collected by Handly Family.

HANEY (HANY, HENEY, HEANY), DAVID   Dearborn County
Born—About 1761.
Service—Enlisted with Capt. Church in Penn., 1775, in Regt. of Infantry, under Col. Francis Johnston. Served until end of war, 7 yrs. Was in battles of Brandywine, Germantown, Paoli and Yorktown. Wounded several times in the thigh by British bayonet at battle of Paoli.

Proof—Pension claim S. 36507, B. L. Wt. 1152-100; Penn. Archives, Series 2, vol. X, p. 550.
Died—March 10, 1834, Dearborn County.
Wife and one child, names unknown.
Collected by Mrs. Walter Kerr, Aurora, Indiana.

HANKS, ABNER   Johnson County
Born—1763, Richmond Co., Virginia.
Service—Enlisted in April, 1780, and served 3 mos. in Capt. George Harrison's Virginia CO., then 3 mos. in Capt. George Sisson's CO., Virginia.
Proof—Pension claim S. 31729.
Died—Sept. 5, 1846. Buried Lick Spring Cemetery, Ninevah Twp. Government marker placed by Alexander Hamilton Chapter D. A. R.
Married—Five times. First W. Elizabeth Dale, m. 1787. Ch. Matilda; Thomas; Susan; Mary; Elizabeth; Ailsie; John Dale; Maria. Second W. Mary, m. 1807. Ch. Sarah. Third W. Frances Milton, m. 1810. Ch. Signor; Milton; Washington; Martha; Caroline; Grace. Fourth W. Sarah Goodman, m. 1821. Ch. Amanda; America. Fifth W. Sally Shouse, m. 1832. Ch. David. There were three other children, making 21 for the soldier.
Collected by Mrs. I. E. Tranter, Franklin, Indiana.

HANNA, ROBERT   Union County
Born—Dec. 10, 1744, Prince Edwards Co., Virginia.
Service—Fought from S. C. to Vermont. In battle of Cowpens, which was fought on his Uncle Joseph Hanna's plantation. Also at Bennington and King's Mt.
Proof—House of Hanna; O'Hart's Irish Pedigree, vol. 2, p. 551; Certificate of service from Secretary of State and S. C., Stub Book 65.
Died—Jan. 24, 1821. Lived in Franklin Co., but buried across the line in Union Co., Sims Cemetery. Stone.
Married—Mary Parks, 1748-1834. Ch. Mary, m. John Templeton; Joseph, m. Sarah Adair; Margaret, m. Wm. Byrd; Katharine, m. John Hitch; Janet, m. Solomon Manwaring; Robert, m. first Sarah Mowery, second Olive Catherine Wood; Graem, m. first Agnes Taylor, second Mary McKinney; James, m. Nancy Laird; John, m. Sarah Jones.
Collected by Mrs. Elnora P. Campbell, Liberty, Indiana.

HANNAMAN, WILLIAM   Vermillion County
Born—Nov. 14, 1763, New York.
Service—Entered service early part of 1778, when only 14 yrs. of age, as a volunteer for 9 mos. in Capt. James Booth's CO. of Vir. Militia. Volunteered to keep Garrison at Nuttlesford on Elk

Creek, under Col. Wm. Louden. In 1781-82 was an Indian Spy
under orders of Col. Louden.
Proof—Pension claim S. 32299.
Died—Sept. 17, 1839. Probably buried in Helt Twp., Vermillion Co.
Married—Wife unknown. Ch. George, m. Margaret Mack; Christopher,
m. 1831, Elizabeth McDowell.
Collected by Mrs. Ora A. Doyle, Clinton, Indiana.

HANNIS, HENRY   Switzerland County
Born—May 12, 1757, Ulster Co., New York.
Service—Pri. in New York Troops as follows: Sept., 1775, 9 mos.
   Capt. John Aker's CO.; July, 1776, Capt. John Deyo's CO., Col.
   Pawling's Regt., discharged 1776; 1777, 6 mos. in Capt. Harden-
   bergh's CO.; Aug., 1777, 3 mos. Capt. Peleg Ranson's CO., and
   was in the battle of Saratoga; Sept., 1779, 4 mos. Capt. Conklin's
   CO., Col. Owen's Regt.
Proof—Pension claim S. 32288.
Died—Sept. 23, 1835.
Married—Hannah ——. Ch. Sarah, m. James A. Stewart; William
   (War of 1812), m. Ellen Burns; Hannah, m. Wm. Griffith; Lydia,
   m. Wilson Crandell; Polly, m. Thomas Huston; Margaret, m. ——
   Ferguson.
Collected by Mrs. A. V. Danner, Vevay, Indiana.

HARBISON, JAMES   Dubois County
Born—1762, South Carolina.
Service—Virginia Militia, volunteered in Botecourt Co., Vir., 1780, under
   James Robinson. Joined Morgan's Regt. near Ramsour's Mill
   and was in battle at Island Ford, on Yadkin River, 6 mos.
Proof—Wilson's History of Dubois County; War Department; Rocking-
   ham Co., Vir., Records.
Died—Oct. 6, 1841. Buried Dwine Graveyard, N. of Buffalo Trail
   Marker. Government marker placed by Mrs. Wm. E. Cox, Jasper,
   Ind.
Married—1788, first to Ann Hemphill. Ch. Elizabeth; Absalom; Jacob.
   Second W., Rachel Hembree, m. 1825. Ch. Richard; Morgan;
   Johnathan; Mary; Jane.
Collected by George Wilson, Historian of Dubois County, Indiana.

HARDING, EDE   Marion County
Born—1758, near Elizabethtown, New Jersey.
Service—While residing at "Hardin's settlement on George's Creek" in
   Fayette Co., Penn., he volunteered as a pri. with Penn. Troops,
   as follows: from the spring of 1777, 3 mos. in Capt. John Hardin's
   CO., Col. John Hardin's Regt. and acted as guard at a fort in the

summer following, 3 mos. at Lucas' Fort in Fayette Co., Penn., under Capt. John Hardin and Col. Gaddes or Gaddis; in the summer of 1779, under same officers at the same fort, 3 mos.; later about 15 days under same officers against the Indians; 1 mo. under Col. John Minor against the Indians.
Proof—Pension claim S. 32284.
Died—Jan. 14, 1846.
Ch.—Dorcas S. Vanbloricum.

HARDING, HENRY   Marion County
Born—1752, Stafford Co., Virginia.
Service—While residing on Hyco Creek, Vir., he enlisted 1775, served 4 mos. as pri. under Capt. Peter Rogers and Col. Lewis in the Vir. Troops. Re-enlisted in winter 1776, served 6 mos. under Capt. Moore. While a resident of Woodstock, Vir., he enlisted 1780; served 18 mos. in Capt. Holdam's CO., Col. Campbell's Vir. Regt., and was in the battles of Camden, Guilford Court House, and Eutaw Springs.
Proof—Pension claim S. 16145.
Died—"Advanced age." Buried in abandoned cemetery, Marion Co.
Married—Delilah Allensworth. Ch. William; Polly; James; Catherine; John, perhaps Philip; Mary (Polly), m. Elijah Dawson.
Collected by Mrs. Harvey Morris, Salem, Indiana.

HARDING, MICAJAH   LaGrange County
Born—1761, Colchester, Conn.
Service—Commissioned Captain under Washington for a term of 7 yrs.
Proof—The Harding Family History by Forest Harding, p. 28.
Died—1849. Buried on a hill in a field near Cedar Lake.
Married—Betsey ———. Ch. Micajah, Jr.; Daniel; Jessie; Sally; Lucy.
Collected by Mrs. Fred Deal, LaGrange, Indiana.

HARDING, THOMAS   Hendricks County
Born—Jan. 8, 1759, Virginia.
Service—Volunteered at Stradler's Fort on Dunker's Creek in Penn. and served 6 or 8 mos. in Capt. McCleary's CO., Col. McFarland's Regt. of Militia. Also served 8 mos. in Capt. Cross' CO. of Militia under Col. Evins in Gen. McIntosh's Indian Expedition. Served 9 mos. as an Indian Spy under Col. McFarland; 6 mos. under Col. Gaddis; 6 mos. under Col. McCleary and 9 mos. under Col. Evins, all a Spy.
Proof—Pension claim W. 10079.
Died—June 20, 1840. Buried Lingerman Cemetery, S. W. of Brownsburg, Hendricks County.

Married—1784, Sarah Payne, b. 1765. Ch. John, 1785-1854, m. Rachel
Carlisle; Samuel, 1787-1836, m. Annie Shipp; Rebecca, b. 1790;
Sally, b. 1792; Amy, b. 1794; Noah, b. 1797; Ruhamy, b. 1799;
Payne, b. 1802; Aaron, b. 1805.
Collected by Alexander Hamilton Chapter D. A. R.

HARDY (HARDEE), JOHN   Montgomery County
Born—June 2, 1761, Virginia.
Service—Enlisted 1775 or 1776 in Vir. Line, served under Gen. Washington at attack on Hessions, taken a prisoner and placed on prison ship; escaped. Served two years.
Proof—Pension claim S. 16140.
Died—June 2, 1839. Buried on roadside near Offield Creek. Stone.
Married—Second W., Lucy Sears (1770-1829). Ch. Lucinda (a Real Daughter), m. —— McMullen. Soldier's other children—Bella; William; Joseph; Curtis; Frankie.
Collected by Miss Jessie Watson, Crawfordsville, Indiana.

HARPER, EBENEZER   Henry County
Born—Jan., 1740, Chester Co., Pennsylvania.
Service—Enlisted in Philadelphia for 6 mos. in Oct., 1776, under Col. Lowden, Penn. Line.
Proof—Pension claim S. 31728.
Died—Aug. 14, 1835, in Henry Co., Ind.
Married—Phebe ——.

HARRAWAY, OWEN   Jennings County
Born—About 1763, Essex Co., Virginia.
Service—Enlisted April 4, 1781, under Capt. Philip Lee, Essex Co., Vir., Col. James Dabney.
Proof—Pension claim W. 5463, B. L. Wt. 26404-160-55.
Married—Elizabeth ——.

HARRELL, JEREMIAH   Johnson County
Born—Oct. 30, 1756, on Peedee River, South Carolina.
Service—Enlisted April, 1776, at Orangeburg, S. C., and served as pri. for 3 yrs. under Lieut. Alexander Harrington, Col. Thompson, S. C. Troops and was in battle of Brier Creek and Sullivan's Island. Later in battles of King's Mt., Eutaw Spring and Guilford Court House.
Proof—Pension claim S. 17467.
Died—May 6, 1834. Buried Mt. Pleasant Cemetery, White River Twp. Government marker placed by Alexander Hamilton Chapter.

Married—1781, Sarah Osborn. Ch. William; Steven; Moses; Jeremiah, Jr.; Sarah; Jemima; Jane; Comfort.
Collected by Mrs. I. E. Tranter, Franklin, Indiana.

HARRIS, DANIEL   Switzerland County
Born—About 1737.
Service—Enlisted Sheperdstown, Vir., March 2 or April 2, 1777, in Capt. James Kearney's CO., Col. Thomas Hartley's Regt. Was in Sullivan's Indian campaign. Discharged June 1, 1780, from Col. Adam Hubley's Penn. Regt.
Proof—Pension claim S. 36575.
Died—June 7, 1821. Probably buried in Allenville, Cotton Twp.
Married—Elizabeth ——. Had several children.
Collected by Mrs. A. V. Danner, Vevay, Indiana.

HARRIS, JOSHUA   Johnson County
Born—About 1759.
Service—Enlisted in the fall of 1779 as a pri. in Capts. Wallace and Stribling's CO., Col. Campbell's Vir. Regt. Was in the battles of Camden and Guilford Court House and Siege of 96.
Proof—Pension claim R. 4685.
Died—Nov. 6, 1841. Buried in Harris Cemetery, Union Twp.
Married—Martha Herrell, 1788. Ch. Elizabeth; Rachel; Jesse; Casanner; John; Sarah; William; Martha; Lucinda; Joshua; Lettice; James.
Collected by Mrs. I. E. Tranter, Franklin, Indiana.

HARRIS, ROBERT   Switzerland County
Born—Dec. 12, 1766, Preston, Conn. (Son of Daniel.)
Service—Matross in company under Capt. Durkee in Conn. Line, 1 year.
Proof—Pension claim W. 10076.
Died—July 22, 1826. Buried in Quercas Grove, Switzerland Co.
Married—Lucretia Kennedy, 1787, b. 1773. Ch. Robert, b. 1793; Daniel Kennedy, b. 1797; James Hiram, b. 1800; Jacob Rude, b. 1802; Josiah John Nelson, b. 1811; Westley, b. 1818; Lucretia, b. 1789; Dorothy, b. 1791; Alice, b. 1795; Lucretia Whipple, b. 1804; Fanny Morial, b. 1808; Mary Zelphia Anny, b. 1813.

HARROD, WILLIAM   Scott County
Born—Sept. 26, 1764, Berkley Co., Virginia.
Service—Pri. in company of Capt. Paxton, Regt. of Col. Lyon in Penn. and Vir. Line, 6 mos.
Proof—Pension claim S. 16398.
Died—Last payment of pension made on Sept. 18, 1843.
Married—Elizabeth ——.

HARROD, WILLIAM   Clark County
Born—Dec., 1737, Bedford County, Virginia.
Service—Captain under George Rogers Clark, 1778. Land grant in Clark Co.
Proof—Collins History of Ky., vol. 1, pp. 12 and 19.
Died—Oct. 9, 1810, Clark Co., Ind.
Married—Amelia Stephens.

HARRY, CHARLES   Fayette County
Born—About 1761.
Service—Entered service from Washington Co., Penn. Pri. in CO. under Capt. Evans, Col. Marshall's Regt. Penn. Line, 13 mos. from 1779.
Proof—Pension claim S. 16139.
Died—April, 1843, Fayette County, Ind.
Married—1786, Barbara ——, b. 1766. She moved to Cedar Co., Iowa, after the death of her husband to live with a son.

HARSIN, GARRET   Shelby County
Born—June 15, 1753, New York City.
Service—Volunteered June, 1776, as pri. in Capt. Charles Dixon's Co., Col. John Lasher's N. Y. Regt. Was in the battle at Long Island, the retreat from N. Y. and the battle of Harlem Heights and served 5 mos.; in the summer of 1777, volunteered, served 3 mos. in Capt. Moses Cantine's N. Y. CO.; in autumn, 1777, 3 mos. in same CO. About the close of 1777, he entered on board the "Hudson," a public armed vessel, commanded by Capt. John Parmer and served as a sailor for 18 mos. The vessel lay at West Point a part of the time as a guard ship and a part of the time went up and down the river with provisions for the army; later he went into a shop as an artificer under Capt. John Parcels, Quartermaster Gen. Hughs, at Fishkill, N. Y. Length of service, 7 yrs.
Proof—Pension claim W. 10082.
Died—Sept. 24, 1838, Shelby Co.
Married—1784, Elizabeth Doughty, b. 1763. They had eight children. George, b. 1785; Maria, b. 1801.

HART, ADAM   Sullivan County
Born—March 17, 1759, North Carolina.
Service—Pri. and Wagoner in 1st Regt. N. C. Line of Cont'l Line.
Proof—Pension record. Bounty Land Warrant.
Died—Jan. 27, 1847. Buried Bethlehem Cemetery, Haddon Twp. Stone.
Married—Wife's name unknown. Ch. Daniel, m. 1797; Jacob; Henry.
Collected by Mrs. James R. Riggs, Sullivan, Indiana.

HART, JOSEPH   Bartholomew County
Born—June 16, 1761, Loudoun Co., Virginia.
Service—Served in Capt. Holcombs' CO. 4th Vir. Regt., commanded by Col. Thomas Elliott. Also in Capt. Thomas Ridley's CO. Vir. Regt., under Col. Robert Lawson. First name on roll of 4th Vir. Regt., April, 1777. On later roll Feb., 1778, when he is reported discharged, shot through thigh and disabled.
Proof—Pension record.
Died—1841. Buried Garland Brook Cemetery. Stone and D. A. R. bronze tablet placed by Joseph Hart Chapter D. A. R.
Married—Nancy Shanklin, m. 1789. Ch. Edward, b. 1790; Thomas, b. 1791; Joseph, b. 1793; Silas, b. 1796; Gideon, b. 1798, m. Hetty Taylor; Elizabeth, b. 1802. Second W., May Means. Ch. William, b. 1810; Samuel, b. 1813; James Harvey, b. 1815; Isaac Anderson, b. 1817; Charles Coffin, b. 1820.
Collected by Mrs. Laura D. Fix (deceased), Columbus, Indiana.

HARVEY, HENDERSON   Union County
Service—Pri., 1777-1781, in Cumberland Co., Penn. Militia, under Capt. Noah Abraham.
Proof—Penn. Archives, 5th Series, vol. 6, pp. 86, 121, 128, 141, 382, 384. Marriage Proof—Colonial, Revolutionary, County and Church Records in Maryland, vol. 2, p. 531.
Died—Probably buried in the Nelson or Witts Cemetery, Union Co.
Married—Martha McConnell, 1779. Ch. Isabel (1786-1864), m. Rev. John Plummer. There were three other children.
Collected by Miss Ellen Scott, Liberty, Indiana.

HASLET, SAMUEL   Putnam County
Born—1764, Lancaster Co., Pennsylvania.
Service—Pri. in company commanded by Capt. Sloan, Col. Campbell's Regt. N. C. Line, 7 mos.
Proof—Pension claim W. 4377, B. L. Wt. 33730-160-55.
Died—Oct. 6, 1846. Buried Portland Mills Cemetery. Stone.
Married—Nancy Young, 1829. Ch. Samuel; John; James; Joseph; Grissie, m. Wm. Ball.

HATTON, WILLIAM   Hancock County
Service—Enlisted in Virginia as pri. in Capt. Churchill Jones' CO., Col. William Washington's 3rd Regt. of Cavalry. Was at the battle of Bacon's Bridge, S. C., where he was wounded in one leg. Served 2½ yrs.

Proof—Pension certificate No. 17401.
Died—Aug. 27, 1842. Buried on Wesley Williams' farm on bank of Nameless Creek. Government marker placed by James Whitcomb Riley Chapter D. A. R.
Married— —— Kiger. Ch. Jacob; George; John; Nancy; Matilda Catt.
Collected by Mrs. Roy R. Roudebush, Greenfield, Indiana.

HAYES, JOSEPH   Dearborn County
Born—Dec. 16, 1732, Chester Co., Pennsylvania.
Service—On Aug. 28, 1776, mortgaged his two farms for 574 pounds and equipped a company of cavalry of which he was captain for a time under command of Gen. Otho Williams.
Proof—Penn. Archives, 5th Series; History of Dearborn and Ohio Counties.
Died—1812. Buried Limmer Cemetery, Lawrenceburg Twp. Government marker and D. A. R. bronze marker placed by Col. Lochry Chapter D. A. R.
Married—Joanna Passmore. Ch. Solomon; Jane; Phoebe; Joanna; Enoch; Priscilla; Job; Joseph, Jr.
Collected by Mrs. Alta M. Baker, Lawrenceburg, Indiana.

HAYES, SOLOMON   Dearborn County
Born—1755, Chester Co., Penn. (son of Joseph).
Service—Was 2nd Lieut. 7th CO., 1st Battalion, Chester Co. Militia, 1777-1778. Col. John Hannum. Also Lieut. 7th CO., 3rd Battalion, Chester Co., Penn., Militia May 10, 1780.
Proof—Penn. Archives 5th Series, vol. 5, pp. 470 and 559.
Died—1816. Buried Miller Cemetery, Lawrenceburg Twp. Government marker placed by Col. Archibald Lochry Chapter D. A. R.
Married—Mary Craig. Ch. Hannah; Rebecca; Henry; John; Joseph; Jacob; Nancy; Phoebe; Jane; Walter.
Collected by Mrs. Alta M. Baker, Lawrenceburg, Indiana.

HAYNES (HAINES), RICHARD   Union County
Born—Sept. 19, 1763, Prince Edward County, Virginia.
Service—1777, 2 years 6 mos. as private under Capt. Henry Conaway, Regt. of Col. Bedford, Md. Line.
Proof—Pension claim S. 32307.
Died—Feb. 2, 1850. Buried Witt Cemetery, N. E. of Liberty, Ind. Stone.
Married—Margaret Majors, d. 1823. Ch. Tom; Susanna; Harry; Sarah; Richard; Jane; Mary; Jane.
Collected by Mrs. Elnora P. Campbell, Liberty, Indiana.

HEATH, DANIEL Switzerland County
Born—March 26, 1760, Coventry, Conn.
Service—Lived in Albany, N. Y., when he enlisted 1777. Pri. and Serg. in company commanded by Capt. McCalups of Regt. under Col. Blair, N. Y. Militia for 2 years.
Proof—Pension claim W. 7711, B. L. Wt. 40013-160-55.
Died—Oct. 1, 1841. Buried near Enterprise, Cotton Twp.
Married—First W., 1785, Hannah Gates (1765-1797). Ch. James (1794-1864), m. Susannah White; Ann Buckingham; Ira; Asa; Jeremiah; Mary Halford; Daniel; Orra Babit. Second W., Azubah Reynolds, m. 1797. Ch. Arden, b. 1801; Sebvina Ann, b. 1802; Felinda, b. 1804, m. Frances B. McBeth; Charles, b. 1806; Philo Almand, b. 1810; Angeline, b. 1812.
Collected by Mrs. A. V. Danner, Vevay, Indiana.

HEATON, EBENEZER Indiana
Born—June 18, 1750, Morris Co., New Jersey.
Service—A Patriot. Furnished the following substitutes: Benjamin Jennings, 1778, Penn., and Jacob Amboy, 1781, Vir.
Proof—Photostatic Copy on file in Memorial Continental Hall, Washington, D. C.
Died—Jan. 12, 1837. Buried near Waterloo (county not known).
Married—Joanah Sutton (1761-1837). Ch. Abram, b. 1779; Mary, b. 1782; Daniel; Ebenezer; Nancy; Eli; Asa, b. 1798; John; Hannah, b. 1806; David.
Collected by Mrs. Ralph W. Wagoner, Knightstown, Indiana.

HEDGER, STEPHEN THOMAS Parke County
Born—March 25, 1747, Somerset Co., New Jersey.
Service—Pri. in company commanded by Capt. James Thomas, Col. Slaughter, Vir. Line, 6 mos.
Proof—Pension claim S. 32314.
Died—Dec., 1845. Buried Rosedale. Stone.
Children—Malinda Hedger Sale; Elizabeth; Lucy Hedger Evans; Thomas.
Collected by Estabrook Chapter D. A. R.

HEDRICK, PHILIP Henry County
Born—1755, Pennsylvania.
Service—Captain in Col. John Patton's Battalion Berk's Co., Penn., Militia, Jan. 26, 1776. May 12, 1780, is listed as Captain of 5th CO., 2nd Battalion.
Proof—Penn. Archives, 5th Series, vol. 5, pp. 148, 182.
Died—1833. Buried Ebenezer Graveyard, N. W. of Lewisville, Ind. Stone.

Children—By first wife: Margaret, b. 1780, m. John Berger; George, b. 1786, m. Drusilla Ball. Children by second wife: Katherine, b. 1796, m. John Ball; Christopher, b. 1801, m. Zelpha Copeland.
Collected by Joseph Greenleaf, New Castle, Indiana.

HENDERSHOT, ABRAHAM   Wayne County
Born—Oct. 21, 1754, Hunterdon Co., N. J.
Service—While living in Hunterdon Co., N. J., he enlisted in 1776 and served with the N. J. Troops at various times amounting to at least 2½ yrs., as pri. under Capts. Porter, Thomas Jones and Frome and Col. John Stephens. Was in battles of Monmouth, Elizabethtown and Springfield.
Proof—Pension claim R. 4863. Pension rejected as he failed to furnish proof of service as required by law. Name appears on the 1840 census for Wayne Co., Ind.
Collected by Mrs. Carl Caldwell, Milton, Indiana.

HENDERSON, JOHN   Lawrence County
Born—July 20, 1763, Louisa Co., Virginia.
Service—Called into service Sept., 1779, in Virginia Militia, Capt. Thomas Hatcher, Lt. David Rutherford. In 1781, pri. in Militia, Lt. Richard Allen.
Proof—Pension claim W. 10103.
Died—Jan. 11, 1844. Buried Crawford Cemetery, Lawrence Co.
Married—Jemima ——, b. 1763, m. 1787, d. after 1850 in Lawrence Co.

HENDERSON, JOSEPH   Monroe County
Born—March, 1765.
Service and Proof—D. A. R. national number 130353.
Died—March 21, 1849. Buried U. P. Cemetery, Bloomington, Ind. Stone.
Married—Elizabeth Fragier (1767-1841). Ch. Harriett; William; James; Joseph; Polly; Jean; Nancy; Eliza.
Collected by Bloomington Chapter D. A. R.

HENDERSON, WILLIAM   Dearborn County
Born—Aug. 31, 1755, Harrisburg, Pennsylvania.
Service—Entered service in Cumberland Co., Penn., under Capt. McKim, Aug. 1, 1776. Was taken prisoner Nov. 16, 1776. Penn. Line, 8 mos. under Col. Johnson.
Proof—Pension claim S. 32313.
Died—Last payment of pension was made on March 4, 1834.
Collected by Mrs. Walter Kerr, Aurora, Indiana.

HENDRICKSON, MOSES   Dearborn County
Born—Dec. 25, 1755.
Service—July, 1755, drafted under Gen. Lee, Col. Jamison, Lt. Col.
    Bond. Served until last of March, 1777, was on American vessel
    stationed in Baltimore Bay, wounded and sent ashore.
Proof—Pension claim S. 32312.
Died—Aug. 8, 1842, in Dearborn Co.
Married—Jane ——.
Collected by Mrs. Walter Kerr, Aurora, Indiana.

HENNEGIN, JOSEPH   Ripley County
Born—Feb. 6, 1759, Holland.
Service—Entered service from N. Y., 1776, under Capt. Henry O'Hara
    and served two yrs. in Capt. Richard Layden's CO. Later in Col.
    Moses Hazen's Regt. of Penn. Troops. Discharged Jan. 4, 1781.
Proof—Pension claim S. 10097.
Died—April 6, 1833. Buried in Delaware Twp. Stone. Government
    marker and name on bronze tablet in Versailles Court House.
Married—1785, Rhoda Harris, b. 1763. Ch. Peter, b. 1786; Margaret,
    b. 1788; Dorothy, b. 1790; Prudence, b. 1792; Barbara, b. 1793;
    Diadema, b. 1796, m. John Shue; Polly, b. 1799, m. Joseph
    Churchill; Henry, b. 1800, m. Mary Chamberlin; Emily, b. 1806,
    m. John Horton; George, b. 1811, m. Susan Montgomery.
Collected by Mrs. A. B. Wycoff, Batesville, Indiana

HENRY, MOSES   Knox County
Service—Accompanied Gibault and Helm from Kaskaskia to Post
    Vincennes to attempt its peaceful reduction. Moses Henry named
    interpreter and envoy to Indians. Named as one who accompanied Clark into Fort after its capture. Next day was one of
    party sent by Clark up the Wabash to intercept the flotilla of
    British soldiers from Detroit. Name appears on list of Signers
    of Oath of Allegiance, 1778, as Miles Henry.
Proof—English's Conquest of the North West, vol. 1, p. 234; Goodspeed's History of Knox Co., pp. 40, 41, 42, 51, 54.
Died—A bill for digging grave Jan. 9, 1789, paid by widow, is proof
    that he is buried in Knox Co., probably buried in St. Xavier
    Cemetery.
Married—Ann Collins. No trace of children found.
Collected by Mrs. S. G. Davenport, Vincennes, Indiana.

HENTON, GEORGE H.   Orange County
Born—April 8, 1758, Forestville, Shenandoah Co., Virginia.
Service—Served in the Shenandoah Co. Militia and was appointed
    First Lieut. in 1782 and 1783.

Proof—Old Minute Books of County Clerk's Office at Woodstock, Shenandoah Co., Virginia.
Died—Sept. 22, 1837. Buried in Old Murphy graveyard, Stamper Creek Twp. Government marker placed by Lost River Chapter D. A. R.
Married—Mary Rigney, m. 1785. Ch. Deliliah; Ann; Thomas; Mary; Rachel; William; George, Jr.; John Rigney; Guy.
Collected by George E. Henton, M. D., Morgan Bldg., Portland, Oregon.

HERBERT, THOMAS   Tippecanoe County
Born—Oct. 3, 1754, Monmouth Co., New Jersey.
Service—Pri. in battle of Monmouth.
Proof—Listed as a soldier of the revolution in the roster or lists published by the state of New Jersey.
Died—Oct. 25, 1844. Buried Sherry Cemetery, near West Point, Ind. Stone.
Married—Zelpha Murphy (1752-1845). Ch. Amy, b. 1795, m. Jacob Gay, b. 1791.
Collected by Gen. de Lafayette Chapter D. A. R.

HERRING (HERIN, HERRIN, HERRON), ISAAC   Lawrence County
Born—About 1761.
Service—Enlisted 1779, S. C., under Capt. Mason, Col. Merrium, Brigade under Gen. Pulaski. Wounded and taken prisoner. Service 1 yr.
Proof—Pension claim W. 10098.
Died—Oct. 23, 1833, near Leesville, Ind.
Married—Ann Shotwell Gainey, m. 1784. Ch. Sarah, d. infancy; John; Isaac; Dista; Alexander; Joshua; Joel; Lewis.

HIESTED, ABRAHAM   Floyd County
Born—Aug. 11, 1762, Northamton, Pennsylvania.
Service—A private in Capt. Peter Kooken's CO., 1st Battalion, Northampton Co., Penn., Militia, under Lieut. Col. Stephen Balliet, Nov. 1, 1781 to Jan. 1, 1782.
Proof—Family records; marriage records of Covington, Ind.; marriage record of Fairfield, Ohio.
Died—Feb. 13, 1848, near New Albany, Ind.
Married—Magadelina Strickler. Ch. Henry; Abraham; Christian (all were ministers).
Collected by Veedersburg Chapter D. A. R.

HIGGINS, DANIEL   Hendricks County
Born—1763, Augusta Co., Virginia.
Service—Pri. in company commanded by Capt. Harden, Regt. of Col. Logan, Vir. Line, 2 yrs.

Proof—Pension claim S. 17482.
Died—Last payment of pension made on Sept. 17, 1851. Buried on Henry Hunt farm, N. of New Winchester, Ind. Foot-stone.
Children—Thomas, b. 1798, d. 1854, m. Ann, d. 1873; David, d. 1854, m. Helen ——. There were other children.
Collected by Mrs. J. H. Grimes, Danville, Indiana.

HIGH, HENRY   Warren County
Service—Discharge recorded at Court House, Williamsport, Indiana.
Buried—Across road from Redwood school. Stone.
Collected by Mrs. Elmer V. Smith, Williamsport, Indiana.

HIGH, JACOB   Warren County
Born—1753, White Plains, New York.
Service—Volunteered Hampshire Co., Vir., 1777, as pri. in Col. Wm. Foreman's CO., later Capt. Alboah Johnson and Col. Crisip. Building garrison on Big Beaver, Vir. At the Siege of Yorktown.
Proof—Pension claim S. 32322.
Buried—In orchard across the road from Red Wood School. Stone.
Collected by Mrs. Elmer V. Smith, Williamsport, Indiana.

HIGH, JOHN   Warren County
Born—May 10, 1756, Schuylkill, near Philadelphia.
Service—Entered from Romney, Hampshire Co., Vir., June, 1780, as private under Capt. Isaac Parsons, Col. Lawson's Vir. Troops. Battles of Guilford and Yorktown. Discharged Nov. or Dec., 1781. In 1788 volunteered under Capt. Henry Parker one year defending settlements of the Ohio River.
Proof—Pension claim R. 4985.
Died—May 8, 1851.
Married—Second W., Nancy ——. Ch. George; Henry; Isaac; Nimrod; John; Hiram; Frederick; Catherine Price; Christina Sharp; Julian; Amaziah.
Collected by Mrs. Elmer V. Smith, Williamsport, Indiana.

HIGHNOTE (HIGNOTE, HIGNOT), PHILIP   Putnam County
Born—March 15, 1753, Bucks Co., Pennsylvania.
Service—While residing in Richmond Co., Georgia, he enlisted March, 1776, in company of Capt. Green, Lt. Agnatius Few, Maj. Havershand, Col. Elbert, Gen. McIntosh. Sept., 1777, enlisted again as Indian Spy for 1 yr.
Proof—Pension claim W. 10108.
Died—April 18, 1840, in Putnam Co., according to statement of widow in her application for pension.

Married—1786, Agnes Scott. Ch. Alexander, b. 1788; Mary Magdaline, b. 1790; Craft, b. 1792; Charity, b. 1794; Jane, b. 1796, m. Henry Ernhart; Hiram, b. 1798; Philip, b. 1801; Asahel, b. 1805; Nancy, b. 1805; Dorcas, b. 1807.

HIGHT, THOMAS   Morgan County
Born—Sept. 21, 1757, Charlotte Co., Virginia.
Service—Volunteered as a Minute Man. In 1776, enlisted again under Capt. Thomas Collier. In 1778, enlisted for 3 yrs. in Virginia Artillery CO. under Capt. Edward Moody. In 1781, drafted under Capt. King and marched to Camden, thence to Ninety-Six, under Col. Cruger, thence to Salsburg, N. C. Discharged.
Proof—Pension claim S. 32321.
Died—About 1844. Buried near Martinsville, Ind.
Married—Priscilla ——. Ch. Sarah; Lettice; John; William.

HILEY, ABRAHAM   Perry County
Born—Feb. 27, 1757, Hampshire Co., Virginia.
Service—Entered service Dec., 1776, under John Crosap, Capt. of Rifle CO. Volunteered in Fayette Co., Penn. Marched to Hagerstown, Md., to Lancaster, Penn., to Trenton, N. J., joined Gen. Washington. The next spring, marched to Germantown and was sent foraging under Lt. Joseph Jones and discharged by him the last of April or the first of May, 1778, at Valley Forge. Enlisted Feb., 1780, under Capt. Michael Catt in Fayette Co., Penn., joined Gen. Green at Guilford. Was in battles of Camden and Eutaw Springs and was wounded in latter battle and discharged. Entered service again July, 1781, as a substitute for Philip Catt and was taken prisoner by Indians and remained with them for 3 yrs.
Proof—Pension claim S. 31744.
Died—May 1, 1836. Buried Hardingrove, Perry Co.
Married—Mary ——, d. 1837. Only child, Abraham.

HILL, ELI   Dearborn County
Service—Served in Lexington Alarm, 3 days. In 2nd CO., 6th Regt., Conn. Enlisted May 9, 1775, discharged Dec. 16th.
Proof—Conn. Military Record, 1775-1848, pp. 20 and 73.
Died—Probably buried in Old Graveyard at Lawrenceburg, Ind.
Collected by Mrs. Walter Kerr, Aurora, Indiana.

HILL, JAMES   Boone County
Born—Dec. 3, 1767, near Danville, Virginia.
Service—Ensign, 15th Vir. Regt., June 15, 1777; 2nd Lieut., April 1, 1778; 11th Vir. Regt. Served to Oct., 1779.
Proof—Heitman's Historical Register, p. 290.

Died—April 9, 1854. Buried Cedar Hill Cemetery, Lebanon, Ind. Has monument placed by County Commissioners.
Married—Ann Clark. Ch. Sarah, b. 1789; Tauster, b. 1791; Tabitha, b. 1790; Martha, b. 1795; Mary, b. 1798; Pleasant, b. 1800; Joshua, b. 1807.
Collected by Mrs. H. S. McKee, Greensburg, Indiana (a descendant), and James Hill Chapter D. A. R.

HILL, THOMAS   Jennings County
Born—March 17, 1763, New Jersey.
Service—Entered at age of 19 and served 3 mos. as pri. in Vir. Troops.
Proof—History of Coffee Creek Baptist Assoc. Minutes of 1848. Also History of Coffee Creek Baptist Assoc. by Tibbetts, p. 147. Will in Jennings Co. Book 1, p. 77.
Died—April 22, 1841. Buried Old Baptist Cemetery on farm of Sylvester Deputy. Stone.
Married—Mary Stone, 1786, d. 1844. Ch. John, 1787-1852; William, 1789-1817; Thomas, 1797-1876; Allen, 1799-1871, m. Betsey McCrory; Daniel, 1805-1882, m. Jane Dixon.
Collected by John Paul Chapter D. A. R. and Mrs. H. S. McKee, Greensburg, Indiana.

HILLIS, WILLIAM   Jefferson County
Born—1735, Sligo Co., Ireland.
Service—A surgeon in the British Army and came to this country before the war. Became friendly to the Colonies, resigned his commission, entered the Colonial Forces. Served in the Sandusky Expedition. Pri. in Capt. McGiham's CO., Col. Wm. Crawford's Regt.
Proof—Penn. Archives, 6th Series, vol. 2, p. 394; D. A. R. No. 683000.
Died—1818. Buried Ryker Cemetery. Stone.
Married—Jane Carruthers, d 1816. Ch. David, m. Margaret Brook; John; William; Matthew; James; Ebenezer; Jane; Margaret; Nancy.
Collected by John Paul Chapter D. A. R.

HILLS, JOHN   Dubois County
Born—May 16, 1761.
Service—Served in Col. Thomas Eaton's Regt. Enlisted Oct. 10, 1778, for 6 mos. under Capt. Brittain Harris; Jan., 1781, 3 mos. under Capt. Jordan Harris; July, 1782-Oct., 1782, under Capt. Francis Thornton, and in Nov., 1782, for 1 year under Capt. Edmund Gamble. He was in battles of Brier Creek and Guilford. Lived in Warren Co., N. C., at time of enlistment.
Proof—Pension claim S. 16413.

Died—Between Dec. 17, 1834 and Jan. 10, 1835. No record found of
any family.
Collected by George Wilson, Historian for DuBois Co., Indiana.

HILMAN, THOMAS   Henry County
Born—Aug. 22, 1757, Salem Co., New Jersey.
Service—Enlisted in April, 1776, as a pri. at various times in the N. J.
Troops, under Capts. Henry Sparks, Barker, Miller, Smith, Cols.
Holmes, Smith, Potter, and Dick; he was in engagements at
"Cuckletown" and Quinton's Bridge and served until Oct., 1778—
22 mos. 20 days. Eight mos. of his service was as a substitute
for his brother, John.
Proof—Pension claim S. 32320.
Died—May 5, 1835. Henry Co.

HINES, JACOBAS (JACOB)   Park County
Born—Oct. 28, 1752, Newcastle Co., Delaware.
Service—While a resident of Chester, Kent Co., Md., in April, 1775,
he joined a company of minute men commanded by Capt. John
Watkins and about one month after entering, he went on an expedition to a point on Chesapeake Bay about 12 miles from
Chester and served four days. Was called into active service,
Aug., 1777, in Capt. Watkin's Md. CO., and was in the battles
of Paoli and Germantown, and was discharged just before
Christmas, 1777; enlisted again March, 1779, served two or three
months in Capt. Marmaduke Tilldan's CO., Col. Alexander Anderson's Md. Regt. Later served 6 or 8 mos. as assistant to John
Batten, Purchasing and Issuing Commissary.
Proof—Pension claim S. 16401. Allowed pension 1832 from Parke
Co., Indiana.

HINKLE, NATHAN   Sullivan County
Born—March 31, 1759, Lancaster Co., Pennsylvania.
Service—Pri. in Capt. Christ's CO., Lancaster Co., Penn. Enlisted
April, 1776, and was in Trenton in 1776; wintered in Philadelphia,
thence to Staten Island. Was in battle of Long Island where all
of the company except himself, Capt. Christ, and five others were
taken prisoners. Was in battles of Brandywine and Paoli and
wintered at Valley Forge, 1778. Discharged at Red Lion.
Proof—Penn. Archives, 5th Series, vol. 2, pp. 49-50; Pension record.
Died—Dec. 25, 1848. Buried Hymera, Jackson Twp. Stone placed by
Historical Society.
Married—Maria Magdeline Zureker. Ch. Margaret; Mahala; Rebecca;
Phoebe; William; Samuel.
Collected by Hinkle Family.

HINKLE, WENDLE   Sullivan County
Born—1755, Lancaster County, Penn.
Service—Pri. in Capt. James McConnell's CO., 5th Battalion, Penn. Militia.
Proof—Penn. Archives, 5th Series.
Died—1838. Buried Pleasantville, Jefferson Twp. Stone.
Married—1784, Elizabeth Fox. Ch. Mary Magdalina; Philip; Anthony; John W.; Amelia; Elizabeth; Margaret; Nathan; Susan; Sarah; Martha; Katherine.
Collected by Hinkle Family.

HINMAN, ASABEL   Warrick County
Born—March 23, 1742. Southbury, Conn.
Service—Served one year. Was with Benedict Arnold on famous march through Maine to aid Gen. Montgomery in his attack on Quebec in 1775. He commanded a company of New Jersey troops at Long Island. Was at Yorktown, was severely wounded in battle of Brandywine, losing one leg. Then served as Quartermaster and was in command of the supply trains. Often paid for supplies himself.
Proof—Early Puritans, vol. 2; Stryker's History of N. J., p. 848.
Died—Sept. 5, 1825. Buried on Old Stevens Farm, S. of Boonville. Government marker placed by Vanderburg Chapter D. A. R.
Married—Mary Harris Hinman (a cousin). Ch. Rhoda, m. Romney Perigo; Anna Harris, m. Ephraim Brashears; Samuel, m. Nancy Hedges; Maria, m. Richard Stevens; George.
Collected by Mrs. H. K. Forsythe, Newburgh, Indiana.

HITE, JACOB, SR.   Rush County
Born—Feb. 14, 1761. Frederick Co., Maryland.
Service—Enlisted from Frederick Co., Vir., under Capt. Gilkison. Was in the company of Generals McIntosh, Armistead, and Newall. As a pri., served 2 mos. in 1778, from Oct. 1, 1781, served 6 mos. Present at Yorktown.
Proof—Pension claim S. 16414.
Died—1839. Buried Richland Cemetery. Name on bronze tablet in Rush Co. Court House.
Married—Catherine Shimer. Ch. John; George (War of 1812); William; Jacob, Jr.; Polly, m. Archibald Crowdy; Alexander.
Collected by Mrs. Willard Amos, Rushville, Indiana.

HOBAUGH, PHILIP   Madison County
Born—About 1763.
Service—Enlisted 1779, at Pittsburgh, in Capt. Samuel Brady's CO., 8th Penn. Regt., Col. Byard. Discharged at Ft. Pitt Nov., 1783. In battles of Guilford Court House, Siege of 96, and Eutaw Springs.

Proof—Pension claim W. 10125, B. L. Wt. 212-100. Soldier asked for bounty in 1804 from Ross Co., Ohio; 1818 to 1820, he was living in Madison Co., Ohio; 1822, asked for transfer of pension to Randolph Co., Ind.; 1840, his widow applied.
Died—Aug. 6, 1836, in Madison Co., Indiana.
Married—Christine Huverin. Ch. Molly, b. 1797; Michael, b. 1806; Elizabeth, b. 1808; Susannah Longacre, b. 1810; Peter, b. 1813.
Collected by Mrs. Orville Dailey, Albany, Ohio.

HODGES, RICHARD   Ripley County
Service—Pri. in Capt. Joshua Miles' Regt., the 6th Maryland under Col. Williams. Enlisted Sept. 9, 1778, for one year. Later was a member of Chaplain's CO. Discharged Jan., 1780.
Proof—Pension record.
Died—Buried in Blair Cemetery, Brown Twp. Stone crumbled. Name appears on bronze tablet in Versailles Court House.
Descendants are: Mrs. Nora Newman Crouch, Osgood, Ind.; Mrs. Madge Crouch Franke, Spades, Ind.; and J. L. Hodges, 1432 N. 17th St., Philadelphia, Penn.
Collected by Mrs. A. B. Wycoff, Batesville, Indiana.

HOFFMAN, HENRY   Indiana
Born—About 1760.
Service—Enlisted June, 1776, under Capt. Grant, Col. Holler, Maj. Bird in Flying Camp, Penn. Line. Served 6 mos. In battles of Long Island and White Plains. Served 2 mos. as Militiaman under Lt. Stahley.
Proof—Pension claim W. 10127.
Died—April 1, 1834, at Dentown (from statement of widow), Indiana.
Married—First to Margaret Boo, d. 1788. Ch. Catherine, b. 1775. Second to Mary Ann Drum, m. Dec. 25, 1788.

HOGAN, PROSSER   Harrison County
Born—1764.
Service—In 1777, he enlisted in Guilford Co., N. C., under Capt. Anthony Sharp and Col. Clarke, in N. C., for 3 yrs. Served and enlisted again in same company then commanded by Capt. Tatum. Taken prisoner at Charleston, S. C., but escaped.
Proof—Pension claim S. 36592.
Died—Last payment of pension made on Jan. 20, 1830.

HOLBROOK, GEORGE SR.   Gibson County
Service—"In 1842 the Board of County Commissioners exempted George Holbrook, Sr., from paying tax on 160 acres of land on which he resided in this county, on giving proof of his having

served in the Rev. War." Tart's History of Gibson Co., p. 105. He applied for pension, Gibson Co., May 15, 1828, age 84. Applied again on Feb. 13, 1837, age 93. States he entered as a Lieut. in CO. commanded by Capt. John Armstrong, 3rd Regt. N. C. State Troops. Entered April or May, 1776, at Surry Court House, N. C. Left Regt. at Winchester and entered Morgan's Regt. as Capt. about 1777—thence to Fredericktown, Md., for the winter—thence to Phila. After the battle of Germantown, marched south through Md. and Vir., stopping at Staunton, thence through S. C. and on to Cowpens and Eutaw Springs.

Proof—Pension claim R. 5120. Pension rejected—no reason given.

HOLE, DANIEL   Washington County
Born—April 5, 1757, Essex County, New Jersey.
Service—Enlisted in Hampshire Co., Vir., Aug., 1777, with Vir. Troops under Gen. Hand. In spring of 1780, moved to Falls of Ohio and engaged in Indian Warfare. Enlisted March 1, 1781, under Capt. Richard Chennoth and served under George Rogers Clark for 3 mos. Enlisted again 1782 in Capt. Samuel McAfie's CO.
Proof—Pension record.
Died—March 3, 1839. Buried Mill Creek Cemetery, near Salem, Ind. Marked by Christopher Harrison Chapter D. A. R.
Married—Mary Bedell. Ch. Phoebe; Esther; Nancy; Lydia; Stephen; Catherine; Aaron; Mary; Elizabeth.
Collected by Miss Mary Brittain, Vincennes, Indiana.

HOLLOWAY, LEVI   Hamilton County
Born—April 9, 1735, Worcester Co., Maryland.
Service—Enlisted 1777 in Capt. James Lane's CO., under Capts. George Bell, James Faucett and Josiah Deal. Served as guard on eastern shores of Md.
Proof—Pension claim S. 32332.
Died—Buried in Carey Cemetery, White River Twp.
There are numerous descendants living in county.
Collected by Mr. Perry A. Bray, Noblesville, Indiana.

HOLMAN, GEORGE   Wayne County
Born—Feb. 11, 1762, Maryland.
Service—Served under George Rogers Clark as pri. in Ky. Militia.
Proof—Pension record; English's History of North West Territory, vol. 2, p. 985.
Died—May 22, 1859. Buried Maple Grove Cemetery, removed to Elkorn Cemetery, S. of Richmond, Ind. Government marker placed by Richmond Chapter D. A. R.

Married—Jane Rue (1757-1831). Ch. Joseph; William, m. Rue Meek; John; Benjamin and Joel; Patsey, m. William Meek; Rebecca, m. John Woodkirk; Sarah, m. John Odell; Greenup, m. Lethe Druley; Jesse, m. first, Nancy Galbraith, second, Sarah Julian; Catherine, m. Adam Porter; Isaac.
Collected by Mrs. Paul L. Ross, Richmond, Indiana.

HOLMAN (HOLEMAN), ISAAC   Clark County
Born—March 20, 1757, Rowan Co., North Carolina.
Service—Private. Enlisted 1777 or 78, from Rowan Co. Served 95 days under Capt. Samuel Reed. Re-enlisted 1780 or 81, serving 3 mos. under Capt. Ritchie Grimes, Col. Luke. Again served 2 mos. under Col. Luke. In battle of Cowans Ford and Guilford Court House.
Proof—Holman Branch in "Ancestry of Grafton Johnson" by Knobe. D. A. R. No. 182117.
Died—April 5, 1843. Buried New Chapel Cemetery, N. E. of Jeffersonville. Stone.
Married—First to Catherine Wilcox. Ch. Rachel; Elizabeth; Eda; Isaac; William; Polly; Aaron; Moses; Catherine; Matilda. Second to Lillas Mitchell (1775-1866). Ch. Andrew Mitchel; Matilda.
Collected by Mrs. Keplar W. Barnes, Charlestown, Indiana.

HOLMES, WILLIAM   Knox County
Born—Jan., 1751, Carlisle, Pennsylvania.
Service—Pri. in Capt. Matthew Gregg's CO., Second Battalion Cumberland Co. Militia, July, 1777. Also in Capt. Asa Hill's CO.
Proof—Penn. Archives, 5th Series, vol. 6, pp. 157-199.
Died—Aug. 21, 1836. Buried Upper Indiana Cemetery. Stone. Bronze tablet placed by Holmes Family.
Married—Elizabeth Love, d. 1836. Ch. Jane, m. Thomas Emison, 1802; Hetty, m. William Bruce, 1819; Andrew, m. Delilah Tyler Bruce, 1819; Josiah, m. Margaret McClure, 1818.
Collected by Miss Estelle Emison, Alice Manor, Vincennes, Indiana.

HOOD, WILLIAM   Jennings County
Born—1753.
Service—Enlisted in N. C. prior to battle of Guilford; pri. in Capt. Alex. Brevard's CO., Col. Archibald Lytle's N. C. Regt. In battles of Santee and Ashley River. Discharged after 18 mos. or 2 yrs. service.
Proof—Pension claim W. 25781.
Died—April 6, 1829, Jennings County.

Married—Kitty Dephery (Dephens), b. 1785, m. 1812. Ch. Hannibal, b. 1813; Jesse, b. 1815; Sally, b. 1817; Ellenor, b. 1819, m. 1833, William Lee. Second W., Frances Ragan, m. 1827.
Collected by John Paul Chapter D. A. R.

HOOKE (HOOK), GEORGE   Monroe County
Born—Oct., 1751, Guilford Co., North Carolina.
Service—Sergeant Orderly in CO. commanded by Capt. Nelson, Col. Polk's Regt. in N. C. Line for 2 yrs.
Proof—Pension claim W. 10112.
Died—March 7, 1835, Monroe Co.
Married—Pension application states that Agnes Hook, widow applied for pension and that Jane Hook received it. Lineage, vol. 113, p. 73, gives wife, Jean Bright. All state married 1789. Ch. given in pension application—Anne R. A., b. 1789; James, b. 1790; Thomas, b. 1793; Betsey, b. 1796; John, b. 1798; George B., b. 1800; John C. B., b. 1803; Rebeccakah, b. 1806; William, b. 1808.
Collected by Mrs. I. E. Tranter, Franklin, Indiana.

HOOVER, ANDREW (HUBER, ANDREAS)   Wayne County
Born—Sept. 21, 1752, on Pipe Creek, Frederick Co., Maryland.
Service—Furnished supplies for the troops and received pay for them.
Proof—From Accounts of the United States with North Carolina, War of Revolution, Book C, p. 117, found in custody of N. C. Historical Commission.
Died—Dec. 29, 1834. Buried "Friends Cemetery," now Starr Park, Richmond, Ind. Bronze tablet on stone at his grave—"In memory of Andrew Hoover and his wife, Elizabeth Waymire Hoover, patriots of the Revolutionary War, who settled in Wayne County in 1806 and were parents of Mary Hoover Newman, Elizabeth Hoover Bulla, David Hoover, who laid out and named the City of Richmond; Frederick Hoover, Susannah Hoover Wright, Henry Hoover, Rebecca Hoover Julian, Andrew Hoover, Catherine Hoover McLane, Sarah Hoover Sanders. Tablet erected by de-descendants and dedicated by Richmond Chapter D. A. R.
Collected by Mrs. Paul Ross, Richmond, Indiana.

HOPEWELL, JOHN   Sullivan County
Born—1751, Virginia.
Service—Enlisted near Winchester, Vir., spring of 1777, in Capt. Charles Porterfield's and Gabriel Long's CO., Col. Morgan's Vir. Regt. Was at taking of Burgoyne and Monmouth. Served until spring of 1780.
Proof—Pension claim S. 63591.

Died—Sept. 6, 1826. Buried New Lebanon, Sullivan Co.
Married—Sarah Edwards (1756-1829). Ch. Lewis; Henry; Porter; Samuel; Deliliah; Margaret, b. 1787; Sarah, b. 1791; John, Jr.
Collected by Miss Edna Calvert, Sullivan, Indiana.

HOPPER, JOHN   Owen County
Born—About 1751.
Service—Enlisted in Wilkes Co., N. C., last of March, 1781; served as pri. in Capt. Alexander Brevard's CO., Col. John Armstrong's N. C. Regt. Was in battles of Ninety-Six and Eutaw Springs. Discharged in March, 1782.
Proof—Pension claim W. 7785.
Died—March 11 or 12, 1852, in Owen Co., Ind.
Married—1842, Mrs. Catherine Piles, in Martin Co., Ind. (She was no doubt a second wife for soldier came to Indiana to live with his children in 1829.)
Collected by Mrs. Wm. Mavity, French Lick, Indiana.

HOPPER, WILLIAM   Scott County
Born—Nov. 21, 1764, Culpepper Co., Virginia.
Service—Drafted 1781 in company of militia under Capt. Hardin of Caswell Co., N. C., Col. Wm. Moore, Gen. Butler. Served 3 mos. Discharged. Later in 1781, volunteered for 2 mos. under Capt. Mullin, Col. Moore, horse man.
Proof—Pension claim R. 5221. Applied from Scott Co., Ind., in 1832.

HORNBACK, ABRAHAM   Spencer County
Born—About 1758.
Service—Enlisted in Hampshire Co., Vir., Feb. 9, 1776. Served as a pri. in Capt. Abel Westfall's CO., Col. Muhlenberg's 8th Vir. Regt.; he was at the taking of Burgoyne, was in several skirmishes under Col. Morgan. Discharged by Capt. Van Swearingen, Feb. 9, 1778, at Valley Forge.
Proof—Pension claim W. 10120.
Died—Nov. 16, 1834. Buried Baker Creek graveyard, near Eureka, Luce Twp. Government marker placed by Spier Spencer D. A. R.
Married—Hannah Cleaver, d. 1842. Ch. William; Daniel; Elizabeth; Mary, m. 1809, James Sallee.
Collected by Miss Laura M. Wright, Rockport, Indiana.

HORRALL (HORRELL), WILLIAM   Daviess County
Born—1754, Amherst County, Virginia.
Service—Enlisted Aug., 1776. Served 3 mos. as pri. in Capt. Higginbottom's CO., Col. Mason's Vir. Regt. Enlisted Aug., 1777, for 6 mos. in Capt. Thomas Morrison's and Capt. Alexander Hen-

derson's CO., Col. Gibson's and Col. Boyer's Vir. Regt. Enlisted Aug., 1780, for 3 mos. in Capt. John Morrison's CO., Col. Meage's and Col. Randall's Vir. Regt. In 1781, served in Capt. David Shelton's CO. and in Capt. John Lovin's CO., Col. Richardson's and Col. Randall's Vir. Regt. Discharged Dec., 1781.

Proof—Pension claim S. 17472.

Died—1851. Buried Old Bethel. Government marker placed by White River Chapter D. A. R.

Married—First to Priscilla Calvert Houghton (1757-1823). Ch. James, m. Elizabeth Capehart; William, Jr., m. Peggy Stone; John, m. Rebecca Banks; Nancy, m. John Ellis; Sarah, m. William Wallace; Thomas, m. first to Nancy Wallace, second to Sarah Jones; Rachel, m. first to John Stafford, second to John Jones; Priscilla Calvert, m. William Jones. Soldier, m. second to Elinor Morgan Wallace, widow of John Wallace (Rev. S.). No issue.

Collected by Mrs. Roy Bogner, Washington, Indiana.

HORTON (HOOTEN), THOMAS   Decatur County
Born—1752, Virginia.

Service—Enlisted in Virginia, June 22, 1776, served as pri. in Capt. Glen Drayton's CO., Col. Charles Cotesworth Pinckney's 1st Continental Regt., S. C.; March 25, 1777, was appointed Corporal; May 1, 1777, sergeant; June 2, 1778, sergeant major; discharged Aug. 4, 1778, at Charleston and his discharge signed by Col. Charles Cotesworth Pinckney.

Proof—Pension claim W. 670.

Died—July 24, 1841. Buried Sandcreek Cemetery. Stone.

Married—Orender (Orander) Bush, m. 1802. Soldier stated he had four infant children.

Collected by Mrs. H. S. McKee, Greensburg, Indiana.

HOSKINSON, JOSIAH   Shelby County
Born—1759, Maryland.

Service—"Return of the Lower Battalion of Militia of Montgomery County, Md., made by Col. John Murdock July 15, 1780, appears the name of Josiah Hoskinson, 3rd Sergeant of Capt. Aaron Harris' CO."

Proof—Maryland Historical Society.

Died—1836. Buried in an abandoned cemetery on farm now owned by J. A. Amos in Jackson Twp.

Married—First Wife name unknown. Her Ch. Thomas; Charles; John; James; Kathryn; Enos. Second Wife, Alcy Brent. Ch. Josiah; Elisha; Elizabeth; Hugh; Sarah; Isabel, m. —— Quick.

Collected by Mrs. Walter Kerr, Aurora, Indiana.

HOUCK (HAWKE), MICHAEL   Sullivan County
Born—1751, Maryland.
Service—Served as a gunner in Capt. William Born's CO., also designated as Capt. William Brown's CO. of Maryland Artillery Regt., Continental Troops, commanded by Col. Charles Harrison. Enlisted Nov. 22, 1777; was promoted to the grade of corporal Jan., 1780. Name last on pay roll March and April, 1783.
Proof—War Department, Adjutant-General's Office.
Died—Buried, Cass. Twp., Sullivan Co.
Married—Katie ———. Ch. Philip.
Collected by Mrs. James R. Riggs, Sullivan, Indiana.

HOWLETT, WILLIAM   Jennings County
Born—About 1767.
Service—First enlistment under Capt. John Facet, Lieut. Rufus Perry. Second, under Col. Samuel Robinson, Col. Whitcomb, Maj. Wait, Capt. Wm. Buchanan, Lieut. Jacob Ferman in Vermont Militia. Third, 1779, under Capt. Huntington, Col. Seth Warren. Was in the battle of Bennington and at surrender of Burgoyne. 15 mos. Fourth enlistment, volunteered at New London, Conn., as mariner on "trumbull," Capt. Nichols, Lieuts. Malby and Starr.
Proof—Pension claim R. 5305, rejected for insufficient proof.
Died—Aug. 27, 1852, Jennings County.
Married—1815, Martha Jack.

HUBBELL, JOHN   Henry County
Born—Sept., 1754.
Service—Enlisted 1777 under Col. Matthew Ogden, N. J. Line. Sergeant in N. J. Line, 5 years.
Proof—Pension claim W. 9484.
Died—April 17, 1834. Buried Wisehart Cemetery, New Lisbon, Dudley Twp. Stone.
Married—1778 to Mary Robertson, b. 1759. Ch. John, Jr., b. Nov., 1778; Isaac, b. 1780; Daniel, b. 1782; Sarah, b. 1784; Abigah, b. 1786; Rachel, b. 1788; Anna b. 1790; David, b. 1792.

HUCKLEBERRY, GEORGE   Clark County
Born—About 1730, Wurtemburg, Germany.
Service—Enlisted from Penn., Westmoreland Co. His name appears as a pri. on a miscellaneous list of soldiers.
Proof—Penn. Archives, 5th Series, vol. 4, p. 745.
Died—After 1782. Buried on his farm in Grant 75, Clark County, near where Fourteen Mile Creek empties into the Ohio River. Stone.
Married—Rosanna Wise. Ch. Jacob; John; Martin; Susannah; George; Daniel; Abraham; Elizabeth; Henry.
Collected by Mrs. Thomas N. Todd, Charlestown, Indiana.

HUFFMAN, JOHN Knox County
Born—Jan. 1, 1759, Pennsylvania.
Service—Pri. in Capt. Weaver's CO., 4th Battalion, Lancaster Co. Militia, Oct. 4, 1779. Appears on rolls as pri. in Capt. Thomas Robertson's 3rd CO., 7th Battalion, Lancaster Co. Militia commanded by Lieut. Col. Alexander Lawry and pri. in 10th Battalion Militia, 1782.
Proof—Penn. Archives, 5th Series, vol. 7, pp. 393, 785, 1025.
Died—1824. Buried Herman Cemetery, Knox County.
Married—Margaret Upp, and 2nd W. Nancy Sprinkle, m. 1786. The soldier's will mentions the following children: George; Michael; Betsey; Polly; Peggy; Sally; Caty (a dau.); Solomon; Samuel; James; Jacob; Nancy; Hannah; Eliza; Harriet; William.
Collected by Miss Frances Lloyd and Mrs. S. G. Davenport, Vincennes, Indiana.

HUFMAN (HUFFMAN), HENRY Switzerland County
Born—About 1750.
Service—Enlisted 3 yrs. March, 1777, in Maryland company under Capt. McMahon, Col. Nevel, to serve until March, 1781. Discharged at Lancaster, Penn.
Proof—Switzerland County, Ind., Civil Order Book 1828, p. 117.
Married—Fanny ——. Ch. Ann; Sarah; Lewis, m. Elizabeth Glenn.
Collected by Mrs. A. V. Danner, Vevay, Indiana.

HUGHES, JOHN Jennings County
Born—About 1760.
Service—Pri. in Capt. Nathaniel Fox's CO., 6th Vir. Regt., Col. James Hendricks, Lieut. Col. Charles Simms. Enlisted July, 1777; discharged Feb., 1778. On July 19, 1783, he received a certificate amounting to 101 pounds, 3 shillings, 9 pence. Received Bounty Land in Clark's grant, Indiana, for services under George Rogers Clark.
Proof—Vir. State Library has photostat copy; W. D. 127,4; English Conquest of N. W. Territory, vol. 2, p. 846.
Died—Feb. 19, 1831. Buried near Graham Church, which is close to Jefferson County line. Government marker.
Married—Mildred Bland (1764-1809), m. 1795. Ch. John; Mildred; James; Isaac; Evaline; Vardoman.
Collected by Mrs. Anna Hughes Andres, Madison, Indiana.

HUMPHREY, EBENEZER Switzerland County
Born—May 8, 1763. Worcester Co., Massachusetts.
Service—Pri. in CO. of Capt. Tucker, Regt. of Col. Tyler in Mass. Militia, 15 mos.

Proof—Pension claim S. 18040.
Died—March 23, 1841. Buried Inercus Grover Cemetery, Posey, Twp. Stone.
Married—Hulda Keeney. Ch. Stephen, b. 1791; Arthur, b. 1796; Indianus H., b. 1824. There were other children.
Collected by Mrs. A. V. Danner, Vevay, Indiana.

HUNT, JOSIAH   Martin County
Born—May 4, 1763, Delaware.
Service—Pri. in CO. commanded by Capt. Brady, Penn. Line, 9 mos. Also under Gen. Anthony Wayne against the Indians.
Proof—Pension claim W. 1289.
Died—April 9, 1839, Truelove Cemetery.
Married—1796, Bethia Reeve.

HUNT, MESECH   Sullivan County
Born—Dec. 16, 1762, Maryland.
Service—Pri. in Maryland Militia and statement "Revolutionary Soldier" on his tombstone.
Proof—D. A. R. No. 139634 and inscription.
Died—Nov. 30, 1840. Buried Camp Ground Cemetery, Gill Twp. Stone.
Married—Sarah Roby (1770-1854). Ch. Jane; Anna; Martha; Mary; Millie; Sarah; Elizabeth; John, Jr., b. 1802, m. Hannah Davidson; Jetson; Dory.
Collected by Mrs. James R. Riggs, Sullivan, Indiana.

HUNTER, JOHN   Daviess County
Born—Dec. 2, 1755, New Castle, Delaware.
Service—Enlisted from Cumberland Co., Penn., Dec. 16, 1776, 4 mos. as pri. in Capt. Robert Culbertson's CO. under Majors Smith and Miflin. In 1777, 5 mos. in Capt. Thomas Askey's and Alexander People's CO. under Col. James Dunlap. July, 1778, 4 mos. against Indians under Capt. Young and Col. James Dunlap.
Proof—Pension claim S. 32334.
Died—Aug., 1836. Buried Mt. Olive Cemetery, Barr Twp. Government marker placed by White River Chapter D. A. R.
Married—Mary ——. Ch. Reuben; James; Edmund; William; Roswell; John; David. (From soldier's will.)
Collected by Mrs. Roy Bogner, Washington, Indiana.

HUNTER, PATRICK   Harrison County
Born—1760, North Ireland.
Service—Enlisted Aug. 1, 1781, Penn., under Lieut. Isaac Anderson, Col. Archibald Lochry. Aug. 24, 1781, was captured by Indians on Ohio River and carried to Detroit, Montreal and Quebec, thence to N. Y., where he was paroled in Jan., 1783.

Proof—Pension claim S. 17501.
Died—May 9, 1848. Buried Rehoboth Cemetery. Stone.
Married—Nancy Jack, b. 1764, m. 1883. Ch. Eleanor, b. 1790, m. Martin Miller; Nancy, b. 1803, m. Benjamin Jordan; Finwell; Marshall; Mary; William; David.
Collected by Mrs. Louise Miller Bulleit, Corydon, Indiana.

HUME, JOHN   Marion County
Born—1761, Lancaster Co., Pennsylvania.
Service—Volunteered as pri. with Penn. troops as follows: From Feb. or March, 1777, 6 wks. in Capt. Wm. Grimes CO., Col. Philip Marsteller's Regt. From Oct., 1777, in Capt. Ambrose Crain's CO., Col. Roger's Regt. Marched to the neighborhood of White Marsh and was in an engagement at Barnhill Church, 2 mos. From spring 1778, 1 mo. in Capt. John Barnet's CO. From fall of 1779, 2 mos. in Capt. James Johnson's CO., Col. Allen's Regt., and was stationed at Fort Schwartz on the west branch of the Susquehanna River in defense of the frontier against the Indians. From the summer of 1780, 1 mo. as a ranger in Capt. John Barnet's CO.
Proof—Pension claim S. 31765.
Died—1840. Buried near Trader's Point.
Married— —— Crawford, m. 1787. Ch. James; Margaret; Thomas; Martha.
Collected by Irvington Chapter D. A. R.

HURLBUT, CALEB   Jennings County
Born—1753, Litchfield, Connecticut.
Service—Name appears in a list of soldiers in a volume of Sick Soldiers' Bills, 1775, being itemized accounts of expense of individual soldiers during illness. Enlisted Sheenboro, Washington Co., N. Y.; was a sergeant under Col. Webster and Capt. Tozer.
Proof—Conn. Rev. Rolls of the Conn. Historical Society Collection, vol. 8, pp. 16-21; Hurlbut Genealogy, p. 112; Roster of N. Y. State Troops, by Fernow, p. 401.
Died—1824. Buried Paris Crossing, Jennings Co.
Married—Lydia Mitchell. Ch. Caleb, b. 1792; Louis; Thankful, m. John Ballard; Jerusha, m. Mandeville; Rachel, m. Able Benjamin; Cyremia, m. James Chandle; Polly.
Collected by Caroline Scott Harrison Chapter D. A. R.

HURT (HERT, HIRT), JAMES, JR.   Lawrence County
Born—1766, Prince Edward Co., Virginia.
Service—Enlisted at the age of 15 in Virginia Line on Continental Establishment, 1781-3.

Proof—Manuscript War 4. Virginia State Library.
Died—Oct. 9, 1834. Buried Ferguson Cemetery.
Married—Polly Wommack. Ch. Judith, 1802-89, m. John Hurt, 1802-48.
Collected by John Wallace Chapter D. A. R.

ICE, ANDREW   Henry County
Born—1758, Hampshire County, Virginia.
Service—Pri. in Vir. Troops, 1777; 6 mos. under Capt. Owen Davy and Col. Zaccheus Morgan. In 1778, 6 mos. under Capt. Brinton and Col. Charles Evans and was out against the Indians in the "Northwest." Also served 2 mos. under Capt. Jacob Prickett at Scott's Mills and 2 mos. under Capt. Warman at Harrison's Fort.
Proof—Pension claim S. 32336.
Died—March 13, 1848. Buried Mt. Summit Cemetery. Government stone and S. A. R. marker placed by Patrick Henry Chapter S. A. R.
Married—Mary ——. Ch. Jesse, b. 1786, m. Sarah Hickman; Abram, b. 1790; Elizabeth, b. 1792; Frederick, b. 1796; Mary, b. 1799, d. 1802; Andrew, b. 1803, d. 1805.
Collected by Clarence H. Smith, New Castle, Indiana.

ILES, SAMUEL   Rush County
Born—Aug. 17, 1745, near Bristol, England.
Service—Volunteered May or June, 1777, at Churchill, Queen Anne Co., Md., for 9 mos. in a company under Capt. Hanokin. Was at Germantown.
Proof—Pension claim R. 5474 (Record shows him to be a deserter).
Buried—Fairview Cemetery, Union Twp. Name on tablet in Rush Co. Court House.

INGRAM, ANDREW   Floyd County
Born—1758, Fentress County, North Carolina.
Service—Enlisted Sept., 1779, in Montgomery Co., Vir., under Capt. Charles Morgan, Col. Arthur Campbell. Served 4¼ mos. in infantry and 2½ mos. in cavalry.
Proof—Pension claim S. 32338.

IRVIN (IRWIN), JENNETTE BREWSTER   Monroe County
Born—1761, Augusta Co., Virginia.
Service—A Patriot. Wove, spun, and knit to supply clothing for the soldiers.
Proof—Revolutionary services of the Brewster Sisters by Ann S. Alexander; The Maxwells, Houstons, and Allied Families.

Died—1839. Buried Cemetery on I. U. Campus, Bloomington, Ind. Stone.
Married—Samuel Irvin, a Rev. S. For children, see his record.
Collected by Mrs. Charles Emery, Bloomington, Indiana.

IRVIN (IRWIN), SAMUEL   Harrison County
Born—Feb., 1760, Virginia.
Service—With Gen. Greene in S. C. and in his retreat into Virginia. In battle of Cowpens.
Proof—History of Maxwell, Dunn, Doak, Campbell and Allied Families.
Died—Aug. 3, 1837. Buried Cedar Hill Cemetery, Corydon, Ind. Stone.
Married—Janet (Jennette) Brewster, a patriot, b. 1761. Ch. Mary, m. Joseph W. Doak; Williamson, m. Polly Davis; Bryson, m. Martha Davis; Sarah, m. William Frost; Samuel Williamson, m. Jane Doak; Jane, m. Austin Seward; James, m. Anna Davis; Elizabeth, m. Williamson Alexander.
Collected by Mrs. N. B. Mavity, French Lick, Indiana.

IRVINE, WILLIAM   Orange County
Born—Sept. 26, 1763, Halifax County, Virginia.
Service—In Halifax Co.; served 3 mos. as 1st sergeant in Capt. Peter Rogers' CO., Col. Mason's Vir. Regt. Discharged Aug. 12. This service was as a substitute for his brother Samuel. Enlisted May, 1780; 3 mos. as a wagoner in Capt. Paul Waddleton's CO., Col. Richardson's Vir. Regt. 1781, served as orderly sergeant in Capt. James Hill's CO.; was transferred to Capt. Watkin's CO., Col. Joseph Crockett's Vir. Regt., in which he acted as ensign. Was at surrender of Cornwallis and marched with British prisoners to Noland's Ferry on Potomac River, where he was discharged. In 1782, served as wagoner under Major McCray.
Proof—Pension claim S. 16422.
Died—Sept. 25, 1850. Buried Finley Cemetery, Orleans Twp. Stone.
Married—Mary —— (1775-1835). Ch. James D.; Samuel; Jane; Jesse; William W.; Martha A.; Lucinda; Nancy.
Collected by Mrs. N. B. Mavity, French Lick, Indiana.

ISHAM, GEORGE J. (or I.)   Henry County
Service—Enlisted at Colchester, Conn., for 3 yrs. and served under name of Jonathan Isham. Honorably discharged at Morristown, N. J. In battles of Stony Point, Monmouth. Wounded in left arm.
Proof—Pension claim S. 41682.
Died—Aug. 17, 1843, Henry Co., Ind.
Pension application mentions several children but no names given.

ISREAL, JOHN Johnson County
Born—1765, Albemarle County, Virginia.
Service—Enlisted in Wilkes Co., N. C., served 3 mos. from May, 1781, in Capt. Pendleton Isbel's CO., Col. Isaac's Regt., in expedition against the Tories; from Sept., 1781, 3 mos. in Capt. John Beaverly's CO., Col. Benjamin Harrington's Regt., went on an expedition against the Cherokee Indians. From Feb., 1783, 3 mos. in Capt. Finnezee's CO. of Light Horse.
Proof—Pension claim S. 17510.
Died—Last payment of pension was made Sept. 21, 1837. Buried in Hamner Cemetery. Government marker placed by Alexander Hamilton Chapter D. A. R.
Collected by Mrs. I. E. Tranter, Franklin, Indiana.

JACKSON, ANDREW Franklin County
Born—May 30, 1754, Loudoun County, Virginia.
Service—Enlisted Oct., 1779. Served 2 yrs., 5 mos. under Capt. David Scott and Col. Ivins (Evens) Vir. Line. Indian warfare. In battle of Dunkaid's Creek near Morgantown, also Fish Creek, Vir.
Proof—Pension claim R. F. 5510.
Died—April 30, 1837. Buried on what is now Franklin County Infirmary Farm, S. of Brookville, Ind. Stone.
Married—1772, Elizabeth Sargent (1754-1782). Ch. Thomas; Rachel; James, b. 1776, m. Mary Marshall; Catherine; Elizabeth, m. —— Jones.
Collected by Mrs. Leo Schultheis, Vincennes, Indiana, and Mrs. Roscoe C. O'Byrne, Brookville, Indiana.

JACKSON, JAMES Jefferson County
Born—Rutherford County, North Carolina.
Service—Pri. in Sharp's CO.; enlisted 1781. Left service April 12, 1782. Land warrant of 228 acres for 30 mos. service. Served in Salisbury Dist.
Proof—Roster of Revolutionary Soldiers of North Carolina.
Died—1846. Buried Old Cemetery, 2 miles N. W. Kent, Ind. Government stone by John Paul Chapter D. A. R.
Married—1817, Mary Arbuckle (probably this was second wife).
Collected by John Paul Chapter D. A. R.

JACKSON, SOLOMON Jefferson County
Born—Dec. 3, 1760, Warren Co., North Carolina.
Service—Pri. in CO. of Capt. White, Col. Johnson's N. C. Regt. for 18 mos. Substituted spring of 1779 for 7 mos. under Col. Lincoln, Col. Johnson, Capt. White. Drafted 1780, 7 mos. under Gen.

Gates, Gen. Green. Drafted Feb., 1781, under Gen. Green, Capt. Nazery. In the battles of Camden and Guilford Court House.
Proof—Pension claim S. 16424. Applied from Scott Co., Ind.
Died—Jan. 12, 1848.
Children—Pension application names son, Jesse. Gen. Accounting Office shows two children, James and Sarah Jackson Hogue.

JACOBS, SAMUEL   Johnson County
Born—March 23, 1760.
Service—Enlisted as a pri. in 1776, at Culpepper Court House, in Capt. Field's CO., Col. Trotter's Regt. Was in battle of Monmouth. Discharged winter of 1777.
Proof—Pension claim W. 11921.
Died—1840. Buried on Hardin Farm, Nineveh Twp. Stone.
Married—1782, Elizabeth Martin. Ch. Bennett; James; Elizabeth; Martin; Phebe; Sarah; Milburn; Julia; Frances. Second W. Lydia Groves, m. 1824. Ch. Mason; George Arnold; Amanda.
Collected by Mrs. I. E. Tranter, Franklin, Indiana.

JAMES, THOMAS   Rush County
Service—Pri. in CO. of Capt. Bupy in Md. Line, 6 mos. Enlisted July, 1776, from Baltimore. Taken prisoner at Fort Lee, escaped, taken ill, then discharged.
Proof—Pension claim S. 16423. Ind. Cert. 13804. Was a Baptist clergyman in Rush Co., Ind.
Died—The last payment of pension was made on Sept. 12, 1842.

JAMESON, THOMAS   Jefferson County
Born—Nov., 1733, York County, Pennsylvania.
Service—Took the Oath of Allegiance in Henry Co., Vir., 1777. Also served as a private.
Proof—Vir. Mag., vol. 9, pp. 152 and 414; Rev. War Records of Vir., by Brumbaugh, p. 205.
Died—1830. Buried Hebron Cemetery. Government stone placed by John Paul Chapter D. A. R.
Married—First W. unknown. Her Ch. Samuel; John; Martha; William. Second W. Hannah Taggart (1745-1830), m. 1764. Ch. Mary; Jane; Nancy (1770-1838) m. John Holcombe; Alexander; Hannah; Rhoda; Thomas (1783-1843), m. Sally Humphries.
Collected by John Paul Chapter D. A. R.

JAQUESS, JONATHAN   Posey County
Born—April 28, 1753, Middlesex County, New Jersey.
Service—Two years on land and 3 yrs. on sea. Second N. J. Regt. under Col. Sheldon. In battles of White Plains, Long Island, King's Mt. Aided in loading some vessels with rocks or stone and then

sinking them in the North River to prevent the British fleet from passing up the river. Also detailed to carry messages to and from Gen. Washington and his officers.
Proof—Report of Adjutant-General of N. J.; Stryker's Officers and Men of N. J., p. 644.
Died—June 29, 1843. Buried on Homestead one mile from Poseyville, Ind. Stone.
Married—First W. Sally Jaquess (a cousin); Second W. Esther E. Coy. Ch. Sarah; Grace; Christian; John. Third W. Rebecca Fraser Rankin (1762-1849). Ch. Garrison J., m. 1773, m. Mary Smith; Elizabeth, m. 1st Samuel Herons, 2nd Christopher Ashworth; George F., b. 1796, m. Charlotte Copeland; Rebecca, b. 1798; Pamela, b. 1800, m. Rev. John Schrader; John Wesley, b. 1801, m. Judith Smith; Ogden J., b. 1803, m. 1st Matilda Nesbet, 2nd Anna Hamilton; Fletcher, b. 1806, m. Roxanna Stewart; Asbury.
Collected by Mrs. Charles T. Johnson, Mt. Vernon, Indiana, and Gen. John Gibson Chapter D. A. R.

JEFFRIES, GOWIN   Vigo County
Born—1756, King and Queen Co., Virginia.
Service—Enlisted from King and Queen Co., Vir., for 3 yrs. as fifer in CO. of Capt. Wm. Spiller, Col. Thomas Marshall's State Artillery Regt. Discharged at Richmond, Vir., after Gen. Gates' defeat.
Proof—Pension claim S. 32341. Moved to Ind., 1847, and applied for pension from Vigo Co. Cert. No. 25326.

JENKINS, EZEKIEL   Clark County
Born—About 1763.
Service—Enlisted 1779 in April for 3 yrs., in the 4th Regt. of Vir. Troops under Gen. Morgan, Col. Stanhope, Capt. Calam. Discharged April, 1782.
Proof—Pension claim S. 16163.

JENNINGS, AUGUSTIN   Knox County
Born—Sept. 24, 1724, Virginia.
Service—Enlisted as a pri. in 12th Vir. Regt., under Col. James Wood, in Capt. Stephen Ashby's CO., Oct. 12, 1776. Served 2 yrs. and was honorably discharged Oct. 10, 1778.
Proof—Wither's Family Bible and descendants Louise Withers Lowry and Jessie R. Lowry.
Died—Dec. 18, 1786. Buried on farm in Johnson Twp., Knox Co.
Married—1748, Hannah Williams (1728-1780). Ch. Nancy, b. 1753, m. Mathew K. Withers; Jemima.
Collected by Mary Penrose Wayne Chapter D. A. R.

JENNINGS, ISREAL Lawrence County
Born—March 10, 1752.
Died—Jan. 4, 1841. Buried Mt. Zion Cemetery. Inscription on stone reads "Soldier 1776."
Collected by Mrs. Ellen Hoover, Bedford, Indiana.

JERAULD, DR. GORTON Gibson County
Born—Feb. 22, 1752, East Greenwich, Rhode Island.
Service—Surgeon First Battalion Rhode Island Militia, 1780-83.
Proof—"Samuel Groton, His Life and Times. A History of Providence and Rhode Island," by Adelas Groton, p. 270.
Died—July 5, 1822. Buried Warnock Cemetery, Princeton, Ind. Stone.
Married—First W. Elizabeth Stafford. Second W., 1778, Phoebe Rice, b. 1757. Ch. Henry, b. 1779, m. Lucy Arnold; John, b. 1780, m. Nancy Westcott; Edward Gorton, b. 1782, m. Sophie Baker; Sylvester, b. 1783, d. 1803; Elizabeth, b. 1786, m. Werdon Underwood; Candace, b. 1790, m. Gordon Byron Bingham; William, b. 1793, m. Ada Bucklin; Phebe Ann, b. 1797, m. Charles Harrington; Duty, b. 1799, m. Ruth Ann Waters; Sylvester Tiffany, b. 1804, m. Irene Harrington.
Collected by Gen. John Gibson Chapter D. A. R.

JESTER, NIMROD Wayne County
Born—Oct. 15, 1762.
Service—While residing in Guilford Co., N. C., he enlisted April, 1780, and served 3 mos. as a pri. in Capt. John McDow's N. C. CO. In battle of Camden. Enlisted Sept., 1780, and served 6 wks. as a pri. in Capt. John Gillespie's CO. of Light Horse, Col. Daniel Gillespie's N. C. Regt. Served 2 mos. in Capt. Philip's N. C. CO. Late in 1781 served 1 mo. in Capt. Salathiel Martin's N. C. CO. Enlisted 1782 and served 1 yr. in Capt. Charles Gordon's CO., Col. Armstrong's N. C. Regt. He guarded prisoners at Salisbury, N. C., for 3 mos.
Proof—Pension claim W. 275999.
Died—Oct. 8, 1854. Buried Mt. Zion Cemetery, Williamsburg, Wayne County.
Married—1841, Mary Bishop.
Collected by Mrs. Paul L. Ross, Richmond, Indiana.

JINES, JACOB Jefferson County
Born—1764.
Service—Served as a fifer in Rev. Was wounded while marching to meet Gen. Ross.
Proof—Biographical Souvenir of Jeff. Co., Ind., p. 234.

Died—Aug. 8, 1864. Buried Marble Church graveyard, Monroe Twp. Stone.
Married—Elizabeth —— (1778-1857). Son, Silas, b. 1812.
Collected by John Paul Chapter D. A. R.

JOHN, JEHU   Franklin County
Born—Dec. 2, 1759, Chester Co., Pennsylvania.
Service—Served as pri. in Capt. John Scott's CO., Lieut. Col. John Gardner's Penn. Regt.
Proof—Lineage, vol. 102, p. 65.
Died—Jan. 30, 1837. Buried Brookville Cemetery. Stone.
Married—1781, Eliza David (1763-1846). Ch. Elizabeth, b. 1799, m. Bethual Franklin Morris; Robert; Enoch D.; Jehu, Jr.; Isaac.

JOHNS, HENRY   Boone County
Born—April 21, 1757, in Wales.
Service—Pri. in a company designated at various times as Capt. John Hunter's CO., and Capt. Thomas Lucas' CO., in Col. Wm. Malcom's Regt., Cont'l Troops. Enlisted Aug., 1777, for period of war. His name is last borne on muster roll of the late Capt. Lucas' CO. under Lieut. A. Neely for May, 1778, dated June 15, 1778. Records do not show from which state he entered service but the officers mentioned were from N. Y.
Proof—Office of Adjutant-General; War Department
Died—March 26, 1833. Buried Johns Cemetery, Union Twp., Boone Co. Stone.
Married—First W. unknown, except she was born in Wales. Son, George. Second W. Nancy Duncan. Ch. Joseph; John; Frank; Renny; Robert, b. 1803, d. 1846; Jacob, b. 1801, m. Harriet Stevens; Elizabeth, b. 1791, m. Jesse Lane.
Collected by Mrs. C. M. McClaine, Lebanon, Indiana.

JOHNSON, ABRAHAM   Sullivan County
Born—Oct., 1754, Hampshire Co., Virginia.
Service—Served near 6 mos. as Capt. under Col. Stephen Riddle, Major Vanmeter, Gen. McIntosh, in 1777. In 1781 about 2 mos. as Capt. under Col. Elias Posten, Major John Higgins, Vir. Line.
Proof—Pension claim S. 16427.
Died—Aug., 1833. Buried in a field near Bethlehem Cemetery.
Married—Elizabeth Bogardus. Ch. Abraham; Peter; John; Elizabeth; Ruth; Bailey.
Collected by Mrs. Elizabeth Pirtle, Sullivan, Indiana.

JOHNSON, ARCHIBALD   Washington County
Born—June 18, 1763, North Carolina.
Service—Served as a "droven" in the Revolutionary War, as certified
    by the Historical Commission of N. C.
Proof—North Carolina Historical Commission; D. A. R. No. 235553;
    Will and Cemetery Records of Washington Co., Ind.
Died—Feb. 2, 1822. Buried Pugh Cemetery N. of Salem, Ind. Stone.
Married—1782, Mary Idol. Ch. William; Elizabeth; Henry; Cloy;
    Grace; Francis; Nancy; Mary; Archibald; Sarah; Martha; John.
Collected by Mrs. Joseph Cummings, Brownstown, Indiana.

JOHNSON, DANIEL   Clark County
Born—Nov., 1763, Maryland.
Service—Pri. in Capt. William Winter's CO. of Militia, 26th Battalion,
    Charles Co., Md. Pri. in 8th Class, in Capt. Parramore's CO.,
    Worcester Co., Militia, Md., 1780.
Proof—Manuscript Revolutionary War Militia List in the Library of
    the Maryland Historical Society.
Died—May 31, 1847. Buried Old Cemetery near New Washington,
    Clark Co. Stone.
Married—First two wives unknown. Ch. McKinley; Anna, m. ——
    Long. Third W. Elizabeth Mosley. Ch. Alfred, b. 1820, m. Nancy
    Robbins; James; Mary, m. Allen Deputy; Priscilla, b. 1827, m.
    Samuel Robbins; Gideon, m. 1st Martha Wilson, 2nd Mary Duke,
    3rd Eliza Duke.
Collected by Mrs. Wm. R. Sellers, Franklin, Indiana.

JOHNSON, DAVID   Jackson County
Born—Oct. 10, 1759 or 1760, Frederick Co., Virginia.
Service—Served under Col. Shelby, Maj. Thomas Quirk, Capt. Thomas
    Martin.
Proof—Pension claim S. 32349.

JOHNSON, HENSON   Harrison County
Born—Feb. 25, 1763, Frederick Co., Virginia.
Service—Drafted 3 mos. Virginia Militia, before Cornwallis surrendered,
    under Capt. Bell. In Feb., drafted, Capt. Reynolds, Col. Willis
    Regt. Marched to Winchester Barracks to guard provisions, then
    to Philadelphia to guard British prisoners. Enlisted again under
    Capt. Frost, Col. Edmonds in Vir. State Line; marched to join
    Gen. Lafayette at Richmond.
Proof—Pension claim S. 16171, B. L. Wt. 26778-160-55.
Died—Jan. 9, 1858. Buried Blunk Cemetery near Elizabeth, Harrison
    County.

Married—Jane ———— (1772-1846), m. 1798. Ch. Elizabeth, b. 1810, m.
John Lemmon; Amos, b. 1810, m. Charlotte Shuck; Nellie; Levi;
Anna; John; Mary.
Collected by Mrs. Margaret Ordner, Corydon, Indiana.

JOHNSON, JAMES   Knox County
Born—1745, probably in Virginia.
Service—"I give to my son James my library of books, my rifle, guns,
and powder horn. I give the powder horn, not because of its
value, but because it was carried by his grandfather, James
Johnson, in and during the whole of the Revolutionary War, and
is a silent witness of many of the hardest fought battles." From
the will of John Johnson, still in existence, and also a copy in Knox
County Records, signed July 10, 1817. Powder horn still
preserved.
Died—April 7, 1817. Buried Indiana Church Cemetery, Harrison Twp.,
Knox Co. Stone.
Married—Margaret ————, d. 1825. Ch. John, b. 1776, d. 1817, m.
Margaret.
Collected by Mrs. S. G. Davenport, Vincennes, Indiana.

JOHNSON, JAMES   Ripley County
Born—About 1760.
Service—Enlisted spring 1782 in Vir., in company of Lieut. John
Harres of Vir. Cont'l Line commanded by Gen. Steuben at Point
Fort on James River. In same year he re-enlisted in Light Dragoon Service, under Col. Wm. Washington; continued in service
until 1784. Received bounty land.
Proof—Pension claim S. 36664, B. L. Wt. 1963-100.
Died—After 1843. Buried Cliff Hill Cemetery, Johnson Twp., Ripley
Co., on an Indian mound near center of cemetery (S. A. R.
Records).
Children—Mary; Sarah; Nancy; Able.

JOHNSON, JOHN   Fulton County
Born—May 14, 1762, Hanover Co., Virginia.
Service—In Feb., 1779, drafted in Capt. John Anderson's CO.; served
3 mos. In fall of 1780, drafted in Capt. John Dandridge's CO.,
3 mos. In Aug., 1781, drafted in Capt. John White's CO., 2 mos.,
20 days. Was at the siege of York.
Proof—Office of Adjutant General, War Department. Applied for pension from Marion County, Ind.
Died—Aug. 7, 1860. Buried Shelton Cemetery, S. of Rochester, Ind.
Stone.
Dau.—Elizabeth, m. Thomas Shelton.
Collected by Mrs. Emma E. Bitters, Rochester, Indiana.

JOHNSON, OTHNIEL Fayette County
Born—About 1755.
Service—Belonged to the company commanded by Capt. Joseph Bloomfield in the Regt. of Col. Elias Dayton. Enlisted from Cumberland Co., N. J., in March, 1776. Discharged May, 1777, at Morristown, N. J.
Proof—Pension claim No. 41709.
Buried—Orange Twp.
Children—Lawrence; Lewis; Mary; Eunice.

JOHNSON, PHILIP Jennings County
Born—1758, in Scotland or Virginia.
Service—Enlisted at Hale's Hole, Essex Co., Vir., April, 1777, and served for 6 years as matross in Capt. James Pendleton's CO. In battles of Monmouth, Stony Point, Gates' Defeat, and Petersburg.
Proof—Pension claim S. 36657.
Died—July 11, 1835. Buried on West Bank of Big Otter Creek, in an old garden on farm now owned by Mat Kibler, Jennings Co.
Married—1782, Susannah —— (1766-1834). Ch. Jane, b. 1783; William M., b. 1786 (War of 1812); Giles, b. 1788; Elizabeth, b. 1791; James R., b. 1793; Lemmy S., b. 1795; Joel W., b. 1798; Mary, b. 1800; Berry, b. 1802; Lankston, b. 1804; Clement, b. 1807.
Collected by Mrs. I. E. Tranter, Franklin, Indiana.

JOHNSON, ROBERT Pike County
Born—Feb. 2, 1750, Virginia.
Service—Enlisted in Sept., 1775, in Greenbrier Co., Vir., and served 1 yr. under Capt. Albie Chile, Major John Newal. Discharged at Ft. Randolph, Vir.
Proof—Pension claim rejected for want of witnesses.
Died—Aug. 1, 1835. Buried in Johnson graveyard, S. of Petersburg, Indiana.
Married—Martha Ralston (1765-1835). Ch. Elizabeth; Rebecca, m. Wm. Coleman; Patsy; Peggy; Mary, m. James Kinman; Sarah; Robert, Jr., b. 1803, m. Caroline McClannahan; Nancy, b. 1806, m. Thomas English.
Collected by Cradle of Liberty Chapter D. A. R.

JOHNSON, ROSWELL Ripley County
Born—Aug. 14, 1769, Montgomery Co., Virginia.
Service—Drummer-boy with the Vir. Troops in the Continental Army for 3 mos. in 1782.
Proof—Family records furnished by Mrs. Otto F. Thum, 677 S. Sherman, Denver, Colo.
Died—July 14, 1837. Buried near Versailles, Ind. Stone and bronze tablet placed by Ripley Co. Historical Society.

Married—Polly Barnet. Had 17 children. These names obtained—
Sarah Jane, m. Obed Wilson; John; Wesley J.; Eliza Baker; Bettie
Cole; Betsey Pate; Amanda Blackwell.
Collected by Mrs. A. B. Wycoff, Batesville, Indiana.

JOHNSTON, JAMES   Carroll County
Born—Oct. 5, 1755, on the Delaware River.
Service—Volunteered from Mecklenburg Co., N. C., 1780, under Capt.
Samuel Flanegin. Fought in S. C. in battle of Hanging Rock.
Enlisted 1781, under James Osburn, Col. Hobert Ervine, Regt. of
riflemen.
Proof—Pension claim S. 16168. Applied in Carroll Co., Ind., March 16,
1835, for transfer from Tenn. to Ind. Rolls. Had a son.
Died—Last payment of pension was made on April 28, 1838.

JOHNSTON, THOMAS   Ripley or Dearborn County
Born—1755.
Service—Enlisted April, 1777, in Capt. Henry McKinley's CO., Col.
Cook's Regt., Penn. Line, on the Continental Establishment; was
wounded in his left leg Oct. 4, 1777, while in the battle of Germantown, was moved to Bethlehem Hospital for 3 mos. then to
Shavertown Hospital, Lancaster Co., Penn., for 3 mos., then to
Lebanon, Penn., where he was employed in preparing ammunition
cartridges. Discharged April, 1780.
Proof—Pension claim W. 10158.
Died—May, 1823. Buried either in Ripley or Dearborn Co. Soldier
applied and received pension while living in Dearborn Co. Name
is on bronze tablet in Versailles Court House.
Married—1793, Sarah Foster (1777-1846). Ch. Nancy; Isaac; James;
Wayne; Nathaniel; Thomas; Elizabeth Rider.
Collected by Mrs. A. B. Wycoff, Batesville, Indiana.

JONES, DAVID   Jefferson County
Born—1759, King George Co., Virginia.
Service—Enlisted in Aug. or Sept., 1776, as pri. in Capt. Matthew
Arbuckle's Vir. CO. and was stationed at Point Pleasant for about
2 yrs., after which he enlisted in Capts. Dawson's and Heath's
CO., Col. Gibson's Vir. Regt., at Fort Pitt and was discharged
at expiration of service of 1 yr., 17 days.
Proof—Pension claim W. 10050.
Died—May 6, 1836. Buried in Indian Kentuck Cemetery near Canaan,
Jeff. Co. Government marker placed by John Paul Chapter
D. A. R.
Married—Rebecca Rutherford. Ch. Sarah, m. John G. Ryker; David.
Collected by John Paul Chapter D. A. R.

JONES, EPAPHRAS Floyd County
Born—Feb. 10, 1764.
Service—Enlisted 1777, in Hartford Co., Conn., 3 yrs. as pri. under Capt. Thos. Woster, Col. Sam. B. Webb, Lieut. Col. Wm. Livingston, Maj. Ebenezer Huntington, Conn. Line.
Proof—Pension claim S 16789.
Died—Feb. 14, 1847. Buried Jones Burial Ground, now abandoned.
Married—First W. —— in New England. Second W. Ann Sillman.
Collected by Mrs. V. R. Conner, New Albany, Indiana.

JONES, FRANCIS Wayne County
Born—1763 or 1768.
Service—States he was in the company commanded by Henry Sharpe, Col. Archibald Lytle's N. C. Regt.
Proof—Pension claim S. 36653. Moved to Wayne Co., Ind., 1839, to live with children.
Died—Jan. 31, 1841.
Married—Christiana ——.

JONES, JAMES Spencer County
Born—July 4, 1760, York County, Pennsylvania.
Service—Sept., 1778, volunteered as pri. in Capt. Wm. Wilson's CO., Col. Francis Loche's N. C. Regt. Discharged March 10, 1779. Summer and fall, 1780, served a tour of 3 mos. in Capt. Thos. Cowan's CO. In 1781, 3 mos. under Capt. Richard Simmons' CO., Col. Smith's Regt.
Proof—Miss Bonnie J. Jones, a descendant, Rockport, Ind.
Died—Sept. 22, 1851. Buried in a field near Dale, Ind.
Married—1783 Susanna Kinkaid. Ch. John W.; James; Jessie; Gilbert; William K.; Andrew; Thomas; Hannah; Mary Ann; Susan; Elizabeth; Kate; Jennie.
Collected by Miss Bonnie J. Jones, Rockport, Indiana.

JONES, MATTHEW Hendricks County
Born—March 18, 1758, Southampton Co., Virginia.
Service—Enlisted Aug., 1778, as pri. under Cols. Goskins, Wells and Dick; 6 wks. in 1778, 18 wks. in 1779, 8 wks. in 1780, 6 wks. in 1781, in all 9 mos. Was in battle of Petersburg, Vir., and at the surrender of Cornwallis.
Proof—Pension claim S. 32348.
Died—July 18, 1836. Buried Baptist Cemetery at Center Valley. Stone.
Married—Mary Crump (or Crumpler), 1768-1826. Ch. Thomas, b. 1785 (oldest son); John; Berryman.
Collected by Mrs. A. E. Austin, 215 Third Street, Woodburn, Oregon.

JONES, RICHARD LORD Floyd County
Born—May 15, 1767, Colchester, Connecticut.
Service—A fifer in CO. under Capt. Watson in Col. S. B. Webb's Conn. Line, for a term of 3 yrs., from June 20, 1777, to June 20, 1780.
Proof—Pension claim W. 765, B. L. Wt. 5469-160-55.
Died—July 23, 1852. Buried Fairview Cemetery, New Albany, Ind. Stone.
Married—1806, Elizabeth Clark (1776-1871). Ch. Pensioner states he had four daughters and one son. Only name given is Sarah, m. —— O'Conner.
Collected by Mrs. V. R. Conner, New Albany, Indiana.

JONES, THOMAS Putnam County
Born—About 1745.
Service—Enlisted fall of 1775. 3 yrs. as pri. under Capts. William Fontaine and Clough Shelton and Col. Stevens, Virginia Militia. Discharged at Norristown, Penn., 1779. In battles of Brandywine, Germantown.
Proof—Pension claim S. 36656.
Died—Last payment of pension was in 1837. Buried on Burton farm, Madison Twp.
Collected by Miss Minnetta Wright, Greencastle, Indiana.

JONES, THOMAS Spencer County
Born—1751.
Service—Enlisted under Capt. Kirkpatrick from Virginia.
Proof—Mrs. A. J. Wedeking, a descendant, Dale, Ind.
Died—1832. Buried Brown Cemetery near Dale, Ind.
Married—Ann Thompson. Ch. Mary; Lawrence; John; Sarah; Nellie; Margaret; Martha; Thompson; Hannah.
Collected by Miss Laura Wright, Rockport, Indiana.

JONES, WILLIAMSON Morgan County
Born—1759, Essex Co., Virginia.
Service—Enlisted 1776, as fifer in Caroline Co., Vir., under Gen. Nelson, Col. Mathews, Capt. Daniel Coleman.
Proof—Pension claim S. 17516. He had two brothers, James and John.

JUDD, JOB Dearborn County
Born—Oct. 21, 1757, Farmington, Connecticut.
Service—While living in Farmington, he enlisted in the Conn. State Troops, Jan., 1780, under Gen. Waterbury, Maj. Shipman, Capt. Matthews, Lieut. Goodin and Ensign Hotchkiss.
Proof—Pension claim W. 10160, B. L. Wt. 26116-160-55.

Died—July 23, 1846. Buried Bright, Dearborn Co. Stone. Bronze tablet placed by Col. Archibald Lochry Chapter D. A. R.
Married—1782, Mary Andrew, b. 1757. Ch. Joseph, 1787; Mary, b. 1789; Job, b. 1790; Phinehas (1792-1830), m. Elizabeth Coverdale; Sally, b. 1794; Orrin, b. 1796; Prue; Selah; Roswell and Susannah, b. 1802.
Collected by Mrs. Walter Kerr, Aurora, Indiana.

JUDD, JOHN   Parke County
Born—About 1761.
Service—Served in Regt. of Conn. Line commanded by Elisha Sheldon of the Light Dragoons in the 4th CO., under Capt. Halbert, afterwards the 6th CO., under Capt. Staunton and Lieut. Bull. Discharged June, 1783.
Proof—Pension claim W. 26707.
Died—April 3, 1826, in Parke Co., Ind.
Married—1793, Hannah —— (1775-1840). Ch. Lyman, b. 1793; Ariel; John; Hannah, m. —— Faircloe; George; Mary, m. —— Goble.

JUSTICE, JAMES   Fayette County
Born—May 15, 1751, Cumberland Co., Pennsylvania.
Service—Enlisted July 1, 1776, as pri. in James McConnell's CO., Cols. Stewart and Clark from Cumberland Co., Penn. Enlisted Aug., 1777, in Thomas Ashey's CO., Col. Clark. Enlisted 1778 in Matthew Jack's CO., Col. Brodhead. In battles of Trenton and Brandywine.
Proof—Pension claim S. 16898. Penn Archives, 5th Series, vol. 6, p. 605.
Died—Oct. 17, 1843. Buried Schillinger farm, S. of Connersville, Ind.
Married—1787, Nancy Campbell. Ch. John, m. Rose Hood; James; Joseph, 1792-1858, m. Deliah Fuell; Thomas; Hannah, m. John Egan.
Collected by Olde Towne Chapter D. A. R.

KEESLING, (KEISLING, KIESLING), JOHN   Henry County
Born—March 25, 1758.
Service—Enlisted at Reading, Berk's Co., Penn., and served with Penn. troops as follows: from Sept., 1776, 2 mos. in Capt. Jacob Whetstone's CO. as substitute for his father, Jacob; from Nov., 1776, 2 mos. in Capt. Lindemoot's CO., Col. Hiester's Regt.; in 1777, 2 mos. in Capt. Lindemoot's CO., and in 1779 2 mos. as wagoner.
Proof—Pension claim S. 16434 and Penn. Archives, 5th Series, vol. 5, p. 240.
Died—Dec. 25, 1840. Buried Fatic Cemetery, Fall Creek Twp. Government stone.

Married—First W. 1788, Eve Miller (1765-1806). Ch. Jacob, b. 1789, m. Catherine Sheffer; Elizabeth, b. 1791, m. John Raper; Catherine, b. 1792, m. Daniel Sheffer; Mary, b. 1795, m. Benjamin Fisher; John, b. 1796, m. Linna Bulla; Daniel, b. 1797, m. Catherine Zeek; Peter, b. 1800, m. first to Nancy Bosworth, second to Margaret Broombaugh; George, b. 1804, m. Elizabeth Miller; Susanna, b. 1806, m. Adam Carter.
Collected by Indiana S. A. R. and John Conner Chapter D. A. R.

KEIPHART (KEPHART), GEORGE   Jackson County
Born—About 1754, Maryland.
Service—He enlisted in 1776 and served 1 yr. as a pri. in Capt. George Strickler's CO. in Col. Smallwood's Maryland Regt., and was in the battles of Long Island and White Plains. He enlisted Feb. 22, 1776, and served in Capt. Bowyer's CO. in Col. Weltner's Regt., and was in a battle at Catherinetown on the Tioga River, length of this service 3 yrs.
Proof—Pension claim S. 36673.
Died—Aug. 18, 1824.
Married—Margaret ——, 64 yrs. old in 1820.

KEITH, ALEXANDER   In Indiana
Born—1746.
Service—Enlisted in fall of 1775 as pri. in Capt. Morgan Alexander's CO., Col. Alexander Spottswood's 2nd Vir. Regt., later in Capt. Marquis Calme's CO. until the close of war.
Died—May 14, 1828. In 1820 he was living in Orange Co., Ind., was one of the early settlers of N. West Twp. He died in State Prison at Jeffersonville, Ind. Letters of adm. were granted to David Jones by Clerk of Circuit Court of Crawford Co., Ind., on July 28, 1828. Arrears of pension due paid at Agent's office, Corydon, Ind., on Sept. 27, 1828, to David Jones.
Proof—Pension claim S. 36672.
Married—Phebe ——. Ch. Polly; Nancy; James; Susannah.
Collected by Mrs. N. B. Mavity, French Lick, Indiana.

KEITHLEY, JOHN   Harrison County
Born—Jan. 1, 1755, Germany.
Service—A Patriot. Gave service by hauling supplies for the army from N. C. through Penn.
Proof—D. A. R. No. 153574.
Died—July 28, 1835, Harrison Co., Ind.

Married—1781, Mary Ann Riblen. Ch. Catherine, b. 1783; Elizabeth, b. 1784; Anna, b. 1786; John, b. 1788; Polly, b. 1789; Sarah, b. 1790; Rachel, b. 1793; James, b. 1796; Joseph, b. 1799; Susannah, b. 1801; William, b. 1803; Jacob, b. 1805.
Collected by Mrs. Ruth Stewart, Brookville, Indiana.

KELLAR, DEVAULT   Morgan County
Born—1749, Germany.
Service—Enlisted 1776. Served 4 yrs. 6 mos. as pri. in S. C. Troops under Col. Beard and Capt. Waters. Parents came to Charleston, S. C., 1755. He resided in S. C., N. C., Vir., Ky., Washington Co. and Morgan Co., Ind.
Proof—Pension claim S. 32358.
Died—Last payment of pension was made on April 5, 1844.

KELLEY, JOSHUA   Owen County
Born—1751, Maryland.
Service—About July 13, 1775, enrolled in Baltimore Co., Md., under Capt. Isaac Hammond, Lt. Samuel Merryman, Maj. Chas. Carmand, Col. Thos. Guest. At the end of year Christopher Owens was elected Capt. by the company and Joshua Kelly, Ensign. He served as Ensign 4 yrs.
Proof—Pension claim R. 21706, rejected.
Died—Buried on his farm N. of Spencer, Ind. Not marked.

KELLY, ELIAS   Clark County
Born—Aug. 3, 1762, Newcastle Co., Delaware.
Service—Served as pri. in Penn. Line, 1778, under Capt. Enoch for 6 mos.
Proof—Pension claim S. 16175. Moved to Clark Co., Indiana Territory, 1791.
Died—Last payment of pension was made on Sept. 9, 1843.

KELLY (KELLEY), WILLIAM   Spencer County
Born—Jan. 10, 1760, Virginia.
Service—Entered service at age of 16 on eastern shore of Virginia under Col. Simpson, who died and was succeeded by his son Selby or Shelby Simpson, Maj. Wm. Young, Capt. Richard Justinson (Justis). After close of war he lived in Virginia, then Maryland, then Kentucky and on to Indiana.
Died—March 18, 1846, Spencer Co., Ind.
Children—William, Jr.; Jacob; Elizabeth Ruble.
Proof—All found in pension application 5833, rejected.

KELLY (KELLEY), WILLIAM   Switzerland County
Born—Nov. 2, 1755, Chester Co., Penn.
Service—Pri. in Virginia Militia, 9 mos. from 1777, Capt. Baldwin, Col. Steele. Resided in Winchester, Vir., when he enlisted.
Proof—Pension claim W. 10165.
Died—Jan. 21, 1834, Posey Twp., Switzerland Co. Probably buried Lostutter Cemetery.
Married—1786, Sarah Preysor. Ch. Nancy, b. April 13, 1787; Catherine, b. Dec. 30, 1789; Mary Ann, b. Feb. 17, 1792; Elizabeth, b. Sept. 20, 1795; Thomas (m. Dorthea) and Rachel, b. July 31, 1798; Lydia Ann, b. Nov. 11, 1800, m. 1824 Wm. Hess; William, b. March 26, 1802, m. Sept. 6, 1837, Mirea Craig.
Collected by Mrs. O. V. Danner, Vevay, Indiana.

KELSEY, THOMAS   Dearborn County
Born—March 12, 1754, New York.
Service—Enlisted Ulster Co., N. Y., May, 1776, served 7 mos. Capt. Samuel Clark's CO. Re-enlisted in 1777, served 7 mos. in Capt. Peleg Ransom's CO., Col. Pawling's Regt.
Proof—Pension claim S. 2687.
Died—April 30, 1834. Buried near Cole Chapel, near Dillsboro, Ind. Stone. Bronze tablet placed by Col. Archibald Lochry Chapter D. A. R.
Married—Eunice Thomas St. John. Ch. Mathew; Eliphalet; Susan; Thomas; Sarah; Eunice; Rebecca; John; Daniel, m. Eunice Cole; Joseph.
Collected by Mrs. W. M. Green, Rising Sun, Indiana.

KELSO, ALEXANDER, JR.   Morgan County
Born—March 30, 1758, Augusta, Virginia.
Service—Pri. in N. C. Militia under Cols. Richardson, Shelby, Sevier and Dorothy, Capts. John Bartley, Maxwell and Hubbard.
Proof—Pension claim W. 9493.
Died—Sept. 1, 1835. Buried Morgantown, Ind.
Married—1721, Margaret Balch (1752-1848). Son, James Balch, 1796-1876.

KEMP, REUBEN   Crawford County
Born—1754.
Service—Enlisted as pri. under Capt. Edward Worthington, Col. George Rogers Clark, in Vir. Line.
Proof—Pension claim S. 16901.
Died—1834. Buried Sheckle's graveyard on Little Blue River N. of Alton, Ind. Government marker placed by George R. Wilson.

Married—First to Patsy ——. Ch. Virginia Jane; Samuel; Reuben; William, b. 1874; Charles; Polly Ann; Henry, b. 1804. Second W. ——. Ch. Asa; Solomon, b. 1806. (Mrs. Isabell Kemp Simmons, age 97, of Holland, Ind., 1937, is a granddaughter.)
Collected by Robert Kemp, Holland, Indiana (a descendant).

KENDRICK, HETH   Jennings County
Born—Dec. 22, 1764, Brattleboro, Vt.
Service—Enlisted Brattleboro, Vt., June, 1780, as a substitute for his father, Lemuel Kendrick. Served under Col. Wm. Fletcher, Capt. James Blakely, Lt. Cochran.
Proof—Pension claim S. 16176.
Died—Aug. 24, 1843.
Pension application names Maj. Kendrick as soldier's heir.

KEPLER, JOHN   Randolph County
Born—1763, Sweden.
Service—Pri. in Capt. John Arndt's CO., 1st Battalion, Northampton Co., Penn., Militia.
Proof—D. A. R. Lineage, vol. 137. Cemetery record in Randolph Co. history 1882, p. 128.
Died—Jan. 24, 1848. Buried Pleasant Ridge Cemetery, West River Twp.
Married—Helen De Avarie. Ch. John Long, 1804-86.
Collected by Mrs. Oren E. Ross, Winchester, Indiana.

KEPLER, MATTHIAS   Wayne County
Born—1726, Germany.
Service—April 8, 1776, enlisted in Capt. Andrew Long's CO. of Penn. Rifle Regt. under Col. Miles, served in French and Indian War and was with the Virginia Troops under Washington at Braddock's defeat.
Proof—Penn. Archives, 5th Series, vol. 2, pp. 435 and 437; History of Wayne Co., Ind. (1884), p. 575; Young's History of Wayne Co., p. 241.
Died—1822. Buried family graveyard on old Kepler Farm, Harrison Twp. Son, Peter, m. Elizabeth Shafer.
Collected by Mrs. Paul L. Ross, Richmond, Indiana.

KERR, WILLIAM   Dearborn County
Born—June 2, 1756.
Service—While residing in Guilford Co., N. C., he enlisted and served as a substitute for his brother David, 18 mos. in Capt. Patrick McGibbony's CO., Col. Alexander Martin's N. C. Regt.; soon after his discharge he enlisted and served 6 wks. in Capt. Arthur Forbe's CO., Col. James Martin's N. C. Regt., later served 3 or 4 mos. in Col. Jon Paisley's N. C. Regt.

Proof—Pension claim R. 5892, rejected for failure to prove 6 mos. service. Military Record No. 174435; History of Dearborn Co.
Died—Jan. 1, 1843. Buried Ebenezer Cemetery, Manchester Twp. Government marker and bronze tablet placed by Col. Archibald Lochry Chapter D. A. R.
Married—1784, Elizabeth Aiken (1757-1814). Ch. Jane, b. 1785, m. Wm. Brown; David, 1787-1870, m. Sarah Flake; Mary, b. 1789, m. —— McBride; Catherine, b. 1791; Robert, b. 1793; John, 1795-1874; William Akin, b. 1797; Walter, 1799-1900, m. Elizabeth Russell; Nancy, b. 1806.
Collected by Mrs. Walter Kerr, Aurora, Indiana, and Mrs. H. S. McKee, Greensburg, Indiana.

KERSEY, JOHN   Boone County
Born—March 11, 1764, Pittsylvania Co., Virginia.
Service—Enlisted from Lexington Station, Ky., about Sept. 1, 1780. Served 2 yrs. 2 mos. as pri. in Capt. Robert Patterson's CO., Col. Daniel Boone's Vir. Regt. and in Capt. Wm. McConnell's CO. In skirmishes against the Indians.
Proof—Pension claim S. 16435. Pension allowed Nicholas Co., Ky., 1832, then transferred to Boone Co., Ind.
Died—Last payment of pension was made on Sept. 27, 1852.

KESLER, JACOB   Tippecanoe County
Born—July 14, 1757.
Service—Enlisted in York Co., Penn.
Proof—Indiana Magazine of History, vol. VIII, p. 15.
Died—Aug. 12, 1843. Buried Coe Cemetery, Laramie Twp. Stone.
Married—Katherine ——. Son, George.
Collected by General De Lafayette Chapter D. A. R.

KESTLER, FREDERICK   Clark County
Born—1760, Lancaster Co., Penn.
Service—Pri. for 20 mos. from 1776 in Penn. and Vir. Militia under Capt. John Clarke, Regt. of Col. Potter.
Proof—Pension claim S. 16177.
Died—March 9, 1836.
Married—Catherine ——, d. 1837. Ch. Susannah Giltner; Samuel; Emanuel.

KEVER (McKEVER), JAMES   Franklin County
Born—1759, Ireland.
Service—During the Rev. War he was living on Bush River in Ninety-Six District, S. C. He was taken prisoner by the British and held from April to June, when he made his escape and reached

the Army under command of Gen. Greene. He volunteered and served from July, 1780, to Sept., 1780, as a pri. in Capt. George Dockin's S. C. CO. Was in battle of Camden. Volunteered in Dec., 1781, served 6 mos. as a ranger in Capt. Hugh Leaton's (Seaton) S. C. CO.
Proof—Pension claim W. 10166.
Died—Oct. 15, 1835, Franklin Co., Ind.
Married—1791, Jane Craig. Ch. Mary, b. 1791; Elinor, b. 1795; Sary, b. 1806; John, b. 1808.
Collected by Mrs. Roy Bogner, Washington, Indiana.

KEYTE, JOHN   Washington County
Born—Oct. 20, 1755, Essex Co., N. J.
Service—Pri. under Capt. Hendrick Smock, Col. Michael S. Taylor. Enlisted again in June, 1778, under Burrows of N. J., Col. David Trumen. Captured and carried to New York, held prisoner 8 mos. Enlisted again at Chaptauk, Md., in April, 1781, and served 9 mos. under Capt. John Cain, Col. Henry Downs of Md.
Proof—Pension claim S. 32354; Steven's History of Washington Co.
Died—Feb. 13, 1834. Buried Mill Creek Cemetery, Washington Twp. Government marker placed by G. A. R.
Married—1782, first to Elizabeth Carter. Ch. Jesse; Hosea; Nathan; Louis (1790-1852), m. Catherine Colglazier; Hiram; Icabod; Joel; Emily Jane, m. Jacob Colglazier; Margaret Ann, m. John Gaskins, soldier; m. second to Sally Carnes, 1827.
Collected by Mrs. Harvey Morris, Salem, Indiana.

KILGORE, CHARLES, JR.   Daviess County
Born—Jan. 4, 1764, Orange Co., N. C.
Service—Enlisted in Washington Co., Vir., in 1778, 6 wks. in Capt. Joseph Martin's CO.; summer of 1779, 3 mos. in Capt. Snoddy's CO.; spring of 1781, 2 mos. in Capt. Cowan's CO.; from March, 1782, 6 wks. in Capt. Cowan's CO. and on an expedition against the Cherokee Indians.
Proof—Pension claim W. 7994.
Died—Nov. 28, 1844. Buried Kilgore Cemetery near Ragesville, Ind. Stone.
Married—Avarilla Simpson, 1766-1857. Ch. Hiram, b. 1790, m. Nancy Grant; Reuben, b. 1795, m. Catherine Veale Arrell; Stephen, m. Catherine Fulkerson; Charles, d. 1884, m. Lucy Ann Pence; Simpson, m. Christianna ——; John, m. Locia Angeline Williams; Winnie, m. Joseph Lee.
Collected by Mrs. Roy Bogner, Washington, Indiana.

KIMBAL, JESSE   Gibson County
Born—March 19, 1760, Preston, Conn.
Service—Served under Capt. Adam Shapely at New London, Conn. Served 3 mos. of his brother Samuel's time, who was home on sick leave. Application for pension rejected because he did not serve 6 mos.
Proof—The Kimball Family; vol. 18, Ind. Magazine of History. Family Bible.
Died—Nov. 18, 1857. Buried Kimball graveyard near Owensville, Ind. Stone.
Married—1794, second to Elizabeth Roelofson, d. 1843. Ch. Mary, b. 1794, m. Jas. Gates; Sarah, b. 1796; Elisha, m. Mary Boyle; Amy, b. 1799, died young; Margaret; Esther, m. Sam Miller; Isaac, m. Phillis Low; Cynthia, 1809-1845, m. Ephriam Knowles; Enoch, m. Sarah Boyle; Mahalah.
Collected by Gen. John Gibson Chapter D. A. R. and G. W. Courter, 8818 Nelson St., New Orleans, Louisiana.

KIMMER (KEIMER), NICHOLAS   Fayette County
Born—Probably in Germany.
Service—Corporal in Infantry in Penn. Line, Capt. Finney's 4th Regt., April 23, 1777-81.
Proof—Pension claim W. 10179; Penn. Archives, 2nd Series, vol. 10, p. 515.
Died—Oct. 19, 1841, age 83. Buried Cole Cemetery, Posey Twp., Fayette Co. Stone.
Married—1784, Sarah Taylor. Ch. Elizabeth, b. 1786; Catherine, b. 1788; Susannah, b. 1791; Peter, b. 1793; John, b. 1795; Mary, b. 1797; Sarah, b. 1799; Samuel, b. 1801; Abigail, b. 1803; Daniel, b. 1805; Margaret, b. 1807.

KING, CORNELIUS   Morgan County
Born—Nov. 21, 1753, New Castle, Del.
Service—Enlisted at Tegart's Valley, Vir. In expeditions against Indians. Served under Lt. White, Capt. John Lewis, Col. Andrew and Charles Lewis.
Proof—Pension certificate S. 17527.
Died—Jan., 1840, Morgan Co., Ind. William Cemetery, Green Twp., Road 37.
Children—Fancillo King (was a grandson of Cornelius K.).

KING, GEORGE   Decatur County
Born—May 12, 1751, Berkeley Co., Vir.
Service—Served under Capt. William Kieford in Washington and Maj. Lee's Cavalry, 2 yrs. Also detailed in forage department. Enlisted again April, 1781, and served as Orderly Sergeant under Capt. McIntyre and Col. Darke.

Proof—Pensioner; Rev. War Records of Vir., by Brumbaugh, pp. 174, 206, 250.
Died—Sept. 11, 1838. Buried Milford, Ind. Government stone. Bronze tablet by Dr. Bernays Kennedy (a descendant).
Married—1775, Mary Sanders, d. 1842. Ch. Elizabeth; George; John; James; William; Edward; Jeremiah; Phebe; Sarah; Esther.
Collected by Miss Kate Cooper, Kokomo, Indiana.

KING, JAMES   Jefferson County
Proof—Rev. Soldiers of Vir., p. 255; Bounty Warrants; War Mss. 5, p. 13; Chesterfield Supplement; Court House Vir., Ill., Dept. D, 321 Romney, p. 20; War Mss. 4, pp. 242-245; Journal of House of Delegates, Dec., 1818, p. 80, Rockbridge Co., Vir.
Children—Phebe, b. Jefferson Co., Ind., m. Wm. DeLapp 1816; Jacob, m. Frances Shelton; Joseph, m. Mary A. Russell; James T., m. Mary Hunt.
Collected by John Paul Chapter D. A. R.

KING, JESSE   Wayne County
Born—About 1755.
Service—Entered Vir. Militia 1776, and served under Capt. Wm. Seward; later under Capt. John Walker, 4th Vir. Regt. In 1777 under Capt. Wm. Bailey and served as Corporal for 6 wks. under Capt. John H. Cocke.
Proof—Pension claim 201; Rev. Soldiers of Vir., Eckenrode, p. 255.
Died—Buried on Mendenhall Farm, Clay Twp., Wayne Co., Ind.
Children—Samuel; Daniel, m. Marie McAlister; Elisha; Lorenzo D., m. Betsey Way; John; Newton; Isaac; Levi; Milton; Mary Jane.
Collected by Mrs. Paul L. Ross, Richmond, Indiana.

KINNEY (KENNY), RICHARD   Scott County
Born—About 1749.
Service—Enlisted in Vir. in Company of Capt. Waggoner, 12th Vir. Line. Discharged at Winchester Barracks. In battles of Brandywine and Germantown. Served 2 yrs.
Proof—Pension claim W. 10175; B. L. Wt. 2415-100.
Died—April 25, 1838, Scott Co.
Married—1782, Susan Shadd. Ch. Mary, b. 1783; Sarah, b. 1784, m. —— Wilkerson; Saul or Sol, d. before 1843, left 5 ch.; Rachel, b. 1790, m. —— Dean; John; George; Claborne, d. before 1847, left 4 ch.; Catherine, m. —— Morgan; James; Rosa.

KIRKHAM, ROBERT   Harrison County
Born—1754, Augusta Co., Vir.
Service—Volunteered June 10, 1779. Was a member of John Holder's CO. at or near Boonesborough, Madison Co., Ky.

Proof—Collin's History of Ky., vol. 1, p. 13.
Died—After 1800, Harrison Co., Ind.
Married—Jane Boyd. Ch. Margaret; Henry; Jane; Anna; Elizabeth; Sarah; Polly; John; Prudence; Michael; Robert; William.
Collected by Miss Mabel Claxton, French Lick, Indiana.

KIRKPATRICK, DAVID   Blackford County
Born—1758, Maryland or Virginia.
Service—Enlisted at age of 18 years.
Proof—Name listed in 1840 census as a pensioner, but no record has been found by Veteran's Adm.
Died—About 1849. Buried in Stewart Cemetery S. E. of Hartford City.
Children—Francis and seven others, whose names are unknown.
Collected by descendants. Given by Mrs. Otis Beal, Hartford City, Indiana.

KNIGHT, MOSES (a Negro)   Knox County
Also known as Moses Sharper and Moses McIntosh. Reared by Gen. Alexander McIntosh, who lived on the Big Peedee River, S. C.
Service—Enlisted in 1779 and served until 1782 as a pri. in Capt. James Fauntleroy's CO., Col. John McIntosh's S. C. Troop of Horse. In 1782 he was made "press master" and took a boat load of corn from Culp's Ferry to Gen. Green's Army.
Proof—Pension claim W. 10182.
Died—April 2, 1848, at Vincennes, Ind.
Married—Marian Hopewell, 1795 or 1796. Ch. Abraham; Isaac; Analiza; Aaron; Catherine.
Collected by Mrs. Roy Bogner, Washington, Indiana.

KRIDER, CHRISTIAN   Cass County
Born—Jan. 22, 1757, Lancaster Co., Penn.
Service—Member of the Second Class, Capt. Baltzer Orth's CO., Lancaster Co., Penn., Militia, Dec. 25, 1781.
Proof—Penn. Archives, 5th Series, vol. 7, p. 145.
Died—Dec. 23, 1847. Buried Bethlehem M. E. Cemetery, Cass Co. Stone.
Married—Susanna Elebarger. Ch. Christian, Jr., 1783-1839 (War of 1812); Henry, 1799-1868.
Collected by Miss Laura D. Henderson, Logansport, Indiana.

KUNTZ, GEORGE   Clark County
Born—Before 1760, Germany.
Service—Pri. in Capt. Mathias Henning's CO., Second Battalion, Lancaster Co. Militia, 1782.

Proof—Penn. Archives, 5th Series, vol. 7, p. 185.
Died—Feb. 4, 1842, near Jeffersonville, Ind.
Married—Leah Corbin, d. 1830. Ch. John; Matilda; Mary; Frederick; Ellen; Rachel, 1814-1877, m. Joshua Jones; Jacob; Nancy; Hulbert; Catherine.
Collected by Ann Rogers Clark Chapter D. A. R.

KYSER, FREDERICK   Jennings County
Born—1761, Burks Co., Penn.
Service—Resided in Montgomery Co., Md. In 1780 he and his team pressed into service by Gen. Lacy's Brigade, wagon loaded with ammunition driven to Norfolk to York, to Norfolk to Md. In 1781 removed to Ky. Enlisted in Sullivan's Fort, Capt. James Patton, Gen. Clark.
Proof—Pension R. 6061. Claim rejected. Applied from Jennings Co., Ind., 1834.

LACY, ELIJAH   Morgan County
Born—Oct. 14, 1764, Hanover, Vir.
Service—Enlisted 1778, Goochland Co., Vir., as pri. in Vir. Militia under Cols. Bland and Taylor, Capts. Parrish, Timberlake and Hatcher.
Proof—Pension claim W. 10189.
Died—April 25, 1846. Buried Mt. Zion Cemetery S. of Hall, Morgan Co. Stone.
Married—Frankey Holland. Ch. Jesse; probably others.
Collected by Miss Ura Sanders, Gosport, Indiana.

LADD, JOSEPH   Wayne County
Born—June 2, 1760, Guilford Co., N. C.
Service—Served 6 mos 21 days as a pri. in N. C. Troops.
Proof—Pension claim W. 3565.
Died—June 12, 1834. Buried Jacksonburg, Wayne Co.
Married—First to Catherine Bacey Damon (1771-1797). Ch. Anna, b. 1785, m. John Vaughn; Elizabeth Smith, b. 1787, m. Abel Lomax; Constantine, b. 1789, m. Nancy Carr; Nancy, b. 1790, m. Tristian Starbuch; Noble, b. 1792, m. Mary Burton; Judith, b. 1794, m. John Green; William, b. Feb. 1, 1797, m. Isabel Boyd. Soldier m. second time, Dec. 25, 1797, Mary Angel. Ch. Mary Davis, b. 1802, m. Paul Frazier; Isaac Newton, b. 1804, m. Elizabeth Hutchens; Bethany, b. 1807, m. Samuel K. Boyd; Amos, b. 1809, m. Hannah Slack; Catherine, b. 1811, m. Samuel Johnson; Charles, b. 1813, m. Charlotte Way and Sarepta Cummings; Joseph D., b. 1816, m. Matilda Clement and Eliza Britton; Susannah, b. 1816, m. Seth Way; Benjamin, b. 1819.
Collected by Mrs. Paul Ross, Richmond, Indiana.

LA FOLLETTE, JOSEPH   Putnam County
Born—1745.
Service—Pri. in Capt. Henry Balkins' Troop of Light Dragoons in
    Gen. Count Pulaski Legion. Enlisted May 24, 1779, for 3 yrs.,
    and his name appears on the roll of the troops to April, 1780.
    Stationed Dec. 13, 1779, at Morristown, N. J., and March 13, 1780,
    at Westfield, N. J.
Proof—Adjutant General's Office; History of LaFollette Family in
    America; Morristown, N. J., First Presbyterian Church History,
    1742-1881, and combined Register, 1742-1899.
Died—Jan., 1834. Buried Racoon, Franklin Twp. D. A. R. marker.
Married—1771, Phoebe Goble, b. 1743. Ch. Usuel, b. 1773, m. Nancy
    Lee; Robert, b. 1776; Abigal, b. 1779; Jesse, b. 1781; Isaac, b.
    1783; Jacob, b. 1785; John, b. 1787.
Collected by Miss Mary Hostetter, Indianapolis, Indiana.

LAMB, JAMES   Wayne County
Born—July 15, 1754 or 56, Perthshire, Scotland.
Service—Sergeant in Capt. David Stephenson's CO., 8th Vir. Regt. of
    foot under Col. Abraham Bowman. Enlisted March 21, 1776, 2 yrs.
Proof—War Department.
Died—1841. Buried Elkhorn Cemetery. Government marker placed by
    Richmond Chapter D. A. R.
Married—Hannah Boone, 1769-1839. Ch. Anna; James; William, m.
    Fanny Gaar; John, m. Catherine Boone; Thomas, m. Sarah Smith;
    Joseph Boone, m. Janet Mustand; Elizabeth, m. Smith Hunt; Cath-
    erine, m. Stephen G. Hunt; Jane, m. Samuel Spahr; Hannah.
Collected by Mrs. Paul Ross, Richmond, Indiana.

LAMB, JOHN   Perry County
Born—May 22, 1757, Albany Co., N. Y.
Service—Pri. in Capt. Barent J. Ten Eyck's CO., 2nd N. Y. Regt.,
    Cont'l Troops from May 5, 1778, to Feb. 5, 1779. Re-enlisted,
    served 1779-81 in Gates' Regt. of N. Y. Militia.
Proof—War Department.
Died—1818. Buried Upper Cemetery at Tobinsport, Ind. Government
    marker placed by Lafayette Springs Chapter D. A. R.
Married—1779, Beulah Curtis, 1760-1848. Ch. Solomon; Beulah; John,
    Jr.; Katherine; Ezra; Israel; Bathsheba; John Willis; William B.;
    Dorastus; Rudolphus.
Collected by Mrs. Vernice A. Conner, Tell City, Indiana.

LANCASTER, WILLIAM   Switzerland County
Born—Nov. 17, 1746, Hanover Co., Vir.
Service—Enlisted Orange Co., Vir., in Wm. Buckner's CO., Col. Harvey's
    Regt.; guarded British and Hessian prisoners at Albemarle Bar-
    racks; 1780, was 80 days in Capt. Berry Johnson's CO., Maj. Na-

thaniel Welsh; July and Aug., 1781, under Abner Porter, commissary, collecting cattle for army.
Proof—Pension claim S. 16902.
Died—Nov. 4, 1843. Buried on Napoleon Miller's Farm, Switzerland Co.
Married—First W. unknown. Second W. Mrs. Sarah Blades, d. Feb. 18, 1848. Ch. Isabel, m. Evan Miller; Catherine, m. Patrick E. Porter.
Collected by Mrs. A. V. Danner, Vevay, Indiana.

LANDERS, KIMBROW   Switzerland County
Born—1757, Albemarle Co., Vir.
Service—Enlisted 1777, 2 yrs., 9th Vir. Regt. under Col. George Mathews. Enlisted again under Capt. Powell of 13th Vir. Regt. for 3 yrs. Discharged at Winchester, Vir. In battles of White Marsh and Germantown.
Proof—Pension claim W. 1623.
Died—May 26, 1831. Buried Cotton Cemetery, Jefferson Twp.
Married—Second W. Keziah Humbles, m. July 21, 1798. Daughter Martha, m. Aaron Sturgeon. Sons named in soldier's Will are Nathaniel, William, Benjamin, John, Kimbrow and Bradley.
Collected by Mrs. A. V. Danner, Vevay, Indiana.

LANE, JACOB   Tippecanoe County
Born—May 27, 1760, Lynchburg, Vir.
Service—Served in Lieut. Col. Melane's CO. of the 1st N. C. Battalion under Col. Thomas Clark. Enlisted Aug. 2, 1777, for 3 yrs.
Proof—D. A. R. National Nos. 262396, 268611; Tombstone Records, Tippecanoe Co., Ind., and Marriage Records.
Died—Sept. 15, 1830. Buried Greenbush Cemetery, Lafayette, Ind. Stone. Bronze tablet placed by Gen. de Lafayette Chapter D. A. R.
Married—Susan Leigh. Ch. William; Gideon; Eleanor; Thomas; Samuel; Louis; James; Marthe; Margaret.
Collected by Mrs. Arthur McQueen, West Lafayette, Indiana.

LANE, JAMES   Rush County
Born—About 1749.
Service—Enlisted July 8, 1777, in Uniontown, Penn., for 3 yrs. in Capt. James O'Harra's Independent CO. Was in several skirmishes against the Indians. May, 1778, he went with part of his CO. and part of 9th Vir. Regt. down the Mississippi River with a cargo of continental provisions to barter with the Spaniards for clothing for the troops at Pittsburg.
Proof—Pension claim S. 35517. Had 6 children, all married in 1820. He moved to Rush Co., Ind., in 1827.

Died—May 2, 1827, in Rush Co.
Collected by Mrs. Willard Amos, Rushville, Indiana.

LANE, LARKIN   Parke County
Born—Feb. 22, 1762, Spotsylvania Co., Vir.
Service—While a resident of Spotsylvania Co., Vir., he enlisted in
   July, 1781, and served 3 mos. as pri. in Capt. Frank Colman's
   CO., Col. Thomas Merriwether's Vir. Regt.; he enlisted in Nov.,
   1781, and served 3 mos. 7 days as pri. in Capt. John Legg's CO.,
   Col. Merriwether's Vir. Regt.
Proof—Pension claim S. 16442.
Died—About 1847. Buried on his farm in Greene Twp. Stone.
Married—1780, Sarah Price, 1763-1837. Ch. Alexander; Lucinda, 1793-
   1854, m. Floyd Burks, 1787-1862.
Collected by Mrs. H. L. Hancock, Rockville, Indiana.

LANE, SAMUEL   Fulton County
Born—1769, Beaver Co., Penn.
Service—A member of Capt. Pittman Gower's Militia.
Proof—Penn. State Library Archives; biographical sketch of second
   wife.
Died—Sept. 21, 1845. Buried Old Cemetery, Akron, Ind. Stone.
   D. A. R. marker placed by Manitou Chapter D. A. R.
Married—First to Jane Homes. Ch. Martha, 1788-1878, m. Jacob Sippy
   (War of 1812) and had 10 children; a daughter and a son died in
   childhood. Soldier m. second to Lucretia Johnson Sippy in 1832.
Collected by Mrs. Ina Brundige, Akron, Indiana.

LANG, FRANCIS   Greene County
Born—About 1760.
Service—Entered July 18, 1780, Charles Co., Md., Company of Capt.
   Charles Smith, Regt. of Col. Smith, Continental Establishment.
   Capt. Bluff, Col. Ford, Md. Line, to Nov., 1783. Discharged by
   public proclamation. Battles of Guilford Court House, Camden,
   Siege of Ninety-Six.
Proof—Pension claim W. 10188; B. L. Wt. 343-60-55.
Died—July 19, 1847. Buried 6 miles east of Bloomfield.
Married—First W. unknown. Ch. Nancy, b. 1803; Nehemiah, b. 1806;
   Stansbury, b. 1807; Sarah, b. 1809; James, b. 1811. Second W.
   —— Kennedy. Third W. Susannah Hunter Philip (a widow), m.
   1828.

LANGDON, DANIEL, JR.   Knox County
Born—May 9, 1757, Southington, Conn.
Service—Capt. of 3rd Company of Cavalry under Col. Asa Bray.

Proof—Conn. Historical Society Collection, vol. 8, p. 210.
Died—May 21, 1841. Buried Langdon Cemetery, Knox Co. Stone.
Married—Sally Coles, 1762-1815. Ch. Sophia; Samuel; Betsy; Luther; Harriet; Leonard Coles; Sally Smith; Phoebe; Nancy; Henry.
Collected by Mrs. S. G. Davenport, Vincennes, Indiana.

LANGDON, PHILIP   Washington County
Born—1760, Somers, Conn.
Service—Enlisted Somers, Conn., March 6, 1777, in Col. Sheburn's Regt. Discharged Morristown, N. J., March 4, 1780.
Proof—Pension claim S. 35513.
Died—Sept. 1, 1853. Buried Franklin Cemetery. Government marker placed by Christopher Harrison Chapter D. A. R.
Married—Dorcas ———. Ch. Philip, Jr., and others, names not known.
Collected by Mrs. Harvey Morris, Salem, Indiana.

LANGUEDOC, CHARLES LACOSTE DIT   Knox County
Service—A Patriot. Signed oath of allegiance to the Republic of Virginia, July 20, 1780. The name in the list is Charle x. Languedoc.
Proof—George Rogers Clark's Papers, 1771-1781; Ill. Hist. Coll., vol. VIII, pp. 52-59.
Died—Buried in Old Cathedral Cemetery.
Married—Felicite Mignaux, d. 1794. Ch. Charles Lacoste dit Languedoc, bapt. Nov. 29, 1794, m. Marcelite Valle, b. 1814. Probably other children.
Collected by Mrs. Leo Schultheis, Vincennes, Indiana.

LANMAN, JAMES   Perry County
Born—1752, Fairfax Co., Vir.
Service—Enlisted at Charleston, S. C., July, 1776, as Orderly Sergt., 1 yr. in 1st Regt. of Riflemen in S. C. Line under Capt. John Hampton. Enlisted second time as Orderly Sergt. March 3, 1781, for 2 yrs. under Capt. Wm. Butler in 1st Regt. of Horse, Col. Wm. Henderson.
Proof—Pension claim S. 31812. Last payment of pension, March 4, 1841.

LASH, ADAM   Bartholomew County
Born—About 1738.
Service—Enlisted in Amboy, N. J., in June, 1776, in Capt. Andrew Pottinger's CO. under Col. Richard McCollister of Gen. Green's Brigade. Discharged Dec. 25, 1776. Re-enlisted in the department for the manufacture of arms and to do blacksmith work. Discharged Dec. 24, 1779. In battles of Long Island, Trenton, Brandywine and Germantown. Was wounded at Germantown.

Proof—His sworn statement made in Bartholomew Circuit Court, March, 1824, found in Civil Order Book A, pp. 162-164.
Married—And children (four), names unknown.
Collected by Mrs. Laura D. Fix (deceased), Columbus, Indiana.

LASHLEY, GEORGE   Daviess County
Born—About 1738, Prince Georges Co., Md.
Service—Enlisted Aug., 1776, as pri. in Capt. Jared Bristow's CO., Col. Francis Deakin's Md. Regt. Discharged Feb., 1777.
Proof—Pension claim S. 3184.
Died—March, 1847. Buried Lashley graveyard. Government marker and tablet placed by White River Chapter D. A. R.
Married—Mary Bradford. Ch. named in Will are Delilah; Patsy, m. Jacob Freeland; Sarah, m. Henry Mattingly; Sidney, m. —— Colbert.
Collected by Mrs. Roy Bogner, Washington, Indiana.

LAWLER, NICHOLAS   Jefferson County
Born—Sept. 10, 1743, Northumberland Co., Vir.
Service—Enlisted in Fauquier Co., Vir.; pri. in Virginia Troops; Sept., 1777, 3 mos. Capt. James Winn, Col. Elias Edmund's Regt.; April, 1778, 3 mos. Capt. Leonard Sharp, Col. Armistead Churchill's Regt.; Aug., 1781, Capt. Winn, Col. Edmund; marched to Yorktown, was at surrender of Cornwallis, guarded prisoners to Winchester, Vir.
Proof—Pension claim S. 32372.
Died—1837. Probably buried on land he entered.
Collected by John Paul Chapter D. A. R.

LAWRENCE (LARENCE), ISAAC   Hendricks County
Born—1762, Camden District, South Carolina.
Service—Pri. in CO. under Capt. Goodwin, Col. Williams' Regt., S. C. Line for 11 mos.
Proof—Pension claim S. 32373.
Buried—Fox Cemetery, N. of Plainfield, Indiana.

LAWRENCE, JOSEPH   Greene County
Born—Nov. 1, 1755, Albemarle Co., Virginia.
Service—Volunteered and entered Militia of Virginia "Minute Men" under Capt. Dabney Carr. Served about 1½ years. In 1777, volunteered as ranger in N. C. under Capt. Wm. Underwood. Discharged in Surrey Co., N. C. Again enlisted under Capt. David Umphrey. In 1779, volunteered in Militia of N. C. In battle of Guilford Court House.

Proof—Pension claim S. 31810.
Died—Pension paid to March 4, 1839. Buried near Sylvania Church, Cincinnati, Green Co.

LAWRENCE, VOLANTINE — Dearborn County
Born—1758.
Service—Served under Col. Archibald Lochry at the Lochry Massacre, Aug. 24, 1781, and was taken prisoner.
Proof—Name on list of Soldiers serving with Col. Archibald Lochry. Copy of the original list is on file Registrar General's Office.
Died—Nov. 29, 1827. Buried St. Leon Cemetery. Stone. Government marker placed by Col. Archibald Lochry Chapter D. A. R.
Married—Mary Stone, d. 1838.
Collected by Mrs. Walter Kerr, Aurora, Indiana.

LAWRENCE, WILLIAM — Clark County
Born—1766, North Carolina.
Service—Served as private soldier.
Proof—North Carolina Revolutionary Army Accounts, vol. 11, p. 23, folio 1.
Died—July 12, 1822. Buried on Oscar Hutching's Farm, near New Washington. Stone.
Married—Catherine Bland. Ch. Jane; Mary; John; Winnie; Margaret.
Collected by Mrs. Roscoe Leak, Lizton, Indiana.

LEABO, ISAAC — Monroe County
Born—1754, Normandy, France.
Service—Came to America with Gen. Lafayette, enlisted Normandy, France, 1779. Served in CO. Saint Leger Regiment de Soissonais.
Proof—D. A. R. national No. 191760.
Died—About 1840. Buried Van Buskirk Cemetery, Gosport, Ind. Government marker placed by Miss Ura Sanders.
Married—Sarah Jennings. Ch. Noah, b. 1786; Josiah, b. 1788; Susan, b. 1790; Rachel, b. 1792; Jacob, b. 1794; Sarah, b. 1796; Elizabeth, b. 1798; Catherine, b. 1799; Zinnie, b. 1800; Lucinda, b. 1802.
Collected by Miss Ura Sanders, Gosport, Indiana.

LEAP, JOHN — Boone County
Born—1735, Germany.
Service—Served under Capt. John Jameson of 4th Regt. Penn. Militia, Col. Arch. McIlroy, from Sept., 1775, to Jan., 1778, as private. Enlisted while living in Springfield Twp., Bucks Co., Penn. Discharged at Morristown, N. J.
Proof—R. 6225.

Died—Sept. 16, 1845. Buried Mountabor Cemetery, Fayette, Indiana. Government marker.
Married—Barbara Dirth Leap. Ch. David, m. Frances Shandy; Isaac C., m. Sarah Woollen; Andrew J.
Collected by Mrs. J. H. Duchemin, Sheridan, Indiana, and Mrs. Sarah Leap Acton, Seattle, Washington.

LEE, DAVID   Tippecanoe County
Born—January 27, 1766, New Jersey.
Service—Enlisted in spring of 1781 at Sturgess Station, Kentucky, in the company of Capt. Sturgess. This was a volunteer company serving 3 mos. guarding the forts and frontier. Then enlisted in Capt. Samuel Pottenger's CO. and joined Cark's campaign in spring of 1782. Assisted in building the block house where Cincinnati now stands. In 1784 drafted in Capt. Pottenger's CO.
Proof—Pension papers.
Died—Jan. 10, 1852. Buried 12 miles S. E. of Lafayette, Ind., on Road 52. Stone.
Married—1785, Mary Osborn, b. 1764. Ch. Katherine, b. 1788; David, Jr., b. 1791; William, b. 1793; Joseph, b. 1796; Mary Ann, b. 1798; Nathaniel, b. 1801; Ezra.
Collected by Mrs. Grace Lee Slayback, 17 S. 4th St., Lafayette, Indiana.

LEE (ALIAS SEE), JOHN   Henry County
Born—1757, near Charleston, West Virginia.
Service—Enlisted 1776, in Greenbrier Co., Vir., for 1 year to defend western frontier. Discharged Sept., 1777. Enlisted 1779, in Botetourt Co., Vir., in Gen. Scott's Brig. 12th Vir. Regt., joined the main army in Penn. under Gen. Washington, went into winter quarters at Valley Forge. In battles Stony Point and Germantown. Three years' service.
Proof—Pension claim S. 17538.
Died—Last payment of pension was made Jan. 2, 1837. Buried on his farm near Lewisville, Ind.
Married—Margaret Jarrett. Ch. Mary, b. 1787; David; Charles; Michael; George.
Collected by Maj. Hugh Dinwiddie Chapter D. A. R.

LEE, JOSEPH   Decatur County
Born—April 22, 1762, Hunterton Co., New Jersey.
Service—Private in company commanded by Capt. Conover of the regiment under Col. Chambers in N. J. Line for 14 mos. Entered service in Huntington Co., N. J., 1778.
Proof—Pension claim R. 6245. Ind. certificate 19316.
Died—Aug. 24, 1837. Buried at Shiloh, Decatur Co. Stone.

Married—1787, Eleanor Davison or Davidson, d. 1844. Ch. Andrew b. 1789; Ann b. 1790; Hannah b. 1793; Elizabeth b. 1796; Rebecca b. 1798; Mary b. 1801; Joseph b. 1803; Davison b. 1805; Eleanor b. 1807; Martha b. 1810; Susannah b. 1813; Perry b. 1817.

LEEDS, JAMES   Dearborn County
Born—1762, Gloucester Co., New Jersey.
Service—Pri. in CO. commanded by Capt. Higby, N. J. Militia, 6 mos.
Proof—Pension claim S. 31817.
Died—Last payment of pension was made on April 12, 1841.
Collected by Mrs. Walter Kerr, Aurora, Indiana.

LEER, JACOB   Elkhart County
Born—1765, Montgomery Co., Ohio.
Service—Pri., in Capt. Robert Samplis' CO., 10th Penn. Regt., under Col. Richard Humpton, 1778.
Proof—Penn. Archives, Series 5, vol. 3, pp. 499, 517, 440, 576; vol. 5, p. 669.
Died—1827. Buried in abandoned cemetery, Elkhart Co. (John Bainter farm, N. W. of Goshen). Government marker placed by William Tuffs Chapter D. A. R.
Married—Frances Stutsman 1769-1860. Hannah b. 1788, m. John Lindiman; Abraham b. 1801, m. Mary Esther Miller; Catherine b. 1802; Jacob b. 1803; David b. 1809; Samuel b. 1810; Mary b. 1820.
Collected by Mrs. F. C. Wherly, Elkhart, Indiana.

LEFLER, GEORGE   Harrison County
Born—About 1752.
Service—Pri. in CO. commanded by Capt. Bell of the Regt. of Col. John Gibson in Vir. Line for 2 yrs., March, 1780 to March, 1782.
Proof—Pension claim S. 35522. Ind. certificate 19630. Several ch.

LE GORE, JOHN   Rush County
Born—1755.
Service—Enlisted April 1, 1776, in Lancaster, Penn., in the CO. of Capt. Zebulon Pike of 4th Penn. Regt. Discharged Dec., 1783. In battles of Brandywine and White Plains.
Proof—Pension claim S. 35521.
Died—July 7, 1829. Name is on bronze tablet in Rush Co. Court House. Records in General Accounting Office show he died in Marion Co., Indiana.
Married—First W. Margaret Funk. Ch. Dan b. 1803, m. Sarah Orr. Second W. Esther ——.

LE GRAND, GABRIEL CHRISTOPHER   Knox County
Born—About 1721, Normandy.
Service—A Patriot. Signed the Oath of Allegiance to the State of
    Virginia, July 20, 1778. Name appears as "Le Grand, juge."
Proof—Ill. Hist. Coll., vol. VIII, pp. 52-59; Clark's Papers.
Died—Feb. 10, 1789, age 68. Buried Cathedral Cemetery. Date and
    names from Church Records.
Married—Veronique Raume. Ch. Francis b. 1785, d. 1788; Gabriel Jr.
    d. 1789; Benjamin bapt. 1788; Charlotte; Joseph; Delle Veronique,
    m. 1788; Michel Auge; Babine; Jean Marie (son).
Collected by Mrs. Leo Schultheis, Vincennes, Indiana.

LEGRAS (LEGRACE), JEAN MARIE PHILIPPE   Knox County
Born—Not known, but came to Post Vincennes by 1774.
Service—Colonel of Militia; Commandant and 1st Magistrate of Vincennes. Signed the Oath of Allegiance.
Proof—Goodspeed's Hist. of Knox and Daviess Cos., pp. 47-55; Clark's
    Papers, 326, 333, 356; St. Xavier Cathedral Records; Ill. Hist.
    Coll., vol. VIII, Clark's Papers, pp. 52-59.
Died—Feb. 10, 1788. Buried "in the Church, on the Epistle side."
Married—Marie Devegnais, d. 1790, age 57. Ch. J. M. Legras, Jr.
Collected by Mrs. Leo Schultheis, Vincennes, Indiana.

LEMMON, JOHN   Harrison County
Born—Nov. 6, 1740. Ireland.
Service—Joined the artillery in the Province of Maryland in 1776 commanded by Capt. Nathaniel Smith, Lieut. William Woolsey, Lieut.
    Alex. Fornval, Serg. George Keepott. Received a grant of land
    in Clark County, Ind., for his services under Gen. George Rogers
    Clark.
Proof—English's History of Northwest Territory, vol. 1, p. 846.
Died—March 31, 1811.
Married—1760, Sarah Stansburg. Ch. Lemuel b. 1761; Martha b. 1764;
    Hannah b. 1766; Alex b. 1768; Thomas b. 1770; John b. 1772;
    Benjamin b. 1774; Eleanor b. 1777; Charles b. 1786.
Collected by William Henry Harrison Chapter D. A. R., Valparaiso,
    Indiana.

LEMON, MATTHIAS   Greene County
Born—Feb. 18, 1762, Lancaster Co., Pennsylvania.
Service—Enlisted June, 1778, at Sunbury, Penn., in Capt. Geddis' CO.,
    which was not attached to any regiment and as mounted ranger
    did duty along the Susquehanna River to protect the settlers
    against Indians and was discharged in the fall; March, 1779, enlisted at Northumberland, Penn., as substitute for his brother
    James, who was drafted and served in Capt. Thos. Gaskins CO.,

3 mos. It also appears from statement of his widow, in her claim
for bounty land that Matthias Lemon was paid for service as
Lieut. Col. in Gen. Davis' Brigade, N. Y. Militia from Sept.
1-16, 1814.
Proof—Pension File No. 6277. Rejected for lack of proof of 6 mos.
service. Lineage, vol. 62, p. 322.
Died—Dec. 15, 1841.
Married—First W. unknown. Second W. Mary Hunnel. Ch. Francis
M., m. Mary Kilgore. Other children of the soldier: William, m.
Phoebe Jenks; Brutus; Thomas; Matthias Jr.; Clinton; Lucien.

LEONARD, NATHANIEL   Henry County
Born—Dec. 10, 1748, Trenton, New Jersey.
Service—Early in Rev. War he drove a baggage wagon, was afterwards assistant wagon master and forage master. He was subsequently promoted to Capt. in N. J. Militia and served until the close of war. In battle of Monmouth.
Proof—Pension claim W. 24513.
Died—Oct. 15, 1823. Buried Chris Herr Cemetery, Dudley Twp. Stone and S. A. R. marker by Patrick Henry Chapter S. A. R.
Married—Esther Heath. Ch. Zephaniah; Mary; Thomas; Elizabeth; James; Nathaniel; Esther; Nancy; John; Lavina; Samuel.
Collected by Patrick Henry Chapter S. A. R. and Sarah Winston Henry Chapter D. A. R.

LEVI, ISAAC   Ripley County
Born—1751, Germany.
Service—While resident of Lexington, Ky., he enlisted in 1780. Pri. in Capt. Robert Patterson's and Benj. Harrison's CO., a troop on expedition against Indians on Big Miami under Gen. George Rogers Clark. In the battle of Pickaway Town, defeated the Indians. Stationed at Post Vincennes. Served two years.
Proof—Pension claim W. 773.
Died—Sept. 21, 1850. Buried near Osgood, Ripley Co. Bronze tablet at Versailles Court House.
Married—Last W. Mary Tucker (widow of John Tucker, a Rev. S.), m. Nov. 14, 1841. Descendants of former marriages settled about Osgood, Indiana.
Collected by Mrs. A. B. Wycoff, Batesville, Indiana.

LEWIS, DAVID   Orange County
Born—1740. Probably Maryland.
Service—Served as private in Capt. Cuthbert Harrison's Troop, also designated 2nd Troop, 1st Regiment Light Dragoons, Continental Troops; also designated 1st Regiment Virginia Light Dragoons,

commanded by Col. Theodorick Bland. His name first appears on the pay roll of the company for Nov., 1777, and is last borne on the company muster roll for Nov., 1778.
Proof—War Department.
Died—Dec. 5, 1816. Buried Lewis Cemetery in Paoli Twp. Stone.
Married—Agnes Abraham, m. Sept. 9, 1766. Ch. John M. b. 1771, d. 1852, m. Elizabeth Younger (dau. of a Rev. S.), d. 1859.
Collected by Dan B. Bishop, Mitchell, Indiana.

LEWIS, JOHN   Rush County
Born—1749, Loudoun Co., Virginia.
Service—May, 1777, he was drafted at Cox's Fort at the mouth of Crop Creek on the Ohio River, 1 mo. under Capt. Mason and was stationed at Fort Wheeling under Col. Abraham Shepherd. Later drafted for 6 mos. in service commonly called the Wood Rangers under Maj. Henry Taylor, Capt. Isaac Pierce. In 1780 he was drafted, 1 mo. to guard and pack provisions to the army at Ft. Lawrence on the Muskingum River under Capt. Bates.
Proof—Pension File No. 16448.
Died—1847. Buried Flat Rock Cemetery, Rush Co.
Married—Second W. Mary Powers. Ch. Phebe; Stephen; Nancy, m. Wm. Thompson; Margaret b. 1781, m. Andrew Guffin; Jane; John.
Collected by Mrs. Blanche Brookover Spencer, Globe, Arizona.

LEWIS, THOMAS   Switzerland County
Born—Dec., 1764, Caroline Co., Virginia.
Service—Enlisted as a pri. in Capt. Coleman Sutton's or Capt. Taylor's CO., Col. Andrew Thornton's Vir. Regt. This was in March or April, 1781, served 2 mos. Enlisted in June, 1781, 2 mos under Col. Thomas Matthews. In Aug. or Sept., 1781, served as 2nd Serg. under Major Carey in the Vir. Troops for 2 mos. and 2 wks.
Proof—McAllister, Virginia Militia in the Rev. War, p. 138; Pension Claim W. 8032, B. I. Wt. 27672-160-55.
Died—July 28, 1832. Switzerland County.
Married—1804, Sarah Condly. Had 9 children, names not given in pension papers.
Collected by Mrs. Harvey Morris, Salem, Indiana.

LINDLEY, JONATHAN   Orange County
Born—June 15, 1756, Pennsylvania.
Service—A Patriot—"In 1787 to Jonathan Lindley, sundries for military services 50 L. 2.6." In 1783 for sundries furnished and cash paid Militia of N. C., etc., as allowed by auditors of Hillsborough Dist. as per report, 83 L. 19.90.

Proof—N. C. Hist. Com. From Accounts of U. S. with N. C.; War of
Rev., Book C., Page 91; N. C. Rev. Army Accounts, vol. VI, p. 1,
folio 3.
Died—April 5, 1828. Buried Old Lick Creek Cemetery, 3 miles E. of
Paoli. Stone.
Married—First W. Deborah Dicks, b. 1752. Ch. Zachariah (Col. in
War of 1812), m. first Mary Mosier, second Anne Braxton, third
Theresa Potter; Hannah, m. Thomas Braxton; Ruth, m. Joseph
Farlow; Thomas, m. Amy Thompson; Elinor; William, m. first
Michel Hollowell, second Anna K. Fisher; Deborah, m. Jonathan
Jones; Mary, m. Silas Dixon; Queen Esther, m. Alexander Clark;
Catherine, m. Edward McVey; Sarah, m. William Hadley; Jonathan; Soldier second W. Martha Henley. Ch. Guilielma, m. Levi
Woody.
Collected by Mrs. N. B. Mavity, French Lick, Indiana.

LINDLY (LINDLEY), MOSES   Dearborn County
Born—About 1752.
Service—Enlisted Morristown, N. J., Feb., 1776, in Col. Elias Dayton's
Regt., 1 yr. Discharged at Morristown.
Proof—Pension claim S. 36685.
Died—Last payment of pension was made on Sept. 17, 1829.
Collected by Mrs. Walter Kerr, Aurora, Indiana.

LINDSAY, WILLIAM   Knox County
Born—April 15, 1760, Chester Co., Pennsylvania.
Service—1776, 1 mo. pri. under Capt. Nathaniel Vernon, Col. George
Pierce. 1776, 6 mos. pri. under Capt. McClure, Wm. Price, Col.
Montgomery. 1777, 3 mos. pri. under Capt. Copeland, Col. Sharp
Deleny. 1777, 3 mos. Spy, Capt. Thomas Lewis, Col. Sharp
Deleny. April, 1778, 1 yr. wagoner under Capt. James Kinkade,
Col. Francis Waid. April, 1779, 1 yr. wagoner under Capt. James
Kinkade, Col. Clemet Biddle.
Proof—Pension record.
Died—Oct. 8, 1836. Buried Old City Cemetery, Vincennes, Ind. Stone.
Married—First W. Elizabeth Mace. Ch. Susanah; James; Amelia;
Jane; Elizabeth; Martha; William; George; Levina. Second W.
Clarissa Prior, 1785-1883. Ch. Esther Jones b. 1825, m. John Wm.
Nelson; Benjamin Franklin; Elizabeth Mace, m. Joseph Joyce;
Eunice Sarah, m. George Bedell; Hiram Hunter.
Collected by Miss Mary A. Brouillette, Vincennes, Indiana.

LINN (LYNN), PATRICK   Marion County
Born—About 1753.
Service—Served in 5th Penn. Regt. under Col. Johnson, Capt. Benjamin
Bartholomew, 3 yrs.

Proof—Pension claim S. 36688; Penn. Archives, 2nd Series, vol. 10, p. 552.
Died—April 7, 1829, Marion Co., Indiana.

LIPPERD, WILLIAM   Ripley County
Born—1760.
Service—Enlisted from South Carolina in February, 1780. Discharged in March, 1781. Re-enlisted on same date; discharged in March, 1782.
Proof—Pension claim W-10199.
Died—May 5, 1834. Cliff Hill Cemetery, Versailles, Ripley Co., Ind. Bronze tablet in Versailles C. H. 1928, by Ripley Co. Ind. Historical Society.
Collected by Mrs. A. B. Wycoff, Batesville, Indiana.

LIST, JOHN   Owen County
Born—March 2, 1753.
Service—Pri. N. Y. Militia. Enlisted Clavernack, N. Y., under Capt. John TenBroek, Gen. Van Schaick.
Proof—Pension claim S. 35523.
Died—Jan. 18, 1834, Owen County.

LITTELL (LITTLE), ABSALOM   Clark County
Born—Sept. 12, 1751, Fayette Co., Pennsylvania.
Service—Pri. in Capt. James Knox's CO., Morgan's Rifle Regt., Continental Troops under Col. Daniel Morgan. Name first appears on pay roll, July, 1777, and was last on pay roll, Dec., 1778.
Proof—Adjutant-General's Office War Department.
Died—March 17, 1824. Buried Stony Point Cemetery, near Sellersburg, Clark Co. Stone.
Married—Mary Norris. Ch. Amos; Abraham; Absalom; John Thompson; Ann; Josiah Tremble; Margaret.
Collected by Mrs. I. E. Tranter, Franklin, Indiana.

LLOYD, SAMUEL   Decatur County
Born—May 27, 1747.
Service—Pri. in Regt. commanded by Capt. Sowitt, Col. Lee in N. C. Militia, 1776.
Proof—Pension claim S. 32382.
Died—April 24, 1834.
Children—Son James.

LOCHRY, ARCHIBALD   Dearborn County
Service—Colonel of the Penn. Rangers sent to the aid of George Rogers Clark.
Proof—Heitman's Historical Register, p. 355.

Died—Aug. 24, 1781. Was killed in what is now known as Lochry Massacre. Buried Riverview Cemetery, Lawrenceburg, Ind. Bronze marker placed by Col. Archibald Lochry Chapter D. A. R.
Married—Elizabeth ——. Ch. Elizabeth.
Collected by Mrs. Walter Kerr, Aurora, Indiana.

LOCKMAN, VINCENT   Jackson County
Born—1760 or 1762, North Carolina.
Service—Served under Gen. Gates and Col. Malmaday. Taken prisoner at or near Hillsboro, N. C.
Proof—Above taken from statement of widow in her application for pension North Carolina Rev. Records, Vol. 12, p. 53, Folio 4, and p. 54, Folio 1.
Died—Oct. 23, 1843. Buried Old Heighton Hill Cemetery, near Medora, Ind. Stone.
Married—First W. Anna Kirkland. Second W. Christian Miller Hagan. Soldier's Ch. Lucinda; Mary; Vincent; William; Polly; Washington; Patsy; Nancy; Elizabeth; Emily; Melinda; Minerva.
Collected by General Jacob Brown Chapter D. A. R.

LODER, DANIEL   Dearborn County
Born—July 11, 1750, Cumberland Co., New Jersey.
Service—Private in company commanded by Capt. Foster in Regt. of Col. Preston in N. J. Line for 8 mos.
Proof—Pension claim S. 32884.
Died—May 14, 1833. Dearborn County.
Married—Hannah ——.
Collected by Mrs. Walter Kerr, Aurora, Indiana.

LOGAN, PATRICK   Rush County
Born—May 6, 1752, Ireland.
Service—Enlisted at Redstone, Penn., in Dec., 1776, or Jan., 1777; served as pri. in Capt. Robert Beall's CO., Col. Russell and John Gibson, 13th Vir. Regt. and in Capt. James O'Hara's CO. In Battles of Brandywine. Discharged about 1779. Name appears as pri. in Capt. Moore's CO., 4th Battalion of Chester Co. Militia, 1783.
Proof—Pension claim S. 41778, and Penn. Archives, vol. 5, p. 683.
Died—July 1, 1828. Buried Flat Rock Cemetery. Stone. Name on tablet in Rush County Court House.
Married—1780, Sarah Nancy Harper, 1763-1800. Ch. Thomas, 1781-1847, m. first Mary Stroughton, second Elizabeth Frazier, third Mary Parker; Henry, 1783-1866, m. Margarette Crum; Catherine, 1786-1856, m. Daniel McDonald; Charles, 1788-1822, m. Elizabeth Knight; John Jones, 1790-1817; Mary, 1793-1856, m. Joseph

Stoughton; Samuel, 1795-1868, m. first Zena Brigg, second Sarah Snodgrass; Rachel; Robert; William.
Collected by Mrs. Harvey Morris, Salem, Indiana.

LOGAN, WILLIAM   Union County
Born—Aug. 2, 1762, Ireland.
Service—Enlisted June or Aug., 1780, 3 mos. as pri. in Capts. Kilgore's and Robert Lard's CO,, Col. William's S. C. Regt. In Nov. or Dec., 1780, served 1 mo. in Capt. Lard's S. C. CO., and was in some skirmishes. In 1781 served in Capt. James Dillard's CO. of Light Horse Rangers, Cols. Joseph Hayes' and Levi Casey's S. C. Regt.; went on a tour to the Cherokee Nation and was in the battle on the Edisto River. Served to the close of the war.
Proof—Pension claim S. 32385, and Family Bible.
Died—Sept. 12, 1838. Lived in Franklin County, Ind., but buried across the line in Union Co. in Sims Cemetery. Stone. Government marker.
Married—Eleanor Craig d. 1844. Ch. John b. 1789; Robert b. 1792; Mary b. 1794; David b. 1797; Alexander b. 1799; Nancy b. 1801; Jane b. 1803; Nelly b. 1805; William C. b. 1810; James b. 1814; Nancy J. b. 1826.
Collected by Mrs. Elnora P. Campbell, Liberty, Indiana.

LONG, CHRISTOPHER   Henry County
Born—1746, Culpepper Co., Virginia.
Service—Private at Great Bridge, Norfolk, Vir., Dec., 1775, Dunsmore's War; Col. Wm. Woodford, Lt. John Marshall. Pri. in N. J., 1776. At Valley Forge 1777-1778, Guilford Court House, Color Sergeant Yorktown, 1781; Name appears in list of 6 Long Brothers of Culpepper Co., Vir., who served throughout the War.
Proof—Genealogy of War Long of Culpepper Co., Vir., Vol. E.; Chicago Hist. Society, pp. 5, 9, 10, 13-15.
Died—Aug. 14, 1829. Buried near Devon School, Liberty Twp. Stone.
Married—Sarah Turner. Ch. Reuben, m. Martha Witt; Ellis, m. Margaret Cherry; Ellen, m. Henry Fee; Dicy, m. Morris Humphries; Gabriel, m. Sarah Humphries; Benjamin, m. Rebecca Jenkins; Elisha, m. Malinda Hale; Joel, m. Jane Sharp Boggs.
Collected by Mrs. Florence Burgess Grosvenor, Richmond, Indiana.

LONG, JOHN   Harrison County
Born—Dec. 25, 1755, Louisa Co., Virginia.
Service—Private in Regt. commanded by Col. Muhlenburg of Vir. Line, 4 years, 1776.

Proof—Pension claim W. 10200.
Died—May 20, 1828. Buried Highfill's burying ground near Corydon, Ind. Stone.
Married—1780, Delila Elliot, b. 1765. Ch. Jesse b. 1782; Leve b. 1784, m. Susan Elliott; William b. 1795; Thomas b. 1796; John E. b. 1805; Delilah b. 1807.
Collected by Mrs. W. C. Adams, Corydon, Indiana.

LOSEY (LACEY), MOSES   Ohio County
Born—About 1760.
Service—Pri. in CO. commanded by Capt. Wilkinson, Regt. Col. Shreeves, N. J. Line, 9 mos. 5 days.
Proof—Pension claim S. 16257.
Died—Feb. 23, 1836. Buried Randolph Twp.
Married—Rachel ——, d. 1840. Ch. Marian Gise; Rhoda Walker; Mary Mevey; Jemima Hart; Rebecca Moulton.
Collected by Mrs. Walter Kerr, Aurora, Indiana.

LOTT, JOHN   Jefferson County
Born—Oct. 22, 1742, Carolina Co., Virginia.
Service—In Albemarle Co., Vir., Militia; was ordered by Col. Thomas Jefferson into service; joined Capt. James Harris' CO., Col. Brookings, Vir. Regt.; served 2 mos. 5 days. Enlisted in Oct., 1780, 2 mos. 15 days in Capt. Bennet Henderson's CO., Col. Holt Richardson's Vir. Regt.; June, 1781, served 2 mos. 12 days in Capt. Elijah Hambler's CO., Col. Reuben Lindsay's Vir. Regt. Served 31 days in Capt. Robert Sharp's Vir. CO., and was present at surrender of Cornwallis. Was a sergeant.
Proof—Pension claim S. 18089, and Jefferson Co. Records.
Died—Jan. 30, 1844. Buried Ryker's Ridge.
Children—Elijah of Massas Co., Ill., and Phebe, m. John Lott.
Collected by John Paul Chapter D. A. R.

LOVEJOY, SAMUEL   Decatur County
Born—1753, Essex Co., Mass.
Service—Private under Capts. Holt, Johnson, Buffington. One of the Minute Men. On Lexington Alarm April 19, 1775. Enlisted Aug. 19, 1777. Discharged Nov. 30, 1777.
Proof—Records Secretary of the Commonwealth of Mass., vol. 12, p. 136; vol. 17, p. 65; vol. 20, p. 105. Letters of Enoch Morse, Boston, Mass. Pension claim R. 6472. Widow's application rejected for lack of proof of 6 mos. service.

Died—Sept. 13, 1822. Buried Downeyville, Decatur Co.
Married—1788, Esther Morse, 1766-1854. Ch. Nanny b. 1789, m. Ebenezer Watson; Samuel; Thaddeus; Benjamin; Abigail; William b. 1803; Esther; James S. b. 1806.
Collected by Caroline Scott Harrison Chapter D. A. R.

LUCAS, FRANCIS   Gibson County
Born—March 10, 1753.
Service—Pri. in Regt. of Col. Green of Vir., 1 yr.
Proof—Pension claim S. 36687. Ind. Cert. 7900. Pension discontinued.
Married—Fanny ———. Ch. Mary; Jemima; William; Francis Jr.

LUMPKIN, ROBERT   Randolph County
Born—1756.
Service—Wagoner in the Revolutionary War.
Proof—Randolph County history 1882. Listed as pensioner on 1840 census but no record found by Vet. Adm.
Died—Nov. 12, 1842. Buried Losantville Cemetery, Nettle Creek Twp. Stone.
Married—1785, Elizabeth Forrest (1766-1846). Ch. John b. 1786; Mary b. 1788; James b. 1791; Robert b. 1793; Sarah b. 1796; Richard b. 1798; William b. 1800; Elizabeth b. 1803; Washington b. 1806; Nancy b. 1809; Anderson b. 1812.
Collected by Mrs. James P. Goodrich and Mrs. Oran E. Ross, Winchester, Indiana.

LUNSFORD, MASON   Harrison County
Born—About 1765.
Service—Resident of the Falls of Ohio, State of Vir., when he enlisted. Pri. in CO. commanded by Capt. Bailey of Regt. of Col. Montgomery of Vir. Line, 2 yrs.
Proof—Pension claim S. 32387. Ind. Certificate 25031.
Died—Last payment of pension was made on Sept. 2, 1843.

MACK, RICHARD   Vermillion County
Born—1765.
Service—Fifer in Capt. Kimberly's CO., 2nd Regt., Conn. Line.
Proof—Pension claim W. 9910—B. L. Wt. 1447-100.
Died—July 4, 1847. Probably buried Helt Twp.
Married—1787, Betty Harvey b. 1773. Ch. Erastus b. 1788, m. Martha Benton; Lovina b. 1791; Betty P. b. 1793; Dudley b. 1795; Asa H. b. 1797; Wareham b. 1801; Hutoah b. 1803; Samuel b. 1805.

MADDEN, WILLIAM   Harrison County
Born—Feb. 27, 1762, Frederick Co., Virginia.
Service—Enlisted Jan., 1781, in Frederick Co., Vir. Ordered out to
    guard prisoners at Winchester, Vir. Served 3 mos., under Capt.
    Reynolds. Enlisted May, 1781, in Col. Edmonds' Regt. Enlisted
    again under Capt. Bell.
Proof—Pension claim W. 9902, B. L. Wt. 26908-160-55.
Died—Oct. 17, 1834, in Harrison Co.
Married—1800, Jane Haney (Hainey).

MAGRUDER, NORMAN BRUCE   Switzerland County
Service—While resident of Georgetown (now D. C.), enlisted 1781 and
    served as pri. in Capt. George Bell's CO., Cols. Wm. Murdock's
    and Wm. Dickey's Md. Regt., 6 mos.
Proof—Pension claim W. 9542.
Died—Feb. 16, 1836. Switzerland Co.
Married—1783, Nancy Paugh. Ch. Mary b. 1784; James b. 1786; Sally
    b. 1789, m. Amos Gilbert.
Collected by Mrs. A. V. Danner, Vevay, Indiana.

MAHL, FREDERICK   Knox County
Born—Nov. 16, 1757, in Germantown, Pennsylvania.
Service—Enlisted 1776 in Germantown, as pri. in Capt. James Hazlett's
    CO., Col. Halker's Penn. Regt. In battles of Princeton and Ger-
    mantown. Served 1 yr. In 1778 or 79 entered on board the
    armed ship "Fair America." Served 6 mos. as landsman, during
    which time 18 prizes were captured on coast between N. Y. and
    Charleston. Early in 1778 he went to Pittsburgh, hence down
    Ohio River and joined George Rogers Clark and was present at
    Capture of Vincennes Feb., 1779.
Proof—Pension claim S. 33035.
Died—Sept. 20, 1835. Buried on Mahl farm.
Married—First W. Marie Thorn. Ch. John; Charles; Solomon; Isaac;
    Mary; Harriett; Elizabeth; Frederick. Second W. Polly Foster.
Collected by Mrs. H. D. McCormick, 518 N. 4th St., Vincennes, Indiana.

MAHONEY, JAMES   Washington County
Born—1763, Virginia.
Service—Served in Capt. Wales CO., Col. Abraham Buford's Virginia
    Regt. In battles of Camden, Cowpens, Guilford, Eutaw Springs,
    and Ninety-Six, where he was wounded. Discharged at Win-
    chester, Vir., 1783.
Proof—Pension claim S. 36056; Early Minutes of Sharon Baptist
    Church.

Died—1821. Buried Sharon Baptist Cemetery, S. E. of Salem, Ind.
Government marker placed by Christopher Harrison Chapter
D. A. R.
Children—Taliferreo; Bennet; Polly Fisher; Arthur.
Collected by Mrs. Harvey Morris, Salem, Indiana.

MAHORNEY, BENJAMIN   Putnam County
Born—1760.
Service—Enlisted March 4, 1779, Fauquier Co., Vir. Served until Oct.
    25, 1780, under Capts. William Wales and Thomas Hoard and
    Epps, and Col. Buford and Gen. Washington. 3rd Vir. Regt.
Proof—Pension claim S. 32393.
Died—Dec. 25, 1854. Buried Smuthe Cemetery, E. of Fillmore. Government marker placed by Washburn Chapter D. A. R.
Son—Owen.
Collected by Miss Minnetta Wright, Greencastle, Indiana.

MALLORY, LEMUEL   Perry County
Born—May 22, 1763, Stratford, Conn.
Service—Enlisted in Stratford, Conn., 1778, under Capt. John Yates,
    Col. Heman Swift, 8 mos. March, 1780, enlisted as pri. under
    Lt. Pinto, Ensign Daggett. Stationed opposite West Point, N. Y.,
    then marched to Orangetown, N. J. Discharged at Orangetown.
    Enlisted 1781, battles at New Haven and Fairfield.
Proof—Pension claim W. 6785.
Died—Feb. 16, 1851. Buried Shoemaker Cemetery at Rome, Ind.
Married—1819, Rebecca Long. Dau. Edna, m. Charles Roff.

MALONE, FRANCIS   Vermillion County
Born—1760, Lancaster, Pennsylvania.
Service—Enlisted under Capt. Wm. Morrow in Penn. Militia as a volunteer and Indian Spy, April, 1777. Served 5 yrs. under Col. James
    Morrow, Capts. Dougherty and Boon.
Proof—Pension claim S. 16942.
Died—Sept., 1841. Probably buried in Helt Twp.

MANNON (MANNAN), JOHN   Harrison County
Born—Oct. 15, 1752, King George Co., Virginia.
Service—While residing in King George Co., Vir., enlisted April 15,
    1777, as pri. in Capt. Wm. Bombaree's CO., Cols. Townsend Dade
    and Robert Stith, Vir. Troops. Was stationed along the Potomac
    River. Wounded. Discharged June 25, 1779.
Proof—Pension claim W. 9538.
Died—Nov. 10, 1833. Buried in Blunk's Cemetery, Webster Twp.
    D. A. R. marker placed by Hoosier Elm Chapter D. A. R.

Married—Letice (Lettice, Letitia) —— (1765-1851). Ch. William b. 1785; James b. 1787; Nancy b. 1789; John b. 1791; Sary b. 1793; Mary b. 1795; Lucy b. 1798; Susannah b. 1800; Robert b. 1800.
Collected by Hoosier Elm Chapter D. A. R.

MARLATT, ABRAHAM — Wayne County
Born—1761, Winchester, New Jersey.
Service—Private in Capt. Hunn's CO. 1st Regt., Monmouth Militia, N. J.
Proof—Pension claim W. 21771.
Died—July 23, 1828. Buried Franklin Cemetery, E. of Milton. Government marker and bronze tablet placed by National Old Trails Chapter D. A. R.
Married—1785, Ann Linder, b. 1767. Ch. George b. 1786; Thomas b. 1790, m. Elizabeth Bellar (Ballard); Rachael; Mary, m. Connover; and eight other children.
Collected by Mrs. Paul Ross, Richmond, Ind., and Mrs. Glenn Beeson, Cambridge City, Indiana.

MARSH, SAMUEL — Dearborn County
Born—About 1761, Thompson, Windham Co., Conn.
Service—Enlisted under Capt. Low at Cheshire, Berkshire Co., Mass. In 1777, enlisted again at Brattleboro, Vt., under Capt. Weaver of Militia for 6 mos. as Minute Man. In 1780, enlisted for 3 mos.
Proof—Pension claim S. 16943.
Died—July 12, 1840.
Married—Elizabeth —— (who survived soldier).
Collected by Mrs. Walter Kerr, Aurora, Indiana.

MARSH, WILLIAM — Harrison County
Born—1747, England.
Service—Capt. in 8th Battalion, Penn. Militia, under Col. Patterson Bell, 1778.
Proof—D. A. R. No. 141178.
Died—1823. Buried Marsh Cemetery, near Laconia.
Married— —— Cornwallis. Son, Nathaniel (1788-1864), m. Sally Battershell.

MARTIN, JACOB — Washington County
Born—Feb., 1749, Ireland.
Service—Pri. in Capt. Andrew Graff's CO., Lieut. Christopher Crawford's detachment of the 1st Battalion. Standing guard at Lancaster, 1776.
Proof—Penn. Archives, Fifth Series, vol. 7, p. 13, 1073.

Died—Oct. 19, 1828. Buried Lavonia Cemetery. Government stone.
Married—Catherine Wilson. Ch. Alexander; Elizabeth.
Collected by Mrs. H. L. Buckles, Hartford City, Indiana.

MARTINDALE, WILLIAM   Miami County
Born—March 8, 1753, Philadelphia, Pennsylvania.
Service—First service 1777 or 78, Union District, S. C. When first
    drafted, hired a substitute. Later volunteered as a ranger.
Proof—Pension claim R. 6980.
Died—Jan. 24, 1854. Buried at Chile, Ind. Bronze tablet placed by
    Nineteenth Star Chapter D. A. R.
Married—Martha Bishop, d. 1817. Ch. John; Moses; James; Sarah;
    Polly; Nancy; Rachel; Patsy; Ruth.
Collected by Mrs. Charles Wolf, Peru, Indiana.

MASON, GEORGE   Dearborn County
Born—1757 or 1758, Hampshire Co., Virginia.
Service—Enlisted July, 1781, Fayette Co., Penn., under Col. Dougherty.
    Taken prisoner and kept in Canada 1 year and 5 mos.
Proof—Pension claim S. 33053.
Died—Last payment of pension was made March 27, 1837.
Collected by Mrs. Walter Kerr, Aurora, Indiana.

MASON, PETER   Jay County
Born—Aug. 22, 1764, Virginia.
Service—Volunteered Oct. 24, 1778, from Lancaster Co., Vir., as pri. in
    Capt. Wm. Chouning's CO., Col. Henry Towles' Vir. Regt. Served
    3 yrs. and 1 mo.
Proof—Pension claim S. 32394. Applied for pension from Campbell Co.,
    Ky. Moved to Jay Co., Ind., 1839, to live with children.
Died—Last payment of pension was made on Sept. 12, 1843.
Collected by Mrs. Oscar Finch, Portland, Indiana.

MASON, THOMAS   Montgomery County
Born—About 1761.
Service—Enlisted under John Rhoades, Col. Hall's Regt. in 1778, Dela-
    ware Line, 1 yr. In battles of Guilford Court House, Camden,
    and Eutaw Springs.
Proof—Pension claim S. 36691.
Died—Last payment of pension was made on Sept. 8, 1846. Buried in
    "Old Town" Cemetery. Marked by Indiana S. A. R.
Children—Eliza —— b. 1807; Jefferson b. 1810; Polly b. 1815; Malin
    Jackson b. 1816; Margaret b. 1818; Wilson Campbell b. 1821;
    Mary; William, m. Nancy Lambert; John; Priscilla.

MASTEN, MATHIAS   Hendricks County
Born—March 9, 1765, Delaware.
Service—Private the last 6 mos. of the war and was present at Yorktown.
Proof—D. A. R. Nos. 106069 and 194224; A Portrait and Biographical Record of Boone, Clinton, and Hendricks Counties of Indiana, p. 1042.
Died—Nov. 9, 1856. Buried in Coatesville Cemetery. Stone.
Married—Sarah Stanley. Ch. Darius b. 1795, m. Polly Fair; Mary b. 1797, m. Coleman Jenkins; John b. 1799, m. Sarah Cosner; Hezekiah b. 1801; Sarah b. 1803, m. Joseph Bodenhamer; Ruben b. 1806, m. Peggs Garrison; Mathias b. 1809; Charlotte b. 1812, m. Morgan Johnson; David b. 1816, m. Elizabeth Appablee.
Collected by Mrs. R. W. Brown, Richmond, Indiana and Miss Guila Masten Newlon, Coatesville, Indiana.

MASTERS, JOHN   Franklin County
Born—About 1759.
Service—Enlisted near Petersburg, Virginia, in 1779 or 1780; served as pri. in Capts. Loveley's, Wilson's and Coward's companies, Cols. Davies', Hawes' and Green's Vir. Regts. Was in the battles of Guilford Court House, Camden, Siege of Ninety-Six and Eutaw Springs, and was discharged by Major Snead, having served at least 18 mos.
Proof—Pension claim S. 36057.
Died—1836. Buried Old Franklin Cemetery, Fairfield Twp. Stone.

MATHERS, WILLIAM   Monroe County
Born—1757, Ireland.
Service—In Cumberland Co., Penn. Militia; on roll of Capt. Askey's CO. on guard at Frankstown, this being the 6th Battalion commanded by Col. Jas. Dunlap, reported April 15, 1781. Again he marched with Capt. John Hodge, Cumberland Co., Militia.
Proof—Penn. Archives, 5th Series, vol. VI, p. 410; vol. IV, pp. 298, 634.
Died—Nov. 30, 1844. Buried Clear Creek Cemetery, Perry Twp. Stone and Government marker.
Married—Esther Thorn. Ch. Gavin; James; William; John; Isabella; Benjamin; Thomas.
Collected by Mrs. Lura Bell Mitchell Emery, Bloomington, Indiana.

MAUZY, WILLIAM   Rush County
Born—1755, Virginia.
Service—Served 1776-1780 in Girard's Vir. Regt.
Proof—Rev. Soldiers of Virginia, Eckenrode List, p. 209.

Died—1837. Buried East Hill Cemetery, Rushville, Ind. Government marker.
Married—1772, Ursula Arnold (1753-1823). Ch. Elizabeth; James; George; Sallie; John; Arnold; Silas; Peter b. 1793, m. Sallie Gooding; William; Henry.
Collected by Mrs. Jessie Spann Gary, Rushville, Indiana.

MAVITY, WILLIAM   Ripley County
Born—About 1750, Ireland.
Service—Sergeant-Major of 2nd Battalion, 4th Regt., Vir. Troops, under Col. Walker. It was his duty to make daily reports. These he set down in a pocket diary. This was in possession of a great-great-grand daughter, Mrs. Carrie Mavity Riggins of St. Helens, Cal., in 1922. This diary contains a description of siege of Yorktown and the surrender of Cornwallis.
Died—1832. Buried near New Marion, Ripley Co., Ind.
Married—Mary Jones. Ch. John; William; Jesse; James; David Jones; Morton; Wesley.
Collected by Mrs. N. B. Mavity, 223 Summit Circle, French Lick, Indiana.

MAY, ABRAHAM   Green County
Born—1762, Virginia.
Service—While living in Tigers Valley, Vir., he volunteered for 3 mos., as pri. under Capt. Scott, Lt. Maxwell. Drafted 1781 for 6 mos., pri. under Capt. Cunningham, Lt. Biddinger, Gen. Morgan. Marched through Winchester to Williamsburg to Richmond.
Proof—Pension claim S. 17562.
Died—1840. Buried Bloomfield Cemetery. Government marker.
Married—Martha ——.

MAY, JOHN   Jefferson County
Born—1755.
Service—At Salisbury, N. C. Served 9 mos. as pri. in Capt. Micajah Lewis's N. C. CO. In 1782, pri. in Capt. Anthony Sharp's CO., Col. Archibald Lytle's N. C. Regt. Discharged at close of war, 18 mos. In battle of Stono and Guilford.
Proof—Pension claim S. 36690. Jefferson Co. Records, Order Book B.-316. Probate Book C.-362; Deed Book C.-362.
Died—Jan. 1, 1822.
Child—Jane, m. Dudley Beebe.
Collected by John Paul Chapter D. A. R.

MAYFIELD, MICHAJAH   Sullivan County
Born—1748, Virginia.
Service—Enlisted in Vir., Jan., 1779; served one yr. as pri. in Capt. Jesse Evans CO., Col. John Montgomery's Vir. Regt., under Gen. George Rogers Clark and marched to Ill. Re-enlisted and served as pri. a part of the time under Capt. Richard Brashears, Capt. George of the Artillery, and Capt. Holmes. Discharged March, 1783.
Proof—Pension claim S. 36692.
Died—Feb. 22, 1838. Buried Pleasantville.
Married—Wife died in Ky. Ch. James b. 1784; William.
Collected by Mrs. James R. Riggs, Sullivan, Indiana.

MAXWELL, BEZELEEL   Jefferson County
Born—Dec. 20, 1751, Albemarle Co., Virginia.
Service—Fincastle Co., Vir., Militia. As a member of Capt. Doak's CO. that was organized 1774, enlisted in the Continental Army under Gen. Anderson and was in the battle of Point Pleasant. Was at Yorktown.
Proof—War Department Records; History of S. W. Virginia.
Died—Jan. 9, 1828. Buried in old cemetery close beside Hanover Church; cemetery abandoned. Government marker erected in present Hanover cemetery by John Paul Chapter D. A. R.
Married—1775, Margaret Anderson (1755-1834). Ch. Anne b. 1781; Elizabeth; Fannie; Margaret b. 1795; Mathilda b. 1800; John; Samuel b. 1777; James Anderson; Hervey b. 1786; William; Edward.
Collected by John Paul Chapter D. A. R.

MEAD, JOHN   St. Joseph County
Born—April 10, 1764, New York.
Service—Enlisted for 9 mos. under Capt. Joseph Harrison. Re-enlisted in same CO. for 2 yrs., 1782-1784.
Proof—Pension claim S. 32409; Certificate No. 22341.
Died—December 21, 1845 (General Accounting Office).
Married—Elizabeth ——.

MEAD, THOMAS   Pike County
Born—1754, Frederick Co., Virginia.
Service—Enlisted Feb., 1776; served 18 mos. as pri. under Capt. Thomas Hutchins, Col. Muhlenburgh. From fall of 1778 to 1779 under Capt. William T. Cole, Col. Thos. Polk, N. C. Served as wagoner and later as forage master for 11 mos., 14 days in Gen. Ashe's Brigade.
Proof—Pension record.

Died—Jan. 14, 1835. Buried in Old Town graveyard, Petersburg, Ind. Bronze tablet placed by Cradle of Liberty Chapter D. A. R.
Married—Sarah ——.
Collected by Cradle of Liberty Chapter D. A. R.

MEDOCK (MEDDICK, MEDAUGH), EMMANUEL   Jefferson County
Born—1760.
Service—3 yrs. in 2nd Regt. of New Jersey, under Capt. John N. Cummings. Enlisted Jan. 11, 1779. Discharged Feb. 12, 1782.
Proof—Original certificate of service and discharge in Jefferson Co. Ind. Historical Society. Pension claim W. 9563.
Died—Jan. 11, 1829. Probably buried in Fugit Cemetery at Manville.
Married—1787, Leah Ryker, d. 1844. Ch. Catherine; Magdelany; James and Geradus.
Collected by John Paul Chapter D. A. R.

MEEK, JACOB   Wayne County
Born—March, 1755, Elkridge, Maryland.
Service—While residing in Westmoreland Co., Penn., he enlisted April 1, 1776, and served as pri. in Capt. John Stinson's CO. of Penn. Militia and helped to build Fort Wheeling; after 3 mos. service, he re-enlisted in Capt. Hugh Stinson's CO. and served as pri. until discharged Christmas Day, 1776. He enlisted in summer of 1779 and served 3 mos. as pri. in Capt. Ralph Cherry's Penn. CO.
Proof—Pension claim S. 16480.
Died—May 23, 1840. Buried Pri. cemetery on Lashley Farm, S. of Richmond, Ind. Government marker placed by Richmond Chapter D. A. R.
Married—1778, Nancy Marcus (Warcins). Ch. John; Jeremiah Lee b. 1780, m. Rebecca Grimes; Isaac m., first Nancy Perkins, second Mary G. Davidson; William, m. Patsey Holman; Patsey, m. Elijah Fisher; Effie, m. William Grimes; Rue, m. Capt. Wm. Holman; Joshua.
Collected by Mrs. Paul L. Ross, Richmond, Indiana.

MEEK, THOMAS   Decatur County
Born—1756, Maryland.
Service—A Patriot. In Commissary Department, having charge of a wagon train.
Proof—Statement made by grandson of Patriot.
Died—1838. Buried Springhill Cemetery, Decatur Co. Stone.
Married—Martha Davis, b. 1760. Ch. James; Samuel; Adam; Sarah; Priscilla; Tirzah; Martha; Mary; Sophia; Davis; Gemimia; Ann; David.
Collected by Vessie Riley, Greensburg, Indiana.

MENEFEE, SPENCER   Decatur County
Born—1762, Culpepper Co., Virginia.
Service—Volunteered under James Browmen, Culpepper Co., Vir.,
    July, 1779. Drafted, 1780, Capt. Noll, Col. Muhlenburgh, 8 mos.
    Drafted 1781, 8 mos. Discharged.
Proof—Pension claim S. 16191.
Died—Last payment of pension was made on April 10, 1834.

MEREDITH, SAMUEL   Union County
Born—Dec. 25, 1758, Delaware.
Service—Served 7 yrs. Enlisted in Vir., under Capt. George Handy
    of Maryland, Col. Henry Lee. Also classed as a dragoon. Served
    under Gen. Green.
Proof—Pension claim W. 9565.
Died—Nov. 29, 1840. Crawford Cemetery, Union Twp. Stone.
Married—Mary Breadley, m. 1788, d. 1844. Ch. Ruth, m. William
    Cleaver. Possibly other children.
Collected by Mrs. Elnora P. Campbell, Liberty, Indiana.

MERRY, CORNELIUS   Knox County
Born—July 1, 1763, Litchfield Co., Conn.
Service—Conn. Militia. Enlisted in 1778, as substitute for Samuel
    Merry, of Hartford Twp., Hartford Co., Conn.; served 2 mos. as
    pri. in Capt. King's CO. In 1779, 2 mos. as pri. in Capt. Will's
    CO., Col. Bebey's Conn. Regt. In 1779, 6 mos. with Conn. troops,
    under Lt. Owings, and was stationed at Simsbury mines in Conn.,
    where he was engaged guarding prisoners. In 1781, pri. in Capt.
    Sheppard's Conn. CO. and was discharged on receiving news of
    surrender of Cornwallis.
Proof—Pension claim S. 16479.
Died—Feb. 25, 1842. Buried Upper Indiana Church Cemetery. Stone.
Married—1813, Anna —— (1780-1845). Ch. Cornelius Jr., m. America
    Thompson; Calvin, m. Isbel Hanks.
Collected by Mrs. S. G. Davenport, Vincennes, Indiana.

MESSERVE, WILLIAM   Jennings County
Born—April 6, 1750.
Service—Enlisted 1781, under Col. Crane, Capt. Thorpe, and Col. John
    Brooks, Mass. Line.
Proof—Pension claim W. 802. B. L. Wt. 91996-160-55.
Died—July 6, 1850. Buried Kellar Cemetery, Sandcreek Twp. Stone.
Married—1821, Zeporah Beacham, d. 1864 in Hamilton Co., Ohio.

MIKESELL, JACOB   Clark County
Born—Nov. 2, 1758, Frederick Co., Maryland.
Service—Enlisted in Frederick Co., Md., July, 1776, as pri. in Capt.
    Daniel Dorsey's CO., Col. Josias Carvil Hall's Md. Regt. of the
    Flying Camp. Discharged Dec., 1776. Enlisted Aug., 1777, 2 mos.,
    pri. in Capt. Martin Derr's CO., Col. Baker Johnson's Md. Regt.
    Served 1 week as teamster in 1781.
Proof—Pension claim S. 16202; Jefferson Co. Ind. Records, Deeds Book
    B, pp. 226, 228, 229.
Died—Buried on Albert Mills' farm near Bethlehem, Clark Co. A
    broken slab marked the grave in 1912.
Collected by John Paul Chapter D. A. R. of Madison and Ann Rogers
    Clark Chapter D. A. R. of Jeffersonville, Indiana.

MILES, THOMAS   Blackford County
Born—1769, England.
Service—Enlisted first after the Battle of Bunker Hill. Lived in Steuben Co., N. Y., and came to Fayette Co., Ind., 1835, and in 1841, moved to Washington Twp., Blackford Co. At the Dec. term, 1843, of the commissioner's court of Blackford Co., he was exempted by the Co. Commissioners from the payment of any taxes on his real estate by reason of his army services.
Proof—Family record.
Died—1849. Buried in Miles Cemetery, northwest of Hartford City, Ind.
Married—Mary Underwood. Ch. William, m. Caturrah Casterline; possibly other ch.
Collected by Miss Wilma Hendricks, Hartford City, Indiana.

MILLER, ABRAHAM   Knox County
Born—1762, Pennsylvania.
Service—Private in Capt. Bernard Mains (Manns) CO., 4th Battalion,
    Lancaster Co. Penn. Militia, 1782.
Proof—Penn. Archives, Series 5, vol. 7, p. 428; D. A. R. No. 110343.
Died—1822, Knox County, Indiana.
Married—1797, Elsie Thomas (1767-1844). Son, Daniel (1807-1893), m.
    1828 Nancy English (1810-1890).
Collected by Mrs. S. G. Davenport, Vincennes, Indiana.

MILLER, EDWARD   Shelby County
Born—1739, Shenandoah, Virginia.
Service—Enlisted in Augusta Co., Vir., Feb., 1779; pri. in Capt. Adam
    Wallace's and Gray's CO. In many skirmishes and taken prisoner
    in Charlestown; held until June, 1781. Discharged July 31, 1781.
Proof—Pension record.

Died—Jan. 12, 1836. Buried in Miller Cemetery, Hendricks Twp., Shelby Co.
Married—Rebecca ——. Ch. William b. 1788; Catherine b. 1790; Christina b. 1791; Polly b. 1793; John b. 1795; Jacob b. 1796; Rebecca b. 1798; Henry b. 1801; Alexander b. 1803; Andrew b. 1805; Isaac b. 1807; Elizabeth b. 1809; Edward b. 1813.
Collected by Mrs. Mildred W. Moberly, Shelbyville, Indiana.

MILLER, HENRY   Lawrence County
Born—1750, Richmond, Virginia.
Service—"Soldier in the Revolutionary War under George Washington."
Proof—From inscription on stone at grave.
Died—1834. Buried in Guthrie Creek Church. Stone.
Daughter—Mary, m. Adam Zollman.
Collected by Miss Nell Malott, Bedford, Indiana.

MILLER, HENRY   Tippecanoe County
Born—Dec. 6, 1759, Augusta Co., Virginia.
Service—March to July, 1776, in Capt. Henry Burford's CO., under Col. Wm. Christie, against Cherokee Indians. From Feb. 18, 1778, in Capt. Jacob Ellis and Robert's CO., Col. Wm. Davis's Vir. Regt. Marched to Monmouth, later to West Point; in winter quarters near Bound Brook, N. J., and discharged Feb. 20, 1779. From Feb., 1781, 2 mos. in Capt. David Beard's CO., Col. Lynch's Regt.
Proof—Pension claim S. 16481.
Died—Jan. 18, 1846. Buried Oxford Cemetery, E. of Lafayette, Ind. Stone and bronze marker placed by Mrs. E. E. Reynolds.
Married—Sarah —— "died Feb. 1, 1838, age 74 yrs. 4 mos. 21 days" from stone.
Collected by Gen. de Lafayette Chapter D. A. R.

MILLER, JACOB   Montgomery County
Born—1755, Virginia.
Service—Enlisted in Loudoun Co., Vir., in spring or summer, 1781; served as pri. in Capts. Abraham Kirkpatrick and Luke Cannon's CO., Col. Thomas Posey's Vir. Regt., and was at the siege of Yorktown, after which he marched to Georgia and served there until after evacuation of that state by the British and was discharged at the close of war.
Proof—Pension claim W. 9569. B. L. Wt. 13717-160-55.
Died—July 25, 1839. Buried Masonic Cemetery, Crawfordsville, Ind. Stone.
Married—Margaret Dick, m. 1782, d. 1863. Ch. John d. 1844; George d. 1846; Isaac; Mary; Teny; Eliza.
Collected by Miss Jessie Watson, Crawfordsville, Indiana.

MILLER, JOHN   Rush County
Born—Dec. 10, 1752, Pennsylvania.
Service—Enlisted Aug., 1776, Penn.; 3 yrs. as pri. under Capts. Montgomery and Finley, Col. Brodhead. Engaged in taking of Burgoyne.
Proof—Pension claim S. 16974.
Died—1841. Buried in Hurst graveyard, Walker Twp. Name on bronze tablet in Rush Co. Court House by Rushville Chapter D. A. R.
Married—Margaret Bowier d. 1838. Ch. John, Jr. (1767-1863), m. Ellen Beckett; Mary; Jane; Oliver; Sarah; William.
Collected by Mrs. Williard Amos, Rushville, Indiana.

MILLER, MORDECAI   Hendricks County
Born—Dec. 22, 1755, North Carolina.
Service—1 mo pri. with Capt. Wm. Boskins 1770. From 1777 served in various troops with Capt. Wm. Boskins, Thos. McCall, Moses Lidle, John Norwood, and Gen. Andrew Pickens. In battles of Kettle Creek, Cowpens, Eutaw Springs. Served 2 yrs. and 4 mos. With Gen. George Rogers Clark in expedition to Kaskaskia and Ft. Sackville.
Proof—Pension record; Memoirs of R. M. Hazelett, Sr.
Died—1841. Buried Walnut Cemetery, close to Hendricks-Morgan Co. Line.
Married—Isabel Adair. Daughter, Nancy, m. —— Hazelett.
Collected by Mrs. R. M. Hazelett, Veterans Adm. Hospital, Marion, Indiana.

MILLER, NOAH   Ohio County
Born—Aug. 6, 1756, New Jersey.
Service—Entered in Isaac Morrison's CO., Col. Ogden, May, 1778, in Essex Co., N. J., to March, 1779. Discharged Morristown for 9 mos. service. In battle of Monmouth.
Proof—Pension claim S. 36129.
Died—Sept. 12, 1838. Buried Rising Sun Cemetery. Stone.
Children—Cornelius; Joseph; Pamela; Polly; Susan; William; Sarah.
Collected by Mrs. Walter Kerr, Aurora, Indiana.

MILLS, JOHN   Blackford County
Born—March 15, 1753.
Service—Enlisted from some one of the southern states under another name, therefore not much can be learned of his service.
Proof—Inscription on tombstone, "A Revolutionary Soldier."
Died—May 15, 1850. Buried in Shields Cemetery, N. W. of Hartford City.
Immediate family not known but there are descendants.
Collected by Pearl Casterline Smith (a descendant), Hartford City, Indiana.

MILNER, AMOS   Fayette County
Born—July 9, 1760, Pennsylvania.
Service—Served 4 yrs. as pri., under Capts. Jesse Pigman and Joseph
    Van Metre, in the Monongahela country; Vir. Line, Col. John
    Miner.
Proof—Pension claim R. 7252½; D. A. R. No. 272746.
Died—Sept. 1, 1851. Buried Mount Garrison Cemetery, Jennings Twp.
    Stone.
Married—Hannah Rice. Ch. Sarah; John; Nancy, m. James Woster.
Collected by Miss Florence N. Evens, Greencastle, Indiana.

MINGLE, JOHN   Madison County
Born—Feb., 1758, Bedford Co., Pennsylvania.
Service—Pri. in Bedford Co., Penn., Militia.
Proof—Penn. Archives, 5th Series, vol. 4; pp. 246 and 610.
Died—Aug. 18, 1842. Buried Menden Cemetery, S. of Pendleton.
Married—Martha ——. Ch. Lewis; John; David; Elizabeth; Eva;
    George.
Collected by Kentland Chapter D. A. R. and Mrs. Ida L. Mayse,
    Anderson, Indiana.

MINNEAR (MINNIEAR, MINNEGER), ABRAHAM   Indiana
Born—About 1762.
Service—While living in Northumberland Co., Penn., he volunteered
    1778, in Capt. Thomas Camplain's CO. of rangers, Col. Samuel
    Hunter's Penn. Troops. Discharged 1779, served 9 mos.
Proof—Pension claim S. 16969, Certificate 7387. In 1821, lived in
    Shelby Co., Ohio; 1830, in Vermillion Co., Ill. Applied for pen-
    sion 1832, from Montgomery Co., Ind.
Died—Last payment of pension was made Nov. 23, 1846.
Collected by Mrs. Ernest A. Brown, Lafayette, Indiana.

MITCHELL, ABRAHAM   Lawrence County
Born—Aug. 23, 1761, Pennsylvania.
Service—Enlisted 1778, as militia man at Guilford Co., N. C., for 9
    mos., under Capt. Sharpe, Col. Martin.
Proof—Pension claim S. 33102.
Died—April 17, 1856. Buried Tanksley Cemetery.

MITCHELL, AMASA   Scott County
Born—May 29, 1761, Vermont.
Service—Fifer. Not old enough to carry a gun, being a fair musician
    at that time, he was made a fifer. Served 7 yrs.
Proof—Pension records.
Died—Jan. 11, 1851. Buried Old Friendship Cemetery.

Married—1786, Mary Frymier (1770-1836). Ch. Daniel b. 1788, m. 1st Elizabeth McCan and 2nd Nora Calhoune; Catherine b. 1790; John b. 1792; William b. 1794; Mary b. 1796; John b. 1800; James b. 1806; Harvy b. 1810; Eliza b. 1814. (From family Bible.) Collected by Mrs. Margaret Mitchell Sieboldt, New Albany, Indiana.

MITCHELL, ELIJAH   Huntington County
Born—March 6, 1761, Ireland.
Service—Enlisted in Mecklenberg Co., N. C., and served the following enlistments: April 8, 1779, 3 mos. in Capt. James Barr's CO., Col. McDowell's Regt.; 1780, 2 weeks in Capt. Ezra Alexander's CO.; fall of 1780, 2 weeks; later, 4 weeks in Capt. McRee's CO.; two other terms of 1 mo. each; 1781, 3 mos.
Proof—Pension record.
Died—Aug. 1, 1847. Buried in Good Cemetery, near Warren, Ind. Stone. Bronze marker placed by Huntington Chapter D. A. R.
Married—Sarah Ireland. Ch. Martha b. 1786 d. 1851, m. Andrew Morrison; Sarah b. 1788, m. David Parson Purviance; Mary (1797-1878), m. Elam Purviance; Eli (1793-1876), m. Kiziah Purviance; Lewis (1796-1857), m. Sarah Mitchell; Elizabeth (1798-1863), m. Lewis Wasson Purviance; Fleming (1802-1880), m. Malinda Morrison; Nancy (1805-1874), m. Thomas Brawley; Kiziah (1807-1868), m. James Paul.
Collected by Miss Mildred M. Parvin, Huntington, Indiana.

MITCHELL, JAMES   Harrison County
Born—Sept. 28, 1738, Pennsylvania.
Service—Was a pri. in the Fifth Class of Capt. Benjamin White's CO. of 5th Battalion of Washington Co., Penn., Militia, under Col. Thomas Crooks.
Proof—Penn. Archives, 6th Series, vol. II, pp. 201 and 210.
Died—June 1, 1827. Buried Old Cedar Hill Cemetery, Corydon, Ind. Stone.
Married—1769, first W. Esther Gibson (1740-1815). Ch. Mary; William and James (twins); Sarah. Second W. Margaret McPheeters. Ch. John G.; David L. W.; Mary Margaret.
Collected by William Mitchell (descendant) Corydon, Indiana.

MITCHELL (MIKLE), JOHN   Marion County
Born—July 29, 1758, Middletown, Pennsylvania.
Service—Enlisted 1776. Capt. Godfrey, Col. Flowers, Penn. Line, 3 yrs. Discharged Philadelphia.
Proof—Pension claim S. 33114.
Died—Jan. 11, 1851, Marion Co., Ind.

Married—Judith Hollinger. Ch. Sarah Ann b. 1796; Barbara b. 1805; Michael b. 1808.
Collected by Caroline Scott Harrison Chapter D. A. R.

MITCHELL, WILLIAM — Parke County
Born—Oct. 20, 1746, Essex Co., Virginia.
Service—While a resident of Amelia Co., Vir., he enlisted as pri. in the Vir. Troops, served as follows: In May, 1778, 9 weeks in Capt. Rowland Ward's CO., Col. Rowland Ward's, Sr. Regt. In Aug., 1778, 9 weeks in Capt. John Dennis' CO., Col. Abraham Green's Regt. In Oct., 1778, 9 weeks in Capt. John Knight's CO., Col. Haw's Regt.
Proof—Pension claim R. 7269.
Died—1836. Buried New Discovery Cemetery. Marked by G. A. R.
Married—Choe Nance (1755-1842). Ch. Oliva; William; Giles; James; Frederick; Ann.
Collected by Mrs. H. L. Hancock, Rockville, Indiana.

MITCHELLER (MICHELLER), JACOB — Ripley County
Service—Enlisted from N. C. in Aug. 1778. Discharged Sept., 1778. Re-enlisted July, 1779. Discharged Nov., 1781.
Proof—Pension claim W. 25706.
Died—1844. Name on bronze tablet in Versailles Court House.
Collected by Mrs. A. B. Wycoff, Batesville, Indiana.

MIZNER, HENRY — Rush County
Born—Sept. 22, 1759, Bucks Co., Pennsylvania.
Service—Volunteered April 1, 1777, 6 mos. as Indian Spy under Capt. Joseph Green of Penn. Troops. On March 1, 1778, again served as spy until Dec., 1778. Enlisted April 2, 1779, as boatman with Penn. troops under Capt. Henry Dougherty and went with Gen. Sullivan on his Indian Expedition. Volunteered again May 1, 1781, spy under Capt. Reddick, Penn. troops.
Proof—Pension claim S. 16482. Moved to Rush Co. in 1821 and was still living there in 1832.
Collected by Mrs. Willard Amos, Rushville, Indiana.

MODERELL, ADAM — Owen County
Born—July 5, 1755, Lancaster Co., Pennsylvania. (Son of Robert.)
Service—Pri. in Vir. Militia. Enlisted 1780 under Capt. Lewis Hickman, Gen. George Rogers Clark, Capt. James Davis, Col. Floyd.
Proof—Pension claim S. 35523.

MONROE, ALEXANDER Marion County
Born—1758, Virginia.
Service—Served as private, corporal, and sergeant in the Vir. Troops.
Proof—Bounty Land Warrants No. 6225; Rev. War Records of Virginia by Brumbaugh, p. 476.
Died—Nov. 20, 1842. Buried Southport, Ind. Stone.
Married—1782, Betsy Chenoworth (1764-1829). Ch. Elizabeth (1804-1874), m. Joseph Wallace; William.
Collected by Mrs. Ira E. Tranter, Franklin, Indiana.

MONTGOMERY, HUGH Decatur County
Born—Feb. 29, 1754, Ireland.
Service—Enlisted Feb., 1777, in Capt. James Sullivan's CO., Col. Russell's 9th Vir. Regt. in the Continental Establishment. Received discharge from Col. John Gibson at Pittsburgh. In battles of Germantown, Brandywine.
Proof—Pension affidavit in Decatur Co. Circuit Court, pp. 2, 3, April term, 1832.
Died—May 20, 1830. Buried N. E. of Greensburg, Ind. Stone.
Married—1784, Eva Hartman. Ch. Mary b. 1785, m. Alexander Grant; Elizabeth b. 1787, m. —— Thompson; Thomas b. 1788, m. Elizabeth Bingham; Henry b. 1790, m. Polly Howard; Margaret b. 1792; William b. 1793, m. Ann Davine; Sally b. 1795, m. —— Martin; Hugh b. 1797, m. Elizabeth Montgomery; Nancy b. 1799, m. —— Hindman; George b. 1801, m. Elizabeth Jackson; Peggy b. 1803, m. —— Kercheval; Michael b. 1806, m. Ann F. Robison; Robert b. 1807, m. Louisa Robison.
Collected by Mrs. H. S. McKee, Greensburg, Indiana.

MONTGOMERY, SAMUEL Gibson County
Born—1743, Virginia (son of Hugh and Caroline).
Service—Pri. in Vir. Troops.
Proof—D. A. R. Lineage 86, pp. 287, 288.
Died—1815. Buried on Benson farm near Owensville, Ind. Stone.
Married—Polly McFarland. Ch. Dorcas b. 1787, m. Thomas Stone; Polly; Rachel; Katie; Robert; James; Benjamin; John, Samuel, Jr.
Collected by Gen. John Gibson Chapter D. A. R.

MONTGOMERY, THOMAS Gibson County
Born—1745, Roanoke Co., Virginia (son of Hugh and Caroline).
Service—Served as pri., then Lieut. in Capt. John Martin's CO., of Clark's Ill. Regt. of Vir. State Troops under Gen. George Rogers Clark. A muster roll of the organization dated March 22, 1783, shows that his services commenced Oct. 22, 1780, terminated Nov. 26, 1782.

Proof—Pension record. D. A. R. No. 208561.
Died—1818. Buried near Owensville, Ind.
Married—1767, Martha Crockett (1740-1803). Ch. Molly b. 1770, m. Mathias Mounts; Jane (1774-1846), m. Capt. Jacob Warrick; Hugh b. 1768; Thomas and Isaac (twins) b. 1776; Patsey b. 1780, m. Col. Robert McGary; Walter Crockett b. 1784, m. Nancy Roberts.
Collected by Mrs. Roy Bogner, Washington, Indiana.

MOORE, GEORGE   Jasper County
Born—Oct. 10, 1749, Frederick Co., Maryland.
Service—Enlisted April 15, 1775, as pri. in Capt. Michael Cresap's Md. rifle CO. Was in battle of Bunker Hill and discharged April 15, 1776. Re-enlisted for 2 yrs. in Capt. Joseph Smith's CO., Col. James Smith's Md. Regt. In battles of Long Island, White Plains and Trenton, Princeton, Brandywine and Germantown. Discharged 1778. Several later enlistments.
Proof—Pension record.
Died—July 18, 1848. Buried Smith Cemetery, Jasper Co. Stone. Bronze marker placed by Gen. Van Rensselaer Chapter D. A. R.
Married—1780, Nancy Ball, and had 21 ch. Only following known: William; George; John; Mahala; Nancy Dowden; Phebe; Mary Standage.
Collected by Mrs. Art Hopkins, Rensselaer, Indiana.

MOORE, JONATHAN   Bartholomew County
Born—Aug. 2, 1754.
Service—Enlisted in N. Y., June 28, 1775, for 6 mos., pri. in Capt. William Goforth's CO. of the First N. Y. Regulars commanded by Col. Alexander McDougall. Discharged at Albany, N. Y., Dec. 28, 1775; re-enlisted at Hopewell, N. J., April, 1776, for 1 yr. in Capt. Thomas Paterson's CO., 3rd N. J. Regulars, Col. Elias Dayton. Re-enlisted at Ticonderoga, N. Y., Jan. 13, 1777, for the war. Was at battle of Brandywine; transferred at Valley Forge, March 19, 1778, to the Commander-in-Chief's guard. Was at battle of Monmouth, Connecticut Farms; Kings Bridge; Yorktown. Discharged Nov. 3, 1783.
Proof—Inscription on marker; County Records; Lossing's second volume.
Died—Sept. 25, 1853. Buried Sharon Cemetery, N. E. of Columbus, Ind. Stone. Bronze marker placed by Joseph Hart Chapter D. A. R.
Children—Hugh; Hannah; Jonathan.
Collected by Mrs. Laura D. Fix (deceased), Columbus, Indiana.

MOORE, RODERICK   Switzerland County
Born—Feb. 9, 1761, Salisbury, Connecticut.
Service—Enlisted from Salisbury in June or July, 1777, pri., 6 mos. in
    Capt. Roger's CO., Col. Enos' Conn. Regt. Enlisted 1778, 2 mos.
    in Capt. Roger Moore's Conn. CO.
Proof—Pension claim W. 9578.
Died—June 16, 1841, Switzerland Co.
Married—1787, Mary Guthery b. 1770. Ch. Cynthia b. 1788; Erastus
    b. 1790; Lucretia (1792-1860), m. Ethol B. Lyon; William b. and d.
    1795; Jeremiah (1796-1800); Almon b. 1800, m. 1825 Laura Pearson; Mary Ann (1802-1823); Philena b. 1805, m. 1824 John Barker;
    Roderick, Jr. b. 1808, m. 1838 Mary Phillips; Charlotte b. 1811.
Collected by Mrs. A. V. Danner, Vevay, Indiana.

MOORE, SAMUEL   Putnam County
Born—July 14, 1761, Staunton, Virginia.
Service—While residing in Greenbrier Co., Vir., he enlisted Feb. 1,
    1781, as pri. in Capt. James Armstrong's CO., under Major Andrew
    Hamilton in Vir. Troops. Discharged Sept., 1781.
Proof—Pension claim S. 16983.
Died—Buried in Putnam County.
Collected by Miss Minnetta Wright, Greencastle, Indiana.

MOORE, WILLIAM   Washington County
Born—1758, Delaware.
Service—Served from S. C. under Gen. Rutherford, Col. John Armstrong, Capt. Free.
Proof—Pension claim W. 2152, B. L. Wt. 26485-160-55.
Died—July 15, 1844. Buried near Livonia.
Married—1777, Olive Free. Ch. William; Amy; Jacob; Edward; James;
    George; Elizabeth. Second W. 1798 Anna Quiard. Ch. Jonathan
    b. 1800; Silas; Samuel; John; Olive; Joshua; Nancy; Mary;
    Catherine; Polly Ann; Joseph b. 1824.
Collected by Mrs. I. E. Tranter, Franklin, Indiana.

MOORE, WILLIAM   Orange County
Born—1754, Botetourt Co., Virginia.
Service—Enlisted Dec. 25, 1780, in Randolph Co., N. C.; pri. Capt.
    Charles Goldston's CO., Col. John Luttrell's N. C. Regt. Again
    1781. Discharged March 16, 1782.
Proof—Pension claim S. 17592.
Died—April 15, 1833. Buried Stampers Creek Church Cemetery, Paoli
    Twp. Stone.
Married—Rachel —— (1762-1839). Ch. Edward b. 1792 (War of 1812),
    m. Abigail Reed; Rachel, m. Joel Vandeveer.
Collected by Mrs. N. B. Mavity, French Lick, Indiana.

MORGAN, NATHAN   Switzerland County
Born—Oct. 22, 1752, Delaware.
Service—Volunteered 1777, served 3 terms, 6 mos. in all as pri. in
   Capt. Wm. Love's CO., Col. Preston's Vir. Regt. Most of his
   service he was stationed at "Chizels" Lead Mine in Montgomery
   Co., Vir.
Proof—Pension claim S. 16985.
Died—Sept. 4, 1839. Buried McKay Cemetery, Craig Twp. Stone.
Children—Lewis Howell, m. Elizabeth Freeman.
Collected by Mrs. A. V. Danner, Vevay, Indiana.

MORRIS, CORNELIUS   Tippecanoe County
Born—Oct. 2, 1759, Augusta Co., Virginia.
Service—Pri. recruited by Capt. Lloyd Beall.
Proof—Pension record; Archives of Maryland, vol. 18, Muster Roll.
Died—Aug. 6, 1834. Buried Benton Cemetery, N. W. of Lafayette, Ind.
   Bronze tablet placed by Gen. de Lafayette Chapter D. A. R.
Married—Sarah Dudley. Ch. Mary; Catherine; Annie; William; Hurley; Sarah; Jane; Cornelius, Jr.; Harriett; Elizabeth.
Collected by Mrs. Arthur McQueen, West Lafayette, Indiana.

MORRIS, JACOB   Henry County
Born—March 22, 1762, Middlesex Co., New Jersey.
Service—Enlisted at age of 16 in 1778 as pri. in CO. of Capt. Jacob
   Piatt for 6 mos.
Proof—Pension claim S. 33122. In 1838 applied for transfer from
   Bracken Co., Ky., to Indiana to live with children.
Died—Last payment of pension was made Oct. 27, 1840. On Sept. 15,
   1840, he was living in Henry Co., Ind.

MORROW, JOHN   Marion County
Born—Nov. 27, 1760, Chester Co., Pennsylvania.
Service—Enlisted as pri. in Capt. Thorne Ashley's CO., 1st Battalion,
   Cumberland Co. Militia. Served under Capt. Wm. Blaine 3 mos.,
   1776. April, 1778, 3 mos. under Capt. Bohannon and Col. Fred
   Watt. 1 mo. in 1779 in Capt. Wm. Blaine's CO.
Proof—Penn. Archives, vol. 6, p. 61.
Died—Aug. 24, 1835. Buried Crown Hill Cemetery.
Married—First W. Elizabeth Pollock (1753-1813). Ch. Alexander b.
   1783, m. Mary P. Coffey. Second W. Abigail Miller (1781-1842).
   Ch. Priscilla b. 1817, m. James Grant McMahan.

MOSIER, TOBIAS   Fountain County
Born—North Carolina.
Service—Enlisted fall of 1776, Randolph Co., N. C., 6 mos. in Capt.
   John Barnet's CO., Col. Littorell's N. C. Regt.

Proof—Pension claim S. 16487.
Died—1835. Buried Rob Roy Cemetery, Shawnee Twp. Government marker placed by Mrs. George E. Foster.
Married—Nancy Myers. Ch. Robert; Elizabeth.
Collected by Mrs. A. S. Dolch (deceased), Attica, Indiana.

MOUNTS, THOMAS   Switzerland County
Born—July 5, 1764.
Service—Enlisted from Westmoreland Co., Penn., 1779, and served 3 mos. under Lieut. Lewis Fleming and Col. Caleb Mounts. From May, 1780-1781, 3 mos. in Capt. James Wallace CO. and 3 mos. in Capt. John Minters' CO., and under Col. Providence Mounts in 1781-82.
Proof—Pension claim S. 17594.
Died—July 8, 1822. Buried Lostetter Cemetery near Grant's Creek Baptist Church. Stone.
Married—Nancy Crawford. Ch. Nancy, m. Henry Wallick; Rachel, m. Wm. Scott; Cynthia, m. John Lampton; Mary, m. Alexander Leggett; Thomas, m. Vina Palmer; Josena, m. Isaac Pogue.
Collected by Mrs. A. V. Danner, Vevay, Indiana.

MURPHY, BUTLER   Marion County
Born—1756, Virginia.
Service—The name appears on a list of soldiers in the Virginia Line in Continental Establishment who received certificates for the balance of their full pay. The list indicates that the sum of 50 pounds, 5 shillings, 6 pence was received on account of his service.
Proof—Certificate from the War Department; family records loaned by S. Hasley's grandson.
Died—1840.
Married—Lydia ——. Ch. Sarah.
Collected by Mrs. May Kaufman, Indianapolis, Indiana.

MURPHY, JAMES   Orange County
Born—1751, Virginia.
Service—Enlisted 1776 in Capt. William Edmund's CO. and Col. Edmunds' and Gaskin's Vir. Regts.; transferred to Gen. Morgan's rifle corps. In battle of Brandywine, at the taking of Burgoyne, Monmouth, Jamestown, Eutaw Springs, at the surrender of Cornwallis, and was discharged at Winchester, Vir.
Proof—Pension claim S. 35532.
Died—1826. Buried on the farm he entered, Stampers Creek Twp. Stone.
Married—First W. —— Newland, had three children, youngest was Daniel (War of 1812). Second W. Margaret ——.
Collected by Mrs. N. B. Mavity, French Lick, Indiana.

MURPHY, WILLIAM   Union County
Born—May 14, 1742, Salem County, New Jersey.
Service—Served as pri., Gloucester Co., N. J., Militia. Received certificate No. 258 dated May 1, 1784, amounting to 1 pound, 16 shillings for the depreciation of his Continental pay in Gloucester, N. J.
Proof—Office of Adjutant General of New Jersey.
Died—Aug. 20, 1830. Buried Bath Cemetery. Stone.
Married—Phebe Sherry (1744-1828). Ch. Samuel (1774-1862), m. Elizabeth Hitchener; William, Jr. (1776-1863); Rachel b. 1780, m. David Ogen.
Collected by Mrs. Elnora P. Campbell, Liberty, Indiana, and Miss Mildred M. Parvin, Huntington, Indiana.

MUSGRAVE, SAMUEL   Warrick County
Born—1747, Lancaster County, Pennsylvania.
Service—Enlisted July, 1776, in "Cannonkachick" Settlement, Cumberland Co., Penn. Served 3 mos. as pri. in Capt. Patrick Jack's Penn. CO. Enlisted in July, 1777, served 3 mos. as pri. in Capt. George Crawford's CO., Col. Irvines' Penn. Regt. and was at the battle of Brandywine. In 1782 served 12 mos. as Indian Spy under Lieut. Robert Ritchie in Penn. Troops.
Proof—Pension claim W. 9211.
Died—Sept. 2, 1834. Buried Davis Cemetery, N. W. of Yankeetown. Stone.
Married—1767, Elizabeth ———. Ch. Huldah b. 1768; Moses b. 1770; Mary b. 1772; Samuel Davies b. 1775; David b. 1776; James b. 1779; Elizabeth b. 1781; Sarah b. 1783; Jane b. 1785; William b. 1788; Ann b. 1790.
Collected by Mrs. H. K. Forsythe, Newburgh, Indiana.

MUSGROVE, SAMUEL   Parke County
Born—June 27, 1760, Loudoun Co., Virginia.
Service—While residing in Loudoun Co. near Leesburg, he enlisted in May, 1776, and served as a pri. in Capt. Thomas West's CO., Col. Rawlings' Vir. Regt.; he was taken prisoner at the capture of Fort Washington, held for 6 or 8 weeks, when paroled and returned home in the spring of 1777. Volunteered later in 1777 and served 2 mos. as pri. in Capt. Joshua Wilson's CO. in a campaign against the Indians.
Proof—Pension claim W. 9583.
Died—April 3, 1847. Buried family graveyard in Bilbo, Howard Twp.
Married—1790, Elizabeth ———. Third child was John b. 1797, and fourth was Samuel b. 1800. There were several others.

MYERS, HENRY   Ripley County
Born—1747, Pennsylvania.
Service—Enlisted from Penn. in 1778 under Col. George Wilson. Served
    2 yrs., 5 mos.
Proof—Pension claim S. 31876. Family records in Ripley Co., Ind., and
    Montgomery Co., Ky.
Died—Dec. 20, 1842. Buried Myers Cemetery, W. of Cross Plains.
    Stone. Government marker placed by Ripley Co. His. Society.
Children—Lewis; George; Daniel; Rebecca, m. Jacob Overturf. Probably others.
Collected by Mrs. A. B. Wycoff, Batesville, Indiana.

MYERS, JACOB   Franklin County
Born—About 1741.
Service—Enlisted in Guilford Co., N. C., in June or July, 1777, served
    as pri. in Capt. Wm. Lytle's N. C. CO. and in Col. Archibald
    Lytle's N. C. Regt. Was in the battles of Brier Creek and Stono
    and in an engagement about 12 miles from Charleston, S. C.,
    where he received several wounds. Was discharged in Sept.,
    1779. Later he served 9 mos. in Capt. John Ramsey's N. C. CO.
Died—About 1838 in Posey Twp.
Married— —— Milberry. Ch. Isaac; Abraham; Sally; Jacob; John.

McAFEE, MATHEW   Clark County
Born—About 1760.
Service—Enlisted Aug. 10, 1776, by Capt. Moses Carson in 8th Penn.
    Line. Served as Corporal. Discharged by Stephen Bayard.
Proof—Pension claim S. 36697, B. L. Wt. 100-95.
Died—Last payment of pension was made on April 17, 1823.

McANELLY (McNELLY), PETER (Negro)   Knox County
Born—1758, Louisa County, Virginia.
Service—Enlisted in spring of 1781 and served 3 tours of 3 mos. each
    as pri. with Vir. Troops, under Capts. James Watson, Anderson,
    and Johnson, in Col. White's Regt.
Proof—Pension claim S. 16467.
Died—Last payment of pension was made Nov. 19, 1846.
Collected by Mrs. S. G. Davenport, Vincennes, Indiana.

McBRIDE, ISAAC   Clark County
Born—1757 Shippies Town, Maryland.
Service—Pri. in Capt. Joseph Bowman's CO. with Gen. George Rogers
    Clark in the expedition against Vincennes. Enlisted April 6,
    1778, and was discharged Aug. 8, 1778. Was allotted land in
    Clark Co., Ind., in payment of his services.

Proof—Virginia State Library List of Rev. Soldiers of Vir., p. 280; English's Conquest of N. W. Territory, vol. 2, pp. 847 and 1035; Original Survey Book in Recorder's Office of Clark Co. showing allotment of land to Rev. Soldiers.
Died—1830. Buried on the land allotted him. Stone.
Married—1793, his brother's widow, Mary Carr d. 1806. Ch. Isaac, Jr.; David; Mary (1798-1877).
Collected by Ann Rogers Clark Chapter D. A. R.

McCAMMON, MATTHEW   Sullivan County
Born—1757, Ireland.
Service—Enlisted in Camden District, S. C., 1779, served 9 mos. in Capt. James Knox's CO., Col. E. Kershaw's S. C. Regt. Enlisted 1780, 1½ mos. in Capt. Henry Bishop's CO., Col. Henry Hampton's and Wade Hampton's S. C. Regt. Was at the taking of Forts Congaree, Thompson, and Orangeburg, was in a skirmish with the Tories under Simon Girty and in battle of Eutaw Springs, where he received a slight wound.
Proof—Pension claim S. 17578.
Died—Oct. 6, 1841, Carlisle, Ind.
Married— ——Trimble. Ch. Hugh; Richard; John; Zerilda; Margaret; Nancy.
Collected by Miss Edna Calvert, Sullivan, Indiana.

McCASLAND, WILLIAM   Jefferson County
Born—March 8, 1758, Chester Co., Pennsylvania.
Service—Enlisted in Cumberland Co., Penn., July, 1776; 3 mos. in Capt. Culbertson's Penn. Co.; enlisted in Dec., 1777, and served 3 mos. in Capt. Young's Penn Co.; enlisted in 1781, and served 3 mos.
Proof—Pension claim W. 21790; Will in Jefferson Co., Ind.; Entered land in Jefferson Co., Ind., 1813.
Died—May 3, 1839.
Married—1781, Eleanor —— b. 1761. Ch. Jain b. 1782; Dorathia b. 1784; Susana b. 1786; John b. 1788; Mary b. 1790; Elenor b. 1793; Sarah b. 1795; William b. 1797, m. Mary G. Cochran; Pheby b. 1800; Lovina b. 1802; James H. b. 1804.
Collected by John Paul Chapter D. A. R.

McCLELLAN, DANIEL, SR.   Jefferson County
Born—1760.
Service—Volunteered in spring 1776 in Guilford Co., N. C., under Capt. Mahan, Col. Montgomery's Regt. Was in battle of Blackwater-Bridge. Discharged at Hillsborough. Moved in 1776 to Mifflin Co., Penn. Enlisted Aug., 1777, and was captain of a company under Col. Irwin. In battles of Brandywine and Germantown,

discharged spring of 1778. Captain of another company under Col. Watts and Gen. Lacy; discharged in June. Organized a company of rangers in 1778; received commission from Gov. Mifflin; served 1778-81 under Col. Purdy, Turbalt and Major Elliot.
Proof—Shelby Co., Ky., records and Jefferson Co., Ind., records.
Died—Oct. 18, 1847. Buried Pisgah Cemetery, Graham Twp. Stone.
Married—Nancy ——. Ch. John b. 1784; Daniel, Jr.; Joseph.
Collected by John Paul Chapter D. A. R.

McCLELLAND, JAMES   Clark County
Born—March 29, 1759, County Derry, Ireland.
Service—Came to Fayette Co., Penn., in 1771 and enlisted in Sept., 1776, served 1 mo. under Capt. James Doherty, stationed in a fort on Dunkark Creek. Enlisted in Sept., 1777, served 5 weeks under same captain against the Tories. Enlisted Aug. 10, 1778, under same captain in Gen. McIntosh's campaign.
Proof—Pension claim W. 2315.
Died—Jan. 24, 1840, at his home in Saluda Twp., Jefferson Co., but buried across the county line in Clark Co., Antioch Cemetery.
Married—First W. —— Hughes (1757-1798). Ch. Richard b. 1792. Second W. Sarah McKinley, m. 1815.
Collected by John Paul Chapter D. A. R.

McCLURE, DANIEL   Knox County
Born—Feb. 13, 1754, Ireland.
Service—Pri. under Col. George Rogers Clark, aiding in the capture of Vincennes from the British. Also in 2nd Battalion of the Cumberland Co. Militia of Penn. in 1780, under Capt. John Carrothers.
Proof—Penn. Archives, 5th Series, vol. 6, p. 181.
Died—Dec. 27, 1825. Buried Upper Indiana Cemetery. Stone.
Married—Martha Baird. Ch. John, m. Elizabeth Elliott; James; Thomas, m. Elizabeth Handley; Charles, m. Margaret DcDonald; Joseph, m. Mary Goenz; Mary, m. Charles Archer; Martha, m. 1st Mr. Balch, 2nd Charles Armstrong; Daniel, m. 1st Esther Thompson, 2nd Mary Jane Bartmas; Elizabeth, m. James Elliott; Ester, m. John Stockwell.
Collected by Mrs. S. G. Davenport, Vincennes, Indiana.

McCLURE, GEORGE   Knox County
Born—June 4, 1757, Londonderry, Ireland.
Service—Pri. in Capt. Thomas Kennedy's CO. in the 2nd Battalion of Cumberland Co. Militia, Penn., Col. John Davis. He enlisted at age of 21 in 1775.
Proof—Penn. Archives, 5th Series, vol. 6, p. 158; D. A. R. No. 116965.

Died—1824. Buried Upper Indiana Cemetery. Stone.
Married—Jane Gilmore. Ch. Catherine; Mary; Robert G.; Margaret; Cynthia; Matilda; George; William; James S.; John.
Collected by Mrs. S. G. Davenport, Vincennes, Indiana.

McCLURE, JOHN   Knox County
Born—July 12, 1745, Ireland.
Service—Pri. in Capt. John Campbell's CO., 2nd Battalion, Cumberland Co. Militia, 1778, Col. John Davis.
Proof—Penn. Archives, 5th Series, vol. 6, p. 31.
Died—June 14, 1814. Buried Upper Indiana Cemetery. Stone.
Married—1786, Jane McGuire McClinton (1756-1820). Ch. James; Mary; Elizabeth; Margaret; John (1797-1871), m. Eliza Armstrong.
Copied by Mrs. S. G. Davenport, Vincennes, Indiana.

McCLURE, ROBERT   Marion County
Born—June 10, 1753, Richmond, Virginia.
Service—Private under General Sumter.
Proof—Documents Relating to the History of South Carolina during the Revolutionary War by A. S. Salley, pp. 7 and 8.
Died—Sept. 11, 1830. Marion Co., Ind.
Married—1772, Margery Buffington. Ch. Ann, m. —— Pearson; Sarah; William; Samuel b. 1777, m. Mary Stewart; John, m. Elizabeth Buffington; Margaret b. 1787, m. 1st Robert Speer, 2nd David Ingle; Mary, m. Barclay Benbow; Margery b. 1791, m. Stephen Julien; Robert, Jr., b. 1795, m. 1st Esther Gerard, 2nd Jane Gillispie; Rosanna b. 1798, m. Enoch Pearson.
Collected by Mrs. Harry Moltz, Decatur, Indiana.

McCLURE, WILLIAM   Knox County
Born—Dec. 14, 1749, Ireland.
Service—Unassigned ensign, Col. Burd's Cumberland Co., Penn., Regt., 1760, age 11 years. Capt. in 5th CO., 2nd Battalion, Davis' Penn. Militia under Col. John Davis. Quartermaster and wagon conductor in Penn. from July 5, 1777, to May 14, 1778, age 28 yrs. Served 6 mos. as Capt. under Col. George Rogers Clark in 1780.
Proof—Records of Cumberland Co.; Records in Adjutant General's Office; Pension record.
Died—Dec. 14, 1811. Buried Upper Indiana Cemtery. Stone.
Married—1787, Margaret Mossman (1771-1853). Ch. John; Elizabeth; Archibald Mossman; Charles; Mary; William, Jr.; Louisia; Melinda; Caroline Jeane.
Collected by Mrs. S. G. Davenport, Vincennes, Indiana.

McCOMB, WILLIAM   Clark County
Born—May 20, 1750, Augusta Co., Virginia.
Service—Drafted Augusta Co., Vir., Sept., 1777, under Capt. Wm.
    Anderson. Served 3 mos. Drafted again for 3 mos. 1778 under
    Capt. Cannon. Drafted 1780, 3 mos. Volunteered 1781, 3 mos.
    Drafted 1781, 3 mos. All in Regt. of Col. Huggert, Vir. Line.
Proof—Pension claim S. 16198.
Died—Last payment of pension was made on April 18, 1846.

McCONNELL, HUGH   Fountain County
Born—Jan. 1756, Newcastle Co., Delaware.
Service—Pri. in Capt. John Maxwell's CO. and Col. Oliver Spencer's
    Regt. Enlisted May, 1777, for duration of war and was on the
    rolls to July 1, 1779.
Proof—Pension claim S. 74760.
Died—1835, Fountain Co., Ind.
Married—Elizabeth Jolly. Ch. James; John; David; Samuel; Elizabeth; Martha; Hettie; William; Hugh; Thomas.
Collected by Col. Isaac White Chapter D. A. R.

McCORD, WILLIAM   Knox County
Born—1762, Frederick County, Virginia.
Service—Enlisted in Winchester, Vir., in 1780 or 81, pri. in Capt.
    Rice's CO. Col. Edmund's Vir. Regt., served 3 mos. And 3 mos.
    in Capt. Jacob Grimes' CO. Next year 3 mos. in Capt. Taylor's
    CO.
Proof—Pension claim S. 16194.
Died—March 20, 1846. Buried in Price Cemetery. Stone.
Children—Margaret, m. Michael Starner; William, Jr., m. Sarah Hollingsworth; George; Asa.
Collected by Mrs. S. G. Davenport, Vincennes, Indiana.

McCORMICK, JOHN   Jackson County
Born—1750, Virginia.
Service—Pri. in Capt. John Mark's CO., 14th Vir. Regt. commanded
    by Col. Charles Lewis. He was enlisted Jan. 6, 1778, and in Dec.
    was transferred with his CO. to the 10th Vir. Regt. under Col.
    William Davis. His name last appears on the roll for Nov., 1779.
Proof—War Department records; Church certificate from East Penseborough, Vir., dated Oct., 1783. Jackson Co., Ind., Probate "C"
    Will Book, p. 57.
Died—Sept., 1822. Buried on McCormick Farm near Brownstown, Ind.
    Stone. Government marker.
Married—Rebecca Findley. Ch. Samuel; James; Nancy; Hudson;
    Thomas; Sallie; Jane.
Collected by Gen. Jacob Brown Chapter D. A. R.

McCORMICK, JOHN   Fayette County
Born—Aug. 30, 1754, Virginia.
Service—Enlisted 1776 in Vir. as pri. under Capt. James Robinson, Col.
    Christie. Second enlistment under Capt. James Shelly. Third
    enlistment from Penn. for 3 mos. in Capt. McCall's CO.
Proof—Pension record; Rev. Soldiers of Vir. by Eckenrode, p. 195.
Died—April 8, 1837. Buried City Cemetery, Connersville, Ind.
Married—1785, Catherine Drennen (1769-1862). Had 8 sons and 6
    daus. John, Jr. (1791-1825), m. Bethiah Case; William b. 1793, m.
    Susannah Woolverton; James (1797-1858), m. Patsy Perkins;
    Catherine b. 1808; Mary (1813-1815).
Collected by Mrs. S. G. Davenport, Vincennes, Indiana.

McCOY, ROBERT   Knox County
Born—Nov. 26, 1761, Augusta County, Virginia.
Service—Volunteered 1777 in Capt. Andrew Lockridge's Vir. CO., 3
    mos. Enlisted 1778, 3 mos. in same CO. under Col. Dickenson.
    In 1779 was ordered by Col. Abraham Smith to carry an express
    to his father, Capt. John McCoy. Volunteered 1781 in Capt.
    David Gwinn's Vir. CO. In battle of Guilford Court House.
Proof—Pension claim S. 16197.
Died—Oct. 30, 1852. Buried McCoy Cemetery, near Monroe City.
    Stone. The inscription gives him the title "Captain."
Married—Margaret —— (1767-1841). Ch. (named in will) Alexander,
    1802-72; Robert, 1809-72; Nancy Junkins; Sarah Reel; Margaret
    Ray d. 1838; Malinda Jordan.
Collected by Mrs. George McCoy and Mrs. S. G. Davenport, Vincennes,
    Indiana.

McCOY, WILLIAM   Clark County
Born—1754, "McCoy Fort," Fayette Co., Pennsylvania.
Service—Pri. in Col. David Williamson's CO., Capt. Andrew Swearington, Penn. Troops.
Proof—Penn. Archives, 6th Series, vol. 2, p. 123.
Died—Aug. 2, 1813. Buried Old Silver Creek Churchyard, Clark Co.
    Stone.
Married—1775, Elizabeth Rice (Royce) 1758-1834. Ch. James b. 1776,
    m. Nancy Johnson; John, m. Jane Collins; Isaac; Sallie; Lydia;
    Rice b. 1789, m. Malinda Pounds.
Collected by Mrs. John Logan Marshall (descendant), State Regent of
    S. C. Clemson College, South Carolina.

McCULLOUGH, JOHN   Owen County
Born—Jan. 17, 1755, Lancaster Co., Pennsylvania.
Service—Pri. N. C. Militia. Enlisted 1776 in York Co., Penn., and
    again Sept., 1777, Mecklenburg Co., N. C., in "Regulators." Served

under Col. Frances Holton, Capt. Wm. Ross, Lieut. Joseph Morrison, Capt. Osburn, Capt. James Reese, Maj. James White, Col. George Alexander, Gen. Rutherford.
Proof—Pension claim S. 32404.
Grave—Probably buried in Surber Farm, N. W. of Gosport, Indiana.

McCUNE, JOSEPH   Jefferson County
Born—Jan. 11, 1760, Lancaster County, Pennsylvania.
Service—Enlisted in Dec., 1776, served as substitute for his brother, Alexander McCune, as pri. in Capt. Ross' Penn. CO. and was in battle of Trenton; in 1777 served again for his brother, was stationed at Lancaster guarding prisoners. Enlisted in S. C. under Capt. McClure, Gen. Sumter in S. C. Troops; was in battles of Rocky Mount and Hanging Rock.
Proof—Pension claim S. 16465.
Married—1824, Maria Redenbaugh.
Collected by John Paul Chapter D. A. R.

McDANIEL, WILLIAM   Vigo County
Born—1732, Scotland.
Service—Pri. in Capt. Joseph Spencer's CO., 7th Vir. Regt. under Col. Alexander McClenachan. Enlisted April 10, 1775, and discharged April 10, 1778.
Proof—War Department, Adjutant General's Office.
Died—March 10, 1817. Buried McDaniel's graveyard, Vigo Co.
Married—Mary Duff Fard. Ch. Elizabeth; Harriette; George; Alemara; Aaron.
Collected by Caroline Scott Chapter D. A. R.

McDONALD (McDONIELDS), JOSEPH   Ripley County
Born—1760, Frederick County, Maryland.
Service—Volunteered May, 1779, served on frontier of Penn. under Ensign Joseph Sparks, Lieut. Johnson. From Aug. to Nov., 1779, served as substitute under Col. Ashmon, Capt. Thomas Norton. Total service 6 mos. and 18 days.
Proof—Pension claim S. 33065.
Died—June 15, 1841. Buried Old Washington Cemetery, Versailles, Ind. Government marker.
Daughter—Mary, m. John Grimes.
Collected by Mrs. A. B. Wycoff, Batesville, Indiana.

McDONALD, PETER   Clark County
Born—1753, Cape May, Virginia.
Service—Private 8th Vir. Regt. of Infantry. In service under Gen. Lee. In battles of Brandywine and Germantown. Taken prisoner in latter battle and was confined in Philadelphia prison. Served 3 yrs. exclusive of imprisonment and was discharged 1781.

Proof—Pension claim W. 9554.
Died—March 6, 1825. Buried near Charlestown, Indiana.
Married—Catherine Wise, d. 1841. Ch. James b. 1789; Martha; Mary b. 1784; John b. 1785; Sarah b. 1787, m. Andrew Mitchell; Catherine b. 1791, m. John F. Dietz; Daniel b. 1793; Elizabeth b. 1795; Rachel b. 1798; Permeley b. 1800, m. David Copple; David b. 1803; Peter b. 1806.
Collected by Mrs. Gertrude Rosenbarger, Corydon, Indiana.

McENTIRE, WILLIAM　　　　　　　　　　　　　Gibson County
Born—June 3, 1756.
Service—Entered under Capt. Wm. Rippy of Shippensburg, Penn., for 1 yr. in 1776. Again Feb. 15, 1777, under Capt. Sam. Montgomery, Col. Sam. Hayes' Regt., Gen. Wayne's Brigade, 3 yrs. Discharged March 27, 1780, at Morristown, N. J.
Proof—Pension claim S. 36693.
Died—July 8, 1821. Gibson Co. (Penn. Archives, Series 2, vol. 10, p. 471).
Married—Mary ——. Ch. William; James.

McGAHEY, WILLIAM　　　　　　　　　　　　　Putnam County
Born—1762.
Service—Enlisted in Carlisle, Cumberland Co., Penn. Served 2 yrs. in Capt. Pratt's CO., in Col. Wm. Butler's 3rd Penn. Regt., Continental Line; in Capt. Thomas Church's CO., 4th Penn. Battalion under Col. Anthony Wayne; also spoken of in the Rangers on Frontiers, 1778-83, from Cumberland Co. and in Capt. Boal's CO., 1782.
Proof—Pension claim S. 36696; Penn. Archives, 5th Series, vol. 11, pp. 153 and 1005; 3rd Series, vol. 23, p. 596.
Died—Sept. 4, 1829. Buried Skillman graveyard, Russell Twp. Government marker placed by Washburn Chapter D. A. R.
Married—1788, Prepare Clark. Ch. Frances b. 1789, m. Zadoc Connor; John C. b. 1791; Andrew b. 1793; William b. 1796; James b. 1798, d. 1800; Margaret b. 1800 or 1801; Martha b. 1803; Samuel b. 1805; James b. 1808; Michael D. b. 1812.
Collected by Miss Sara Bridges and Miss Minnetta Wright, Greencastle, Indiana.

McGANNON, DARBY　　　　　　　　　　　　　Jennings County
Born—May 18, 1756, in Virginia or Ireland.
Service—Enlisted April 3, 1777; served 3 yrs., ranked as corporal under Capt. Moore Fauntleroy and Col. Stephen Maylen. Battles engaged in, Monmouth and Brandywine.
Proof—Pension record. Applied from Gallatin Co., Ky. Entered land in Jennings Co., Ind., in 1821.

Died—Feb. 1, 1830. Buried on farm across from Freedom Church, S. of Vernon. Stone.
Married—Sallie Cogswell (1769-1833). Ch. Zachariah (1790-1865), m. Lucy Coleman; Mary E., m. John Moreland; Thomas, m. Eleanor Tanner; Damsel, m. Daniel Lattimore; Jane, m. 1827 Walter Lattimore; John, m. 1824 Polly Carney; Alexander, m. 1834 Sally Butler; Hugh, m. 1840 Elizabeth Furgerson; Sally, m. Manlove Butler; Alsey; Ruben, m. —— Branham.
Collected by John Paul Chapter D. A. R.

McGILL, ROBERT   Jennings County
Born—April 2, 1758, Somerset Co., New Jersey.
Service—Enlisted Sept., 1776, Col. Hunt, Capts. Seaburn, and Goyn McCoy, Somerset Co., N. J. Enlisted second time under Col. Winds, Maj. Davis, Capt. Parker. Third time under Col. Frelinghuyser, Maj. Butler, Capt. Parker. Fourth time, Col. Ellis. In battles of Monmouth, Piscataqua, Bound Brook.
Proof—Pension claim S. 16946.
Died—July 17, 1835, Jennings County.

McKAY, ALEXANDER   Jefferson County
Born—Feb. 2, 1752, Scotland.
Service—Pri. in N. C. Line.
Proof—Clark's State Records, N. C., vol. 22, p. 233; Roster Rev. Soldiers N. C., pp. 498-500; D. A. R. No. 144517; Will Book A-204 Jefferson Co, Ind.
Died—Aug. 31, 1819. Buried McKay-Stites Cemetery, Jefferson Co. Stone.
Married—Barbara —— (1759-1931). Ch. James d. 1845; Margaret, m. Ross Sharpe; John, m. Mary Francis; George, m. Elizabeth Francis; Jennet; Angus; Jane, m. George S. Thompson; Mary; Marjorie.
Collected by John Paul Chapter D. A. R.

McKAY, ROBERT   Jefferson County
Born—Feb. 12, 1760.
Service—Enlisted from Shenandoah Co., Vir., where he lived, Oct. 1779. Served 3 mos. in Capt. Wm. Jennings' Vir. CO., and guarded prisoners at Albemarle Barracks; enlisted Oct., 1780, and served 3 mos. under same capt.; 3 mos. in Capt. George Prince's Vir. CO.
Proof—Pension claim S. 16956.
Died—Last payment of pension Sept. 28, 1835. Probably buried on his farm.
Married—1782, Lydia Leith. Ch. David, m. 1804 Sophia Smith; John, m. 1801 Isabel Gaines; Enoch, m. 1799 Clary H. Smith.
Collected by John Paul Chapter D. A. R.

McKAY, THOMAS   Jefferson County
Born—1750, Scotland.
Service—Served in North Carolina with brothers Alexander, William, George and Angus.
Proof—Information from Mrs. Minnie Shumate, a descendant of Alexander McKay.
Died—1835. Buried McKay-Stites Cemetery. Stone.
Son—Thomas, Jr., m. Mary McKay, a cousin, dau. of Alexander. (From deeds in Jefferson Co., Ind.)
Collected by John Paul Chapter D. A. R.

McKINNEY, ALEXANDER, SR.   Orange County
Born—1753 or 4, Augusta Co., Virginia.
Service—Pri. in Capt. Ambrose Madison's CO., in Vir. Regt. of guards at Albemarle Barracks, commanded by Col. Francis Taylor. His name appears on a pay roll for April or May, 1799, time of service, 2 mos. Records also show his name as a sergeant of Vir. Cavalry.
Proof—War Department, Adjutant General's Office.
Died—March 18, 1822. Buried Trimble Cemetery, N. East Twp. Stone.
Married—Mary McClure 1795. Ch. Alexander; Polly; Elizabeth.
Collected by Mrs. N. B. Mavity, French Lick, Indiana.

McKINNEY, DAVID   Orange County
Born—1755, Augusta Co., Virginia.
Service—Oct. 15, 1777, Court Martial Record, Augusta Co., Vir., David McKinney, Capt. Moffett's CO., Vir. Militia, returned as a delinquent for not appearing at a pri. muster, Oct. 3, 1777, and was fined. Oct. 27, 1778, David McKinney of Capt. Trimble's CO., Vir. Militia, returned as a delinquent for not appearing at a pri. muster Oct. 6, 1778, and was to appear at next Court Martial. April 13, 1779, it was shown he had removed to Rockbridge Co. Oct. 16, 1779, David McKinney of Capt. Simpson's CO., Vir. Militia, returned delinquent for not appearing at pri. muster in Dec., 1778, and was acquitted.
Proof—Adjutant General's Office, War Department.
Died—May 7, 1822. Buried Trimble Graveyard, N. East Twp. Stone.
Married—First W. Mary Stuart, and second W. 1785, Margaret Wallace. Ch. James; Esther; Elizabeth; Margaret; John; Robert; Alexander; Mary; Thomas; David; William W.; Cynthia Ann.
Collected by Mrs. N. B. Mavity, French Lick, Indiana.

McKINNEY, JOSEPH   Randolph County
Born—1748, Virginia.
Service—Enlisted 1776 as a pri. in Capt. Harry Terrill's CO., 5th Vir. Regt. of Foot under Col. Josiah Parker.

Proof—D. A. R. Lineage, vol. 56, p. 216 Randolph Co. History of 1882. And inscription of tombstone.
Died—1838. Buried Fairview Cemetery, Green Twp. Stone.
Married—Susan F. McVey. Son, Anthony Wayne.
Collected by Mrs. James P. Goodrich and Mrs. Oran E. Ross, Winchester, Indiana.

McKINZEY, JESSE   Knox County
Born—About 1763.
Service—Enlisted at Frederick, Md., about April 1, 1780; served as pri. in Capt. Michael Boyer or Bowyer's CO., Col. Weltner's Regt.; a few days before revolt of Penn. Troops, the companies enlisted from Maryland were separated from this Regt., and soldier marched back to Frederick; thence to Baltimore in Capt. William's CO., at which place he joined Capt. Hamilton's CO.; went to Annapolis and served under Capt. Trueman; was ordered to Yorktown, where he served under Baron Steuben until the capture of Lord Cornwallis, after which he went to S. C., and served in Capt. Price's CO., Col. Stewart's Md. Regt., until fall of 1783, when discharged.
Proof—Pension claim W. 7432.
Died—Nov. 3, 1818. Probably buried Greenlawn or Old City Cemetery, Vincennes.
Married—1784, Catherine ———. Ch. John b. 1788; Bennet b. 1791; Elenor b. 1793.
Collected by Mrs. S. G. Davenport, Vincennes, Indiana.

McKNIGHT, JOHN   Washington County
Born—1730, Ireland.
Service—Pri. in Chester Co. Penn. Militia, serving under Capt. Cochran in the 8th Battalion, Col. Mathew Boyd. His name appears on list of retirement March, 1781.
Proof—Militia Records of Chester Co., Penn.; S. A. R. of Ill. No. 42578; Charles McKnight; Cemetery, Court and County Records, Washington Co., Ind.
Died—April 16, 1826. Buried McKnight Family Cemetery, W. of New Philadelphia, Ind. Stone.
Married— ——— Hazelit, b. and d. in Ireland. Ch. William (1764-1825), m. Agnes.
Collected by Mrs. Harvey Morris, Salem, Indiana.

McMANNIS, JOHN   Boone County
Born—1760, Chester Co., Pennsylvania.
Service—While residing at Wheeling, Vir., he volunteered in March, 1778, as a pri. in Capt. Leonard Helms' CO., Col. Rogers Clark's

Vir. Regt., went by boat to the falls of the Ohio, built a fort on an island at that place and was discharged in Sept. following.
Proof—Pension claim S. 17574.
Died—Dec. 31, 1842.
Son—John. Three other children.
Collected by Cradle of Liberty Chapter D. A. R.

MacMILLEN, DANIEL   Ripley County
Born—1757, Ireland.
Service—Enlisted from Maryland in spring of 1778. Discharged Sept., 1781.
Proof—Pension claim W. 6800.
Died—April 15 or 16, 1838. Buried near Correct, Ind., on a farm, now owned by Everett Pickett. Government marker. Name on bronze tablet in Versailles Court House.
Married—1811, Jane Sconce. Ch. Julia Ann b. 1814, m. 1st Edwin Johns, 2nd John Green; Franklin b. 1816, d. young; Stephen b. 1818, m. Eliza Wade; Margaret b. 1819, d. young.
Collected by Mrs. A. B. Wycoff, Batesville, Indiana, and Mrs. Daisy McKenzie, Louisville, Kentucky.

McMILLON (McMULLEN), ROWLEY   Union County
Born—About 1750, Ireland.
Service—Enlisted in Abbeville District, S. C., March 13, 1781, in Capt. Morrison's CO., Col. James Jackson's Georgia Regt., called the "State Legion." Discharged June 13, 1782. In battle of Midway, Ga., and several skirmishes under Gen. Wayne.
Proof—Pension claim S. 16945. Pensioned 1832 from Union Co., Ind.
Died—Sept. 7, 1843.
Married— —— Wallace. Ch. Rowley; Elizabeth; Margaret Shook; Jane Wilson; Nancy; James.
Collected by Mrs. Elnora P. Campbell, Liberty, Indiana.

McMURTREY (McMURTRIE, MURTNEY), JOHN   Allen County
Born—1740, near Philadelphia, Pennsylvania.
Service—Pri. and Corp. in 1st Regt. Penn., 1777, Oct., 1779. Sergeant-Major and Ensign of 1st Penn. Regt. Resigned 1780. He was Capt. in Ky. Militia, 1779, under Gen. Harmer in the western country in the expedition against the Miami Indians.
Proof—Heitman's Historical Register, p. 374.
Died—Killed in action at Miami Towns (Fort Wayne, Ind.) Oct. 22, 1790. Probably buried in trench along the Maumee River, Fort Wayne, Ind.

Married—Mary Todd Hutton (a cousin). Son James.
Collected by Mrs. T. J. Hindman, 1214 West Jefferson, Fort Wayne, Indiana.

McPHEETERS, JOHN   Washington County
Born—About 1762.
Service—Drafted Sept. 18, 1780, Augusta Co., Vir. Capt. Patrick Buchanan, Lieut. James Bratton. Marched to join troops of Gen. Morgan. Was with Col. Washington, who captured about 300 Tories at Rugeleys Mills. At Cowpens. Discharged Jan. 17, 1781. Drafted 1781, 2 mos. under Capt. Buchanan, Col. Huger.
Proof—Pension claim S. 17576.
Died—1842. Buried Horner's Chapel near Salem, Ind.
Married—Margaret Anderson. Ch. Samuel; Robert; James; Wallace; Cameron; Jennie; Sarah; Rebekah; Nancy; Margaret, m. David G. Mitchell.
Collected by Miss Gladys Mitchell, Corydon, Indiana.

McQUEEN, THOMAS   Bartholomew County
Born—Dec. 2, 1761. Baltimore, Maryland.
Service—Pri. under Capt. Hogan, Col. Williamson. Helped destroy Indian towns on Muskingon River under Capt. Charles Balderback and Col. Crawford, and engaged in the battle of Crawford's Defeat. On May 18, 1782, was taken prisoner by the Cherokee Indians, detained 1 yr., escaped and recaptured twice. Was prisoner for nearly 2 yrs.
Proof—Pension claim S. 33080.
Died—1838. Buried in Clifford Cemetery. Stone.
Married—1785, Sarah Vaughn. Ch. Mary; Uriah; Joshua; Elizabeth; Nancy; Jennie; Sallie; Debora; Benjamin; John; Thomas.
Collected by Mrs. Lenore M. Blackledge, Bloomington, Indiana.

McREYNOLDS, JOSEPH   Posey County
Born—Dec. 12, 1762, Caswell Co., North Carolina.
Service—Entered service Dec. 16, 1778, and served 3 mos. as pri. under Capt. Porter, Col. Harrison, N. C. In Nov., 1780, served 3 mos. as pri. under Capt. Coleman, Col. Archibald Murphy. In 1781 served 3 mos. under Capt. Wm. Saunders, Col. Wm. Moore. 3 mos. under Capt. Haroldson and was in battles of Guilford Court House, Eutaw Springs.
Proof—Pension claim S. 33070.
Died—Nov. 30, 1840. Buried Mt. Pleasant Cemetery near Poseyville. Stone.
Married—Henrietta Browning. Ch. Joseph; Edward; Margaret.

McWHINNEY, THOMAS   Wayne County
Born—1755, Ireland.
Service—Aug. 28, 1780, enlisted in Capt. Samuel Patton's CO., 4th
    Battalion, Penn. Militia, under Col. Samuel Culbertson. May 13,
    1782, enlisted in 8th CO., 4th Battalion Penn. Militia under Capt.
    Walter McKinney.
Proof—Penn. Archives, 5th Series, vol. 6, pp. 278-297, 305.
Died—Feb. 25, 1828. Buried Beulah Cemetery near the Indiana-Ohio
    State Line. Government marker placed by Richmond Chapter
    D. A. R.
Married—Eleanor Fryar. Ch. William (1789-1824), m. 1812 Elizabeth
    Kendrick; John (1790-1845), m. 1st Mary Doughan, 2nd Pamela
    Adams Alexander; Matthew b. 1792, m. Temperance Kendrick;
    Samuel; Stephen (youngest son); Stephen (War of 1812); Margaret; Elizabeth; Eleanor.
Collected by Mrs. Paul Ross, Richmond, Indiana.

NAY, SAMUEL   Johnson County
Born—1760 or 1763, in Culpepper County, Virginia.
Service—Enlisted in 1778 and served 18 mos. as a substitute for William
    Nay. Enlisted in 1781 as a substitute for Joseph Nay, served 3
    mos. in Captain Waugh's CO., Col. Thomas Barbour's Vir. Regt.
    Served 3 mos. from Oct. 1, 1781, in Capt. Kid Slaughter's CO.,
    Col. John Slaughter's Regt.
Proof—Pension claim R. 7563. Rejected for lack of 6 mos. service.
Died—Oct. 1, 1848. Buried Nay or Tremaine Cemetery, Nineveh Twp.
    Stone.
Married—Nancy ——. Catherine; Bennett; James; John; Mary; Nancy;
    Samuel; Asa B.; Rhoda; Elizabeth; Presley; Phebe; Lucy.
Collected by Mrs. Ira E. Tranter, Franklin, Indiana.

NEELEY, JOSEPH   Sullivan County
Born—1759, Orange Co., North Carolina.
Service—Volunteered 1776, served 3 mos. Capt. Douglas' CO., Col. Folsom's N. C. Regt. Re-enlisted served 3 mos. under same officers.
    March, 1777, served Capt. Benjamin Walkers, Cooper's and Farri's
    companies, Col. Leonard Marbury's Regt., Light Dragoons. Served
    guarding frontiers Georgia. Taken prisoner, escaped, was discharged, served 3 yrs.
Proof—Pension claim S. 31879.
Died—July 14, 1836. Buried Antioch Cemetery, Cass. Twp. Stone.
Married—Nancy Ann Horton, 1774-1851. Ch. Mary b. 1797.
Collected by Mrs. James R. Riggs, Sullivan, Indiana.

NEELY, JOSEPH   Gibson County
Born—1758 on ship.
Service—Enlisted in Capt. Marshall's CO., Col. Miles' Battalion, March
    19, 1776, which was raised in Hanover Twp., Lancaster Co., Penn.
    They were called Penn. Rifle Regulars. He was at Brandywine
    and Yorktown.
Proof—D. A. R. No. 241160; Penn. Archives.
Died—Oct. 26, 1806. Buried Neely Hill near Patoka, Ind. Bronze
    marker by Gen. John Gibson Chapter and Cradle of Liberty Chapter D. A. R.
Married—1781, Martha Johnston. Ch. Thomas; John I., m. Jane Montgomery; Patsy b. 1792, m. Andrew D. Ralston; Katherine, m.
    Henry Reel; Jane b. 1798, m. Thomas Jefferson Evans; Margaret
    b. 1798, m. Samuel Adams; Julia, m. Thomas Johnson; Anna;
    Joseph, m. Lydia Montgomery.
Collected by Gen. John Gibson Chapter D. A. R.

NEW, JETHRO   Jennings County
Born—Sept. 20, 1757, Kent Co., Delaware.
Service—Enlisted 1778, in Capt. Richard Dolliver's CO., 2nd Delaware
    Regt., Col. Henry O'Neill. Saw execution of Major Andre, was
    at battle of Cowpens, and at the siege of Yorktown.
Proof—Delaware State Archives, vol. 2, p. 766.
Died—1827. Buried Vernon Cemetery, Vernon, Ind.
Married—Sarah Bowman, b. May 25, 1764. Ch. William; George W.;
    Jeptha; Mary; Elizabeth; John B.; Amelia; Sarah; James; Hickman; Nancy; Robert A. b. 1798, m. Susan Taylor.
Collected by John Paul Chapter D. A. R., Madison, Indiana.

NEWCOMER, PETER   Ripley County
Service—Pri. in Capt. John Black's Company. Col. Hasterman's 3rd
    Battalion, Northumberland Co., Penn. Militia. Entered service
    Oct. 12, 1779, and was discharged on Nov. 4, 1779.
Proof—Pension records in War Department. Bronze tablet in Versailles Court House, 1928.
Collected by Mrs. A. B. Wycoff, Batesville, Indiana.

NEWELL, SAMUEL   Owen County
Born—Nov. 4, 1754, Frederick Co., Virginia.
Service—Pri. and Lieut. in Vir. Militia. Enlisted 1776, Washington
    Co., Vir. Served under Capt. John Shelby, Capt. Cocke, Capt.
    James Shelby, Capt. James Thompson, Capt. John Campbell, Capt.
    Wm. Buchannon.
Proof—Pension claim R. 7617. D. A. R. No. 138344.
Died—Sept. 21, 1841.

Married—Jane Montgomery, d. Feb. 11, 1843. Ch. Samuel; John M.; Joseph B.; Margaret E., m. Wm. Owens; Jane, m. Jas. Evans; Susanna, m. Andrew Evans; Esther, m. Jesse Evans; William Tell Newell.

NEWLAND, HARROD Marion County
Born—1766, Bartley Co., Virginia.
Service—Volunteered March, 1779, from Washington Co., Penn., with a company of militia formed by Jesse Pigman for purpose of pursuing Indians. From April, 1780, served 6 mos. From April, 1781, served 6 mos. and in 1782 served 6 mos. under Capt. Hughes, Col. Crawford in Penn. Line.
Proof—Pension claim S. 16494.

NICHOLS, JOSHUA Orange County
Born—July 10, 1758. Rowan Co., North Carolina.
Service—A pri. in the CO. of his father, Capt. Nichols, Rowan Co. Militia, commanded by Gen. Rutherford. Was with a detachment under Gen. Ashe in battle of Brier Creek, where Gen. Ashe was defeated. Later served 6 mos. under his father. Enlisted as pri. under Capt. Wm. Alexander, Col. Wm. Polk's N. C. Regt. In battles of Orangeburg, Eutaw Springs.
Proof—Pension claim S. 32414.
Died—Sept. 7, 1841. Buried on farm owned by Norman Ballard.
Ch.—Martin; Jacob; Thomas.
Collected by Mrs. N. B. Mavity, French Lick, Indiana.

NICHOLS, WILLIBE Carroll County
Born—Dec. 25, 1762, Pasquotank Co., North Carolina.
Service—Entered service from N. C. for 5 mos. Discharged. Entered again March, 1781, from Norfolk Co., Vir., as substitute for Joel Sawyer, in CO. of Rufus Williams, in Maj. Davis Battalion, Col. Doshier's Regt. and served as sergeant for 3 mos. Discharged June. Enlisted again in Aug. as substitute for John Wood. Discharged Nov., 1781.
Proof—Pension claim S. 32415. Applied for pension Aug. 12, 1838, from Carroll Co., Ind.

NIGHT, JACOB Owen County
Service—Pri. Penn. Militia. Enlisted 1776 Berks Co., Penn. Served under Capt. Olespaw and Capt. Hester.
Proof—Pension claim S. 31881.
Died—April 30, 1839.

NITHERCUT, WM. Franklin County
Born—About 1763.
Service—Enlisted May 25, 1781, served 12 mos. as pri. in Capt. Doherty's CO., Cols. Armstrong and James Little's N. C. Regt. In battle of Eutaw Springs.
Proof—Pension claim S. 35539. Living in Franklin Co., 1823.
Died—After 1823. Had a family.

NORMAN, JOHN Putnam County
Born—1743, Sussex Co., Delaware.
Service—Volunteered for 6 mos. service at Johnston, Sussex Co., Del., as pri. under Capt. Polk, Del. Line.
Died—1833. Buried Putnam Co.

NORRIS, DANIEL Switzerland County
Born—About 1762.
Service—Inscription on marker reads "Daniel Norris, a Revolutionary Soldier, Died March 11, 1828, in the 66th year of his age."
Died—Buried Loshetter Cemetery, Posey Twp.
Ch. Hugh L., m. Nancy Powell May 8, 1830.
Collected by Mrs. A. V. Danner, Vevay, Indiana.

NORTH, LOT (Brother of Thos. of Switzerland Co.) Ohio County
Born—Jan. 10, 1756, Farmington, Connecticut.
Service—Drummer boy in Conn. Regt.
Proof—Hist. Dearborn, Switzerland and Ohio Cos., 1885.
Died—Oct. 8, 1825. Graveyard on North's farm, near North's Landing. Same graveyard as brother Thos. North, but Co. line runs through graveyard.
Married—Silence Horsford.
Collected by Mrs. Walter Kerr, Aurora, Indiana.

NORTH, THOMAS Switzerland County
Born—Aug. 29, 1748, Farmington, Connecticut.
Service—Pri. from May 12-Dec. 18, 1775, in 2nd CO., Capts. Samuel Wylls, and later Ezekiel Scott; 2nd Regt., Cols. Joseph Spencer and later Samuel Wylls.
Proof—Record of Conn. Men in the Rev., p. 46.
Died—Oct. 30, 1830. Cemetery on North's farm near North's Landing. The cemetery is in Switzerland Co. Stone.
Married—Bathsheba ——, 1773-1847. Ch. Royal F.; George W., m. 1827 Saby B. Lampton.
Collected by Mrs. A. V. Danner, Vevay, Indiana.

OARD, WILLIAM   Clay County
Born—Sept. 22, 1754, in Charles Co., Maryland.
Service—Enlisted Feb., 1776, for 3 mos. as a pri. in Capt. Garret
    Bond's CO., Col. Jeremiah Jourdan's Md. Regt. Enlisted 1780 for
    2 mos. in Capt. John Sandford's CO., Col. Blackburn's and Col.
    Tipp's Vir. Regt.
Proof—Pension claim S. 16496.
Died—Sept. 15, 1833, in Park Co., Ind. Buried in Old Hill Cemetery
    in Brazil, Clay Co., Ind. Stone. Bronze tablet placed by Ft.
    Harrison Chapter S. A. R. and William Oard Chapter D. A. R.
Collected by Mr. Cornelius F. Possons, Indianapolis, Indiana, and Miss
    Pearly Finley, Brazil, Indiana.

OGDEN, JEDEDIAH   Union County
Born—Feb. 17, 1750, in Cumberland Co., New Jersey.
Service—Pri. in company under Capt. Sam Ogden (his brother), Col.
    Newcomb N. J. Regt. for 9 mos.
Proof—Pension claim S. 32419.
Died—1840. Buried Bath Springs Cemetery. Stone.
Married—First W. unknown. Second W. 1782, Polly Whitacre (1757-
    1806). Ch. Daniel (1797-1871), m. 1816, Harriet Lummis. Third
    W. Judith, d. 1838.
Collected by Mrs. Elnora P. Campbell, Liberty, Indiana.

OLINGER, JOHN   Carroll County
Service—Inscription on stone read "Pa. Mil. Rev. War."
Buried—In Nebo Cemetery, Jackson Twp.
Collected by Mrs. Julia H. Irelan, Delphi, Indiana.

O'NEAL, JOHN   Ripley County
Born—1760 in Essex Co., Virginia.
Service—Enlisted June, 1777, from Virginia. Served 1 yr., 1 mo., 20
    days.
Proof—Pension claim S. 32422.
Died—Nov. 7, 1832. Name appears on bronze tablet in Versailles
    Court House.
Collected by Mrs. A. B. Wycoff, Batesville, Indiana.

ORME, CHARLES   Morgan County
Service—Served 6 yrs. as pri. in Maryland's 7th Regt. under Col.
    John Gunsby, Capt. John Courts Jones. Enlisted June, 1778, in
    Montgomery Co., Md.
Proof—Pension claim S. 35543.
Died—Pension paid to Aug. 18, 1840.

OSBORN, WILLIAM   Warrick County
Born—1763.
Service—Drafted at age of 15 yrs. from Rowan Co., N. C., for 3 mos.
    under Gen. Green. Next tour was as volunteer under Capt.
    Neghtors, Col. Colwell, Gen. Retherwood. Discharged at end of
    that time.
Proof—Order Book 3, p. 215, in Warrick Co., Ind., Clerk's Office.
Collected by Mrs. H. K. Forsythe, Newburg, Indiana.

OSBORNE, WILLIAM   Fountain County
Born—Jan. 10, 1764.
Service—Enlisted from N. C. in 1779. Served 3 mos. as a pri. under
    Capt. William Adams. In 1780 served 6 mos. as a pri. under
    Capt. Wm. Fabre and Col. Moffitt.
Proof—Pension records.
Died—April 5, 1835. Buried in DeHaven-Osborne Cemetery, 6 miles
    E. of Covington, Ind. Stone.
Married—Elizabeth Redden. Ch. Peggy, m. James Sherrill; Abner,
    m. Eliza Glass; Ipsley, m. Granville Adkins; Katherine, m. Gilbert
    Cook; William, m. Susanna Cook; Susan, m. Jacob DeHaven;
    John Taylor, m. Permelia De Haven; Ruben Lyle; Patsy Ann,
    m. 1st Joseph Miller, 2nd Mathew Barkley.
Collected by Mrs. Mary DeHaven, Covington, Indiana.

OTIS, EDWARD   LaPorte County
Born—April 6, 1766, Lyme, Connecticut.
Service—Pri. Conn. Troops, under Capt. Lord and Col. Star. Wounded
    at Bunker Hill.
Proof—Pension claim S. 32425.
Died—June, 1852. Buried Biglow's Mills, LaPorte Co., Ind. Stone.
Married—1787, Mary Merrill (1770-1822). Ch. Lois; Ezekiel; Jesse, m.
    Charlotte Davy; Phoebe; Mary; Merrill; Edward.
Collected by Mrs. Carrie H. Tourne, LaPorte, Indiana.

OVERLIN, WILLIAM   Spencer County
Born—Dec. 12, 1755, England.
Service—Served from Dec., 1777, to summer of 1783 as a fifer pri.
    under Capts. Robert Beall and Benjamin Biggs, Col. John Gibson.
    Was in battles of Brandywine and Germantown.
Proof—Pension records.
Died—Feb. 24, 1837. Buried Old Baker Creek's graveyard, Luce Twp.
    Stone placed by Spier Spencer Chapter D. A. R.
Married—1787, Letitia McKinney. Ch. Jonathan; William; Eli; Polly;
    Delilah; Lelah.
Collected by Miss Laura M. Wright, Rockport, Indiana.

OVERTURF, MARTIN Ripley County
Born—1756.
Service—Pri. in Continental Line, Washington Co., Penn., Militia.
Proof—Penn. Archives, 5th Series, vol. 4, pp. 415 and 723.
Died—About 1850. Buried Old Whitham Cemetery, Brown Twp. Government marker placed by Ripley Co. Historical Society.
Married—Catherine Deitch. Ch. Jacob b. 1785, m. Rebecca Myers; Samuel b. 1787, m. Sarah Cole; Catharine b. 1789, m. George Myers; Conrad b. 1791, m. Pelina Steele.
Collected by Mrs. A. B. Wycoff, Batesville, Indiana.

PAGES, GUILLAUME Knox County
Born—Cap Jante Parish, Quebec.
Service—A Patriot. Signed the Oath of Allegiance at Post Vincennes, July 20, 1778.
Proof—Ill. Hist. Coll., vol. VIII, Clark's Papers, 1771-1781, pp. 52-59.
Died—1801. Buried Old Cathedral Cemetery, Vincennes, Ind.
Married—First W. 1770, Josette Schabart (Chaffard, Chapart). Ch. John Baptiste b. 1772. Second W. 1778, Marie Victoire Huneau. Ch. Dominick b. 1783, d. 1868 (War of 1812); Marie, m. Simon Gonzales; Joseph d. 1800; Guillaume.
Collected by Mrs. S. G. Davenport and Mrs. Leo Schultheis, Vincennes, Indiana.

PALMER, JOHN Pike County
Born—1766, Union Co., South Carolina.
Service—Enlisted from Union Co., S. C. Pri. 2 mos. under Capt. Putnam, Col. Brandon; 2 mos. under Capt. Butler, Col. Hammond; 2 mos. under Capt. McDougal and 2 mos. under Capt. Bailey.
Proof—Pension record.
Died—1839. Buried near Petersburg, Ind. Bronze marker placed by Cradle of Liberty Chapter D. A. R.
Married—Mary Howell. Ch. Thomas.
Collected by Cradle of Liberty Chapter D. A. R.

PALMER, WILLIAM Posey County
Born—About 1757.
Service—Enlisted Prince William Co., Vir., under Capt. Wm. Johnson as corporal in 10th Vir. Regt., Brig. Gen. Woodford, 1776. Taken prisoner at battle of Brandywine, where he lost a leg.
Proof—Pension claim W. 5476.
Died—About 1828.
Married—1787, Sarah Berry. Pension application speaks of eldest dau.

PARK (PARKS), SAMUEL			Posey or Perry County
Born—About 1759.
Service—Pri. in CO. commanded by Capt. Talmage, Col. Hopkins' Regt., N. Y. Line, 1 yr.
Proof—Pension claim S. 32434. Posey Co. Probate Court Records C and D, p. 255. Applied for pension Nov. 18, 1833, Breckenridge Co., Ky. Filed again 1842 at Rome, Perry Co., Ind.
Died—After 1842.

PARKINSON, ABRAHAM			Switzerland County
Born—About 1758.
Service—Enlisted July, 1777, under Capt. Thomas Lookus, 14th Regt. Penn. Line, called "Penn Blues," Col. Richard Butler, Capt. Thomas Campbell. Served 5 yrs. 3 mos. 11 days. Discharged at Amboy, N. J. In the battles of Long Island, Stony Point and Brandywine.
Proof—Switzerland Co. Civil Order Book 1820, p. 378.
Married—Elizabeth ——. Peggy; Ester; John; Martin; Samuel; Abram.
Collected by Mrs. A. V. Danner, Vevay, Indiana.

PARKS, GEORGE			Monroe County
Born—Aug. 5, 1759, Amherst Co., Virginia.
Service—Enlisted at the age of 17 yrs. in Wilkes Co., 1776, as sergeant under Capt. Lenoir, Col. Isaac ——; in 1777 under Capt. Johnson, Col. Benj. Cleveland; in 1779, under Capts. Lenoir and Richard Allen, all N. C. Regts.
Proof—Pension claim W. 27457, B. L. Wt. 53670-160-55.
Died—Dec. 7, 1837. Buried Ellettsville, Ind. Stone. Bronze marker placed by Bloomington Chapter D. A. R.
Married—First W. Millie Davidson. Ch. Elizabeth; James; Samuel; Polly; Benjamin; Pleasant b. 1789, m. Esther Carlton; Nancy; Milly. Second W. Catherine Reed (1777-1860). Ch. Hannah, m. Wm. Pluett; Meredith; Alfred; Curtis; Sarah b. 1812, m. Johnston Sharp; Rebeccah; Carlton.
Collected by Mrs. Clarence Forsythe, 548 N. Audubon Road, Indianapolis, Indiana.

PARKS, HUGH			Scott County
Born—Feb. 15, 1757.
Service—Enlisted for 6 mos. under Capt. Roger More, N. C. Line. Later enlisted for 3 yrs. under Capt. Wm. Goodman and Regt. of Col. Polk. Discharged in N. J. Was in battles of Brandywine, Germantown.

Proof—Pension claim W. 9591.
Died—Dec. 13, 1838, Scott Co., Ind.
Married—1781 or 2, Elizabeth Barnhill. Ch. John; Mary; Samuel; James; Hugh; Robert b. 1793; Alexander b. 1795; William b. 1789; Margaret; Pleasant b. 1803; Jesse b. 1818; Elizabeth b. 1806; Sarah b. 1809.

PARR, ARTHUR Washington County
Born—July 5, 1758, Guilford Co., North Carolina.
Service—Drafted March 1, 1776, from Fairfield Dist., S. C., Pri. in CO. under Capt. Hancock, Col. Beard's S. C. Regt., 2 yrs. from 1776. In Augusta campaign, also under Gen. Lincoln in battle of Stone Creek. Horse service under Gen. Pulaski at siege of Savannah.
Proof—Pension claim S. 16219; sworn statement by soldier in 1832, now a record in Washington Co. Court House.
Died—March 21, 1833. Buried Franklin Cemetery, Washington Twp. Stone.
Married—Mary Morgan, d. 1837. Ch. Enoch (1785-1851), m. 1st Nancy Carr, 2nd Ruth Lindley; Morgan; Jemima; Elizabeth; Martha; David; John; Mary; Susanna.
Collected by Mrs. Harvey Morris, Salem, Indiana.

PARR, JOHN Johnson County
Born—June 14, 1759, Morris Co., New Jersey.
Service—Enlisted middle of Feb., 1776, as a pri. in Capt. Thomas Reading's CO., Col. Elias Dayton's N. J. Regt., for 12 or 13 mos. Served 2 mos. under Capt. Abraham Dickerson. In summer of 1778, 9 mos. in Capt. Henry Luce's CO., Col. Shreves' N. J. Regt. 1 mo. in 1780, under Capt. Isreal Luce. In battles of Monmouth and Springfield.
Proof—Pension claim S. 17617.
Died—Sept. 7, 1850. Buried in Nolin Cemetery near Greenwood, Ind. Stone.
Children—David; Matthias; Moses; Mary.
Collected by Mrs. I. E. Tranter, Franklin, Indiana.

PARR, MATHIAS Johnson County
Born—Sept. 19, 1757, Morris Co., N. J.
Service—Enlisted early in 1776 as pri. in Capt. Thomas Patterson's CO., Col. Elias Dayton's 3rd N. J. Regt. Length of service 1 yr. 2 mos. Volunteered in spring of 1777, served 4 mos. as pri. in Capts. Nathaniel Horton's and Sharp's CO. In fall of 1777, served 2 mos. as pri. in Capt. Stephen Brown's N. J. CO. In 1778, 3 mos. in Capt. Peter Dickerson's CO.

Proof—Pension claim S. 17001.
Died—April 17, 1846. Buried Pisgah Cemetery, Hensley Twp. Government marker placed by Alexander Hamilton Chapter D. A. R.
Married—Mary ———. Ch. James; Abner; Mary Parr Finley; Hannah Parr Ashley; Neaty Parr Isreal; Amy Parr Isreal; Elizabeth Parr Alexander.
Collected by Mrs. I. E. Tranter, Franklin, Indiana.

PATRICK, JOSHUA   Vigo County
Born—Feb. 24, 1762, Vollentown, Connecticut.
Service—Enlisted as a fifer in militia of Capt. Josiah Gibbs about 1776, served 4 mos. Later served as a substitute for several men. Jan., 1777, pri. 3 mos. under Capt. Moses Branch. Again served as substitute for 2 mos. Present at the surrender of Burgoyne. Joined Sheldon's Light Horse in N. Y. in 1780. In service at Forts Edwards, Ann and George in 1781-2-3.
Proof—Pension claim S. 32431.
Died—Jan. 10, 1842. Buried in Woodlawn Cemetery, Terre Haute, Ind. Stone.
Son—Dr. Septer Patrick (probably only son to come to Indiana).
Collected by A. R. Markle, Terre Haute, Indiana.

PATRICK, ROBERT   Jefferson County
Born—1753.
Service—Enlisted for 18 mos. in Penn., Capt. Thomas Church's CO. In Jersey line in Cont'l Establishment. Served to end of war. Discharged at Philadelphia from Capt. George Trumbourn's CO., Col. McGaw's Regt. In battles of Staten Island. Was taken prisoner.
Proof—Jefferson Co., Ind., Order Book B. 337.
Collected by John Paul Chapter D. A. R.

PAUL, JOHN   Jefferson County
Born—Nov. 12, 1758, Germantown, Pennsylvania.
Service—Served through entire campaign with George Rogers Clark. Enlisted at Red Stone Old Fort, now Brownsville, Penn., when 19 yrs. of age in CO. of Wm. Harrod. Was one who stood firm at Corn Island and served at reduction of British forts on the Wabash. Was at Kaskaskia and Vincennes.
Proof—English "Conquest of the Northwest," vol. 2, p. 848; Collins Hist. of Ky.
Died—June 6, 1830. Buried at Fairmount. Government marker placed by John Paul Chapter D. A. R.

Married—1794, Sarah Thornberry Grover. Ch. Ann Parker b. 1799, m. William Hendricks; John Peter b. 1800, d. 1835; Sarah b. 1802, m. Dr. Robert Cravens.
Collected by John Paul Chapter D. A. R.

PAULEY, WILLIAM   Boone County
Born—March 2, 1762. Spottsylvania Co., Virginia.
Service—Pri. in company commanded by Capt. English of Regt. by Col. Preston, Vir. Militia.
Proof—Pension claim W. 10233.
Died—Nov. 22, 1838. Buried Precinct Cemetery. Stone.
Married—1787, Margaret Munsey (1768-1845). Ch. John; Margaret b. 1822; Joseph b. 1801, m. Sarah Blaine.
Collected by James Hill Chapter D. A. R.

PAYNE (PAIN), JOHN   Washington County
Born—1754, Kent Co., Delaware.
Service—Pri. in infantry commanded by Capt. Fountain and Capt. Skelling, 1777.
Proof—Pension certificate No. 7098; Farabees in America, pp. 1, 18, 21, 37; D. A. R. No. 187719.
Died—Aug., 1837. Buried Old Hebron Cemetery, Washington Twp.
Married—1789, Jane Farabee. Ch. Amy Payne (Pain) b. 1790, m. John Farabee; Harry d. young; Nehemiah b. 1795; Susanna b. 1798, m. Henry Pitts, Sr.
Collected by Mrs. Harvey Morris, Salem, Indiana.

PAYTON, LEWIS   Harrison County
Born—March 8, 1763, Amherst Co., Virginia.
Service—Enlisted shortly after surrender of Cornwallis, as pri. in Capt. Kirkpatrick's CO., Col. Hawes' Vir. Regt., 7 mos.
Proof—Pension claim S. 17003.
Died—April 10, 1838. Buried on farm now owned by George Kraft, Webster Twp. Stone. Government marker placed by Hoosier Elm Chapter D. A. R.
Married—Winefred Folwell. Ch. Abraham; Augustus; Blueford; Mark; Nelson; Nancy; Francis; Dorthey; Lewis; Nimrod.
Collected by Pearl Shuck Lottick, Corydon, Indiana.

PEACHEE, BENJAMIN   Daviess County
Born—Dec. 25, 1756, New Jersey.
Service—Enlisted May 24, 1778, for 9 mos. as pri. in Capt. John C. Cumming's CO., 2nd N. J. Regt., Col. Isreal Shreve. Discharged May 1, 1779.

Proof—Pension claim S. 35552.
Died—Aug., 1837. Buried Bethany Cemetery, E. of Washington, Ind. Government marker placed by White River Chapter D. A. R.
Married—First W. Anna Abbot. Son, Benjamin. Second W. Elizabeth Cinderella Brandus. Ch. George W.; James b. 1784, d. 1867.
Collected by Mrs. Roy Bogner, Washington, Indiana.

PEAK, NATHAN   Switzerland County
Born—About 1752.
Service—Enlisted at Annapolis under Capt. Henry Gaitor, Col. Stone. Discharged near Philadelphia. In battles of White Plains and Trenton. Auditors Office, Annapolis, shows he enlisted as pri. in Md. Regt. Dec. 10, 1776. Discharged Nov. 14, 1780. Received $136.60 from John Hamilton, Agent Md. Line, for pay from Aug. 1, 1780, to Jan. 1, 1782. Also $69.70 from Jan. 1, 1782, to Jan. 1, 1783.
Proof—Pension claim S. 35550.
Died—Dec., 1824. Buried on his farm now owned by Charles Haskell.
Married—Catherine ———. Ch. Samuel, m. Polly Butler; Eleanor, m. ——— Keith; Nancy, m. ———Fenton; Catherine, m. Wm. Keith, Jr.
Collected by Mrs. A. V. Danner, Vevay, Indiana.

PEARCE, BENJAMIN   Fayette County
Born—Sept. 28, 1757.
Service—Pri. in company commanded by Capt. Hadley (Headly) in Col. Ford's Regt., N. J. Line, 6 mos.
Proof—Pension claim S. 32438.
Died—July 17, 1847.

PEARSON, MAHLON   Fountain County
Born—April 7, 1761, Bucks Co., Pennsylvania.
Service—Enlisted June, 1777, served 1 yr. 8 mos. 10 days. Prisoner while on furlough, detained 6 wks., released on parole. At the siege of Savannah, Capts. George Avery, Young and Joseph Hughes; Maj. Benj. Jolly; Cols. Brannon, Wm. Fair, Henderson, S. C. Troops.
Proof—Pension record.
Died—Jan. 28, 1839. Buried Bethel Cemetery, E. of Attica, Ind. Stone.
Married—Amelia Cain. Ch. John Cain b. 1784, m. Margaret Burns; Marjery, m. George Parnell; Elvira, m. Thomas Pearson; Margaret; Delilah; Barbary; Lydia, m. John Campbell; Enoch, m. Jane Ann Colvert.
Collected by Mrs. Jesse Martin, Attica, Indiana, and Rev. Harry E. Martindale, Oxford, Indiana.

PEARSON, SHADRACH — Owen County
Born—1754, Virginia.
Service—Pri. 1st Vir. Regt. Enlisted 1776 in Vir. under Capt. Richard Taylor, Gen. Muhlenburg, Col. Hendricks, Col. Wm. Russell, Col. Richard Parker, Gen. Wayne. In battles at Germantown, Brandywine, Monmouth, Trenton, Princeton and Stoney Point.
Proof—Pension claim S. 35551. B. L. Wt. 14129-100.
Died—Pension last paid on March 4, 1838. Buried near Paragon, Owen County.
Married—Rachel ——. Ch. Casindanea; Henry C.

PEARSON, THOMAS — Warren County
Born—1741, England.
Service—Enlisted Feb., 1776, Carlisle, Penn. Pri. Capt. William Rippy's CO. Col. Irvine's Penn. Regt. In battle of Three Rivers, taken prisoner. Escaped July 22, 1776. In battle at Trenton. Service 13 mos. Enlisted at Philadelphia for 15 mos. Next service was 2 yrs. under Capt. Howard, Col. Hampton's Penn. Regt.
Proof—Pension claim S. 32440.
Died—Aug. 4, 1835. Buried Green Hill Cemetery.
Son—John W.
Collected by Mrs. Elmer V. Smith, Williamsport, Indiana.

PELHAM, DR. WILLIAM — Posey County
Born—1759, Williamsburg, Virginia.
Service—Served 3 yrs. as surgeon's mate and Jr. Surgeon in Cont'l Hospital established in Vir. under direction of Dr. William Rickman about March, 1780. Later entered as surgeon, Vir. State Hospital. Allowed claim for bounty-land.
Proof—Pension claim S. 3678.
Died—Feb. 3, 1827. Maple Hill Cemetery, New Harmony, Ind. Stone.
Son—William C.

PELL, WILLIAM — Harrison County
Born—Jan. 1, 1760, Kent Co., Maryland.
Service—Pri. in CO. of Capt. Johnson, Col. Crawford's Regt., Vir. Line, 1 yr.
Proof—Pension claim S. 16503.
Died—Jan. 17, 1839.

PEMBERTON, JOHN — Decatur County
Service—Pri. in company commanded by Capt. Leech, Col. Stubblefield's Vir. Regt., 14 mos.
Proof—Pension claim S. 16223.

Died—June 5, 1845, age 82 yrs. 10 mos. 15 days. Buried in Sandcreek Cemetery. Inscription on stone states he was a Rev. Soldier.
Son—Thomas.

PENDERGAST, EDWARD   Ripley County
Born—1765 Winchester, Virginia.
Service—Enlisted from Carlisle, Cumberland Co., Penn., in 1779. Served 1 yr. under Maj. Wilson and Lieut. Holmes, Capt. Samuel Postlewait.
Proof—Pension claim S. 16505.
Died—1843. Buried Old Washington Cemetery, Versailles, Ind. Government marker and name on bronze table in Versailles Court House by the Ripley Co. Historical Society.
Collected by Mrs. A. B. Wycoff, Batesville, Indiana.

PENDOCK, SAMUEL   Crawford County
Born—About 1765.
Service—Pri. in Regt. commanded by Col. Olnay of Rhode Island Line for 2 yrs.
Proof—Pension claim W. 26297. B. L. Wt. 239-60-55.
Died—July 20, 1833, Crawford Co., Marengo, Ind.
Married—First W. unknown. Second W. Anna Blevins, m. 1825.
Daughters—Levina and Melissa, neither married.

PENNETENT, JOHN   Ripley County
Born—About 1748.
Service—Pri. in Regt. commanded by Cols. Bluford and Haws of Vir. Line, 18 mos. service.
Proof—Pension claim S. 35554.
Died—Oct. 24, 1821, Ripley Co.
Married—Catherine —— d. 1834.

PERCIVAL, JABEZ   Dearborn County
Born—July 16, 1760, Chatham, Connecticut.
Service—Pri. in Capt. Abel King's CO., Col. Sears' Regt. for 3 mos. Was also one of the "Sugar House" prisoners.
Proof—Conn. Archives, vol. 30, p. 56; Ind. Mag. of History, vol. VIII, p. 19.
Died—June 28, 1841. Buried under the Lawrenceburg Levee.
Married—1786, Elizabeth Stearns (1768-1835). Daughter, Elvira (1790-1835).
Collected by Mrs. Walter Kerr, Aurora, Indiana.

PERIN, LEMUEL   Fayette County
Born—Oct. 21, 1749, Rehoboth, Massachusetts.
Service—Pri. in Capt. John Perry's CO., which marched on the Lexington alarm.
Proof—D. A. R. Nos. 138320 and 120397.
Died—1822, Connersville, Ind.
Married—First W. 1773, Martha Nasel. Ch. John (1774-1866), m. 1st Hepsabah Williams, 2nd Rachel Rice; Samuel (1785-1865). Soldier m. second W. 1792, Amelia Dickinson. Soldier's other children were Rachel; Anthony; Lucy, m. —— Carpenter; Hannah, m. —— Hathaway; Patty, m. —— Fountain; Glover.

PHELPS, ABIJAH   Jay County
Born—Feb. 13, 1759 (date on tombstone) or Feb. 13, 1762 (date given in pension).
Service—While a resident of Simsbury, Hartford Co., Conn., he enlisted in 1778 and served 1 mo., acting as one of a guard to Burgoyne's prisoners; he enlisted in 1779, and served 1 mo. as pri. under Lieut. "Hollyburt" and Gen. Mead, at Horseneck; he enlisted July 1, 1780, and served 6 mos. as pri. in the 2nd Conn. Regt., under Col. Zebulon Butler, stationed most of the time near West Point. Also with Gen. Wayne when the British occupied New York. Discharged Dec. 3, 1780.
Proof—Pension claim S. 4648.
Died—Aug. 24, 1851. Buried Daugherty Cemetery, Bear Creek Twp. Stone. Bronze marker placed by Mississinewa Chapter D. A. R.
Collected by Mrs. Oscar T. Finch, Portland, Indiana.

PHELPS, ASAHEL   Jackson County
Born—About 1762.
Service—Pri. in Regt. of Col. Sheldon of Conn. Line, for 3 yrs.
Proof—Pension claim W. 6866. B. L. Wt. 13718-160-55.
Died—April 2, 1839.
Married—1818, Margaret Stowers. Ch. Asahel; Celestina; Daniel.

PIERCE (PEIRCE, PEARCE), CHARLES   Clark County
Born—About 1760.
Service—Enlisted Feb., 1777, in 6th Mass. Regt. under Capt. Adam Wheeler and Col. Thos. Nixon. Discharged Feb. 9, 1780. Original discharge filed with pension application.
Proof—Pension claim S. 36735.
Died—Buried in Cemetery 2, Charlestown, Ind. Government marker.
Married—Lucy ——.
Collected by Miss Mary Carr Guernsey, Charlestown, Indiana.

PIERCY, JACOB   Putnam County
Born—1759, Virginia.
Service—Fifer in Capt. John Bankson's CO., Penn. Continental Line, 1776-1779.
Proof—Pension records; Indiana S. A. R. records.
Died—Aug. 28, 1831. Buried Cloverdale Cemetery, Cloverdale Twp. Stone.
Married—Abby McDowell (McDonell). Ch. Hannah.
Collected by Caroline Scott Harrison Chapter D. A. R.

PIERSON, JAMES   Crawford County
Born—Oct. 13, 1757, Salisbury, North Carolina.
Service—Enlisted from Wilkes Co., N. C., 1776 or 1777 in Capt. Benjamin Cleveland's N. C. CO. Was stationed at Carter's Fort as guard. Served 3 mos. Enlisted later for 3 mos. in Capt. Jesse Franklin's CO. in N. C. Troops.
Proof—Pension claim S. 32446.
Buried—At Alton, Crawford Co., Indiana.

PIETY, THOMAS   Knox County
Born—1763, Pennsylvania.
Service—In 1780 served from vicinity of Fort Pitt, Penn., to Jefferson Co., Ky. Served at various times, 1790-91, as Sergeant and pri. under Capt. William Hall and Presley Gray, Cols. J. Hardin, Wilkerson, Scott and Oldham.
Proof—Pension claim R. 21475; D. A. R. No. 144194.
Died—May 17, 1835. Buried Old Maria Creek Cemetery.
Married—1792, Mary Duncan. Ch. Nancy (1805-1837), m. David Ruble; William D.
Collected by Mrs. S. G. Davenport, Vincennes, Indiana.

PIGMAN, JESSE   Fayette County
Born—1765, Hagerstown, Maryland.
Service—Enlisted in militia 1780 in Washington Co., Penn. Drafted as pri. under Capt. Jesse Pigman (father). Served term, then acted as Ensign of a Spy CO.
Proof—Pension claim R. 8250. Thought to be buried in Mt. Garrison Cemetery, near the Fayette-Union Co. line.

PIKE, ZEBULON   Dearborn County
Born—Sept. 18, 1751, Woodbridge, New Jersey.
Service—Cornet 4th Continental Dragoons, 1st March, 1777; Regimental Adjutant, 20th Nov., 1777; Lieut. 15th March, 1778; Captain, 25th Dec., 1778; Regimental Paymaster, 1st June, 1780, and served to close of the war. Continued army service until 1815.

Proof—Heitman's Historical Register, p. 442; Pension claim S. 637; Penn. Archives, Series 2, vol. 11, p. 128.
Died—July 27, 1834. Buried Lawrenceburg Cemetery. Bronze tablet placed by Col. Archibald Lochry Chapter D. A. R.
Married—Isabella Brown b. 1753, m. 1775. Ch. James Brown (1784-1855), m. Elizabeth Carberry.
Collected by Mrs. Walter Kerr, Aurora, Indiana.

PILE, RICHARD — Clark County
Born—1760, Richmond, Virginia.
Service—Served as a member of Capt. Joseph Mitchell's CO., 12th Vir. Regt., Col. James Wood. He is reported as having been enlisted Jan. 17, 1777, for 3 yrs. His name last appears on the CO. roll dated at Scon River, Newark, Dec. 1, 1779, with remark "On Guard." He was at Valley Forge from Feb. to May, 1778.
Proof—Pension record; Waddell's Annals of Augusta Co., Vir.
Died—March 23, 1816. Buried Jeffersonville, Ind.
Married—Rebecca Clifton. Ch. Burdet Clifton.
Collected by Ann Rogers Clark Chapter D. A. R.

PILES, ELIJAH — Decatur County
Born—March 13, 1757.
Service—Served a total of 2 yrs. 8 mos. from 1776 under Col. Gibson, Capt. Freeman. Was a Spy.
Proof—Pension claim S. 32447.

PINNICK, JAMES — Orange County
Born—1747, Pennsylvania.
Service—Served from Jefferson Co., Ky., 1780.
Proof—Archives in State Library, Richmond, Vir.; Manuscript IPD77, a pay roll of the Lincoln Militia under Capt. Joseph Kincaid in 1782.
Died—1831. Buried abandoned graveyard, Log Creek Valley, Paoli Twp. Government marker placed by Lost River Chapter D. A. R.
Married—1782, Elizabeth Farris (Ferris). Ch. William; John; Agnes; Nathan; Lucinda; James; Rosanna; Isaac; Mary; Eliza; Elizabeth.
Collected by Mrs. N. B. Mavity and Miss Anna J. Maris, French Lick, Indiana.

PLEW, ELIAS — Boone County
Born—1762, New York.
Service—Enlisted in N. Y. July 1, 1871, and served to Jan. 1, 1782, under Capt. Neal and Col. Menawicher.

Proof—D. A. R. No. 242996.
Died—Feb. 5, 1843. Buried Pleasant View Cemetery. Stone.
Married—Lucinda Hall. Ch. Moses, m. Vena Ann Smith; Aaron, m. Christiana Eshnger; Martha Ann, m. Jonathan Wall; Abe, m. Cornelia Rangel.
Collected by James Hill Chapter D. A. R.

PLOUGH, ALBERT   Sullivan County
Born—1762.
Service—Enlisted 1781 at Westbrook Fort on the Delaware River, served 6 mos. in Capt. Westbrook's CO., Col. Rosekranz. Was Discharged 1781.
Proof—Pension claim R. 8284, not allowed for want of information but soldier died before he could supply it.
Died—Sept., 1852. He had applied for pension in Aug., 1852. Buried Little Flock Cemetery, Hamilton Twp. Stone.
Collected by Mrs. James R. Riggs, Sullivan, Indiana.

PLOUGH, JACOB   Knox County
Born—About 1754, probably in New Jersey.
Service—Served 9 mos., enlisted as Regular, June 18, 1778, at Mount Holly, N. J., a few days before Gen. Clinton left Philadelphia, in CO. under Col. Shreaver, Capt. William Hellam, Lieut. Nigley.
Proof—Pension claim S. 36738.
Married—Lydia ———.
Collected by Mrs. S. G. Davenport, Vincennes, Indiana.

PLUMMER, SAMUEL   Dearborn County
Born—Sept. 16, 1742, Scarborough, Maine.
Service—Pri. Capt. Samuel Thomas CO., Col. Benjamin Tupper, 1778. Pri. under Capt. Benjamin Larabee, Col. Mitchell, 1779.
Proof—Historical and Genealogical Register, vol. 1, p. 169; Essex Institute, Plummer Genealogy, pp. 17, 59, vol. 50; Mass. Soldiers and Sailors, vol. 12, p. 476; History of Durham, Maine.
Died—March 5, 1820. Buried Zion Cemetery near Manchester. Stone. Bronze marker placed by Col. Archibald Lochry Chapter D. A. R.
Married—Sarah Bragdon. Ch. Arthur; Joseph: Daniel; Luther; and several daughters.
Collected by Lela Schooley Twining, 2115 Holly Street, Austin, Texas.

POE, JOHN   Johnson County
Born—1758, Guilford County, North Carolina.
Service—Pay roll of Capt. Turner's Company from Caswell Co., and Chatham Co., N. C., under the command of Col. McDowell from March 15th to July 30, 1779. Under "Men from Chatham Co." is found John Poe.

Proof—Roster of Soldiers from N. C. in the American Revolution, p. 597.
Died—Oct. 9, 1834. Buried in Pisgah Cemetery. Government marker placed by Alexander Hamilton Chapter D. A. R.
Married—Mary Newan. Ch. Samuel; Christopher; Betsey; Polly; Natty; John and Elijah.
Collected by Mrs. I. E. Tranter, Franklin, Indiana.

POINDEXTER, GABRIEL Floyd County
Born—1758, Louisa Co., Virginia.
Service—Volunteered in Virginia Infantry. He is reported in the list of Virginia men and officers who had not received their bounty land.
Proof—Virginia Military Records; D. A. R. No. 110842.
Died—1831 in Clark Co., Ind., but is buried across the county line in Floyd Co. on the old Shirley Farm.
Married—Mary Swift (1760-1820). Ch. Moses; Clevins; Merriweather; Lucy; Harriet; Polly; Elizabeth; Margaret.
Collected by Mrs. V. R. Conner, New Albany, Indiana.

POLK, CHARLES Knox County
Born—Feb. 2, 1745, Frederick Co., Maryland.
Service—Captain under Col. George Rogers Clark in the campaign of 1780-81. Capt. in Regt. of Minute Men of Mecklenburg Co., N. C., under Col. Thomas Polk, his uncle.
Proof—North Carolina Archives, State Records, vol. 10, p. 954; Genealogy of Macy Family (April, 1902); Alexander's History of Mecklenburg, N. C., p. 108.
Died—Oct. 11, 1823. Buried Polk Cemetery on Maria Creek (cemetery now destroyed).
Married—1774, Delilah Tyler (1755-1797). Ch. William b. 1775; Sarah; Elizabeth b. 1777, m. Spear Spencer; Nancy; Charles b. 1782, m. Margaret McQuade; Edward; Eleanor b. 1786-1859, m. John H. Hollingsworth; Thomas; Mary; Robert.
Collected by Miss Frances Lloyd and Mrs. S. G. Davenport, Vincennes, Indiana.

POLLARD, JAMES Spencer County
Born—1762, Culpepper Co., Virginia.
Service—While a resident of Amherst Co., Vir., he enlisted and served 3 yrs. as pri. in Capt. Booker's CO., in Col. Kirkendall's Vir. Regt. Discharged about the time of surrender of Cornwallis.
Proof—Pension claim S. 32449.

Died—July 4, 1840. Thought to be buried in Conrad graveyard, Mt. Zion Church.
Married—1789, Annie Rediford. Ch. Jesse, 1794-1846, m. Mary Lynch.

POLLEN, WILLIAM   Delaware County
Born—Oct. 14, 1762, New Jersey.
Service—Pri. in company of Capt. Sisler, Vir. Line, 7 mos.
Proof—Pension claim S. 32453.
Died—Feb. 19, 1837. Probably buried in Rees Cemetery.
Married—Elizabeth ——. Ch. Nancy; Rebecca; Margaret Patterson; Daniel; Peter; William.

POMEROY, ETHAN   Vigo County
Born—1744, Hadley, Massachusetts.
Service—Sergeant in Capt. Samuel Cook's CO., Col. Woodbridge's Mass. Regt., 3 mos. 21 days.
Proof—History and Genealogy of the Pomeroy Family by Albert A. Pomeroy.
Died—1825. Buried Terre Haute, Ind.
Married—1774, Esther Parsons. Ch. Celinda Pomeroy Cherry b. 1779.
Collected by Estabrook Chapter D. A. R.

POPE, SAMUEL   Shelby County
Born—March 25, 1761, near Warrick, New York.
Service—Enlisted in Oct., 1776, and served as a substitute for Cornelius Bogart, to whom he was apprenticed, as a pri. in Capt. Glover's N. Y. CO.; during this tour of 3 mos. he was engaged in three skirmishes with the Tories and refugees, one at New Bridge, one near his home, and one near Paramus; volunteered June, 1778, and served 9 mos. as a pri. under the same Capt. at different times.
Proof—Pension claim R. 8332.
Died—Feb. 3, 1837. Shelby Co.
Married—1790, Phebe Lee, and had several children—only one named —Catharine Pope Weir.

PORTER, DAVID   Dearborn County
Born—1736, Rockbridge Co., Virginia.
Service—Served in 13th Vir. Regt. as pri. Also served in French and Indian Wars.
Proof—Virginia State Library Report, p. 244, 9th Annual Report; War Department.
Died—1810, Dearborn Co.

Married—First W. unknown. Ch. James; David; Mary. Second W. Nancy Longwell. Ch. John; Alexander b. 1799, m. Elizabeth Elder.
Collected by Mrs. H. S. McKee, Greensburg, Indiana.

PORTER, ELI (ELIAS)   Randolph County
Born—About 1760.
Service—Pri. in CO. under Capt. Nose, Col. Wood's Regt., Vir. Line for 3 yrs., 1777-1780.
Proof—Ohio Certificate No. 20249. Applied from Clermont Co., Ohio, 1830.
Died—Nov. 4, 1848. Buried on farm N. of New Salem, Ind. Proof of death in Randolph Co., Ind., is given in records in General Accounting office, Washington, D. C.
Married—Mary ——, 1817.
Collected by Mrs. Oren E. Ross, Winchester, Indiana.

PORTER, THOMAS   Switzerland County
Born—Nov. 29, 1761.
Service—Pri. in CO. under Capt. Chapman in Conn. Line, for 9 mos.
Proof—Pension claim S. 17640.

PORTLOCK, JOHN   Franklin County
Born—July 7, 1765, Shenandoah Co., Virginia.
Service—While residing in Augusta Co., Vir., he volunteered in 1781, served in Capt. David Givinn's CO., Col. McCreary's Vir. Regt., marched to the South and joined Gen. Green's Army. Was in battle of Guilford Court House, and was slightly wounded. Served 6 mos.
Proof—Pension claim S. 17636.
Died—Jan. 30, 1849. Thought to be buried at Andersonville, Franklin Co.
Children—John, m. Amy Moore; Barrnet, m. Sarah Line.

POSEY, ZEPHANIAH   Rush County
Born—1753, Virginia.
Service—Entered service Nov. 5, 1776, as pri., afterwards made Sergeant. Served as pri. in Capt. Charles Gallahue's CO., 11th Vir. Regt., under Col. Daniel Morgan, Lieut. Col. John Cropper. Was transferred to Capt. George Ricis' CO., and was discharged Nov. 1, 1779.
Proof—Pensioned June 23, 1819, as Sergeant of Vir. Continental CO. in Hamilton Co., Ohio; D. A. R. No. 75240.

Died—Oct. 21, 1826. Hamilton Co., Ohio. Buried Hopewell Graveyard, Richland Twp., Rush Co., Ind. Government marker.
Married—Mary Jackson, 1760-1839. Ch. Nancy b. 1782; William b. 1784; Frances b. 1786; Sarah b. 1788; Armstead b. 1793; Alfred b. 1796; Cecelis b. 1799; Louisa b. 1801; Albert b. 1805.
Collected by Mrs. Willard Amos, Rushville, Indiana.

POST, EBENEZER   Lawrence County
Service—Pri. in Col. John Durkee's Regt. in Conn. Line of Cont'l Army from Jan. 1, 1780, to Jan. 1, 1781.
Proof—Pension claim S. 36741.
Married— —— W. died 1822. Ch. Nancy b. 1790; Phebe; James; Sally; Richard; Calvin; Alexander and Fanny (twins) b. 1803.

POWELL, NATHAN   Dearborn County
Born—1754, Chester Co., Penn.
Service—Served as pri. in Col. Patterson Bell's Regt., 8th Battalion, Chester Co. Militia, Penn. Line.
Proof—D. A. R. Lineage, vol. 86, p. 133.
Died—1831. Buried Busse farm, Hogan Twp. Stone.
Married—Sarah Nickels, 1780-1850. Ch. Erasmus, 1788-1843, m. 2nd Polly Allen.

POWERS, LEWIS   Dubois County
Born—About 1754.
Service—Pri. Jones' Co., 1st Regt. Light Dragoons. In battles of Brandywine, Germantown, Monmouth. Enlisted July, 1776, served 2½ yrs.
Proof—Pension claim S. 16414.
Died—Aug. 16, 1833. Buried Evan's Graveyard, W. of Jasper, Ind. Government marker placed by Luther A. Parker.
Married—Martha ——. Ch. Major T.; Anderson; Dorothy; and several others.
Collected by George Wilson, Historian of Dubois County.

PRATHER, THOMAS   Jackson County
Born—Mar. 26, 1756, Prince George Co., Md.
Service—Enlisted 1776 at Will's Court House at Mulberryfields, N. C., pri. in Capt. Cleveland's CO., Col. Love's Regt., N. C. Line, 2 yrs.
Proof—Pension claim 17032.
Died—Pension last paid to March 4, 1841.
Children—Pension mentions son, Bazil, and a daughter. Early marriage records of Jackson Co. show a number of Prather marriages.

PRATT, JONATHAN Ripley County
Born—1764, Needham, Massachusetts.
Service—Enlisted in March, 1781, served to Oct., 1785, as a pri. Enlisted at Templeton, Mass. Served under Capt. Daniel Lunk, Col. Tupper, Col. Vose.
Proof—Pension record.
Died—Jan. 13, 1850. Prattsburg, Ripley Co. Government marker placed by Hist. Society.
Married—Betsey ——, 1775-1849. Ch. Lucy b. 1802; Samuel b. 1805; Dyer b. 1808; Jonathan b. 1809; Eben b. 1815; Elijah b. 1817.
Collected by Mrs. A. B. Wycoff, Batesville, Indiana.

PRENTICE, NATHANIEL Noble County
Born—March 14, 1764, New London, Connecticut.
Service—In battles of Bennington, Saratoga, Monmouth. He was confined on the prison ship, "Jersey," from which he was sent as a prisoner to Jamaica. Exchanged at the close of the war.
Proof—Pension record.
Died—1839. Buried in Ligonier, Ind. Marker and bronze tablet.
Married—Second W. Margaret Hedden Boyer (1776-1861). Ch. Nathaniel; William; John; Nelson; Eliza Prentice Johnson.
Collected by Mrs. H. G. Misselhorn, Kendallville, Indiana.

PRICE, JOSEPH Posey County
Born—Feb. 7, 1758, Huntington Co., New Jersey.
Service—Pri. under Capt. Campbell, 3rd Regt. N. J. Line. In 3rd Regt. Penn. Line under Col. "Chay," Capt. Stewart, 1 yr. Served 3 mos. in S. C.
Proof—Pension claim R. 8470.
Died—Buried on Dirt Road between No. 669 and Harmony Way.
Children—Heirs named in pension application, Maxey; Lolly; Gillison; Larkin.

PRICE, THOMAS Monroe County
Born—April 22, 1750, Frederick Co., Virginia.
Service—Pri. in CO. under Capt. Rader, Col. Gibson's Regt., Vir. Line, 9 mos.
Proof—Pension claim S. 31917.

PRICE, THOMAS Posey County
Born—1763, Culpepper Co., Virginia.
Service—Pri. under Capt. Dan Smith. In battle of Point Pleasant.
Proof—Military District of Ohio, Cont'l. Line Warrant No. 3203; Rev. War Records of Vir. by Brumbaugh, p. 486.

Died—1828. Buried Bethsaida Cemetery.
Married—Sarah Jane Mosby (1740-1820). Ch. Reuben (1780-1855), m. Mary Linden.

PRITCHARD, JOHN   Decatur County
Born—July, 1759.
Service—Pri. in CO. under Capt. Douglas, Regt. of Col. Mathews, Vir. Line, 1 yr., 1781.
Proof—Pension claim S. 32456.
Died—March 28, 1847. Buried Sandcreek Cemetery.
Married—Ann ———. Ch. Elizabeth; Margaret; Mary; Harriet; Fanny; and several sons.

PRITCHETT, JOHN   Gibson County
Born—April 6, 1767, Loudoun Co., Virginia.
Service—Served 3 yrs. and 15 days as a pri., corporal and sergeant in Capt. Lipscomb's CO., also known as Capt. Young's CO., in the Regt. variously known as 1st, 3rd, 7th, 5th, and 11th Vir. Regt. Also as a sergeant in Capt. John Steed's CO., 2nd Vir. Brigade, Col. Christian Febiger. Enlisted Feb. 14, 1777, and discharged in 1780.
Proof—Pension claim R. 20182; Ind. Cert. 3751.
Died—June 21, 1842. Buried Blythe Chappel Cemetery, W. of Fort Branch. Stone.
Married—1781, Elizabeth Hayhurst (1767-1830). Ch. Presley b. 1782; Charles b. 1784; Lydda b. 1786; Sally b. 1788; Patsey b. 1791; Betsey b. 1793; Juda b. 1796; Elisha b. 1799, m. Elizabeth Mead; Polly b. 1802; Nancy b. 1804; Wright B. b. 1806.
Collected by Gen. John Gibson Chapter, D. A. R.

PROCTOR, JOHN   Elkhart County
Born—Feb. 10, 1752. Stafford Co., Virginia.
Service—Tombstone bears inscription, "A Revolutionary Soldier." Served in Vir. Regt. throughout the war. In battle of Stony Point under Gen. Wayne and at siege of Yorktown.
Proof—Pension claim R. 8496; Elkhart Co. History, p. 856.
Died—Jan. 11, 1856, age 104 years. Buried Heaton Cemetery. Stone.
Children—John Jr. d. 1882, m. Rebecca Spangler; William.
Collected by Mrs. Fred C. Wherly, Elkhart, Indiana.

PROTSMAN (PROTZMAN), JOHN   Switzerland County
Born—July 10, 1763, New Jersey.
Service—Served in 5th CO., 2nd Battalion, Northampton Co., Penn. Militia under Capt. Henry Alshouse, Col. Roup. Received pay for service from 1778 to 1783.

Proof—Penn. Archives, 5th Series, vol. 8, pp. 369, 121, 135, 133, vol. 13, p. 217.
Died—Aug. 10, 1841. Buried Vevay Cemetery. Stone.
Married—Nancy Barbara Reckner (1766-1841). Ch. David b. 1791, m. Maxey McMillen; John b. 1793, m. Elizabeth Mitchell (both were soldiers of 1812); Elizabeth b. 1795, m. Stephen Stewart; Samuel b. 1797, m. Jemima Campbell; Nancy b. 1799; William b. 1801, m. Polly Campbell.
Collected by Mrs. A. V. Danner, Vevay, Ind., and Nellie Protzman Waldenmaier, Washington, D. C.

PULEE, JOHN   Cass County
Service—Soldier in the Rev. War.
Proof—History of Cass County, p. 127; One Hundred Years of Tipton Lodge No. 33, F. and A. M., p. 155. These are considered authentic.
Collected by Miss Laura Henderson, Logansport, Indiana.

PURCELL, EDWARD   Sullivan County
Born—March, 1759, Hampshire Co., Virginia.
Service—Enlisted in 1775, served 7 mos. as a pri. under Capt. James Parsons of Virginia. Enlisted 1781, served 6 mos. under Capt. Mull, Major Williams, Virginia.
Proof—Pension record.
Died—1851. Buried Old Town Cemetery, Carlisle, Ind.
Married—Abigail Williams. Ch. Nancy, m. Thomas Holder.
Collected by Mrs. James R. Riggs, Sullivan, Indiana.

PURCELL, JONATHAN   Knox County
Born—Hampshire Co., Virginia.
Service—In Virginia Militia who were paid off at Romney, Va.
Proof—Special Report of Dept. of Archives and History of J. H. Echenrode, pp. 361-362.
Died—March 4, 1813 (from Administrator's papers). Buried West Salem Cemetery.
Married—Catherine —— d. 1803. Ch. Johnathan; John (1780-1856), m. Hanna Hollingsworth.
Collected by George Purcell, Bloomington, Indiana.

PURCELL, WILLIAM   Knox County
Born—July 31, 1761, Hampshire Co., Virginia.
Service—Enlisted from Hampshire Co. as pri. and served from Apr., 1781, 3 mos. in Capt. Michael Stumpt's CO. In Nov., 1781, 3 mos. in Capt. Isaac Parson's CO. under Col. Willis.
Proof—Pension claim S. 16229; McAllister's Virginia Militia in Rev. War, p. 286.

Died—About 1842. Buried McCleskey Farm, just off Bruceville Road. Stone.
Married— —— Benefiel. Ch. Edward; probably others.
Collected by Mrs. Leo Joice and S. G. Davenport, Vincennes, Indiana.

PURCILL, LAWRENCE   Harrison County
Born—About 1756.
Service—Enlisted Feb., 1777, Loudoun Co., Vir., 3 yrs. in Capt. Windsor Brown's CO. of 1st Vir. Regt., Col. Gibson, served 6 mos. transferred to Capt. Armstead's CO. of Grenadiers. Discharged at Alexandria. Battles, Monmouth, Stony Point.
Proof—Pension claim R. 8524 rejected.

RACINE, FRANCOIS   Knox County
Born—Oct. 16, 1758, Vincennes, Indiana Territory.
Service—A Patriot. Signed Oath of Allegiance to the State of Virginia, July 20, 1778. Listed as Fransoy X. Rassine.
Proof—Clark's Papers; Ill. Hist. Coll., vol. VIII, pp. 52-59.
Buried—In cemetery adjoining St. Francis Xavier Cathedral.
Married—Teresa Compagnotte. Ch. Celeste b. Feb. 29, 1783, m. 1803; Francois Valle b. 1785; probably other children.
Collected by Mrs. Leo Schultheis, Vincennes, Indiana.

RAGIN (REAGAN), THOMAS   Clinton County
Born—May 6, 1749.
Service—Pri. and Capt. in CO. commanded by Capt. Watts, Regt. by Col. Glenn in Penn. Line, 18 mos.
Proof—Pension claim W. 9244.
Died—July 25, 1838.
Married—1776, Hannah —— b. 1754. Ch. Rezin b. 1777; Jesse b. 1779; Daniel b. 1783; William b. 1786; Rebecca b. 1780; Thomas b. 1791; Hannah b. 1795.

RAILSBACK, DAVID   Wayne County
Born—Dec. 12, 1769, in Loudoun Co., Virginia, or Rowen Co., North Carolina (both places given in county histories).
Service—He was assistant wagon boy for his brother, Edward, in the Colonial army.
Proof—Young's History of Wayne Co., pp. 150 and 354.
Died—Oct. 17, 1856. Buried Elkhorn cemetery. Stone.
Married—Sarah Stephens b. 1774. Ch. Mary, m. Wm. Lewis; Enoch, m. Nany Fouts; Judith, m. Thomas Cobb; Edward, m. Francis Hunt; William, m. Mary Rhodes; Caleb and Matthew (twins),

m. Nancy and Sarah Barnhill; Joel, m. Elizabeth Fouts; David, m. Mary Smith; Nathan, m. Sina Hunt; John, m. Pamelia Davenport; Sarah, m. Larkin Gaar.
Collected by Mrs. Paul L. Ross, Richmond, Indiana.

RAINBOLT, ADAM — Greene County
Born—1757, Cape Fear, North Carolina.
Service—While residing in Burke Co., N. C., served as pri. with N. C. Troops as follows: from Oct., 1780, 3 mos. in Capt. Mordecai Clark's CO., Col. Holmes' Rgt. Was in battle at Cowpens. Served at various times under Capt. Bakerstaff and Cols. Cleveland, Williams and Washington, 6 mos.
Proof—Pension claim S. 32466.
Died—Nov., 1834, at his home in Lawrence Co. Buried in Storm Cemetery in Green Co. Stone.
Married—1787, Jane Potter (1765-1834). Ch. John b. 1788; Jesse b. 1797; Adam b. 1824; Joe.
Collected by Mrs. Mary A. Stonaker, Bedford, Indiana.

RAMER (REAMER, RAYMER), HENRY — Dearborn County
Born—About 1750.
Service—Pri. in company under Capt. Bendlelow, Regt. of Col. Conat, Penn. Line for 1 yr., 5 mos.
Proof—Pension claim W. 9615.
Died—Dec. 1, 1835.
Married—Mary —— d. 1849. Ch. Susan Whelstone; Polly Spangler; Mary Helmz; Ule Whelstone; Betsey Johnson; Peter (6th child); Henry (8th child).
Collected by Mrs. Walter Kerr, Aurora, Indiana.

RAMSAY, THOMAS — Jefferson County
Born—1739, Bucks Co., Pennsylvania.
Service—Served as a pri. in Capt. Thomas Craig's CO., 3rd Penn. Regt. His name first appears on the pay roll of the company Aug., 1775, and is last found on the pay roll of Capt. Banner's CO. same Regt. under Col. Joseph Wood for Nov., 1776.
Proof—From original records on File in War Department, not from bound vol.
Died—June, 1829. Buried Point Pleasant, near Kent, but government marker placed in Greenbrier cemetery by John Paul Chapter, D. A. R.
Married—Hannah Lochard (1771-1829). Ch. Martha, m. John Hunt; William b. 1779, d. 1820; Jane (1795-1835), m. William White. Will Book C., pp. 287-289, gives the following heirs: Asenath

Mounts; William Ramsay; Benjamin Ramsay; Robert R. Ramsay; John Ramsay; Thomas Ramsay; Levi Ramsay; Jane White; Mary Humphries.
Collected by John Paul Chapter, D. A. R.

RAMSAY, WILLIAM   Hendricks County
Born—1748, Caroline Co., Virginia.
Service—Volunteered 1779. Served 4 mos., 10 days under Gen. Butler, Capt. Camplin, Col. McDowell. Enlisted 1781 for 3 mos. as sergeant under Capt. Umphries, N. C. Line.
Proof——Pension claim S. 17035.
Died—Sept. 4, 1836. Possibly buried on farm near Morgan Co. Line.
Son—Bartholomew.

RAMSEY, SAMUEL   Clark County
Born—June 2, 1760, Lancaster, Pennsylvania.
Service—Pri. in CO. commanded by Capt. Boyd, Penn. Line, 6 mos.
Proof—Pension claim S. 31920. Lived in Clark Co., 1836.

RAND, THOMAS   Dearborn County
Born—July 19, 1746, Belfast, Ireland.
Service—Pri. in Vir. Infantry Continental Establishment.
Proof—Rev. War Records of Vir. by Brumbaugh, pp. 186, 265; D. A. R. No. 147661.
Died—Oct. 29, 1825. Buried Rand Cemetery, Caesar Creek Twp. Stone. Bronze marker placed by Col. Archibald Lochry Chapter, D. A. R.
Married—Elizabeth Carder (1767-1821). Ch. Elizabeth (1802-86), m. Thomas Froman; James (1791-1864).
Collected by Mrs. Wymond I. Beckett, 22 E. 52nd St., Indianapolis, Indiana, and Mrs. Walter Kerr, Aurora, Indiana.

RANEY, JEREMIAH   Martin County
Born—About 1765, Maryland.
Service—Serg. Enlisted for 3 yrs. in 5th Regt., N. Y. Line, commanded by Col. Lewis Dubois.
Proof—State Archives of N. Y.; Documents relating to colonial history of N. Y., vol. I, p. 220.
Buried—Mt. Pleasant, Martin County.
Married—Mary Joan Sheenan. Ch. Elizabeth Hester, m. James Andrew Crooks; John Felix, m. Mary Nail; Sarah, m. Charles Fewell; James, m. Mary Holland; Jonathan, m. Patsy Beck.
Collected by Miss Virginia Davis, Loogootee, Indiana.

RANK, GEORGE Tippecanoe County
Born—Cumberland Co., Pennsylvania.
Service—Pri. in Capt. John Herkerider's CO., 9th Battalion, Lancaster Co., Penn. Militia, 1782.
Proof—Penn. Archives, 5th Series, vol. 7, p. 955.
Died—1845. Buried Greenbush Cemetery, Lafayette, Ind. Stone. Name placed on bronze tablet by Gen. de Lafayette Chapter, D. A. R.
Married—Martha ——. Had 12 children; two known, George Washington and William.
Collected by Gen. de Lafayette Chapter, D. A. R.

RANSFORD, JOSEPH Sullivan County
Born—1763.
Service—Fifer in Capt. Robert Walker's CO. in 2nd Artillery Regt. Cont'l Troops under Col. John Lamb. Enlisted March 11, 1777, for 3 yrs. Was transferred Feb., 1778, as a gunner to Capt. Eustis' CO., 3rd Artillery Regt., under Col. John Crane. Discharged April 11, 1780.
Proof—War Department.
Died—1849. Buried Drake Cemetery, Fairbanks Twp. Stone.
Collected by Mrs. James R. Riggs, Sullivan, Indiana.

RANSOM, ISREAL Harrison County
Born—July 22, 1760.
Service—Enlisted Dec., 1780 or 1781, in Marlborough, Conn., under Capt. John Darkee. Served until Sept., 1783. Pri. in CO. under Col. Grosnover of Conn. Line. Discharged West Point.
Proof—Pension claim W. 9616. B. L. Wt. 80031-160-55.
Died—Sept. 18, 1839. Buried Snyder's Chapel, Harrison Co., 12 m. from New Albany, Ind.
Married—1786, Lois Newton (1769-1859). Ch. Russell; Alfred; Gadson; John; Isreal; Francis Henry b. 1796, m. Sarah Allen and Nancy Budd; Louisa; Hiram; Julia Ann; Montgomery.

RANSTEAD, JOSEPH St. Joseph County
Born—1767.
Service—Pri. in Regt. commanded by Col. Sprouts in Mass. Line, 2 yrs., 9 mos.
Proof—Pension claim W. 26352. B. L. Wt. 57784-160-55.
Died—Aug. 20, 1836. Buried Hamilton Cemetery. Bronze tablet placed by Schuyler Colfax Chapter, D. A. R.
Married—First W. unknown. Dau. Elizabeth; second W. 1793, Jane McMullen. Ch. Leonard; John; Minerva; Joel; Jane; James; Sarah; Susan, m. Jesse Frame; Mary Ann.
Collected by Miss Amanda McComb, South Bend, Indiana, and Mrs. Orville Dailey, Albany, Ohio.

RASOR, PETER   Spencer County
Born—Oct., 1758, Culpepper Co., Virginia.
Service—Enlisted from Culpepper Co., Virginia, as pri. in Vir. Militia.
    Served several tours of duty in 1781, under Capt. Clark and Maj.
    Groves. Present at surrender of Cornwallis.
Proof—Pension claim R. 8600. Rejected for lack of 6 mos. service.
Died—Nov. 11, 1831. Buried Hackleman graveyard, Rockport, Ind.
    Stone.
Married—Frances Adair. Ch. Simeon b. 1787; Elizabeth b. 1788;
    George; Anne.
Collected by Miss Laura M. Wright, Rockport, Indiana.

RAY, JONATHAN   Marion County
Born—March, 1759, Frederick Co., Maryland.
Service—Pri. in CO. under Capt. Price, Col. Rollins' Regt. in Md. Line
    for 6 mos.
Proof—Pension claim S. 16513.

RAY, THOMAS   Shelby County
Service—Lived in Wake Co., N. C., when drafted. Was not quite old
    enough but did serve 3 mos. Later served in 5 tours of 3 mos.
    in N. C. line.
Proof—Pension claim W. 9614.
Died—Nov. 16, 1829.
Married—1782, Elizabeth Pearce d. 1844. Ch. Hudson; James; Gilley;
    Sarah; Susanna; Martha; Chaney.

RAY, WILLIAM   Vigo County
Born—Nov. 26, 1740, Belfast Co., Ireland.
Service—Enlisted after battle of Bunker Hill in a CO. under Anthony
    Wayne. Later served as Lieut. for 3 yrs. and 3 mos. Was at
    Valley Forge.
Proof—Pension claim S. 32470.
Died—July 28, 1840. Buried Riley, Ind. Bronze marker placed by In-
    diana S. A. R.
Married—Ann Brown. Ch. William II; John; Rev. Robert; Josa; Eliz-
    abeth; Sarah; Martin M.; Gov. James B.; Jane; Polly; Mary Etta.
Collected by Caroline Scott Harrison Chapter.

REA, ROBBIN   Jefferson County
Born—June 7, 1762, Lancaster Co., Pennsylvania.
Service—Enlisted in Mecklenburg, N. C., in Nov., 1778. Served 6 wks.
    in Capt. James Harris' N. C. CO.; in Capt. Wiley's CO., Col. Har-
    ris' Regt.; Dec. 27, 1780, was in Capt. Wiley's CO., Col. Hender-
    son's Regt.; in April, 1781, served under Capt. Thomas Shelby,
    Wm. Hutchinson, Samuel Martin. Discharged April 17, 1782.

Proof—Pension record.
Died—Nov. 4, 1852. Buried Underwood Cemetery. Government marker placed by John Paul Chapter, D. A. R.
Married—1786, Nancy Patton. Ch. James b. 1786; Jane b. 1788; Samuel b. 1790; Margaret b. 1792, m. Huston Patton; Matthew b. 1794; Silas b. 1796; John b. 1798, m. Margaret Swan; Nancy; Martha.
Collected by John Paul Chapter, D. A. R.

REAMER, DAVID   Switzerland County
Born—Dec., 1754, Somerset Co., New Jersey.
Service—Enlisted in fall of 1779. Served until March or April, 1783, in Capt. Thomas Wylies' CO. of Artificers, Continental Army. Also served under Col. Gibson.
Proof——Pension claim W. 9621; Doc. 1st Session of 23rd Congress.
Died—Sept. 21, 1836. Buried Lostutter's Cemetery, near Ohio Co. Line. Stone.
Married—1780, Nancy Smith d. 1848. Ch. Catherine b. 1782, m. George March; Jane b. 1784; George b. 1786; Elizabeth b. 1788, m. Peter Lostutter; James b. 1791; Mary b. 1783; David; Rebecca, m. Calip Hayes; Henry b. 1812; Sarah, m. Henry Kelley; Nancy, m. James A. Kelley.
Collected by Mrs. A. V. Danner, Vevay, Indiana.

REANY (REINEY), JOSEPH   Greene County
Born—About 1754, near Burlington, New Jersey.
Service—Served as pri. in N. C. troops as follows: Oct., 1779, 5 mos. in Capt. John Donald's CO. in Col. John Locke's Regt.; July, 1780, 3 mos. in Capt. Peter O'Neil's CO. under Col. Paisley and was in battle of Camden; from Oct., 1780, 3 mos. in Capt. James Robinson's CO. in Col. John Littrel's Regt.; in 1781, 2 mos. in Capt. Thomas Dugan's CO.
Proof—Pension claim W. 11127.
Died—Sept. 8, 1846. Probably buried in Cass Twp.
Married—First W. about 1787, name unknown. Second W. Mary Ward.
Collected by Mrs. Roy Bogner, Washington, Indiana.

RECTOR, CHARLES   Miami County
Born—March 26, 1761, Fauquier Co., Virginia.
Service—Drafted under Capt. Tapley in Hampshire Co., Vir., in spring of 1781. Sent to Ft. Pleasant on S. Branch of Potomac under Col. Joseph Nevel, Capt. Teverbaugh.
Proof—Pension claim R. 8637, rejected.
Died—Jan. 1, 1852. Buried Mt. Hope Cemetery, Peru, Ind.
Married—1824, Catherine Haynes Marshall. Ch. Elizabeth (1825-1892).

REDDEN, GEORGE — Fountain County
Born—1746.
Service—Served with New Jersey Troops.
Proof—War Department.
Died—1838. Buried on Charles Smith farm near Sterling, Van Buren Twp. Government marker placed by Veedersburg Chapter, D. A. R.
Children—William; Elizabeth Osborn.
Collected by Miss Edith Miller, Veedersburg, Indiana.

REDDICK, WILLIAM — Marion County
Born—About 1760.
Service—Enlisted Philadelphia under Capt. Lawrence Kain, 1777, Col. Patton's Regt., served until 1783. Discharged at Philadelphia by Capt. Doyle. In battles of Brandywine, Germantown, Monmouth and at surrender of Cornwallis.
Proof—Pension claim W. 9620. B. L. Wt. 40674-160-55.
Died—Oct. 3, 1831. Buried Reddick graveyard, Lawrence, Ind.
Married—Margaret Trump. Ch. Joshua; Helia; Lucinda; Rachel; William (3rd child) b. 1790; Richard (oldest) b. about 1786.

REDINGTON, DANIEL — Dearborn or Decatur County
Born—1763.
Service—Pri. in CO. under Capt. Ephraim Cleaveland, Col. Jackson's Regt. of Mass. Line for 22 mos., 27 days.
Proof—Pension claim W. 9623.
Died—Aug. 17, 1834.
Married—1786, Anna Prince. Ch. John; Margaret.

REDMAN, AARON — Gibson County
Born—About 1760, Loudoun Co., Virginia.
Service—Pri. in Capt. Porterfield's CO., 11th Vir. Regt. 1776, for 3 yrs.
Proof—Pension claim W. 9622.
Died—Aug. 27, 1840, Gibson Co.
Married—1784, Nancy (Ann) Craig. Had 14 children. Two known, Margaret b. 1784; John.

REDMAN, BENJAMIN — Bartholomew County
Born—Maryland.
Service—Pri. 4th CO. Militia, Montgomery Co., Maryland.
Proof—Record from Col. John Long, Genealogist, Garden Apartment, Baltimore.
Buried—Carter's Cemetery, 5 mi. N. of Columbus, Ind. Stone. Died while on a visit to his daughter, Mrs. Carter.
Collected by Mrs. Laura D. Fix (deceased), Columbus, Ind.

REED, DAVID   Orange County
Born—Morris Co., New Jersey.
Service—Pri. in CO. of Capt. Springer. Was at Fort Prichett, Monongahela Co., Aug. 3, 1777. His name also appears as ranger on the frontier, Capt. Ichabod Ashcraft's CO.
Proof—Penn. Archives, 6th Series, vol. 2, p. 268; series 3, vol. 23, pp. 212, 317.
Died—After 1820. Buried on land entered by Wm. Reed, E. East Twp.
Married—Rachel ——. Ch. William (oldest son) b. 1779, m. Ruth Glover.
Collected by Mrs. N. B. Mavity, French Lick, Indiana.

REED, GEORGE   Warrick County
Born—June 12, 1760, King William Co., Virginia.
Service—Enlisted N. C. under Capt. John McClamma, Maj. James Love, Col. Thomas Bloodworth. Served 73 days, was taken prisoner near Wilmington, paroled by British Major Craig. Enlisted in militia under Capt. Amos Love, Maj. Snead.
Proof—Order Book 3, p. 190, of Warrick Co. Probate Records. Received pension in 1832.
Died—1855. Buried Floyd Cemetery, 3 mi. N. of Boonville, Ind. Government marker placed by Vanderburgh Chapter, D. A. R.
Married—Grace Utterbach. Ch. Henderson; Jim; Joe; Claybourn; Minard; George; Armer; Waldon; Bill; Alfred; Susie, m. Thomas Leslie; Nancy, m. Bill Abshire; Betsey, m. Tom Robinson.
Collected by Mrs. H. K. Forsythe, Newburgh, Indiana.

REED, ISAAC   Wayne County
Born—1757.
Service—Pri. in Capt. Cookson Long's CO. and Battalion of Northumberland Co., Penn. Militia under Col. James Potter. In 1777 he signed the Oath of Allegiance.
Proof—D. A. R. Lineage, vol. 74, p. 23.
Died—1823, Richmond, Ind.
Married—1782, Margaret Baker (1763-1850). Ch. John b. 1783, m. Mahettable Kinnan.

REED, JOHN   Clinton County
Service—Enlisted Feb. 17, 1776, in Capt. Thomas L. Moore's CO. of 3rd Penn. Militia.
Proof—Penn. Archives, Series 2, vol. 10, pp. 96 and 100.
Buried—Kirklin Cemetery.

REED, JOSEPH   Harrison County
Born—About 1760.
Service—Enlisted May 30, 1776, as substitute for David Elder in 13th
    Penn. Regt. under Capt. Matthew Scott. After battle of Monmouth the Regt. combined with 2nd under Col. Stewart. Discharged 1780 or 1781 at Princeton.
Proof—Pension claim W. 9618; Penn. Archives, Series 2, vol. 10, p. 435.
Died—Aug. 26, 1826, Harrison Co.
Married—Margaret Quick. Ch. John; Robert; James; Nancy; Kress
    (Tress); Betsey Charles; Rebecca Roberts; Polly Reed; Dennis.

REED, JOSHUA   Orange County
Born—Oct. 29, 1757, Morris Co., New Jersey.
Service—Enlisted in Vir. Troops as follows: Nov., 1775, under Capt.
    Johnathan Paddocks, marched to a station at mouth of Fish
    Creek on Vir. side of Ohio River. Served 2 mos. in Capt. Samuel
    Mason's CO. guarding the frontiers. In Oct., 1776, served 2 mos.
    in Capts. Thomas Gaddis' and Springer's CO. In 1777, served 4
    mos., assisted in building Forts McIntosh and Tuscarawas. In
    1782 under Gen. Wm. Crawford, was in battle of Sandusky.
Proof—Pension claim S. 32476.
Died—May, 1838. Buried Stampers Creek Church Cemetery, Paoli Twp.
    Stone.
Married—Johannah —— d. 1823. Ch. Rachel, m. Thomas Phillips;
    Martha, m. Jacob Marts; Mary, m. Peter Mahan.
Collected by Mrs. N. B. Mavity, French Lick, Indiana.

REED, THOMAS   Crawford County
Born—Oct., 1753, Lancaster, Co., Pennsylvania.
Service—While living in Lancaster Co., Penn., he enlisted as pri. with
    Penn. troops as follows: From July or Aug., 1776, 2 mos. in Capt.
    John Patton's CO., Col. Porter's Regt.; from Dec., 1776, 2 mos. in
    same Regt.; from Nov., 1777, 2 mos. in Capt. Paxton's CO., Maj.
    Brown's Battalion; June, 1778, 2 mos. in Capt. Reim's CO.,
    guarded prisoners at Lancaster.
Proof—Pension claim S. 31926.
Died—After April, 1834. Had family but no names given in pension
    application.

REESE, JOHN   Clark County
Born—About 1752 in Wales.
Service—Served under Lieut. David Enoch at Fort Pitt. Had served
    132 days, Oct. 2, 1775.
Proof—P. 45, Manuscript Book Pitts. Revolutionary Pay Roll, in the
    Vir. State Library; P. 76, Pioneer Preachers of Indiana, Evans.

Died—Jan. 2, 1827. Buried near New Washington, Ind.
Married—Jane —— (1749-1822). Ch. Catharine, m. Robert Tilford; Sarah, m. Thomas Davis; Benjamin, m. Sarah Davis; John, m. Elizabeth Simenton.
Collected by Mrs. Ira E. Tranter, Franklin, Indiana.

REID, ALEXANDER   Lawrence County
Born—June 11, 1755.
Service—Enlisted 1776 in Greenbrier Co., Vir., as pri. and orderly-sergeant in 12th Vir. Regt. Was in battles of Germantown and Monmouth. Discharged after serving 3 yrs. Re-enlisted in Capt. Andrew Wallace's Vir. CO. Captured at siege of Charleston, detained a mo. and made his escape.
Proof—Pension record.
Died—Dec. 10, 1851. Buried Tanksley Cemetery, Bedford, Ind. Stone.
Married—Wife's name unknown. Ch. Hannah b. 1786, m. 1809 Alexander Wright Mitchell; John; Thomas; Sallie; Ann.
Collected by Mrs. Ellen Hoover, Bedford, Indiana, and W. R. Alexander, Parkville, Missouri.

REID, JAMES   Sullivan County
Born—1762, Pennsylvania.
Service—Pri. in Capt. Isaac Thomas CO. of Foot Militia belonging to the 1st Battalion of Chester Co., Penn.
Proof—Penn. Archives, Series 5, vol. 5, p. 507.
Died—1855. Buried Pleasantville Cemetery, Jefferson Twp. Stone.
Married—1788, Jean Black (1762-1852). Ch. Martha b. 1789; Robert b. 1792; Jean b. 1795; Backes b. 1797; Betesia b. 1800; James S. b. 1802.
Collected by Mrs. H. K. Ross, Sullivan, Indiana

REILEY, JOHN   Rush County
Born—Dec. 9, 1751, Cecil Co., Maryland.
Service—Was in Lord Dinsmore's expedition against the Indians in 1774. First enlistment was for 6 mos., then re-enlisted for 3 yrs. Was in battle of Bound-brook and another near Morristown. He was one of Morgan's selected corps of riflemen. In battle of Saratoga and at the surrender of Burgoyne.
Proof—Pension allowed while living in Campbell Co., Ky.; Ind. Mag. of Hist., vol. VIII, p. 16; D. A. R. Lineage, vol. 61, p. 135.
Died—Dec. 22, 1845. Buried Hopewell cemetery, Richland Twp. Stone.
Married—1785, Elizabeth McCulloch d. 1840. Ch. John Jr., m. Levina Morlan; Mary, m. Samuel Alley; Robert.
Collected by Mrs. Willard Amos, Rushville, Indiana.

REILEY (RIELY), JOHN   Orange County
Born—About 1758, Carlisle, Pennsylvania.
Service—Enlisted in Carlisle, Penn., Nov. 2, 1776, as pri. and musician in Capt. Henry McKinley's CO., Col. Cooke's 12th Penn. Regt. Also served in 3rd Penn. Regt. In battles of Monmouth, Jamestown and siege of Yorktown. Was in 1st Vir. Regt. when discharged Nov. 3, 1783.
Proof—Pension claim S. 36781.
Died—Nov., 1838. Buried Old Cemetery at Paoli, Ind. Government marker placed by Lost River Chapter, D. A. R.
Married—Mary McIlvaine d. 1840. Had 11 children, but names only four, David; Thomas; Robert; Charles, in pension application.
Collected by Mrs. N. B. Mavity, French Lick, Indiana.

RENEAU, THOMAS   Harrison County
Born—April 4, 1760, Frederick Co., Virginia.
Service—Enlisted in CO. under Capt. Ford for 1 mo., 1776. Next tour was 3 mos. under Capt. May, Col. Stinson. Built Ft. McIntosh and did scouting. Penn. Line, 10 mos.
Proof—Pension claim S. 32477.

REYNOLDS, JOSEPH   Franklin County
Born—Jan. 11, 1762, Dutchess Co., New York.
Service—While residing in Orange Co., N. Y., he enlisted April 10, 1776, and served as a sailor on board the schooner, "Olive Branch," under Capt. Jacob Swim. Schooner captured by British Oct. 28, 1776. Enlisted April 12, 1778, as pri. in Capt. Van Duzer's N. Y. CO., discharged July 12, 1778. Enlisted May 15, 1779, as pri. in Capt. Smith's N. Y. CO., acted as guide to Gen. Wayne's Army. Was at Stony Point. Discharged July 22, 1779. Enlisted April 1, 1780 under Lieut. Dow in N. Y. Troops, discharged Oct. 1, 1780.
Proof—Pension claim S. 31928. Moved to Franklin Co., Ind., 1811, and received pension while living in Whitewater Twp., 1834.

RHOTEN (RATTAN), THOMAS   Putnam County
Born—1755.
Service—While residing in Northumberland Co., Penn., he enlisted in Penn. Troops. Served from November, 1776, until January 15, 1781, as pri. under Capts. John Harris and Christie and Cols. Cook and Craig. In battles of Brandywine, Germantown, and Stony Point.
Proof—Pension claim S. 16232.
Died—Last payment of pension Sept. 4, 1838. Buried Beech Grove Cemetery, Madison Twp.
Collected by Miss Minnetta Wright, Greencastle, Indiana.

RICH, ELIJAH   Dearborn County
Born—Jan. 3, 1762, Weston, Worcester Co., Massachusetts.
Service—Enlisted June or July, 1777, discharged June, 1780. Served
   under Col. Daniel Keyes, Major Boyd, Mass. Line.
Proof—Pension claim S. 17048.
Died—1839. Thought to be buried in Manchester Twp.
Collected by Mrs. Walter Kerr, Aurora, Indiana.

RICHARDSON, THOMAS   Warrick County
Born—1762, Loudoun Co., Virginia.
Service—Enlisted 1780, Bedford Co., Vir. Militia 3 mos., Capt. Jacob
   Earley, Col. Lynch's Regt. 3 mos. as substitute for George Con-
   duff. 1781, substitute for John Ayers, 3 mos.
Proof—Pension claim R. 8767. In. Cert. 25103.
Died—Jan. 15, 1840.
Married—1781, Elizabeth ———. Ch. Jacob.

RICHEY, GILBERT   Rush County
Born—Between 1750 and 1760.
Service—Penn. Militia, 1st Class, called on duty July 10, 1782.
Proof—Penn. Archives, Series 6, vol. 2, p. 342.
Died—About 1858. Rader Cem. Orange Twp.
Married—Wife unknown. Ch. John b. 1792; Adam and Eve (twins)
   b. about 1795.
Collected by Mrs. Helen R. Osburn, Greensburg, Indiana.

RICHMOND, NATHANIEL   Madison County
Born—March 26, 1760, Taunton, Massachusetts.
Service—Served as pri. under Capt. Abner Hayard's CO., 2nd Mass.
   Regt. Enlisted Aug. 9, 1779, July 20, 1780, April, 1781. Served
   four years.
Proof—Adjutant Gen. Office, War Dept., Washington. Certified copy
   of the discharge of Nathaniel Richmond from the Army of the
   Revolution in 1783. This copy was dated Jan. 25, 1823.
Died—Sept. 1, 1829, Pendleton, Ind.
Married—Second W. Susannah Lambert (1763-1845), m. 1784. Ch.
   John Lambert b. 1785, m. Lorane Sprague Patchin; Sylvester b.
   1797, m. Electa Bell; Zebulon; Nathaniel; Gideon; Philena; Digh-
   ton; Priscilla; Abiezer; Molly; Thankful.

RICKETTS, NATHAN   Switzerland County
Born—Aug. 26, 1759, Antietam, Maryland.
Service—Pri. in CO. commanded by Capt. McCormick, Regt. of Col.
   Piper, 11 mos., 14 days.
Proof—Pension claim S. 32480.

Died—Will probated Jan., 1847. Buried Mt. Carmel Cemetery, Posey Twp. Stone.
Married—Jane ———. Ch. William Rebecca Neal; Edward; Susannah Neal; Abram; Nathan; Elizabeth Rich; Jane Shepherd; Ann; Ephraim. (All named in Nathan Sr. Will, probated 1847, in Ohio Co.)
Collected by Mrs. A. V. Danner, Vevay, Indiana.

RICKETTS, ROBERT   Ohio County
Born—Jan. 15, 1765.
Service—Pri. in CO. commanded by Capt. Johnson, Regt. of Col. Piper, Penn. Line, 6 mos., 7 days.
Proof—Pension claim S. 17047.
Died—Feb. 14, 1853. Left widow and 11 children.
Collected by Mrs. Walter Kerr, Aurora, Indiana.

RINKER, GEORGE   Henry County
Born—1752, Lancaster Co., Pennsylvania.
Service—Enlisted Oct., 1780, in Vir. Served 6 mos. as Lieut. under Capt. Jacob Rinker. Marched to Cheraw Hills, S. C. Enlisted again in May, 1781, for 3 wks. as pri. under Capt. Jacob Rinker and Col. Darke in Vir. Enlisted Sept., 1781, for 2 mos. as 1st Lieut. under Capt. Auld (Dee) and Col. Darke of Vir. Present at Yorktown.
Proof—Pension claim S. 32485 (applied for pension 1832 in Union Co., Ind.).
Died—Dec. 11, 1835, Henry Co.
Married—Mary Coffman b. 1766-1863. Ch. Phillip; John; Jacob b. 1810, m. Cynthia Anna Clevenger; Catherine; Betsy; Rebecca, m. George Painter.
Collected by Mrs. H. L. Buckles, Hartford City, Indiana, and Mississinewa Chap., D. A. R.

ROBBINS, EPHRAIM   Ohio County
Born—1759, Kellingly, Connecticut.
Service—Entered service from Connecticut in 1775 and served 14 months under Gen. Putnam and Lieut. Robbins.
Proof—Pension claim S. 17052; Conn. Hist. Society Collections, vol. 12, p. 128 (1775-83).
Died—1836. Buried Rising Sun, Ind. Stone. Name on bronze tablet in Versailles Court House. (Ripley Co.)
Married—Lusina Webster. Ch. Rhoda 1790-1859, m. Morris Merrill.
Collected by Mrs. A. B. Wycoff, Batesville, Indiana.

ROBBINS, JOHN Wayne County
Born—1741, North Carolina.
Service—History of Wayne Co. published in 1884, page 358, says he was a soldier of the Rev. War.
Died—1834, Wayne Co., Ind. Methodist Cemetery called Locust Grove, near Abington. Stone.
Married—Sarah ——. Ch. Moses b. 1765, d. 1850.
Collected by Mrs. Paul L. Ross, Richmond, Indiana.

ROBBINS, WILLIAM Decatur County
Born—Oct. 21, 1761, Randolph Co., North Carolina.
Service—Oct., 1777, enlisted and served till 1781 under Capt. Joseph Clark, Col. Dugan, and Col. Anthony Sharp.
Proof—Pension records. Hist. of Decatur County, Ind., p. 537.
Died—1834. Buried Mt. Pleasant. Stone. Government marker.
Married—Bethiah Vickery b. 1760. Ch. Marmaduke and Jacob b. 1783; Elizabeth b. 1788; Polly b. 1791; Nathaniel b. 1793; John b. 1795; William b. 1797; Dosha b. 1804.
Collected by Mrs. H. S. McKee, Greensburg, Indiana.

ROBERT, JOHN Switzerland County
Born—March, 1753, Morris Co., New Jersey.
Service—Volunteered New Jersey Troops 1776-8, 8 mos. as Sergt. under Capt. Seeley, Col. Martin's Regt. In battle of Long Island and White Plains, 1777, commissioned Lieut. Stationed at Haddonfield, 3 mos.
Proof—Pension claim S. 16239.
Died—Aug. 6, 1837. Buried Craig Twp.
Married—1814, Mary ——.
Collected by Mrs. A. V. Danner, Vevay, Indiana.

ROBERTSON, JESSE Boone County
Born—1758.
Service—Enlisted in Louisa Co., Vir., in 1780. Served 6 mos. under Capt. Bins. In 1781, served 4½ mos. In battle of Camden and siege of Yorktown.
Proof—Virginia State Pension Records, vol. 514, p. 88: Statements of Estill Co., Ky., vol. 3.
Died—1846.
Married—1795, Sally White. Ch. John; Julia; Ozias; Lucinda; Malenda; Bridget; Susannah; William.
Collected by James Hill Chapter, D. A. R.

ROBINSON, JOHN, SR.   Rush County
Born—Virginia, 1755.
Service—Enlisted in Loudoun County, Vir., in March, 1776, and served 3 yrs. with the Virginia Troops in Capts. Charles Porterfield's and Long's Companies in Colonel Daniel Morgan's Regiment.
Proof—Pension Certificate No. 7150.
Died—1842. Buried East Hill Cem., Rushville.
Children—John Robinson Jr. b. 1800; William b. 1802; Martha b. 1805; Milly b. 1806; Jane b. 1809; Agnes b. 1810; Daniel b. 1813; Ivy b. 1817.
Collected by Wm. Henry Harrison Chapter, Valparaiso, Indiana.

ROBINSON, JOSEPH   Clark County
Born—April 6, 1763.
Service—1779, drafted, served as pri. in CO. commanded by Capt. Moon, Col. Lynch Regt., Vir. Militia, 1 yr.
Proof—Pension claim W. 9635.
Died—Sept. 11, 1834.
Married—1789, Methany Wright. Ch. Mary b. 1790; James and Wm. b. 1792; Nancy b. 1794; Betsy b. 1796; John b. 1799; Martha b. 1801; Jemima b. 1803; Miller b. 1806; Methany b. 1809; Jackson b. 1806.

ROBINSON, WINTHROP   Switzerland County
Born—April 22, 1761, Stratham, New Hampshire.
Service—Served 1777 as a drummer in CO. commanded by Capt. Parsons in Col. Sentre's N. H. Militia. 1778 pri. in CO. commanded by Capt. Worthen, Col. Peabody's N. H. Militia. 1779, orderly-sergeant in CO. commanded by Capt. Worthen, Col. Mooney, N. H. Militia. 1780, orderly-sergeant in CO. commanded by Capt. Gordon as Lieut. on board ship, "Buccanier."
Proof—Pension claim W. 9637.
Died—Dec. 5, 1836, by statement of widow in Cotton Twp., Switzerland Co.
Married—1784, Beulah Rice. Ch. Isabella b. 1785; Algernon Sidney (1787-1862), m. Abigail Harding; Winthrop b. 1792; William N. b. 1794; Anthony W. b. 1796; Azubah b. 1798 d. 1800; Daniel L. b. 1801 d. 1811; Eliza L. b. 1804 d. 1810; Jermiah b. 1806.
Collected by Mrs. Walter Kerr, Aurora, Indiana.

RODMAN, HUGH, SR.   Dubois County
Born—Northumberland Co., Pennsylvania.
Service—Served from May 1, 1778 to 1783, as frontier ranger under Capt. James Thompson.
Proof—Penn. Archives, 5th series, vol. 4, pp. 378 and 692.

Died—May 7, 1815. Buried Armstrong's Graveyard, South of Ireland, Ind. Government Marker.
Married—Elizabeth Hearst. Ch. William; John; Hugh Jr.; James; Thomas; Rachel.
Collected by Mr. George R. Wilson, Historian of Dubois Co., Indiana.

ROGERS, ETHAN Steuben County
Born—Oct. 22, 1756, Connecticut.
Service—Served as a pri. in Col. Josiah Starr's Company, 1st Conn. Regt. He enlisted July 15, 1780, for 6 mos., and was discharged Dec. 5, 1780.
Proof—Records in War Department.
Died—Sept., 1849. Buried Wright's Cemetery, Salem Twp. Government Marker. D. A. R. Marker placed by Pokagon Chapter, D. A. R.
Married— —— Fisher. Ch. Daniel; Mary; Clarissa; Nancey; Ethan;
Collected by Mrs. Ernest D. Kemery, Angola, Indiana.

ROGERS, HENRY Monroe County
Service—Ranger on the frontier of Westmoreland Co., Penn. Militia, 1778-1783. In John Van Meeter's Co., and in Philip Roger's Company.
Proof—Penn. Archives, Series 3, vol. 23, pp. 282, 285, 314, 317; series 6, vol. 2, p. 349; series 5, vol. 4, pp. 451, 754.
Grave—Is said to have been buried on Roger's farm.
Married—Margaret Jenkins. Ch. Sallie R., m. Simpson Coatney; Rebecca, m. Judge Aquilla Rogers; Hannah, m. Stephen B. Seall; Benjamin Franklin b. 1795 d. 1870; David b. 1780 d. 1856; Phillip; Aquilla; Johnathan b. 1775 d. 1834.
Collected by Mrs. Myra Esarey Mayse, Bloomington, Indiana.

ROGERS, STEPHEN Switzerland County
Born—1760.
Service—Pri. in Regt. commanded by Col. Taylor in Vir. Line, 3 yrs.
Proof—Pension claim W. 5729, B. L. Wt. 18372-160-55.
Died—Nov. 30, 1846. Buried Long Run Cemetery. Stone.
Married—First W. Nancy —— d. 1837. Ch. Henry, m. 1829 Lucinda Crandell; Stephen, m. 1822 Ruth Todd; Elizabeth, m. 1824 John Lock; Nancy, m. 1830 John Graham. Second W. of the soldier, Villa McPhearson Todd.
Collected by Mrs. A. V. Danner, Vevay, Indiana.

ROLLF, JAMES Ripley County
Born—1764.
Service—Entered service from Vermont in 1781. Served 2 yrs.

Proof—Pension claim S. 36876.
Died—September, 1837. Name on bronze marker in Versailles Court House. Many descendants still living in Ripley County, Indiana.
Collected by Mrs. A. B. Wycoff, Batesville, Indiana.

ROLLINS, HANNANIAH   Ohio County
Born—1761, Kent Co., Delaware.
Service—Pri. in Continental Troops.
Proof—Delaware Archives, vols. 1 and 2; Military List.
Died—1836. Buried Randolph Twp.
Married—1787, Martha ——, b. 1762. Ch. Elizabeth b. 1805, m. 1822 John Barker.
Collected by Mrs. Walter Kerr, Aurora, Indiana.

ROOF (ROUF), PETER   St. Joseph County
Born—January, 1753.
Service——Served as a pri. from Bedford Co., Pennsylvania.
Proof—Penn. Archives, 5th Series, vol. 5, pp. 90 and 105; 5th Series, vol. 4, pp. 249, 612; 6th Series, vol. 3, p. 29; vol. 22, pp. 213, 616.
Died—Oct. 25, 1834. Buried City Cemetery, South Bend, Ind. Stone. Bronze marker by Schuyler Colfax Chapter D. A. R.
Married—Margaret Replogle. Ch. Jacob, m. Mary Bainter; Peter, m. Sarah Spurgeon; David, m. Rebecca Shaw; Daniel; Henry; Margaret, m. Frederick Bainter and Jacob Witter and Christian Holler; Eva, m. John Cripe.
Collected by Miss Amanda McComb, South Bend, Indiana.

ROOTS, BENAJAH GURNSEY   Fayette County
Born—Nov. 13, 1758.
Service—Pri. in Capt. John Smith's CO., Vt., Feb., 1779. Scout in Capt. Simeon Wright's CO.; 1780, in Capt. Nathaniel Blouchard CO. of Militia. Corporal in a detachment raised as a levy from Col. Thomas Leis Regt. of Militia for defense of the frontier Oct., 1781.
Proof—Certified by F. S. Peck, State Adjutant General at Montpelier, Vt., June 18, 1897.
Died—Sept. 11, 1842, Connersville.
Married—Louis Higley.

ROSE, EZEKIEL   Union County
Born—About 1765.
Service—Served as a private, 1st Regt. Hunterdon CO. Militia, under Capts. William Tucker and Henry Phillips; in active service in detachment under the command of Capt. Tucker. Entered Oct. 15, 1777, and mustered Oct. 31, 1777.

Proof—Adjutant General Office, Trenton, N. J.
Died—Dec. 5, 1824. Buried Bath Springs Cemetery, Harmony Twp. Government Marker.
Married—Three times.
Collected by Elnora P. Campbell, Liberty, Indiana.

ROSE, WILLIAM   Union County
Born—April 24, 1757, New Jersey.
Service—Served as pri. and Corporal, in 1st Battalion, Second Establishment, N. J. Continental Line; Jan. 1, 1779, Sergeant, and March 1, 1780, Sergeant in Capt. De Hart's CO., First Regiment, N. J. Continental Line.
Proof—Office of Adjutant Gen. of N. J.
Died—April 30, 1830. Buried Bath Springs Cemetery, Harmony Twp.
Married—Hannah Buroughs. Ch. Abraham; John B.; Mary; Phoebe; Cornelius. Second W. Rachel Dubois. Ch. William Jr.
Collected by Mrs. Elinor P. Campbell, Liberty, Indiana.

ROSS, DANIEL   Jackson County
Born—About 1755.
Service—Enlisted 1775, Mass. CO. of Capt. Geo. Miller, 2nd Regt. Cont'l Line, Col. Joseph Devoice, 1 yr. 6 mos. Afterwards enlisted for duration of war, served to June 19, 1782. Discharged Richmond, Vir. Battles, White Plains, Newport Rd., Monmouth.
Proof—Pension claim W. 10237. B. L. Wt. 87019-160-55.
Died—July 19, 1835.
Married—Avy Jones (2nd w.). Ch. Patsey; Lewis; John.

ROSS, ISAAC   St. Joseph County
Born—May 7, 1760, New Jersey.
Service—While residing in Essex Co., N. J., he enlisted 1776. Served at various times on short tours until sometime in 1781, amounting to at least 3 yrs. in all, as a pri. under Capt. Crame and Jonathan Dickerson, Major Hayes, Oliver Spencer, John Mauritius Goetschius and Lee and Cols. J. Smith, Edward Thomas, Potter and Crame in the N. J. Troops. He was in the Battle of Monmouth.
Proof—Pension claim W. 4575.
Died—Jan. 31, 1843. Buried City Cemetery, South Bend, Ind. Stone. Bronze marker by Schuyler Colfax Chapter D. A. R.
Married—1789, Elizabeth Pembroke. Ch. David b. 1790; Experience b. 1792; Ichabod b. 1793; Mary b. 1795; James b. 1796; John b. 1798; William b. 1800; Daniel M. b. 1801; Isaac b. 1803; Benjamin b. 1806, m. Rachel Helmick; Ann b. 1808, m. Abraham West (a Rev. S.); Susannah b. 1811; Thomas b. 1813.
Collected by Miss Amanda McComb, South Bend, Indiana.

ROSS, THOMAS   Monroe County
Born—Jan., 1755, Albemarle Co., Virginia.
Service—Enlisted Bedford Co., Vir., Jan. 1, 1777, as pri. in Col. Lewis
    Regt. of Vir. Line. Served 6 yrs. in battles of Brandywine,
    Germantown and Trenton.
Proof—Pension claim S. 36877.

ROSSEAU, ANTOINE (ANTHONY)   Fountain County
Born—1760, in France.
Service—Enlisted under LaFayette and fought under him during his
    service in America, and returned with him to France. Enlisted
    in the Navy and returned to America on the ship Scorpion, one
    of the fleet of Comte de Grasse, which took part in the battle of
    Chesapeake Bay. Also in the siege of Yorktown, when Cornwallis surrendered.
Proof—From the French Consul at Chicago.
Died—June 25, 1855. Buried two miles east of Covington, Ind. Government marker by Richard Henry Lee Chapter D. A. R.
Collected by Mrs. Worth Reed, Covington, Indiana.

ROUSH, JOSEPH   Monroe County
Born—Feb. 15, 1751, Culpepper Co., Virginia.
Service—Enlisted under Col. James Barbour, Capt. Harry Tolls, Vir.
    Militia. Drafted for 2 mos., marched about 10 days then discharged. Again ordered out for 2 mos., Gen. Muhlenburg. Went
    to Petersburg, attached to Hospital, then back to Richmond.
Proof—Pension claim R. 9036—rejected—did not serve 6 mos.

ROWE, GEORGE   Posey County
Born—1750—On the ocean.
Service—Lieut. in Capt. Trappen's CO., North Hampton Co., Penn.
    Served 7 yrs.
Proof—Penn. Archives, 5th Series, vol. 8, p. 447.
Died—1818. Buried on Mr. Fuhrer's farm on the Upton road, N. W.
    of Mt. Vernon, Ind.
Married—1770, Margaret Wever. Ch. John; George; Martin; Michael;
    Simeon; Andrew; Daniel; Samuel; Jacob b. 1779; Mary; Elizabeth; Julia.
Collected by Mrs. W. R. Davidson, Evansville, Indiana.

ROWLAND, THOMAS   Jefferson County
Service—Captain Botetourt's Militia, Virginia.
Proof—Botetourt Pets. A 2187; House of Delegates 1777, 69; War
    Mss. 23, 1778 (Rev. Soldiers of Vir.).
Buried—Pisgah Cemetery, Deputy, Ind. Government marker placed
    by John Paul Chapter D. A. R.

Son—Thomas, m. 1832 Isabella Wilson.
Collected by John Paul Chapter D. A. R.

RUE, RICHARD   Wayne County
Born—1760, Kent Co., Maryland.
Service—Enlisted under George Rogers Clark. Pri. in Kentucky Militia.
Proof—Pension Record. The History of the North West Territory (English), vol. II, p. 985.
Died—Dec. 12, 1844. Buried Elkhorn Cemetery, south of Richmond, Ind. Stone.
Married—Elizabeth Holman d. 1833. Ch. Mary 1785-1858, m. Joseph Cox; Polly Elizabeth; Rachel; Sally; Nancy; Henry; Samuel; Nelly Jane.
Collected by Mrs. Paul L. Ross, Richmond, Indiana.

RUSSELL, JOHN   Clark County
Born—1765.
Service—Enlisted Feb. 6, 1776, in 3rd Vir. Regt. under Col. George Weeden, Capt. Philip Lee. In battles of White Plains, Brandywine, Germantown. Discharged from Valley Forge by Brig. Gen. William Woodford.
Proof—Pension claim S. 36878.
Married—Elizabeth ———. Ch. Eliza; Polina; Mahala; Nancy.

RUTLEDGE, PETER   Ripley County
Born—1756.
Service—Entered service from Maryland in 1776 under Capt. Joshua Miles, served 6 mos. and 16 days.
Proof—Pension claim R-9115.
Died—May 29, 1844. Buried near Olean, Brown Twp. Name on Bronze tablet in Versailles Court House.
Married—1818, Ruth ———. Ch. Sarah; American and Benjamin (twins); Elijah.
Collected by Mrs. A. B. Wycoff, Batesville, Indiana.

RYAN, GEORGE   Jefferson County
Born—1756.
Service—Served on Continental Establishment about 5 yrs. Enlisted in 1776, Capt. Jonathan Clark, 8th Vir. Regt., Col. Peter Muhlenburg. Served 2 yrs. Enlisted under John Steed for 3 yrs. Capt. Abraham Kirkpatrick, Capt. James Curry. Discharged by Col. Bluford at Charlotte, S. C.
Proof—Oath of service, Jeff. Co. Records, Order bk. B-352.

Died—March 10, 1831.
Married—Had wife, and four ch. in 1820.
Collected by John Paul Chapter D. A. R.

RYKER, JOHN   Jefferson County
Born—Jan. 18, 1764, New Jersey.
Service—Served as pri. from Essex Co., N. J.
Proof—Stryker, N. J. Soldiers in the Rev., p. 734.
Died—Nov. 22, 1848. Buried Rykers Ridge Cemetery, near Madison, Ind.
Married—First W. 1784, Martha Van Cleave b. 1756. Ch. Rachel b. 1786; Ruth b. 1788; Jerodus b. 1791, m. Martisha Wilhoite; Deborah b. 1793; Sarah b. 1795; Samuel J. 1797-1881; Leah b. 1799; Malinda b. 1801; John b. 1803. Soldier m. second to Amelia Littlejohn, 1838. Ch. Mary Ann.
Collected by John Paul Chapter D. A. R.

SAMPLE, THOMAS   Gibson County
Born—June 22, 1747.
Service—Enlisted in S. C. Regt. under Col. Hughes for 18 mos. Discharged at Ft. Charlotte. Enlisted again under Col. James Wilson at White Horse, in Chester Co., Penn., in 1st Penn. regular line for 12 mos. Discharged at Jockey Holler, N. J., by Col. James Chambers. Battles of Stony Point.
Proof—Pension claim S. 36750. He was in Gibson Co., Ind., 1818.
Married—Margaret ——.

SAMPSON, SAMUEL   Clay County
Born—About 1762.
Service—Pri. in CO. under Capt. Johnson, Penn. Line for 15 mos. Received 200 acres of land and sold them to Bethuel Covalt.
Proof—Pension claim S. 32506.

SAMPSON, WILLIAM   Harrison County
Service—Pri. in CO. under Capt. Price, Regt. of Col. Taylor, in Virginia Militia, 8 mos.
Proof—Pension claim S. 17067.

SAMUELS, GILBERT   Franklin County
Born—Aug. 5, 1755.
Service—An account of his death states that he was a soldier in the Revolutionary War.
Proof—"Brookville American" issue of Feb. 20, 1835; Family Bible.
Died—February 11, 1835. Buried Asbury Cemetery, Springfield Twp.

Married—Cathern ——, d. Feb. 2, 1830. Ch. John b. Sept. 21, 1787; Mary b. Sept. 11, 1790, d. 1791; James b. March 18, 1793; David L. b. Nov. 26, 1796, d. Feb. 24, 1830; Gilbert b. July 29, 1799, d. May 8, 1832.

SANBORN (SANBURN), RICHARD   Clark County
Born—About 1761.
Service—Volunteered 1779-1780. Pri. in Capt. David McGregor's CO., Cols. Henry Dearborn and Geo. Reid's N. H. Regt., was in a battle with Indians on the Mohawk River. Discharged 1783.
Proof—Pension claim S. 36749.
Died—Feb. 2, 1829, Clark Co.
Married—Eunice ——. Ch. Matthew P.

SANDERS, HENRY   Monroe County
Born—Oct. 26, 1751, Perquimans Co., North Carolina.
Service—Enlisted in S. C. Militia and served under Capts. Lewis and Bayliss and Gen. Greene. Received pension for 2 yrs. service.
Proof—Pension records.
Died—Feb., 1834. Buried Vernal Church Graveyard, 3 miles west of Bloomington, Ind. Stone.
Married—1779, Dicy Blake. Ch. Isaac; Feribae b. 1781; Henry b. 1790; John b. 1792; Wright b. 1795; Joseph; Dica; Priscilla; Morning; Benjamin.
Collected by Miss Ura Sanders, Gosport, Indiana, and Newell Sanders, Lookout Mountain, Tennessee.

SAPPENFIELD, MICHAEL   Harrison County
Born—Dec., 1761, Rowan Co., North Carolina.
Service—Pri. and sergt. in CO. commanded by Capt. Grimes, Regt. by Col. Locke in N. C. Line, 6 mos. pri. and 6 mos. Sergt.
Proof—Pension claim S 17068.
Died—April 14, 1837, Harrison Co., Ind.
Married—1785 or 86, Sarah Myers, d. 1839. Ch. John, 1805-64; Mary.

SAUNDERS, JAMES   Allen County
Born—About 1756, Gloucester, Virginia.
Service—Enlisted in Berkeley Co., Vir., Aug., 1781. Served as pri. 6 mos. 15 days in Capt. George Cooke's CO., Col. Willis' Regt. of Virginia Troops.
Proof—Pension records.
Died—Feb. 2, 1834. Name placed on bronze tablet by Mary Penrose Wayne Chapter D. A. R.
Married—Martha ——. Ch. Sarah; Dorothy; Elizabeth.
Collected by Mrs. Sue Vesta Hanna (deceased), Fort Wayne, Indiana.

SAURMAN, PETER   Ohio County
Service—Enlisted winter of 1775 at Philadelphia in Capt. Harman's
   CO. of Infantry, Col. De Hames' Regt., for 1 yr. Served other
   times as volunteer on board the Letter of Marque, the Lady of
   Washington, commanded by Capt. Josiah.
Proof—Pension claim S. 36748. In 1823, he owned property in Rising
   Sun, Indiana, Ohio County.
Married—Sten ——.

SAXON, JOHN   Blackford County
Born—Nov. 17, 1761, England.
Service—Entered at age of 16 yrs. as drummer boy. Served through-
   out the war.
Proof—Pension records.
Died—Sept. 24, 1862. Buried I. O. O. F. Cemetery, Hartford City, Ind.
   Stone.
Married—Elizabeth Evans. Ch. James; Lydia; Ellis; Malinda Caster-
   line; Mary Townsend.
Collected by Mrs. Cora Covault Tuttle, Hartford City, Indiana.

SCOTT, ALEXANDER   Cass County
Born—Oct., 1762, Hardy Co., Virginia.
Service—While residing in Hardy Co., Vir., he served in 1780, 3 mos.
   as spy in Capt. Robert Craven's CO. Enlisted March, 1781, served
   2 mos. in Capt. Michael Stump's CO. Sept., 1781, in Capt. Fisher's
   CO. Was at Yorktown and assisted in guarding 700 Hessians to
   Winchester Barracks.
Proof—Pension claim S. 16244.
Died—1844. Buried Spring Creek Christian Cemetery in Clay Twp.
   Stone.
Married—Sarah ——. Ch. Reverend Alexander (War of 1812); David
   (1784-1837); Sarah A. Dunbar (1795-1875); Rev. John (1797-
   1866); Cynthia Wilson (1807-1861); Margaret Boyd (1809-1850);
   Polly McLucas.
Collected by Miss Laura D. Henderson, Logansport, Indiana.

SCOTT, BENJAMINE   Jackson County
Born—May 29, 1754, Augusta, Virginia.
Service—Enlisted in Augusta Co., Vir., March, 1777, and served as 1st
   sergeant for 6 mos. in Capt. Moses Hutton's CO. of Vir. Troops,
   Lt. Silvester Ward. Was discharged at Wheeling, Vir., Aug.,
   1777. May 1, 1781, he enlisted and served as an orderly-sergeant
   for 2 mos. in Capt. Michael Stumps' CO., Lt. Michael Hornbeck
   by Major McPherson. Discharged July 1, 1781.

Proof—Pension claim 17076.
Died—Oct. 5, 1840. Buried on Scott farm, Owen Twp.
Married—Nancy ——. Ch. John; James.
Collected by Gen. Jacob Brown Chapter D. A. R.

SCOTT, JAMES   Dearborn County
Born—May, 1758, on Ocean.
Service—Enlisted 1776, Winchester, Vir., in John Patton's CO., Col. William Heath's Regt. In battles of Brandywine, Monmouth and Germantown.
Proof—Pension claim S. 32511.
Collected by Mrs. Walter Kerr, Aurora, Indiana.

SCOTT, JOHN   Jefferson County
Service—Volunteered July 1, 1776, at Shippenburg, Cumberland Co., Penn., in Capt. Culbertson's CO. Marched to Amboy, N. J., where he was appointed commissary by Col. Lowrie; in fall went to Staten Island, had an engagement with British and Hessians; was with army in retreat through N. J. to Trenton, then crossed the Delaware to 4 mi. above Trenton; served here as brigade commissary till after battle of Princeton, returned home; in June, 1777, appointed quartermaster by Col. Dunlop; was in battle at Chad's Ford on Brandywine, Sept. 11, 1777; later, under Col. Jones was brigade commissary till Jan., 1778. Sometime later, volunteered in the light horse, and served near Philadelphia. Served 1 mo. and 3 or 4 days as private; 4 mos. as assistant commissary; 2½ mos. as quartermaster; 6½ mos. as brigade commissary.
Proof—Penn. Archives, Series 2, vol. 10, p. 590; Pension claim R. 9294.
Died—March 24, 1834, in Jefferson Co., Ind.
Married—1790, Hannah —— b. 1758.
Collected by John Paul Chapter D. A. R., Madison, Indiana.

SCUDDER, ABNER   Switzerland County
Born—June 17, 1764, in Essex Co., New Jersey.
Service—While residing in Roman Co., N. C., he enlisted in May, 1781, and served 1 yr. as a private in Capt. Alexander Brevard's CO., Cols. Dickson's (Dickinson) and Blount's N. C. regiments, was in battle of Eutaw Springs, where he was slightly wounded by a gun shot. Left service April 18, 1782.
Proof—Pension record.
Buried—Bethel Cemetery in York Twp. Stone.
Married—Kathrine ——. Ch. William b. 1793-1872 (War of 1812), m. Kate Cox.
Collected by Mrs. A. V. Danner, Vevay, Indiana.

SCUDDER, JOHN A.   Daviess County
Born—1759.
Service—Surgeon in 18th Regiment, Monmouth Co., New Jersey.
Proof—Taken from D. A. R. papers.
Died—Nov. 6, 1836. Buried Old City Cemetery, Washington, Ind. Stone.
Married—Elizabeth Foreman (1772-1848). Ch. Dr. Charles, m. Mary Hord; Fenwick, m. Mary Ann Hyatt; William; Anderson; John, m. Alice Jane Arrell; Jacob, m. Matilda Arrell; Henry, m. Jane Beasley; Ellen, m. Jesse Crabb and Vance Jones; Emma, m. David Wood.
Collected by Mrs. Roy Bogner, Washington, Indiana.

SEAL, JOSEPH   Franklin County
Born—1738, Pennsylvania.
Service—Enlisted at commencement of war, as a volunteer in Capt. Weekley's CO. of Dragoons and served throughout the war. Was in battles of Brandywine, Monmouth, Cowpens, and Yorktown. Received two severe wounds, one in the face and one in the hip.
Proof—"Brookville American" issue of Sept. 5, 1834.
Died—Sept. 1, 1834. Buried James Cemetery, Springfield Twp., Franklin Co., Ind.
Married—Mary Montgomery. Ch. James; William; Martha; Joseph; Mary; Benjamin.

SETZER, JOHN   Knox County
Born—April 9, 1760, Germany.
Service—A pri. for three yrs., joined the regt. in Ky., went to Kaskaskia, thence to Post St. Vincennes, in 1779, and aided in the reduction of the British Garrison at said Post. He was with George Rogers Clark.
Proof—House Doc. 1833, 34 Vir. Archives.
Died—Dec. 13, 1836. Buried Indiana Cemetery, 5 mi. west of Vincennes. Stone.
Married—Mary Schwartz. Ch. John; Rebecca; Sarah; Samuel.
Collected by Mrs. Elizabeth Scott, Independence, Kansas.

SEWARD, SAMUEL   Fayette County
Service—Enlisted for 1 yr., Oct., 1775, in N. J. Capt. Silas Hoel, Col. Henez (?) Regt. Discharged. Enlisted for 9 mos. Capt. Mead, Col. M. Ogden.
Proof—Pension claim S. 36751.
Died—1829.

SHADBURN, RICHARD   Clark County
Service—Inscription on marker reads "Richard Shadburn, War of the
    Revolution 1776." Buried Cemetery 2, Charlestown, Ind.
Collected by Miss Mary Carr Guernsey, Charlestown, Indiana.

SHADDAY (SHADDY), JOHN   Switzerland County
Born—Feb. 26, 1754, Orange Co., North Carolina.
Service—Pri. in Cav. and Inf. in CO. commanded by Capt. Allen, Regt.
    by Col. O'Neal, N. C., 14 mo. from 1779.
Proof—Pension claim W 9647; B. L. Wt. 26115-160-55.
Died—Feb. 21, 1859. Buried Slawson Cemetery, Bennington, Ind.
    Stone.
Married—1795, Mary Fogleman. Ch. Elizabeth; Polly, m. John Low;
    Barbara, m. Martin R. Cope; Lucinda, m. Alexander Thompson;
    Emsley, m. Polly Leap; George W., m. Louise Green; Wm. Hardin,
    m. Francis Dyer; Jacob; John, m. Francis A. Neal; Turley; Jordon, m. Louise Brenson.
Collected by Mrs. A. V. Danner, Vevay, Indiana.

SHAFFER (SHAVER), FREDERICK   Clinton County
Born—Dec. 14, 1755, Woodstock, Virginia.
Service—Enlisted from Woodstock, Vir., Oct. 15, 1779, as pri. under
    Capt. Thomas Kirk and Col. Campbell. Served 2 yrs. and 9 mos.
Proof—Pension claim S. 32517.
Died—Dec. 19, 1855. Buried Gray's Cemetery, near Middlefork, Clinton Co. Stone.
Married—Barbara Ann Fry. Ch. Henry; Solomon; John; Sarah; Mary;
    Catherine; Sina; Elizabeth; Benjamin; and three others.
Collected by Mrs. Lillian K. McClure, Frankfort, Indiana.

SHANNON, GEORGE   Jefferson County
Born—March, 1759, Lancaster Co., Pennsylvania.
Service—Served under Capt. Greathouse in 1778, patrolling the Ohio
    River. In 1779, 6 mos. under Gen. McIntosh, Col. Gibson, assisted
    in building Fort Lawrence. In 1782, in expedition against Indians at Sandusky.
Proof—Pension record; Penn. Archives, Series 2, vol. 14, p. 708; Bracken
    Genealogy, p. 32.
Died—Dec. 4, 1840 (Dates on stone 1753-1844). Buried Bethel Cemetery, south of Hanover, Ind.
Married—1785, Ann Reid (1764-1847). Ch. Sarah, 1786; Mary, b. 1790;
    Jean b. 1797; Ann b. 1799; Margaret 1802; George; John; Thomas.
Collected by John Paul Chapter D. A. R. and Mrs. W. S. Denham,
    Charlestown, Indiana.

SHANNON, WILLIAM   Knox County
Born—In Ireland.
Service—Capt. with George Rogers Clark. Present at taking of Fort
    Sackville.
Proof—English's Conquest of North West, vol. I, pp. 531 and 532; vol.
    II, pp. 1050, 1052, 1065; Historical Sketches of Old Vincennes,
    pp. 283, 284.
Died—1782 or 1783. Probably buried in Cemetery of Francis Xavier
    Church.
Married—About 1769 ——. Ch. Elizabeth b. 1770, m. Col. Francis
    Vigo; Mary b. 1775, m. Capt. Robert Buntin; Sarah b. 1777, m.
    Doctor Samuel McKee; William b. 1779; Nancy b. 1781; Margaret
    b. 1782.
Collected by Miss Ruth Jordan and Mr. Hiram Foulks, Vincennes,
    Indiana.

SHAVER, JOHN   Switzerland County
Service—Enlisted for 3 yrs., about Feb. 14, 1781, in Vir. CO. under
    Capt. Reuben Field, Col. Thomas Gaskins' Regt. Served until
    Sept., 1783.
Proof—Pension claim S. 36753. Wife and three children mentioned in
    application but names not given.

SHAW, HENRY   Spencer County
Born—1762.
Service—Enlisted sometime in 1776 in Leesburg, Vir., as pri. in Capts.
    Peyton Harrison's, Adam Wallace's and Kirkpatrick's CO., and in
    Cols. Febeger's and Abraham Buford's Vir. Regt., also in Capt.
    William Beatty's Md. CO. and in Col. Smith's Md. Regt. In the
    battle of Buford's Defeat, Cowpens, Guilford and Yorktown. Dis-
    charged May, 1783, having served 7 yrs. and 4 mos.
Proof—Pension claim S. 36756.
Died—Feb. 1, 1829.

SHAW, JAMES   Parke County
Born—About 1763.
Service—Enlisted in Greenbrier Co., Vir., in 1780, as pri. in Capt. Ben-
    jamin Brigg's CO., Col. Gibson's 9th Regt. Was in an engagement
    near Fort McIntosh in Ohio, and was discharged Jan., 1782, having
    served 18 mos. Later served under Capt. Samuel Brady.
Proof—Pension claim S. 36757.
Married—Elizabeth ——. Ch. James; Thomas; Joseph; Rachel.

SHAW, JONATHAN   Fayette County
Born—Feb., 1759.
Service—Enlisted at Connecticut Farms, N. J., spring 1777, as pri. in
    Capt. John Holmes' CO., Col. Matthias Ogdens' 1st N. J. Regt. In
    the battles of Springfield and at Yorktown and was discharged
    June, 1783.
Proof—Pension claim S. 36754. Children are referred to in application
    but names not given.

SHED, DANIEL   Dearborn County
Born—April, 1749.
Service—Entered service in Brookline, formerly called Rabi, N. H. First
    attached to CO. of Capt. Fry and Col. Baldwin. Enlisted spring
    1778, served 1 yr., discharged at West Point. Battles Bunker
    Hill and Bennington.
Proof—Pension claim S. 36755.
Died—April 10, 1820.
Collected by Mrs. Walter Kerr, Aurora, Indiana.

SHEPHERD (SHEPPARD), WILLIAM   Putnam County
Service—Enlisted by Capt. John Shepherd of Col. John Baldwin's Regt.
    of Artificers about April 1, 1780 or 81, transferred to Capt. Thos.
    Patton's CO., artillery artificers. Discharged 1783. Yorktown.
Proof—Pension claim S. 32413; B. L. Wt. 566-100.
Died—Sept. 13, 1843 (?).
Children—William; Moses; Rebecca; Joseph.

SHIELDS, JAMES   Orange County
Born—About 1754.
Service—Received land for service of 3 yrs. as a soldier in the Vir. Line.
    Inscription on stone reads "James Shields, who fought for liberty
    in 1776, and died, upwards of 70 yrs. of age."
Proof—Old Kentucky Entries and Deeds, by Jillson, Warrant No. 1240.
Died—Aug. 10, 1824. Buried Bethel Cemetery, 1 mile north of Orange-
    ville, Ind.
Married—Ann Brown. Ch. Daniel; David; Ambrose; Jane Ware; Nancy
    Southern; Lydia Glenn.
Collected by Mrs. N. B. Mavity, French Lick, Indiana.

SHIRK, ANDREW   Franklin County
Born—Sept. 7, 1753, Switzerland.
Service—Pri. in Capt. George Nagle's CO. of Col. William Thompson's
    Battalion of Riflemen and in active service from June, 1775, for
    1 year. Pri. in Capt. Henry Bicker's CO. of 10th Regt. of Penn.
    Line in 1776-1777 and 1778.

Proof—Penn. Archives, 2nd Series, vol. 10, pp. 33 and 727.
Died—Jan. 14, 1829. Buried Big Cedar Cemetery. Stone.
Married—Martha Hamilton, d. 1820. Ch. John; David; Andrew; Joseph; Samuel b. 1792-1859, m. Elizabeth Stout; Isaac; Nancy; Martha.

SHIVELY, HENRY   Orange County
Born—June, 1760, Germany.
Service—Pri. in Capt. Martin Huey's Company, 1st Battalion, Lancaster Co. Militia, 1782.
Proof—Penn. Archives, 5th Series, vol. 7, pp. 67, 80, 82, 99.
Died—June 14, 1842. Buried Johnson Cemetery on Hannigan Cornwell farm, Paoli Twp. Stone.
Married—Mary Banta. 12 Ch. Those known are Nancy; Elizabeth; Sarah; Mahala; Jacob Banta; Philip; Henry Jr.; John M.
Collected by Mrs. N. B. Mavity, French Lick, Indiana.

SHORES, CHRISTIAN   Clark or Floyd County
Born—July 11, 1744.
Service—Enlisted Dec. Served a tour of 3 mos. under Capt. Robertson and Col. Martin Armstrong in S. C., a tour of 2 mos. in Stokes Co., N. C., as pri. under Capt. Henry Smith.
Proof—Pension claim S. 32514.
Died—Jan. 8, 1836.
Married—Mary ——.

SHORT, JOHN   Lawrence County
Born—Feb. 15, 1756, Shenandoah, Virginia.
Service—Enlisted for 5 mos., Aug., 1776, under Capt. William Nail; for 4 mos. Sept., 1778, under Capt. McCutcheon; for 2 mos July, 1781, under Col. William Nail.
Proof—Pension record.
Died—May 15, 1836. Buried Mayfield Cemetery. Stone.
Married—1780, Mary Hansford. Ch. Wesley; William; John; Thomas; Samuel; Rhuben; Ezekiel; Hansford; Sarah.
Collected by Mrs. Ellen Hoover, and Mrs. Lula Short Bowden, Bedford, Indiana.

SHUCK, PHILIP   Harrison County
Born—1760, Berks Co., Pennsylvania.
Service—Entered as a substitute for his father, John Shuck, in 1776. Served 2 mos. Drafted for 2 mos. Volunteered as a Minute Man.
Proof—Pension claim S. 31958.

SHUEMAKER (SHEWMAKER), LEONARD   Jackson County
Born—May 19, 1757, Goochland Co., Virginia.
Service—Pri. in CO. commanded by Capt. Evans of Regt. by Col. Montgomery, Vir. Line, 2 yrs.
Proof—Pension claim S. 17082.
Died—About 1837. Buried Harrell Cemetery, Driftwood Twp. Stone.
Married—Polly ——. Ch. Sarah Goodwin James; Nancy Haret; John R.; Josiah; Evans; Leonard.
Collected by Mrs. D. J. Cummings, Brownstown, Indiana.

SHUPE, JOHN   Switzerland County
Born—April 14, 1764, Bucks Co., Pennsylvania.
Service—Enlisted Bucks Co., Penn., 1776 or 77, served 8 mos. pri. in John Jameson's CO. in Col. Keichline's or S. Dean's Penn. Regt.
Proof—Pension claim S. 16247.
Died—Feb. 24, 1833, probably buried Vevay Cemetery.
Collected by Mrs. A. V. Danner, Vevay, Indiana.

SIMMONS, JOEL   Henry County
Born—June 10, 1757, Albemarle Co., Virginia.
Service—Enlisted in 1776 for 3 mos. under Lt. James Darland. Reenlisted in 1777 for 1 mo. under William Davis. In 1779 or 1780 served 6 mos. under Henry Burke, James Martin, Col. Hola Richardson.
Proof—Pension claim S. 17677.
Died—Sept. 4, 1838. Buried Sulphur Springs Cemetery, Jefferson Twp. Government marker and Bronze S. A. R. marker.
Children—Robert b. 1779; Ephrium b. 1782; Sally b. 1784; Joab b. 1787; David b. 1796; Peggy b. 1794; Elizabeth b. 1797; Joel b. 1800; Thompson b. 1802; Polly b. 1805.
Collected by Mrs. H. S. McKee, Greensburg, Indiana and Ind. S. A. R.

SIMMS, PRESLEY   Montgomery County
Born—1753, Stafford Co., Virginia.
Service—Pri. in CO. commanded by Capt. Williams, Regt. of Col. Montroy, Vir. Line, 2 yrs.
Proof—Pension claim S. 32546.
Buried—Mt. Pleasant Cemetery. Stone.
Married—Nancy Bridewell. Ch. Presley Jr.; Charles.
Collected by Miss Jessie Watson, Crawfordsville, Indiana.

SIMPSON (Negro)   Gibson County
Service—Was body servant of Washington. Brought to Gibson Co. by Robert Archer and given his freedom April 17, 1816, by the legal heirs of Robert Archer.

Proof—Tart's History of Gibson Co., Indiana, p. 78.
Died—1850. Buried Archer Cemetery, Princeton, Ind. Stone.
Collected by Gen. John Gibson Chapter D. A. R.

SIMS, WILLIAM   Union County
Born—May 14, 1760, Culpepper Co., Virginia.
Service—Pri. in Capt. Andrew Wallace's CO., 12th Vir. Regt. Enlisted March 1, 1777, for 3 yrs. Transferred to Lt. Col. William Heth's CO. 3rd and 7th Vir. Regt. in June, 1778, and to Capt. Henry Young's CO., 5th and 11th Vir. Regt. in May, 1779. Appointed sergeant Feb. 16, 1778. Signed the Hanover Petition in Vir., 1783. Was at Valley Forge.
Proof—Pension record. Eckenrode's List. Rev. Sol. of Vir., p. 277.
Died—1843, in Franklin Co., Ind., but buried across Co. line in Union Co., Sims Cemetery. Stone.
Married—Amelia Russell (1760-1822). Ch. Larkin b. 1780; Mary b. 1781; Joshua b. 1783; William b. 1785; Elizabeth b. 1787; Sarah b. 1788; Stephen 1790; Thomas b. 1792; Ann b. 1797; Martha b. 1799; Lewis b. 1802. Soldier m. second to Fear Strudevant, 1779-1840.
Collected by Mrs. Elmora P. Campbell, Liberty, Indiana.

SIPES, DANIEL   Harrison County
Born—About 1761, Lancaster Co., Pennsylvania.
Service—Pri. in CO. commanded by Capt. Ogler, Regt. of Col. Johnson, Md. Militia, 10 mos.
Proof—Pension claim S. 17092.
Died—Feb. 14, 1834. (Lived in Blue River Twp., Harrison Co.)

SIX, JOHN   Posey County
Born—Aug. 18, 1758.
Service—Enlisted in Vir., Aug. 5, 1776, served as a pri. in Capt. Matthew Arbuckle's CO., Col. John Nevill's Vir. Regt. and was discharged at "the great Kanawha," having served 14 mos.
Proof—Pension claim S. 36758.
Died—1826. Buried Maple Hill Cemetery. Marked by New Harmony Chapter D. A. R.
Married—Wife died 1825. Daughter, m. John Grant.
Collected by New Harmony Chapter D. A. R.

SKINNER, THOMAS   Franklin County
Born—May, 1759, Kent Co., Delaware.
Service—Served with Delaware Militia, as follows: from the Spring of 1777 to the Spring of 1779 as pri. in Capt. Edward Dyer's CO.; from the Spring of 1779 to the Spring of 1780 in Capt. John Gray's CO.; from the Spring of 1780 to Nov., 1783 in Capt. Edward Dyer's CO.

Proof—Pension claim R. 9635.
Died—1843. Buried Ebenezer Churchyard, Bloomingrove Twp. Government marker placed by Twin Fork's Chapter D. A. R.
Married—First W. Maria ——. Ch. Nancy; Esther; William; Thomas; Daniel. Second W. 1797, Anne Caton. Ch. Mary; Elizabeth; James; Eleanor; John; Anne; Stephen; Catherine.
Collected by Mrs. Z. R. Peterson, Detroit, Michigan.

SLANSON, EZRA   Dearborn County
Born—Jan. 10, 1758, Stamford, Fairfield Co., Conn.
Service—Volunteered at Stamford early in 1776, under Capt. Brown. In Conn. Line, 2 yrs. In battle of White Plains.
Proof—Pension claim S. 171701.
Collected by Mrs. Walter Kerr, Aurora, Indiana.

SLAVENS, ISAIAH   Putnam County
Born—June 14, 1762, Augusta Co., Virginia.
Service—Enlisted Oct., 1780, for 50 days in CO. of Col. Moffett's Vir. Regt. For 3 mos., 1781, Capt. Thomas Hecklin's CO., Col. Simpson Mathias' Vir. Regt. For 3 mos. in June, 1781, in Capt. Chas. Cameron's Regt.
Proof—Pension claim S. 16529.
Died—Sept. 8, 1848. Buried Brick Chapel Cemetery, north of Greencastle. Stone.
Married—First Martha Stuart. Ch. Reuban b. 1786. Second, Barbara. Ch. Henry and others.
Collected by Col. Isaac White Chapter D. A. R.

SLEETH, ALEXANDER   Fayette County
Born—Aug. 20, 1750. New York.
Service—Scout and Indian fighter in W. Vir.
Proof—D. A. R. No. 76866; History of Shelby Co., Ind., p. 717; "Four Rev. Soldiers and Their Descendant's" by Eloise M. Roberts.
Died—May 14, 1820, probably buried Waterloo Cemetery, Fayette Co.
Married—First —— Montgomery. Ch. John. Second, Anne Smith. Ch. David; Alexander Jr.; Thomas; Jonas; James; Mary and Ann (twins); William H.; Robert P.; Caleb; Nancy; Albert; Susanna.

SLIKER, LUCAS   Franklin County
Born—1752, Sussex Co., New Jersey.
Service—While living in Bedford Co., Penn., he enlisted in the spring of 1776 and served 9 mos. as pri. in Capt. Jeremiah Cott's CO. in Col. Piper's Penn. Regt. One yr. later he enlisted and served

6 mos. as pri. in Capt. Nehemiah Stokeley's Penn. CO. and was in several small engagements with the Indians.
Proof—Pension claim S. 32523.
Died—After 1833.

SMITH, ASA   Floyd County
Born—Feb. 8, 1761, Conn.
Service—Enlisted April, 1777, in Col. Samuel Webb's Conn. Regt., from Hartford Co., Conn. Served as pri. in CO. under Capt. Wells, Col. Stark's Vt. Line for 9 mos.
Proof—Floyd Co. Probate Court Records 1830-1836, p. 92; Pension claim S. 32528. Lived in New Albany Twp., Floyd Co., Ind., 1832.
Collected by Mrs. V. R. Conner, New Albany, Indiana.

SMITH, EDWARD   Harrison County
Born—1754, England.
Service—Lieut. 7th Vir. Regt.; was a prisoner in 1780; retired Feb. 12, 1781, on account of being absent as prisoner.
Proof—Heitman Historical Register, p. 502; Adjutant General's Office.
Died—1828. Buried near Corydon, Ind.
Married—1779, Nancy Black. Ch. Jenny; Mary; Sally; Rachel; Isabelle; Nancy; James; John; Samuel.
Collected by Mrs. Kate Highfill Stevens, Corydon, Indiana.

SMITH, EZEKIEL   LaPorte County
Born—1760, Orange Co., New York.
Service—Enlisted at age of 16 from Orange Co., N. Y.
Proof—Robert's N. Y. In The Revolution.
Died—Sept. 28, 1838. Buried Door Village Cemetery. Stone. S. A. R. Bronze marker.
Married—Rhoda ———, d. 1838. Ch. Charlotte, m. 1824 Aaron Earl.
Collected by Miss Elvira Oakes and Arthur Stewart, LaPorte, Indiana.

SMITH, HENRY   Rush County
Born—About 1765.
Service—Pri. under Capt. Brady at Pittsburg, March 2, 1782, and served in Regt. CO. by Capt. John Gibson in Penn. Line on the Continental Establishment. Taken prisoner by Indians near Ft. McIntosh and held 3 mos., and 9 mos. by British.
Proof—Pension claim S-40467. Penn. Archives, Series 2, vol. 10, p. 663.
Died—After 1834. Buried Pleasant Run Graveyard, Noble Twp. Name on tablet, in Rush Co. Court House.
Children—James; Mahala; and 9 others.
Collected by Mrs. Willard Amos, Rushville, Indiana.

SMITH, HEZEKIAH   Marion County
Born—April 18, 1753, Delaware.
Service—Enlisted at Granby, Mass., in Col. Marshal's Regt. 4th Hampshire Co. Regt.
Proof—Mass. Soldiers and Sailors, vol. 14, p. 412; Thompson's Hist. of Marshall Co., Ind., p. 268.
Died—April 26, 1824. Buried near Trader's Point.
Married—Mary Ann Rector, d. 1836. Ch. Daniel; Peter; Hezekiah Jr. 1805-79; Miles C.; Simeon; Carlton; Marquis L. b. 1815; Elizabeth; Susan; Deborah; Nancy.
Collected by Caroline Scott Harrison Chapter D. A. R.

SMITH, JAMES   Gibson County
Born—1754, Virginia.
Service—Enlisted in the year 1776 for two years in Capt. Bowyer's CO. which was part of the 12th. Vir. Regt. He afterwards re-enlisted for 3 yrs or during the war. He was in service until sometime in the year 1780 when he was on his march to join the Southern Army.
Proof—Records of the War Department.
Died—1837. Buried on James Mount's farm near Owensville, Ind. D. A. R. marker placed by Gen. John Gibson Chapter D. A. R.
Married—Margaret Truax. Ch. John, m. Jane Alcorn and Patsey Daugherty; James, m. Betsy McCray; Andrew, m. Ezenith Stone; Isaac, m. Susan Martin; David, m. Eliza Clark; Polly, m. Durham Creel; Betsy, m. Absalum Redman; Jane, m. Stephen Daugherty; Lidia, m. Painter Marvel; Ann, m. Robert Redman.
Collected by General John Gibson Chapter D. A. R.

SMITH, JOHN ANDREW   Lawrence County
Service—Enlisted Fauquier Co., Vir., Capt. Elias Edmonds, Col. Thos. Marshall. Regt. Artillery for 3 yrs. Discharged Aug. 22, 1780.
Proof—Pension claim S. 36775.
Died—Nov. 22, 1836.
Married—Margaret —— (1798-1870). Ch. Elizabeth; Rejoice; Sally; Alexander.

SMITH, MICHAEL   Rush County
Born—About 1762.
Service—Pri. in CO. of Capt. Springer of Pittsburgh in 1777 and served in Regt. commanded by Col. John Gibson in Vir. Line on Continental Establishment. Served 6 yrs. and 6 mos. and was discharged at Pittsburgh in July, 1783.
Proof—Pension certificate 16451.

Buried—Pleasant Run Graveyard, Noble Twp. Name on Bronze tablet in Rush Co. Court House.
Children—Elizabeth; Hugh; Mary.
Collected by Mrs. Willard Amos, Rushville, Indiana.

SMITH, REUBEN   Floyd County
Born—1758.
Service—Enlisted 1777, near Brownsville, Penn., for term of 3 yrs. Attached to 13th Vir. Regt. Later belonged to 7th Vir. Regt. under Col. John Gibson. Stationed at Fort Pitt.
Proof—Pension claim W. 9659.
Died—1843. (Will probated Nov. 14, 1843), probably buried Greenville Twp.
Married—Mary ——. Ch. John.
Collected by Mrs. V. R. Conner, New Albany, Indiana.

SMITH, RICHARD   Franklin County
Born—1757.
Service—Enlisted in Prince Edward Co., Vir., in Feb., 1780, in Capt. Parson's CO., Col. William Washington's Regt. of Light Dragoons. He was in the battle of Guilford Court House, was in the siege of Ninety-Six and was wounded in battle of Eutaw Springs. He was discharged in June, 1782.
Proof—Pension claim S. 16254.
Died—July 1, 1840. (Five in his family in 1821.)

SMITH, SAMUEL   Jennings County
Born—Oct. 24, 1760, Fishkill, N. Y.
Service—Enlisted as pri. in N. Y. Line, first under Gen. Skyler, Col. Gansevourt, Capt. Thomas Hicks; second, transferred to Capt. Switz; third under Maj. Denie, Capt. Ellsworth; fourth, Maj. Vanderhover, Capt. Ellsworth.
Proof—Pension claim S. 32530.
Buried—Brewersville, Indiana.
Married—Elizabeth Peters. Ch. James Peters Smith.

SMITH, THOMAS   Johnson County
Born—1763, Pittsylvania Co., Virginia.
Service—Enlisted 1780, Orange Co., N. C., as a pri. in 2nd N. C. Regt. under Col. Tilgman Dixon, Lt. Col. Henry Dixon, Maj. Francis Graves, Capt Henry Cannady, Col. Thomas Wilkerson, Capt. Cornelius Sayler. Discharged 1782.
Proof—Pension claim 32524.
Died—Last date of pension made on Oct. 8, 1842.
Collected by Mrs. I. E. Tranter, Franklin, Indiana.

SMITH, THOMAS   Washington County
Born—1749 or 1750, Virginia.
Service—Enlisted in Amherst Co., Virginia, under Capt. Samuel Cobbile (Cavil), Col. Buckner's 6th Vir. Regt. Served 1 yr. then transferred to Col. Morgan's Regt. Discharged March 4, 1778. In battles of White Marsh, Saratoga.
Proof—Pension claim S. 36771; Senate Documents, vol. 3, p. 75; Washington Co. Ind. Minute Book A, p. 208.
Died—Feb. 27, 1829.
Married—Kesiiah —— (aged 55 in 1820). Children not known.
Collected by Mrs. Harvey Morris, Salem, Indiana.

SMITH, WILLIAM   Rush County
Service—Feb. 1, 1777, he enlisted as a pri. in CO. commanded by Capt. Uriah Springer in Vir. Line on the Continental Establishment. He resided in Westmoreland Co., Penn., when he enlisted. After enlistment he joined 2nd Vir. Regt. under Col. John Gibson and was discharged July 25, 1783.
Proof—Pension claim S-40465.
Buried—Pleasant Run Graveyard, Noble Twp. Name on Bronze tablet in Rush Co. Court House.
Collected by Mrs. Willard Amos, Rushville, Indiana.

SMITHERS, WILLIAM   Dearborn County
Born—Dec. 22, 1741, Stafford Co., Virginia.
Service—Pri. in CO. commanded by Capt. Leg. Regt. by Col. Williams in Vir. Line, 6 mos.
Proof—Pension claim S. 17682.
Died—May 14, 1833.
Collected by Mrs. Walter Kerr, Aurora, Indiana.

SMYTH, PHILIP D.   Switzerland County
Service—Enlisted for 3 yrs. Aug. 18, 1776, in Hagerstown, Md., under Capt. Wm. Hirer, Regt. of Col. Hooicker, Col. Sticker, Maj. Wiltner, Md. Line, attached to Gen. Mechlenberg's Brigade, Continental Establishment. Discharged. Volunteered for 2 or 3 mos. tour under Gen. Sullivan to go up Susquehannah River. In battles of Princeton, Brandywine and Germantown, and Monmouth.
Proof—Switzerland Count Court—Order Book D., p. 627. Declaration made Oct. 5, 1825. His wife was 75 yrs. old.
Collected by Mrs. A. V. Danner, Vevay, Indiana.

SNAPP, GEORGE   Knox County
Born—Feb., 1752, Bucks Co., Pennsylvania.
Service—While residing in Frederick Co., Vir., enlisted in spring 1778,
    served 4 mos. in Capt. Joseph Longacre's CO. guarding prisoners
    in Winchester and at Barracks near there. Later served 1 mo. in
    Capt. Bell's CO., 2 mos. in Capt. Gilkerson's CO. A part of his
    service was under Colonel Hoalmes (?).
Proof—Pension claim S. 32531.
Died—1845. Buried Snapp Cemetery, Busseron Twp.
Children—Jacob Rudolf, d. 1842; Joseph d. 1843; Elijah d. 1863; Elizabeth.
Collected by Mrs. S. G. Davenport, Vincennes, Indiana.

SNODDY, JOHN   Owen County
Born—Feb. 23, 1758, in Rowan Co., North Carolina.
Service—Enlisted Jan., 1775, for 3 mos., pri. under Capt. James Purvines and Gen. Rutherford, N. C.; enlisted Jan., 1778, for 2 yrs.,
    pri. under Capt. Gass and Col. Cleveland, N. C.; enlisted Jan.,
    1780 for 3 mos., pri. under Stuart and Col. Martin, N. C.; for 3
    mos., pri. under Capt. Lenoir and Col. Isaacs, N. C.
Proof—Pension record.
Died—March 22, 1843. Buried Surber Farm, northwest of Gosport, Ind.
    Stone.
Married—Nancy Niblick. Ch. Fergus b. 1780 and others. Second, m.
    1796, Mary McNeil. Ch. Julia, m. John Bryant; Elizabeth, m.
    Henry McAlister; Samuel, m. Jane Shields; James, m. Rachel
    Errman; Thomas, m. Sarah Raper; Barton, m. Elizabeth Petit;
    Martin, m. Eliza Steel; Amanda, m. Joseph Warren; Nancy, m.
    David Shields.
Collected by Miss Ura Sanders, Gosport, Indiana.

SNOW, LEMUEL   Franklin County
Born—Dec. 7, 1759, Barnstable, Cape Cod, Massachusetts.
Service—Enlisted at age of 16 from Boston, Mass., and served continuously until end of war. Made Lieut. when 18 yrs. old. Discharged Oct., 1781. Was engaged in several major battles, was at
    Valley Forge the entire winter, witnessed the execution of Major
    Andre, the evacuation of N. Y. by the British, and was with the
    Army at Newburgh when it was disbanded by Washington.
Proof—Mass. Soldiers and Sailors, vol. 4, p. 617; vol. 37, p. 207. Pierce's
    Register; Heitman's Historical Register, p. 509.
Died—Sept. 3, 1824. Buried Snow Hill Cemetery, White Water Twp.
    Stone. S. A. R. marker placed by Harry Gale Nye, a descendant.

Married—1785, Lydia Hodges. Ch. Anna; Lydia; Joseph; Lemuel; Hannah; Hercules; Betsey Dinnie; Betsy; Mary Hussey; Salome and Sophronie (twins); Crocker; Nymphas Hinckley; Abigail Phinney.

SNYDER, JOHN   Knox County
Born—Probably in Germany.
Service—Pri. 5th Class, 3rd CO., 3rd Batt., Lancaster Co. Militia, 1781. Adjutant, 1783, 3rd Batt., Lancaster Co. Served under Lieut. Col. James Ross.
Proof—Penn. Archives, Series 5, vol. 7, pp. 265, 321, 323.
Buried—In Harrison Twp.
Children—Leonard, m. Juliana ——; William, m. Susanna Barkman; John Jr.
Collected by Mrs. S. G. Davenport, Vincennes, Indiana.

SNYDER, LEONARD R.   Knox County
Born—Pennsylvania.
Service—Pri. in Capt. John Rutherford's CO. 4th Batt., Col. Robert Elder, Aug. 12, 1777. Pri., Nov. 5, 1777, Capt. Martin Weaver's CO. of Lancaster Co. Militia under Col. John Rogers. Discharged Dec. 13, 1777.
Proof—Penn. Archives, Series 5, vol. 7, pp. 358, 527, 1009.
Died—After 1840. Buried Old Hamline Chapel, Harrison Twp.
Married—Juliana ——; Ch. John R. 1803-1853, m. Nancy Wily Sampson; Samuel R.; David R.; James R. 1817-1875, m. Rebecca Sampson; Martin; Solomon; Andrew Catherine; Polly.
Collected by Mrs. S. G. Davenport, Vincennes, Indiana.

SNYDER, WILLIAM   Knox County
Service—Return of those ordered to march in the 1st class of the 3rd Batt., Lancaster Co. Militia in 1780. Payroll of men of 1st class of 3rd Batt., Lancaster Co. Militia under Capt. John Sleter. A return of Lieut. Samuel Elliot's CO. 1779, 1782, 8th class, 1783, Ensign in 4th CO., 6th Batt.
Proof—Penn. Archives, Series 5, vol. 7, pp. 234, 281, 469, 495, 613, 978, 1118.
Died—1822. Buried probably in Harrison Twp.
Married—Susannah Barkman (Barekman). Ch. Henry, m. Amanda Whitcomb; John; James; George; William.
Collected by Mrs. S. G. Davenport, Vincennes, Indiana.

SOLSBY (SOLSBE), DANIEL   Vigo County
Born—April 15, 1755.
Service—Enlisted Sept., 1776, for 3 yrs. in 8th Regt. Penn. Discharged 1779 at Ft. Pitt.

Proof—Pension claim W. 9666.
Died—1841, March 4. Buried Honey Creek Twp. Government marker.
Married—1781, Rachel Bircham (1765-1844). Ch. John b. 1782; Susannah b. 1785; Margaret b. 1787; Daniel Jr. b. 1789; Rachel b. 1791; Mary b. 1794; Sarah b. 1795; Samuel b. 1797; Martha b. 1799; William b. 1801; Asenath b. 1803.

SPADER, BERGEN   Scott County
Born—Dec. 5, 1762, Somerset Co., New Jersey.
Service—Pri. in CO. under Capt. Quick, New Jersey, and Md. Line for 15 mos. Col. Crane's Regt.
Proof—Pension claim S. 31979.

SPANN, JESSE   Jefferson County
Born—1756.
Service—Inscription on marker reads "Scout."
Proof—D. A. R. No. 221765. Stone.
Buried—Craig's Cemetery at Middlefork.
Married—Mary Leighton.
Collected by John Paul Chapter D. A. R.

SPARKS, JAMES   Jackson County
Service—Served from beginning of war until 1782 in Westmoreland Co., Penn.
Proof—Pension claim S. 32,533.
Died—May 25, 1834. Statement of daughter, Alicy Newkirk.

SPARLING (SPARLIN), GEORGE   Orange County
Born—About 1752.
Service—Served 1 yr. in 1st Regt., N. J., commanded by Capt. Daniel Piatt, 3 yrs. Capt. Longstreet. In battles of Brandywine and Monmouth.
Proof—Pension claim S. 36783.

SPENCE, JAMES   Sullivan County
Born—1755, North Carolina.
Service—Enlisted in Raleigh, N. C., in May, 1776, served 2½ yrs. in Capts. James Jones' and de Medidi's Companies, Col. Sumpters, N. C., Regt. of Cavalry and was in a battle at Charlestown and several small skirmishes.
Proof—Pension claim S. 36782.
Died—1837. Buried Gill Twp.
Child—James.
Collected by Mrs. James R. Riggs, Sullivan, Indiana.

SPENCER, AMASA Jennings County
Born—1760, Albany, N. Y.
Service—Enlisted Charlotte Co., Vir. Served under Capt. Wm. Morton, Col. Joel Watkins, Capt. Thos. Williams, Col. Lucas, Col. Cocke, Capt. John Fewkway, Col. Lynch. In battles of Camden and Guilford, Court House.
Proof—Pension claim W. 2017.
Died—July 10, 1846. Buried on Moses Spencer farm, Spencer Twp.
Married—Priscilla Fitzgerald.

SPENCER, WALTER Scott County
Born—April 14, 1760, Hartford Co., Connecticut.
Service—Enlisted 1776 under Col. Nathan Denison. In battle of Wyoming Co. Re-enlisted. Served in Conn. Line, 2 yrs.
Proof—Pension claim S. 16533.

STAGG, JOHN Jennings County
Born—1760, Bergen Co., New Jersey.
Service—Enlisted Haverstraw, N. Y., under Maj. Van Houton, Capt. Abraham Vanderdunk, Capt. John Bell, Col. Shreve's 2nd Jersey Regt., Lt. Talmage.
Proof—Pension claim W. 2267; B. L. Wt. 8166-160-55.
Died—July 9, 1846.
Married—1833, Martha Phillips. Ch. Sarah, m. Philip Stoat.

STEEL, JOHN Morgan County
Born—Jan. 25, 1761, Hampshire Co., Virginia
Service—Enlisted in April or May, 1781. Served 3 mos. as a pri. in Capt. Michael Stump's CO., Col. Muhlenberg's Vir. Regt. In skirmish at Silver Creek. Enlisted July or Aug. of 1781, served 3 mos. under Lieut. Blue and was at the siege of Yorktown.
Proof—Pension claim S. 17706.
Died—Received last pension on April 1, 1836.
Collected by Mrs. Ira E. Tranter, Franklin, Indiana.

STEELMAN, JOHN Floyd County
Born—1757, Gloucester Co., New Jersey.
Service—Drafted under Capt. Jeremiah Smith, 3 mos. Again for 3 mos. Vol. under Capt. John Summers, 6 mos., N. J.
Proof—Pension claim W. 9684. B. L. Wt. 86033-160-55.
Died—April 10, 1836, Floyd Co
Married—1824, Elizabeth Smith.

STEINBERGER (STONEBARGER, STEEN-
BARGER), JOHN — Bartholomew County
Born—1760, in Shenandoah Valley, Virginia.
Service—Served with Old Dunmore County Militia, in Capt. Michael Reader's CO. under Lieut. Richard Branham. Service date: prior to April 30, 1778.
Proof—D. A. R. No. 294583.
Died—1821. Buried Old Union Cemetery, near Taylorsville, Ind.
Married—Elizabeth Norman. Ch. Henry b. 1786; George; Frederick b. 1791; John; David; Elizabeth; Gideon; Catherine; Reuben.
Collected by Mrs. Wm. R. Johnson, Franklin, Indiana.

STEINSUFFERT (STONESEIFER, STONESYPHER),
HENRY — Harrison County
Born—Feb. 4, 1755, Germany.
Service—Enlisted in 1782, 3rd CO., Capt. Wm. Heaffer, 1st Class, 5th Batt., York Co. Penn. Militia.
Proof—Penn. Archives, 6th Series, vol. 11, p. 528.
Buried—1841. Jordan Cemetery, 3 miles South of Corydon. Stone.
Married—Elizabeth Hoffheinze. Ch. John; George; Elizabeth; Henry; Catherine; David; Joseph; Adam.
Collected by Miss Amanda Bottorff, Charlestown, Indiana.

STEPLETON, ANDREW — Switzerland County
Born—About 1752.
Service—Enlisted at Ronney, Vir., 1777. Served in Capt. William Vause's CO., Col. James Wood's 12th Vir. Regt. In battle of Brandywine and Monmouth. Wounded. Served 6 yrs. and 2 mos. Discharged at Winchester, Vir., by Col. Neville.
Proof—Pension claim S. 36799.
Buried—Probably at Allensville, Cotton Twp.
Married—Barbara ———. Ch. John, m. Polly Johnson; Betsy, m. Daniel Cole; Andrew, m. Huldah Spencer.
Collected by Mrs. A. V. Danner, Vevay, Indiana.

STERRIT (STERRITT), STEWART — Harrison County
Born—1762, Londonderry, Ireland.
Service—Enlisted 1781, Frederick Co., Md., as a substitute for his father, James Sterritt, who was drafted for 6 mos. under Capt. Daniel Smith.
Proof—Pension claim S. 31991.
Married—Rebecca ———.

STEVENS (STEPHENS), ISAAC   Vigo County
Born—About 1754.
Service—Served in 3rd Regt., N. J. Line, in Capt. Sharp's CO. for 1 yr. Present at surrender of Cornwallis. Discharged after 5 yrs. 8 mos.
Proof—Pension claim S. 36798.

STEVENS (STEPHENS), SAMUEL   Ripley County
Born—June, 1768, Carlisle, Pennsylvania.
Service—Drafted March, 1777. Marched against Shawnees and Wyandottes under Col. John Cannon, 3 mos. Served 3 mos. from July, 1777, as substitute for Anthony Boli under same officers. May, 1778, served 3 mos. at Mentuers Bottom. Total of 9 mos.
Proof—Pension claim W. 22332.
Died—July 1, 1834. Name on bronze tablet in Versailles Court House.
Married—Mary —— b. 1760. Ch. Mary b. 1780, m. Joseph Harber; other Ch.
Collected by Mrs. A. B. Wycoff, Batesville, Indiana.

STEVENSON (STINSON), JAMES   Wayne County
Born—Dec. 10, 1754, Lancaster Co., Pennsylvania.
Service—Served as follows: June, 1776, in Capt. Jacob Wolmack's CO. of Rangers, N. C. Troops; Oct., 1776, as First Sergt. in Capt. Joseph Wilson's CO., Col. John Carter's Regt; June, 1778, as Lieut. in Capt. Gess's CO., Col. Carter's Regt.; 1779, commissioned Capt. Served till Jan., 1781, in Col. Servier's Regt.
Proof—Draper's King's Mt. and Its Heroes, p. 424.
Died—May 24, 1845. Buried Jacksonburg, Ind. Government marker.
Married—Mary Gess, b. 1755. Ch. Nancy; Polly; Sally; Amy; John, 1783-1845, m. Elizabeth Simms; Narcissa; Samuel; James.
Collected by Mrs. Paul L. Ross, Richmond, Indiana.

STEWART, CHARLES   Jefferson County
Born—1759.
Service—While residing in Spotsylvania Co., Vir., enlisted in 1775, marched to Hobbs Hole under Lt. Stubblefield, went into the marine service, served 18 mos. Enlisted Dec. 20, 1776, for 3 yrs. served in Capt. Gabriel Jones' CO., Col. George Gibson's Regt. Was furloughed May 17, 1779, on account of sickness.
Proof—Penn. Archives, Series 2, vol. 10, p. 637. Pension claim S. 16261.
Died—1840, in Switzerland Co. May be buried across the line in Ripley or Switzerland.
Married—Ann ——.
Collected by John Paul Chapter D. A. R., Madison, Indiana.

STEWART, JAMES, JR.   Floyd County
Born—June 8, 1743, Berkley Co., Vir.
Service—Pri. in Capt. Andrew Lynn's CO. of Rangers on the frontiers, 1778-1783, Westmoreland Co., Vir., now Penn.; also a pri. in Capt. William Harrod's CO., 1780, at stations near the falls of the Ohio River, now in Jefferson Co., Ky.
Proof—Penn. Archives, 3rd Series, vol. 23, p. 326. Collin's Hist. of Ky., Vol. 1, p. 12.
Died—Dec. 29, 1812. Probably buried near Greenville, Ind.
Married—Rebecca Marchant (1748-1815). Ch. William; James; John; Pricilla; David; Anna; Rebecca; Marchant; Stephen; Elizabeth; Isaac.
Collected by Mrs. V. R. Conner, New Albany, Indiana.

STILWELL, DAVID   Gibson County
Born—Oct. 29, 1755.
Service—Entered Guilford Co., N. C., under Capt. John Summers of 1st Regt., Col. Thomas Clark. Enlisted May, 1777, served to 1781. In battles of Monmouth and Charlestown.
Proof—Pension claim S. 36816.
Married—Mourning ———. Ch. Osbourne.

STILL, MURPHY   Washington County
Born—1758, near Charleston, S. C.
Service—In same company with Arthur Parr of Washington Co. Served 5 yrs. Was a scout on many occasions.
Proof—Was recognized as Rev. Soldier and talked over service many times with Arthur Parr, Micajah Callaway and James Garrison as soldiers. Buried in Washington Co. Received land from government.
Died—1831. Buried on Still Farm, later known as Joseph Johnson Farm, in Gibson Twp. Stone.
Married—1795, Phoebe Rives. Ch. George and eight others, names not known.
Collected by Mrs. Harvey Morris, Salem, Indiana.

STILLWELL, RICHARD   Dubois County
Born—1732, probably England.
Service—Served as ensign in Capt. Peter Van Sant's 3rd Associated CO. for lower Wakefield Twp., Buck Co. Militia, in 1775. 1st Lieut. 1777, in Capt. Joshua Anderson's 6th CO., 5th Battalion, Buck Co. Militia. 1780, Capt. of the 2nd CO., 3rd Battalion, Buck Co. Also served as Capt. 1781 and 1783.
Proof—Penn. Archives, 5th Series, vol. 5, pp. 304, 354, 390, 421, 422, 433, 436, 444.

Died—1836. Buried Simmon's Graveyard 3 miles southeast of Holland, Ind. Government marker, placed by Mrs. George E. Norman of Jasper, Ind.
Married—1784, Sarah Enlow. Ch. Henry, b. 1786, d. 1817. 2nd w. Elizabeth Simmons. Ch. Richard; Moses; Elizabeth; William.
Collected by George R. Wilson, Historian, Dubois Co.

STINE, PHILIP   Harrison County
Born—Oct., 1762.
Service—Drummer in CO. commanded by Capt. Millingers, Penn. Line, 1 yr.
Proof—Pension claim S. 17122.
Buried—Pott's Cemetery, W. of Corydon, Ind. Bronze marker placed by Hoosier Elm Chapter D. A. R.

STINGLEY, GEORGE   Tippecanoe County
Born—Sept. 12, 1763.
Service—While residing in Hampshire Co., Vir., he enlisted about Nov. 4, 1781, served as sergeant under Capts. Joseph Berry, Stinson and James Simeral, Cols. Vincent Williams and Niswonger, was stationed at the garrison at Winchester, Frederick Co., Vir., as one of the guards over the British prisoners taken at Cornwallis' surrender and was discharged May 4, 1782, by Col. Hugh Holmes.
Proof—Pension claim S. 32543. Pensioned 1834, Tippecanoe Co., Ind.

STINSON, ELIJAH   Vanderburg County
Born—May 15, 1762, Vir.
Service—Pri., served in Capt. Smith's N. C. CO., and was in an engagement near Purysburg as Sergt. in Capt. SyCathaelt Martin's CO. At siege of Charleston and battle of Camden. As spy under Capt. Joel Lewis.
Proof—Pension claim W. 9678.
Died—March 21 or 23, 1835. Buried Evansville, Ind.
Married—1780, Rachel Cobb. Ch. James, b. 1781; Sarah, b. 1783, m. Manassa Chaney; John B., b. 1785; Elizabeth, b. 1787; Lewis Cobb, b. 1789; William, b. 1793; Martin, b. 1795; Beuoni, b. 1798; Nancy, b. 1801.
Collected by Mrs. W. R. Davidson, Evansville, Indiana.

STODARD, PHILO   Floyd County
Born—1765, Lanesborough, Mass.
Service—Enlisted 1779 in Richmond, Berkshire Co., Mass., under Col. Hagaboom. 1780 under Capt. Ford, Col. John Brown, Lieut. Levi Spencer. 1781 under Capt. Josiah Gale.
Proof—Pension claim S. 31992.

STONE, NIMROD H. Vermillion County
Born—Oct. 1, 1764, Fauquier Co., Vir.
Service—Enlisted April 28, 1781, Light Horse Inf., Capt. Wm. Triplett, Col. Francis Triplett. Discharged Nov. or Dec., 7 mos. service.
Proof—Pension claim S. 32535.
Died—1841, Laudersdale, Ind.
Married—Sarah Craig. Ch. Delilah, 1798-1883, m. Wm. Landers.

STONE, SAMUEL Dearborn County
Born—About 1759.
Service—Enlisted Mass. Line, Jan. 1, 1776, in Capt. Barnes' Inf., Regt. of Col. Nixon, for 1 yr. Enlisted again summer of 1779 under Col. Smith and served to end of war. In battles of Princeton, Trenton, Harlem Heights.
Proof—Pension certificate No. 9033; Pension claim S. 36808.
Collected by Mrs. Walter Kerr, Aurora, Indiana.

STONEBRAKER, SEBASTIAN Montgomery County
Born—1757, near Philadelphia.
Service—Pri. in Col. Elder's Penn. Regt., Lancaster Co.
Proof—Pension claim S. 32540.
Died—July 6, 1836. Buried Bunker Hill Cemetery near Alamo. Stone.
Married—Susan Yeakle. Ch. William; Mary Watson; Catherine Fruits; Christina Smith; Joseph; Jacob; George; Henry.
Collected by Miss Jessie Watson, Crawfordsville, Indiana.

STONER, PETER, SR. Putnam County
Born—June 6, 1764, in Penn.
Service—Enlisted various times in 1780 and 1781 from Mecklenburg Co., N. C. Served under Capts. Rease, Wm. Hutchinson and Samuel Martin, and Cols. Caleb Phifer and Wm. Polk, in N. C. and S. C. In battles of Eutaw Springs, Monks Corner, Hanging Rock, King's Mountain and Cowpens.
Proof—Pension record.
Died—April 7, 1851. Buried Pleasant Hill Cemetery, Madison Twp. Government marker, placed by Washburn Chapter D. A. R.
Married—1793, Eva Cotner. Ch. Henry; Daniel, m. Mary Wells; Jonathan, m. Mrs. Mary Holmes Askew; Solomon; Sarah, m. Joseph Wells; Rosa, m. Stephen Wells; Eva, m. Mr. Henshaw; Mary, m. Jesse Burnett; Peter, Jr., m. Mary E. Wells.
Collected by Miss Minnetta Wright, Greencastle, Indiana.

STORK (STURK), JOHN   Knox County
Born—Penn.
Service—Muster Roll of Capt. Sampson Thomas' CO., Chester Co., Dec.
    26, 1780; pri. 4th Class in same CO. and 1781; 1782 under Capt.
    Samuel Roberts.
Proof—Penn. Archives, Series 5, vol. 5, pp. 603, 620, 637, 876, 879, 411.
Died—Dec., 1828.
Married—Nelly ——. Ch. Jacob; Margaret, m. Sebastian Frederick;
    Katherine, m. Charles Pressey; John; Polly, m. Thomas Beard.
Collected by Mrs. S. G. Davenport, Vincennes, Indiana.

STORM, JOHN   Greene County
Born—Feb. 3, 1760, Penn.
Service—Served as pri. under Capts. Smith and Boyer, 1st Vir. Regt.,
    also under Capt. Robert Morrows, Col. William Washington's
    Continental Dragoons.
Proof—Pension claim W. 1953.
Died—1835, Dec. 13. Buried on farm near Hobbieville, Ind.
Married—1798, Anne Parsons (1776-1854). Ch. Leah, b. 1798; Martha,
    b. 1800; Margaret, b. 1803, m. Jacob Young; Joseph, b. 1807;
    Peter, b. 1809; Nancy, b. 1811; Harrison, b. 1813, d. 1814; Mary
    Ann, b. 1815; Anne, b. 1819; Hannah, b. 1821; Washington, b.
    1824.
Collected by Mrs. E. A. Hammack, Dugger, Indiana.

STORY, JOHN   Jennings County
Born—About 1760 in Southhampton Co., Vir.
Service—Served as a pri. from Jan. to Oct., 1781, under Capts. Joshua
    Nicholson, Arthur Boykin, Jesse Whitehead, Simmons, Rodgers,
    Mitchell, Cols. Wells Reddick and Benjamin Blount. Enlisted at
    Southhampton, Vir., and was in the siege of Yorktown.
Proof—Pension claim S. 6155.
Died—Sept. 12, 1845. Buried Vernon Cemetery, Vernon, Ind. Stone.
Children—Thomas J. (War of 1812).
Collected by Mrs. Ira E. Tranter, Franklin, Indiana.

STOUT, JOB   Franklin County
Born—Feb. 21, 1763, Hopewell, N. J.
Service—Enlisted June 15, 1780, as pri. in Capt. Johannes Van Ellen's
    CO. of volunteers of Northampton Co., Penn. Inscription on stone
    reads "In memory of Job Stout, a Rev. Soldier."
Proof—Penn. Archives.
Died—Feb. 28, 1833. Buried Big Cedar Cemetery. Stone.
Married—1771-1847, Rhoda Howell. Ch. Jonathan; Mary; Rachael;
    Elizabeth; Abner; Margaret; Joab; Rebecca; David; Sarah; Ira;
    Aaron; Anna.

STOTTS (STOUT), MICHAEL　　　　　　　　　Fountain County
Born—Penn.
Service—Pri. in Lieut. Samuel Elliott's CO., Lancaster Co. Militia, for 1 yr, 1778.
Proof—Penn. Archives, 5th Series, vol. 7, p. 468. Pension record.
Died—1834-1835. Buried Baptist Cemetery, Richland Twp. Government marker.
Children—Elizabeth; Lucretia; Ann; Mary.
Collected by Mrs. A. S. Dolch (deceased), Attica, Indiana.

STRINGHAM, DANIEL　　　　　　　　　　　Parke County
Born—1764, Wallkill, N. Y.
Service—While residing in Wallkill, N. Y., he volunteered Oct., 1777, and served 1 mo.; the next year he served 2 mos.; in 1779 he served 3 mos.; all of his service was rendered as a pri. in Capt. Samuel Watkin's CO., Col. Moses Phillip's N. Y. Regt., and he was out against the Indians, who were burning towns and committing depredations against the inhabitants.
Proof—Pension claim S. 32536.
Died—Aug. 6, 1841. Buried on farm owned by Mrs. Essie Strong, Florida Twp. Stone.
Married—Abagail Horton, d. 1842.
Collected by Mrs. H. L. Hancock, Rockville, Indiana.

STUCKY, JOHN FREDERICK　　　　　　　　Warrick County
Born—1761.
Service—From May 25 to Oct. 26, 1777, pri. in Capt. John Volick's (George Volick's) CO., 9th Battalion of Lancaster Co. Militia, commanded by Col. John Huber. 1779 same CO. 1780 1st CO., 3rd Battalion, under Capt. Philip Duck, same CO. 1782.
Proof—Penn. Archives, vol. 7, pp. 233, 268, 289, 292, 325, 885, 890, 905.
Died—1856. Buried Mt. Zion Cemetery, Lynnville. Government marker.
Married—Barbara Skeemp (1765-1861). Ch. Catherine; James; Martin; Rose; Ann; Margaret; John (1798-1875), m. Polly Miller; Elizabeth; Jacob.
Collected by Dr. H. I. Meyer, 104 S. Michigan Ave., Chicago, Ill.

SUDETH, ISAAC　　　　　　　　　　　　　Grant County
Service—Buried Bethel Cemetery, Wilson's Ford. Inscription on stone reads "Old Revolutionary Soldier, age 99."
Daughter—Nancy, b. 1799, d. 1856, m. Gabriel Johnson, b. 1797, d. 1869.
Collected by Gen. Francis Marion Chapter D. A. R. and Mrs. H. G. Ervin, Hartford City, Indiana.

SUGGAN, JAMES   Jefferson County
Born—About 1744.
Service—Enlisted in Leesburg, Loudoun Co., Vir., Oct., 1776, in Capt.
    Thos. West's Vir. CO., in Col. Rawling's Rifle Regt.; was at the
    siege and capture of Fort Washington and in several small skirmishes; discharged in 1779. Received a wound in one of his arms.
Proof—Pension claim S. 36821.
Died—Sept. 4, 1830. Probably buried in Milton Twp.
Married—Prissa ——.
Collected by John Paul Chapter D. A. R., Madison, Indiana.

SULCER, WILLIAM   Greene County
Born—1756, in Shenandoah Co., Vir.
Service—Enlisted 1775 as substitute for his father and served 6 mos.
    under Capt. Lewis in Col. Lewis' Vir. Regt. In battles of Trenton
    and Princeton. Wounded. Total service 18 mos.
Proof—Pension claim W. 9687.
Died—Dec. 14, 1836.
Married—1793, Jane Johnston. Seven children. Only one known,
    Henry, b. 1794.
Collected by Mrs. S. G. Davenport, Vincennes, Indiana.

SULLIVAN, DANIEL   Clark County
Born—Oct., 1740.
Service—While a resident of Md. enlisted 1776-7 as pri. in Capt. Benjamin Stoddard's CO., Col. Hartley's Regt., and in Capt. Geo.
    Bush's CO., Col. Hartley's Regt. (3rd Penn. Regt.).
Proof—Pension claim W. 25169; Penn. Archives, Series 2, vol. 10, p.
    477.
Died—1820 or 1821.
Married—Sarah ——, d. 1845. Ch. John; Daniel, Jr.; Mary, m. Abraham Miller.
Collected by Ann Rogers Clark Chapter D. A. R.

SUMMERS, GEORGE   Clark County
Born—1764, Little York, Penn.
Service—A drummer in Capt. John Doyle's CO., Col. Josiah Harmar's
    6th Penn. Regt.
Proof—D. A. R. Lineage, vol. 122, p. 156.
Died—1841. Buried near Utica, Clark Co.
Married—1804, Prudence Gross (1781-1853). Ch. Elizabeth Elinor
    (1820-1902).
Collected by Mrs. Harvey Morris, Salem, Indiana.

SWAIM, ISAAC   Marion or Hendricks County
Born—Staten Island, N. Y.
Service—Pri., Capt. Simon Duryea's CO., First Battalion, Somerset Co.,
    N. J. Militia.
Proof—Stryker's Jersey Men in the Revolution, p. 776.
Died—Feb. 2, 1829. Buried on the Swaim Farm, located where the
    Clermont Girls' School is now. This is near the line of the two
    counties.
Married—Hannah ——, d. 1817. Ch. Anthony, b. 1784; Hannah, b. 1788,
    m. John Craig Jones.
Collected by Miss Frances E. Emerson, Plymouth, Indiana.

TAFF (TAFFE), JAMES   Marion County
Born—Dec. 4, 1755, Hampshire Co., Vir.
Service—Enlisted in the 8th Vir. Line under Capt. Abel Westfall and
    detached to Col. Morgan's Rifle Corps at Middle Brook, N. J.; a
    powder maker by occupation; enlisted in Hampshire Co., Vir., for
    2 yrs. Was in an engagement at Rising Sun, N. J., at Brunswick
    and the taking of Burgoyne in N. Y. and at Edge Hill.
Proof—Pension claim S. 36825.
Died—June 13, 1832, Indianapolis, Ind.
Married—Elizabeth Reed Radcliff. Ch. Benjamin; John; Nancy; Elizabeth.

TAYLOR, DAVID   Jefferson County
Born—1755, Augusta Co., Vir.
Service—Enlisted at Staunton, Augusta Co., Vir., in Feb., 1776, and
    served until Dec., 1776.
Proof—Pension certificate 17488.
Died—Before 1832. Buried Woodfill Cemetery.
Married—Nancy Hingston, b. 1752. Ch. David; James; Isaac; John;
    Jeremiah; Abigail; Anna; Sarah; Hannah; Elizabeth; Nancy
    (1784-1853), m. David Taylor (son of Joseph).
Collected by Mrs. Virginia H. Buck, Madison, Indiana, and Mrs. Wm.
    D. Pence, Evanston, Illinois.

TAYLOR, IGNATIUS   Wayne County
Born—Sept., 1742, St. Mary Co., Md.
Service—Commissioned Capt. of Militia in St. Mary Co., Md., in 1776.
    At the close of the war he retired with the rank of Major.
Proof—Maryland Archives, vol. 11, p. 529. Journal of Correspondence
    of Md. Council of Safety during 1776, by William H. Brown.
Died—Sept., 1809, Hagerstown, Ind.
Married—Anne Wilkinson. Ch. Francis; Elizabeth Field Taylor.
Collected by Caroline Scott Harrison Chapter D. A. R.

TAYLOR, JACOB Franklin County
Born—1759, Vir.
Service—Inscription on stone reads "Jacob Taylor, of Vir., a Revolutionary Soldier. Aged 89 years. Nov. 12, 1848, he left the shores of time."
Died—Nov. 12, 1848. Buried St. Johannes Ev. Prot. Church, Highland Twp. Stone.

TAYLOR, JACOB Dearborn County
Born—Nov. 12, 1758 or 1759, Winchester, Vir.
Service—Enlisted at Winchester, 1777, as pri. in Capt. Steele's CO. Was transferred to Capt. Merriwether's CO., Cols. Morgan's and Lee's Regts. In battles of Monmouth and Cowpens. Wounded. Later served 3 mos. in Capt. George Bell's CO., Vir. Militia. Present at Yorktown. Discharged Dec., 1781.
Proof—Pension claim R. 10416½. Rejected for want of proof.
Died—Aug. 23, 1849, in Kelso Twp. (May be the Jacob Taylor who is buried in Franklin Co.)
Collected by Mrs. Walter Kerr, Aurora, Indiana.

TAYLOR, JOSEPH Jefferson County
Born—1747, Augusta Co., Vir.
Service—Enlisted at Staunton, Augusta Co., Vir., Feb. 1, 1766, and served 11 mos. as wagoner in Capt. John Hays' CO., Cols. Thomas Fleming's and George Matthews' Vir. Regt.
Proof—Pension certificate 2075. Buried Woodfill Cemetery. Government marker. Placed by John Paul Chapter D. A. R.
Married—Susan Wooden. Ch. Anna; Margaret; Nancy; Susan; Mary; David, b. 1780-1851, m. Nancy Taylor (daughter of David); John; Joseph.
Collected by Mrs. Virginia H. Buck, Madison, Indiana, and Mrs. Wm. D. Pence, Evanston, Illinois.

TAYLOR, OBADIAH Lake County
Born—1762, Deerfield, Mass.
Service—Name appears in list of men raised to serve 6 mos. under Brig. Gen. John Glover, Mass., July 10, 1780. Name appears on several other lists for the year 1780.
Proof—Mass. Soldiers and Sailors in the Rev., vol. 15, p. 415.
Died—Buried Old Indian Burial Ground, East Cedar Lake.
Married—Abigail Williams. Ch. Obadiah; Adonijah, b. 1792, m. Lucy Winchester; Horace, b. 1801, m. Sarah A. O'Dell; Leander; Seymour; Mrs. Dorothy Lilley; Mrs. Betsey Edgerton; Mrs. Almira Palmer; Mrs. Miranda Stillson; Mrs. Rhoda Gifford; Mrs. Rachel Hurlburt.
Collected by Miss Ethel A. Vinnedge, Creston, Indiana.

TEEPLE, JACOB Clark County
Born—June 19, 1763, Somerset Co., N. J.
Service—While living in Northumberland Co., Penn., enlisted as a substitute for his father, who was lame. Served as a fifer from 1778 to 1780. Frequently engaged in scouting parties. Served under Capt. John Nelson. Total service 18 mos.
Proof—Pension claim S. 16552.
Died—July 7, 1835. Buried Robertson Church Cemetery, near Charlestown.
Married—Hannah ——.
Collected by Anne Rogers Clark Chapter D. A. R.

TEMPLETON, ROBERT Franklin County
Born—Sept. 6, 1762, in Ireland.
Service—Enlisted Feb., 1780, for 3 mos.; Dec., 1780, 3 wks.; 1781, 2 wks.; Oct., 1781, 1 mo.
Proof—Pension record.
Died—Nov. 10, 1841. Buried on the Fred H. Miller Farm, Brookville Twp. Stone.
Married—Mary Hannah (1766-1845). Ch. William; Mary; Robert; David; Elizabeth Ann; Jane; Nancy Agnes.
Collected by Mrs. Charles Masters, Brookville, Indiana.

THOM (THOMES), JOSEPH Jefferson County
Born—1748, North Ireland.
Service—Enlisted in 1782. In official return of 4, 5, 6 classes of Capt. White's CO. of 5th Battalion of Washington Co., Penn., Militia. Return signed by Nathan Powell, Lieut.
Proof—Penn. Archives, 6th Series, vol. 11, p. 189. Inscription on stone: "5th Battalion, Pa. Rev. War."
Died—Nov. 23, 1829. Buried Marling Cemetery. Government marker. Placed by John Paul Chapter D. A. R.
Married—Elizabeth Craig (1758-1826). Ch. Jane, b. 1780, m. Robert Cathcart; Sarah, b. 1781, m. Aaron Aimes and James Travis; Samuel, b. 1783, m. Sarah Travis; John, b. 1786, m. Margaret Culbertson and Mrs. Nancy Wallace Nintner; William Wilson, b. 1788, m. Charlotte Austin; Robert, b. 1790, m. Lydia Moorhead; James, b. 1793; Elizabeth b. 1795, m. Alexander Armstrong; Alexander Craig (1797-1864), m. Elizabeth Taylor; Joseph, b. 1800.
Collected by John Paul Chapter D. A. R. and Miss Amanda L. Bottorff, Charlestown, Indiana.

THOMAS, DAVID Union County
Born—1761, Dinwiddie Co., Vir.
Service—While a resident of Warren Co., N. C., he entered service as a substitute for his brother, Wm. Thomas, and served 6 mos. as a pri. in Capt. Chas. Allen's N. C. CO., and was in the Battle of

Brier Creek. Later served 3 mos. as a pri. in Capt. John White's N. C. CO. Next he volunteered in Mecklenburg Co., Vir., and served 3 mos. in Capt. Chas. Davis' CO., Col. Alexander Dick's Vir. Regt.
Proof—Pension claim S. 32552. Allowed pension Sept. 9, 1833, Harrison Twp., Union Co.
Died—1834.

THOMAS, EVAN   Jennings County
Born—Feb. 22, 1757, Frederick Co., Vir.
Service—Enlisted pri., William Co., Vir., 1775. Capt. Philip Lee against Dunmore; 1776, Capt. Charles West, Col. Weeden, Major Leach; 1781, Hampshire Co., Vir., substitute for James Magraw; battles of White Plains, Harlem Plains, Germantown, Brandywine, Piscataqua.
Proof—Pension claim S. 17728.
Died—Feb. 11, 1840. Buried Jennings Co., Ind.
Married—Third W., Mary ——, d. March 3, 1843. Booth Thomas, heir of the soldier. (Newspaper account of death states the soldier had 14 children, 82 grandchildren, 37 great-grandchildren.)

THOMAS, HENRY   Rush County
Born—May 3, 1756, Tulpehocken, Penn.
Service—Enlisted Sept., 1781, in Northumberland Co., Penn.; served 7 mos. as orderly-sergeant in Capt. John Ingram's Penn. CO.
Proof—Pension claim W. 9851.
Died—Sept. 4, 1836.
Married—1780 or 1781, Mary ——. Ch. Jacob, b. 1784; Henry, b. 1786; Margaret, b. 1787; Elizabeth, b. 1790 (?); Barbara, b. 1792; Mary, b. 1795; George, b. 1798; Susannah and Anna E., b. 1802.
Collected by Mrs. A. B. Wycoff, Batesville, Indiana.

THOMAS, JOHN   Shelby County
Born—Nov. 11, 1763, N. J.
Service—Entered service from Fauquier Co., Vir., under Capt. James Winn; drafted for 6 mos., 1778, as militia man, Gen. Morgan. In Battle of Cowpens.
Proof—Pension claim S. 16271.
Died—Last payment made March 4, 1837. Buried Lewis Creek Baptist Church Cemetery.
Three children living in Shelby Co., Ind., in 1837; no names given.

THOMAS, WILLIAM   Vigo County
Born—1758, Vir.
Service—Engaged in the battles of Trenton, Germantown and Brandywine. He enlisted Feb. 17, 1776, and served as pri. under Capt. Andrew Russell in the 5th Vir. Regt.

Proof—Records office of Adjutant General, War Department. Pension record.
Died—1828. Buried in Prairie Creek Cemetery, Prairie Creek Twp. Stone.
Children—Joseph; Abijah; Elijah; William; Rebecca; Nancy; Emmett; Elizabeth; Polly.
Collected by Fort Harrison Chapter D. A. R.

THOMPSON, DAVID St. Joseph County
Born—May, 1766, in East Windsor, Conn.
Service—1780, served as drummer boy, as substitute for Philip Dimick, under Col. McSarin, stationed at Fort Griswold. Later volunteered under Gen. Putnam for 3 mos.
Proof—Pension record.
Died—1846 or 1847. Buried Olive Chapel Cemetery, South Bend, Ind.
Married—Sally Fisk. Ch. David, m. Susan Fuller; Johnathan, m. Sally Pool; Sally, m. Asel Savory; Nancy, m. Boswell Fuller; Orrin E., m. Catherine Roe; Charles, m. Peggy Bradley; Isaac, m. Betsy Friscus; Lydia, m. Abram Goble; Polly, m. William Parnell.
Collected by Miss Amanda McComb, South Bend, Indiana.

THOMPSON, JOHN Knox County
Born—1760, Caroline Co., Vir.
Service—1776, volunteered in CO. of horsemen, commanded by Capt. John Fitzhugh, Vir. Line, 1 mo. 10 days. Pri. cavalry 10 mos. 20 days. Pri. Inf.
Proof—Pension claim S. 17144.
Died—Dec. 20, 1835.
Married—Anne ———.
Collected by Mrs. S. G. Davenport, Vincennes, Indiana.

THOMPSON, LAWRENCE Clay County
Born—1755, Dunmore Co., Vir.
Service—Enlisted 1777, served 6 mos. Discharged Dec., 1777. Rank 1st Sergeant under Capt. Alfred Moore of Col. Moore's N. C. Regt. Soldier resident in Rowan Co., N. C., at time of enlistment.
Proof—Pension claim S. 32554.
Died—About 1863, age 108 yrs. Buried Zenor Cemetery, near Prairie City School House. Stone placed by Clay Co. Commissioners.
Married—Martha ———. Ch. Frances, m. Thomas Wheeler; John D., m. Elizabeth Elsey.
Collected by Miss Pearl Finley, Brazil, Indiana.

THORN, MICHAEL, JR.   Knox County
Born—1764, on South Branch, Potomac, Vir.
Service—While residing on Turtle Creek, Penn., enlisted 1779 or 1780 for 3 mos. in CO. under Capt. Ellison, and acted as guard for the frontier; later served 3 mos. under Capt. Ford and Col. McIntosh, and assisted in building Fort McIntosh.
Proof—Pension claim S. 16272.
Died—After Sept. 16, 1844. Probably buried in Decker Twp.
Married—Cassandra ——. Ch. Esau and probably others.
Collected by Mrs. S. G. Davenport, Vincennes, Indiana.

THORP, TIMOTHY   Allen County
Service—Ensign in 4th Vir. Regt., 1776 to the close of the war.
Proof—Heitman's Historical Register, p. 542, War Department.
Died—Oct. 22, 1790 (killed in action by Indians in Harmer's defeat at Miami Towns). Probably buried in trench.
Collected by Mrs. T. J. Hindman, Fort Wayne, Indiana.

THRELKELD, THOMAS   Allen County
Born—1734, King George Co., Vir.
Service—Served in King George Co., Vir., Militia, 1778; in Stafford Co., Vir., 1779 and 1782.
Proof—Col. Hansford Threlkeld, U. S. A., retired, Morgansfield, Ky. (descendant).
Died—Killed in action Oct. 22, 1790, in Harmer's defeat at Miami Towns.
Married—Prior to 1786, Mrs. Nellie Long. Ch. Thomas, b. Oct. 30, 1790.
Collected by Mrs. T. J. Hindman, Fort Wayne, Indiana.

THURSTON, JASON   Indiana
Born—1762, Dutchess Co., N. Y.
Service—Enlisted 1778 under Capt. Tate, 1 mo. Entered again for 3 mos. under Capt. Roger Sutherland. Enlisted 1780, N. Y. Levees for 9 mos. under Col. Spaulding, Capt. Levingston.
Proof—Pension claim S. 32556. Ind. certificate 25459.

TIBBETTS, GEORGE   Rush County
Born—1765, Lebanon, York Co., Maine.
Service—Enlisted from Gouldsborough, Maine, in June for 6 mos. under Capt. Reuben Dyer and Lieut. Abraham Allen; 2 yrs. later he enlisted at Bangor, Maine.
Proof—Pension claim R. 10592; Mass. Soldiers and Sailors, vol. 15, p. 726; Bangor Hist. Mag., vol. 4, p. 21; vol. 6, p. 294.
Died—1844. Buried Fairview Cemetery.

Married—Lucretia Doe (1766-1853).
Collected by Mrs. Lucretia Ann Clifford Aneshaensel, 615 East 54th St., Indianapolis, Indiana.

TILFORD, WILLIAM   Jefferson County
Born—Nov. 2, 1750, Rockbridge Co., Vir.
Service—Sergeant in Capt. Samuel McDowell's CO., Col. Andrew Lewis' Vir. Regt.; pri. in Capt. Andrew Moore's CO., Col. John Bowyer's Vir. Regt.; pri. in Capt. Gray's Vir. Regt. at the siege of Yorktown.
Proof—Pension record; D. A. R. No. 225006.
Died—1835. Buried Slippery Point Cemetery, south of Kent.
Married—1780, Isabella Weir. Ch. Samuel, b. 1781; Alexander, b. 1782, m. Elinor McCullough; Mary, b. 1785; Sarah, b. 1787, m. Samuel Maxwell.
Collected by John Paul Chapter D. A. R.

TISDALE, CUDBARD   Daviess County
Born—Nov. 23, 1750, Chesterfield Co., Vir.
Service—Enlisted Mecklenburg Co., Vir., May 4, 1776, Capt. James Anderson's CO., Col. Wm. Meredith's Vir. Regt. Discharged Dec. 20, 1776. Enlisted Jan., 1781, Capt. Asa Oliver's CO., under Major Jones in Vir. Troops. Discharged April 11, 1781. Enlisted Sept. 5, 1781, Capt. Thompson Fulk's CO. in Col. Lewis Burrill's Vir. Regt. Discharged Nov. 1, 1781, in Mecklenburg Co., Vir.
Proof—Pension claim S. 16554.
Buried—Alexander Hill, Veale Twp. Government marker by White River Chapter D. A. R.
Married—Martha ——, d. 1822. Ch. Renison, m. Nancy Pry, and other children.
Collected by Mrs. Roy Bogner, Washington, Indiana.

TODD, JOSEPH   Switzerland County
Service—Inscription on stone reads "Revolutionary Soldier."
Died—1834. Buried Long Run Cemetery. Stone.
Married—First W. unknown. Ch. Nancy, m. James McClanahan; Ruth, m. Stephen Rogers, Jr.; Joseph, Jr., m. Eleanor Lock; John, m. Nancy Lock; David. Second W., Villa McPhearson. Ch. Jesse; Adaline; Catherine.
Collected by Mrs. A. B. Danner, Vevay, Indiana.

TODD, THOMAS   Lawrence County
Born—June 3, 1761, Easton, Penn.
Service—Served 14 mos. Enlisted June 3, 1779. Enlisted from Rowan Co., N. C. Substituted for his brother, Benjamin, 3 mos. Battle of Stone.

Proof—Pension record.
Died—April 5, 1843. Buried Gilgad, near Heltonville. Stone.
Married—Zipphora Conger, b. 1761, d. 1833. Ch. Isaac, b. 1782; Jane, b. 1784, m. Michael Woolery; Jonathan, b. 1786, m. Jane Dodds; Hannah, b. 1788, m. Jacob Woolery; Peter, b. 1791; Daniel, b. 1793; Henry, b. 1796; Thomas, b. 1799; Sally, b. 1801; Moses, b. 1803; Sally, b. 1805, m. William Morran.
Collected by Mrs. B. E. Myers, Connersville, Indiana.

TONEY, JESSE   Floyd County
Born—1760, Albemarle Co., Vir.
Service—Enlisted as pri. under Capt. Holman Rice at Albemarle Barracks, Vir. He was detailed to guard prisoners, Burgoyne's men. Honorably discharged from Col. Taylor, Gen. Bland in command.
Proof—Pension claim W. 11794; B. L. Wt. 101695.
Died—March 17, 1848 or 1849, Floyd Co., Ind.
Married—Second W., Nancy Craig. Ch., but no names given.

TORRONS (TORRENS), SAMUEL   Hamilton County
Born—About 1757, New Castle Co., Del.
Service—While residing in Berkeley Co., Vir., he volunteered 1777, served over 3 mos. as 1st Sergt. in Capt. William Morgan's Vir. CO. Later served 3 mos. as 1st Sergt. in Capt. Nicholas McIntire's CO., Col. Scott's Vir. Regt.
Proof—Pension claim W. 9860.
Died—Jan. 17, 1836.
Married—1785, Anna ———. Ch. Elizabeth, b. 1787; Nancy, b. 1789, m. William McCaw. Possibly other children.

TOWER, GIDEON   Dearborn County
Born—April 11, 1753, Cumberland, Providence Co., R. I.
Service—Enlisted 1775 in CO. of Conn. Militia under Capt. Cleft, Parson's Regt.; 1776, pri. in CO. of R. I. Troops, under Capt. Wilcox, Dyer's Regt.; 1778, substitute; 1779, pri. in CO. of Vt. Militia, Capt. Noble; 1780, orderly-sergt. in CO. of Vt. Militia, Capt. Hutchins.
Proof—Pension claim S. 1735.
Died—1847. Probably buried in Ceasar Creek Twp.
Married—1775, wife unknown, had 13 ch.; John and Gideon are only names known.
Collected by Mrs. Walter Kerr, Aurora, Indiana.

TOWNSEND, JOHN   Wayne County
Born—1763, Penn.
Service—Served under Gen. Greene for 3 yrs. Enlisted at the age of 17, pri. of the 2nd class.

Proof—Fox's History of Wayne Co., p. 492; History of Wayne Co., 1884, p. 678.
Died—1853. Buried Quaker Cemetery at Middleboro; later moved to cemetery at Fountain City, Ind.
Married—Elvira Cain, b. 1767. Ch. Stephen, b. 1810 (youngest child).
Collected by Mrs. Paul L. Ross, Richmond, Indiana.

TOWNSEND, WILLIAM Morgan County
Born—April 5, 1760, N. C.
Service—Pri. in N. C. Troops. Enlisted for 9 mos., Mecklenburg Co., N. C. Served under Gen. Ashe, Col. Archibald, Capts. James Jack, Goodman, Craig, Cowan, Thomas Harris, Gen. Gabes, Capts. Wm. Hughston and Reese.
Proof—Pension claim S. 17152.

TRACY, SOLOMON Bartholomew County
Born—About 1759.
Service—Enlisted Halifax Co., Vir., 1781, under Capt. Thomas Bowyer in Col. Campbell's Regt., Vir. Cont'l Line. Discharged 1782 at Salisbury, N. C. In battles at Guilford Court House, Camden and Eutaw Springs.
Proof—Pension claim S. 36830.
Died—1839. Buried Liberty Cemetery, near Clifford, Ind.
Family—Had wife and 2 children in 1820.

TRAMEL, SAMPSON Morgan County
Service—Pri. in N. C. Troops. Enlisted first in Rutherford Co., N. C., and later 1781 in S. C. Served under Col. Wm. Grimes, Lt. George Taylor, Col. Middleton and Capt. Philip Waters.
Proof—Pension claim W. 6313.
Died—March 28, 1838, Morgan Co., Ind.
Married—Susan ——.

TRINKLE, CHRISTOPHER Washington County
Born—About 1751, Montgomery Co., Vir.
Service—Enlisted in 1777 as pri. in the Vir. Line and served 5 yrs. under Capts. Triplett, Sirbling, Sheperd, Col. Campbell. In battles of Brandywine, Camden, Roolsford, Grueford and Eutaw Springs.
Proof—Pension claim S. 36829; Patton Genealogy.
Died—March, 1820. Buried Trinkle Farm.
Married—Elizabeth Hickman. Ch. Elizabeth, m. Sampson Patton; Stephen; Polly, m. Burris, Clark, Kester; Henry, m. —— Shellabarger; John; Fred, m. Sallie Hickman; Adam, m. Hannah Rutherford; Jacob, m. Peggy Hickman.
Collected by Mrs. Mattie Hardin McKrill, Decatur, Indiana.

TROUT, ANTHONY DANIEL   Harrison County
Born—Dec. 12, 1751.
Service—Enlisted while resident of Tyron Co., N. C., 1777, and served
    5 yrs. Served in Capt. Henry Hampton's CO., Col. Sumter's A. C.
    Regt. Was in battles of Charlestown, Eutaw Springs, where he
    was wounded, and at Guilford Court House. Served 6 mos. in
    Col. Elijah Clarke's G. Regt.
Proof—Pension claim W. 9863.
Died—1844.
Buried—Luther's Chapel Cemetery. Stone.
Married—1790, Mary Catharine Grubb (1766-1870). Ch. Catharine Elizabeth, b. 1791, m. James Vaughn; Mary, b. 1799, m. John Blume;
    David, b. 1802, m. Harriet Conrad; Marion Sophier, b. 1808.
Collected by Hoosier Elm Chapter D. A. R.

TRUE (TREW), ARTHUR   Randolph County
Service—Inscription on stone reads "War 1776."
Died—Dec. 12, 1857. Buried New Pittsburg Church Cemetery. Stone.
Married—Phebe ——.
Collected by Mrs. James P. Goodrich and Mrs. Oren Ross, Winchester,
    Indiana.

TRUE, ROBERT   Clark County
Born—1758, Spotsylvania Co., Vir.
Service—Enlisted in Spotsylvania Co., Vir., Oct., 1776, as pri. in Capt.
    Francis Taliferro's CO., Col. Thos. Towles' Vir. Regt. Discharged
    Oct., 1777. Enlisted in March, 1778, served 3 mos. as pri. in
    Capt. John Craig's CO. Enlisted Aug., 1781, in Capt. Thomas
    Clayton's CO., Col. Merriwether's Regt. Present at Yorktown.
Proof—Pension claim W. 9526.
Died—Aug. 7, 1833, in Jefferson Co., Ind. Buried Bethlehem Cemetery,
    in Clark Co.
Married—1777, Nancy Crookshank (1760-1842). Ch. Mary Ann, b. 1778,
    m. James West; Ezikiel, b. 1780, d. 1832; John, b. 1784; Lucy, b.
    1786, d. 1832; Robert, b. 1788; James, b. 1790; Nancy, b. 1792;
    Elizabeth, b. 1794, d. 1833; Phebe, b. 1798.
Collected by John Paul Chapter D. A. R.

TRUSLER, JAMES   Franklin County
Born—Nov. 7, 1755, Amherst Co., Vir.
Service—Pri. for 7 mos. in Vir. Regt. under Capt. Ezeriah Martin,
    Col. Smith.
Proof—Pension claim W. 9528.
Died—Sept. 5, 1844. Buried Ebenezer Cemetery, Blooming Grove Twp.

Married—1776, Susannah Wilson (1775-1852). Ch. Sarah, b. 1782, m. John Adair; Edmund, b. 1804, m. Parmelia Moore; John; Samuel Wilson, b. 1795, m. Martha Curry; and 7 others' names unknown.
Collected by Mrs. Irene Baumheckel (descendant), Connersville, Indiana.

TUCKER, JOHN   Parke County
Born—1751, Gloucester, R. I.
Service—Enlisted as a Minute Man under Capt. Stephen Winsor, and served 4 mos. 18 days in 1776; 3 mos. 9 days in 1777; 2 mos. in 1778; 40 days in 1779. This service under Capt. Aaron Arnold, Capt. May and Col. Chad Brown in R. I. Troops.
Proof—Pension claim S. 17739. Pension allowed 1832 while living in Liberty Twp., Parke Co.

TUCKER, JOHN, SR.   Ripley County
Born—About 1753.
Service—Enlisted June, 1782, as pri. in Capts. Brinkley's and John Coleman's CO., Col. Archibald Lytle's N. C. Regt. Battles of Eutaw Springs and James Island. Discharged July, 1783.
Died—Dec. 20, 1840. Buried near New Marion. Name on bronze tablet in Versailles Court House.
Married—First W. unknown. Second W., 1833, Mary ———. Had 2 sons.
Collected by Mrs. A. B. Wycoff, Batesville, Indiana.

TUCKER, THOMAS   Putnam County
Born—Feb. 11, 1757, Halifax Co., N. C.
Service—Enlisted as a Volunteer Militia Man in March or April, 1779, under Capt. Hardy Griffin, from Nash Co., N. C. In July, 1781, enlisted under Capt. Kidand, served 1 yr. guarding and defending the town of Halifax.
Proof—Pension claim S. 16556.
Died—1840.
Children—Amos; Thomas; Benjamin; Solomon; Piety (1798-1873); Amy; Elizabeth and Rachel.
Collected by Ft. Harrison Chapter D. A. R.

TUCKER, WILLIAM   Allen County
Born—July 2, 1761, Maryland.
Service—While residing in Mecklenburg Co., N. C., enlisted May, 1780, as pri. in Capt. David Wilson's CO., Col. Mathew Lock's N. C. Regt. In the battles of Gates' Defeat, Cowan's Ford, Guilford Court House. Wounded.
Proof—Pension claim R. 18574 (rejected because he did not serve 6 mos.). N. C. Archives show his heirs received land for his services.

Died—Sept. 30, 1846. Buried Huntertown Cemetery. Stone.
Children—John; James; Thomas, b. 1810; Samuel.
Collected by Mrs. T. J. Hindman, Fort Wayne, Indiana.

TUFFS, WILLIAM   Elkhart County
Born—Sept. 20, 1740, near Boston, Mass.
Service—Enlisted from Mystic, Mass., April, 1775, and served 3 mos. in Capt. Wm. Wentworth's CO., Col. Gill's Mass. Regt. Enlisted May, 1776, in Capt. Cornelius Sanford's Mass. CO. Later served 3 mos. in Capt. Samuel Tucker's Mass. CO., and was in battle of Rhode Island.
Proof—Pension claim S. 32026.
Died—Sept. 19, 1848, aged 108 yrs. Buried Bonneyville Cemetery, E. of Bristol. S. A. R. marker.
Married—Wife unknown. Son, John. Eliza Dexter of Elkhart Co. made affidavit that she was a granddaughter.
Collected by Mrs. F. C. Wherly, Elkhart, Indiana.

TULL, HANDY   Jefferson County
Service—Served under Capt. Henry Shade, 1st Battalion Riflemen, under Col. Brodhead, Penn. Regt.
Proof—Penn. Archives, 5th Series, vol. 2.
Died—After 1830.
Married—Eleanor ———. Ch. Anna M., m. William Smith.
Collected by John Paul Chapter D. A. R.

TULLIS, MICHAEL   Franklin County
Born—Feb., 1756, New Jersey.
Service—Enlisted for 1 yr. in Berkeley Co., Vir., under Capt. Hugh Stinson, 8th Regt. Inf., Col. Wm. Darke. 1776 enlisted again in 8th Regt. under Capt. Daniel Culp for 3 yrs. In battles at Staten Island, Brandywine and Germantown.
Proof—Pension claim W. 26558.
Died—About 1832 in Franklin Co., Ind., according to statement of widow.
Married—1791, Elizabeth Jones. Soldier stated he had 18 children. Widow's record shows Moses, b. 1792; Thomas B., b. 1794; Samuel, b. 1796; David, b. 1800; Isaac, b. 1802; Aaron, b. 1804; Mary, b. 1807.
Collected by Mrs. Orville Dailey, Albany, Ohio.

TURNER, ROBERT   Ohio County
Born—Oct. 8, 1760, Penn.
Service—Volunteered in Chester Co., Penn., under Capt. James McDowell, Col. Montgomery, using his own team. He was wagon master 1778-1781 under Henry Saunderson.

Proof—Pension claim R. 10762; D. A. R. No. 29138.
Died—1838. Buried at Aberdeen.
Married—Ann Carlisle (1760-1850). Had a son.

TURNER, SMITH   Switzerland County
Born—1750.
Service—Enlisted 1776 under Capt. Thomas Palmer of 9th Vir. Regt. under Gen. Muhlenburg, served to March, 1778. Discharged by Gen. Muhlenburg at Valley Forge. In battles of Brandywine and Germantown.
Proof—Pension claim S. 36832.
Died—March 7, 1831. Probably buried in Jefferson Twp.
Married—Abigail ———. Had a daughter.

TURNHAM, THOMAS   Spencer County
Born—1749, Tennessee.
Service—Enlisted 1775, served in Capt. Wm. Taliaferro's CO., Col. Woodford's 2nd Vir. Regt. In 1776 served in Col. Steven's Vir. Regt. Was in battles of Norfolk, Brandywine, Germantown, Monmouth, Savannah, Cowpens and at Yorktown. Discharged Oct. 25, 1781.
Proof—Pension claim S. 36831.
Died—Oct. 28, 1834. Buried near Dale and Lincoln City, Carter Twp.
Married—Second W., Eva Liston. Ch. David, b. 1805, m. Mary Emmick and Nancy Jones; Betsey.
Collected by Miss Laura M. Wright, Rockport, Indiana.

TURPIN, FRANCOIS   Knox County
Service—A Patriot. Signed Oath of Allegiance to the State of Virginia, July 20, 1778. Name appears as Francois Turpans.
Proof—Clark's Papers; Ill. Hist. Coll., vol. VIII, pp. 52-59.
Died—After May 9, 1795. Buried Cathedral Cemetery.
Married—Josette Levront. Ch. Rosalie, bapt. 1791, m. Charles Grimard; other children.
Collected by Mrs. Leo Schultheis, Vincennes, Indiana.

TURPIN, OBEDIETH (OBADIAH)   Hendricks County
Born—1761, Prince Edward Co., Vir.
Service—Enlisted from Vir. in spring of 1779 and served in Capt. Richard Worsham's CO., Col. Merriwether's Vir. Regt. Marched to Petersburg, then served as wagoner, went to Charleston, S. C., and continued in service 18 mos. In 1781 served 3 mos. in Capt. Francis De Graffenreid's CO. and later 3 mos. in Capt. Jary's or Gery's CO. Discharged after surrender of Cornwallis.
Buried—East Cemetery, Danville, Ind.

TUTTLE, ENOS   Clark County
Born—Aug. 11, 1762, New Haven, Conn.
Service—Pri. in CO. commanded by Capt. Todd of Col. Lyon's Regt., Conn. Line, 15 mos. Enlisted July, 1779.
Proof—Pension claim S. 17740; Collection of Conn. Hist. Society, vol. 12, p. 34.
Died—1843. Buried on his farm near Memphis. Stone.
Married—Candace Hotchkiss, b. 1763. Ch. Lewis; Enos Starling; Maria; Solomon; probably others.
Collected by C. C. Wamsley, 229 S. Berendo St., Los Angeles, California.

ULRICH, JOHN   Wayne County
Born—Oct. 14, 1764, Germany.
Service—A pri. on a general return of the First Partisan Legion under Col. Armand Marquis De La Rouerie, with the altercations that happened from Jan. 1 to July 1, 1782. Enlisted April 11, 1778.
Proof—Penn. Archives, vol. 3, pp. 857-872.
Died—Aug. 23, 1838. Buried Ulrich Cemetery, near Hagerstown, Ind. Stone.
Married—Christana Brombaugh. Ch. Daniel; John; David; Jacob; Christana; Elizabeth.
Collected by Mrs. Virginia Falls Beeson, Cambridge City, Indiana.

UPDIKE, ISAAC   Franklin County
Born—1762, New Jersey.
Service—Pri. in Capt. James Moore's CO., 2nd Regt., Somerset Militia, 1777, 1778 and 1780. Received certificate from Quartermaster General's Department for carting in the Rev. War.
Proof—Adjutant General's Office at Trenton, N. J.
Died—1825. Buried in Franklin Co., Ind.
Married—1784, Nancy ——. Ch. Peter, b. 1784, m. Nancy Smith; Elijah, b. 1791, m. Elizabeth Snook; Lutetia, b. 1795, m. Samuel Smith; Elizabeth, b. 1798, m. Abraham Smalley.
Collected by Mrs. H. S. McKee, Greensburg, Indiana.

URTON (ERTON), PETER   Orange County
Born—April 22, 1765, Fairfax Co., Vir.
Service—Enlisted March, 1781. Served 3 mos. 20 days as pri. in Capt. Charles Little's CO., Col. Ramsey's Vir. Regt. Served 3 mos. 10 days in Capt. O'Bannion's CO., Col. Churie's Vir. Regt.
Proof—Pension claim S. 16561.
Died—Soldier's Will probated Nov. 28, 1835. Buried on Old Bedster Farm in N. West Twp. Stone. Government marker placed by Lost River Chapter D. A. R.
Children—As named in Will—Matilda, m. Thomas Bedster; Henry.
Collected by Mrs. N. B. Mavity, French Lick, Indiana.

UTTER, ABRAHAM   Boone County
Born—May 9, 1765, Boston, Mass.
Service—While residing in Cumberland Co., Penn., he enlisted May 1,
    1777, as pri. in Capt. Dougherty's Penn. CO. Went on Gen. Sullivan's Indian expedition for 6 mos. Enlisted 1780 or 1781 for 2
    mos. in Capt. McCallister's Penn. CO. Enlisted March, 1782,
    served 2 mos. 14 days in Capt. Harrell's Penn. CO.
Proof—Pension claim S. 32563.
Died—Jan. 14, 1851. Buried Cox Cemetery, Boone Co. Stone.
Married—Martha Lycan. Ch. Samuel (1792-1863), m. 1816, Jane Vance;
    Jane, m. Samuel Moore.
Collected by James Hill Chapter D. A. R.

UTTERBACK, BENJAMIN   Morgan County
Born—1755, Fauquier Co., Vir.
Service—Enlisted at Fauquier Co., Vir., Court House, Oct., 1777. Served
    as Orderly-Sergeant in Capt. Elias Edmond's CO. and Capt. Samuel Blackwell's CO., Col. Thomas Marshall's Vir. Regt. Marched
    to Williamsburg and from there fought in many battles in the
    South as a gunner in the artillery. Discharged at Hillsboro, N. C.,
    1780.
Proof—Pension record. The original discharge papers are now in Virginia State Archives at Richmond, Vir.
Died—About 1842. Buried on Cherry Farm, 5 miles E. of Gosport,
    Ind. Government marker placed by Miss Ura Sanders.
Married—1780, Elizabeth Snelling. Ch. James Benjamin (1790-1836),
    m. 1820, Mariam Collett; Nancy; Joel.
Collected by Mr. William I. Utterback, 1810 Kite Ave., Huntington,
    West Virginia.

VANARSDALL, LAWRENCE (LAURENCE)   Hendricks County
Born—Near Somerset Court House, New Jersey.
Service—Enlisted in May, 1776, Princeton, N. J., and served 6 mos. in
    Capt. Wm. Piatt's CO., Col. Forman's N. J. Regt. Was in battle
    of Long Island. Was a Minute Man. Drove a baggage wagon
    under Capt. Beatty from Trenton to Valley Forge.
Proof—Pension claim W. 6359.
Died—March 10 or 12, 1836, Hendricks Co.
Married—First W. unknown. Son, Laurence. Second W., Mrs. Tabitha
    Curry.
Collected by Mrs. Ira E. Tranter, Franklin, Indiana.

VAN BIBBER, PETER   Ripley County
Born—1757.
Service—Enlisted from Vir. in Oct., 1775. Discharged in June, 1777.
    Served 1 yr. 8 mos. Re-enlisted Nov., 1780. Discharged Sept.,
    1781. Drafted July, 1782, for 6 mos. Discharged Nov., 1782.

Proof—Pension claim S. 32566.
Children—Sarah, m. John Yocum; Rachel, m. Samuel Kincart.
Collected by Mrs. A. B. Wycoff, Batesville, Indiana.

VAN BUSKIRK, ISAAC — Monroe County
Born—Oct. 7, 1760, Loudoun Co., Vir.
Service—Pri. in Vir. Militia. Enlisted in 1778 and served 1 yr. under Capt. Wallace. In battle of Monmouth.
Proof—Pension record; inscription on stone.
Died—Oct. 27, 1843. Buried Van Buskirk Cemetery, near Gosport, Ind. Stone. Bronze marker by Bloomington Chapter D. A. R.
Married—Jerusha Little. Ch. James; Isaac; John; Michiel; Absolem; William; Polly; Sallie; Priscilla; Jerusha.
Collected by Ora Van Buskirk, Gosport, Indiana.

VANCLEAVE, JOHN — Jefferson County
Born—New Jersey.
Service—Served as pri. in Capt. Chenoweth's CO. of Jefferson Co., Ky., Militia on tour of duty at building of Fort Nelson, April 20 to May 12, 1782. Served in Ky. Militia in 1780. Received military grant from Vir: in 1790 for 300 acres on Muddy River.
Proof—Illinois Papers have name on payroll of Capt. Chenoweth's CO.; Will in Jefferson Co., Ind.
Died—May, 1812, in Jefferson Co., Ind.
Married—First W., Mary Shepard, d. 1781. Ch. Rachel; John; Elizabeth; Aaron; Benjamin; Nancy and Sallie (twins). Second W., Mrs. Rachel Ryker. Soldier's Will also names sons, Peter and David.
Collected by John Paul Chapter D. A. R.

VAN DALSEM, HENRY — LaPorte County
Born—Aug. 12, 1757, New York City.
Service—Served as follows: fall of 1775 to June, 1776, as pri. under Capt. Wm. W. Gilbert, N. Y. Troops; June, 1776, for 5 mos. as pri. under Capt. Viner VanZandt, Col. John Lasher, N. Y. Troops; Jan., 1777, for 1 mo. as pri. under Capt. Abraham Blauvelt, Col. Day; April, 1777, 1 mo. as pri. under Capt. Hogancamp; July, 1777, 1 yr. as Orderly-Sergt. under Capt. Abraham Haring, N. J. Troops.
Proof—Pension records. Applied from Fayette Co., Ind.
Died—March 10, 1835. Buried Oak Grove Cemetery, Wills Twp. Stone. S. A. R. marker.
Married—1781, Eunice Zabriskie, b. 1759. Ch. William.
Collected by Miss Margaret Oakes and Dr. S. Arthur Stewart, LaPorte, Indiana.

VANDERBURGH, HENRY   Knox County
Born—1760, Troy, N. Y.
Service—Capt. of 2nd Regt. of Cont'l Troops in N. Y. Enlisted and
    appointed Lieut. 1776. Made Capt. 1780. Was one of the origi-
    nal members of the Society of Cincinnati.
Proof—Heitman's Historical Register, p. 555.
Died—April 12, 1812. Buried at Bellevue, now suburb of Burnett
    Heights, Vincennes, Ind.
Married—Frances Cornoyer (1775-1860). Ch. Julia; Cornelia; Helen,
    m. George Rogers Clark Sullivan; Elizabeth; Mary; Sydney;
    Henry; James; Ferdinand; Frances, b. 1810, m. Joseph Somes.
Collected by Mrs. S. G. Davenport, Vincennes, Indiana.

VAN DEVANTER, BARNABAS   Grant County
Born—1761, Bucks Co., Penn.
Service—Enlisted 1778, 1779, 1781 from Rockingham Co., Vir., as a pri.
    in the lower Rockingham Regt. under Capt. Abraham Lincoln, Col.
    Harrison. Present at Yorktown and in McIntosh Campaign.
Proof—Furnished by Hon. Willis Van Devanter, Judge of the Supreme
    Court of U. S.
Died—Jan. 4, 1851. Buried on Paxton Farm, E. of Veterans' Hospital.
Married—1801, Elizabeth Siler. Ch. Christian; Elizabeth; and others.
Collected by Mrs. Charles A. Priest, Marion, Indiana.

VANDEVENTER, PETER   Harrison County
Born—About 1740.
Service—Pri. in Capt. Savage's Vir. Line. Enlisted at Millerstown, Vir.
Proof—Pension claim S. 36833.

VAN SANTE, JOHN   Parke County
Born—May, 1762, Fishkill, Dutchess Co., N. Y.
Service—Pri. in CO. commanded by Capt. Wright, Col. Courtland's N. Y.
    Regt. Served 12 mos. 5 days.
Proof—Pension claim S. 17172.

VAN WINKLE, JOHN   Franklin County
Born—March 16, 1754, Essex Co., N. Y.
Service—Enlisted Jan., 1776, as pri. under Capts. Jonathan Parsons,
    Britten and Aaron Clark, Cols. Dayton, Ogden, Spencer and Bar-
    ber in N. J. Troops. Discharged Dec., 1781. In battles of Tren-
    ton, Princeton, Brandywine, Germantown, Monmouth, Conn. Farms,
    Springfield, Yorktown.
Proof—Pension claim S. 32564.
Died—After 1833. Buried on Louis Hinds Farm.

VAWTER, JESSE   Jefferson County
Born—Dec. 2, 1755, Vir.
Service—Enlisted 1777 in Capt. John Camp's CO., 1st Vir. Regt., under
    Col. George Gibson.
Proof—Vir. Mag. of History and Biography 1893-1894; D. A. R. No.
    113765.
Died—March 20, 1838. Buried Wirt Cemetery. Government marker
    placed by John Paul Chapter D. A. R.
Married—1781, Elizabeth Watts (1762-1830). Ch. Frances, b. 1785, m.
    John Branham; Mary, b. 1787, m. Linsfield Branham; John, m.
    four times; William, m. Frances Vawter; James, m. Sarah Watts;
    Sarah, m. Thomas Stribling; Julia, m. Matthew Wise; Achilles, m.
    Martha Smith; Ann, m. Abner Moncrief.
Collected by John Paul Chapter D. A. R.

VEALE, JAMES CARR   Daviess County
Born—March, 1763, Loudoun Co., Vir.
Service—Volunteered in Chester Dist., S. C., as a pri. in Capt. Hol-
    lingsworth's CO., Col. Brandon's S. C. Regt. Served to close of
    war.
Proof—Pension claim W. 9586.
Died—Jan. 4, 1839. Buried on farm now owned by T. C. Singleton,
    Veale Twp. Government marker placed by White River Chapter
    D. A. R.
Married—1782, Lavina Towns. Ch. James Carr, Jr., b. 1786, m. Eleanor
    Aikman; Daniel, m. Mary Coleman; Catherine, m. James Arrell
    and Reuben Kilgore; Alsey, m. Josiah Wallace; Nancy, m. James
    Lett; William, m. Elizabeth Stephenson.
Collected by Mrs. Roy Bogner, Washington, Indiana.

VEST, SAMUEL   Washington County
Born—April 7, 1759.
Service—Enlisted Bedford Co., Vir., 1779, under Capt. James Adams,
    Lieut. Mathew Artee, Col. Wm. Callaway. Called to guard lead
    mines in Vir. Served 3 mos. 12 days, Nov., 1779. Enlisted as a
    drafted militiaman under Capt. Robert Adams and served less
    than 9 mos.
Proof—Pension claim S. 16563.
Died—After 1840. Buried Cavetown Cemetery, N. of Campbellsburg.
    Stone.
Married—Jane ——. Ch. Samuel, Jr., and others.
Collected by Mrs. Harvey Morris, Salem, Indiana.

VIGO, FRANCIS   Knox County
Born—1747, Italy.
Service—A Patriot. Furnished funds for the campaign of Gen. George
    Rogers Clarke upon Vincennes.

Proof—"Vigo, the Forgotten Patriot," by Dr. Rosseli.
Died—1836. Buried Greenlawn Cemetery, Vincennes, Ind. Stone placed by Francis Vigo Chapter D. A. R.
Married—Elizabeth Shannon. No children.
Collected by Miss Frances Lloyd, Vincennes, Indiana.

VINCENT, JOHN   Franklin County
Born—Aug. 24, 1750, London, England.
Service—Enlisted from Culpepper Co., Vir. Received 200 acres of land for service for 3 yrs. as a corporal in Vir. Cont'l Line. Made a Lieut. of Militia of Hampshire Co., Vir., March 15, 1782.
Proof—Pension record S. 16566; McCallister's "Virginia Militia in the Rev.," p. 293.
Died—Jan. 26, 1837. Buried on Stoops Farm, Brookville Twp.
Married—Sarah Johnson (1758-1822). Ch. Nancy; Beckey; Caty; Betsey; Polly; William; Jeremiah; Samuel; Sarah; John.
Collected by Harry M. Stoops (deceased).

VOORHEES, GARRET   Martin County
Born—March 11, 1748.
Service—Enlisted Sussex Co. Court House, N. J., April 20, 1777, as pri. in Capt. Abraham Lyons' CO., 4th N. J. Regt.; transferred to 2nd Regt., 1779. Discharged at New Windsor, N. Y., 1783.
Proof—Pension claim S. 47189.
Died—Dec. 20, 1848. Buried Old Salem Cemetery, McCameron Twp. Inscription on stone reads "Garit Voris, born March 11, 1748, died Dec. 20, 1848, a Soldier of the Revolution."
Collected by Mrs. N. B. Mavity, French Lick, Indiana, and Mr. Oscar Boruff, Owensville, Indiana.

WALDEN, JOHN, SR.   Putnam County
Born—March 6 or 8, 1756, Middlesex Co., Vir.
Service—While residing in Middlesex Co., Vir. Enlisted in the Vir. Troops during the summer of 1777 and served to the end of the war (1783) as a pri. He served under Capts. Thos. Ewell, Spellman, Dudley, Augustin Tabb, Eggleston and Armstrong, and under Cols. William Brent, Abraham Buford and Henry Lee. He was in the battles of Monmouth, Stony Point and the Evacuation of Charleston.
Proof—Pension claim W. 9878.
Died—Dec. 22, 1835. Buried Manhattan Cemetery, S. W. of Greencastle. Stone.
Married—Mary Collins. Ch. Sallie; John; Henry; Elizabeth; Richard; Dollie; Nancy; Patsy.
Collected by Beulah Long, Greencastle, Indiana.

WALKER, JOHN Posey County
Born—Dec., 1754, Antrim Co., Ireland.
Service—Enlisted 1775 from Chester District, S. C., and served as pri. in Capt. Michael Dixon's CO., Col. Edward Lacy's Regt., S. C. Troops. Served other enlistments under different commands.
Proof—Pension claim W. 9875.
Died—Oct. 14, 1844. Buried family graveyard, near Stewartsville. Stone. Bronze marker placed by New Harmony Chapter D. A. R.
Married—1790, Nancy Stuart (Stewart), (1761-1853). Ch. John; Joseph; Margaret; William (1802-1880); and three others.
Collected by Mrs. Charles T. Johnson, Mt. Vernon, Indiana.

WALKER, OBADIAH Jackson County
Born—May, 1760.
Service—Enlisted at Wyoming, Penn., Sept. 2, 1776; served in Capt. Robert Durkee's Independent CO. and in Capts. Simon Spalding's and Benton's COS. Col. Durkee's 1st Conn. Regt. In battles at King's Bridge, N. Y., Millstone, Bound Brook, Mud Fort and Monmouth, N. J. Discharged at West Point, June 10, 1783. Served as pri. and as non-commissioned officers and received two badges of merit.
Proof—Pension claim S. 36834. Owned land in Grassy Fork Twp., Jackson Co., in 1837.
Wife—Elizah ——.
Collected by Mrs. D. J. Cummings, Brownstown, Indiana.

WALKER, SAMUEL Wayne County
Born—1758, Rockbridge Co., Vir.
Service—Pri. in Vir. Troops; in the fall of 1777 or 1778, for 3 mos. in Capt. Wm. Paxton's CO., and soon after this he served 3 mos. in Capt. Charles Campbell's CO., Col. Downman's Regt. He served at various times as a spy in Capt. William McConnell's Co., amounting in all to 6 mos.
Proof—Rev. War claim S. 16567.
Collected by Mrs. Paul L. Ross, Richmond, Indiana.

WALL, WILLIAM Madison County
Born—1758, Vir.
Service—Entered in Capt. Morgan's CO., Col. Wood's Regt., Vir. Line. In Col. Taylor's Regt. 2 yrs.
Proof—Pension claim S. 17179; D. A. R. Lineage 59, p. 103.
Married—Nancy Elkins. Ch. Martha Ellen, m. Zimre Moon.

WALLACE (WALLIS), BENJAMIN Delaware County
Born—Jan. 12, 1758, Caswell Co., N. C.
Service—Pri. in CO. of Capt. Sanders, Maj. Taylor's Regt. of N. C. Line, 11 mos.

Proof—Pension claim S. 32571.
Died—Aug. 24, 1838. Buried Miller Cemetery, Harrison Twp.
Married—Mary ——. Ch. Ann, b. 1774; David B., b. 1776; William, b. 1778; Mary (1780-1782); John, b. 1782; Sarah, b. 1785; Zebulum, b. 1787; Ruth, b. 1789; Benjamin, b. 1792; Jane, b. 1794; Joseph, b. 1797; Polly, b. 1801.
Collected by Mrs. Lue R. Spencer, Washington, D. C.

WALLACE, JOHN   Daviess County
Born—1754.
Service—Enlisted in Fredericksburg, Vir., in 9th and 11th Troops, Western Division, in Gen. John Gibson's Detachment; discharged March 29, 1780.
Proof—W. F. R. Laffel's record of Rev. War, second column, p. 282.
Died—1822. Buried Old Bethel, Shanks Cemetery. Government marker. Placed by White River Chapter D. A. R.
Married—Elinor Morgan. Ch. William, b. 1786, m. Sarah Horrall; Mary, m. Moses Morgan; Nancy Calvert, m. Thomas Horrall; Josiah, m. Elsie Veale; Elizabeth, m. Jesse Chapman; Nicholas, m. Mary Ballow; Coleman, m. Sarah Chapman; Wesley, m. —— McKinley and Rachel Chapman; Morgan, m. Elizabeth Ballow; Sarah, m. John Newcomb.
Collected by Mrs. Roy Bogner, Washington, Indiana.

WALLACE, JOHN   Owen County
Born—About 1746.
Service—Pri. N. C. Militia. Enlisted 1777 for 3 yrs., Duplin Co., N. C., under Capt. Joseph Rhodes, Capt. Charles Steward, Col. Patton, Capt. Armstrong, Gen. DeKalb.
Proof—Pension claim W. 25897; B. L. Wt. 18209-160-55.
Died—Aug. 24, 1834. Buried Owen Co.
Married—First W. unknown. Ch. Mary Ann; Ellen; John; Geo. Washington. Second W., Frances Meador (widow with 3 children). Ch. Isaac; Elias H.; Angus R.; John; Eli H.

WALLACE, NATHANIEL   Jefferson County
Born—1752, in Maryland.
Service—Penn. records show service in Washington Co. Name occurs in several companies.
Proof—Certified copy of Oath of Allegiance, Montgomery Co., Md. Penn. Archives, 5th Series, vol. 3-956; vol. 15-2-2364.
Died—Jan. 24, 1841. Buried Greenbriar Cemetery, N. of Hanover. Stone.
Married—Mary Wallace. Ch. Mary, m. 1806, Amos Butler; Frances, m. David Loring; Ann, m. Richard Loring; Nathaniel.
Collected by John Paul Chapter D. A. R.

WALLS, JOHN   Putnam County
Born—April 4, 1762, in York Co., Penn.
Service—Enlisted at York Co., Penn., 1776, for 1 yr. as Drummer; 1780 for 6 mos. Served under Capts. James Wright and William Wall, and Col. Henry Miller, also Capt. John Washington. Was wounded on the head in the battle of Germantown.
Proof—Pension claim S. 17762.
Died—1836. Buried Old Cemetery, Greencastle. Stone. A government marker. Name on bronze tablet in Putnam Co. Court House.
Married—Mary or Elizabeth Patterson. Ch. Washington; Jefferson; Clinton; Elizabeth; Lucy; Sarah.
Collected by Lela Esther Walls, Greencastle, Indiana.

WARD, DANIEL   Union County
Born—1763, Morris Co., N. J.
Service—Served as Minute Man in Morris Co., N. J. Later served with "Jersey Blues" and again as pri. in N. Y. Troops under Capt. Lynn and Col. McDougal. In the battle of Springfield and Short Hills.
Proof—Pension claim S. 36836.
Died—About 1825. Probably buried in Union County.
Married—Ruth Bigelow. Ch. Jonathan, b. 1808, m. Mary A. Hammil.
Collected by Benjamin Du Bois Chapter D. A. R.

WARD, JOHN   Cass County
Born—Aug. 24, 1752, Morristown, N. J.
Service—Enlisted at Morristown, N. J., 1776, in Capt. Benoni Hathaway's Regt. under Capts. Augustine Bayles and Marshal, Col. Seeley.
Proof—New Jersey Archives; inscription on stone.
Died—May 13, 1839. Buried in Spring Creek Christian Cemetery, Clay Twp. Stone. Government marker.
Married—1806, Pamelia Bridge (1779-1820). Ch. Samuel, b. 1784; Sarah Richardson, b. 1788; William; John, Jr., b. 1800; Thomas; Pamelia; Julia Bennet; Elizabeth Sellers, b. 1803. Soldier m. second to Elizabeth Shipman.
Collected by Miss Laura D. Henderson, Logansport, Indiana.

WARD, JOHN   Ripley County
Born—1760, North Carolina.
Service—While living in Surry Co., N. C., entered service Nov., 1777, for 3 mos. as a substitute. Served short time as volunteer in N. C. Militia under Gen. Rutherford, Col. Bernard, Capt. Henry Smith, Col. Isaac, Capt. Bostick, Col. Little. In battle of Camden, S. C.

Proof—Pension claim S. 16284. Since Rev., resided in Ky. and Tenn. and Ripley Co., Ind.
Buried—Near Versailles, Ind. Name on bronze tablet Versailles Court House.
Collected by Mrs. A. B. Wycoff, Batesville, Indiana.

WARD, THOMAS — Randolph County
Born—May 3, 1759, in Guilford Co., N. C.
Service—Enlisted 1777 as pri. in Capt. Depon's CO., 1st Regt., N. C., Col. Thomas Clark.
Proof—N. C. Rev. Soldier, vol. XII, p. 70, folio 4; p. 71 and folio 1. Land Grant N. C. Record.
Died—Feb. 11, 1839. Buried White River Cemetery, near Winchester. Stone.
Married—Mary Margery Pigott (1759-1843). Ch. Sarah, m. Joshua Moffet; Nancy, m. Ellis Kizer; Margery; Mary, m. Joseph Moffet; Elizabeth, m. Burkett Pierce; Joel; Joab; Lydia, m. Thos. Pierce.
Collected by Mrs. James P. Goodrich and Mrs. Oren Ross, Winchester, Indiana.

WARD, TIMOTHY — Ohio County
Born—March 10, 1760, Essex Co., N. J.
Service—Drafted in Capt. Reeves CO., Col. Courtland's Regt., spring of 1777, in N. J. Battles of Springfield, Conn., Fields, Elizabethtown, Second River.
Proof—Pension claim S. 1775.
Died—June 3, 1845. Buried Olive Branch Graveyard, Pike Twp. Stone.
Collected by Mrs. Walter Kerr, Aurora, Indiana.

WARD, WILLIAM — Fountain County
Born—March 15, 1758, Vir.
Service—Served 3 yrs. as pri. in Col. Russell's Detachment of the Vir. Line.
Proof—H. J. Eckenrode, Manuscript of Vir. Rev. Soldiers, p. 457.
Died—May 25, 1833. Buried N. E. of Covington, Ind. Government marker placed by Richard Henry Lee Chapter D. A. R.
Married—Verlinda Harrison (1758-1831). Ch. Samuel (1779-1803), m. Sarah De Haven; Ann (1781-1834); Elizabeth; William Harrison; Sarah; John (1790-1853), m. Tamer Masterson; Thomas; Mary; Benjamin.
Collected by Mrs. W. B. Coffing and Mrs. Worth Reed, Covington, Indiana.

WARD, ZEBEDIAH   Clark County
Born—Dec., 1755, Essex Co., N. J.
Service—Enlisted in N. J., Dec., 1775; was appointed Sergt. Col. Ogden's N. J. Regt.; went to N. Y. and was discharged Dec. 14, 1776; reenlisted and served 4 mos. as ranger in Capt. Elijah Squere's CO. under Maj. Samuel Hayes in N. J. Troops. Enlisted in Capt. John Peck's CO., Col. Jeremiah Smith's N. J. Regt.; served to Nov., 1778.
Proof—Pension claim S. 16285.
Died—1837. Buried Clark Co., Ind.
Married—July 16, 1828, Harriet Jones.
Collected by Ann Rogers Clark Chapter D. A. R.

WARDELL, ROBERT FOWLER   Scott or Clark County
Born—About 1759.
Service—Musician in Regt. of Col. Shreve of N. J. Line for duration of war. Enlisted 1778. Discharged June 3, 1783, by Capt. Abel Wayman.
Proof—Pension claim S. 36839; B. L. Wt. 155-100. Applied for pension in Clark Co., 1818. Lived in Scott Co., 1820.
Died—Sept. 23, 1836.
Children—Sarah; Rebecca; Robert; Thomas; Charles; and 5 others, all older.
Collected by Miss Mary Carr Guernsey, Charlestown, Indiana.

WARDEN (WORDEN), BARNARD   Switzerland County
Service—Enlisted in July, the year Maj. Andre was hanged at Johnstown on Mohawk River, N. Y., in Capt. Norton's CO., 4th N. Y. Regt., Capt. Smith, Col. Wisenfelt's Regt., Cont'l Establishment. Discharged at Albany, N. Y. Enlisted again in May for 9 mos. in Dutchess Co., N. Y.
Proof—Switzerland Co., Ind., Civil Order Book, 1826, p. 660.
Collected by Mrs. A. V. Danner, Vevay, Indiana.

WARREN, GEORGE   Allen County
Born—1758, Maryland.
Service—Served as pri. from Md.
Proof—Maryland Archives, vol. 18.
Died—Dec. 16, 1842. Buried Huntertown Cemetery. Stone.
Collected by Mrs. A. V. Flint, Fort Wayne, Indiana.

WASSON, JOSEPH   Wayne County
Born—1744, England.
Service—Served under Gen. Nathaniel Greene.
Proof—Pension record; Young's History of Wayne County, p. 357.

Died—1822. Buried Beulah Cemetery, east of Richmond.
Married—1770, Sarah Smith (1753-1832). Ch. Archibald, m. Elizabeth Smith; Joseph; David, m. Elizabeth Fleming; Nathaniel McCoy, m. Jane Strong; John, m. Mary Smith; Ezra, m. Jane Campbell; Lemuel; Mary, m. Josiah Campbell; Elizabeth, m. Jonathan Lambert.
Collected by Mrs. Paul L. Ross, Richmond, Indiana.

WATSON, JOHN   Rush County
Born—Dec. 11, 1760, Bedford Co., Penn.
Service—Entered service 1775. Discharged 1777 in Washington Co., N. C., under Capt. James Wilson. In battles of King's Mt.
Proof—Pension claim S. 16287. Moved to Rush Co. 1834 to live with children.

WATTS, MASON   Jennings County
Born—About 1765.
Service—Pri. in CO. under Capt. Edmonds, Regt. of Col. Marshall; Vir. Line 3 yrs. from 1778.
Proof—Pension claim S. 17760.
Died—1850.
Heir—Peter Watts (so stated in pension papers).

WAY, ISAAC   Dearborn or Ripley County
Born—1763.
Service—Enlisted from Vir. in spring of 1780. Served 1 yr., left the service in 1781.
Proof—Pension claim S. 16568.
Buried—Either in Ripley or Dearborn County. Name on bronze tablet, Versailles Court House.
Collected by Mrs. A. B. Wycoff, Batesville, Indiana.

WAYMAN, HARMAN   Boone County
Born—Aug., 1750, Culpepper Co., Vir.
Service—While residing in Culpepper Co. he enlisted as a pri. in Vir. Troops; from Sept., 1777, 2 mos. and 12 days in Capt. Wm. Chapman's CO.; in summer 1778, 2 mos. in Capt. Henry Hill's CO.; in Dec., 1778, 14 days; in summer 1779, 2 mos. 4 days in Capt. Henry Tool's CO.; in fall 1781, in Capt. Rice's CO., went to Albemarle Barracks where he was engaged in mending wagons. Returned home about Jan. 2, 1782.
Proof—Pension claim S. 32618. Pensioned 1834, Boone Co., Ind.
Collected by James Hill Chapter D. A. R.

WEATHERHOLT, JACOB   Perry County
Born—1758, in Lehigh Co., Penn.
Service—Virginia Continental Line under Col. John Gibson from 1780-1784.
Proof—W. T. R. Saffell's "Records of the Revolution."
Died—April 23, 1837. Buried Upper Cemetery at Tobinsport, Perry Co., Ind. Stone.
Married—Catherine —— (1764-1816). Ch. Jacob, Jr., b. 1784; John, b. 1786; William, b. 1792; Sarah, b. 1794; Henry, b. 1795; Milley, b. 1799; Betty, b. 1802. Second W., Sarah Jane Miller. Ch. Mildred Jane, b. 1817.
Collected by Wallace Weatherholt, Monticello, Indiana.

WEAVER, PHILIP   Harrison County
Born—Oct. 19, 1764, Loudoun Co., Vir.
Service—Enlisted from Loudoun Co., Vir., as pri., Aug., 1781, to Nov., 1781, under Capt. Josiah Moffet and Col. West; Dec., 1781, to March, 1782, under Col. West.
Proof—D. A. R. Lineage.
Died—1835. Buried Potato Run, Scott Twp.
Married—Ann Swartz. Ch. John.
Collected by Estabrook Chapter D. A. R.

WEEKS, CHARLES   Allen County
Born—1759, Upper Vir.
Service—Served under his father. He refused a pension.
Proof—Obituary in News and Sentinel, 1842.
Died—April 2, 1842. Possible Perry Twp. or Springfield. Name on bronze tablet on boulder. Placed by Mary Penrose Wayne Chapter D. A. R.
Married—Jane ——, d. 1843. Had a large family.
Collected by Mrs. Joseph Hanna, deceased.

WEIR, MARKHAM   Monroe County
Service—Inscription on stone reads "A Soldier of Revolution." Buried Liberty Cemetery, near Gosport, Ind.
Died—Jan., 1831, age 96.
Collected by Miss Ura Sanders, Gosport, Indiana.

WELCH, DANIEL   Dearborn County
Born—1763.
Service—Entered service from Conn. Enlisted at Sandy Hill, Fort Edwards, N. Y. State, with Capt. Burris, June, 1778, and served 4 yrs.
Proof—Pension claim S. 36841; B. L. Wt. 919-100.

Buried—Mt. Siani. Government marker placed by Col. Archibald Lochry Chapter D. A. R.
Married—1827, Nancy Hancock Davis.
Collected by Mrs. Walter Kerr, Aurora, Indiana, and Mrs. A. B. Wycoff, Batesville, Indiana.

WELCH, SAMUEL   Jefferson County
Born—1763, Penn.
Service—Springer Legion. Served as drummer boy in 1776 in Cumberland Co., Penn., Capt. John Cambell's CO.
Proof—Pension records, Family Bible, Jefferson Co. Probate Book, F. 66.
Died—Dec. 30, 1842. Buried Caledonia Cemetery. Stone. Government marker placed by John Paul Chapter D. A. R.
Married—1797, Jane Cunningham, d. 1846. Ch. Samuel Green; Mary, m. Robert Jamison; Nancy, m. Alvin Lindley; Rebecca, m. John Scott; Elizabeth, m. Robert Mackared; Jane, m. Isaac Banta; Sarah; Louisa, m. Miller Robinson; Margaret; James.
Collected by John Paul Chapter D. A. R.

WELLS, JOHN   Clinton County
Born—1764, Williamsburg, Vir.
Service—Enlisted from Surry Co., N. C., Nov., 1780, as pri. in Capt. Jones' CO. Served 6 mos. in commissary department under Gabriel Jones, later as pri. in Capt. Andrew Hampton's CO., Col. Absolom Bostick's Regt.
Proof—Pension claim S. 32581. Lived in Clinton Co., Ind., in 1839.
Died—About 1845.

WELLS, JOSEPH   Orange County
Born—Unknown.
Service—In Militia of N. C. Also furnished supplies and money.
Proof—Accounts of the United States with N. C., War of Revolution, Book C, p. 93.
Died—1823. Buried in Orange County.
Children—Isaac; Zacharia; Nathan; Levi; Peter; Jonathan; Jesse; Charity Freeman.
Collected by Miss Mabel Claxton, French Lick, Indiana.

WELLS, NATHANIEL (NATHAN)   Orange County
Service—Served in Stephen Lee's CO., Col. John Starkey's Regt., N. C. Troops. Also furnished supplies and money.
Proof—War Department Records; Accounts of the United States with N. C. War of Revolution, Book C, p. 93.
Died—April 26, 1817. Buried Lick Creek Cemetery, near Paoli, Ind. Government marker placed by Lost River Chapter D. A. R.

Married—Esther ——. Ch. Elizabeth; Susannah; Charity; Sarah; Esther; Joseph; Stephen; Nathan; John; William.
Collected by Miss Mabel Claxton, French Lick, Indiana.

WELLS, WILLIAM   Floyd County
Born—1760, Colbert Co., Md.
Service—Pri. in CO. of Capt. Sharp, N. C. Regt., for 6 mos.
Proof—Pension claim S. 32583. Resided in New Albany, Ind., 1834, when he made application.

WELTON, JONATHAN   Knox County
Born—July 18, 1756, Vir.
Service—He was under Capt. Fisher at the surrender of Cornwallis at Yorktown. A part of the time was under Capt. Stump. A pri. in the Vir. Militia. Was granted 300 acres of land in Knox Co.
Proof—Pension claim R. 11320.
Died—March 9, 1823. Buried in the Helderman Cemetery, near Monroe City. Stone.
Married—Margaret Miles. Ch. David; William; Martha Finley; James; Elizabeth; Sally.
Collected by Mrs. Norman E. Beckes, Vincennes, Indiana.

WEST, JOHN   Jefferson County
Born—1748.
Service—Enlisted in 1780 in Spotsylvania Co., Vir.; served as a pri. in Capt. Mark Thomas' and Benjamin Roberts' COS. under Maj. Slaughter and Col. William Davies in the Vir. Troops, and left the service in Oct., 1782, having served 2 yrs.
Proof—Pension record S. 16573. Will in Jefferson Co., Ind. Entered land.
Died—Aug. 11, 1833.
Married—Susannah Robinson. Ch. John T., m. Ursley ——; Nancy, m. Thomas Glover; James, b. 1773; William.
Collected by the John Paul Chapter D. A. R.

WESTFALL, CORNELIUS   Greene County
Born—March 9, 1756.
Service—Enlisted in 1776 as orderly-sergeant in Capt. Abel Westfall's CO., Cols. Peter Muhlenburg's and Abraham Bowman's Vir. Regt. Appointed ensign 1777. Served until 1778.
Proof—Pension claim S. 36842.
Married—Sarah ——. Ch. Josephine; Susanna.
Collected by Ura Sanders, Gosport, Indiana.

WESTFALL, JACOB   Putnam County
Born—Oct. 10, 1755, Hampshire Co., Vir.
Service—Entered service June 30, 1781, 6 mos. as First Lieut. of Capt.
    George Jackson's CO., Col. Zachariah Morgan's Regt., Vir. Troops.
    Served in Gen. George Rogers Clarke's expedition against Indians.
Proof—Pensioned Sept. 18, 1833, No. 141947.
Died—1835.
Married—1777, Mary King (1758-1841). Ch. Annie; Elizabeth; Levi;
    John; Janet; Mary; Cornelius, b. 1778.
Collected by Caroline Scott Harrison Chapter D. A. R.

WESTON (WESSON), LEVI   Decatur County
Born—May 27, 1753, Grafton, Mass.
Service—Enlisted from Grafton, Mass., serving with the Northern Army
    in Capt. Edmund Brigham's CO., Col. Job Cushing's Regt., in
    1777-1778. He was at the surrender of Burgoyne.
Proof—Crane's Genealogical History of Worcester Co., Mass., vol. 1, p.
    228; Hopkinton, Mass. Vital Records, pp. 199, 385, 386; Sutton,
    Mass. Vital Records, p. 305; Mass. Soldiers and Sailors in the
    Revolution, vol. 16, p. 881.
Died—About 1852. Buried South Park Cemetery, Greensburg, Ind.
    Stone.
Married—Olive Locke, b. 1753. Ch. Susannah, b. 1771, m. John Stevison;
    Olive, b. 1773; Patience, b. 1775; Levi, b. 1776, m. Lucy Freeland;
    Humanity, b. 1778, m. Amelia Aldrich; Olive, b. 1780, m.
    Capt. Jason Haywood and Elijah Fitch; Experience, b. 1781; Jubal,
    b. 1786, m. Claussa Mellen; Samuel, b. 1787; Ethan, b. 1789; Martha,
    b. 1791.
Collected by Mrs. H. S. McKee, Greensburg, Indiana.

WHEATLEY, JOSEPH   Boone County
Born—Jan. 4, 1761, England.
Service—Enlisted Feb. 14, 1777, in N. J., Capt. Marmaduke Curtis' CO.,
    Col. Israel (Shreve), in Jersey Line in Cont'l Establishment.
    Served till end of war. Discharged at Rocky Hill, N. J. Battles
    of Germantown, Monmouth, Springfield and Yorktown.
Proof—Pension claim W. 1683; Order Book B-338, Jefferson Co.
Died—July 30, 1844. Buried farm of Clem Hixon. Stone.
Married—Alice Norris, b. 1771. Ch. George; William, b. 1795; Catherine.
Collected by John Paul and James Hill Chapters D. A. R.

WHEELER, BENJAMIN   Clay County
Born—1758, Baltimore Co., Maryland.
Service—Enlisted 1777 for 3 mos. as a pri. under Capt. Thomas Marshall and Capt. Robert Lemon's CO. of Col. Darby Lux's Maryland Regt. Enlisted 1777 for 4 mos. in Capt. Wm. Philip's CO. Engaged in skirmishes with Indians. Residence of soldier at enlistment, Baltimore, Md.
Proof—Applied for pension 1833 from Clay Co. Allowed.
Buried—Sloan Cemetery, west Bowling Green.
Child—Thomas (War of 1812), m. Frances Thompson.
Collected by Miss Pearl Finley, Brazil, Indiana.

WHEELER, JAMES   Gibson County
Born—1753.
Service—Served in CO. of Inf. under Capt. Patterson, 6th Vir. Regt., Col. Buckner. Battles of Trenton, Princeton and Guilford. Served 5 yrs. and 10 mos.
Proof—Pension claim W. 9887.
Died—July 4, 1843. Buried S. E. of Princeton, Ind. Stone.
Married—Elizabeth Welch.
Collected by Gen. John Gibson Chapter D. A. R.

WHEELER, SIMEON   LaPorte County
Born—Jan. 30, 1761, Cheshire, New Haven Co., Conn.
Service—Enlisted in Capt. Sanford's CO., Conn. Troops, in 1777, at Woodbridge, Conn., and again in Capt. Basil's CO. in 1778. Was present at the burning of Stratford and Fairfield.
Proof—Pension claim S. 17776.
Died—1841. Buried Low's Cemetery, Coolspring Twp. Government marker and S. A. R. marker.
Married—1782, Anna Sanford, d. 1836. Ch. David; Alma; Jane; Miles; Alfred, b. 1800; Candace.
Collected by Miss Margaret Oats, LaPorte, Indiana, and Mrs. Orville Daily, Albany, Ohio.

WHETSTONE, DANIEL   Dearborn County
Born—1750, near Hagerstown, Md.
Service—Pri. in CO. commanded by Capt. Shearer, Regt. of Col. Davis, Md. Line, for 8 mos. 28 days.
Proof—Pension claim S. 32591.

WHICKER, WILLIAM   Delaware County
Born—Aug. 27, 1760, near Richmond, Vir.
Service—Entered service at age of 14 without enlistment. Enlisted later with his brother James and served under Capt. Hester with Gen. Taylor. Later served under Gen. Richard Caswell. In 1779

enlisted for 3 mos. under Capt. Pearce and transferred to command of Gen. Davidson as 1st Sergt. Was in 5 battles.
Proof—Pension record, D. A. R. No. 157480.
Died—Nov. 2, 1841. Buried Strong Cemetery. Stone.
Married—1778, Sarah Bingaman. Ch. Matthew; Asa; Luke; Berry (1758-1840), m. Lillice Campbell; Susan; Elizabeth.
Collected by Mrs. Horace G. Murphy, Muncie, Indiana.

WHITE, ABRAHAM (ABRAM) Vermillion County
Born—June 21, 1762, Washington Co., Md.
Service—Entered service in 1777 and served 2 mos. as pri. under Capt. Springer. In 1778, served 4 mos. as pri. under Capt. Daugherty, Col. Evans. Aug., 1780, served 3 mos. under Capt. Ashcraft, Col. McLeary, Penn. Troops. March, 1782, served 2 mos. Pri. of Inf. 1 yr. 10 days.
Proof—Pension claim W. 6473.
Died—June 22, 1853. Buried Vermillion Co., Ind.
Married—1808, Milly Hopewell (3rd wife). Ch. Abram, Jr., b. 1811, m. Ada Maria Blakesley.
Collected by Mrs. Anna Ora Doyle, Clinton, Indiana.

WHITE, NATHAN (NATHANIEL) Tippecanoe County
Born—July 25, 1759, Dutchess Co., N. Y.
Service—Sergt. in Col. Marivanus Willett's CO. of N. Y. State Militia; raised in and about the city of Albany, 1781.
Proof—Pension record; Probate Court record, 1833, Tippecanoe Co.
Died—Jan. 24, 1836. Buried Greenbush Cemetery, Lafayette, Ind. Name on bronze tablet, by Gen. de Lafayette Chapter D. A. R.
Married—First W. 1785, Hannah Finch (1766-1832). Ch. Annie, b. 1789; Sarah, b. 1791, m. Robert Williams; Lodema, b. 1794, m. saac Reid and Hezekia Hunter; Patience, b. 1796; Lanson, b. 1801, m. Mary Daugherty; George C., b. 1804, m. Julia A. Noel; Lucinda and Lucia (twins), b. 1806; Samuel F., b. 1812. Second W. 1834, Priscilla Goldsberry.
Collected by Mrs. Arthur McQueen, Lafayette, Indiana, and Col. Isaac White Chapter D. A. R.

WHITE, ROBERT Marion County
Born—Dec. 17, 1760, Penn.
Service—Served from 1776 to 1783, a total of 21 mos., as pri. under Capts. John Shearer, Joseph Cisney, Andrew Hood, Cols. Crawford and Williams. Enlisted from Westmoreland Co., Penn.
Proof—Records of War Department.
Died—Jan. 1, 1835. Buried New Bethel Cemetery.
Collected by Miss Marion May Carr, 2356 N. New Jersey St., Indianapolis, Indiana.

WHITE, WILLIAM   Dearborn County
Service—From Penn.
Proof—Pension certificate S. 26902; Dearborn Co. History 1885, p. 199.
Collected by Mrs. Walter Kerr, Aurora, Indiana.

WHITEHEAD, ROBERT   Putnam County
Born—1762.
Service—Enlisted near Holstein River, Western N. C., Oct., 1779, and served until Oct., 1782, as a pri. under Capt. Bailey in Col. John Montgomery's Regt. of Illinois; also under Gen. George Rogers Clarke in the Vir. Line Regt.
Proof—Pension claim S. 25999.
Died—Feb. 20, 1852. Buried Monroe Twp., near Bainbridge Town.
Collected by Miss Minnetta Wright, Greencastle, Indiana.

WHITTAKER (WHITACRE), JOHN   Ripley County
Born—1760.
Service—Enlisted in Vir., Dec., 1776, as pri. in Capt. George McCormick's CO., Col. John Gibson's Vir. Regt., 3 yrs.
Proof—Pension claim S. 36845.
Died—Sept. 12, 1825. Buried Benham, Ind. Bronze tablet in Versailles Court House.
Married—Martha ———.
Collected by Mrs. A. B. Wycoff, Batesville, Indiana.

WIGGINS, WILLIAM   Franklin County
Born—1748, Bucks Co., Penn.
Service—Enlisted from Bucks Co., Penn., in the early part of the war and served 6 mos. in Capt. Lott's CO., in Col. Penrose's Penn. Regt. Later he was placed in a leather factory in Philadelphia to make shoes for the soldiers.
Proof—Pension claim S. 17781.
Died—Sept., 1840. Buried McKindrie Church Burial Ground in Metamora Twp. Government marker placed by Twin Forks Chapter D. A. R.
Child—Mary, m. Rev. Wm. Sherwood.

WILEY, WILLIAM   Hendricks County
Born—1762, Penn. or Guilford Co.
Service—Pri. in N. C. CO. under Capts. John McAdoo, Forbish, Paisley and Steward, Col. Armstrong. Enlisted April, 1780, for 4 mos.; Sept., 1780, 3 mos.; 1781, 6 wks.
Proof—Pension record, D. A. R. No. 142416.
Died—1842. Buried Old Cemetery, south of Avon, Ind. Stone.

Married—Anna A. Shannon. Ch. Abney, b. 1789; Shannon, b. 1791; Samuel, b. 1793; William, b. 1796; Izarrah, b. 1801, m. Miss Jenkins; Alfred, b. 1802, m. Suzannah Thomas.
Collected by Mrs. H. C. Sears, Danville, Indiana.

WILKERSON, DAVID — Warren County
Born—About 1764.
Service—Pri. in CO. under Col. Wm. Washington, Vir. Line, for 3 yrs. In battles of Eutaw Springs, Guilford Court House and Cowpens.
Proof—Pension claim S. 36847.
Children—Lucretia and two sons, names not given in pension application.

WILKERSON, JOSEPH — Jennings County
Born—1757, Vir.
Service—Pri. in Capt. Ralph Faulkner's CO., 5th Vir. Regt., Col. Chas. Scott. He enlisted Jan. 27, 1776, for 2 yrs. His name last appears on a roll of 5th and 9th Vir. Regts., dated June 11, 1778. Enlisted again. Entire service, 6 yrs.
Proof—Pension claim S. 17795.
Died—Oct. 7, 1841. Buried on a farm near Scipio, Geneva Twp.
Married—Nancy Meek. Ch. Emma.

WILKERSON, WILLIAM — Brown County
Born—1740, King George Co., Vir.
Service—Served in N. C. Troops under Capt. John Henderson, Capt. Joseph Gill, Capt. Micajah Bullock, and Capt. Jones Fuller.
Proof—Pension claim S. 32602.
Died—1842.
Married—Twice and had 21 children—15 sons and 6 daughters. Son, Soloman.

WILKINS, GEORGE — Parke County
Born—March 6, 1758, Philadelphia Co., Penn.
Service—While residing in Orange Co., N. C., volunteered about Christmas, 1782; served as a pri. in Capt. Clement Hall's N. C. CO. and in Cols. Lytle's and Dixon's N. C. Regts., and was discharged by Col. John Armstrong, having served more than 1 yr.
Proof—Pension claim S. 32605.
Children—James and 5 others.
Collected by Estabrook Chapter D. A. R.

WILLEY, BARZILLAI — Clark County
Born—June 10, 1764.
Service—Drummer in Capt. Samuel H. Parson's CO., 6th Regt. Pri. in Capt. Amos Jone's CO.

Proof—Conn. Men in the Revolution, pp. 72, 506.
Died—May 22, 1851. Buried Bowery Churchyard, near Memphis, Ind. Stone.
Married—Elizabeth McCough (McCaugh), (1765-1843). Ch. Jonn Fletcher, m. Paulina Garner; Elizabeth.
Collected by Miss Bertha F. Poindexter, Jefferson, Indiana.

WILLIAMS, CONSTANT   Crawford County
Born—1763, in Plainfield, Conn.
Service—While residing in Williamstown, Mass., he enlisted 1776 and served as a pri. in Capt. Samuel Williams' Mass. CO., in Capt. Dewey's Vermont CO., under Gen. E. Allen, and under Capt. or Col. Benjamin Samuels in the Mass Troops. He was in the battle of White Plains at Saratoga when Gen. Burgoyne was captured and on some scouting parties against the Cowboys. His entire service amounted to about 9 mos.
Proof—Pension claim S. 32594.
Died—Sept., 1835. Buried Leavenworth, Ind.
Married—Alsa Barnett, June 30, 1828.

WILLIAMS, ISAAC   Harrison County
Born—Feb., 1760, Craven Co., S. C.
Service—Pri. and Sergt. in CO. commanded by Capt. Chapman, Regt. by Col. Crackett, in Vir Line for 2 yrs. from 1780. Signed Oath of Allegiance.
Proof—Pension claim S. 16297.

WILLIAMS, JAMES   Sullivan County
Born—Feb. 26, 1764, Plainfield, Conn.
Service—Enlisted in Stephentown, Albany Co., N. Y., Oct. 1, 1779, as pri. under Capt. James Magee and Cols. Graham, Malcolm and Woolsey with the N. Y. Troops and was discharged Oct. 29, 1780.
Proof—Pension claim S. 32070.
Died—After 1833, Gill Township, Sullivan Co.
Collected by Mrs. James R. Riggs, Sullivan, Indiana.

WILLIAMS, JAMES   Vermillion County
Born—May 24, 1762.
Service—Pri. in CO. commanded by Capt. Rice, Col. Weeden's Regt., Vir., 2 yrs.
Proof—Pension claim W. 9895.
Died—Jan. 29, 1837.
Married—July 29, 1784, Mary ——, b. 1764. Ch. Sally, b. 1786; Agthew D., b. 1789; Catey M., b. 1792, m. Wm. Humphrey; John M., b. 1795, m. Mary Good; Polly C., b. 1797, m. Russel Grace; James D.,

b. 1800, m. Ruth Peckenpaugh; Rachel H., b. 1804, m. Solomon Peckenpaugh; Thos. T., b. 1806.

WILLIAMS, JOHN — Washington County
Born—1765, Orange Co., N. Y.
Service—Volunteered June, 1781, in CO. of Rangers under Capt. Atwater. Served 9 mos.
Proof—Pension claim S. 32069. Pensioned from Floyd Co., Ind.
Died—1844. Buried near Greenville, Fredericksburg, Washington Co.
Married—Mary Donaldson. Ch. William, b. 1793, d. 1879.

WILLIAMS, REMEMBRANCE — Jefferson County
Born—1758.
Service—Pri. under Gen. MacIntosh, Col. Crawford, and Capt. A. Wiggins; drafted in Aug. In Sept. marched from Hampshire, Vt., to Fort Pitt, assisted in building Fort MacIntosh, then to Hampshire Co. and discharged. Campaign of 6 mos., 1778-1779. Served to close of war.
Proof—Vir. records; inscription on marker "Vir. Militia."
Buried—On family cemetery Williams Farm, near Dupont. Government marker placed by John Paul Chapter D. A. R.
Married— —— Marshall. Ch. John Garrett; Robert, m. Elizabeth Blue; Remembrance; Jesse; Peggy, m. David Branham; Hannah, m. Gideon Moncrief.
Collected by the John Paul Chapter D. A. R.

WILLIAMS, RICHARD — Lawrence County
Born—Oct. 16, 1747, Scotland.
Service—Served as Pri. in 1st Battalion of Militia of Orange Co., N. C., under Col. Ambrose Ramsey.
Proof—N. C. Revolutionary Army Accounts, vol. VI, p. 14; Colonial Records of N. C., vol. X, p. 753.
Died—Jan. 16, 1827. Buried Breckenridge Cemetery, near Bedford, Ind. Government marker.
Married—Elizabeth Andrews Edwards. Ch. Vinson, b. 1787, m. Sarah Carter; John; Henry.
Collected by John Wallace Chapter D. A. R.

WILLIAMS, WILLIAM — Delaware County
Born—March, 1762, S. C.
Service—Pri. in CO. of Capt. Boyd, Regt. of Col. Kilgore, S. C., for 6 mos.
Proof—Pension claim S. 32595.

WILLIAMS, WILLIAM D.   Warrick County
Born—1760, Brunswick Co. [State not given].
Service—Entered service Vir. State Militia, April, 1777, under Capt. Thomas Edmonds. Enlisted 1777 under Capt. Ephraim Peoples and Capt. John Mackling. Served as Minute Man for 12 mos. under Capt. Peter Pelloson.
Proof—Warrick Co. Order Book 3, p. 212.
Died—Aug. 18, 1846. Buried Old Wesley Chapel Cemetery, north of Boonville, Ind. Stone. Government marker by Vanderburg Chapter D. A. R.
Married—Susannah ——. Ch. Calvin M.; James L., m. Elizabeth Lynn; Henry; Isabel; Rachel.
Collected by Mrs. Harold K. Forsythe, Newburgh, Indiana.

WILSON, EPHRAIM   Ripley County
Born—July 18, 1756, Sussex Co.
Service—Enlisted from Penn. in May, 1774. Drafted in 1778 and served 1 mo. Had been discharged in July, 1774, from first enlistment. Served as substitute for 1 mo. in 1779. Re-entered in March, 1778, as a substitute again. Discharged in April, 1779. Total service, 5 mos.
Proof—Pension claim S. 32609.
Died—March 22, 1850. Buried Wilson Cemetery, Johnson Twp. Stone. Name on bronze tablet in Versailles Court House.
Married—Catherine ——, d. July 28, 1819.
Collected by Mrs. A. B. Wycoff, Batesville, Indiana.

WILSON, ISAAC   Marion County
Born—1747.
Service—A Patriot. Name appears as member of the Watanga Association in their petition to the N. C. Provincial Council about Aug. 22, 1776.
Proof—Ramsay's Annals of Tenn., published at Charleston by John Russell, pp. 134-138.
Died—Nov. 12, 1823, Indianapolis, Ind.
Married—Sarah Neal. Eight children by first wife and nine by second wife. Only names known: Elizabeth Glaze; Patsy Dowe; Charles Wesley; Lorenzo.
Collected by the Caroline Scott Harrison Chapter.

WILSON, JAMES   Lawrence County
Born—Aug. 28, 1761, Frederick Co., Vir.
Service—Pri. in CO. under Col. Edmonds, Vir. Line, for 7 mos.
Proof—Pension claim W. 10000.
Died—Sept. 7, 1834.
Married—1783, Sarah Brown.

WILSON, JOSEPH   Orange County
Born—1742 or 1744, N. Y.
Service—Commissioned as 1st Lieut. May 6, 1777, Capt. Matthew Grier's 2nd CO., Col. Arthur Erwine, 2nd Battalion.
Proof—Penn. Archives, 5th Series, vol. 5, pp. 334, 444.
Died—1826. Buried family cemetery, north of Orangeville. Stone.
Married—Mary Britton, d. 1843. Ch. Margaret, b. 1787; Andrew, b. 1789 (War of 1812); Rachel, b. 1791; Nathaniel, b. 1794 (War of 1812); Joseph, b. 1797.
Collected by Mrs. Ida Bonner, Orleans, Indiana.

WILSON, MICHAEL   Switzerland County
Born—About 1757, probably Vir.
Service—Enlisted at Romney, Hampshire Co., Vir., in 1777 as pri. in Capt. William Voss's CO., Col. Wood's Vir. Regt. In battles of Brandywine, Germantown, Monmouth, Stony Point. Discharged 1780 by Col. Febeger. Served 3 yrs.
Proof—Pension claim S. 36849.
Died—1824 (estate settled Switzerland Co.). Buried Vevay, Ind.
Collected by Mrs. A. V. Danner, Vevay, Indiana.

WILSON, NATHANIEL   Jefferson County
Born—Oct. 18, 1766, Cumberland Co., Penn.
Service—Served as pri. in the 3rd Battalion, 7th class of Cumberland Co. Militia, 1778-1780.
Proof—Penn. Archives, 5th Series, vol. 6, pp. 209, 218, 224; Jefferson Co. records.
Died—Jan. 9, 1828. Buried Underwood Cemetery. Stone.
Married—Susan Riddle (1760-1835). Ch. John; James; Nathaniel; Anna, m. Hezekiah Patton; Susan, m. Daniel Baxter; Mary, m. Joseph Steele; Jane, m. James Steele (children named in Soldier's Will).
Collected by John Paul Chapter D. A. R.

WILSON, WILLIAM   Jefferson County
Born—Nov. 7, 1765, Cumberland Co., Penn.
Service—While residing in Northumberland Co., Penn., he volunteered March 15, 1780 or 1781.
Proof—Family record; Pension record.
Died—Sept. 20, 1834, Jefferson Co., Ind. Buried Underwood Cemetery, north of Madison. Stone.
Married—1793, Sarah Riddle. Ch. Polly Woodfill, b. 1794; Nancy, b. 1795; Anne Stewart, b. 1798; Sarah Brisben, b. 1800; Eliza Adkinson, b. 1808; Gean Woodfill; Mathilda, b. 1809; Jane, b. 1812;

Marshall, b. 1802; William R., b. 1805 (children named in Soldier's Will).
Collected by John Paul Chapter D. A. R.

WILSON, WILLIAM   Indiana
Born—1739, County of Armagh, Ireland.
Service—Volunteered June 1, 1780, at Philadelphia as Boatswain on board the sloop of war "Luzerne", under Capt. Thomas Bell. On voyage to West Indies, captured 3 British boats. "Luzerne" was captured by the frigate "Enterprise" from London. Held prisoner until 1783 in London, then released.
Proof—Pension claim S. 32606.
Died—Last payment of pension was made on Oct. 11, 1843. Lived in Wayne Co., Ind., in 1822, then moved to Henry Co., at which place he made application for pension in 1832. On Oct. 3, 1843, pensioner certified that he had been a resident of St. Joseph, Ind., for the space of 1 yr., and that previous thereto he had resided in Elkhart Co., Ind.

WIMMER, JACOB   Henry County
Born—1762, Somerset Co., N. J.
Service—Volunteered 1778, Somerset Co., N. J. Served terms under Capt. Stout, Capt. Murphey, Gen. Winan's command. Following year he served 6 mos. under Capt. Lott, Col. Seeley and Capt. Taylor. In 1780 he served under Lieut. Garrison and Maj. Baird. He was in several skirmishes.
Proof—Pension record.
Buried—Ashland, Ind., by a railroad.
Collected by Mrs. G. K. Hewit, Newcastle, Indiana.

WINCHELL, ROBERT RUGGLES   Franklin County
Born—1750, Farmington, Conn.
Service—Drummer, Sergt., Sergt.-Maj., in Capt. Sackett's CO., Col. Woodbridge's Regt., Mass. Troops. He kept the CO. rolls.
Proof—Winchell Genealogy, by Alexander Winchell, 2nd ed., 1917.
Died—Aug., 1820. Buried probably in Old Brookville Cemetery.
Married—1777, Martha Hubbard (1749-1826). Ch. John, b. 1779; James; Nathaniel, b. 1781; Stephen, b. 1789; Peter; Lydia; Benjamin Franklin; Betsey.

WINSHIP, JABEZ LATHROP   Franklin County
Born—1752, Norwich, Conn.
Service—Member of Capt. John Lattimer's CO., Col. Samuel H. Parsons' Regt., Conn. State Militia. Served 6 days on Lexington Alarm.
Proof—Conn. "Men in the Revolution."

Died—1824 (Will probated Feb. 14, 1824, Brookville, Ind.). Probably buried Old Cemetery, Brookville.
Married—Hannah Forsythe. Ch. Joseph, b. 1771; Elizabeth, b. 1785; Jessie, b. 1787; Lovina; Lura, b. 1789.
Collected by Ernest B. Cole, Indianapolis, Indiana.

WISEMAN, JAMES   Miami County
Born—Jan., 1759.
Service—While residing in Rowan Co., N. C., he enlisted and served with the N. C. Troops as follows: for 3 mos. in Capt. Richard Graham's CO. and was discharged a few days before the siege of Charleston; he served a second tour in Capt. Merick Davis' CO.; again enlisted and served for 3 mos. in Capt. E. Gamble's CO., Col. Locke's Regt.; and again enlisted and served 4 mos. in Capt. John Lopp's CO.
Proof—Pension claim S. 16298 (application mentions a family).
Died—In Peru, Ind. Buried Reyburn Cemetery.

WITHAN, PETER   Owen County
Born—March 9, 1763, Culpepper Co., Vir.
Service—Pri. Vir. Militia. Enlisted March, 1781, Culpepper Co., Vir., under Capt. Fisher Rice, Col. Robert Alcock, Gen. Edward Stephens, Capt. Ambrose Bohannon, Col. Slaughter, Adjt. Welch. In battle of Yorktown.
Buried—Spencer Cemetery.

WITHERSPOON, JOHN   Gibson County
Born—Dec. 11, 1756, York Co., Penn.
Service—Pri. in CO. commanded by Capt. Osbourne, Regt. by Col. Polk, N. C. Line, for 9 mos. 10 days.
Proof—Pension claim S. 32601.

WOOD, ABRAHAM   Washington County
Born—About 1758, Penn.
Service—Pri. in Regt. of Col. Patten, Penn. Line, for 3 yrs. In battles of Ft. Washington, Brandywine, Germantown, Monmouth, and at Yorktown.
Proof—Pension claim W. 6563; Probate Court Records, Washington Co., Ind., p. 420.
Died—Dec. 18, 1839 (Court Records); Dec. 22, 1840 (statement of widow in her application for pension).
Married—1807, Nancy Bolin, d. 1853. Ch. John; Rachel Wright; Nancy Guy; Elisha (these named in settlement of estate); another son, David, is given by descendants.
Collected by Mrs. Harvey Morris, Salem, Indiana.

WOODS, JOSEPH Gibson County
Born—Aug. 22, 1745, Vir., Charlottesville, Albemarle Co.
Service—Served as pri. in Capt. Benjamin Briggs CO., 7th Vir. Regt. His name was last borne on muster roll for June, 1783. At Fort Pitt.
Proof—Rev. Soldiers of Vir., Eckenrode List., p. 482.
Died—Jan. 16, 1835. Buried White Church Cemetery, near Princeton. Stone.
Married—Mary Hamilton (1747-1829). Ch. John, b. 1769, m. Polly Dickson; James, b. 1770, m. Nancy Dickson; Margaret, b. 1772, m. Samuel Hogue, Sr.; Patrick, b. 1775, m. Jane Hannah; Joseph L., b. 1776, m. Elizabeth Hannah; William P., b. 1778; David, b. 1780, m. Esther Witherspoon; Isaac, b. 1783, m. Elizabeth Witherspoon; Jane, b. 1785, m. Samuel Hogue, Jr.; Elizabeth, b. 1787, m. William Embree; Samuel H., b. 1791, m. Ann McMillan.
Collected by John Gibson Chapter D. A. R.

WOODWORTH, DANIEL Greene County
Born—Jan. 14, 1752, Ulster Co., N. Y.
Service—Pri. in CO. of Capt. Johnson, Col. VanHorn's Regt., N. Y., for 10 mos.
Proof—Pension claim S. 32612.
Child—Daniel, Jr.

WOODWORTH, DYER Franklin County
Born—Nov. 20, 1757, Salisbury, Conn.
Service—Enlisted while a resident of Oblong, N. Y., as an Armorer in the CO. commanded by Capt. Increase Childs, in the Regt. of Col. Livingston of the New York State Troops. In the 2nd year of the Rev. enlisted for 12 mos., most of which time he worked in the Armory Shops under the direction of Jacob Rieder. About a year after, while a resident of Salisbury, Conn., again enlisted for about 6 mos. in the CO. commanded by Capt. Ensign in the Conn. State Troops.
Proof—Pension claim S. 17799. Last payment of pension was Sept. 27, 1833.
Died—Prior to Feb. 18, 1842, when administrator appointed. Franklin Co. records. Perhaps buried N. E. of Brookville.
Married—Anne ——. Ch. Mehitable, m. Amos Baldwin; Hannah, m. Philip Shay; Charity; Almira, m. Joseph Shay; Rileigh, m. Keturah Newkirk; Artemidorus C., m. Polly Stull.
Collected by Mrs. J. W. Holter, Connersville, Indiana, and W. H. Brewer, Terre Haute, Indiana.

WRIGHT, JAMES   Jennings County
Born—May 12, 1752, Cumberland Co., Penn.
Service—While resident of Penn. enlisted June, 1779. Made Ensign. Served in Capt. Samuel Todd's CO., Bedford Co., under Col. Davis and Maj. John Woods. Served 3 tours.
Proof—Pension claim S. 16378.
Died—Aug. 26, 1839, Jennings Co.
Heir—Robert Elliott (named in pension application).

WRIGHT, JAMES   Fayette County
Service—Enlisted in Vir. under Capt. John Green, 8th Vir. Regt., Col. Wm. Preston. Application for pension made in Vir. and was paid to March, 1827. He then moved to Fayette Co., Ind., to better his conditions.

WRIGHT, JEREMIAH   Crawford County
Born—March 29, 1762, Hampshire Co., Vir.
Service—Enlisted as pri. when only 14 yrs. of age, Capt. Sullivan, Col. Gibson, 13th Regt., Vir. Vol. Inf. Served 4 mos. as pri., 9 mos. as Lieut., under different Capts.; 3 mos as spy (Indian) under Capt. James Marshall. Served with Col. McIntosh's CO. in Ga.
Proof—D. A. R. Lineage, vol. 57, p. 28.
Died—May 18, 1833. Buried Public Cemetery, Fredonia, Crawford Co.
Married—Mary Cunningham. Ch. Elizabeth; Jeremiah.
Collected by Mrs. V. R. Conner, New Albany, Indiana.

WRIGHT, ROBERT   Dearborn County
Born—1762, New York.
Service—Enlisted in N. Y. in 1780 as a pri. under Capts. Tiebout and Bleeker, Cols. Gausevart and Van Schaick of N. Y., and served to the close of the war. He was in siege of York and several skirmishes. June 5, 1818, applied for a pension from Dearborn Co. Allowed.
Proof—Pension claim S. 26852; D. A. R. No. 241221.
Died—Oct. 23, 1823.
Married—July 2, 1786, Juda ——, b. 1763. Ch. Ira (1787-1867), m. Elizabeth Carpenter.
Collected by Mrs. Roy Bogner, Washington, Indiana.

WRIGHT, ROBERT   Clinton County
Born—1755, Ireland.
Service—Volunteered 1776, 2 mos. as pri. in Capt. Thomas Brewster's CO., Col. Thomas McKean's Penn. Regt. Several other enlistments. In the battle of Princeton.

Proof—Pension claim S. 3620.
Died—1841. Buried Providence Cemetery.
Married—Second W. 1799, Agnes Holmes. Ch. Thomas J., m. Elizabeth B. Wright.
Collected by Capt. Harmon Aughe Chapter D. A. R.

WRIGHT, WILLIAM   Washington County
Born—March 25, 1760.
Service—Enlisted Randolph Co., N. C., 1780. Served 3 mos. as pri. under Capt. James Robinson, Col. John Litteral. In 1781, 3 mos. under Capt. John Raves and 3 mos. under Capt. William Gray, Col. Thomas Dugan.
Proof—Pension claim S. 16301; Stevens History of Washington Co., Ind., p. 632.
Died—1838. Buried Wright Family Cemetery, on Harrison Deeny Farm. Government marker placed by Christopher Harrison Chapter D. A. R.
Married—Betsey Morgan, m. about 1780. Ch. Celia; Sally; Betsey; Samuel; Elijah; Arwin; Morgan; Wesley.
Collected by Mrs. Harvey Morris, Salem, Indiana.

WYATT, JOHN   Rush County
Born—1748, London, England.
Service—Enlisted 1778 under Capt. Joseph Crockett's CO., Col. Abraham Bowman's Regt., Vir. Troops. Was at Monmouth and Yorktown.
Proof—Pension claim S. 16303.
Died—1833. Buried near Milroy, Ind.
Married—First W. 1772, Susan Summitt (1751-1823). Ch. John; Jess; Sam; William; James; George (1795-1862); Susan; Nancy; Elizabeth; Priscilla; Mary (1784-1863).
Collected by Rushville Chapter D. A. R.

WYATT, WILLIAM   Jefferson County
Born—England.
Service—Vir. Service.
Proof—Brumbaugh "Rev. War Records," vol. 1, p. 517. Received bounty land.
Buried—Probably in Ryker's Ridge.
Married— —— Kitchen. Ch. Mordecai, b. 1791, m. Cynthia Kidd; George; John; Parmelia; Emily.
Collected by John Paul Chapter D. A. R.

WYCOFF, JACOB Ripley County
Born—Nov. 3, 1754, N. J.
Service—Entered service from Monmouth Co., N. J., in July, 1775. Served 2 yrs.
Proof—Pension claim S. 32619.
Died—Feb. 18, 1835. Buried Versailles, Ind. Government marker. Name on bronze tablet in Versailles Court House.
Married—Susannah Allen, b. 1762. Ch. John, b. 1785; Daniel, b. 1787; Robert, b. 1791, m. Hannah Allen; Allen, b. 1802, m. Eleanor Simpson.
Collected by Mrs. A. B. Wycoff, Batesville, Indiana.

WYLLYS, JOHN PALSGRAVE Allen County
Born—Aug. 11, 1754, Hartford, Conn.
Service—Adj. of Wolcott's Conn. State Regt., Jan., 1776; Brigade Maj. to Gen. Wadsworth, Aug. 7, 1776; taken prisoner Sept. 15, 1776, on the retreat from New York; exchanged Dec. 20, 1776; Capt. of Webb's Additional Cont'l Regt., Jan. 1, 1777; Maj., Oct. 10, 1778. Served to Dec. 25, 1783. Major United States Inf. Regt., June 9, 1785; Maj. 1st Inf. United States Army, Sept. 29, 1789.
Proof—Heitman's Register, p. 608.
Died—Killed in action with Indians on the Miami, Oct. 22, 1790. Probably buried in trench along the Maumee River, Fort Wayne, Ind.
Married—Jerusha Talcot, d. 1783.
Collected by Mrs. T. J. Hindman, Fort Wayne, Indiana.

YARBAUGH (YARBROUGH), JOHN Decatur County
Service—Enlisted in Caroline Co., Vir., in fall of 1775; served in Capt. Samuel Hawes' CO., Col. Woodford's 2nd Vir. Regt., for 2 yrs., then re-enlisted in same CO. and served until close of war. In battles of Monmouth, Brandywine, Germantown and Stony Point.
Proof—Pension claim S. 36861. Applied from Nicholas Co., Ky., 1818, and in 1826 had moved to Decatur Co., Ind.
Died—March 2, 1834.
Married—Mary ——. Had children.

YOCUM, JOHN Clay County
Born—1747, Vir.
Service—Enlisted May, 1780, and served 6 mos. as pri. in Capt. George Jackson's CO., Col. Morgan's Vir. Regt. Later served 2 mos. guarding the frontier under Capt. Rowland Thomson.
Proof—Pension record.
Buried—On the John Foulke Farm, S. of Brazil, Ind. Stone placed by the Clay County Commissioners.

Children—George; Sarah Yocum Hansley.
Collected by Miss Pearl Finley, Brazil, Indiana.

YORK, JEREMIAH   Perry County
Born—June 22, 1762.
Service—Served as substitute for James Tucker in Capt. David Scott's
    CO., 1780, 8th Regt. Penn., Gen. Gibson, for 2 yrs.
Proof—Pension claim W. 10006; B. L. Wt. 94059-160-55.
Died—Sept. 10, 1835.
Married— —— Brown. Ch. Jeremiah; Job; Ezekiel; Thomas; and
    others. Second W. 1825, Joanna Allsworth. Third W., Letitia
    Boyer.

YOUNG, JARET (JARRETT)   Knox County
Born—1762, Vir.
Service—Enlisted 1780 in Camden District, S. C.; served 6 mos. as pri.
    in Capt. John McCool's CO. and Capt. Amos Davis' CO., S. C.
    Regt.
Proof—Pension claim S. 16304.
Died—Jan. 10, 1835, in Knox Co.
Children—Sarah, m. Peter Hollingsworth; Nancy, m. William Howard;
    William, m. Betsey Jones; Sparling, m. Peggy Cochran; Robert,
    m. Polly Snyder; Garret, m. Susannah Crook; Mariah, m. James
    Boyd; John.
Collected by Mrs. S. G. Davenport, Vincennes, Indiana.

YOUNG, JOHN   Clark County
Born—1757, Scotland.
Service—Enlisted 1780 and served 3 mos. as pri. in Capt. George Houston's CO., Col. Nall's Vir. Regt. Served 1 mo. as substitute. Enlisted 1781 as pri. in Capt. Wm. Herron's CO., Col. Benjamin Harrison's Vir. Regt., 3 mos. Wounded.
Proof—Pension claim S. 16588.
Died—Feb. 23, 1844, in Clark County.
Married—Ann Margaret ——, d. 1844. Ch. James.
Collected by Ann Rogers Clark Chapter D. A. R.

YOUNG, MATTHIAS   Clinton County
Born—About 1760, Frederick Co., Md.
Service—Pri. in CO. commanded by Capt. Creger, Col. Johnson, Md.
    Regt.
Proof—Pension claim R. 11949, Ind. certificate No. 26861.
Died—Aug. 11, 1838. Buried on Young Farm, now Wallace Farm.

Married—1783, Anna Barbara Christ. Ch. Matthias, Jr. (1789-1844), m. Hannah Aughe; Catherine, m. John B. Coleman; David; Solomon, m. Deboree Ann Hevelin; John; Mary, m. Edward Ryan.

YOUNG, MORGAN LaGrange County
Born—1762, Morris Co., N. J.
Service—Enlisted 1776 as pri. in N. J. Troops; 1 mo. in Capt. Ezekiel Crane's CO., Col. John Stark's Regt.; 9 mos. under Gen. Maxwell; 1778, 3 mos. in Capt. Robert Young's CO.; 1780, 2 wks. on Staten Island; 1781, 3 mos.
Proof—Pension claim S. 17804.
Died—Jan. 21, 1852. Buried Pretty Prairie Cemetery. Stone.
Married—Jane —— (1757-1847). Ch. Losey.
Collected by Mrs. Fred Deal, LaGrange, Indiana.

YOUNG, PHILLIP Shelby County
Born—1766, Monmouth, N. J.
Service—Enlisted 1781 as pri. in Capt. Cornelius Carhart's CO., Col. Sylvanus Seely's Regt., Hunterdon Co., N. J., Militia.
Proof—Sworn statements of children.
Died—July 1, 1840. Buried Blue River Cemetery (not Little Blue River Baptist Church Cemetery as stated on tablet in Shelbyville Public Library). Stone. Bronze marker by Mary Motte Green Chapter D. A. R.
Married—Amelia Youngs (1783-1860). Ch. Martha; Mary (both "Real Daughters"); Benjamin.

YOUNGBLOOD, JACOB Fountain County
Born—June, 1750, N. C.
Service—Enlisted from Edgefield Co., S. C., Jan., 1775, under Capt. John Ryan, Col. LeRoy Hammer, Lt. Col. John Perviel, for 6 mos.
Proof—Pension claim S. 17219.
Died—About 1839. Buried Mill Creek Twp. Government marker placed by Veedersburg Chapter D. A. R.
Collected by Mrs. Worth Reed, Covington, Indiana.

YOUNGER, JOSHUA Lawrence County
Born—May 11, 1755, Vir.
Service—Pri. in Capt. William Vanse's CO., Col. James Wood's 12th Vir. Regt. Wounded. Discharged May, 1779.
Proof—Pension claim W. 10009.
Died—Aug. 2, 1834. Buried Leatherwood Cemetery. Government marker placed by John Wallace Chapter D. A. R.

Married—First W., Lizzie Lee. Ch. Lizzie. Second W. 1787, Catherine Yoter. Ch. Stephen; Polly; Nimrod; Sallie; Mary; John; Garrett; Lewis.
Collected by John Wallace Chapter D. A. R.

ZABRISKIE (ZEBRISKY), CHRISTIAN — Vermillion County
Born—Sept. 19, 1754, Paramus, N. J.
Service—Pri. in Third CO., 6th Battalion of Northampton Militia, under Capt. Thos. Sillyman, Col. Lavall.
Proof—Penn. Archives, 6th Series, vol. 3, p. 839.
Died—Sept. 26, 1830. Buried Eugene Twp.
Married—Elizabeth Morgan. Ch. Sarah; Henry; Mary; Lewis; Abraham.
Collected by G. O. Zabriskie, 623 Tewkesbury Place, N. W., Washington, D. C.

LIST OF MEN IN COMPANY OF COL. ARCHIBALD LOCHRY

Who were massacred by the Indians near the mouth of Lochry Creek (now Dearborn Co., Ind.) on Aug. 24, 1781. These names all appear on a bronze tablet in Riverview Cemetery, Dearborn Co., Ind., erected by Col. Archibald Lochry Chapter D. A. R. This list is furnished by the Registrar General, D. A. R. Office.

Col. Lochry (Col. Archibald Lochry)
Capt. Campbell (Capt. William Campbell)
Ensign Ralph
Ensign Maxwell
Ensign Cahel
Sergt. Galaher (Hugh Gallaher)
Sergt. Evens (Samuel Evans)
Sergt. Burris (Ebenezer Burus)
Sergt. Fursyth (John Forsyth)
Sergt. Black (James Black)
Sergt. Allison (William Allison)
Corp. Paton (Isaac Patton)
John Gibson
John Young
Robt. Dongan (Robert Duncan)
John Straiton (John Stratton)
John Burns
Wm. Hudson
John Phesant (John Pershing)
Zenis Hardon
John Milegan
John Corn
Mathew Lamb
Joseph Baily
John Smith
Wm. Cain (William Kean)
Adam Ewin (Adam Ewing)
Peter McLin
Archibald Askin
David Elinger (David Dillinger)
George Butcher
Peter Bareckman
Josia Brooks
John Row (John Rowe)
Jonas Peter
Jas. McRight
John McKinby

The following list of men in the Company of Col. Archibald Lochry were taken prisoners on Aug. 24, 1781. Only a few are known to have died in Indiana, but the entire list is given.

Major Craigraft (Charles Craecroft)
Capt. Stokley (Widow Elizabeth Stokeley, W. 4079)
Capt. Orr (Capt. Robert Orr, S. 4631)
Capt. Shannon (Samuel Shannon)
Lt. Robison (James Robinson)
Lt. Anderson (Isaac Anderson, W. 4628)
Lt. Craig (Widow Elizabeth Craig, W. 3075)
Lt. Scott (John Scott)
Lt. Baker (Melcher Baker)
Ensign Hunter (Patrick Hunter, d. Harrison Co., Ind.)
Adjt. Guthrie (John Guthrie)
Quartermaster Wallace (Richard Wallace)
Sergt. Trimble (John Trimble)
Sergt. McCloud (Norman McLeod)
Patrick Johnson
Richard Fleming
Robert Watson
Abm. Anderson
Micl. Harie (S. 39645)
Wm. Mars
John Sence
Micl. Miller
Patrick Murphy (Samuel Murphy, S. 22413)
Jas. Cain (James Kean, S. 22342)
Jas. McPherson (James McPherson, S. 9008)
Wm. Martial
Peter Conoly
John Farrel
Denis McCarty (Dennis McCarty, S. 22388)
Solomon Atkin
John Lavear
Mathias Fisher (S. 22239)
George Dice (George Hice, S. 22423)
John Porter
John Smith
Adm. Oury (Adam Owry, W. 2964)
Sam. LeFever
John Hunter
Joseph Erwin
Manasa Coyl (Manasseh Coyle, W. 2759)
Hugh Stear (Hugh Stears, S. 6108)
John Cat
Volantine Lawrence (d. in Dearborn Co., Ind.)
Jacob Lawrence (S. 4521)
Christian Fast (Christian Fast, S. 4195)
Charles McLin
Wm. Roach (William Roark, S. 32495)
Henry France (Henry Franks, W. 4956)
Abm. Highly (Abraham Hiley, d. in Perry Co., Ind.)
George Mason (d. in Dearborn Co., Ind.)
Wm. Witherenton (William Worthington, S. 1722)
Cairy Cuighly (Cary Quigley, S. 22452)
Thos. James

Thos. Atkison
John Stackhouse
Wm. Clark
Eliha Risly
Jas. Dunseith
Dal. Cain

Wm. Husk
Robert Wilson
Isaac Lewis (Ezekiel Lewis, S. 4533)
Alex. Burns
Hugh More

Proof—The Original List is in the British Museum and a copy in the office of the Registrar General, N. S. D. A. R.

LIST OF MEN WHOSE SERVICE IN REVOLUTIONARY WAR HAS NOT BEEN VERIFIED AT PRESENT TIME

ANDREWS, ARTHUR   Boone County
Born—Mar. 10, 1753, Lancaster Co., Penn.
Died—1834. Buried Hopewell Cemetery. Stone.
Collected by Mrs. C. M. McClaine, Lebanon, Indiana.

BEATY, ANDREW   Lawrence County
Born—1747.
Died—Nov. 19, 1819. Buried Mayfield Cemetery. Stone placed by John Wallace Chapter D. A. R.
Service—Served throughout the war. Was at Yorktown.
Married—Nancy —— (1765-1838). Youngest ch. James.
Collected by Mrs. Ellen Hoover, Bedford, Indiana.

BOYD, JOHN   Hendricks County
Born—1761.
Died—Jan. 6, 1840. Buried at Clayton, Ind. Stone. Applied for pension from Hendricks Co., Nov., 1833.
Service—Enlisted from N. C., served under Capt. Joseph White, Col. Charles McDowell. Enlisted Aug., 1782, for 3 mos. Discharged Nov., 1782. Feb., 1783, served under Maj. Armstrong. Discharged at Guilford Court House, 1783. Interior Department declares his declaration to have been false.
Married—Mary Roberts, 1784 or 1785. Ch. Alexander Smith; William, b. 1787; John; James; Martha; Elizabeth; Spencer; Joshua; Jane; Susan; Elisha; Hugh; Matilda; Susan; Matthew.
Proof—Pension claim R. 1089. This man is not to be confused with the John Boyd in Lawrence Co., Ind.

BROWN, ROBERT   Ohio County
Born—1734.
Died—1816. Buried at Rising Sun, Ind. Dearborn Co. Hist., p. 446, states he gave service in Conn.
Child—Ethan Allen Brown (1776-1852). Was Governor of Ohio.
Collected by Mrs. Walter Kerr, Aurora, Indiana.

BUCK, WILLIAM   Switzerland County
Born—1764.
Died—1844. Buried at Patriot, Ind. Stone. Is listed on 1840 census as pensioner, but name cannot be found by Vet. Adm.

CANNON, ISAAC — Dearborn County
Service—Dearborn Co. Hist., p. 199, states he gave service in Delaware. Probably buried on Holman Hill.
Married—Mary Bathhurst. Ch. Isaac, Jr.; Charles B.; Mary Ann; Evaline; Rebecca.
Collected by Mrs. Walter Kerr, Aurora, Indiana.

CRAWFORD, WILLIAM — Wayne County
Born—1745, in Belfast, Ireland.
Service—Served under Gen. de Lafayette as a message bearer. Young's Hist. of Wayne Co., p. 176.
Died—Dec. 30, 1826. Buried Bryant's Chapel, near Centerville, Ind.
Married—1766, Martha Cooper, d. 1824. Ch. James; William; John, m. Nancy McCoy; Nathan; Elizabeth; Jane; Mary; Margaret.
Collected by Mrs. Paul Ross, Richmond, Ind.

DAY, JOHN — Dearborn County
Service—Dearborn Co. Hist., p. 199, states he gave service in Penn.
Collected by Mrs. Walter Kerr, Aurora, Indiana.

DYCKMAN (DIKEMAN), JOHN — Dearborn County
Service—Dearborn County Hist., p. 199, states he gave service in N. Y.
Collected by Mrs. Walter Kerr, Aurora, Indiana.

ENDSLEY, ANDREW — Wayne County
Born—Ireland, d. 1826. History of Wayne Co., 1884, p. 283, states he was a Rev. Soldier.
Married—Jane ——, d. 1810. Ch. Abraham; James; John; Andrew, m. Sally Willams; Hugh; Thomas; Samuel; Peter, m. Mary Wright; Sarah; Elizabeth, m. Edward Hunt; Jane, m. Joseph Hunt. Ch. are named in soldier's Will and marriages are found in marriage record.
Collected by Mrs. Paul Ross and Mrs. Fred Gennett, Richmond, Indiana.

GIBSON, JOHN C. — Dearborn County
Born—Aug. 28, 1765.
Died—Aug. 2, 1845. Name listed in 1840 census as a pensioner, but cannot be located by Vet. Adm. Buried Bright's Cemetery.
Married—Nancy Mills. Ch. William; Joshua; Robert; Whalen; David; John; George; Charles; Elizabeth; Nancy; Polly; Charlotte; Sarah.
Collected by Mrs. Walter Kerr, Aurora, Indiana.

HATHAWAY, RICHARD — Daviess County
Service—Hist. of Daviess Co. states he was a Rev. Soldier.
Died—Killed by Indians about 1812. Buried Maysville Cemetery.
Collected by Mrs. Roy Bogner, Washington, Indiana.

JONES, JOHN   Wayne County
Service—Hist. of Wayne Co., 1884, pp. 342-344, states he was a Rev.
    Soldier and refused a pension.
Child—Levi M., b. 1787, m. Mary Thomas.
Collected by Mrs. Paul Ross, Richmond, Indiana.

JONES, MOSES   Porter County
Buried in Cornell Cemetery, E. of Hebron, Ind. Bronze marker placed
    by William Henry Harrison Chapter D. A. R.
Collected by Mrs. E. R. Bryant, Hebron, Indiana.

KELLY, AMOS   Clay County
Born—1755.
Died—1842. Buried Zenor Cemetery. County Commissioners of Clay
    Co. marked this grave in 1906 on the tradition of early settlers
    that he was a Rev. Soldier.
Collected by Miss Pearly Findley, Brazil, Indiana.

KITCHEN, JOSHUA   Gibson County
Buried—Mt. Moriah Cemetery. Tart's Hist. of Gibson Co., p. 105,
    states he was a Rev. Soldier.
Married—Julia Duff, b. 1819.
Collected by Miss Anne Hudleson, Princeton, Indiana.

MOORE, ALEXANDER L.   Wayne County
Born—S. C. Hist. of Wayne Co., 1884, p. 796, states he was a Rev.
    Soldier.
Married—Phoebe Edwards. 6th ch. James, b. 1798.
Collected by Mrs. Paul Ross, Richmond, Indiana.

MOORE, MORDECAI   Wayne County
Born—Penn. Hist. of Wayne Co., 1884, p. 796, states he was a Rev.
    Soldier.
Child—Alexander L., m. Phoebe Edwards.
Collected by Mrs. Paul Ross, Richmond, Indiana.

McMULLIN (MAXWELL), RAWLEY   Jefferson County
Service—Served under Lafayette. Buried Hebron Cemetery. Govern-
    ment marker placed by John Paul Chapter D. A. R.

RICHARDSON, SAMUEL   Dearborn County
Service—Hist. of Dearborn Co. states he served from Vermont.
Collected by Mrs. Walter Kerr, Aurora, Indiana.

ROBERTS, JOHN   Boone County
Born—July 14, 1760.
Died—Oct. 7, 1840. Buried Mechanicsburg Cemetery. Stone.
Collected by Mrs. C. N. McClaine, Lebanon, Indiana.

ROGERS, WILLIAM   Jefferson County
Buried—Pisgah Cemetery at Deputy. Government marker placed by John Paul Chapter D. A. R.

SACKETT, ENOCH   Dearborn County
Service—Hist. of Dearborn Co., p. 199, states he was a Rev. Soldier.
Collected by Mrs. Walter Kerr, Aurora, Indiana.

SACKETT, JOHN   Dearborn County
Service—Hist. of Dearborn Co. states he was a Rev. Soldier.
Collected by Mrs. Walter Kerr, Aurora, Indiana.

SMITHSON, DRUMMOND   Randolph County
Born—July 12, 1754.
Died—Dec. 31, 1844. Buried Union Cemetery. Stone.
Married—Mary ——, d. Jan. 16, 1851, aged 97. Listed in 1840 census as a pensioner, but name cannot be found by Vet. Adm.
Collected by Mrs. James P. Goodrich and Mrs. Oren Ross, Winchester, Indiana.

STEVENSON, GEORGE   Wayne County
Born—Aug. 18, 1757.
Died—Aug. 31, 1828. Hist. of Wayne Co., 1884, states he was a Rev. Soldier.
Married—1782, Sarah Cropper (1763-1830). Ch. Vincent; Rachel; Joseph, m. 1811, Sarah Martin; George; Sarah; James; Levi; Thomas. Moved to Wayne Co. in 1807.
Collected by Mrs. Paul Ross, Richmond, Indiana.

TWIBELL, JOHN   Blackford County
Born—March 14, 1760, Monahan Co., Ireland.
Died—July 21, 1853. Buried Twibell Cemetery, near Montpelier, Ind. Stone. Was first a British soldier, then deserted and joined the American Army.
Married—Elizabeth ——. Ch. David; Josiah.
Collected by Nancy Knight Chapter D. A. R.

THOMAS, JOHN   Wayne County
Born—1743.
Died—Nov., 1814. Buried New Garden Cemetery. Stone. Was a
    Quaker, opposed to war and refused to serve except as compelled.
    Young's Hist. of Wayne Co., pp. 302-303.
Married—Molly Clark (1748-1840). Ch. John, m. Lydia Sneed; Isaac,
    m. Rachel Knight; Mary, m. Moses Mendenhall; Elijah, m. Susannah Sneed; Stephen, m. Hannah Mendenhall; Francis, m. Lydia
    Woodward; Christina, m. Thomas Knight; Benjamin, m. Anna
    Moorman; Sarah, m. Charles Baldwin.
Collected by Mrs. Paul Ross, Richmond, Indiana.

THOMAS, JOSEPH   Wayne County
Service—Served directly under Gen. Washington. Wayne Co. Hist.,
    1884, p. 344.
Child—Mary, b. 1784, m. Levi M. Jones.
Collected by Mrs. Paul Ross, Richmond, Indiana.

WALLACE, JOHN   Wayne County
Born—Virginia. Hist. of Wayne Co., 1884, p. 757, and Fox's Hist. of
    Wayne Co., p. 869, states he was a Rev. Soldier.
Died—1829.
Child—John (War of 1812), m. Mary Banks.
Collected by Mrs. Paul Ross, Richmond, Indiana.

WARD, JOHN   Hendricks County
Buried in a private cemetery—the only grave. Inscription on stone
    reads "John Ward—U. S. Soldier—Revolutionary War".
Collected by Mrs. J. Harold Grimes, Danville, Indiana.

REVOLUTIONARY SOLDIERS WHO WERE PENSIONED IN INDIANA AND LATER TRANSFERRED TO OTHER STATES

Babcock, Sherman	Harrison Co.	d. in Knox Co., Mo.
Barnes, James	Vigo Co.	Trans. to Tenn.
Brees, Timothy	Franklin Co.	Trans. to Ohio
Brooks, Henry	Orange Co.	Trans. to Mo.
Brown, Timothy	Franklin Co.	d. in Iowa
Brown, William	Franklin Co.	Trans. to Ohio
Campbell, William	Crawford Co.	d. in Ill.
Cannon, John	Daviess Co.	Trans. to Ky.
Caswell, Samuel	Rush Co.	Trans. to Ky.
Colyer, John	Franklin Co.	Trans. to Mo.
Coy, Christopher	Harrison Co.	d. in Ill.
Culton, Joseph	Morgan Co.	Trans. to Mo.
Cunningham, Richard	Clay Co.	Trans. to Ohio
Edleman, Leonard	Rush Co.	Trans. to Ky.
Erwin, David	Hendricks Co.	d. in Daviess Co., Ky.
Findley, David	Clark Co.	Trans. to Ill.
Galbreath, William	Scott Co.	Trans. to Ill.
Hamman, Isaac	Hamilton Co.	d. in Ohio
Hanlon, Matthias	Montgomery Co.	d. in Ohio
Haycock, Daniel	Switzerland Co.	Trans. to Ill.
Hicks, John	Washington Co.	Trans. to Tenn.
Hough, William	Warren Co.	Trans. to Ohio
Humphreys, George	Gibson Co.	Trans. to Ill.
Hurst, William	Washington Co.	d. in Ill., 1835
Irwin, David	Morgan Co.	d. in Daviess Co., Ky.
Jackson, Samuel	Floyd Co.	Trans. to Ill.
Johnson, Arthur	Gibson Co.	Trans. to Ill.
Johnson, David	Parke Co.	Trans. to Knox Co., Ohio
Jones, George	Vigo Co.	d. in Ohio or N. Y.
Kilgore, Charles, Sr.	Daviess Co.	Trans. to Tenn.
Killion, Jacob	Scott Co.	Trans. to Ill.
Kitchen, James	Warren Co.	Trans. to Ill.
Mead, William	Vanderburgh Co.	Trans. to Ill.
Miller, John A.	Floyd Co.	Trans. to Mo.
Montgomery, John	Parke Co.	d. in Ill.
McClellan, Joseph	Harrison Co.	Trans. to Tenn.
McClerkin, Matthew	Union Co.	d. in Preble Co., Ohio
McCoy, William	Decatur Co.	d. in Louisville, Ky.
McDonald, John	Henry Co.	Trans. to Iowa

McIntire, Robert	Fountain Co.	d. in Neb.
McMickle, Peter	Crawford Co.	d. in Ill.
McPhester, Andrew	Putnam Co.	Trans. to Mo.
Osburn, John	Fountain Co.	Trans. to Iowa
Penn, Benjamin	Jefferson Co.	d. in Ky.
Rhoades, Daniel	Vigo Co.	d. in Edgar Co., Ill.
Ryan, Richard	Lawrence Co.	Trans. to Tenn.
Scarborough, John	Posey Co.	Trans. to Ill.
Scott, Samuel	Parke Co.	d. in Ky., 1820
Skates, James	Dearborn Co.	Trans. to Ohio
Stephenson, James	Floyd Co.	Trans. to Ohio
Stiles, Hezekiah	Franklin Co.	d. in Ohio
Thompson, James	Vigo Co.	Trans. to Ill.
Williams, Thomas	Fountain Co.	d. in Ill.
Wilson, Robert	Hancock Co.	Trans. to Ill.

LIST OF INDIANA PENSIONERS IN OTHER WARS, GIVING THE COUNTY IN WHICH THEY WERE LIVING WHEN PENSIONED

Almon, Thomas	Posey Co.	War of 1812
Antis, George	Gibson Co.	War of 1812
Baldwin, Pollard	Warren Co.	Not Rev. War
Banks, James	Knox Co.	War of 1812
Barnes, Hugh	Owen Co.	War of 1812
Bartholomew, Joseph	Clark Co.	Indian War, d. in Ill.
Bedford, Elias	Tippecanoe Co.	War of 1812
Bevens, David	Bartholomew Co.	War of 1812
Blue, David	Parke Co.	Indian War
Boone, Joseph	Shelby Co.	Indian War, 1791
Bradford, John	Monroe Co.	War of 1812
Briggs, Robert	Harrison Co.	War of 1812
Budd, Daniel	Franklin Co.	Not Rev. War
Burton, George	Jefferson Co.	Indian War
Byrnes, Matthew	Floyd Co.	War of 1812
Carr, Samuel	Clark Co.	War of 1812
Christy, David	Clay Co.	War of 1812
Collins, Stephen	Marion Co.	War of 1812
Collins, William	Knox Co.	War of 1812
Coltrin, John	Vigo Co.	War of 1812
Colvin, Samuel	Bartholomew Co.	Not. Rev. War
Conger, Zachariah S.	Dearborn Co.	War of 1812
Crist, William	Marion Co.	War of 1812
Cunningham, Christopher	Fayette Co.	War of 1812
Curry, William	Franklin Co.	Not Rev. War

Davis, Joseph	Randolph Co.	War of 1812
Douglas, Jeremiah	Montgomery Co.	War of 1812
Durham, John	Dearborn Co.	War of 1812
Dye, George	Boone Co.	War of 1812
Emmery, Edward	Washington Co.	War of 1812
Evans, James	Gibson Co.	War of 1812
Ferby, E.	Randolph Co.	War of 1812
Foster, James	Marion Co.	War of 1812
French, Micah	Hamilton Co.	War of 1812
Godfrey, Zachariah	Lawrence Co.	War of 1812
Grass, Daniel	Spencer Co.	War of 1812
Hall, Jacob	Dearborn Co.	War of 1812
Hardin, George W.	Monroe Co.	War of 1812
Harrington, Charles	Vanderburg Co.	War of 1812
Hendricks, Thomas	Wayne Co.	War of 1812
Holden, Richard	Daviess Co.	War of 1812
Houston, Leonard	Lawrence Co.	War of 1812
Irvine, Alexander	Rush Co.	War of 1812
Jacob, George W.	Vanderburg Co.	War of 1812
Keyser, Jacob	Floyd Co.	War of 1812
Kiles, John	LaGrange Co.	War of 1812
Lee, Arza	Posey Co.	War of 1812
Lindley, Zachariah	Orange Co.	War of 1812
Little, Samuel	Harrison Co.	War of 1812
Mallory, Timothy	Jefferson Co.	War of 1812
McBride, Patrick	Harrison Co.	Not Rev. War
McDonough, Francis	Dearborn Co.	Regular Army
McKinney, Robert	Washington Co.	Wayne's Campaign, 1791
Nelson, George	Posey Co.	War of 1812
Norris, John	Clark Co.	War of 1812
Parker, John	Floyd Co.	Indian War, 1791
Peabody, Stephen G.	Switzerland Co.	War of 1812
Pearce, John	Henry Co.	War of 1812
Philips, Thomas	Orange Co.	Indian War, 1791
Pierce, James	Switzerland Co.	War of 1812
Pitts, Stephen	Marion Co.	War of 1812
Potter, Samuel	Knox Co.	War of 1812
Ricketts, William	Dearborn Co.	Indian War, 1791
Roberts, Ebenezer	Dearborn Co.	War of 1812
Ruminer, Daniel	Daviess Co.	War of 1812
Rumsey, Charles	Rush Co.	War of 1812
Russell, John	Perry Co.	Regular Army
Ryan, James	Franklin Co.	War of 1812
Ryon, James	Hancock Co.	War of 1812
Samuels, William	Crawford Co.	War of 1812

Sedgwick, Thomas ....Martin Co. ....War of 1812
Shields, Joshua ....Cass Co. ....War of 1812
Stroud, Isham ....Orange Co. ....Not Rev. War
Sutton, David ....Jefferson Co. ....Regular Army
Swift, Socrates ....Ripley Co. ....War of 1812
Taylor, Isaac ....Vermillion Co. ....War of 1812
Thompson, David ....Fountain Co. ....War of 1812
Thompson, John ....Harrison Co. ....War of 1812
Todd, Joseph ....Switzerland Co. ......War of 1812
Tongate, Meredith ....Orange Co. ....Not Rev. War
Toothman, Jacob ....Dearborn Co. ....War of 1812
Turner, Julius ....Washington Co. .....War of 1812
Wheeler, John ....Clay Co. ....War of 1812
Williams, John ....Decatur Co. ....Not Rev. War
Wilson, James ....Orange Co. ....Not Rev. War
Worrell, Robert ....Orange Co. ....War of 1812
Wyatt, Mordecai ....Jefferson Co. ....War of 1812
Wyatt, Thomas ....Wayne Co. ....War of 1812

www.ingramcontent.com/pod-product-compliance
Lightning Source LLC
Chambersburg PA
CBHW071142300426
44113CB00009B/1050